MW00650706

To Br. Muhammad Qazzafi
and family,

Dr. Yahia Abdul-Rahman
4-1-2016

The Art of RF (Riba-Free) Islamic Banking and Finance

The Wiley Finance series contains books written specifically for finance and investment professionals as well as sophisticated individual investors and their financial advisers. Book topics range from portfolio management to e-commerce, risk management, financial engineering, valuation and financial instrument analysis, as well as much more. For a list of available titles, visit our website at www.WileyFinance.com.

Founded in 1807, John Wiley & Sons is the oldest independent publishing company in the United States. With offices in North America, Europe, Australia, and Asia, Wiley is globally committed to developing and marketing print and electronic products and services for our customers' professional and personal knowledge and understanding.

The Art of RF (Riba-Free) Islamic Banking and Finance

Tools and Techniques for Community-Based Banking

Second Edition

YAHIA ABDUL-RAHMAN

WILEY

Cover image: ©Exotica.im/Getty Images; bottom: ©Dimitri Otis/Getty Images
Cover design: Wiley

Published by John Wiley & Sons, Inc., Hoboken, New Jersey.
Published simultaneously in Canada.

The First Edition of this book was published by John Wiley & Sons, Inc. in 2010.

Library of Congress Cataloging-in-Publication Data:

Abdul-Rahman, Yahia, 1944-
[Art of Islamic banking and finance.]
The art of RF (Riba-Free) Islamic banking and finance + website : tools and techniques for community-based banking / Yahia Abdul-Rahman. — Second edition.
1 online resource. — (Wiley finance)
Includes index.
First Edition of this book was published by John Wiley & Sons, Inc. in 2010.
ISBN 978-1-118-77096-2 (cloth); ISBN 978-1-118-77115-0 (ebk);
ISBN 978-1-118-77090-0 (ebk)
1. Banks and banking—Islamic countries. 2. Banks and banking—Religious aspects—Islam. 3. Finance—Islamic countries. 4. Finance—Religious aspects—Islam. I. Title.
HG3368.A6
332.10917'67—dc23

2014021659

Printed in the United States of America.

10 9 8 7 6 5 4 3 2

Contents

Preface to the Second Edition

In 2009, John Wiley & Sons called me, stating that they were looking for an American to author a book on RF (riba-free) Islamic finance and banking because most books authored on the subject, until then, were in fact authored by authorities who live outside the United States. I welcomed the idea. *The Art of Islamic Banking and Finance* was published in 2010. I am thankful to all those readers who chose to buy the book and who were kind enough to critique and rate the book on Amazon.com.

We at the LARIBA RF Movement, are most indebted to God, the Lord of all people, for creating this opportunity to publish the book, to make it successful worldwide and to help popularize the RF Movement. This movement aims at inviting people of all religions, nations, and beliefs to live riba free. This RF lifestyle is a lifestyle that is free of debt, of overconsumption, of trying to use extravagance and "cool" looks to impress others, and of thinking that money can be rented at a price called interest by using credit cards, excessive borrowing, and the equity of one's home as a source of extra money to extinguish consumptive spasms created by slick advertising campaigns. The RF Movement is out to popularize a new RF lifestyle—a lifestyle that is free from the abuse of credit cards to consume more. It is a movement that promotes the goal of paying debt as soon as one possibly can. The movement also entices students, the leaders of the future, not to take the easy way out by borrowing their tuition using student loans. The RF Movement promotes that it is better for a student not to borrow money, find a part-time job, and graduate in six years debt free in contrast to graduating in four years with the heavy burden of debt.

The second edition includes:

- Many of the recommendations and feedback that were received from many of the readers of the first edition. I thank all of those readers who invested their time to carefully read the book and to communicate their critiques, valuable feedback, and insightful advices to me.
- Rearrangements of chapters to present the new ideas that cast a new light on the RF banking, finance, and monetary disciplines presented in the book for the first time in the history of RF Islamic banking. This, I hope, will make these RF disciplines and the real added value of applying the

RF banking, finance, and monetary disciplines crystal clear. For example, Chapter 5 in the first edition was divided into two chapters—Chapters 5 and 6. In addition, a new Chapter 12 was added to integrate and wrap up all the research findings, the RF disciplines, and the pioneered models presented in the book and how this integrated process is applied in practice.

- New chapters added to cover:
  - RF capital markets to include a detailed study of financial products that were not fully covered in the first edition of 2010.
  - The financing products available in the riba-based conventional banking and their applicability in an RF domain.
  - How to handle nonperforming loans in an RF setting based on the 10-year RF operating experience at the LARIBA Bank of Whittier since 2003.

It is hoped that the reader of this second edition will find these additions enriching and most useful:

- A set of review questions at the end of every chapter. These questions can be useful to students if the book is taught at a university campus. The review questions also will help give an intriguing quick insight about what to expect to learn by reading each of the chapters.
- The use of a dedicated website for the book. See the page at the back of the book for details.

Now to a personal note and some words of advice:

In 2014 at the age of 70, I want to leave a message to the new generation of RF bankers—Muslims and non-Muslims—before I return to God:

- Try your hardest; never lose hope, which is a manifestation of believing in God; and try your best by starting from the idea that it is possible to achieve what others tell you is impossible.
- Remember that we, the believers in the RF lifestyle, are not out to discredit nor do away with the riba-based banking and finance system. We are out to offer an alternative lifestyle and system that we hope will shine when contrasted with the riba-based system.
- Never give up or feel defeated when you face a setback or if you could not achieve a dream. You will be criticized by Muslims and non-Muslims with good intentions and sometimes from people who lack experience and vision for the future. Never let these criticisms get you down. Listen carefully and fix the problems they bring to your attention as much as you can within the limitations at hand. Never discount the criticism of others to your work. Always pay respect and close attention to what others say about your work—good and bad.

- Always associate with the optimists and the constructive well-meaning criticizers, but never hate those who criticize you or position them as your enemies. Remember never to burn your bridges with others. You will never know when you will need others in the future.
- Communicate with people in the language they understand, including presenting RF banking disciplines, products, and contracts in a way that can be easily compared, evaluated, contrasted, and litigated with the riba-based conventional banking and finance disciplines.
- Continue to build institutions and not a one-person organization. Institutions live for generations, but one-person shows expire when that man or woman disappears from the scene.
- Hold to your RF beliefs and disciplines and always be frank, sincere, and straight in your communications with the public; what comes out of the heart reaches people's hearts.
- Deal with all people with a humble attitude and respect. Never be boastful about what you, your staff, and/or your company have done by serving others in the community. Never complain because people do not appreciate your work. The ultimate goal you and we all should be working for is to please God.
- Remember that when it seems that it is over, God will bring His rescue from the least expected source.
- Make sure never to use ruses and circumventions of the RF disciplines and the law, including the laws of the land.
- Always be clear in explaining the added value of the RF disciplines. Remember that the RF Movement is out to serve all people: Jews, Christians, Buddhists, Sikhs, Zoroastrians, and those who do not believe.

Remember that no one, regardless how pious that person is, holds the keys to paradise and to God's kingdom. We are all servants of God and His people, who were created by Him. We at the RF Movement are thankful because the first edition of this book made it to the top 10 bestsellers list in its category on the Amazon.com book list for a period of over six months. The book was bought by many customers around the world—in the United States and Canada, as well as in many countries around the world, mainly in Asia and Europe.

The success of the book prompted John Wiley & Sons to issue another printing in 2012, and with the success and the almost sellout of the second printing, it was decided to produce this expanded second edition.

Our hard work in publicizing and promoting the book worked. John Wiley & Sons, thankfully, did its share of marketing the book in the media by arranging radio and print media interviews and Internet publicity. To complement these efforts, we at the RF Movement decided to create a road show to present the book to universities, government regulatory authorities, and different communities around the world. The book was presented with signing events in many cities in the United States, Canada, Europe, Asia, the Middle East, and Africa.

In the United States, we arranged book-signing seminar events at the University of Wisconsin; California State University in San Bernardino; University of Southern California; Southwest Law School in Los Angeles; University of Texas at Dallas (UTD); Bradley University in Peoria, Illinois; Whittier College; George Washington University; and Columbia University, to mention a few. We visited most states'/provinces' major cities in the United States and Canada.

Internationally, book-signing events were conducted in many countries around the world.

In the United Kingdom, we presented at Oxford University, London School of Economics, and Durham University. In addition, we presented the book to the communities in Manchester and in East London at one of the larger Islamic Centers of London. These events were arranged by my dear friends, gifted RF monetary regime researcher Tarek El Diwany, and Afzal Chaudhary, who has moved to Manchester from southern California after retirement. We at the RF Movement thank them for their efforts and sincere help.

In the rest of the world, the book was presented at many universities and many government financial authorities in Malaysia, Singapore, Turkey, Saudi Arabia, Egypt, United Arab Emirates, Lebanon, Tunisia, Jordan, Switzerland, South Africa, Ethiopia, Argentina, and Trinidad. In addition, the book was promoted in Kazakhstan, where we had a successful full-service RF banking operation—LARIBA Bank of Kazakhstan—from 1993 to 2006. The bank was sold in 2006 due to the new excessive capital requirements of the government at that time because we simply did not have $100 million. LARIBA Bank of Kazakhstan was the first bank ever in the history of Kazakhstan and the former Soviet republics in Central Asia to introduce and publicize, using TV interviews and lecture series, mortgages in general and, for that matter, RF mortgages. The book was also introduced and promoted by the Egyptian Islamic Banking and Finance Association. It is important to note the successful introduction of LARIBA—LARIBA Misr Al Arabiya—in Egypt between 2004 and 2010, when its services were temporarily frozen due to political turmoil that led to the events that took Egypt to the January 25, 2011, revolution. It is worth mentioning that half of its finance portfolio was given to members of the Egyptian Coptic and Christian community business entrepreneurs.

It is also useful to report that after the book was released, LARIBA Bank of Whittier opened up a full-service RF banking branch in the City of Richardson, Texas (about eight miles north of Dallas). The new branch, under the able leadership of Mohsin Mandavia, has contributed greatly to our cause and our RF Movement. We all want to thank the Texas community for their wonderful and enthusiastic support of the RF Movement.

To conclude, please remember that "the best of all people are those who benefit people through serving their needs with love and good intentions" as taught by Prophet Muhammad (pp[1]).

NOTE

1. Throughout the book I shall use the abbreviation (pp) to stand for the prayer every Muslim is taught to utter every time he/she hears the name of a prophet mentioned: "May God's peace and prayers be showered onto him."

Preface: My Story with RF (Islamic) Banking and Finance in America

I came to the United States on my own from Egypt to study for my MS and PhD degrees at the University of Wisconsin–Madison in February 1968. I had essentially nothing except my BS degree in chemical engineering from Cairo University and a letter from the University of Wisconsin–Madison accepting me as an International Special Student on a trial basis. I did not have the funds to pay for tuition nor for accommodations, books, and other expenses. It was a big challenge for me, but I made it, through hard work, to where I am today managing a pioneering effort in America to establish what I consider a revival of the banking system that built America. Using a platform we call the LARIBA system (www.LARIBA.com), we offer socially responsible, faith-based, and RF (riba-free) banking. Throughout this book, I will abbreviate it as RF banking.

In 1987, a group of dedicated friends invested $10,000 each to start a small company we called American Finance House LARIBA. We gathered $200,000 as the start-up capital. To my knowledge, this was the first time ever a group of American Muslims who immigrated from India, Egypt, Syria, and Pakistan had bonded together to start a joint project that would eventually become an important force in the American Muslim community and in many non-Muslim communities. Our goal was to start a finance company that would operate without the charging of interest and according to the foundations of Islamic law (*Shari'aa*). Today, in 2009, and after 22 years, the LARIBA shareholders own LARIBA (www.LARIBA.com), the oldest Islamic RF finance company in the United States, and the Bank of Whittier N.A. (www.BankOfWhittier.com), a national bank. The LARIBA System (the finance company LARIBA and the depository institution, Bank of Whittier, N.A.) serves all 50 states in America and services a portfolio of RF Shari'aa-based financing that is worth approximately $400 million. The portfolio includes home mortgages, automobiles, fast food franchises, medical doctors' clinics, dialysis centers, commercial buildings, schools, churches, and Islamic centers. It was, and continues to be, a wonderful journey.

This book is a sincere effort to introduce this new brand of banking—RF banking, which is based on the Judeo-Christian-Islamic value system while upholding the laws of the United States.

I must acknowledge that, after traveling the world and doing business in many nations, I concluded that *only in the United States* can a new immigrant realize his/her dreams, even with a new idea that might have looked unbelievably outrageous at the time. I am deeply indebted to Almighty God, who created the reasons for me to come to America, start a family, and live here. I am thankful to my fellow Americans of all faiths and backgrounds for making our country, the United States of America, what it is. It is unfortunate that America is viewed internationally through the lens of Hollywood movies and the sometimes controversial aspects of our foreign policy. It is unfortunate that the wonderful average American neighbor, colleague, farmer, worker, professional, student, and volunteer do not get a chance to be fully and fairly represented and exposed to the United States and the rest of the world.

My feeling as a Muslim moving to live in the United States was one of curiosity. Moving to America changed my social standing and grouping; I went from being a citizen of a majority Muslim country to being a member of the Muslim minority in the United States, which was an unknown minority belonging to an unknown religion at that time, February 1968. Reflecting on it, I concluded that God in His infinite wisdom wanted us Muslims in the United States to experience living as a minority. If we were wise, we, the Muslims, would learn from this golden opportunity and better understand how to deal with non-Muslim minorities in the Muslim majority countries. At the same time, we might be able to further enrich a country that was—after all—built by successive waves of immigrants, each bringing something new to the broader culture of the nation. Being a member of the small American Muslim minority created an interesting basic feeling, an instinct and need to discover one's roots and to define whom one really is. That was the beginning of our journey, my wife and I, in the service of Islam in America in the form of serving the American Muslim community and the integration of Islam and the American Muslim community to make them part of the unique American mosaic through interfaith and civic activities.

My story with RF (Islamic) finance began in Dallas, Texas, in 1971. I had completed my PhD in chemical engineering, and my wife had completed her MS degree in chemical engineering. I got a job at the Production Research Center of Atlantic Richfield Company (ARCO, which is now owned by British Petroleum). At the time, ARCO had just discovered oil in Alaska and was expanding its research on how to produce that oil and transport it south to the mainland under the most severe operating conditions. We moved from Madison, Wisconsin, to Dallas, Texas, in November 1971. We looked for a *masjid* (mosque) where we could perform our weekly Friday congregational prayers (*jum'aa*). We started by looking for people with a

Muslim last name. The most prevalent and easy name to search for in the phone book was Khan. We called and we got in touch, but we learned sad news: there were no Friday prayers yet in the Dallas/Fort Worth area. We started the first-ever Friday prayers in Dallas, Texas, on Friday, November 26, 1971. Only two persons attended the prayer, which was held at a park behind the Southern Methodist University (SMU) campus—your author and Ghulam Hussein Siddiqui.

The community grew, and we started collecting donations to build an Islamic center of our own, the Islamic Association of North Texas (IANT). We eventually raised approximately $17,000 in donations, and we found a home on a nice-sized piece of land in the city of Grand Prairie, Texas (between the cities of Dallas and Fort Worth), which was selling for approximately $34,000. A medical doctor friend who was on the board of directors, who was more sophisticated because he knew how to borrow from banks, as he had financed his clinic and his convertible Mercedes, suggested that we borrow money from the bank. Members of the community were up in arms because we were entertaining the thought of dealing with interest (riba), which is prohibited in Islam. When I was asked to give an opinion about the issue, I indicated that I was an engineer and a practicing Muslim who takes interest in studying the Qur'aan and Islam, but I knew nothing about money, banking, and finance.

That was the beginning of a journey that gradually took me away from engineering to banking and finance. It was also an amazing coincidence that God created another reason for that transformation. In 1972, the Strategic Planning Group at ARCO was convinced that oil prices would increase drastically because of an impending supply-demand imbalance. ARCO had huge reserves of oil shale in Colorado and "wet" coal in Wyoming. It was decided that the research center would start developing new processes for the production of synthetic oil and gas from shale and coal. I was one of those assigned to the task. I developed a number of processes that were patented by ARCO. The next step was to study the economic feasibility of these new processes. To do that, ARCO, in 1974, agreed to help finance my studies toward an MA degree in international management and finance at the University of Texas at Dallas. There, I chose to study monetary theory, to understand what money is and how money is created, international monetary theory, financial accounting, credit analysis, and international economics.

It was also amazing that God created another reason for me to get a once-in-a-lifetime opportunity to obtain hands-on banking experience. One day in 1974, during the month of Ramadan, while working in my ARCO office in Plano, Texas, I received a phone call from a stranger who said that he was from Kuwait, that he was one of the executive directors of the

World Bank representing Kuwait, and that he was given a mandate from his government to start the Industrial Bank of Kuwait (IBK). When I asked him how he found me, he said that he was looking for an engineer with experience in the petroleum field, preferably one who understood finance and could speak Arabic. It happened that two different persons recommended my name. I went to Washington, D.C., to interview him and was offered a job on the team that would start the IBK. My responsibility was to take care of financing small and medium-sized oil-related development projects and other chemical and petrochemical projects. ARCO management was elated and encouraged me to go. They granted me what the company classified as grade A leave of absence, with a guarantee that my job would be waiting when I was done with the assignment. It was a wonderful experience that introduced me to the process—and the associated challenges—of starting up a bank. The bank developed an industrial development plan for Kuwait. We financed projects ranging from mega-sized petrochemical plants to offshore drilling rigs to projects that were as small as juice packaging facilities and cookie manufacturing plants. In 1975, I returned to Dallas. I became a U.S. citizen in 1976 and completed my MA degree, while my wife completed her MS degree in physics and a PhD in environmental engineering.

At the end of 1976, I was invited to join the ARCO Strategic Planning Group, which took us to ARCO's Los Angeles headquarters. There, I eventually became the senior planning consultant in charge of projecting oil prices based on studies of energy sources, supply, and demand from oil, gas, shale, coal, nuclear, and hydropower, both in the United States and overseas. The group made recommendations to ARCO's management for investing in oil, natural gas, and coal in the United States. This was a wonderful experience that taught me strategic thinking, integrating the thoughts of many experts and executives in their own fields, and translating the conclusions to reach specific, well-defined strategic recommendations and decisions. The experience also gave me a chance to deal with many company executives, leading politicians, and government employees in the field of energy. In 1979, the Islamic Revolution erupted in Iran, and ARCO lost its oil production and supply from Lavon Island (which is off Iran's coast). In 1978, during the peak of the oil crisis, ARCO management assigned me the responsibility of managing the effort to find more than 250,000 barrels of oil per day to supply the shortfall due to the loss of production from the Lavon oil fields. This gave me a chance to see the world. I went to Africa, Asia, and Latin America looking to sign oil supply deals with almost every country that produces oil. In 1982, I received an attractive offer to be an executive vice president of an independent refining company in Houston, Texas. Later on, I started my first company as an entrepreneur trading in oil and petroleum products.

In Houston, I was invited to become a founding member of a new bank, Woodway National Bank (it was acquired by a larger bank later). In 1983, and during our bank board meetings, we were briefed on delinquencies and nonperforming loans that were given to some of the biggest entrepreneurs, companies, and executives in Houston. I also noticed a lot of tension in one of the briefings given by the then-mayor of Houston, Kathy Whitmeyer, and the city's financial manager. Business in Houston had slowed drastically due to the decline in oil prices. Houston was hit as the oil, economic, and real estate bubble burst. (I saw the scars of this crash every time I visited Houston until the early 2000s, 20 years later.)

I went home to discuss this alarming situation with my wife. We decided to sell our house in the expensive Memorial area of Houston. We wanted to sell it fast. We asked a well-educated real estate broker (a former high school mathematics and statistics teacher from Canada) to give us a good estimate for a price that would help us sell it as soon as possible. He invited over 100 real estate agents to our house and polled them. Based on his statistical analysis of the poll, he recommended $595,000, but he hesitated because the house next door was listed for sale at approximately $895,000. We told him to go ahead. We sold the house within weeks for $575,000 and moved to a nice apartment close by until our two daughters finished the school year, at which time we prepared to move back to our house in the city of Altadena near Los Angeles, California (which we hadn't been able to sell because interest rates had risen to nearly 19 percent). We considered ourselves very lucky because we were able to sell our house before the Houston real estate crash, and not being able to sell the California house meant we had a home waiting for us in California. (The next-door neighbor was not able to sell his house until he lowered the price from $895,000 to $300,000.)

Returning home one day in 1984, while still in Houston, I found a telegram from the IBK, the bank I had helped start 10 years before. In 1983, Kuwait was hit by a devastating stock market crash because of a nationally practiced pyramid scheme. I went to interview with the new chairman and received an offer to return to the IBK. I took my family back to California, fixed the house, and settled our children in school. My wife went back to work for CF Braun (Brown & Roots Engineering Company) designing fertilizer plants and oil refineries before she moved later on to work for Northrop, the defense contractor. In September 1984, I started working at the IBK. As the projects manager, my team responsibilities included:

- Taking care of nonperforming assets and recommending a course of action to work out the loan portfolio.
- Identifying new projects that were needed in the economy to help economic growth and to finance them.

- Training a new generation of young Kuwaitis to take over as the new industrial bankers in Kuwait.

Because my daughters were in school, my family did not join me this time; they stayed in the United States. I lived in a half-suite at the Sheraton in Kuwait. During this time, between 1984 and 1986, I had a chance to see how a bank loan portfolio can grow in a fictitious boom and how many took advantage of "easy" credit terms and loose credit standards. I experienced how corruption can change the fiber of a society and how money matters can cause deep feuds between leading families and create irreparable fractures in a society. I also was close to the raging Iran-Iraq war, and I saw daily convoys of hundreds of trucks carrying tanks, military supplies, wheat, and food supplies traveling to Iraq from a Kuwaiti port dedicated to support the Iraqi war efforts (Shua'iba Port). Before I left Kuwait to go back home in 1986, I told my Kuwaiti friends, "Those tanks you are sending to Iraq may come back to threaten your safety and security." Indeed, in 1990, the late President Saddam Hussein invaded Kuwait, and the U.S. Marines came to the Kuwait Sheraton! The rest is history.

In 1986, I returned to California and found a job as a financial consultant with Shearson Lehman (later to merge with American Express and subsequently in many other mergers to become Smith Barney/Citigroup). As I began to work in the financial industry, a dream started forming in my head. My dream was to start a bank or a financial institution for our community.

During all these years, I had remained in close and continuous touch with the community by serving with my wife in the Islamic Center of each city we lived in. My wife and I helped start Sunday schools for the children; I delivered the Friday sermon (*khutbah*) and led the congregational prayers. I also performed and officiated at wedding ceremonies, presided over marriage conflict resolution and family matters, prepared the dead for burial, and taught in the Sunday program to the youths and adults. I was called upon to travel around the United States and Canada to help motivate local Muslim communities to donate generously for the building and financing of *masajid* (mosques) and full-time Islamic schools designed along the same models of Catholic and Jewish schools in the United States, Europe, and the rest of the world.

When we moved from Dallas, Texas, to Los Angeles, California, in 1977, I was elected to the board of directors of the Islamic Center of Southern California. I left the board when we moved to Houston in 1981. In Houston, my wife and I started activating, formalizing, structuring, and institutionalizing the Islamic Sunday school and helped in the organization and operation of the Islamic Center there. After moving back from Houston to Los Angeles, I was again elected to the board and was given the responsibility of chairman of the finance committee at the Islamic Center of Southern California (ICSC). There, I applied what I had been learning all these years. Our team restructured the Center's finances, started a program for automatic donations from members' checking accounts to ensure that the Center employees' salaries and overhead could be provided for on a regular basis, and developed operating policies for the Center. Most important of these policies was to rely only on donations from the American Muslim community. Our policy allowed the acceptance of donations from noncommunity sources and others from outside the United States, but not from governments. It was difficult in the beginning. However, it has been my experience that when you put people to the challenge and articulate your goals to them, you will capture their imagination to join you. Then what seems impossible can become possible. Doing this for all those years gave me the opportunity to understand the community, share its joys and dreams, and feel its pains. It also gave me a chance to meet the youth and children—the new breed of Americans who are Muslim. I saw the future in them, and I had no doubt that it was going to be a very bright and promising future.

During my many fundraising trips, and on my way back home, I started thinking about the future of our community. I asked myself: When were we going to stop "begging" and start building the financial muscles of our community? How could we develop an Islamic finance solution to help solve the problem of many Muslim "puritans," who preferred living in small, crowded, and shabby apartments rather than commit the grave sin of participating in the prohibited riba by borrowing money with interest to finance the purchase of a home? How could we bring these families out of the apartments and into suburban America, where they could meet new neighbors, live a more comfortable life, and send their children to wonderful neighborhood schools, integrating them in America to live a full American life, but without interest (riba)? How could we create an RF financial institution that would be capable and qualified to gather the community's savings and be qualified to invest these savings prudently back in the community, with qualified, dedicated, and honorable community members who have experience, good ideas, and good projects? If we could realize this dream, I knew we could empower the community, help its growth, and create wealth and economic prosperity and job opportunities for many. The answer to this question was to start an RF bank or an RF finance company. The biggest problem was the challenge of operating that institution without riba.

In 1987, I met a visionary who was busy developing RF finance companies and banks around the world. He was in Los Angeles on vacation, and he heard me deliver a Friday prayers' sermon (*jum'aa khutbah*) at the masjid. We became close friends, and I shared with him my dream of starting RF banking services for the community in America. He was another gift from God, because he encouraged me to proceed. He was also instrumental in introducing me to his contacts: significant lawyers, bankers, and religious scholars who specialized in the field of RF finance. He also wanted to start an RF stock portfolio under my management. He further asked our team to develop parameters that would qualify a company stock on world stock markets to meet RF finance investment criteria. In cooperation with a few dedicated and highly qualified Islamic bankers and scholars, we developed these parameters, started the portfolio, and diversified it among different portfolio managers around the world. We reviewed the different screens used to identify RF Shari'aa-compliant stocks and the performance of this $250 million portfolio on a quarterly basis. To my knowledge, that was the first time in history an Islamic RF stock portfolio was developed and brought to life. It would be years before the Dow Jones Islamic Index was developed, made public, and marketed throughout the world.

We started American Finance House LARIBA in 1987. In the beginning, we were not sure if our efforts would be accepted or if they would be misunderstood. We used the name American Finance House: *American* to acknowledge that our company is American, and *Finance House* to imply its nature as an Islamic treasury; in the early history of Islam, the Treasury was called the House of Assets (*Bayt ul Maal*). We also added the word *LARIBA*. In the beginning, we explained to those who did not know about RF financing that LARIBA stood for Los Angeles Reliable Investment Bankers Associates. Those who knew about RF financing also understood that in the language of the Qur'aan (Arabic), *la* means *no* and *riba* means the act of renting money at a price called interest rate (the Old Testament uses the sister word *ribit* for the same concept). We made it very clear that we were not out to change, dismantle, or demolish the conventional banking and finance system in the United States. We simply offered a humble RF alternative that would serve those "puritan" Muslim and other Americans who wanted to live according to their religious beliefs while obeying the laws of the United States. We articulated this at the outset when we made it clear that changing U.S. laws was not one of our objectives.

As we developed LARIBA, we wanted to make sure that it would be a grassroots organization for our community. That meant that we should rely on our own resources, not go hat-in-hand soliciting capital from the oil-rich communities in the Gulf. We believed that if we were really serious, we could entice many of our community members, starting with each one of us putting our own money where our mouths were. We also wanted to train members from our community on RF Islamic banking and finance. We made sure that we did not use the American Muslim as a marketing front for the same conventional finance operations to take advantage of a market niche. The strict guidelines were severe and challenging. They meant that we would have a steep uphill battle to develop and achieve what we wanted. However, we believed that the turtle approach would be much more effective than the jumping frog approach. A turtle goes slowly to its target; and if a hurdle stands in its way and prevents it from progressing, it takes a sidestep and proceeds. Compare this to the frog, which jumps up and down and back and forth and often ends up where it started. Yes, it took us a long time, but that time helped us develop a system, learn from our mistakes, sharpen our models, train a new generation of Americans who believe in our LARIBA concepts that abide by RF disciplines, and prove ourselves to the community at large.

We started LARIBA in 1987 (in the month of Ramadan) out of a box. We slowly grew it out of the box and moved it to the apartment above the garage in my house. Then we moved to Pasadena, California, where we expanded three times, ending with almost four times the initial square footage and now to its current location in Whittier, California. We started with one part-time employee and grew to 22 employees. One thing that helped us grow was the Internet. In 1997, LARIBA was contacted by a young man who was doing his master's degree at USC (University of Southern California) in computers and Web development. He needed a $3,000 loan to buy a powerful computer to help him in his studies, but no one would finance him. We financed him at LARIBA. We asked him to develop the first LARIBA portal, www.AmericanFinance.com, which later became www.LARIBA.com. The LARIBA site became very popular. From the time we started keeping track of the number of unique visitors in the year 2000 through July 2009, the LARIBA site has attracted more than 1 million unique visitors. It became the most information-rich site available on the subject of RF Islamic banking.

In 1994, I authored and self-published my first book: *LARIBA Bank—A Foundation for a United and Prosperous Community*. It was a simple book that summarized what I had learned and read over the years about Islamic banking, and in it, I also articulated our community dreams. The demand for the book was great. We printed it twice and distributed more than 6,500 copies in the United States. A publisher in Malaysia acquired the printing rights and continues to distribute it on a large scale in Malaysia and Indonesia. LARIBA became an important household name in the United States and Asia, as well as the Middle East. The brand name LARIBA is now considered to be like "Coca-Cola"—recognized throughout the world as the brand of RF (Islamic finance). We were invited to speak at universities such as Harvard University, the University of Illinois, the University of California at Los Angeles (UCLA), Claremont Graduate College, and many others, in addition to Islamic centers, churches, and synagogues all over the United States and Canada. In addition, we were invited to present at international conferences in Malaysia, Bahrain, Brunei, Saudi Arabia, Kuwait, Singapore, Canada, England, Turkey, South Africa, and Egypt. The media began taking notice. *ABC Nightly News* (with Peter Jennings) had a segment on LARIBA, as did the Voice of America, Malaysian television, National Public Radio (NPR), and American Public Media's *Marketplace*. The *Los Angeles Times* had a front-page article on LARIBA, with a full-page inside report. Since that time, we have been reported about in *USA Today*, the *Dallas Morning News*, the *Wall Street Journal*, the *Washington Post*, the *Houston Chronicle*, the *Chicago Tribune*, and the *Detroit Free Press*, to mention a few.

One day, we received a phone call from the U.S. State Department to thank us at LARIBA. They explained that when they had published an article about LARIBA in their newsletter to the Middle East, many media outlets in the Middle East had picked up the story and republished it. The caller remarked that this was one of the few times they had been able to forward a positive story from the United States that appealed to the press in the Middle East.

In our effort to popularize the concepts we used, we started a new tradition. The tradition was to have an annual recognition award for significant distinguished contributors to the field of RF banking in the world. We awarded every "who's who" leader in the field, and we tied the award dinner attended by almost 500 members of the community and leaders of southern California to an annual seminar on Islamic banking. This effort ran for 12 years. The event was designed to be graceful, but full of subliminal notions that underlined our American affiliation and our respect for the U.S. political system and its laws. For example, we invited color guards to start our events. We were the first Islamic organization in the history of American Muslims to start its events not only with an invocation and recitation from the Holy Qur'aan but also with the national anthem, sung by a professional singer and later by a wonderful young lady, an American Muslim from the community. We invited our congressmen, state representatives, mayors, and many other public figures to the dinner. The awards that were handed out were not only awards from LARIBA but also included certificates of commendation from the Congress of the United States, the California State Assembly, the Los Angeles Board of Supervisors, and the Mayor of Pasadena, California (a city 20 miles northeast of Los Angeles, where our LARIBA offices were first located).

We also did something very bold in the year 2000. After the currency crisis of Southeast Asia, Malaysia, under the leadership of Dr. Mahathir Muhammad, was the only country in the region that weathered the storm and was able to contain the problem without sacrificing its foreign currency reserves or resorting to heavy borrowing from the International Monetary Fund (IMF). The board of LARIBA decided to create a new award called the Lifetime Achievement Award, and we gave it to the then–Prime Minister of Malaysia, Dr. Mahathir Muhammad. Dr. Mahathir came to Chicago to receive his award. We at LARIBA also did something unique for the ceremony. Instead of holding the function at a local prestigious, brand-name hotel, we held it in a Chicago suburb, in the auditorium of a prominent and well-appointed Islamic center built by American Muslims who emigrated from Bosnia. This move gave LARIBA wide coverage in the community and in the world press, as well as good political and operating credibility.

LARIBA had very humble means, and it lacked enough capital. We used to finance a home once every two to three months (the terms of financing were onerous: 40 percent down and a seven-year term) and a car every month, because we had a tough time convincing our friends to invest in the company. The U.S. regulations regarding solicitation of funds are strict and in general do not allow solicitation unless an offering is registered with the government. The process of registering for a public offering with the U.S. Securities and Exchange Commission (SEC) is lengthy and very expensive. However, we persevered, and our patience paid off. The community learned more about us, and the volume of calls started to increase. However, we could not meet all that growing demand.

In 2000, we received an e-mail from a banker who used to work for Freddie Mac (an American government-sponsored entity devoted to investing in long-term mortgages to enhance home ownership in America[1]) to obtain information about LARIBA. We explained to him what we do. In response, he introduced us to an executive at Freddie Mac, Saber Salam, who was interested in growing its mortgage finance activities among minorities in America. We talked, and he loved what we were doing. A delegation from Freddie Mac came to evaluate the company and its operations. We explained to them that for every home we finance, we and the customer each have to come up with three rent estimates for a similar home in the same neighborhood to evaluate the rate of return on investing in the house as if it were financing a commercial venture by using the market-measured rental rate to ascertain the economic prudence of the investment. We explained that we do this because our faith prohibits us from renting money at a price called an interest rate, but allows us to rent a tangible and rentable asset like a car, a home, or a business. If the investment (not the lending) makes economic sense, we finance the house mortgage; if not, we do not finance. The analyst in the team was apprehensive; he asked if they could review some of the financing files. They were all impressed when they audited the files.

Freddie Mac gave us approval in less than six weeks (they put out a press release about it on March 26, 2001). This was a record for approval time by Freddie Mac, which usually took an average of six months under normal circumstances. We then were confronted with the issue of the format of the operating relationship and how to do business with them without charging or paying interest. We at LARIBA agreed with Freddie Mac that we would look at them as an investor in each deal and that we would *not* borrow money from them. We felt that it would be hypocritical to borrow money from Freddie with interest and turn around and claim that we were financing mortgages riba free! This *first-time-ever* event in the history of the United States and the American Muslim community helped make LARIBA an important factor in mortgage financing in general and in Islamic RF financing in particular.

In 2002, we were contacted by the larger Fannie Mae,[2] and they also approved us. LARIBA, a year later, became the *only* RF finance company in the history of the United States that issued RF mortgage-backed securities (RF MBS *sukuk—riba-free asset-based bonds*) with Fannie Mae. We are all grateful to God and to the many dedicated men and women, fellow associates at LARIBA, for their dedication and quality work, which made LARIBA among the top 1 percent quality producers for Freddie and Fannie.

It had always been difficult to raise capital for LARIBA. Many of the community members indicated that they would be willing to support us if we were a Federal Deposit Insurance Corporation (FDIC)-insured bank. We, the shareholders of LARIBA, became very interested in buying a bank. We wanted to find a small bank that we could afford and that we could manage and grow slowly. After investing seven years in the search for a bank, we found the Bank of Whittier, National Association (NA). The project of acquiring and working on the change of control of the Bank of Whittier plunged me into another valuable and educational experience. The process was enhanced by the support and encouragement of an expert attorney in the field, Gary Steven Findley, Esq. The Bank of Whittier, being chartered as a national bank, is regulated and supervised by the U.S. Department of Treasury. We learned many lessons in dealing with the U.S. government for the first time. We learned why the United States is what it is, and we all learned why the American banking system has no equal in the world.

We are aware of the unfortunate financial meltdown of 2008. It is known that many politicians claimed that it resulted from the lack of sufficient regulations. That may be partially true in particular and specific situations, but not in general. It is historically known that one of the most important results of the Great Depression was the ratification of the Glass-Steagall Act, which prohibited commercial banks and investment banks from combining their businesses. This act was repealed by the Congress during the Clinton administration. At Smith Barney I was one of those who witnessed the attempts made to combine the two cultures without much success. It is also important to stress here that all the regulations that man can exert in the system will not be able to stop fraud, dishonesty, greed, and the irresponsible behavior of people who are supposed to be the trusted custodians of our assets and savings. Ethics and morality are not instilled in people by regulations but by parents, the school system, the media, and the society at large, starting at an early age.

In 1998, we at LARIBA received approval for change of control of the Bank of Whittier, NA, and were elated to own a bank affiliate. We initially selected community bank managers to run the bank who had a strong background in traditional banking but little familiarity with the community served by the bank and no knowledge of the RF business model.

In July 2003, I attained vesting with Smith Barney, talked to my wife about taking early retirement, and went to reorganize the Bank of Whittier. Today, the Bank of Whittier operates as an RF bank, but in a seamless way. We chose a slogan that described the RF discipline we abide by: *We Do Not Rent Money—We Invest in Our Customers.* We also told people what RF banking and finance is all about. It is a faith-based and socially responsible community effort that is not involved in renting money. We shared with our customers our RF approach to finance, to banking, and to client service, and they experienced our services. Their consistent feedback was: "We have not heard bankers talk like that before!" We shared with our clients what I sincerely believe is the first LARIBA banker in America: George Bailey, the banker played by Jimmy Stewart in the movie *It's a Wonderful Life.*"

The heinous crime of September 11, 2001, shocked us all. I was in the kitchen preparing breakfast and saw it live on TV. I went to the office and received a call from the mayor of Pasadena, California. He asked me what to do. I told him that I have disciplined myself such that when I am in a shocking situation like this, I resort to praying. He and I led an effort to organize, for the first time in Pasadena, the first prayer response to the catastrophe. We invited the leaders of 35 religions and communities in southern California for a prayer at the steps of the Pasadena City Hall. It was heavily attended, and it helped us develop wonderful friendships with many religious leaders of all faiths in southern California.

Reflecting on my personal experience as a naturalized U.S. citizen who has lived in America since 1968, I concluded that I need to pay respects to the rest of America by understanding the majority faith of America, Christianity. I, along with many other American Muslims, was also deeply hurt by the vehement attacks and unfortunate remarks some significant church leaders made about Islam, the God of Islam, and the Prophet of Islam. In response, I decided to work on building bridges of friendship, mutual understanding, and goodwill with the Christian seminary closest to my home—Fuller Theological Seminary in Pasadena. There, we made good friends and participated in a pioneering conflict resolution effort to soothe relations between our two communities. The most important outcome of that effort was a historic announcement that concluded that the Christian God and the Muslim God

(Allah) are indeed the same. This announcement was published in the *Los Angeles Times* on December 3, 2006. We all also discovered in this process of pondering and soul-searching that we at LARIBA had a way to promote better understanding and lasting bridges between the communities of faith: RF faith-based and socially responsible financing.

LARIBA devoted its Annual Awards and Symposium series of 2002 to the subject. We asked professors from the University of Judaism in Los Angeles and a prominent rabbi in North Hollywood (who has a keen interest in the field of ribit/riba-free financing) to present the Jewish view. For two Christian points of view, we invited professors in the fields of lending with interest charging at Loyola Marymount University to present the Roman Catholic view, and professors from Fuller Seminary to present the Evangelical view. It was a wonderful and enriching experience that made us understand more fully and clearly the problem of charging for the use (rent) of money. We also learned the source of the word *usury*, which is now defined as excessive interest—but nobody could answer the question: "Excessive in reference to what?" In fact, usury was defined long ago by the early disciplines of the Catholic Church (before rules were relaxed in the fifteenth century) as the price one pays for renting the right to use money. It was wonderful to hear the metaphor of trying to rent the right of use of an apple, which is impossible because an apple can be owned only when its ownership right is transferred. That is exactly the case with money, which is nothing but a measuring tool. It is not like an automobile, which one can own but can also assign the right of its usage by renting it. Money is a thing—it cannot be rented. We also learned that in the early days, if a person of the Jewish faith charged ribit (interest), he/she could not stand as a witness in a Jewish court; similarly, a Roman Catholic who dealt in (usury) interest was denied the right to a Catholic burial.

Faith-based ribit/riba-free (Islamic) banking and finance—RF banking and finance—is much simpler and must not be more expensive than it is perceived by the public. It is a concept that makes perfect sense. RF banking is based on the belief that credit is a basic human right. It is socially responsible, environmentally compliant, and ethical. RF bankers are trained to make sure that the financing facility makes prudent economic sense to the family because the decision to finance (invest) is based on the prevailing actual market prices. Its bankers are trained *not* to help a community member dig a deeper hole of debt, but rather to help that person get out of debt as soon as possible. RF banking is a system that commits itself to being involved in real economic activities, not simply "renting" money in order to make money on money. Its financing activities involve asset-based or service-based financing—that is, a commodity, a tangible asset, and/or a service must change hands. The primary passion of true RF banking is community service and development. It is interesting to note that this is not much different from the foundation of the well-known U.S. bank regulation titled the Community Reinvestment Act. Our vision is to have an RF banking and finance unit started next to every place of social assembly: trade organizations, clubs, and places of worship (e.g., temples, synagogues, churches, and *masajid*).

Based on our experience since 1987, the outcome has been and will continue to be superior service and a solid credit (loan) portfolio. This is so because the evaluation of the economic viability of each credit facility is based on comparing each asset and/or service with the market to ensure that it is a prudent investment. Because of the low risk and solid products offered by the RF system, the overhead expenses are lower. Because the system is based on the knowledge of each member of a smaller community, the "cardinal" rule of banking (i.e., *know your customer*) is practiced to the fullest. The net result is much higher returns than conventional banks, mainly due to the low levels of nonperforming loans and the deep spirit and culture of voluntarism and service instilled in the RF banker.

This preface has covered a lot of history, experiences, and topics. The book will attempt to introduce the spirit of RF banking as I understand it, as we practice it at LARIBA, and as we have lived it since 1987. I have invested at least 27 years of my life reading, researching, developing finance models, authoring papers, giving lectures all over the world, writing books (including this one), arbitrating between RF (Islamic) banks and businesses holding credits with these RF banks worldwide, and training RF bankers in Malaysia, the United States, Canada, and Turkey. I have the honor of sharing all these experiences with you, the reader of this book.

I have a deep interest in the spirit of Judeo-Christian-Islamic law (Shari'aa, called the law in this book) and the reason this law was put into effect, as revealed to mankind by God of all prophets, including Prophets Noah, Abraham, Ishmael, Isaac, Jacob, David, Solomon, and all subsequent prophets (may the peace and prayers of God be showered on all of them), and by the founders of the three monotheistic faiths, Moses (pp), Jesus (pp), and Muhammad (pp). I have tried the best I can to be educated in my own faith, Islam, as well as Christianity and Judaism. I consider myself as a servant of God and hence a servant of the people who live the life of loving God—God of all people of all backgrounds and walks of life—and this must be translated in disseminating love to all people. It is not enough to lecture people and try to capture their imagination, touch their hearts, and influence their minds. What is important is to touch their pocket and to make a difference in the quality of life they and their families live.

I want to conclude by quoting a *hadeeth* (pronouncement) of Prophet Muhammad (pp), which has been my motto over the years: "The best of people are those who benefit others the most."

NOTES

1. Freddie Mac is a government-sponsored corporation that provides a secondary market for home mortgages and hence helps provide liquidity to mortgage companies.
2. Fannie Mae is a sister company of Freddie Mac, but much larger and older. It provides liquidity for home mortgages in the secondary market.

Acknowledgments

As I sat down to reflect on whom to acknowledge, I found it to be a very difficult task. Many people in many parts of the world contributed to making me the person I am. Mentioning a few names, as is usually done in the front of a typical book, would be unfair to the lands I grew in and the people who contributed to my life and character. That is why I decided to play back my life since I was born in Cairo, Egypt, in a religious district named after the granddaughter of Prophet Muhammad (pp). It is called Al Sayedah Zeinab district, where the masjid (mosque) of the granddaughter of the Prophet—Zeinab—figures prominently. I am deeply indebted to the teachers at this masjid, who instilled the foundations of believing in God in me and the many millions who worshipped there. I am also grateful for the main reason of my being: God. He has given me a wonderful, full life complete with wonderful parents, family, wife, children, grandchildren, teachers, friends, and colleagues.

The Qur'aan teaches that God has ordained never to worship other than Him and to excel in dealing and caring for one's parents and family. The physical reason for my being here goes back to my dear parents.

First, I want to acknowledge my dear, late mother, whose name is also Zeinab. The Qur'aan enumerates to us the hard work a mother goes through from the time of conceiving and bearing a child to the time of delivering that child, weaning him/her, and raising that child. She was educated and ambitious. She was the household financial planner who saved a bit on the side in order to meet the family's extra needs such as buying a refrigerator for the family or paying for a summer vacation in Alexandria. She was widowed at the prime age of 39 and sacrificed dearly to raise a family of five children. I know how difficult it was for her to be standing alone to meet the challenges of a lower income without the support of a husband in these very difficult years, especially when I left Cairo to further my education in America two years after the sudden death of my father. Words cannot express my gratitude and love for her.

My father was a wonderful self-made man. He started his career in the ministry of education as a humble laboratory technician. His ambition prompted him to advance his education and training to become the undersecretary of education in the field of finance and administration when he died. His last post was in an education district that has a high content of non-Muslim—Coptic—Egyptians. I saw him treat all people equally with unconditional love regardless of their faith. During the religious celebrations of our fellow Egyptian Copts, he took the family to their homes to celebrate with them Christmas and other Coptic traditions. He invited them to our house and celebrated together the Muslim festivities. He disciplined us to have a transparent eye, heart, and soul for all people regardless of their faith or stature. His biggest prayer and dream was to die at his desk while serving people. He was a workaholic. He did die of a heart attack at his desk while working late in the evening. His funeral was attended by thousands of people—both Muslims and Christians—many of whom I had never met. Many told me how my father helped them and served them without expecting even a word of thanks. He authored a book on finance and administration that was a useful reference for young finance and administration employees. I remember that we had boxes of the unsold copies stored on our balcony at our house in Cairo, Egypt. As a young man, I did not know why these books were not sold. Now that I am older, I've learned that the average Middle Easterner does not read. I was told by a major Arab publisher in Cairo that a bestselling book in the Middle East prints 7,000 to 10,000 copies! This may be one of the major sources of problems and one of the major reasons of the miseries of the Middle East.

I also was deeply influenced by the character and coaching of my mother's father, Syed Effendi Hegazy. He started as a simple farmer. He learned math and accounting on his own and climbed the ladder to become the chief cashier of the vast agricultural land and real estate properties and estates of Prince Muhammad Ali. He used to take me with him to the office at the Manial palace, which was a block away from our home, and show me how to count the cash and balance the accounts. I shall never forget the scenes of my grandfather wearing his temporary black sleeves to protect his white shirt and the look of the money and vault as well as the sprawling flower gardens and fruit orchards of that palace, which was located in a Cairo suburb called "Manial El Rodah."

I still remember my primary school teacher, Mrs. Fowziyah. She was a kind and astute teacher. I will never forget how one day I went out with my parents and did not do my homework until I came back. My grandfather helped me with the homework since I was so sleepy from being out, and my teacher learned of what happened. She told me privately that a "bird" told her that I did not rely on myself in doing the homework and that she wanted me to promise to not do it again. I gave my promise. As far as I can remember, this was an important lesson and milestone in my life at the tender age of seven. I am indebted to her for her coaching and the promise she took from me. Since that time, I have done my homework and fulfilled my promise to the best of my abilities.

In middle school my character was shaped by two important figures. The first was my English school teacher, Abdel Ghani. He was a big man who carried a small stick with a small rubber hose on its end. He would kid with my best friend at school, but he would also instruct us to respect each other and to not call our friends sarcastic names. One day I did. My friend told him and I had to endure three hits on my palm from that small but hurtful stick. Since that day at the age of nine, I held full respect for everyone I met. To this day, I insist that my associates be called by the name his or her parents chose for each of them. I allow no nicknaming in any of the operations I am involved in. I am also indebted to the gymnastics teacher, whose name I unfortunately do not remember. He trained me to work hard within our team and to help us become the number one gymnastics team in Egypt. We won the most distinguished trophy and recognition in the country that year.

I remember my high school principal, Abdul Samee Bayoumy, who was a very strict school head who wanted his students to be the best in the country. He believed in me and encouraged me to be in charge of the school's radio station. Here, I had fun practicing my preferred hobby of producing radio programs, managing others on the team, leading the morning assembly, planning with others on the team what radio programs would be shared, and, of course, resolving political issues among the team members. I also remember the Arabic language teacher. He was a towering man who was a true reflection of a dedicated Egyptian from the farmlands and was educated at the oldest university in the world—Al Azhar. He was serious, hardworking, and dedicated.

At the university, I met the man who took me as a low-key and shy young man and made all the difference in my character. He knew how to bring out what was concealed inside me. He believed in me and gave me the chance to become the president of the Society of Chemical Engineering at Cairo University. His name was Professor Muhammad Aly Saleh. If there is a person who taught me what life is all about, it was him. He was a wonderful man. He taught us not only chemical engineering but also how to be a citizen in Egypt and of the world. He became a friend and a coach until he died. I also remember a humble man who was an important factor in my life. His name was Professor Yahia Mostafa Al Agamawy. He was a humble servant of the people, and he helped everyone. I learned from him to always stay away from the limelight, especially when you serve your people and those who need help. He worked hard for Egypt, and I was honored to work with him.

As I concluded my life in Egypt and before I left for America at the age of 24 in 1968, I wanted to find my partner in the journey of life. In Egypt, at that time, the only place a man could find his potential wife was at the university. After graduating at the top of my class, I was drafted to teach and do research at the Chemical Engineering Department at Cairo University in July 1965. Because of the death of my father, I decided to rely on myself in saving as much money as I could to help my mother and to save for the airplane ticket and other expenses associated with the impending travel to America. This prompted me to work very hard in order to earn overtime pay. I worked from 7:00 A.M. to almost 9:00 P.M. every day of the six-day week. As a side benefit, this allowed me to see and interact with at least 3,000 students at Cairo University School of Engineering. I was able to know them and their characters. In my pursuit for a wife, I looked for a young lady who was serious, hardworking, sincere, God-loving, reliable, and conservative. I considered many and I settled for the partner of my life, Dr. Magda Muhammad Tantawi Mobasher. I owe Magda many talents that she brought to our family. She worked hard with me in Madison, Wisconsin, with very humble means; she taught me how to plan with the least available resources, how to keep smiling and stay cool under the most severe challenges, how to have fun and plan trips to enjoy time as well as make time to "smell the flowers," how to raise two very accomplished daughters, and how to be loving and helpful to the community and most respected by everyone in the community. She always said that a busy family is a happy family, and she kept us busy with study programs, travel programs, school programs, and many programs that kept us happy and challenged. I am indebted to God, who gave me Magda, the mother of our two daughters, Dr. Maie and Marwa, and their wonderful children Amin, Nadim, Zane, Jude, and Adam. The best description of Magda was given by a very dear couple who are among our best friends, Dr. Ahmad Khalifah and his wife Dr. Aida Gumei. They used to repeat the Egyptian folkloric proverb, "Magda can dig a huge well by only using a simple needle." And she did. She always divided her work into small steps over many days and months until she achieved her ultimate goals. She and I used to dream together of our ultimate home. Sure enough, when we moved to southern California from Plano, Texas (a suburb of Dallas) in 1977, we found exactly that house. It was a gift from God. She practiced her green thumb hobby and applied her stepwise approach to raise a wonderful garden. I am indebted to God and Magda for the wonderful life I've lived. She is a wonderful mother, a loving grandmother, a good wife, a great community servant, a great scholar and employee, a wonderful friend, and a great host. All these talents were acquired from her parents, Dr. Muhammad Tantawi Mobasher, and her wonderful mother, Mrs. Fatima Abdel Rahman—the best mother-in-law one could ever have. I also want to acknowledge my two sons-in-law, Richard St. John and Muhammad Elbeleidy. Richard St. John introduced me to a new way of looking at Islam as the umbrella and the wings that cover and hug all faiths and as an extension of Judaism and Christianity in what I call the Judeo-Christian-Islamic world.

I am honored to have him and his family, Judge Richard and Mrs. Judy St. John, in our family. I also honor Muhammad Elbeleidy for his love, respect, dedication, and graceful statesmanship. I am thankful to God for having met him; his father, the late Mustafa Elbeleidy; and his mother, Nadia Elbeleidy.

I want to conclude this part of my life in Egypt by thanking the people of Egypt for their generosity and their sacrifice. In Egypt, I was educated free of charge, and the government—that is, the people of Egypt—paid me a generous monthly stipend to help me as a reward for my superior performance as a university student. My wife and I owe the Egyptian people a lot, and we hope that we are able to pay it back before we return to God, our creator.

On February 25, 1968, I arrived in America with very little means in order to try to prove myself at the University of Wisconsin in Madison. I was sponsored by Gordon A. and Emilda Bubolz. They took it upon themselves to support my application, to guarantee my educational financial needs for one semester, and to be my family in America. Mr. Bubolz was a senator in the Wisconsin assembly and an insurance company executive. His wife, Emilda, was a Norwegian immigrant who worked as a registered nurse. Magda and I owe this wonderful couple our success story in America. Words will never be sufficient to express our gratitude to God, who made them a part of our life. At the University of Wisconsin, I met a professor who believed in me and in my wife. He supported us and gave us the wonderful example of a humble scholar who lived below his means. Professor E. J. Crosby used his bicycle year-round in the cold, 30-below winters and in the hot, 90-degree summers to bike the 30 minutes to and from his office at the university. We are grateful for all he did for us.

In November 1971, my wife and our little one-year-old daughter Maie packed up and moved to Dallas, Texas, to work for an oil company—Atlantic Richfield Company (now a part of British Petroleum). My bosses were two distinguished engineers. The first was Don Wunderlich, who believed in my abilities and gave me a chance to work on the projects I was hired for and on many other projects that I pioneered after his support and encouragement. He loved innovation, and we produced wonderful research results. I also want to acknowledge my immediate boss, who was a skipper in the U.S. Navy when he was in service. He was sharp, straightforward, sincere, truthful, and to the point. Sometimes his comments could be hurtful, but I looked at him as my coach. I never forgot the day he handed me back my first report with many red lines, comments, and questions. He taught me how to write a memo, how to be specific and to the point. I thank him for his coaching. In Dallas, I met many friends and developed a wonderful community. I shall always remember our friends Ghulam Hussein Siddiqi and Mohammed Solaiman. Mr. Solaiman helped build the first masjid in Richardson, Texas—literally—brick by brick.

In September 1974, my wife, my daughters Maie and the newly born Marwa, and I moved to Kuwait to participate in the start of the Industrial Bank of Kuwait. I want to acknowledge a dear friend who was kind enough to give me the opportunity to know the people of Kuwait on the inside—something that many of the non-Kuwaitis who work in Kuwait did not even consider doing. He also happened to belong to the Muslim Shi'aa school of thought. He introduced me to local scholars who helped me study and broaden my knowledge of Islam to complement what I know based on the Sunni school of thought. I acknowledge Muhammad Abdul Hady Jamal's friendship.

In 1977, we moved to Los Angeles to join the prestigious Corporate Planning Division at Atlantic Richfield Company (ARCO). There, I met a man who had a profound effect on my character. He was Ron Arnault, who was the chief financial officer in charge of strategic planning. His words still ring in my head, "When you go to a meeting, do more than your homework before the meeting and keep the answers in your 'hip pocket'; do not talk until you are asked, and when you are asked, only give 20 percent of what you know." What a wonderful and wise way of living!

Between the fall of 1984 and the spring of 1986, I returned to Kuwait to participate in restructuring the Industrial Bank of Kuwait after a major stock market crash there. In 1986, I came back from Kuwait looking for a job. I want to acknowledge the man who saw my potential and gave me the chance to venture to a completely new field. That was the field of investment banking. Joseph Moure told me after a very long interview that he had decided that I should join the team because I had proven to be successful many times before and that meant I'd be successful in this business as well. I learned from Mr. Moure to focus at will and to read using my finger. This habit has become an important part of the training of any who works on our team.

Perhaps the man who changed the course of my banking career from conventional banking to RF banking is my dear friend Sheikh Saleh Abdullah Kamel. Sheikh Saleh Kamel has given me wonderful opportunities to learn from and meet many of the distinguished scholars, attorneys, and practitioners of RF banking in the world. He believed in my potential, and I thank him for his support and his visionary ideas.

We started LARIBA in 1987 in a humble way. I want to thank all those who believed in the experiment and who invested the very dear $10,000 to start the company. I want to acknowledge Dr. Misbah El Dereiny and Sabry Abdel Azeez, who worked with me to register the company and get it started. I also want to acknowledge some of the partners who helped in making LARIBA the success it is today: Hany El Messiry, Abdullah Tug, Mike Maguid Abdelaaty, Maria Abdullahi, and the founding shareholders and directors of the company, including my dear friends Zubair and Khatija Kazi, Salim and Françoise Shah, Mahmoud and Amal Abdellateef, Mahmoud and Hoda Hassan, Muhammad and Nabila Fahmy, Morsy and Rawya Badawy, Samir and Effat El Kobaitry, Sulaiman El Khereiji, and Ahmad and Magda Hassan.

In 1998, we were successful in acquiring the Bank of Whittier, NA, California, and in July 2003, my wife and I agreed that I take early retirement to run the bank. My life was enriched by the many wonderful people that God has put into my path at the Bank of Whittier. I want to acknowledge the hard work and dedication of the wonderful staff, board of directors, and the bank holding company. I want to thank in particular Alexandra Dang and Wilson Yang for their contributions to the charts and the wonderful research work they conducted on commodity pricing and charting that are included in the book. I also want to acknowledge the trust that was invested in me personally by my dear close friends Zubair and Khatija Kazi, who have chosen to be an important part of the Bank of Whittier project. I also want to thank our attorney, Gary Findley, for all his support and belief in us.

I want to thank all my friends who helped in making this book possible. In particular, I want to acknowledge Shahzad Malik, Esq.; Professor Metwally Amer; and Salim Shah, who spent tireless hours editing and proofreading the manuscript. I sincerely appreciate your time and effort.

Finally, I want to thank a dear friend of mine who lives in London, and who recommended my name to John Wiley & Sons to invite me to write this book. He is Tarek El Diwany, who is a wonderful researcher in monetary issues pertaining to RF banking.

Finally, I want to thank all of our customers, depositors, and investors of all faiths for their trust. I also want to thank my wonderful fellow Americans who are making Islam and the American Muslims part of this wonderful emerging new Judeo-Christian-Islamic America.

About the Book Cover

The book cover was designed by your author to encapsulate, using a metaphor, the banking, financial, and monetary system.

The elephant here represents the whole system: The elephant body reflects the system of banks, financial institutions, regulators, and the economy at large. The head of the elephant represents the Federal Reserve in the United States and the central banks in the country involved. The elephant's head is the most important part of the elephant that directs it and manages its movements. If it is well managed and firmly stirred, it can be driven easily by a small-sized man (or woman). The citizens can sit on top of that elephant and enjoy a pleasant life journey with their homes secured in the background, as seen in the painting. At the bottom of the cover sits a picture containing different currencies of the world, representing the different monetizing fiat currencies used in the world painted in gold as a reference to value, in addition to other precious metals and staple foods as detailed in the book.

RF (Islamic) bankers and the RF scholars in the law (the Judeo-Christian-Islamic Shari'aa law) spent the second half of the twentieth century and the beginning of the twenty-first century in developing and producing finance models with emphasis on contracts using structuring and financial engineering. That is, we concentrated on a small portion of the body but completely ignored the head—the monetary policies, disciplines, and the fair and accurate definition of the real value of fiat (paper) money!

This edition is intended as a wakeup call to RF believers and adherents to develop a complete RF monetary discipline that focuses on defining the value of products and services in the market in real terms by using precious metals and staple foods of each culture as reference and calibrating tools, and not by using fiat (paper) currencies. Paper money, valued properly, can be used only for transactions.

CHAPTER 1

Introduction

This book is for all people of all faiths. Many may think that RF (riba/ribit-free) Islamic banking is for the Muslims only or for the Judeo-Christian-Islamic communities and that Islamic banking is a gateway to the significant wealth amassed by the oil-producing countries in the Gulf.

That is not true! And that is why I am writing this book.

This book is about *riba/ribit-free banking*, or *RF banking*, a new brand of banking and finance service. It can be identified as a faith-based, socially responsible, and community-based approach to banking. It is a service that aspires to serve all people of all faiths and backgrounds. It is believed that there is great demand for RF banking in the United States and the West, as well as in many developing nations worldwide. RF banking is a system that is not built on renting money to those who need it at a price called the interest rate, but is based on renting a tangible asset, such as a car, home, tools and equipment, and businesses at the prevailing actual market lease rates.

In 2001, we at LARIBA (www.LARIBA.com), and later (since July 2003) at the Bank of Whittier, NA (www.BankOfWhittier.com) started a dedicated effort to brand Islamic banking with a new name: *riba-free*, or RF, banking to describe what this new brand of banking and finance really is. The effort we invested has paid off, and the riba-free description and the RF brand name are now used globally. RF is slowly replacing the name "Islamic" banking. After living for more than 46 years in the United States, we came to understand the sensitivities of many in the country toward mixing state and church matters. In the United States, there is a deep-seated belief that the state and church must be separated. The U.S. system of separating church and state implies that a church is not permitted to run the state and, by the same token, the state cannot interfere in and run the affairs of a church. This way, churches (and other places of worship) can keep their independence and focus on producing spiritually, ethically, and morally qualified men and women to send to the state in order to run it.

The name we have advocated and are promoting is *riba-free* and is branded as *RF*. It starts with the word *riba*, a sister-word to the term *ribit* used in the Old Testament. *Riba* means the act of taking advantage of those who need money to meet their basic necessities through the act of renting them money at a price called "interest." RF banking is a brand of banking that is socially responsible and is community based in both spirit and intent. This brand of banking is the manifestation of Judeo-Christian-Islamic values, which are deepening in America and the world. RF banking and finance is a new way of living without having to carry the burden of an ever-accumulating debt through the unnecessary overuse of loans to satisfy the instinct of consumerism (such as the use of credit cards to borrow, home equity lines of credit, and loans of all other types—secured and unsecured).

RF banking pays close attention to whom and what to finance. RF banks do not, for example, finance alcohol- and gambling-related businesses, such as liquor stores or gambling casinos. It also does not finance environmentally irresponsible companies and businesses that are not fair to their employees. It is believed that RF banking will bring back to the United States and the world the characteristics of the banking movement that built America, as dramatized by the famous Hollywood actor Jimmy Stewart in the movie *It's a Wonderful Life*. I believe that Jimmy Stewart was the first American to present, in this movie, the real character of an RF banker. Based on actual operating experience, our customers of all sorts of religious beliefs, including people of Hindu, Buddhist, Judaic, Christian, and Muslim faiths, as well as those who choose not to have a religion, appreciate and love to use the concepts and discipline of RF banking. Their consistent feedback is "we have not heard other bankers who operate and are disciplined like this before . . . we feel that you care about us as members of your family." Escrow company officers love the way we, the RF bankers at the LARIBA System, serve people and our approach to financing. It is interesting to note that a few escrow company employees, after reviewing our closing documents for their customers, voluntarily called us to finance their homes with us. It is important to note that RF banking is cost competitive with conventional riba-based banks.

The modern RF (Islamic) banking movement started in a humble way as a small community finance effort in Egypt (1963) and grew gradually to become a small emerging finance industry in the Middle East (1973). Today, with the increase in demand for oil and gas and the increase in energy prices, many of the Gulf oil-producing countries have accumulated large amounts of cash. Some of the owners of this cash have decided to use RF banks to manage it. This has helped the RF banking industry become better established and a high-growth industry. RF banking came to Europe in the early 1980s. Britain has an Islamic bank (Islamic Bank of Britain [IBB]). Many European municipalities and governments are dealing in *Islamic banking* products, mainly asset-based bonds (*sukuk*). In Asia, many countries have

RF (Islamic) banks and/or finance companies. Malaysia has one of the pioneering and most sophisticated RF (Islamic) banking industry in the world.

At the time of the original writing of the first edition of this book in 2008, the United States and the rest of the world were experiencing a major financial, monetary, and economic meltdown, the likes of which had not been experienced since the Great Depression of the 1930s. The crisis moved the world from the financial and monetary norms of the twentieth century to a new era for the twenty-first century. It is believed that this shift may bring most banks—of all brands—closer to the values, methods, and philosophy of the RF banking brand. In addition, an increasing number of Americans will eventually choose to live a life that is riba free, which reflects the real manifestation of the Judeo-Christian-Islamic value system.

In 2007 and 2008, we in the United States suffered the worst housing crisis in our history when the average home price declined drastically by 20 to 50 percent. This crisis dwarfed the economic meltdown of the Great Depression of the 1930s. This time around, the meltdown involved the major economies of the world. Subprime lending and manufactured riba-based financial securities made by packaging home mortgage promissory notes called mortgage-backed securities (MBSs) were sold to commercial and investment banks around the world as high-quality (AAA) securities. This was not the case. With the decline of the real estate market and the nonperformance of many of the home mortgages, especially the subprime mortgages, investors (many were large international banks and financial institutions throughout the world) discovered that these were not high-quality AAA securities after all. This massive discrepancy created huge historic losses for the largest banks in America and the world, resulting in the failure of major banks and severe declines in the stock markets of the whole world. These events caused the financial system to suffer a deep lack of trust between banks' managers and chiefs of its investment banking units as well as investment banks in general. Many banks in America and around the world ended up holding financial papers that suddenly became illiquid. The result was a liquidity crunch of major proportions, leading to a worldwide credit crunch. This situation has led many banks to refuse to support each other's overnight borrowing needs to provide short-term liquidity. Many banks all over the world woke up to see their capital wiped out or drastically reduced. Some U.S. banking icons, such as Lehman Brothers, were pronounced bankrupt. Others, such as Washington Mutual (now merged with Chase), Wachovia (merged with Wells Fargo Bank), Citibank, and Merrill Lynch (now merged with Bank of America), to name a few, announced hundreds of billions of dollars in write-offs. The U.S. and European governments announced financial rescue packages of more than $2 trillion to help inject fresh capital into the banks, insurance companies, and finance companies. The U.S. government took over the giant mortgage finance institutions Fannie Mae and Freddie Mac, and started devising ways and means to rescue other industries like the automobile industry.

Americans, however, especially the hardworking middle-class families who wanted to realize the American dream of owning a home, to save for a comfortable retirement, or to save in order to be able to send their children and grandchildren to better schools, lost their savings. Their savings were in the form of retirement and pension plans, the assets of which were invested in the failed companies' stock or in mutual funds. Some also lost their homes after losing their jobs. The main reason was the fraudulent mortgage lending practices of many of the unregulated so-called mortgage "bankers," and the new mortgage loan products they manufactured and marketed throughout the United States under glitzy acronyms like:

- *ARMs*, or adjustable rate mortgages, which start at a very low interest rate (and hence a low monthly payment). They are sold to gullible consumers by convincing them that interest rates will not go up! Because families intended to move within two years to a new house (before the interest rates change), ARMs were considered a great financing idea by many, including Alan Greenspan (former U.S. Federal Reserve Board chairman). People acted as though they could predict the future of the financial and housing markets with precision. As has been usually the case, the market has proven them wrong. When interest rates jumped higher and the monthly payments doubled, it became difficult for the consumer to service the home mortgage loan.
- *Interest-only loans* misled the public by promising them low monthly payments on their home mortgages by paying only the interest on the loan and no principal, while enjoying the promise of home price appreciation. The underlying assumption was based on the premise that home prices would rise to no end. This, theoretically, would benefit the consumer by building a "huge" equity at the cost of a very small monthly payment! The rest of the terms were not made clear—for example, one such loan's "fine print" might state that the loan would balloon and would be due in full, in three to five years. This meant that, although it was not explained or forewarned by the mortgage salesperson, the customer would have to either sell the house (and hopefully make a "lot of money" to pay off the loan and keep a handsome profit) or refinance the home. As has been the case, home prices declined, and most of those who used this finance method lost their homes and their hard-saved equity investments.
- *Negative amo (amortization) loans* were engineered so that the home buyer would agree to a monthly payment that would suit his/her budget

needs; if rates were low, then the small monthly payment of the loan would cover the interest and principle. Conversely, if interest rates rose higher, the loan value would increase, because the constant small monthly payments would not cover the needed payment of interest and principal. The shortfall was added to the existing loan, making it bigger. The hope was that home prices would appreciate eternally. Unfortunately, these loans were most often sold to retired senior citizens, who ended up losing their homes.

- *Stated income/no-doc loans*[1] required no documentation to get approval! The only disclosure needed from the applicant was to state his/her income, and the mortgage broker or banker would not even have to verify it. This accommodation was created by commercial banks to be implemented in very special cases. It was meant to be used only by sophisticated and highly experienced bankers for the services and needs of very high-net-worth individuals and entities, which represent a small portion of the population, to reduce the time and the huge efforts necessary to gather and document their vast and diversified assets in full. Instead, this approach was used by the commission-motivated mortgage "bankers" and brokers to lure those with undocumented income—such as those who run cash businesses—regardless of their ability to make the payments and service the loan.
- *Subprime loans* were used when a loan application based on stated income did not qualify for approval because the applicant's credit rating was very low. The idea was to still finance them, but at a premium because of the high risk involved. With the collaboration of investment bankers, a huge *subprime lending* mortgage business started to bloom. In this supposedly win-win business, the mortgage banker won because he or she made a hefty commission that could be as high as 6 to 8 percent of the value of the loan, and the investment banking firm won because it could "package" these loans inside an MBS that combined some of these subprime promissory notes with a certain higher proportion of the low-risk, high-quality mortgage notes. Rating agencies in the United States assigned these packaged MBSs a rating of AAA. This blending of the good-quality mortgage notes with the lower-quality subprime notes helped enhance the yield of the resulting MBSs. Investment bankers sold this higher-yield—supposedly AAA—class of securities to banks in the United States and the rest of the world, pension plans, and finance and investment companies around the world. In the process, the investment banks realized a huge commission. To squeeze more profits, they used additional derivative speculative techniques that turned against them, leading to the crisis. A significant mortgage investment company invited me to a "top executive" industry conference designed to entice

participants to participate in the "booming" and very rewarding subprime market. LARIBA simply refused because our values—based on the Judeo-Christian-Islamic values—require us never to dig a deeper pit of debt for those who we know cannot service that debt.

We have experienced interesting situations in the course of conducting our mortgage banking business at LARIBA. For example, a typical mortgage "banker" in America during the mortgage boom years from 2000 to 2007 was typically a young person, just graduated from—in most cases—high school, with no experience. They introduced themselves as the owner, president, or senior vice president of a loan brokerage or mortgage banking firm. These mortgage bankers were primarily motivated by the commission they make on each loan they fund, which can be up to 8 percent of the loan (e.g., for a $200,000 loan, they would make $16,000). Many of them closed at least 10 loans a month, for an income of more than $160,000 a month! Some of these brokers prospected very low-income families to get them to buy homes and take loans they could not afford. One of these low-income hardworking families was that of our own gardener and his wife. The only thing the mortgage broker asked them for was their Social Security numbers, dates of birth, and signatures on the bottom line of a loan application. Bingo! They got the loan and the young mortgage banker got a fat commission. When our gardener (a U.S. citizen of Latino origins) told us that he had signed up with a mortgage broker to finance a home for $345,000 with no down payment, we suggested that we finance his mortgage at LARIBA to make sure that the process was made easy and inexpensive. In fact, we could not compete. For example, LARIBA required detailed documentation, while his loan broker did not. In addition, the loan pricing offered by Washington Mutual (now merged with Chase) in a special program for minorities was much lower than the market. After 2008, the gardener had a difficult time keeping up with the monthly payments he could have afforded to start with, and the house was foreclosed on. The family went through a turbulent, traumatic emotional experience because they lost their home.

It is believed that two fundamental reasons caused this housing crisis and all previous financial crises and may cause many more future crises if not fixed:

1. *The monetary regime the world is following*. This regime was devised by the Bretton Woods Agreements in 1944 after World War II. It was broken in August 1971 by President Nixon, when he closed the "gold window" and allowed the gold price to adjust to the market forces of supply and demand, instead of fixing it at $35 per ounce as stipulated by the Bretton Woods Agreements. The Bretton Woods system has not

been thoroughly overhauled since. The world has ended up working with an incomplete and broken system since 1971.

2. *Our dangerous culture of greed and selfish consumerism.* The values of responsible citizenry and civilized behavior can only begin at home, with parents (and especially the mother) who set the tone, the ambience, and conscience of the household by insisting that everyone does what is good and what is right. Every Christmas season, the American public watches on television and is deeply touched by Frank Capra's movie *It's a Wonderful Life,* in which actor Jimmy Stewart played the small-town manager of the Building & Loan Society. He had humble means at his disposal, but he and his staff and family made memorable inroads in improving his community and the lifestyle of its families. The movie also dramatizes the way this community banker and his supportive wife were appreciated by their community. That is why this character can be called the character of the first RF banker in America.

In contrast, today's bankers like those enacted by Jimmy Stewart in the aforementioned movie are in short supply, and their passion for helping the community was lost in the maze of trying to manufacture new products and schemes to make money through fees and speculation, aggressive lending practices to meet sales goals, and the excessive use of speculative hedging. One example is hedge funds with mammoth assets, which are active speculators in stock shorting,[2] options,[3] futures,[4] and derivatives.[5] These techniques and the financial instruments used to implement them have prompted the bankers to devise games to corner and outmaneuver competitors, "making" more money on money without a measured productive contribution to the economic well-being of the community or the country. It is true that all these activities have been done with the objective of realizing more profits. There is no problem with earning money and realizing great returns on shareholders' equity while benefiting the shareholders, the community, and the country. However, we must ask how these earnings were realized and whether they added economic value and productivity to the community.

Today's banking, finance, and economic lingo is amazingly descriptive when used to describe what is happening. Some financiers and bankers tell us that they represent the capitalistic system's promise of *making money*. We respectfully submit that this is not true! *Making money* (i.e., manufacturing money) is done at the printing presses by order of the Federal Reserve in the United States or the central bank of the country involved. The words we should use and should train our bankers, our financial officers, and our children to use are *earning money*. The word *earn* implies that the person has gained an income as a reward for a responsible service or an activity he offered. We all remember when parents taught their children to ask themselves before they went to sleep "how much I earned today and what good I have done to earn it."

The culture of making, spending, and wasting money has now become prevalent worldwide. It is based on the false premise of making money on money, which is done by renting money at a rental price called interest rate (called *ribit* in Judaism and *riba* in Islam). Applying this process of reasoning, one can lend money at a rental rate of 8 percent to another person. The borrower is happy, because he/she can pay the money back later, after satisfying his or her consumptive instinct to acquire things so as to be perceived as a respectable member of society and a successful businessperson! Credit cards (which used to be called charge cards when presented first in America in the early 1960s, indicating that they are not cards that can be used to borrow money but to facilitate commerce and to be paid back within a month) have made it even easier to overindulge.

But the ultimate excess of all excesses has been to encourage people, through the culture of money rental (which is riba), to use their home equity as a credit card by taking out *home equity loans*. It is understood that a family would use a home equity line of credit to improve and upgrade their house, for example, to add a new room for their new baby or a growing child. But the home equity line of credit should *not* be used to generate cash through another buzzword (*cash out*); to speculate by buying another home to take advantage of low interest rates and capture the potential of a rising real estate market; or to buy an expensive car, take an expensive cruise or a European tour, or simply gamble with it in the stock market. For these reasons, bankers should be trained to ask, "Why do you need the money?" and decide whether the home equity line of credit is justified and necessary. Of course, we live in a free society, and every citizen is free to do what he/she wishes; we all must respect that freedom dearly. However, each banker is also free to set the rules, policies, and discipline of investing the bank depositors' money and shareholders' capital that will be applied to finance people's needs. Any banker can decide whether he/she is really out to invest in—and, conceptually, with—people in the community, or if he/she is simply renting them money at a rental rate called the interest rate.

The concept of the interest rate and the resulting riba-based culture of renting money is the subject of this book.

It is sincerely hoped that this book will make a humble contribution to a better future for the United States and the world by offering a new brand of banking; RF banking, to the American banking system—the most fair, most sophisticated, and most regulated and governed banking system in the world—which will bring back to the forefront the passion of RF bankers for serving communities' needs.

RF banking has become an important factor in the world of finance. A few years ago, we conducted a nonscientific survey among our friends.

We asked them what came to mind when we said the words "Islamic banking." The answer was: "vast amounts of oil money from the Gulf countries, which are waiting to find investment opportunities!" Unfortunately, what you'll read about in this book is more than just getting hold of these vast resources. It is intended that this book *will* help you understand the basic concepts and discipline of RF (Islamic) banking, which will help your creative mind to develop ideas that can be communicated with the fund managers in these oil-rich Gulf countries and hopefully develop mutually rewarding business relationships. It is hoped that this book will help in achieving better understanding among all people of all backgrounds and of all faiths.

The Jewish Bible, the Christian Bible, and the Qur'aan all prohibit the act of charging rent for the use of money. In the Old Testament, it is called *ribit;* in the Qur'aan, it is called *riba.* So RF (*riba/ribit-free*) banking is involved in investing in and conceptually with people in the community, rather than with renting them money and charging them for the use of that money. In earlier days, the act of charging for the use of money was called *usury* by the Catholic Church in its early days, before the rules were relaxed after the fifteenth century. Unfortunately, today *usury* is defined as *excessive interest.* Sadly, no one offers to complete the definition of the word *excessive* by telling us the reference point above which it becomes excessive!

As outlined earlier, the preferred way to refer to Islamic banking is to call it what it really is. The preferred term must be descriptive and inclusive of all faiths, especially the Abrahamic Judeo-Christian-Islamic cultures, value systems, and faiths. In this book, it is advocated to call it *RF banking and finance* (*R* for riba/ribit, and *F* for free). RF banking is a new alternative banking brand presented to the world by the LARIBA System.

In 1987, when we started the operations of American Finance House LARIBA in Pasadena, California, to deliver RF finance services, we met and interacted with many wealthy individuals, learned scholars, and experienced banking practitioners, as well as accomplished international business and corporate attorneys. Some of us, including myself, were fortunate enough to attend many meetings with distinguished religious scholars, during which various financial, investment, and monetary aspects of modern banking and finance were discussed and explained by practitioners in the presence of expert attorneys. We at LARIBA also were fortunate enough to attend meetings with international corporate attorneys to explain to them the religious scholars' opinions and suggestions regarding making the banking service and/or products RF or riba free (Islamic). This fascinating and educational experience was combined with our dream of establishing an RF financial institution for the community in America and made us think of what is ahead.

The major challenge was to determine how to build an RF finance company or bank that delivers RF banking and finance services to the community, especially in a world that is run using riba. It was a daunting and difficult task to devise an RF banking system that satisfies the requirements of the Judeo-Christian-Islamic law (the Shari'aa law), while simultaneously abiding by and following the laws and standards of the Western banking riba-based system, which has been at least 600 years ahead of RF banking in the sophistication of its standards, systems, and products.

The second edition includes a number of review questions at the end of each chapter. These questions can be used by the reader to utilize it as a reference textbook on the subject in universities and colleges and as quick review of the topics and issues discussed in each chapter.

This book has been organized in two parts. Part One, which consists of eight chapters, focuses on the building blocks of the RF banking system:

- The faith-based aspects of the Judeo-Christian-Islamic value system, which prohibits ribit/riba, will be discussed in Chapter 2.
- The unique principles of the *Commodity Indexation Discipline,* which normalizes prices in the market away from the dollar by valuing these prices using precious metals and/or staple commodities, and the *Mark-to-Market Discipline*, which disciplines RF bankers to evaluate every financing and "lending" operation as an investment, will be discussed in Chapter 3. In this methodology, the real (live) market rent of a car, a home, or a business is used to evaluate the economic prudence and viability of this investment and the monthly payment for a financing deal instead of using riba, which is the straight rental of money at a cost called interest rate.
- The wisdom and processes used to arrive at the faith-based rules, regulations, and laws by applying the Judeo-Christian-Islamic foundations and the methodology of the law (Shari'aa) will be detailed in Chapter 4.
- The definition of money and how money developed from being real, as defined by the law (Shari'aa: gold, silver, and basic food commodities) to becoming paper—*fiat*—money to suit the diversified large transactions' needs of the world (Chapters 5 and 6). The creation and management of money and the monetary system, the role of the central banks and the Federal Reserve System, and the definition of interest designed and implemented by the government to manage the amount of money in the system will be discussed. The foundations of riba in commercial transactions will be reviewed. The new and unique rules and RF monetary and investment discipline put forward by the Prophet Muhammad (pp)[6] to normalize market prices in a standardized fashion, in which he required the use of *Commodity Indexation* process in measuring market prices, and his rule of pricing every item on the basis of its market value using real currency (*noquood*, in Arabic, defined to be in silver or

gold or a commodity that represents a staple and needed staple commodities, like rice, barley, or wheat). Chapters 5 and 6 present very useful and revealing correlations that have been tested thoroughly during the past 28 years for early detection of price and economic bubbles in an economy. The discipline was used as an early warning indicator for fair pricing of consumer needs like cars, homes, and other commodities using the *Commodity Indexation Discipline* pioneered by the Prophet Muhammad (pp). These two chapters will take the reader on a wonderful journey that will provide insight on pricing things in the market using reference basic commodities, and the implications learned from these correlations will be discussed.

- The social responsibility of citizens entrusted with the keeping of people's money and assets—that is, the RF bankers—will be discussed in Chapter 7. The concepts of civility and social responsibility based on the Judeo-Christian-Islamic value system will be presented as a means to establish the most important spirit, substance, and foundation for the RF banking brand.
- The American banking system's tremendous achievements (and its associated banking regulations and acts developed over the years) have been an important force in the world. Chapter 8 details the system and the ways in which it is based on a huge body of human experience rooted in the Judeo-Christian-Islamic value system that cannot be ignored. Chapter 8 also recommends that RF banking religious scholars, regulators, and practitioners understand U.S. banking regulations and systems and build on them. Many of the regulations, as is shown in this chapter, are rooted deeply in the values of the Judeo-Christian-Islamic system.
- Many ask about the difference between RF banking and conventional riba-based banking. Chapter 9 is an attempt to explain the history of RF banking and how it has developed since the early 1950s. In addition, the chapter discusses and articulates the differences between RF banks and conventional riba-based banks.

Part Two, which consists of 10 chapters, attempts to integrate the pieces discussed in Part One to develop a reliable, well-designed, and beneficial RF banking system that is true to the Judeo-Christian-Islamic law in both spirit and substance.

Part Two begins by summarizing the goals defined by two groups of RF (Islamic) bankers. The first group started in good faith and with good intentions from the existing contracts and systems used in conventional banks and tried to sometimes force an RF "Islamic" solution and terminology on the system. This approach has been followed since the early 1960s, and is called *Shari'aa compliant*. The second group, pioneered by the author for the LARIBA System, developed a *Shari'aa-based* approach that uses the spirit and substance of the real intent, discipline, and methodology of RF "Islamic" banking, stressing the fact that it is rooted in the Judeo-Christian-Islamic value system and that it is designed for all people of all faiths without renting money. This Shari'aa-based approach is the basis for the RF banking system.

Following are the issues that will be discussed:

- Chapter 10 focuses on the Shari'aa-compliant techniques and methods used in RF (Islamic) financing in the twentieth century, detailing the most important aspect of the use of form (as in the case of Shari'aa-compliant banking) versus the use of substance (as in the case of Shari'aa-based RF banking detailed in the next chapter). The contract and the way it is structured in the Shari'aa-compliant approach will be contrasted with the Shari'aa-based approach.
- The art of RF banking is developed and analyzed in Chapter 11. This chapter introduces to the reader what is believed to be the new wave of RF banking in the twenty-first century, Shari'aa-based RF banking. This chapter details the many currents involved in the application and implementation of RF banking and the way these currents have been integrated in a way strictly based on the Judeo-Christian-Islamic Shari'aa law, while being operated according to the laws of the land. Perhaps the most important aspect of this twenty-first-century Shari'aa-based RF banking and finance model is that it saves its clients from participating in an economic and speculative bubble by testing the prudence of the investment based on the renting of a tangible asset and not the renting of money. RF bankers help the clients make sure that the investment is prudent and that this investment will make a real difference in people's lives and in the business itself. Eventually, this approach and discipline, when followed, will have a wonderful impact on stabilizing the markets.
- Chapter 12 puts all the RF disciplines presented and discussed in this book together into one integrated RF financing process followed at the LARIBA System.
- The unique and historic experience of restructuring an American bank to operate as an RF bank is detailed in Chapter 13. This chapter gives thorough details on the steps that were taken to change a riba-based bank's fortunes by restructuring the Bank of Whittier, NA, an American riba-based bank, to transform it to operate in an RF format and turning it around to profitability and compliance. In Chapter 13, the operation of an RF bank in the United States will be detailed, including the training and preparation of the RF bankers and descriptions of the different RF products offered at the bank. The challenge in the United States is

to abide by the laws of the land and the American banking regulations, while not violating the tenets of the Judeo-Christian-Islamic Shari'aa law. The other challenge is to develop RF banking products that compete with the products, services, and the huge experience and capital available to conventional riba-based banks in America. We will discuss these challenges as well as strategies for RF banking growth in the United States.

- Chapter 14 discusses the RF capital markets, which include RF asset-based bonds (*sukuk*) and the guidelines for investing in the stock market according to the Judeo-Christian-Islamic Shari'aa law.
- Chapter 15 includes examples drawn from real life to illustrate the development and application RF banking investment products.
- Chapter 16 includes a discussion of the RF credit (loan) products that can be offered in an RF bank and the wisdom associated with it in contrast to those loan products offered by a conventional riba-based bank.
- Chapter 17 includes a discussion on handling nonperforming credits (loan) in an RF bank in contrast to the methods used in a conventional riba-based bank.
- Chapter 18 gives a peek into the future regarding your author's vision of the RF banking brand in the current economic climate, and offers advice to those who are considering living an RF lifestyle.
- In Chapter 19, the author addresses challenges and strategies for the popularization of RF banking in the United States and the world.

It is sincerely hoped that this book will open many eyes and hearts in all fields to realize a better world that will share prosperity fairly and become more peaceful and prosperous.

NOTES

1. Also known as *NINJA loans* (No Income, No Job Application) and *liar loans* because many applicants gave incorrect information while completing the application.
2. *Stock shorting* is a method of profiting from a decline in a stock's price. It is the opposite of investing (or *going long*), in which the investor profits from a rise in the stock's price. *Shorting against the box* means shorting of a stock that one owns to protect against a loss in the value. However, *naked shorts*, or shorting of stocks that are not owned, may create market instability and dislocation that may have a negative impact on the company involved.
3. Trading an *option* on the stock exchange mean giving someone the right to buy or sell a certain stock at a certain price by a specific time. If you

buy an option to purchase securities, it is called a *call option*. If the option you buy is to sell securities, then it is referred to as a *put option*. Some traders even go so far as to purchase both calls and puts on the same stock, with agreed prices and by an agreed date; then it is called a *double option* or sometimes a *put and call option*.

4. *Futures trading* is unlike many other forms of speculating in the markets because one is not required to own or even buy the commodity. All that is necessary is to speculate on where the price of a particular commodity is going and make a decision based on that. If a person were speculating on crude oil, for instance, and he or she expected the price to go up in the future, that investor would buy a *crude oil futures contract*. And if he or she expected that the price would go down, the investor would sell *crude oil futures*.
5. A *financial derivative instrument* is a financial contract whose value is based on, or derived from, another financial instrument (such as a bond or share) or a market index (such as the Share Price Index).
6. The abbreviation *pp* stands for "May God's Prayers and Peace be showered onto them" (in Arabic, "Sallaa Allahu Alayhi Wa Sallam"), a standard idiom that is uttered by all Muslims after mentioning (or writing) any of God's prophets' names like Moses, Jesus, and Muhammad (pp), or hearing any of their names mentioned.

CHAPTER 2

The Faith-Based Judeo-Christian-Islamic Foundation of the Prohibition of Interest and the RF (Riba-Free) Banking System

This chapter studies in some detail the fundamental issue of the prohibition of riba (interest) in Islam and researches its foundations by tracing it back to its origins in the Jewish and Christian faiths and Bibles. An introduction to the religion of Islam is included at the beginning of this chapter to familiarize the reader with an overview of the fundamental foundation of Islam as revealed in the Qur'aan, the teachings of Muhammad (pp) as well as its links to the revelations to the teachings of Moses (pp) and Jesus (pp).

Charging interest (called *riba* in the Qur'aan and *ribit* in the Torah) is divinely prohibited in Judaism and Christianity as it is also clearly and strictly prohibited in Islam. That is why it is believed that this can present the followers of the Abrahamic faiths (Judaism, Christianity, and Islam) with a wonderful window of historic proportions to cooperate together to bring to market a credible, efficient, fair, and equitable financing and banking system—The RF (riba/ribit-free) banking and finance system—which uses the Judeo-Christian-Islamic RF banking and finance discipline. It is important to study, learn, and reflect upon the history of the prohibition of interest from the original teachings of Moses (pp) in the Torah (Jewish Bible), the teachings of Jesus (pp) in the Christian Bible, and the teachings of Muhammad (pp) as revealed in the Qur'aan to discover how these attitudes and disciplines developed over time and eventually produced the more relaxed interest-based banking and finance practices used today.

The main reason for the prohibition of ribit/riba—the prohibition of renting money to those who need it—is to prevent those who have money from taking advantage of and abusing the freedom of the poor and the needy. Slavery became rampant among the Hebrews in ancient Egypt because of the charging of ribit on loans needed by those who did not have the money to buy seeds or to meet their daily needs. When Moses (pp) came to free the Hebrew slaves, he was taught by God to remove ribit from society as revealed in the Torah and later explained and elaborated on in the Talmud by the learned rabbis. It is interesting to note that the rabbinical laws do not allow a Jewish person to stand as a witness in a Jewish court if he is involved in usury/interest. The prohibition of riba/ribit started the transformation process of societies and nations to freedom. It empowered the Hebrews to move out of Egypt behind the leadership of Moses (pp) by crossing the Red Sea to establish new settlements and farmlands. When Jesus (pp) was commissioned to preach God's teachings, the society he was sent to consisted of people who lived in an agrarian society with slavery being practiced. Jesus (pp), as revealed and taught in the Bible (Injeel—the name used for the Bible, in Arabic, among the Muslims), propagated the principle of prohibiting the use of renting money to the poor and the needy as a tool to enslave them and to eventually confiscate their collateral properties, including agricultural lands of the farmers if they could not pay their debt back as agreed. It is interesting to note that in the early days of the Catholic Church, a Catholic who participated in usury/interest through charging it or receiving it is denied a Catholic burial. When Prophet Muhammad (pp) was commissioned by God, the world was experiencing the dawn of the commercial era and international trade. Islam taught, reinforced, and made into law the principles of prohibiting ribit/riba, which involves the rental of money at a price called usury or interest rate and the use of money to take advantage of the unfortunate circumstances of people by confiscating their freedom and eventually turn them into slaves if they do not pay back the principal and usury (riba or interest) at the agreed-upon time. In addition, and in order to meet the demands of the new society of expanding trade and international business, Islamic teaching started a business revolution to define the disciplines, regulations, and rules needed for riba-free business and trade financing, as revealed in the Qur'aan and according to the teaching of Prophet Muhammad (pp).

In Christianity, it is interesting to note that according to the First Century A.D. oral tradition of the Pharisees (a Pharisee is a member of an ancient Jewish sect, distinguished by strict observance of the traditional and written law, and commonly held to have pretensions to superior sanctity) as committed to writing in *Mishnah Sheqalim* 1:3–6, money changers who had "set up in the Temple" exacted "surcharges" for their services. In Christianity, Jesus Christ (pp) stated that one of his goals is to drive the money changers out of the Temple (John 2:15–15; Matthew 21:12–13; Mark 11:15–18).

S. C. Mooney, an author and a leading contemporary Protestant opponent of interest on money, states: "What is being argued here is not a new idea, or a new interpretation of Scripture. It is the historic position. This is not a call to strike out in a new direction; it is a call to return to faithfulness to God. . . ."

It is also interesting to note that under the Biblical concept of the Jubilee (the word *Jubilee* in the Hebrew Scriptures means a year of rest to be observed by the Israelites every 50th year, during which slaves were to be set free, alienated property restored to the former owners, and the lands left untilled), no indebtedness would last longer than the sabbatical seventh year. Visitors to Philadelphia, Pennsylvania, will notice that the key Jubilee passage from Leviticus (25:10) was engraved on the Liberty Bell in Philadelphia by the founders of the United States of America.

History also documents that as late as the fifteenth century, movements abounded to eradicate the renting of money for a price called interest—in other words, to prohibit usury. For example, during the time of the Protectorate that administered the kingdom under England's first fully Protestant monarch, the boy-king Edward VI, the laws of England were returned to their immemorial Catholic position on usury, last implemented by the English Catholic King Henry VII in 1495. All interest on money was declared illegal. The Protestant Edward VI's law banning usury is one of the most stirring documents authored against usury. It is interesting to note that King Henry VII's prohibition of usury in his realm was overthrown in 1545 by his son and successor, King Henry VIII.

As an adherent to Islam and not to Christianity nor to Judaism, the author felt that it would be more appropriate, fair, and credible to study the prohibition of the charging of usury (charging interest to rent money in Judaism and Christianity) is to ask an expert scholar who is also an adherent to each faith and who has demonstrated expertise in the field of finance to summarize the position and the original teachings of his/her faith on usury/the charging of interest on money. It was thought that it would also be useful to discuss how these clear theological injunctions that prohibited the charging of usury/interest were modified, diluted, and/or reconstructed to become in the current acceptable form and which led to the practice of freely and openly charging interest on money.

ISLAM: THE ADDITIONAL AND CLOSING LINK IN THE CHAIN OF JUDAISM AND CHRISTIANITY

This section is thought to form an important foundation to one of the goals of this book, which is to offer a Judeo-Christian-Islamic solution to the problem of renting money at a price called interest rate. It is an introduction to Islam, with an emphasis on how Islam ties itself by the revelations of the Qur'aan to the teachings of Abraham and all his descendants, including Moses (pp) and Jesus (pp).

The basic foundation of faith in Islam is belief in God; in all of God's prophets, including Prophet Abraham (pp[1]) and his children Ishmael (pp) and Isaac (pp) and their descendants; and in subsequent appointed prophets, including Joseph (pp), Moses (pp), Jesus (pp), and Muhammad (pp). A Muslim is a person who submits his/her will to that of God. A Muslim believes that the "people of the book" (as the Qur'aan refers to them) are those brothers and sisters in Judaism and Christianity who received a book of guidance and discipline of living from God: the Torah in the Jewish Bible, the Gospel in the Christian Bible.

It is important to note that part of the creed of a Muslim is that he/she must believe in Moses (pp) and Jesus (pp). Moses (pp) liberated the Hebrews from the slavery practiced against them by the ancient Egyptian Pharaohs and God spoke to him and gave him the Ten Commandments, which were further developed into the Jewish Bible. On that part of the experience of Moses (pp), the Qur'aan[2] reveals:

> *4:164 Of some apostles We have already told thee the story; of others We have not; and to Moses God spoke direct;*

Jesus (pp) was later commissioned to revitalize, deepen, and expand on the teachings of Moses (pp). He taught the words of God and set the ultimate example of offering himself in sacrifice in order for the world to stay the course and for him to leave behind a shining example for all generations to come. This was recorded in the Qur'aan as follows:

> *3:45 Behold! The angels said: "O Mary! God gives thee glad tidings of a Word from Him: his name will be Christ Jesus, the son of Mary, held in honor in this world and the Hereafter and of (the company of) those nearest to God.*

As the world grew, its resources diversified, and its people started traveling to chart new local and international trading routes (resulting in growth in trade and commerce), the Prophet Muhammad (pp) was commissioned by God to expand further on the teachings of Moses (pp) and Jesus (pp) and to offer the people of the world at large a universal working model and various disciplines on how to live, raise a family, build a community, govern, and conduct business with each other.

Prophet Muhammad (pp) was a revolutionary, like Moses (pp), leading a movement to free the slaves and remove slavery of the body and the soul from Arabia and the world. He worked hard to educate and liberate the pagans in Arabia and the rest of the world, to set them free by worshipping only one God. He also followed and built on the example of Jesus (pp) by intensifying people's commitment to God; by softening people's hearts toward those who are poor, deprived, underprivileged, and in need; and by standing up in righteousness to those who abused their riches and powers in the name of religion to take advantage of the helpless poor, the underprivileged and the needy. In doing so, he made it easier for people to live together in peace, with justice and fairness for all.

With the emergence of the Roman/Byzantine Empire and the Persian Empire as the two leading superpowers during the time of Prophet Muhammad's (pp) mission, he was commissioned to offer the world, through the revelations of God's words in the Qur'aan and his living model (the *Sunnah*[3]) a detailed example of a living prophet who was a spiritual leader, the head of a state, and a businessman.

His actions and model of living were all fully documented because he was commissioned in the light of history brought on by the invention of paper and the printing press. He acted as a prophet and as a shepherd (like Jesus [pp] and Moses [pp]) and as a political leader and as head of the state defense forces. He expanded his responsibilities to offer a role model for being a successful merchant, an accomplished money manager, and an admired and trusted investor. Michael Hart, who was born in a Christian family,[4] states: "He [Prophet Muhammad (pp)] was the only man in history who was supremely successful on both religious and secular levels." While studying the Qur'aan and the style of living (the *Sunnah*) of the Prophet Muhammad (pp) depicted in the vastly researched, meticulously authenticated and documented body of his sayings (the *Hadeeth*[5]) and his traditions and story of his life (the *Seerah*[6]), we learn about similar models of living offered by Moses (pp) and Jesus (pp). Prophet Muhammad's life expanded on the examples of Moses (pp) and Jesus (pp) to demonstrate how to live in the more complex world of the sixth century. This new world included more sophisticated communication systems, transportation methods, and trading routes, as well as new businesses, more integrated markets, and expanded villages and cities—and a more sophisticated monetary and economic system. We read in the Qur'aan:

> *2:136 Say: We believe in God, and in that which has been bestowed from on high upon us, and that which has been bestowed upon Abraham and Ishmael and Isaac and Jacob and their descendants, and that which has been sent to Moses and Jesus; and that which has been sent to all the [other] prophets by their Sustainer: we make no distinction between any of them and it is unto Him that we surrender ourselves.*[7]

42:13 The same religion has He established for you as that which He enjoined on Noah—that which We have sent by inspiration to thee—and that which We enjoined on Abraham, Moses, and Jesus.

The religion of Islam as understood from the Qur'aan and the tradition of Prophet Muhammad (pp) reinvigorated the basic religious concepts brought by Abraham, Moses, and Jesus. Being a Muslim means to submit our will to the will of God by worshipping only Him and by abiding by His injunctions, which He revealed to all His prophets.

Conceptually, Islam can indeed be looked upon as part of an encompassing Judeo-Christian-Islamic tradition that extends back to the father and patriarch of all prophets, Abraham (pp). One well-read American Muslim stated that he researched all religions and philosophies to find a faith to which he could adhere. He concluded that Islam was it for him because it did not take away from him Moses (pp) and his Jewish beliefs in the Old Testament or his Christian beliefs in Jesus (pp) and in the Bible. He said that Islam, to him, was the umbrella that covered all and included all God's prophets and messengers. He added that Islam was to him like a tent that brought under it, in one house, the teachings of Moses (pp) in Judaism and Jesus (pp) in Christianity; it did not discredit these teachings, but rather intensified, reinforced, and deepened them.[8] This concept is exactly what is meant in this book by the Judeo-Christian-Islamic lifestyle.

The original teachings of Judaism, Christianity, and Islam prohibit lending money and charging interest/usury (the original word *usury* was used to mean paying a rent for the use of money; the meaning was changed to mean, in today's language, lending at an excessive interest rate), ribit (which means an increase over the original amount of debt, in the language of the Old Testament), and riba (which also means an increase, in the language of the Qur'aan). It is also interesting to note that charging interest is prohibited in Buddhism, Hinduism, and many other faiths and philosophies.[9] Muslims are taught that participating in the culture and practice of charging and/or paying interest (charging interest on lending money, borrowing with interest, and witnessing contracts that involve interest) is divinely prohibited (*haram*) and is one of the worst sins by the Islamic—that is, the Judeo-Christian-Islamic—laws (the term that will be used throughout this book for Judeo-Christian-Islamic law is Shari'aa, "the law"). The act of borrowing money with interest (riba) is not a socially and religiously acceptable behavior. In a typical Muslim society, borrowing money and paying interest is reserved only for meeting a dire need, and it is socially considered a shameful act.

Charging interest is also divinely prohibited in Judaism and Christianity. It is important to study, learn, and reflect upon the history of the prohibition of interest from the original teachings of Moses (pp) in the Torah

(Jewish Bible) and the teachings of Jesus (pp) in the Christian Bible with an eye toward how these attitudes developed into the more relaxed practices involving the renting of money (interest/usury) of today.

It was felt that a more appropriate and credible approach to studying the charging of interest in Judaism and Christianity is to ask an adherent to each faith who is an expert in the field of finance and banking to summarize the position and the original teachings of his/her faith on the charging of interest, and then to discuss how these clear Judeo-Christian-Islamic injunctions that prohibited the charging of interest were modified and reconstructed to become the current acceptable practice of charging interest. In March 2002, the board of directors of LARIBA in Pasadena, California, invited a Jewish rabbi, a Catholic professor, and a Protestant professor to author and present papers on the subject. The following is a summary of their analysis. The next section starts with a summary of the foundations of what I call the Judeo-Christian-Islamic value system and beliefs, followed by an analysis of the prohibition of interest/usury in Judaism, Christianity, and in Islam.

AN INTRODUCTION TO THE JUDEO-CHRISTIAN-ISLAMIC FOUNDATIONS OF FAITH

The following is a brief summary of the building blocks needed to develop a unified understanding of our approach and to study various religions and their position on charging interest.

The Book

Jews: People of the Jewish faith abide by the Jewish Bible, which is called the Torah and is referred to and is acknowledged in the Qur'aan. The people of the Jewish faith believe that it is the book revealed by God to Prophet Moses (pp). It is considered to be the main source of the Jewish law.

Christians: Adherents to the Christian faith abide by the Christian Bible. The Christian Bible comprises the Jewish scriptures in the Torah, which Christians traditionally refer to as the Old Testament, as well as documented writings from the period of Jesus (pp) and just afterward, which are referred to as the New Testament. The New Testament includes four versions of the life of Jesus (pp); each one was written by one of the saints of the Christian faith (St. John, St. Mark, St. Matthew, and St. Luke). The Bible also contains letters from Jesus's (pp) early disciples to various communities and groups; these letters elaborate on the teachings of Jesus (pp).

Muslims: Muslims abide by the Qur'aan. Muslims believe that it is God's last and final revelation to mankind. The Qur'aan affirms the revelation of the book to Prophet Moses (pp), which is referred to in the Qur'aan as the Torah. It also affirms the revelations to Jesus (pp), who came to confirm Moses's (pp) teachings and to expand on such teachings in the Gospel, which is called in the Qur'aan the *Injeel* (a word that is used by Arabic-speaking Christians to refer to the Bible). Muslims are taught that Islam came to affirm the teachings of all the Prophets of God, including the patriarch of all prophets, Prophet Abraham (pp), and all of his children and grandchildren, including Prophets Ishmael (pp), Isaac (pp), Jacob (also known as Israel [pp]), David (pp), Solomon (pp), and the many prophets who preceded the last three (i.e., Moses [pp], Jesus [pp], and Muhammad [pp]). The Qur'aan and the religion of Islam are believed to affirm the messages of Moses (pp) and Jesus (pp) and to expand upon them through the teachings of Prophet Muhammad (pp) in his dual role as the spiritual prophet and the head of the state. Conceptually, Islam and its prophet Muhammad (pp) popularize a Judeo-Christian-Islamic culture and law that are rooted in the teachings of all prior prophets from Abraham (pp) to Moses (pp) and Jesus (pp). A Muslim is required to believe in all of God's prophets, who are all looked upon as equal. The Qur'aan reveals:

> *2:136 Say: "We believe in God, and in that which has been bestowed from on high upon us, and that which has been bestowed upon Abraham and Ishmael and Isaac and Jacob and their descendants, and that which has been vouchsafed to Moses and Jesus; and that which has been vouchsafed to all the [other] prophets by their Sustainer: we make no distinction between any of them. And it is unto Him that we surrender ourselves."*

The People of the Faith

Jews: Ami in the Hebrew language means "my people" (i.e., the people of Moses or the people of the Jewish faith). The Jewish people are also known as the family of Israel, as Israel is another name for Prophet Jacob (pp). The word *Israel* means in Hebrew a person who strives and struggles (just as in the Muslim concept of doing *jihad*). In other words, Prophet Jacob's (pp) name—Israel—means "the struggler" or *mujahid* in Arabic. The word *ami* may be interpreted to mean all God's people, or all followers of the Jewish faith.

Muslims: Ummah in the Qur'aanic language (Arabic) is defined as the people (nation) of the faithful who have chosen to submit their will to the will of God. Notice the similarity between the words *ami* and *ummah*.

The foundation of the teachings of Islam is an affirmation of Judeo-Christian-Islamic values and law. The teachings of Islam state that there is no superiority of a people or a nation over other nations, except through the level of revering God, following His scriptures, and living by the model of all God's prophets, as manifested by the lifestyle and example of all of God's prophets. Muslims are taught that discrimination of any kind is a sin.

Loans

Jews: In the language of the Torah (*Hebrew*), the words *neshek* and *neshah* mean "interest."[10] The word *neshek* literally means a bite. Some other passages also use the words *ribit*, *tarbit*, or *marbit*, which literally mean "increase" and are similar in meaning to the word *riba* used in the Qur'aan. The word *noshem* means lenders. *Noshem* is the term used when speaking of lending to the general public. The word *lawah* is used when speaking of lending to friends and family members, but not for commercial transactions.

Muslims: In the language of the Qur'aan, the word *loan* is *qard*, and it, too, is derived from the verb "to bite" (taking a bite from one's assets). To prevent any circumvention of the Judeo-Christian-Islamic law, Shari'aa, only one type of qard is allowed in Islam—the *qard hassan*, an interest-free (good or benevolent) loan that is extended for a good cause to the poor, the needy, or the distressed.

Usury/Interest

Paying a rent for the right to use something was called *usury* from the early days of the Catholic Church until the fifteenth century. The Roman Catholic Church's original prohibition against usury was slowly relaxed by using the word *interest* instead of the word *usury*. The original meaning of *usury* was to charge a price for using (or renting) money. Today, however, *usury* is defined as excessive interest.

In the case of fungibles (such as wheat, which will be consumed or changes its nature upon use), it would be unjust to pay a price for renting them. This means that fungibles can be sold through a process of title transfer, but not rented. Applying this concept to money, one cannot charge a rent (interest) for the right to use money, because money is a thing.

In the case of nonfungibles, like an owned real estate property, title can be transferred for a price in a buy/sell agreement as defined by the market forces of supply and demand. In Shari'aa, it is called *Milk ul Raqabah* (which means ownership of title). There is also another right that a nonfungible property offers, which is the right of the owner to rent (or lease) the use of that item (such as renting a car or a house) to a lessee. In Shari'aa, it is called *Haq Ul Manfa'aa* (which means the right of usufruct). One can charge for the right to use a nonfungible.

The original teachings of the Old and New Testaments agree with the rules that taking usury on money lent (rent for the use of money) is unjust because this implies selling what does not exist; this evidently leads to inequality, which is contrary to justice. This is not much different from Islam's position on riba.

Riba charging and its divine prohibition (*haram*) in Shari'aa become clearer after learning about the history of the prohibition of interest charging (usury) in the Jewish and Christian Bibles. It also brings to mind an exciting thought: If all faiths of the children of Abraham (pp) agreed on the issue of prohibiting the charging of interest on loans, perhaps we can develop a Judeo-Christian-Islamic window that could lead to cultural unity in the United States and the world. This unity eventually would bring better understanding and cooperation between the people and the leaders of the three Abrahamic faiths, which would eventually lead to a different mind-set and a new style of living that could ultimately lead to peace, fairness, justice, prosperity, and social harmony in the local communities of the United States and the world at large.

All divine revelations in Judaism, Christianity, and Islam started from prohibiting the grievous act of taking advantage of the poor and the needy by charging them interest on the loans that they needed to help them survive and meet their basic needs. Abstaining from cutting out a bite (*qard*) of one's own money and giving it as an interest-free loan to those who are in need is a difficult decision to make, because there is no return on it. The Judeo-Christian-Islamic revelations consider this qard as a loan to God, who promises abundant return on it in this life and the hereafter.

Some of the rich and affluent may lend to the poor and the needy reluctantly, with the intention of showing off in front of others or of using the loan as a tool to control the needy by exploiting their labor or eventually confiscating their lands, houses, and crops. Historically, some of the rich gave their lower-quality assets and foods to the needy and overvalued it when it is returned. They also used harsh language, gestures, and actions to remind the poor and needy of the favors that they have been bestowing on them. All original teachings in Judaism, Christianity, and Islam clearly prohibit such behavior.

Islam advanced and expanded the law (the Judeo-Christian-Islamic Shari'aa law) one step further by divinely institutionalizing the rules of lending to the poor and the needy, pronouncing that the only loan that is recognized is known as *qard hassan* (a good bite/benevolent loan). It is divinely considered the only loan allowed in Islam. The qard hassan can be a term loan, with a time limit for the money to be paid back—in a flexible and merciful way, depending on the specific situation and needs of the borrowing poor and needy—or, in most cases, without a time limit. In fact, in Shari'aa the qard hassan is looked upon as a donation to be paid back by the heavily indebted (for good reasons) whenever they can afford to. The forgiven qard (or the intended bite) that was supposed to be collected out of the owner's assets is considered a loan to God. In Islam, as in the original teachings of Judaism and Christianity, no additional direct or indirect benefit (such as free labor, free use of the indebted person's residence, or receipt of gifts from the person who took the loan) can be drawn out of such a loan because these are considered services that command a value and, hence, are considered payments of implied interest over and above the original value owed. The Judeo-Christian-Islamic Shari'aa law even encourages that the payback be made at the place of residence of the poor borrower or the place the loan was given, whichever is more convenient to the borrower, to relieve that borrower from paying the cost of travel (which itself can be considered an implied interest payment). Judeo-Christian-Islamic law (the Shari'aa law) and rules stress that the dignity of the borrowers should be preserved by never telling others and/or disclosing to the public about the loan given to the poor or their condition in respect of the borrower's privacy. The law also stipulates that the lenders should never try to take advantage of the borrowers, never try to pressure them to expedite the payback of the loan, nor even frowning in their face. The law (Shari'aa) goes further, encouraging the Muslim to forgive the loan in case the borrower is heavily indebted and in no position to pay the loan off. The Department of Treasury of the State (*Bayt ul Maal*) is also made responsible by the law (Shari'aa) to collect alms (*zakah*) from the citizens and use part of this money to relieve those who are heavily indebted and cannot pay the loans back (giving alms in Islam is called *the ritual of zakah*, which means the ritual of purifying one's assets by paying back the right of God in these assets). The law (Shari'aa) requires that if the indebted person dies, the lender forgives the loan as a gesture of good will if the family cannot meet the demand. If the family is able to pay back, the heirs are required to pay the loan off.

By the advent of Islam, the world economic systems had changed from the slavery system of the ancient Pharaonic Egyptians during the time of Moses (pp) and the agrarian systems that were prevalent when Jesus (pp) was commissioned. The world had progressed with the development of sprawling villages, towns, and cities. Larger commercial trading caravans managed by traders and money managers traded commodities and merchandise products and manufactured goods from one country to another. They needed money, not because they were poor and needy but because they wanted to raise additional capital to help them grow their business, finance the goods, and expand their commercial activities. To resolve this demand for capital and to develop divinely accepted rules for financing without riba (in a halal way), the law (Shari'aa), as prescribed in the Qur'aan and the tradition of Prophet Muhammad (pp), expanded on the original teachings of the Jewish and Christian Bibles to develop riba-free (RF) techniques that revolutionized business financing. Prophet Muhammad (pp) was also a businessman and a money manager. He understood the need to finance trading and business activities. Islam presented an expanded Judeo-Christian-Islamic set of rules concerning the financing of trade and business in the seventh century. This expanded on the original teachings of Moses (pp) and Jesus (pp) to develop a unique and complete Judeo-Christian-Islamic law (Shari'aa) concerning finance. This law brought about a pioneering new RF finance system that can be used for just, fair, and equitable RF banking and finance. The RF finance system makes credit available to all people without discrimination (to meet personal credit needs, to finance commercial activities, and/or to finance business) and considers the ability to obtain credit to be a basic human right. This RF Judeo-Christian-Islamic approach comes with an important goal in mind: to bring about peace, justice, fairness, harmony, prosperity, peace of mind, job opportunities, and mutual respect among all people of all faiths and backgrounds, leading to a wonderful future of peace and happiness in the whole world.

THE JUDAIC POSITION ON THE CHARGING OF RIBIT (INTEREST): MONEY, LENDING, AND INTEREST IN THE TORAH AND THE JEWISH TRADITION[11]

Rabbi Yosef Kanefsky leads a Jewish congregation in one of the suburbs of Los Angeles, California. The board of directors of LARIBA contracted him in March 2002 to author a paper that summarizes the prohibition of charging interest on loans in the Jewish tradition. The following is an abbreviated summary of his work published by his permission.[12]

Loans to the Poor

Judaism's teachings about lending money are all based upon the biblical passage in Exodus, Chapter 22, verses 24–26. The verses read as follows:

> *24. When you lend money to any of my people, to the poor among you, you shall not be to him as a creditor, nor shall you impose upon him any interest.*

> *25. If you take your neighbor's [night] garment as a pledge (collateral), you shall return it to him by nightfall*
>
> *26. for that is his only covering; it is his garment for his skin. In what shall he sleep? And it shall come to pass, that if he cries unto Me, I will hear it, for I am compassionate.*

The word that sets the tone for the entire legal discussion is the word *ami*—my people—which is found in verse 24. God specifically regards those in need of loans as being His special people, to whom He is very close. The phrase "you shall not be to him as a creditor" is interpreted to mean that the lender is prohibited from reminding the borrower of his dependent status in any way. The borrower is beloved of God, and the lender must bear this in mind. Even a facial expression on the lender's part can constitute a violation of this prohibition.

But the most concrete expression of God's love for the debtor is, of course, the prohibition against the taking of interest. By rabbinical interpretation, not only is the lender prohibited from charging interest, the borrower is prohibited from offering to pay interest. The Torah rejects the entire notion of a loan as a transaction that brings benefit to the lender. According to the *Halacha* (rabbinical law), a person who either lends or voluntarily borrows with interest is disqualified from being a witness in court.

By rabbinical definition, interest can include considerations aside from cash (Bava Metzia, Chapter 5, Mishna 2). For example, it is prohibited to allow one's creditor to live in and use one's home or workplace rent free. It is even prohibited for the debtor to offer space to his creditor at a discounted rent. These are understood to be gestures through which the creditor realizes benefit from the loan he extended, and therefore are defined as "interest" by rabbinical definition.

It is important to note that all Jewish communities have *Free Loan Societies* that preserve both the spirit and the letter of the laws on dealing in interest. Often, the local Jewish federations or other community-wide organizations administer these interest-free loan societies.

Lending to Non-Jews with Interest

The question as to the permissibility of lending with interest to people who are not part of the Jewish community is debated in the Talmud (Bava Metzia 70b–71a). The Talmud's discussion is inconclusive, and the post-Talmudic rabbis take up the question. Moses Maimonides,[13] in his great Jewish legal code (Laws of Loans, Chapter 5, Law 2), rules that it is permissible for a Jew to charge interest to a non-Jew only when there is a dire need and in the amount necessary to provide himself with a basic living. To charge a usurious (higher-than-normal) rate is prohibited. The great rabbis of medieval France and Germany were somewhat more permissive under circumstances in which Jews were barred from most professions, and Jewish communities were singled out for taxation above the ordinary rates (commentary of Tosafot to Bava Metzia 70b).

Business Financing

In the sixteenth century, as life became much less agrarian and much more commercial, loans were no longer primarily extended for personal reasons, but rather to provide commercial capital. As these kinds of loans were vital for commercial success through business expansion and were not the kinds of loans first envisioned by the Torah, efforts were made to find a permissible vehicle for this kind of enterprise.

Rabbis in Poland and subsequently in other parts of Eastern Europe drafted and refined a document called *heter iska* (this is similar in structure to the *Musharaka* [Joint Venture] RF structure used in RF banking, as will be discussed later.) The essence of this document is to transform the lender-borrower relationship into an investment relationship. The provider of the capital becomes a partner in the venture in which the borrower will be engaging; the borrower will share a specified percentage of the realized profits with the lender/investor. This technical redefinition of the loan as an investment allowed Jewish commercial enterprises to succeed without violating the laws of prohibiting the charging of interest. The heter iska was refined several times to help ensure that the lender/investor would not be exposing himself to an unacceptable level of risk and that some measure of return would be contractually guaranteed. The heter iska is in common use to this day.

THE CHARGING OF RIBIT (INTEREST) IN THE ROMAN CATHOLIC TRADITION[14]: THEN AND NOW[15]

Professor Christopher Kaczor teaches (at the time of preparing this research installment) at Loyola Marymount University in Los Angeles, California. The board of directors of LARIBA contracted him in March 2002 to author a research paper that summarizes the prohibition of charging interest on loans in the Roman Catholic tradition, with an eye toward the history of the relaxation by the Church of the original prohibition. The following is an abbreviated summary of his work.[16]

Lending to the Poor

Jesus (pp) said, as stated in the Bible:

> *When the Son of man comes in his glory, and all the angels with him, then he will sit on his glorious throne. Before him will be gathered all the nations, and he will separate them one from another as a shepherd separates the sheep from the goats, and he will place the sheep at his right hand, but the goats at the left. Then the King will say to those at his right hand, "Come, O blessed of my Father, inherit the kingdom prepared for you from the foundation of the world; for I was hungry and you gave me food, I was thirsty and you gave me drink, I was a stranger and you welcomed me, I was naked and you clothed me, I was sick and you visited me, I was in prison and you came to me."*[17] *Then the righteous will answer him, "Lord, when did we see thee hungry and feed thee, or thirsty and give thee drink? And when did we see thee a stranger and welcome thee, or naked and clothe thee? And when did we see thee sick or in prison and visit thee?" And the King will answer them, "Truly, I say to you, as you did it to one of the least of these my brethren, you did it to me." (Matthew 25:30–42)*

In his *Summa Theologica*, St. Thomas Aquinas writes:

> *To take usury for money lent is unjust in itself, because this is to sell what does not exist, and this evidently leads to inequality which is contrary to justice. In order to make this evident, we must observe that there are certain things the use of which consists in their consumption: thus we consume wine [grape juice] when we use it for a drink, and we consume wheat when we use it for food. Wherefore in such like things the use of the thing must not be reckoned apart from the thing itself, and whoever is granted the use of the thing, is granted the thing itself and for this reason, to lend things of this kind is to transfer the ownership. Accordingly if a man wanted to sell wine [grape juice] separately from the use of the wine [grape juice], he would be selling the same thing twice,*[18] *or he would be selling what does not exist, wherefore he would evidently commit a sin of injustice. In like manner he commits an injustice that lends wine [grape juice] or wheat, and asks for double payment,*[19] *viz. one, the return of the thing in equal measure, the other, the price of the use, which is called usury.*[20]

St. Thomas Aquinas draws a distinction between the use of a thing and the thing in itself. Some items one can use without the item being destroyed by its very use—for instance, a house can be rented out and returned in good condition. However, the use of other things, like an apple, destroys the very thing used. Thus, you could not rent the eating of an apple, but only sell the apple, and in selling it, the transaction would be complete. Since money, on this model, is a thing consumed in its use, to charge a person interest on a loan is to demand payment for selling the money (principal) and another payment for renting the money (interest).[21]

Usury is condemned by St. Ambrose (d. 397), St. Jerome (d. 420), St. Augustine (d. 430), and Pope St. Leo the Great (d. 461), characteristically in connection with taking advantage of the poor. Bishops condemned usury at the Council of Elvira (305 or 306), the Council of Arles (314), and the First Council of Nicea (325). Canon 13 of the Second Lateran Council (1139 C.E.) reads:

> *Furthermore, we [Catholics] condemn that practice. It is looked upon as despicable and blameworthy by divine and human laws, denounced by Scripture in the old and new Testaments. Namely; the ferocious greed of usurers; and we sever them from every comfort of the church, forbidding any archbishop or bishop, or an abbot of any order whatever or anyone in clerical orders, to dare to receive usurers, unless they do so with extreme caution; but let them be held infamous throughout their whole lives and, unless they repent, be deprived of a Christian burial.*[22]

Several popes also condemned usury, including Alexander III, Gregory IX, Urban III, Innocent III, and Clement V. Condemning usury is reflected in the first universal compendium of Catholic teaching in more than 400 years, the Catechism of the Catholic Church, written with the input of all the bishops of the Catholic Church and published by the authority of John Paul II. The Catechism mentions usury in a condemnatory way:

> *The acceptance by human society of murderous famines, without efforts to remedy them, is a scandalous injustice and a grave offense. Those whose usurious and avaricious dealings lead to the hunger and death of their brethren in the human family indirectly commit homicide, which is imputable to them.*[23]

Position of the Contemporary Roman Catholic Church on Allowing the Charging of Interest

Professor Kaczor states that, in his opinion, the Catholic Church maintains that usury is wrong; but does not hold and never did hold that all charging whatsoever of amounts beyond the principal is wrong. Germain Grisez points out:

> *The Church never taught that all charging of interest is wrong, but only that it is wrong to charge interest on a loan in virtue of the very making of the loan, rather than in virtue of some factor related to the loan which provides a basis for fair compensation.*[24]

John Noonan notes:

> *By 1750, then, the scholastic theory and the counter theory, approaching the same problem form different theoretical viewpoints, agree in approving the common practice "of demanding interest on loans."*[25]

As time went on, the majority of theologians approved of taking interest on loans. The Holy Office did not condemn these opinions, and confessors were not obliged to disturb those involved in the practice. In 1917, Canon law actually required Catholic institutions, such as hospitals, schools, or universities, to invest their assets profitably.

According to St. Thomas Aquinas:

1. The lender may require, over and above the amount of the loan, indemnity protection or insurance against loss or damage.
2. The lender may be repaid not just for the principal but also for expenses incurred in making the transaction, including what was "lost" in the transaction. For instance, if the borrower pays back the principal late, the lender may ask for an additional return, since he was deprived of the use of the money during a time when he could have made use of it. As Finnis[26] notes, what is "lost" could therefore include money that could have been generated had the loan not been made. Aquinas apparently considered this possibility and rejected it: "But the lender cannot enter an agreement for compensation, through the fact that he makes no profit out of his money: because he must not sell that which he has not yet *and may be prevented in many ways from having*."[27]

Professor Kaczor argues that the truth of this last phrase would seem to depend greatly upon existing market conditions. In some markets, such as the ones existing in Aquinas's day, the growth of an investment would be highly speculative; in other markets, like the ones existing today, the growth of an investment would be virtually assured (or so it was thought, until the meltdown of 2008). With the rise of such secure ways of investing money, the person who loans money loses what with reasonable assurance he could have made. In other words, Aquinas assumes that money is a sterile, non-fungible commodity; but in contemporary markets, money may be quite productive indeed. John Finnis concludes:

> *Aquinas's account of usury, taken with his general theory of compensation, thus identifies principles (not rules made up by moralists or ecclesiastics) which enable us to see why in his era it was unjust for lenders to make a charge (however described) in the nature of profit, but with the development of capital market for both equities and bonds it was to become fair and reasonable to make precisely such a charge, correlated with (which is not to say identical to) the general rate of return on equities.*[28]

In conclusion, Professor Kaczor states that Aquinas's conclusions about lending at interest were adequate given the financial assumptions and market conditions of his time, but must be adjusted to account for contemporary circumstances.

THE CHARGING OF RIBIT (INTEREST) IN THE TRADITION AND TEACHINGS OF THE EVANGELICAL CHRISTIAN CHURCH[29]

Professor John Goldingay taught at Fuller Seminary in Pasadena, California, at the time of authoring his research paper. The board of directors of LARIBA asked him in March 2002 to author a paper that summarized the laws and regulations regarding the issue of charging interest on loans in the Christian (evangelical) tradition, with an eye toward the history of the relaxation of the original Catholic Church's prohibition. The following is an abbreviated summary of his work.[30] Please note, in contrast to the Catholic thesis, Goldingay's reliance on Moses's (pp) teachings in the Old Testament in addition to the teachings of Jesus (pp) in the New Testament.

Lending to the Poor

The exhortation in Exodus indicates that it is quite possible for creditors to keep the regulation forbidding lending with interest, yet still treat debtors oppressively. The Old Testament refers to this as a personal issue, a community issue, a national issue, and an international issue.

Individual lenders are not to take the necessities of life as pledges, such as an ox or ass, or a garment, or a millstone—or a baby (Deuteronomy 24:6, 17; Job 22:6; 24:3, 9). One oppressive lender is a man who insists on taking away a widow's children (so that they can work for him) because of the family's debt (2 Kings 4:1).

A story about community controversy in Nehemiah 5 concerns oppressive lending: It may refer to charging interest or to other tough actions, such as foreclosing on personal properties. It alludes to two reasons for debt: crop failure and imperial taxation. The two stories also make clear the results of default. One may forfeit fields, orchards, and houses, and/or one may end up in slavery.

The way imperial taxation burdens individuals and leads to debt was anticipated in the way national taxes burdened people. When Israel asked for stronger central government, the prophet Samuel warned them of the burden that such government would be on them (1 Samuel 8:10–17).

Internationally, Habakkuk 2:6–7 warns about the way a major power that has behaved like a creditor, accumulating pledges from weaker and poorer countries, will in due course become the victim of its debtors. The tables will be turned.

The passage in Exodus forbids Israelites to impose interest on poor members of "my people" when lending them "money"—literally, silver, for coinage was a development of the Persian period. Professor Goldingay highlights the fact that in his opinion the reference to the poor indicates that the text does not refer to regular commercial loans.

In Moses's (pp) teaching, Leviticus 25:35–37 expands on the point in Exodus.

> *If any of your kin fall into difficulty and become dependent on you, you shall support them; they shall live with you as resident aliens. Do not take interest in advance or otherwise make a profit from them, but fear your God; let them live with you. You shall not lend them your money at interest taken in advance, or provide them food at a profit.*

Professor Goldingay concludes that the passage supports the ban on lending with interest by speaking of the poor person as "your kin," members of your family, and of the need to "revere God."

Professor Goldingay also states that "people who are doing well are expected to lend freely to the needy and to accept payment in the form of labor, or of the eventual repayment of the debt in money that the person had earned through labor. So debtors would seek to work their way back to solvency by committing themselves to indentured labor for a set period or to paid employment in relation to someone who did have land—the equivalent to getting a job, rather than the norm of being self-employed."[31]

Another passage in Moses's (pp) teaching makes explicit that people must not impose interest on any form of loan, in money or in kind:

> *You shall not charge interest on loans to another Israelite, interest on money, interest on provisions, interest on anything that is lent. On loans to a foreigner you may charge interest, but on loans to another Israelite you may not charge interest" (Deuteronomy 23:19–20 [23:20–21 in Hebrew Bibles]).*

Professor Goldingay states—in contrast to what Rabbi Kanefsky stated (as summarized earlier in this chapter)—that the preceding passage explicitly states that Israelites are permitted to impose interest in lending to a foreigner, someone who is not a member of "the people." This is an example of a number of obligations that did not apply to foreigners.

Beyond Moses's (pp) teaching, Proverbs 28:8 promises that someone who makes a profit by lending with interest "gathers it for another who is kind to the poor" (i.e., they will not see the profit themselves). It is a personal experience of something that the prophet Habakkuk (pp) envisages for the leading world power of his day. Psalm 15 asks the question,

> *LORD, who may abide in your tent?— [i.e., stay in your presence]*

The answer includes the general requirement of a life of integrity and truthfulness, and also some concrete expectations, such as avoiding slander, keeping oaths, refusing bribes—and not lending money with interest. The prophet Ezekiel (pp) speaks in similar terms, listing obligations that people should fulfill if they wish God to treat them as righteous, such as not worshipping by means of images, not defiling their neighbors' wives, not robbing people—and not lending with interest (Ezekiel 18:8, 13, 17). Ezekiel implies that people were not fulfilling these obligations and later makes explicit that the well-to-do in Jerusalem have committed many of the wrongs he lists, including this one having to do with lending with interest (22:12).

Professor Goldingay goes further to say that Christians tend to understand Moses's (pp) teaching as "law," but the word *Torah* has broader meaning. While Moses's (pp) teaching based on the Torah includes regulations that look designed for quasi-legal literal implementation, other material in the writings look more like illustrations of a particular lifestyle. Professor Goldingay argues that one would miss the point if he took it legally—we might fulfill the law's letter, but not its inner demand (the spirit of the law). Similar issues are raised by Jesus's (pp) Sermon on the Mount.

Exodus 22 begins "If you lend . . .," but it presupposes that you will do so. To refuse to lend would contravene other exhortations regarding concern for the needy. The point is explicit in Deuteronomy 15, which urges people to lend generously to poor members of their "family." Righteous people do well in life and are therefore in a position to give and to lend and thus to be a blessing (Psalm 37:25–26). The Bible promises that things go well for the person who deals generously and lends (Psalm 112:5).

The New Testament confirms the stance of the Old Testament without adding to it. Professor Goldingay opines that the New Testament refers to lending with interest only in the context of a parable, about a man entrusting his assets to his servants (Matthew 25:27; Luke 19:23).

Lending to the Enemy

Professor Goldingay also discusses the issue of a Christian lending to the enemy. He states that Jesus (pp) does urge his followers to lend to whomever asks for a loan (Matthew 5:42) and explicitly states that this applies even to enemies and even if you do not expect to gain in any way from the act (Luke 6:34–35). *Maccabaeus*, a Jewish work from about the same period, which some Christians came to treat as near-canonical, claims that when people start conforming their lives to Moses's (pp) teaching, even if they are by nature greedy, they start lending to the needy without charging interest (2:8).

Business Financing and Relaxation of the Rules of Prohibiting the Charge of Interest

Professor Goldingay states: "I imagine that the ban on charging interest would indeed have been intended for literal implementation, but that in asking about its implications for us in a different social context, we need to look at it in the light of the various aspects of its stated rationale (e.g., in its concern for the poor). In more commercial contexts and in a competitive situation." Professor Goldingay concludes that "people might charge interest on commercial loans without infringing the principle underlying this teaching." He further states that through the first millennium of the Common Era, the Christian Church simply affirmed the Old Testament principle that lending with interest was disapproved, on the continuing presupposition that lending was an aspect of care for the needy. But in practice, lending with interest was tolerated, as long as rates were not judged excessive. Where Christians refused to engage in commercial lending, Jewish moneylenders were able to fill the vacuum on the basis of the permission by Deuteronomy to charge interest to foreigners. In the second millennium, commerce began to develop in new ways and the practice of lending with interest became prevalent, despite the church's opposition. In due course, however, in keeping with the usual pattern, the church conformed itself to the secular pattern and provided a theological rationale for it. In the fifteenth century, Italy's public pawnshops developed with Franciscan support to offer loans to the poor more cheaply than those offered by regular moneylenders, charging a very low interest designed simply to cover expenses. In 1516, the Fifth Lateran Council approved these. As years went by, these pawnshops also began to lend for commercial purposes at higher rates.

Feeling unbound by the course of discussion within the medieval church, and perceiving that the Old Testament was concerned with caring for the poor and not with commercial loans, John Calvin[32] removed the ban on lending with interest, with safeguards that predictably were conveniently forgotten. In due course, the Roman Catholic Church also removed its ban on lending with interest.

In conclusion, Professor Goldingay states that as the capitalist world developed, it lost the idea that the point about lending is to be caring toward the needy. In Victorian Britain, the development of the cooperative movement and the building society movement attempted to recover it. In effect, the customers of the co-op (similar to Credit Unions in today's America) were the shareholders, while building societies worked by attracting safe investments from people who hoped eventually to buy a house and lending the money to people who were already in a position to do so.[33]

THE PROHIBITION OF CHARGING OF RIBIT/RIBA (INTEREST/USURY) IN ISLAM

Almost 800 years before St. Thomas Aquinas and John Calvin were researching ways to resolve the prohibition of charging interest as taught by Moses (pp) and Jesus (pp) to accommodate the needs for financing of the growing commercial business, Muslim traders were practicing RF financing to address the financing of the capital needs of Muslims and non-Muslims that are necessary to help in the growth of their trading and commercial activities. The RF finance system and code for financing of commercial transactions needed by Muslim traders and merchants and the non-Muslims who dealt with them was conducted in India, China, central Asian countries, the Middle East, and some European countries. The RF financing rules and codes were based on the Judeo-Christian-Islamic Shari'aa law. This law finalized and detailed RF financing rules, and it was popularized based on revelations of the Qur'aan, which inculcated all God's messages from the Torah and the Gospel when it was revealed between the years 611 and 634 (approximately).

The Development of the Universal RF System in Islam

There is an important fundamental red line in the teachings of Islam—the line that separates what is divinely permissible, called *halal*, and what is divinely not permissible, called *haram*. Every Muslim is trained by his/her parents—regardless of the level of their religiosity—to know these two most important words in the vocabulary of Islam from childhood. It suffices for a mother to tell her child that lying is haram, because the child is trained to know the divine consequences of committing that haram act. These divisions can be called the basis of the Judeo-Christian-Islamic law. Using this concept, one can state that riba is haram. The Qur'aan reveals:

> *3:130 O ye who believe! Devour not usury, doubled and multiplied; but fear God that ye may (really) prosper.*
> *4:161 that they took usury, though they were forbidden; and that they devoured men's substance wrongfully; we have prepared for those among them who reject faith a grievous punishment.*

Charging riba was described as one of the worst and most grievous sins, as reported in the *Hadeeth* (pronouncement) of Prophet Muhammad (pp) that describes "the seven most despicable sins." The Prophet (pp) also was reported to have said that dealing in riba is like committing murder.[34]

The following discussion presents a stepwise development (by the author) that will help in understanding the structure of the RF system.

The Concept of God Owning Everything

In Islam, it is believed that every asset in this world is owned by God. We read in the Qur'aan:

> *31:26 To God belong all things in heaven and earth: verily God is He (that is) free of all wants, worthy of all praise.*

In other words, we, as the servants of God, do not own anything in this world. We are chosen by God in His infinite wisdom to act as His responsible trustees on the assets with which He entrusts us. We are expected to be responsible before God and the public for protecting, preserving, and investing these assets. The individual as a custodian is also expected to invest these assets prudently and successfully back into the community. This type of investment will help to achieve economic prosperity, job opportunities, and peaceful coexistence within the community, in a fair, just, productive, and equitable way. We, in other words, are called upon by our Creator to act as the trustees of these assets on behalf of their real owner—God—and we, as believers, will be accountable before Him for any and all breaches, abuses, or misuses of this trust.

Islam, in its effort to strengthen, deepen, and remind all people of the teachings of God through all His prophets through its revelations and the teaching of Prophet Muhammad (pp) encourages the rich to spend in the way of God to help the poor and needy and not to take advantage of them. The Qur'aan in its revelations covers many of these aspects:

- *Help the poor.* The Qur'aan reinforces the original teachings of Moses (pp) in the Torah and Jesus (pp) in the Bible about caring for the poor and needy and not taking advantage of them.
- *God knows all things:*

  2:270 and if you spend or promise to spend in the way of God, He knows all and those who transgress and practice injustice by not fulfilling their promises have no one to support them.

- *Charity to help the poor can be done in public, but it is better to be done in secret:*

  2:271 If you give charity and declare it in public, that is acceptable, but if you give it in secrecy and give it to the poor, it is better for you, and He almighty will forgive you your misdeeds in return, and He Almighty is the one who knows what you do.

  30:38 and give your kin their rights, the poor and wayfarer.

- *This is a better way of living for those who seek God's acceptance, and those are the real winners, and*
- *Riba (ribit/interest/usury) cannot be charged when you lend to the poor:*

  30:39 that which you lay out for increase through the property of (other) people will have no increase with God. But that which ye lay out for charity, seeking the Countenance of God, [will increase]: it is these who will get a recompense multiplied.

- *A Muslim should help the poor, regardless of whether they are Muslims or non-Muslims:*

  2:272 you are not expected to influence them to be guided to the righteous path [addressing the Prophet Muhammad], but indeed the Almighty guides whomsoever He will and chooses to, and whatever you spend in goodness will be for your own sake and benefit and will be rewarded back to you, and you will never be treated unjustly.

- *The poor and needy must be treated with respect and dignity.* Those who give should not judge the needs by appearance. It is their duty to search for those who are poor and needy but do not show it. God knows all things, and God will reward those who help the poor and needy:

2:273 for the poor who were trapped by their poverty and those who know can recognize them by their sincere attitude. They are not able to work and contribute because they are poor, but they continue to keep their dignity. Those who do not know and the ignorant would expect them to be rich and capable, because they do not extend their hands and beg and ask people to help persistently in a repulsive way, and whatever you spend in goodness is well known by Almighty God.

2:274 Those who spend their money in public and in secrecy will bank their rewards with God, and no one should fear for their future well-being; and they will never grieve or be saddened.

- *God's judgment is on those who charge riba/ribit/interest/usury on loans to the poor and the needy:*

2:276 Almighty God obliterates and destroys riba and He grows the charities paid in the way of God; and God does not like those who disobey His orders and who transgress.

2:278 Oh ye who believe, heed Almighty God and stop all what is left in the practice of riba if you are really believers.

2:279 and if you disobey and continue to charge riba, then expect the permission by God to the believers to stand to fight you by all means representing God and His Prophet; but if you repent, then you can get your original capital with you being treated unjustly or you treating others without justice.

- *Debt forgiveness for those who cannot pay back:*

2:280 And if the debtor who owes the money cannot pay back the principal capital because of his financial condition, then be considerate and work with them with mercy, ease, and compassion; and if you treat those who owe you money with kindness, charitable posture and ease is in fact better for you if you only know.

2:281 And be heedful of the day when you return back to the Creator and each soul will be given what it has earned while on earth and each will be treated with justice and equity.

Developing the Institution of Giving (Zakah) as a Required Islamic Ritual (Like Prayers)

To change the act of giving from being voluntary to being compulsory, and to underline the value of giving to the poor and needy and helping them, alms (called *zakah* in Islam) were included as one of the required five pillars of Islam. In other words, giving alms has the same weight as the pronouncement and witness of the faith, the prayers, the fasting during the month of Ramadan, and the *Hajj* (pilgrimage). It was also given a descriptive name, zakah, which implies that paying out zakah (alms) in fact purifies and cleanses the rest of the assets.

The zakah is the annual obligatory ritual of purifying one's assets and income. The purposes of paying the zakah are to:

1. Foster mutual caring and support between members of the community—both the rich and the poor.
2. Purify the self, the soul, and the assets of each household.
3. Elevate the spiritual soul of purity and excellence.

The Qur'aan contains many verses on a number of topics that relate to giving in the way of God. These are:

- Those who pay out the zakah will be paid back by God and should not fear and consider zakah payment as a loss:

  2:277 Those believers who heed almighty God and do good deeds and pay their obligated zakah (alms) will be paid for their work by God, and there is no fear about their affairs and destiny, and they will not grieve or be sad.

- If you pay the zakah by helping to give the poor and needy without charging riba will multiply their returns on that investment with God:

  30:39 whatever you earned from riba sources to grow in peoples' assets will never grow in the sight of God, and whatever you pay in zakah, seeking the acceptance of God, indeed these are the ones who will multiply their returns and rewards.

Zakah represents the backbone of the Islamic economic system and the Law (the Judeo-Christian-Islamic Shari'aa Law). Abu-Bakr, the first Caliph who assumed the responsibility of running the emerging Muslim State after Prophet Muhammad (pp), waged a campaign to capture those who refused to pay zakah after the death of Prophet Muhammad (pp) and put them on trial.

Prophet Muhammad (pp) also taught that one's assets never reduced because of paying zakah. Prophet Muhammad (pp) pronounced (in the Hadeeth) that whenever the right of God in one's assets (that is, zakah) is not paid and stays mixed with one's assets, it eventually destroys all assets. The zakah system and methods of collecting it are designed to gather and preserve assets in the House of Treasury of the community (*Bayt Ul Maal*) and to reinvest such assets in the community. The amount of zakah required to be paid depends on the way the assets of each household are saved and/or invested. The zakah system encourages community members to reinvest (riba-free or RF) their assets and savings in the community (hence paying less zakah) and not to accumulate their savings as liquid assets (cash) (which requires higher zakah).

The rich who are expected to pay zakah may hesitate to pay it, because they may think that it will reduce their wealth. The Qur'aan teaches that the fulfillment of the zakah obligation (as one of the five pillars of Islam) is one of the best investments one can make, because its return is 700 times, and more, the original investment:

> *2:261 the parable of those who spend their substance in the way of God is that of a grain of corn: it grows seven ears, and each ear Hath a hundred grains. God gives manifold increase to whom He [God] pleases: And God cares for all and He knows all things.*

That is, a $1,000 investment with God (in the form of zakah payment) by paying it to the poor and needy, as described above, is promised to yield 700 times the investment, or $700,000 in this life and more in the hereafter.

This money is used to primarily fulfill the needs of the poor and the needy. The Qur'aan reveals:

> *2:273 [Charity is] for those in need, who, in God's cause are restricted [from travel], and cannot move about in the land, seeking [For trade or work]: the ignorant man thinks, because of their modesty, that they are free from want. You shall know them by their [Unfailing] mark: They beg not importunately from the entire sundry. And whatever of good ye give, be assured God knows it well.*

To further institutionalize zakah (i.e., the ritual of giving), the Qur'aan has defined eight categories that should benefit from the collected zakah. The Qur'aan defines these categories, as revealed in Chapter 9 of the Qur'aan (*Surah Taubah,* which means Repentance), verse 60.

1. *The poor:*
   They are defined as those who cannot afford to feed or clothe themselves and their families. The purpose of paying the zakah is twofold. First is the short-term goal of feeding and clothing the poor. The other purpose, which is a long-term goal, is to teach the poor professions that can help them become gainfully employed. An example is to

teach a poor person how to drive a taxi so that he or she can obtain a drivers' license and qualify as a taxi driver. Working as a driver will allow him or her to earn a halal income, and move him/her from being poor and stationed at the bottom of the social ladder to a higher step up the social ladder and qualify him or her to join those are classified as the needy (miskeen in the language of the Qur'aan).

2. *The needy:*
   They are defined as those who have a job and receive income, but that income is not sufficient to meet all their needs and the needs of their family and dependents. An example is a low-income taxi driver, who does not own the taxi but leases it from another owner because he/she, the needy, cannot get credit. In the system of zakah distribution ordained in the Qur'aan, the needy would be given RF credit that would help him/her to own a taxi, drive it, and eventually grow to own other taxis that would hire the poor (see category 1) to operate that fleet of taxis. This improvement in employment would eventually raise his/her status from being needy to the next step up the social ladder: becoming a small business owner and entrepreneur.
3. *The zakah-collection administrators*:
   They are those who collect and administer the process of zakah collection, distribution, accounting, and investment.
4. *Those who need to be helped, to integrate them and to bring them and their hearts closer to the community:*
   A portion of the zakah funds is paid to this category to build bridges between these people and the community, in an effort to create a dignified, united, prosperous, and peaceful community regardless of faith, color, national origin, political orientation, gender, and/or language.
5. *Freeing the slaves:*
   This category of spending is used to pay for the freeing and liberation of the slaves. This category also applies to many communities that are forced to live under the rule of dictators and who are longing for freedom and liberty.
6. *Relieving the heavily indebted:*
   These members of the community are defined as those who accumulated a lot of debt due to unfortunate circumstances that are out of their hands.
7. *Spending in the way of God:*
   A portion of the collected zakah can be donated to support any charitable effort to please God. Examples include building a school or a place of worship, or helping a student, a refugee, or a new immigrant.

8. *Helping travelers/wayfarers:*
   These are newcomers and travelers who move to new locations or travel to establish a new life, to search for new opportunities, to develop new contacts, relationships, and businesses, and/or to open new markets, but do not have the resources to do it. This money can be used to build hostels, community hotels, and facilities that would make it easier for people to travel and achieve their goals.

It is interesting to note that each of the zakah spending categories/outlet represents 12.5 percent (one-eighth) of the total zakah collected. If an outlet has been satisfied and does not need money, then the money is redistributed as needed to the other remaining categories. The Judeo-Christian-Islamic Shari'aa law allows the head of the state to levy an additional alms payment by those who are capable in case the collected zakah in the treasury cannot meet its obligation.

Other sources of voluntary contributions to the poor and the needy come from voluntary donations to excel over and above the obligatory zakah. This voluntary giving, called *sadaqah*, can be paid through the system of zakah to the treasury of the community or can be managed and paid directly by the givers to the needy.

Yet another source of funds for giving to the poor and the needy is *Nazr*, a promissory donation that is the result of a personal promise between the believer involved and God. It is due and payable once the believer realizes his/her particular goal, dream, and/or wish. Nazr is paid directly by the giver to the specific entity identified while making the promise.

Behavioral Guidelines and the Discipline of Giving

The Judeo-Christian-Islamic Shari'aa law places the following rules for giving. Some of these rules coincide with what was outlined earlier in the Jewish and Christian traditions. These rules are expanded further by the law (Shari'aa) to make them more standardized, fair, and universal:

1. Giving should never be associated with or followed by a grudge, a bad feeling (even in a concealed way), or even a frown. The teachings of Judaism, Christianity, and Islam are essentially similar on this front. The Qur'aan teaches:

   2:264 O ye who believe! Cancel not your charity by reminders of your generosity or by injury—like those who spend their substance to be seen of men, but believe neither in Allah nor in the Last Day. They are in parable like a hard, barren rock, on which is a little soil:

on it falls heavy rain, which leaves it [just] a bare stone. They will be able to do nothing with aught they have earned. And Allah guides not those who reject faith.

2. The motivation behind giving is only to please God by fulfilling the basic tenets of the faith. This will result in self-content, peace at heart, and peace of mind, leading those who practice it to further successes. Giving should not be intended to show off. Giving can be done in public, but it is preferred to be done in secret in order to receive the highest reward from God:

   2:271 If ye disclose (acts of) charity, even so it is well, but if ye conceal them, and make them reach those [really] in need, that is best for you: It will remove from you some of your [stains of] evil. And God is well acquainted with what ye do.

   2:274 Those who [in charity] spend of their goods by night and by day, in secret and in public, have their reward with their Lord: on them shall be no fear, nor shall they grieve.

3. Giving should be from the same stocks that are available to the giver, and not from the lowest quality of products, left over stocks or assets in order to "dump" them on the poor and needy.

   2:267 O ye who believe! Give of the good things which ye have [honorably] earned, and of the fruits of the earth which We have produced for you, and do not even aim at getting anything which is bad, in order that out of it ye may give away something, when ye yourselves would not receive it except with closed eyes. And know that God is Free of all wants, and worthy of all praise.

4. Those who can afford to give but they do not, the Qur'aan compares them to those who follow Satan. And those who follow Satan are promised deep poverty and failure:

   2:268 The Devil and Evil one leads you to poverty and bid you to conduct unseemly. God promises you His forgiveness and bounties. And God/Allah cares for all and He knows all things.

Business Finance

In the early days of Arabia, and with the growth of commerce and inter-community and international commerce and trade, people were in need of capital to finance their growing trading and business activities. Moneylenders would apply a system that stipulates the time at which the loan had to be paid back. The borrower would pay a monthly interest (the cost of using or renting the money, or riba/ribit/interest/usury), and the loan would balloon for the borrower to pay the original amount at maturity. If the borrower could not pay it back for any reason—including reasons that were out of the borrower's control, such as crop failure due to a drought, a windstorm that affected the caravan and resulted in losses, or a severe downturn in the economy—the lender would agree to extend the term of the loan, but the extension would be conditional on increasing the amount of the original loan. In today's banking practices, this is known as an "interest-only term loan with a balloon payment" at the end of the term. If an arrangement is not reached, the lender would immediately foreclose on the collateral property. These loans have been used since the times of Moses (pp) and Jesus (pp) by the moneylenders and money changers. When the loans could not be paid back, the moneylenders would confiscate the farmers' land and properties, rendering them poorer and enslaving them by requiring them to pay the loans back with their labor.

The following is an outline of the RF business law (based on the Shari'aa, which can also be called the Judeo-Christian-Islamic law) as depicted from the Qur'aan and the tradition (Sunnah) of Prophet Muhammad (pp).

1. The law (Shari'aa) requires full documentation in writing and in the presence of witnesses when credit is granted:

   2:282 O You who have attained to faith! Whenever you give or take credit for a stated term, set it down in writing. And let a scribe write it down equitably between you; and no scribe shall refuse to write as God has taught him: thus shall he write. And let him who contracts the debt dictate; and let him be conscious of God, his Sustainer, and not weaken anything of his undertaking. And if he who contracts the debt is weak of mind or body, or is not able to dictate himself, then let him who watches over his interests dictate equitably.

2. In "on-the-spot" trades (called in the law "hand-to-hand") of ready and available merchandise, there is no need for a full contract, but the transaction must be confirmed by witnesses:

   2:282 If, however, [the transaction] concerns ready merchandise which you transfer directly [on the spot] unto one another, you will incur no sin if you do not write it down. And have witnesses whenever you trade with one another, but neither scribe nor witness must suffer harm; for if you do [them harm], behold, it will be sinful conduct on your part. And remain conscious of God, since it is

God who teaches you [herewith]—and God has full knowledge of everything.

2:283 And if you are on a journey and cannot find a scribe, pledges [may be taken] in hand: but if you trust one another, then let him who is trusted fulfill his trust, and let him be conscious of God, his Sustainer. And do not conceal what you have witnessed for, verily, he who conceals it is sinful at heart; and God has full knowledge of all that you do.

3. The law (Shari'aa) strictly prohibits riba in all transactions and encourages an RF lifestyle. The Qur'aan has ruled in a clear way that riba is haram and is strictly prohibited:

   2:275 Those who eat riba stand as those who have been touched and electrified by Satan, because they claim that buying and selling is like charging riba . . . but be on notice that God has allowed buying and selling transactions and He has forbid riba. For those who receive God's admonition and stop the practice of charging riba, they will own what has happened before this admonition reaches them, and his case will be in the custody; and those who return to charging riba (ribit/interest/usury) for the use of money (interest/ usury), they will be the acquirers and owners of hellfire and in there they will remain to eternity.

Prophet Muhammad (pp) has further explained and elaborated on the prohibition of riba in the Qur'aan. In Islam, according to the Judeo-Christian-Islamic Shari'aa law, the offense of charging, taking, paying, or even acting as a witness in a riba-based transaction is considered one of the worst seven offenses in the faith.[35,36,37]

To establish a universal and standardized legal code for and to regulate business transactions, the law (Shari'aa) identifies the following two types of riba, based on the Hadeeth of Prophet Muhammad (pp).

Types of Riba

There are two types of Riba: *Riba al-Jahiliyah* and *Riba al-fadl.*

Riba al-Jahiliyah

Riba al-Jahiliyah means "the riba used during the age of ignorance and paganism." It is also called *riba al-nassee'aa* (the riba that is constrained by a time limit and is time dependent). This type of riba was widely practiced by the pagan Arabs at the advent of Islam. This practice was conducted by the person borrowing money (i.e., renting it at a price called interest) and agrees to return it at a certain date. If the debt was not paid on time, the creditor would levy an additional sum as a penalty in order to agree to prolong the payment term through debt restructuring. This type of lending is similar to what are called today interest-only loans with a balloon payment at maturity. In this type of loan, the borrower pays only the interest (the rent on the money he owes) and, at maturity, he/she pays the original debt. If he/she does not, then a new agreement is concluded that increases the principal amount and prolongs the maturity date.

This type of lending was prohibited in the original sources of Judaism and Christianity, as well as in Islam; reinforcing the thesis advocated in this book that calls the law (Shari'aa) the Judeo-Christian-Islamic law. As the world grew and became more sophisticated, these types of loans were also used by others for business and for other commercial needs. In Islam, there is no doubt that this type of lending is prohibited[38] as ordained in the original sources—the Qur'aan and the Sunnah (tradition and living example)[39] of Prophet Muhammad (pp)—and in adherence to the original teachings of Judaism and Christianity. This makes this type of lending prohibited in the Judeo-Christian-Islamic tradition.

Another interesting practice by the pagan Arabs was of *nass'ee*, or transposing the months of the lunar calendar system they used in order to suit their needs due to the variability in the methods used to cite the crescent of the new month's moon. Nass'ee could involve shifting the end of the calendar year by manipulating the authentication of the new month based on the citation of the moon and to coincide with a special event; in many cases, the calendar could be accelerated or manipulated to render large riba-based contracts in default. By manipulating the calendar and making the loan appearing to have not been paid in the agreed upon payoff time, the lenders could generate a large amount of delinquency payments by the borrowers or can proceed to foreclose on collateral properties through the practice of riba al-nassee'aa or the time–based rental of money as if money is rented on a daily basis at so much money per day. The Qur'aan has in it verses that explain about the prohibition of this type of riba:

> *9:37 Verily the transposing (of a prohibited month) is an addition to Unbelief: the Unbelievers are led to wrong thereby: for they make it lawful one year, and forbidden another year, in order to adjust the number of months forbidden by God and make such forbidden ones lawful. The evil of their course seems pleasing to them. But God guides not those who reject Faith.*

This variety of riba has been prohibited in the original teachings of Moses (pp) and Jesus (pp), but was relaxed later. The law (Shari'aa) still renders these transactions as haram (divinely prohibited).

Riba al-Fadl

This type of riba is defined as taking a loan for payment at a later date for a higher value, or selling an item for a profit (the word *fadl* means an excess or a premium over the original price or the acquisition cost). An example of this type of riba in today's lingo would be taking a $100,000 personal consumer loan from a bank and promising to pay $120,000 back in two years, or borrowing 10 pounds of rice and promising to pay it back in the form of 20 pounds of rice after one year. Another practice in the marketplace was the bartering of goods of different types, natures, and qualities. For instance, one would exchange 10 pounds of small-sized and low-quality dates for 2 pounds of larger, high-quality dates. The critical question in these types of transactions is the level of the premium used, what makes it 20 to 50 percent higher at a later date, and what index should be used to determine that premium. Another factor in these transactions is how to regulate transactions to minimize deception, speculation, and hoarding activities in the marketplace, thus establishing a fair market price. Such practices are all prohibited by the Prophet Muhammad (pp) in order to ascertain healthy open markets that reflect the true market forces of supply and demand. This type of riba has been regulated by the law in order to organize the barter-based trading to ensure that it is riba free, and it prohibited it for items of the same material, element, or food. It is believed that the RF regulation purpose was to achieve the following goals:

- To minimize, if not remove, deceptive practices from the process of business dealings and transactions, such as those involved in barter trading. This prohibition also helps stabilize the market forces of supply and demand, which will eventually help to stabilize market prices and to minimize, and eventually remove, deception or *gharar* (deceptive practices, including misrepresentations about quality, supply/demand factors, pricing, and product types and specifications). The big question and most challenging issue has been (and it is believed that it still is) how to obtain the most fair and representative market value of an item in a free market system and how to price it, especially in a world that was at the time dealing with nonstandardized currencies made of different materials (as opposed to today's world, in which fiat [paper] money is used everywhere). This issue will be discussed in more detail in Chapters 5 and 6.

- To prevent the application and charging of riba al-nassee'aa, in case the indebted person is not able to service his debt due to conditions that are out of his/her control.

The Law (Shari'aa) Prohibits Deceptive and Speculative Activities in Business Transactions (Gharar)

Another strictly prohibited condition of sales transactions is *gharar,* or deception. In fact, calling a transaction riba free or RF implies that it is also gharar free. The word is derived from the Arabic root word *ghoroor*, meaning arrogance and deception. Gharar results in dissatisfaction of one of the parties involved in the transaction when it is discovered and then revealed; it includes defrauding people and improperly taking away people's money and properties[40] (which is haram, meaning divinely prohibited). Another definition that is more attuned to modern economics was given by the late Professor Mustafa Al-Zarqaa. He defined the forbidden gharar sale as "the sale of probable items whose existence or characteristics are not certain, the risky nature of which makes the transaction akin to gambling."[41] The Qur'aan lays the foundations for fair business dealings, stipulating that contracts must fully disclose all aspects and specifications of the items involved in the transaction and such contracts must be fully and clearly documented and must be closed in the presence of qualified witnesses:

> *6:159 . . . give measure and weight with (full) justice; —no burden do We place on any soul, but that which it can bear; —whenever ye speak, speak justly, even if a near relative is concerned; and fulfill the covenant of God. Thus doth He command you that ye may remember.*
>
> *17:35 Give full measure when ye measure, and weigh with a balance that is straight: that is the most fitting and the most advantageous in the final determination.*
>
> *83:1–6 Woe to those that deal in fraud —Those who, when they have to receive by measure from men, exact full measure—But when they have to give by measure or weight to men, give less than due. —Do they not think that they will be called to account? —On a Mighty Day, A Day when (all) mankind will stand before the Lord of the Worlds?*

Professor Elgamal[42] concludes that the meaning of gharar is conceptually "trading in risk, which cannot be defined." Examples are naked stock and commodity (speculating on future market price movements without owning the physical item) options, financial futures, and derivatives that are not backed by a tangible and verifiable asset. Examples are the sale of the catch of a fisherman before he goes fishing or of a calf before it is born.

In conclusion, the Judeo-Christian-Islamic Shari'aa law in consumer and business transactions prohibits both riba and gharar. The RF system advocated in this book should have been in fact labeled a riba- and gharar-free system, but we use the term RF for short. The prohibition of riba, in fact, implies that the transaction must also be gharar-free.

REVIEW QUESTIONS

Judaism

1. Describe the type of society that existed at the time of commissioning Prophet Moses (pp).
2. Why did Prophet Moses (s) teach people to stop dealing in usury/interest? Please reference the verses from the Jewish Bible.
3. What is the basic ruling on interest in the Jewish religion both in the Jewish holy book (Torah) and in the writings of the Jewish scholars (*Talmud* and *Halacha*). Please include your references. Please give examples.
4. What is the name used for interest in the Jewish Bible? What does it mean? What is its definition?
5. Who was Moses Maimonides? Give us a brief summary of his contributions in general and his specific contributions to the prohibition of usury/interest in the Jewish tradition.
6. Are the Jewish people still holding to the prohibition of usury/interest rulings?
7. What are the synagogues doing about solving the problem of usury/interest?

Catholicism

1. Describe the type of society that existed when Jesus (s) was commissioned.
2. What did Jesus teach? Please give references to verses from the Bible and from Jesus's practices.
3. What was the original name used for riba by the Catholic Church?
4. What was the Catholic definition of riba, and what did they call it (in English) and why?
5. What is the meaning of a "fungible" and a "nonfungible?" and how it was used in the Catholic Church to explain the meaning of ribit/riba?
6. How were the rulings on prohibition of riba diluted in the Catholic Church? Please tell us who was responsible, and how did this take place?
7. How did the concept of interest get into being in the Catholic canons and doctrine? Please elaborate using examples.
8. What ruses were used to circumvent classifying a transaction as riba based?

Christian/Presbyterian/Evangelical

1. What are the main sources of law used by the modern Christian Church (Evangelical)?
2. How does the Evangelical Church look at the problem of interest? And how does it allow the charging of interest?
3. Does the Church use the same references used by the Catholic Church and why?

Islam

1. What is the definition of riba in Islam? Does it contradict with the definitions offered by Judaism, Catholic, and Christian traditions and faiths?
2. How many suras (chapters) in the Qur'aan include mention of the subject of riba? Please list the chapters and the verse numbers.
3. Please briefly explain why Sura Rum (Romans) would include a revelation on riba.
4. What were, in your opinion, the most two important contributions made by the Islamic laws regarding the industry of riba?
5. What is the implication of an RF transaction? What other aspect of the transaction it should be free from?
6. What are the two types of riba defined by the Islamic law? Please explain the meanings and where these types were derived from? Please state some examples using today's practices of riba-based banks.
7. What is *gharar*?
8. This book goes to great length to make a case for a new term: "*Judeo-Christian-Islamic*" law, or the law, to have the same meaning as "*Shari'aa.*" Please explain what the book means, and please support your explanation by verses from the Qur'aan. Please tell us how you feel about this approach and why. Please be brief and to the point!
9. When was the last time a European country attempted to outlaw the charging of interest (riba/ribit)? Which country? Who tried to implement it, and what was the end result?
10. Today, many Muslims and many Christians are involved in the "business" of trying to discredit each other. Please:
    a. Explain the stand taken by the book.
    b. Tell us if you agree with this approach.
    c. Explain why you subscribe to your position.

NOTES

1. The abbreviation *pp* stands for "May God's Prayers and Peace be showered onto them." In Arabic: "Sallaa Allahu Alayhi Wa Sallam"—usually

abbreviated as *s*. This is a standard idiom that is uttered by all Muslims after the mentioning or hearing any of God's prophets' names mentioned.

2. Translations of the Qur'aan were obtained from www.Islamicity.com and are from two sources: (1) *The Meaning of the Holy Qur'aan, Eleventh Edition,* by Abdullah Yusuf Ali, Beltsville, MD: Amana, 2009, and (2) *The Qur'an,* a translation by Muhammad Asad (Gibraltar: Andalus Press, 1980). The Islamic City website (www.islamicity.com) is acknowledged for its indexing and search engines of the Qur'aan in different forms, most important of which is the pioneering phonetic search engine.
3. *Sunnah* is an Arabic word for the style, way of life, and tradition of the Prophet (pp).
4. Michael Hart: *The 100: A Ranking of the Most Influential Persons in History* (New York: Citadel Press, 1978).
5. *Hadeeth* is an Arabic word meaning the documented body of sayings of Prophet Muhammad (pp).
6. *Seerah* is an Arabic word that means the documented full life story and autobiography of Prophet Muhammad (pp).
7. The Qur'aan, 2:136.
8. R. St John, Esq: Private communication.
9. Wayne A. M. Visser and Alastair McIntosh, "A Short Review of the Historical Critique of Usury." First published in *Accounting, Business & Financial History*, 8(2) (July 1998): 175–189.
10. Professor John Goldingay, Fuller Seminary, Pasadena, California.
11. Rabbi Yosef Kanefsky, Los Angeles, California: private communication; an invited paper presented at the LARIBA 2002 Annual Symposium and Awards Symposium, Pasadena, California, March 2002.
12. Published by permission from Rabbi Kanefsky.
13. Moses Maimonides (born in Cordoba, Spain, in 1135 and died in Fustat [old Cairo], Egypt, 1204) was a great Jewish scholar, philosopher, and medical doctor who lived in Egypt and was one of the most prominent in the court of Saladin (born in Iraq and died in Damascus in 1193).
14. Professor Christopher Kaczor (http://bellarmine.lmu.edu/~ckaczor/), Department of Philosophy, Loyola Marymount University; private communication: A paper presented at the LARIBA Annual Symposium and Awards, Pasadena, California, March 2002.
15. Professor Kaczor states: "I make no claim to original historical research in this article, but have drawn upon many sources in coming to a deeper understanding of the issues at hand. I have especially drawn upon A. Vermeersche, "Usury," *The Catholic Encyclopedia*, Volume XV, 1912, which is available online at: www.newadvent.org/cathen/15235c.htm and was downloaded on March 5, 2002; A. Vermeersche, "Interest,"

The Catholic Encyclopedia, Volume VIII, 1912, which is available online at www.newadvent.org/cathen/08077a.htm and was downloaded on March 5, 2002; David J. Palm, "Usury," *Encyclopedia of Catholic Apologetics* (San Francisco: Ignatius Press, 2002); and John Noonan, *The Scholastic Analysis of Usury* (Cambridge, MA: Harvard University Press, 1957).

16. Published by permission from Professor Christopher Kaczor, Loyola Marymount University, Los Angeles, California.
17. In Islamic literature, there is a *Qudsi* Hadeeth, or the words of God spoken to Prophet Muhammad, that says exactly the same meanings of the words described here.
18. Two sales in one sale is also prohibited, according to some but not all scholars in Islamic law.
19. The Qur'aan has a verse about those who raise debts in many multiples: 3:130 O ye who believe! Devour not usury, doubled and multiplied; but fear Allah that ye may (really) prosper.
20. St. Thomas Aquinas, *Summa Theologica*, II–II, question 78, article 1.
21. Riba in Islamic law can be defined as the act of renting money at a price called the interest rate; according to the law, money cannot be rented, but fungible and rentable assets and services can.
22. N. P. Tanner, ed., *Decrees of the Ecumenical Councils*, vol. 1, (Washington, DC: Georgetown University Press, 1990), 200.
23. *Catechism of the Catholic Church*, 2nd ed. (New York: Random House, 1997), #2269.
24. German Grisez, *The Way of the Lord Jesus, Vol. II: Living a Christian Life* (Quincy, IL: Franciscan Press, 1993), 834.
25. John Noonan, *The Scholastic Analysis of Usury* (Cambridge: Harvard University Press, 1957), p. 377.
26. John Finnis, *Aquinas* (Oxford, England: Oxford University Press, 1998), 210.
27. St. Thomas Aquinas, *Summa Theologica* II–II, 78, article 2, ad 1, emphasis added.
28. See note 26.
29. Professor John Goldingay, Fuller Seminary, Pasadena, CA.
30. Published by permission of Professor John Goldingay, Fuller Seminary.
31. Based on the Islamic (Judeo-Christian-Islamic) law, it is preferred that the indebted work for a defined wage, then use the wage to pay the debt. This way, the indebted person would be treated fairly and equitably by marking the wage to the market prevailing rates charged in similar situations.
32. French Protestant theologian who lived from July 10, 1509, to May 27, 1564.

33. The Ansar Group started a similar effort in Canada, the Islamic Housing Cooperative; however, its growth was limited because of the lack of liquidity.
34. This was reported by Bukhari, Muslim, and others.
35. In the saying of "... the seven most devastating Sins," the Prophet Muhammad (pp) counted: "believing in partnership with God, murder ... and eating riba ..." as reported by Bukhari, Muslim, and others [al Targhib wa al Tarhib, v. 3, p. 1].
36. The Prophet Muhammad (pp) said: "Four [persons] very truly God will not make them enter Heaven ... and the eater of riba ..." as Al Hakim reported [Al Targhib wa al Tarhib, v. 3, p. 5].
37. The Prophet Muhammad (pp) said that God put wrath on (cursed) the eater of riba and its payer, and those who witness and transcribe the contract involving riba; this was reported by Bukhari and Muslim.
38. From the Farewell Speech Ceremony of Prophet Muhammad (pp) before he died: "Vo, everything of the affair of jahiliyyah (paganism and ignorance) is let fall under my feet, the Riba of jahiliyyah is let fall, and the first Riba I abolish is the Riba of al Abbas son of Abd al Muttalib, it is discarded, all" (principal and increase); reported and authenticated by Muslim.
39. The Hadeeth (sayings of Prophet Muhammad [pp]), narrated by Abu Dawood and Tirmidhzi, reads:

    ... and every Riba of Jahiliyyah is abolished. Neither shall you make [the debtor] suffer injustice [loss], nor shall you be made to suffer injustice, But the Riba of al Abbas son of Abd al Muttalib [the uncle of Prophet Muhammad (pp), who was active in Riba transactions before he became Muslim], it is discarded, all.
40. Mahmoud Elgamal, *Islamic Finance: Law, Economics and Practice* (Cambridge, England: Cambridge University Press), 58. Professor Elgamal's book details the conditions of sale and the types of deceptive practices that are major and minor. This book is a wonderful and very useful reference for those who are interested in the legal Shari'aa aspects of the prohibition of riba and gharar.
41. Ibid.
42. Ibid.

CHAPTER 3

The RF Valuation Disciplines of Commodity Indexation and Marking to the Market

This chapter presents the reader for the first time in the global RF (Islamic) banking and finance domain with two important and fundamental RF disciplines: the Commodity Indexation Discipline and the Marking-to-Market Discipline. In this chapter, the fundamentals of these two disciplines will be laid down and will be detailed later in Chapters 5 and 6, where these two disciplines will be applied using detailed historic stochastic data.

It is well known that Prophet Muhammad (pp), in addition to being God's commissioned Prophet, had been through many life experiences to prepare him for becoming the prophet that changed the course of history to bring the world forward on the courses charted by his predecessors, including Moses (pp) and Jesus (pp). He was a shepherd, a trusted conflict resolution arbitrator, a community leader, and a trusted manager of people's assets in caravan trading and investments. Involvement in business as a trusted, successful, and reputable business leader enabled him to see the world and taught him how the world works and how business is transacted. At the time he was commissioned as the Prophet of God, two major currencies were prevalent in business transactions: the *dirham*, used by the Persian Empire and made out of silver (it was also used by the Greeks and called *drachma*), and the *denarius*, used by the Roman Empire and made out of gold. At that time an important aspect of trading in caravans was transacting business in different local currencies depending on where the trade was conducted. The final step of the trader's transaction was to convert all business proceeds into the local currencies of his/her clients, who entrusted him/her with the management of their money and assets. Naturally, local currency conversion represented a great challenge for the fair-minded and God-revering businessmen and traders to make sure that transactions were expressed fairly in a universal currency without taking away the fair share of the profit or loss to which the investors were entitled.

Prophet Muhammad (pp) came with a simple but revolutionary idea to establish the principles of pricing at fair value and the free market system and to remove deceptive and fraudulent activities in such free markets. The major challenge for caravan trading was to establish standardized rules of exchange because of the variety of local currencies used in the countries they traded in at the time of the Prophet. The other challenge was to determine how to exchange different products for different uses while being fair and while ensuring that the principles of fair value pricing and fair free markets were preserved. Prophet Muhammad (pp) set the rules of a new and innovative system that would bring to bear God's teachings taught by Moses (pp) and Jesus (pp) in one final system that is riba free (RF) and would signify for the first time in history the foundation of an RF Judeo-Christian-Islamic system manifested by the Judeo-Christian-Islamic Shari'aa law.

The system called for relating the price of every item to a standard reference and calibrating commodity that was produced and/or is used in each community. The system called for pricing products and services either in terms of ounces of gold or silver (as metal commodities, called at the time *metal pricing commodities*) or in terms of a food item that was considered a basic staple in the community, such as—at the time of the Prophet—wheat, barley, dates, or salt. He also went on to rule that if one borrowed an ounce of gold, it should be returned to the owner in an equal amount (i.e., only an ounce of gold) even if the repayment was not done hand-to-hand and was made after one year. If the repayment was more than an ounce, the transaction was considered a riba transaction and was considered haram (divinely prohibited). However, one can exchange one ounce of gold into 10 bushels of wheat on the spot (hand-to-hand) or 15 bushels after one year. This transaction would be legitimate based on the RF law (Shari'aa) and would be considered halal (divinely allowed).

The Prophet Muhammad (pp) has ordained, according to his sayings (*Hadeeth*), the following rule regarding buying/selling, exchanges, trading, and bartering:

If a buy/sell agreement involves currency, then one can *only* exchange *without increase*:

- Gold for gold in same weight.
- Silver for silver in same weight.

If the buy/sell agreement involved food items, then one could use only a set of staple food commodities as reference/index commodity items without increase, regardless of the quality or the type of that food item. For example, exchanging 10 small dates for 2 large dates is haram and is considered a forbidden riba-based trade transaction. The rule goes further to stipulate that the rule used for precious metals is also extended to cover the following *Reference Index of Basic Food Staples Commodities*:

- Wheat for wheat
- Barley for barley
- Dates for dates
- Salt for salt

To ensure and to be certain that there is no increase (riba), the exchange must be done on an on-the-spot basis (hand-to-hand) to prohibit the use of speculative futures markets activities in these reference and calibrating items that are used as measuring references for pricing activities.

The illustrative chart in Exhibit 3.1 was devised by a number of RF-interested scientists in 2010. It shows how the Commodity Indexation discipline operates on different commodities trading and barter exchanges.

Please also note that the items listed in Exhibit 3.1 were only for illustration purposes; the Prophet(s) used them because they were either the precious metals' pricing currencies used at that time (in case of the gold denarius or silver dirham) or basic and essential staple foods used then. Based on subsequent jurisprudence, as will be detailed later, and with the change in communities' lifestyle and taste, transacting behavior, important food, and new living needs such as energy, one can expand on the rule while using the same concept and discipline, depending on the prevailing conditions in a certain country or within a certain community.

This concept is similar to using an index of reference commodities as a means of checking the stability of a certain local currency on the international foreign exchange (Forex) markets, especially in a world that is run by fiat or paper money. It is interesting to note that James Baker III, former secretary of the Treasury of the United States, told world financial leaders in 1987 that the Reagan administration "is prepared to consider"[1] using the price of gold in trying to steer its own and the world economies. Baker explained that gold could be used in a specially designed index along with other commodities to help governments discern inflation and then adjust their policies by raising interest rates or taxes, for example.

Further research was conducted by many scholars in the Judeo-Christian-Islamic Shari'aa law to expand on the concept of using the six commodities listed in Exhibit 3.1. Imam Abu Haneefah (the pioneer of a school of jurisprudence carrying his name, the *Hanafi* law) and Imam Ahmad (another well-placed scholar with his own school of jurisprudence—the Hanbali school of jurisprudence oir fiqh) concluded that we could expand the list of reference

EXHIBIT 3.1 RF Rules Governing Sale or Exchange of Items in the Marketplace

	Currency Items				Food Items						Anything Else
	Gold	Silver	Currency 1	Currency 2	Barley	Wheat	Dates	Salt	Food 1	Food 2	Other
Gold	A	B	B	B	C	C	C	C	C	C	C
Silver	B	A	B	B	C	C	C	C	C	C	C
Currency 1	B	B	A	B	C	C	C	C	C	C	C
Currency 2	B	B	B	A	C	C	C	C	C	C	C
Barley	C	C	C	C	A	B	B	B	B	B	C
Wheat	C	C	C	C	B	A	B	B	B	B	C
Dates	C	C	C	C	B	B	A	B	B	B	C
Salt	C	C	C	C	B	B	B	A	B	B	C
Food 1	C	C	C	C	B	B	B	B	A	B	C
Food 2	C	C	C	C	B	B	B	B	B	A	C
Other	C	C	C	C	C	C	C	C	C	C	C

Rule Definitions

Rule A	Exchanged items must be of same amount *and* on-the-spot sale.
Rule B	Amounts of the items could be different but the sale must be a spot sale (e.g., you may trade one pound of wheat for two pounds of barley on the spot).
Rule C	Amounts of the items could be different and does *not* need to be on the spot (e.g., for whatever amounts you agreed to, you can trade on the spot, or deliver goods now and get payment later, or deliver payment now and get the goods later).

Note: The rules are based on two Hadeeth of the Prophet (pp) and the explanation provided in "Fiqh Al-Sunnah" by Sheikh Sayed Sabiq. The Hadeeth explicitly mentioned six items categorized as food or currency. Scholars' opinion is that it also applies to any food or currency.

Source: "Islamic Finance and Capitalism: An Introduction," a presentation prepared by Muhammad Yusuf Dadani, Ahmed Naji, Mohamed Osman, and M. Hashem Sherif. Presented at the Islamic Society of Central Jersey on Sunday, May 23, 2010.

commodities depending on the community in which we live, but with the condition that the reference and calibrating commodity can be weighed or measured accurately without having the ability for transformation over time (as in the case of perishables or metals that are susceptible to being rusted out). Imam Shafi'ee (a scholar who has his own school of jurisprudence—the *Shafi'ee* law) ruled that these indexation items can be eatables that can preserve their value or can be legal tender such as gold and silver (and may be other precious elements). Imam Malik (a scholar with his own school of jurisprudence, the *Maliki* law) suggested that these can be food commodities or items that can offer a lasting and accurately measurable store of value.

The main rule goes like this[2]:

1. In barter exchanges, if the two items are the same in elemental form (e.g., gold for gold, silver for silver, etc.) or are used in the same way (e.g., food, in the case of wheat and barley), then for this exchange to be legal, the quantity (weight, volume, or numbers of units) should be the same, regardless of the quality of the item.

   The exchange must be conducted on the spot (hand-to-hand) and delivery should also be on the spot.
2. If the two items differ in substance but not in use, then fadl (or increase in exchange ratio by adding a premium or by using a multiple or a fraction) can be practiced, but riba al-nassee'aa (the charging of a delinquency penalty in case of not paying back at the promised time as agreed by the two contracting parties, due to conditions that are out of control), cannot be applied. For example, if gold was sold in terms of silver (different substance, but same use as metals used as a value of tender or as an ornament then and now as an important industrial metal) or wheat in terms of rice (wheat and rice are different substances but used for same purpose, i.e., as food), it is permissible to use a ratio that is not 1:1 as established by the free-market forces of supply and demand as required when exchanging gold for gold, silver for silver, small size dates for large size dates, and so on.
3. If the two items differ in substance and purpose of use, then it is halal (divinely permissible) to both practice fadl and defer payment over a certain period of time. For example, one can buy wheat for gold, and the payment can be deferred. There would be two prices: The on-the-spot price (hand-to-hand) can be set at 20 bushels of wheat for an ounce of gold, and the deferred price can be, say, 25 bushels of wheat for an ounce of gold after one year. However, it is very important to note that the rules of riba al-nassee'aa should be implemented (i.e., there should be no late payment penalty if the lateness in payment and settlement of the transaction is justified, as in cases of job loss; crop failure due to, for

example, weather conditions; an unexpected dire need; or a change in the prevailing economic situation).

Conceptually, to be fair to all people both inside a country and internationally, the price of an item—based on the RF Commodity Indexation Discipline pioneered by the Prophet Muhammad (pp)—should always be related to the weight or volume of a reference calibration commodity that is either mined from earth in the form of a natural resource, like gold, copper, salt, oil, or silver, or is a food staple produced by the hard work of the farmer, using earth with its natural nutrients and water provided by rain, flowing rivers, and underground water tables, such as corn, wheat, dates, and barley. The Qur'aan reveals:

> *2:164 Behold! in the creation of the heavens and the earth; in the alternation of the night and the day; in the sailing of the ships through the ocean for the profit of mankind; in the rain which God Sends down from the skies, and the life which He gives therewith to an earth that is dead; in the beasts of all kinds that He scatters through the earth; in the change of the winds, and the clouds which they Trail like their slaves between the sky and the earth;—[Here] indeed are Signs for a people that are wise.*
>
> *7:57 It is He Who sendeth the winds like heralds of glad tidings, going before His mercy: when they have carried the heavy-laden clouds, We drive them to a land that is dead, make rain to descend thereon, and produce every kind of harvest therewith: thus shall We raise up the dead: perchance ye may remember.*
>
> *15:22 And We send the fecundating winds, then cause the rain to descend from the sky, therewith providing you with water [in abundance], though ye are not the guardians of its stores.*

It is interesting to contrast the use of these basic tangible products as calibrating references to price other items in the market. It is well known that commodities such as food, minerals, and metals are produced by the hard work of people. For minerals and metals (and now energy resources like coal, oil, and natural gas), people explore for them and mine them out of the earth. For food, people plant and cultivate it on farms, producing staples like corn, wheat, barley, soybeans, or rice, for which each requires land preparation and special climates. Therefore, there are various products in various locations. Through free trade, people not only make business deals with each other, but also toil to move from one location to another in this wide world to get to know each other and to respect each other's cultures, and in the process discover trading opportunities and start bonding these two communities or nations through trade as they conduct commercial activities together. Combining the hard work of the people with God's gifts to us, like the earth, its fertility, its water resources needed for irrigation, and the specific weather conditions in each geographic location, would produce basic staple food products and other strategic resources like precious metals and energy resources that can be used as a calibrating reference commodity index.

These products were used by the Prophet Muhammad (pp) to set references or indexes for pricing and trading. Compare this concept with the current global practice of governments using a printing press that produces paper banknotes (fiat money) with little effort, except for the smart and highly educated and sophisticated analytical minds and political ideology and domestic currents that decide how much money to print or withdraw from the monetary system, based on economic and monetary statistics. Printing too many of these banknotes (paper money) without paying attention to local economies of production can be a major contributor to inflation and economic instability that would lead to domestic and worldwide instability; the opposite can be true, as well. The system also depends on the great minds of economists, monetarists, statisticians, mathematicians, and computer-based modeling that uses the most powerful computers, modeling techniques, and carefully documented and collected historic data and logistics. Such talents, techniques, and expertise are important but are scarce. In addition, they may not be available in every country. In fact, most countries—except for a few developed nations, led by the United States, Germany, France, and the United Kingdom—are not endowed with a large pool of such talented experts and needed resources.

In an attempt to apply the preceding rules, an effort was invested to study the price history of different commodities and to apply the Commodity Indexation Discipline, introduced earlier, to one of your author's real life investment transactions. For example, in 1974 we bought a house in Plano, a suburb of Dallas, Texas, for $46,000, with a down payment of $3,500. In 1977, it was sold for $65,000. We were very happy to have realized a profit of $19,000 in almost two years by investing in this house. That translates to a price increase of 41 percent in two years on the house in terms of U.S. dollars. The total profit, in dollars, on the original out-of-pocket investment of $3,500 was $19,000, or a 543 percent total profit. It should be noted that all of these wonderful returns were in U.S. dollars. However, if we had measured the total profit in two years as a percentage of the original investment in terms of some of the six reference commodities listed earlier in the Commodity Indexation Discipline, the result would be revealing;

- In terms of wheat, because bread (which is made out of wheat) is a staple food item in the United States: We bought the house for an equivalent of

9,957 bushels of wheat (wheat in 1974 was $4.62 a bushel). We sold it in 1977 for the equivalent of 29,630 bushels of wheat (wheat was $2.16 a bushel). That is a total profit of 300 percent on the value of the house, in terms of wheat. As to the profit made on the invested out-of-pocket capital of $3,500 in terms of wheat, or the equivalent of 757 bushels of wheat, we realized a profit of $19,000, equivalent to 8,796 bushels of wheat—a total profit in wheat terms of 11,620 percent.

- In terms of gold, the picture is different. The value of the house was equivalent to 421 ounces of gold (the price of gold in 1974 was $103 per ounce). We sold it in 1977 for 428.6 ounces of gold (the price of gold was $149.33 per ounce). This translates to an appreciation in the price of the house of 1.8 percent in terms of gold. The total profit made on the invested capital of $19,000, or 127.23 ounces of gold, related to an original investment of $3,500, or 33.97 ounces of gold, yielded a total of 374.7 percent.

Naturally, life 1,400-plus years ago was far simpler than it is today. The matrix of an average citizen's production and demands in a country is more diversified now and is by far more complex and different from one country to another. For example, those who want to think in terms of wheat (in this case, wheat farmers) cannot live on wheat alone because they will need to buy farm equipment, as well as fuel for heating and for operating the farm equipment. They will obtain credit to finance these agricultural activities. However, we cannot live on gold because we cannot eat or drink it. It should be made clear here that in discussing the Commodity Indexation Discipline we do not imply a return to the gold standard. What is strongly recommended here is a pioneering new RF discipline and RF finance and monetary system that uses a reference commodity like gold or a basket of commodities peculiar to each country to calibrate the real value of the local currency. The contents of this basket depend on the country's production and demand matrix. This concept is similar to the concept for the basket used for measuring inflation, for defining the Special Drawing Rights (SDR) currency used by the International Monetary Fund (IMF) and the concept proposed by James Baker III in 1987 to detect economic "bubbles" in a local economy. This RF discipline clearly stipulates that fiat (paper) money can be used, and the U.S. dollar may continue to be the reserve currency of the world along with maybe the euro, but the RF Commodity Indexation Discipline proposed here complements the current fiat money system and may eventually lead to a pioneering RF monetary structure and discipline. This assures all participants that the system and discipline used by government monetary authorities is designed and structured to be fair to all people and all nations. The system also rules that this RF Commodity Indexation

Discipline is implemented in order to price things fairly in the market while detecting any overpricing "bubble" as is usually experienced, for example, in commodities markets such as with energy prices and as was experienced between 2005 and 2007 in the United States housing bubble that led to the 2008 economic and monetary meltdown. This Commodity Indexation Discipline and rules will also help central bankers with their most important jobs and goals of keeping inflation under control, stabilizing currency value on the foreign currency exchanges, and stabilizing as well as optimizing the levels of unemployment. It is interesting to note that the use of this basket of commodities concept can change, not only from country to country, but also from time to time, with changes in the production mix in a certain country. It is felt that this concept will eventually prompt nations to produce more and become efficient producers to improve the value of their currencies on the foreign currency exchange markets.

Finally, it is hoped that economic and monetary research centers around the world conduct focused research on this concept, which has been tested successfully, as will be detailed in Chapters 5 and 6, to come up with useful ideas and propose an RF monetary, economic, and financial policies that can be useful to reflect the real value of local currencies for the good of the world and its citizen in the future. This will eventually create a peaceful world that is fair and just.

DEVELOPMENT OF THE MARK-TO-THE-MARKET RULE

Another issue came up involving barter trading during the time this RF law (the Judeo-Christian-Islamic Shari'aa law) was being developed by the Prophet (pp). The challenge, at the time of the Prophet (pp) as it is today, was how to deal with the challenge of pricing and trading items that could be measured using more than one method—for instance, palm tree dates—as experienced during the time of the Prophet Muhammad (pp). Palm dates can be dry or fresh; they can be measured in size (large, medium, and small) or in numbers of dates, or in terms of weight. Another example, in the case of food items, is that one can exchange rice for rice, but the parties may disagree because one party's rice is inferior in quality to the other party's rice, the length of the grain of one type of rice is longer than another, or the aroma of one type of rice is in more demand than the other type. For dates, it might be that one party had larger dates while the other's dates are smaller and of sweeter quality. In both of these cases, using the Commodity Indexation Discipline required in RF banking and finance, one can only exchange the same weight of rice without increase regardless of size and quality. Another example is the case of dates or grapes.

There are fresh dates or grapes, and there are dried dates and raisins. The question was "Are they the same food items?" The answer was yes, and when they are exchanged they must be in equal amounts: that is 100 small dates for 100 large dates, because the RF Commodity Indexation Discipline rules that dates are dates, regardless. This issue came up when one of Prophet Muhammad's (pp) companions (Bilal, the Ethiopian whose job was to chant the call for the five daily prayers at that time) brought him a gift of large, very high-quality dates. The Prophet (pp) knew that Bilal did not have the means to afford to buy these high-quality large dates. He inquired. Bilal told him that he saved his ration of low-quality small dates for some time and that he went to the market and exchanged them for a smaller number of higher-quality, larger dates. The Prophet Muhammad (pp) told him that this transaction was classified as a riba transaction and that it is divinely prohibited (haram). When Bilal asked what he should have done, the Prophet (pp) said that the small-sized, low-quality dates should have been marked to market by selling them in terms of another reference commodity to satisfy the RF Commodity Indexation Discipline described earlier, such as gold, silver, rice, wheat, or barley, and that he should have used the proceeds to buy the large, higher-quality dates. This way, deception (gharar), misrepresentation, and interference in the free-market forces of supply and demand would be minimized and hopefully eliminated. This process, which we call in this book the RF Marking-to-Market Discipline, helps to fairly define prices and to standardize and stabilize markets, allowing the efficient working of the market forces of supply and demand. This RF discipline has been used by LARIBA since 1988 and is the main reason for its superior portfolio performance over the years.

The Marking-to-Market Discipline is believed to be one of the most important historic developments in the RF finance and banking system and domain. It lays the foundation of fair pricing for products and services, based on real market values within an open and free market operation. The RF Marking-to-Market Discipline is the foundation of the analytical system used by LARIBA[3] to operate in an RF finance mode that is unique.

It is important to stress here that the RF banking brand is not based on renting money at a rental price (interest) but on the actual measured fair market rent of properties, businesses, and services. For example, consider buying a house. The buyer who wants to obtain RF financing and the RF finance institution should mark the house to market. The best way of doing that is to find out how much a similar house in the same neighborhood and with similar specifications would rent/lease for in terms of U.S. dollars per square foot (or euros/square meter). This mutually agreed-upon live market lease rate is used to calculate the rate of return on investment of the proposed purchase and RF Finance transaction, looking at it as an RF investment. If the rate of return on investment makes economic sense (i.e., it is equal to or higher than the expected return by our RF investors), the RF bank proceeds to finance (invest in) the property. In addition, the RF bank does its best to make the monthly payments in the RF mode of financing competitive with those offered by riba-based banks. A very low return implies that this investment would be inferior; the RF banker would advise the customer not to invest.

The RF banking and finance discipline, in an effort to neutralize the effects of the prevailing fiat currency in the local markets, requires that we first apply the Commodity Indexation Discipline to check, in a macroeconomic way, on the existence of a bubble in the business that we are considering to finance. This process is followed by a Mark-to-Market Discipline and approach, evaluating the economic prudence by calculating the real return on investing in this item, using its actual real market rental value. This way, it is affirmed that money is not rented using the prohibited riba—and that the rent is that of the market rent of the facility in the marketplace. For example, in the case of:

- A *car,* the value for which this car is leased in the market (dollars per day), as obtained from actual operating leasing companies.
- A *house,* the actual market rental or lease rate (dollars per square foot) of a similar house in the same neighborhood. It is important to make sure that this house has essentially the same specifications and is located in the same neighborhood as those researched. These rates can be obtained live preferably from real estate agents or from market data on the Web.
- A *commercial building,* the actual market lease rate of the space.
- A *piece of equipment,* the market rental value, in dollars per day.
- A *business,* the lease rate an owner is willing to lease it for in the market.

This rate is used to calculate the rate of return on investment because RF bankers *do not rent money*—in fact, they invest with and in the customer. If the rate of return is higher than the target return for the institution (which is the return expected in the market from shareholders and depositors), then it makes sense to finance/invest with the customer. If the return is lower, then it does not make sense to finance/invest, and the customer is advised and the application may be declined. This rejection is applied even if the customer has fulfilled all standard banking requirements from the creditworthiness test, the appraisal test, and the capacity for servicing the financing obligation. We will discuss this process in more detail in Chapters 11 and 14, and examples will be given.

RIBA-FREE BUSINESS TRANSACTION MODELS

The following is an abbreviated list of the RF finance models used to finance commercial transactions. This is not a comprehensive list. It is designed to familiarize the reader with the concepts used in the different models. A more detailed list with explanation of each model is presented in Chapter 13. It is important to note here that it is preferred to call these models by the names that describe them in English—the language used in this book—and may be in another language that is understood and spoken popularly in the concerned market. The reader will notice that the original Arabic name was included next to the English name of each model for the sake of completion and reference.

Cost-Plus (Murabaha)

The cost-plus (*murabaha*) model is mainly used for commodity and trade financing. In a cost-plus contract, the client would approach the RF finance institution to finance the purchase of a certain item, such as a cargo of soybeans, a car, a house, a commercial building, a business, or a franchise, because the client does not have the funds to purchase it in cash. Here is a brief summary of the steps taken according to this model of financing:

1. The customer issues an order to the RF bank or finance company to buy the items on the customer's behalf.
2. The RF finance institution buys the item in its own name first. The title of that item transfers from the seller to the RF finance institution.
3. The RF finance institution discloses the purchase cost to the ultimate buyer. Then, the RF finance institution sells the item to the customer at a mutually agreed-upon price, which includes a disclosed and agreed-upon profit element, to be paid over a period of time long enough to pay that price back on an affordable monthly basis, for example. The sale price charged by the RF financial institution to the customer is equal to the fully disclosed original purchase price/cost incurred by the RF bank, plus a profit element for the RF bank. As a result of this sales step, the title transfers from the RF finance company, or bank, to the client.

It is important to note here that the profit element should be agreed upon in light of the RF Marking-to-Market Discipline discussed earlier, not to simply take the prevailing interest rate (the price of renting money), calculate the profit element, and proceed to call it profit!

It must be stressed here that the sale price agreed upon between the RF finance institution and the customer, as well as the period of time (term) to pay back, is final, as are the terms of payment. For example, if the term of payment was agreed upon to be five years and the customer had a legitimate excuse to extend it over a longer period of seven years, the agreed-upon sale price would stay the same and there would be no increase—otherwise, the transaction would be deemed a riba (riba-al jahiliyah or riba al-nassee'aa, meaning a time-based prohibited riba), which is divinely prohibited (*haram*).

However, if the customer wants to expedite payments so that he or she pays over a two-year period instead of a five-year period, the agreed-upon price would still be the same unless the RF finance company agrees out of its own free will to reduce the price to accommodate a special request from the customer. This request can be denied, which is acceptable under the Judeo-Christian-Islamic Shari'aa law and is deemed halal, meaning it can be accepted.

There are a number of issues and concerns that are associated with the cost-plus (murabaha) transaction:

- The two buy/sell steps (from seller to RF finance company and then from the finance company to buyer) constitute, theoretically, two changes of title. This will trigger two tax events that would call for the double taxation of the transaction (a tax due on the sale from the seller to the finance institution, and another tax due on the sale from the finance institution to the ultimate buyer who is financed by the RF institution), making it more expensive to finance in many Western societies. The RF finance institution selling to the customer at a higher price may be considered a capital gain, subject to capital gains taxes in the United States and many other countries. The tax burden in this case may be onerous. That is why many of the cost-plus models used by "Islamic" institutions in the West include a *rider* or another contract that contains a condition that makes the ultimate buyer—not the RF bank—responsible for any capital gains taxes that may be applied by the government at any future date if it renders the transaction a taxable transaction. This solution is unfair to those who want to abide by their faiths. It is also unfair that the RF bank claims to be Islamic while throwing all the risk back to the customer.
- Banking institutions are not allowed by the banking laws and regulations in the West to participate in direct transactions as principles or to take title of properties (unless the property is repossessed; however, such properties are handled and recorded on the balance sheet of the RF institution in a special way, and banks are expected to dispose of them as soon as is practical). To get around this rule and to appear to satisfy the legal aspect of the RF law while potentially sacrificing the spirit of RF law, many attorneys resort to using structured financial

tools by involving, in most cases, a separate but expensive-to-operate and maintain offshore company called a special-purpose vehicle (SPV), which buys the property and sells it back to the customer on paper, as is usually done for tax planning that helps some affluent taxpayers in the West to reduce their tax burden. On paper, this approach helps the RF institution to avoid the violation of the banking laws and regulations while appearing to fulfill the requirements of the RF law.

- The well-known banking regulation called Regulation "Z" (Truth in Lending Act; TILA) in the United States requires disclosure of an (*implied*) interest rate that includes in the process of calculating it all costs involved in any consumer lending transaction.
- Cost-plus transactions bear a striking similarity to regular interest-based banking transactions because of the way the profit element is figured out and calculated. This profit is usually tied to the prevailing interest rate in the market. Frankly, it looks like, smells like, and feels like it is riba (a process which includes renting money.)

These issues will be further addressed in Chapters 10 and 11.

Leasing (Ijara)[4] Rules

The Judeo-Christian-Islamic Shari'aa law includes rules about renting (short-term) or leasing (long-term) of the right to use an item (usufruct). The rules that organize the act of leasing are as follows:

- Renting or leasing is defined by the RF law (Shari'aa) as a contract to take advantage of renting the right to use an item. It is important to stress here that the item to be leased must have a usufruct. For example, one can rent the use of a car or a house while keeping title of ownership to the car or the house with the title owner (because these items are non-fungibles meaning that their nature does not change upon use, and they can be returned mostly in the original shape they were when these were first rented out). However, one cannot rent the use of an apple (fungible, meaning that its nature changes upon using it; eating or consuming it in a food recipe) because once it is eaten, it will not exist and one would have infringed on its ownership.
- The two categories of the Commodities Indexation Discipline described as reference calibrating materials are (1) Pricing metals like gold and silver and (2) Staple foods like wheat, barley, rice, dates, salt, and corn, for example.
- These two categories of commodities that are used as calibrating references to establish prices in the market cannot be dealt with in a riba

way, which means that when exchanged, substance for substance, there can be no increase over the original value (riba al-fadl). That is, the calibrating reference commodities including gold or silver and food staples, cannot be leased or rented and cannot be speculated with in the market place because they are references for establishing value, just as we reference the measurement of length with what is agreed to be a "one foot" reference metal located in a special safe in London under controlled weather-conditions in order to use as a standard and global reference scale to what we call a foot in length.

- In addition, one cannot rent something that changes its nature upon using, such as a loaf of bread or an apple. These items are fungibles and cannot be rented. They can only change hands by changing titles of ownership. Another example to demonstrate the ownership versus renting and how it may be confused: one cannot rent a cow in order to collect its milk. That is because when one collects the milk, one acts as if one owns the milk. This is problematic, because the original contract was about leasing the origin (i.e., the cow), not about owning the product (i.e., the milk).
- The usufruct—or the beneficiary use of the subject—can be the use of:
  a. An asset like a home or car.
  b. The facility of an asset, such as the use of a car (for driving), a business like a franchise store (a gas station or a fast food business), a medical clinic, or an X-ray machine.
  c. The work or productive services of an individual, such as an engineer, builder, worker, or any person who can offer defined valuable work. This concept is being used by some institutions, despite the objection of many RF scholars, as a foundation to offer RF student loans.

The RF Legal Foundation on Leasing

Leasing is allowed according to the revelations found in the Qur'aan, the Sunnah (way of life and the tradition) of Prophet Muhammad[5] (pp), and the unanimous opinion of the eminent RF scholars.

In the Qur'aan:

> *43:32 Is it they who would portion out the Mercy of thy Lord? It is We Who portion out between them their livelihood in the life of this world: and We raise some of them above others in ranks, so that some may command work from others [through renting their services]. But the Mercy of thy Lord is better than the [wealth] which they amass.*

2:233 If ye decide on [renting the services of] a foster-mother for your offspring, there is no blame on you, provided ye pay [the mother] what ye offered, on equitable terms. But fear God and know that He sees well what ye do.

28:26 Said one of the [damsels]: "O my [dear] father! Engage him [rent the services of Prophet Moses] on wages: truly the best of men for thee to employ is the [man] who is strong and trusty."

28:27 He said: "I intend to wed one of these my daughters to thee, on condition that thou serve me for eight years; but if thou complete ten years, it will be [grace] from thee. But I intend not to place thee under a difficulty: thou wilt find me, indeed, if God wills, one of the righteous."

Process

- At the request of the client, the RF finance institution would purchase the item registers its title in the institution's name and lease it back to the client for a predefined term.

  The item purchase has two titles: the title of ownership (called, in the Shari'aa law, *Milk ul Raqabaah*) and the right to use it (called, in the Shari'aa law, *Haq Ul Manfa'aa*).
- The RF financial institution, in its capacity as a lessor, would own title to the asset and in turn would lease the right for its use to the lessee, who would proceed to use the item according to the terms of the mutually agreed-upon leasing contract. The client pays a monthly or periodic lease payment at a market rate that is defined by applying the RF Marking-to-Market Discipline discussed earlier and has been agreed upon between the RF finance institution (lessor) and the client (lessee).

The fundamental issue that must be clearly addressed here is the rate at which the asset is leased. In many cases, the "Islamic" banking officer would quote the interest rate of the day as an agreed-upon lease rate. This approach presents a serious problem with the RF discipline. That is why this book advocates that the lease rate used must correspond to the actual live market lease rate as researched by both parties. This is done by asking market practitioners and by live research of market leasing rates of similar items. These appraisals of live market lease rates of similar items must be fully documented and must be part of the leasing contract and necessary documents to complete the RF financing file. These and other issues will be discussed in greater detail in Chapter 11.

In this context, there are two types of riba-based leasing available in the market:

1. *Rental or lease (ijarah):* This finance method, used globally, offers the pure leasing of assets. The asset is leased for a specific period of time and then returned to the title holder at the end of the lease period. These leases are similar to leasing an automobile for two or three years, then returning it to the owner. However, it is important to stress that in today's leasing practices, the monthly lease payment is based on a projected value of the item at the end of the lease term (like the projected value of a car, say, after three years). This practice is not acceptable by the Judeo-Christian-Islamic Shari'aa law because no one can project the future market price of an item; only God knows the future. That is why the price at the end of the lease has to be marked to the active live market at that time by applying the RF Marking-to-Market Discipline. In addition, the difference between the projected value of the item—sale price—at the end of the lease is subtracted from the purchase value at the beginning of the lease. The net is amortized at a defined rental rate of money (interest rate), which renders the transaction a riba transaction.
2. *Lease-to-Own (ijarah-wa-imtilak or ijarah-wa-iqtinaa):* In this method of leasing, the user and title owner agree to a monthly payment that consists of two parts. One part has to do with the gradual purchase of the property by the lessee from the lessor, and the other part has to do with the rental of either the money, as in the riba-based financial leases, or the rental of the actual asset at the prevailing market rate, as in RF leasing where the RF Marking-to-Market Discipline is applied.

This model will be discussed in detail in Chapter 11, and a real case application will be presented in Chapter 14.

Joint Venture (Musharaka) Direct Investment/Equity Ownership or Partnership

In this model, the RF financial institution or its investment subsidiary enters into a direct investment with the customer in the form of equity ownership. Profit or loss would be assigned to each joint venture according to a well-defined distribution formula.

Money Management (Mudaraba)

In this model, the RF financial institution itself can act as a money manager through its investment banking company.

The RF financial institution can also delegate that portfolio management function, as a trusted and appointed representative through a valid proxy, to other qualified money managers.

The money management (*mudaraba*) contract would define the responsibility of the RF institution in its capacity as a money manager (*mudharib*) or as an agent of the client (*wakeel*, which means a representative with discretionary authority) who is responsible to find money manager(s) who will meet the client's defined investment objective, investment time horizon, and the risk tolerance.

Financing Future Production (Ba'i ul Salam)

This model is used to finance the cost of future production of a manufactured product or an orchard. The customer would agree with the RF finance institution to forward the cost of future production. The RF financial institution would come to an agreement to buy the production of an orchard, a farm, or a manufactured product (like equipment or automobiles) before it is produced, at an agreed-upon price. The money is paid in advance to the producer. The producer, in turn, would use the money to purchase the basic services, pay wages, and buy raw materials necessary for the production. This way, the RF financial institution would help in the growth of the economy by providing the liquidity needed by the producing entity. An important guideline that should be guarded against is the possibility of hoarding or "cornering" of free markets by the financing entity.

The preceding RF financing techniques are presented to familiarize the reader with the models used. For a detailed outline and description of these techniques, please refer to Chapter 13 and to an excellent book on the subject: *Understanding Islamic Finance*.[6]

REVIEW QUESTIONS

1. Please explain the "Commodities" Hadeeth (sayings of Prophet Muhammad [pp]). Please elaborate on why he detailed it and how it impacts transactions.
2. Please explain the new Commodity Indexation Discipline proposed in the book and how it was based on the commodities Hadeeth.
3. Please explain how the Commodity Indexation Discipline can be used as a macroeconomic tool in trade, markets, and monetary policy.
4. How can the Commodity Indexation Discipline be used in developing a new monetary regime that is fair to all nations and can replace the Bretton Woods broken monetary regime?

5. What is the *Marking-to-Market Discipline* pioneered by Islam to promote free markets and trading between cities and nations?
6. How does it promote free markets and international trade?
7. What was it based on?
8. A person has a golden ring with a precious stone that weighs 15 ounces. It has gold content of 10 ounces. He wanted to exchange it for a gold bar. Please enumerate the steps and conditions of the exchange:
   a. Can he exchange it today and receive the bar after 3 months?
   b. Can he get the price in gold coins over 12 months in the future?
   c. Can he receive the price in silver? How much silver?
   d. If he gets the silver, can he pay back in 3 months or over 12 months?
9. How do you mark the following items to market?
   a. A car
   b. A house
   c. A kidney dialysis machine
10. Where can we get information on a house that we intend to buy that would be representative to marking that house to market? Please list two sources.

NOTES

1. Peter Kilborn, "Baker Hints at Gold as Guide on Policy," *New York Times*, October 1, 1987.
2. Syed Saabiq, *Fiqh Al Sunnah*, *Arabic*, Vol. 3 (Beirut, Lebanon: Daar Al Kitaab Al Araby for Publishing and Distribution, November 1971), 138.
3. Please visit www.LARIBA.com for more details.
4. See note 2.
5. Prophet Muhammad (pp) was reported to have said, "Give the person you hire his/her wages before the sweat that they invested on the job dries up," meaning to pay them as soon as possible (related by Ibn Majah).
6. Muhammad Ayub, *Understanding Islamic Finance* (Hoboken, NJ: Wiley Finance, 2007).

CHAPTER 4

The Law: The Judeo-Christian-Islamic Shari'aa

An overview on the prohibition of riba/ribit/interest/usury in Judaism, Christianity, and Islam was summarized in Chapter 2. During the early medieval period, the Islamic RF finance models were used by caravan traders conducting business between Arabia and the rest of the world, and in particular in trading through the Silk Road. As commercial and business activities increased, and with the growth of international trade and the creation of money, a sophisticated riba-based banking and finance system emerged and developed in Europe. The prohibition of ribit/riba was relaxed by the rabbinical teachings, the Roman Catholic Church, and the Protestant churches, as detailed in Chapter 2. This chapter is designed to introduce the reader to the tedious, meticulous, and detailed processes used by qualified scholars in the Judeo-Christian-Islamic Shari'aa law to come up with legal rulings (edicts or *fatwas*) that would comply with the teaching of God and His prophets to offer solutions to everyday challenges.

Muslims are required by the Judeo-Christian-Islamic Shari'aa law not to deal in riba. Religious leaders and scholars, who are revered by the faithful in all parts of the world, from the small villages to the largest cities, including those who live as minorities in Asia, Africa, North America, and other parts of the world, are taught that dealing in riba is a major sin.

With the growth of commerce, trading, and industrial development in Europe, more sophisticated riba-based banking operations and trade financing tools were developed to give credit and to help grow businesses. When Europeans began expanding their trade routes into the Turkish Ottoman Empire and colonizing many of their former member states, they brought this new riba-based banking system with them. The riba-based banking system was used only to serve the needs of most of the European businesspeople and their local representatives because the local masses were not trained and equipped to catch up and take advantage of it. Most importantly, the local Muslim public and Muslim business community members did not use it because they believed that banking with interest was divinely prohibited (haram) by Judeo-Christian-Islamic Shari'aa law and was not accepted by the Muslims scholars and thought leaders. This produced, among the local Muslim population, a subculture of avoiding taking a loan altogether. Many may ask how the Muslims have managed their capital needs all these years. It was done in the form of micro-lending cooperatives between friends and family members on the local levels or between businessmen on the commercial level in an informal way; it is still being done now, in the twenty-first century. On the local community level, a group of, say, 10 friends might agree to start an informal small cooperative union, in which each of them places $10 with a trusted member of the group. They then agree, among themselves, as to the schedule of who gets paid in the first month, the second month, and so on. In this way, each member gets a sum of $100 in a certain month. There was no interest charged. The banking needs of the Muslim world, as in all developing countries, have been underserved, especially on the retail level. As these primitive societies began making contact with the world, they woke up to a big surprise. They found that they are at least 600 years behind in the fields of economics, finance, monetary theory, and discipline as well as in banking services. A sophisticated and far-reaching international banking system was slowly installed, and banking with interest became part of normal business transactions in many of these countries. Dissent and concern were expressed constantly by the religious leaders, but no one responded because the religious leaders in the early to middle part of the twentieth century did not have enough stature and were ignored. It is interesting to note here the experience of starting the first Egyptian nationally owned bank, Bank Misr, by the well-known entrepreneur Talaat Harb (1920–1941). Many scholars objected to it because of their concerns about the problem of dealing in riba. However, history records that the well-known progressive religious leader, Imam Muhammad Abduh (1849–1905), issued a fatwa (edict)[1] in 1901 allowing the Egyptian Post Office Savings Department to pay interest on deposits made by the public in its operations with a number of provisions (that were designed as exceptions and conditions to avoid riba) in order for the Post Office to operate and pay interest. That fatwa was called upon and was used as a basis that allowed Bank Misr (Bank of Egypt; *Misr* here is the name for Egypt in many Arabic and old languages) to organize and get started (April 13, 1920). As operations grew, the original provisions stated by Imam Abduh were diluted, and Bank Misr became another riba-based financial institution.

Today, Bank Misr offers a riba-free (RF) window for those interested in Islamic banking in order to compete in the Egyptian market.

With the first oil price jump in 1973 and the use of U.S. dollar as the official and only currency for oil trading came the flow of huge amounts of dollars to the oil-producing Gulf countries. The main concern at that time was the absorptive capacity of the local economies of the countries involved. Armies of commercial bankers and investment bankers landed in these oil-producing countries to expand the existing small riba-based banking operations and to link them efficiently with the international banking system. Many of the business and community leaders went along, but a few were very troubled at the sinful act of participating in riba.

One of them was the late King Faisal of Saudi Arabia. He pledged in 1974 to start a banking system that follows Islamic law (the Judeo-Christian-Islam RF law—Shari'aa). The major problem was the lack of a detailed code in the law that dealt with the existing and sophisticated needs of the customers of the banks and the varied products and services offered by these banks, which were all based on the prohibited riba. This marked the beginning of a brand-new field of RF scholarly research to develop codes of the law that pertains to modern RF consumer and business dealings and banking. Pioneering practitioners of RF banking in Egypt, Turkey, Malaysia, Dubai, Saudi Arabia, and Kuwait began by contacting scholars in the highest-placed Islamic theological seminary, Al Azhar Seminary in Cairo, Egypt. Because the idea was new, the task was very difficult; and because it involved bridging 600 years of a riba-based banking system that uses banking-based English language, which had not yet been mastered by the scholars, a solution was offered. The few leaders of the newly emerging RF banking industry formed a board of scholars that would start the difficult task of developing the RF banking and finance codes of the law. That was the beginning of the creation of what is now known as Shari'aa Board of Islamic Banks.

The religious scholars placed on the Shari'aa Board soon discovered that they did not know much about finance, banking, and monetary issues; they even did not know about the intricacies of bank operations and the riba-based culture and aspects of it. All that was known then were two major rules: interest cannot be charged, and the parties in a consumer or commercial transaction must share the profit and loss. In an effort to bridge the knowledge gap, the RF banking practitioners supplied the Shari'aa Board with riba-based banking practitioners to teach and explain in a crash course format how modern riba-based banks operated and the features of each riba-based banking product and service. Because English was an international banking medium of communication, there was a new demand for scholars who understood and spoke English. Most of these English-speaking scholars did not come from the Arabic-speaking countries; they came from the Asian Muslim countries, such as Pakistan, Malaysia, India, and Bangladesh. Many of these Asian scholars who had mastered English had also mastered Arabic, because it is a prerequisite for Shari'aa scholarship.

This cross-breeding of talents and diversified cultural and educational backgrounds created a rich body of qualified scholars at the Shari'aa Board level. However, because of the diversity in local cultural and educational backgrounds, there were a variety of opinions and levels of flexibility in interpreting the law on what was considered compliant with the Judeo-Christian-Islamic Shari'aa law and what was not. Two major directions were charted. In Egypt and Malaysia (most of the Malaysian scholars had been educated at Al Azhar seminary), Shari'aa opinions were more progressive and understanding of the challenges that were faced then and opted for gradualism in transformation. Scholars from India, Pakistan, and the Arab Gulf countries believed in a more strict approach toward interpreting what was halal (allowed) and what was haram (not allowed). As time went by, new leaders in the field of RF (Islamic/Shari'aa-based) finance law came from Pakistan, India, Egypt, Sudan, the Arab Gulf countries, Malaysia, Syria, Jordan, Lebanon, Europe, and the United States.

THE LAW: SHARI'AA

The word *Shari'aa* has been translated by most as *jurisprudence*. However, it is believed that the word *jurisprudence* does not fully describe what Shari'aa is. It is preferred to translate Shari'aa as "the law." This approach follows the same tradition as the revelations to Moses (pp), which were translated as "the law," and to Jesus (pp) as "the Gospel" (implying "the law"). The use of the terminology "the law" also confirms the Judeo-Christian-Islamic nature of the religion of Islam and hence the RF laws, regulations, and disciplines.

The word *Shari'aa* is derived from the root Arabic word *Shara'aa'*, which means "to introduce," "to enact," and "to prescribe."[2] It is composed of and embodies spiritual beliefs and rules of the religion (based on the Judeo-Christian-Islamic body of laws) that includes ethics, morality, and behavioral admonitions. Shari'aa then is the divine, immutable law. It details the set of rules a Muslim should live, judge, and govern by, and it includes the moral and legal rulings and mandates of Islam. In other words, it is the integration of all the laws sent by God through all of His prophets.

Sources of Shari'aa

The principal sources of Shari'aa are the Qur'aan, which is the unchangeable and the proven inculcation of all of God's messages to all His prophets, including the Torah and the Gospel; and the way of life and example of living (Sunnah) and sayings (Hadeeth) of Prophet Muhammad (pp).[3]

The Qur'aan

Being a Muslim is a description of the state of a person who has chosen to submit his/her will to that of God. Based on this foundation, the Qur'aan teaches that Noah (pp), Abraham (pp), Ishmael (pp), Isaac (pp), and their descendants, as well as Moses (pp), Jesus (pp), and Muhammad (pp) are all Muslims, as they all submitted their will, their way of life, and their style of living to the will of God. It is believed that in order to open up our hearts, our spirits, and our minds here in the United States and in the world, God's messages to His last three brothers in the faith—Moses (pp), Jesus (pp), and Muhammad (pp)—it is preferred and strongly recommended that we should popularize Islam, not as a stand-alone religion, but as a manifestation of the Judeo-Christian-Islamic integration of recorded human religious and spiritual experiences, as taught by God through His revelations to all His peoples and prophets (pp).

The Qur'aan[4] charts out the sequence of truths and its revelation throughout history:

> *3:84 Say: "We believe in God, and in that which has been bestowed from on high upon us, and that which has been bestowed upon Abraham and Ishmael and Isaac and Jacob and their descendants, and that which has been vouchsafed by their Sustainer unto Moses and Jesus and all the [other] prophets: we make no distinction between any of them. [68] And unto Him do we surrender ourselves.*
>
> *3:3 It is He Who sent down to thee [step by step], in truth, the Book [the Qur'aan], confirming what went before it; and He sent down the Law [of Moses] and the Gospel [of Jesus] before this, as a guide to mankind, and He sent down the [Qur'aan] criterion [of judgment between right and wrong].*

The Qur'aan also confirms the sequence of revelation from the Torah (the Jewish Bible) to the Gospel (Christian Bible.) The Qur'aan uses the word *Injeel*, which means the Gospel or the teachings of Jesus Christ, based on the Old Testament and the New Testament. (Christian Arabs also use the word *Injeel* for the Bible).

> *5:46 And in their footsteps We sent Jesus the son of Mary, confirming the Law [of Moses] that had come before him: We sent him the Gospel: therein was guidance and light, and confirmation of the Law that had come before him: a guidance and an admonition to those who revere God.*
>
> *46:12 And before this, was the Book of Moses as a guide and a mercy: And this Book [The Qur'aan] confirms [it] in the Arabic tongue; to admonish the unjust, and as Glad Tidings to those who do right.*

Furthermore, the Qur'aan instructs the believers in an effort to tie together all of God's messages, messengers, and prophets in the chain of life and human development:

> *2:136 Say: "We believe in God, and in that which has been bestowed from on high upon us, and that which has been bestowed upon Abraham and Ishmael and Isaac and Jacob and their descendants, and that which has been vouchsafed to Moses and Jesus; and that which has been vouchsafed to all the [other] prophets by their Sustainer: we make no distinction between any of them. And it is unto Him that we surrender ourselves.*

And referring to Prophet Abraham's offspring, the Qur'aan reveals:

> *6:84 And We bestowed upon him Isaac and Jacob; and We guided each of them as We had guided Noah aforetime. And out of his offspring, [We bestowed prophethood upon] David, and Solomon, and Job, and Joseph, and Moses, and Aaron: for thus do We reward the doers of good.*

As to Prophet Moses (pp), the Qur'aan reveals clearly that he indeed spoke to God, and it details his history in a way very similar to what we read in the Old Testament:

> *2:53 And [remember the time] when We vouchsafed unto Moses the divine writ—and [thus] a standard by which to discern the true from the false—so that you might be guided aright.*

In our efforts as believers in Moses (pp), Jesus (pp), and Muhammad (pp), or the Judeo-Christian-Islamic foundation for building a decent, peaceful, and wonderful society, we are advised by God in the Qur'aan:

> *42:13 In matters of faith, He has ordained for you that which He had enjoined upon Noah—and into which We gave thee [O Muhammad] insight through revelation as well as that which We had enjoined upon Abraham, and Moses, and Jesus: Steadfastly uphold the [true] faith, and do not break up your unity therein. [And even though] that [unity of faith] to which thou callest them appears oppressive to those who are wont to ascribe to other beings or forces a share in His divinity, God draws unto Himself everyone who is willing, and guides unto Himself everyone who turns unto Him.*

That is, the application of the Law of God (the Torah and Prophet Moses [pp], the Gospel and Jesus [pp]) is confirmed, complimented, and expanded on by the Qur'aan; it is the responsibility of all people of all faiths, and especially Muslims. It is not the intent here to make this chapter a detailed study of the Judeo-Christian-Islamic promise of the future; however, it is hoped that this new approach will be researched and expanded upon in the future to popularize this concept in order to build a peaceful and prosperous world.

The Way of Life (Sunnah) of the Prophet

Sunnah means a system, a path, or an example, referring to the example as practiced by the Prophet Muhammad (pp). It is the detailed description of how Prophet Muhammad (pp) put life in the Qur'aan by living according to its teachings and God's inspiration. The details are included in the meticulously researched, documented, and recorded body of the Prophet's (pp) sayings, comments, and actions done with his approval, which is called the *Hadeeth*.[5] The Hadeeth provides information about the Sunnah (the examples provided by Prophet Muhammad of how to live by applying the rules of God revealed in the Qur'aan); it was recorded in the two centuries after Prophet Muhammad's (pp) death, in authenticated Hadeeth collections.

The Science and Foundation of Scholarly Research, or "Usul Ul Fiqh"

Applications of the Shari'aa produce a whole body of scholarly research by a class of scholars called learned scholars (*fuquahaa;* the singular is *faqih*, scholar) in Islamic research circles and institutions all over the world, regardless of the local language. Shari'aa embodies the whole discipline of scholarly research and the detailed authentication of the codes, references, and rulings. It is called *The Science of Origins and Foundation of Scholarly Work* (known in Islamic circles as *Usul Ul Fiqh*). Scholarly research, or the science of Fiqh, is based on the best efforts of the scholars and the scholarly institutions involved in the research.

The opinions and edicts issued by the learned scholars may differ between countries, depending on local circumstances, roots, culture, and intellect. In the United States, one can experience an American federal law that covers the whole country; but at the same time, there are state laws that are specific to each state. That is why Fiqh opinions may vary or change with time and place of implementation, based on new scholarly research examining the applicability of what was ruled earlier in relation to the current needs of the specific situation at hand in a certain particular community or state.

Fiqh classifies human activities into the following five categories:

- *Divinely required duty or obligation* (fard *or* wajib). Every Muslim is required at a minimum to perform these specific rituals, obligations, and actions (such as prayers, fasting during the month of Ramadan, paying zakah [alms], and performing the hajj [pilgrimage to Makkah], for those who can afford it). Failing to do so is classified as divinely disallowed and forbidden (haram); further, it is considered an offense against the faith, because it violates the established limits of what is acceptable (*hudood*). Examples of haram activities are the association in worship with others than one God, the consumption of alcohol, and not caring for one's parent and family.
- *Recommended and encouraged with pleasure, but not mandatory* (mandoob *or* musta'habb). A Muslim is expected to perform these duties only as an extra effort over and above the minimum required, as previously discussed. Those who choose to do it are interested in excelling in the faith, the service of God, and spirituality. The performance of these actions is rewarded, but is not considered a violation if not done. Examples are praying more than the minimum number of required prayers and paying more than is required by the zakah (alms) rulings.
- *Allowed* (mubah). The origin of all Shari'aa rules is that all is allowed, except what has been clearly prohibited. The acceptability of these actions is analyzed by a process of deduction because there was no mention of these activities in the body of the scholarly law (Fiqh), and the books of law (Shari'aa and Fiqh) were silent about such actions.
- *Hated, disliked, disappointing, and frowned upon with disappointment, but not disallowed* (makruh). Although these actions are frowned upon, doing these activities is not prohibited and is not punishable. It is an accepted fact that devout Muslims do not perform makruh.
- *Divinely unlawful* (haram). These actions are clearly prohibited by the law (Shari'aa) and are punishable by penalties specified in the Qur'aan.

The branches of Fiqh (literally, *Fiqh* means "in-depth understanding") include but are not limited to worship rules, family law, inheritance law, commerce and trade transactions law, property law, civil law, criminal law, and laws and regulation covering administration, taxation, constitution, international relations, defense, peace and war ethics, and other categories.

Some of the scholarly scientific approaches used to arrive at a ruling and conclusions reached after comprehensive research, deliberation, and documentation are:

- *The consensus approach* (ijma). This includes rulings or edicts that have been agreed upon by the majority of the fuquahaa (scholars; plural of faqih) in Shari'aa. Consensus (ijma) applies to a situation where no clear conclusion can be made from the Qur'aan and the Sunnah. In this situation, the knowledgeable and well-versed and learned scholars (fuquahaa), in the form of a *Fatwa Board* (a board that includes accomplished scholars and specializes in and is entrusted by the local government with the task of receiving inquiries and issuing edicts or fatwa), will confer and agree on a satisfactory solution to the particular problem by issuing a fatwa (edict—legal Shari'aa-based opinion).
- *The analogy approach* (qiyas). This approach uses reference or comparison of similar circumstances (*qiyas*), in which the fuquahaa use analogies and make comparisons that will allow them to interpolate and/or extrapolate the existing rules of Shari'aa and the body of scholarly research (Fiqh). The concept of qiyas, or analogy, is applied in circumstances where guidance from the Qur'aan and the Sunnah is not directly available. A problem is solved by a process of deduction, comparing the current situation to the ruling passed on a similar situation that occurred earlier.

A number of great Muslim scholars and religious leaders (*imams*)[6] devoted themselves to the collection, compilation, understanding, and application of the scholarly research (Fiqh) and the sources and procedures of the law (Shari'aa) and its practices.

Performing Scholarly Research to Develop and Pass Religious Edicts and Rulings: The Process of Issuing a Fatwa (An Edict)[7]

The law (Shari'aa) describes how Muslims should behave in every aspect of life, from private matters between the individual and God to relationships with others in the family and the wider community. Shari'aa is developed based on Fiqh, the detailed research work conducted by fuquahaa, the highly accomplished scholars who have a tested, proven, and recognized track record and body of accomplishments over many years. The body of detailed laws developed by these fuquahaa is called the Fiqh. Shari'aa is hence the referenced legal and canonical bar used by accomplished and recognized religious fuquahaa in developing detailed legal codes for different societies in different times, depending on local needs, problems, and circumstances, as well as on the time these needs arise.

It is also important to note that Shari'aa is applicable only to people who believe in the Islamic faith. Those who choose to not be believers in Islam are not required to abide by Shari'aa. That is why, for example, zakah, or alms giving, an Islamic ritual ordained by Shari'aa and one of the five pillars of Islam, is replaced by the act of tax collection from non-Muslims who live in a Muslim country; this tax is called *jizyah*, which means taxes.

The Ultimate Intent and Goals of the Law (Shari'aa): *Maqasid* Al Shari'aa[8]

Accomplished and recognized fuquahaa have researched and developed over the years a set of goals that they use to guide believers on how to live comfortably while abiding by the law (Shari'aa.) They developed detailed sets of moral and legal rulings to guide those who are asked to issue an edict (fatwa). These rulings are all assembled in the books of Fiqh, which are similar to books of legal codes and are continually updated with the changes that evolve in a particular society.

To develop a legal canonical system of laws based on the Fiqh that leads to developing the law (Shari'aa) about what is halal (divinely allowed) and what is haram (divinely prohibited), the following fundamental rules must be followed:

- Whatever is not prohibited by the Qur'aan and Sunnah is usually acceptable and is considered allowable (halal).
- The main objective of the law (Shari'aa) is to push away what is harmful to all aspects of life, family, assets, and the faith, and to bring to bear what is good and beneficial to all (in Arabic, the rule is: *Dafu'l Dharar Wa Jalbul Manf'aa*[9]). Based on this important and basic rule, one cannot hurt himself, his family, his wealth, or his faith while attempting to apply the law.
- If a person cannot live by the law in its entirety, he or she cannot be excused for not trying, in a step-by-step approach, until the goal is achieved. The rule states literally that if one cannot achieve the perfect goal of reaching perfect adherence to the law because of conditions and circumstances that are difficult to meet, that would not give that person an excuse for not trying to achieve at least a part of that goal, however small that is (in Arabic, the rule is: *Mala Yudraku Kulluhu La Yutraku Julluhu*).

As explained earlier, the legalistic expression of the law in a canonical fashion is called the Fiqh. Fiqh is changeable, depending on circumstances of places, people, specific experiences, and the accepted customs, which is known in the Islamic research and scholarly circles as *urf*. The science that organizes the process of generating edicts is called Usul Al Fiqh, or foundations of Fiqh. In general, Fiqh rulings that would lead to a set of canonical laws are concerned with achieving five basic goals. These goals are, in order of priority, concerned with the maintenance of:

1. Religion, faith, and the Islamic way of life called *deen* (meaning religion or a way of life)
2. Life
3. Family and offspring, including children, grandchildren, and relations of kin
4. Intellect
5. Wealth

By applying these goals in sequence, one would conclude that:

1. Wealth should be spent and invested in gaining knowledge.
2. Knowledge and advances in the field of intellectual accomplishment lead to better knowledge and the advancement of intellect.
3. Knowledge and intellect are used to serve the family.
4. The family is provided with a better, healthy, and honorable life.
5. The ultimate achievement will be a faith-based, capable community that upholds the faith and lives by the law (Shari'aa.) As a result, faith in the process of issuing a fatwa (edict) will be held in highest regard, will be made attractive to many, and will be accepted and followed by the community as the preferred religion, system, and a way of life.

For example, the solicitation of an edict or a question for an opinion of Shari'aa regarding wealth takes a second priority behind the benefits to the intellect, knowledge, and life. That is why the fuquahaa (learned scholars) permitted the use of alcohol-based antiseptics in surgical procedures to preserve and protect life, despite the fact that alcohol is divinely prohibited as haram. The reason it is allowed in surgical situations is that preserving life has a higher priority (priority 2) than preserving the capability of the mind and intellect (priority 4), which is needed by the faithful to know God and to exercise good judgment and is waived if alcohol is consumed.

Scholars indicated that they must not only classify and prioritize the aim of the law based on the different levels of importance, but they must also consider another dimension of prioritization, and that is levels of urgency of the matter in the following three levels:

1. Basic requirements and needs (*dharuririyat*) of those who need a ruling on a certain matter.
2. Complementary additions to further refine the basic requirements in priority (1), based on the need of the inquirer (*hajjiyat*).
3. Improvements, modifications, and further refinements of the complementary requirements defined in item 2 (*tahsinaat*).

Working in this two-dimensional domain, and combining the five levels of goals with the three levels of urgencies, one gets at least 15 combinations of priorities. In other words, the scholar (faqih), in his or her pursuit of an edict (fatwa or opinion), should meticulously consider the 15 possibilities and carefully analyze the situation at hand before reaching an edict. When competing rulings occur, the ruling that belongs to a higher block in the table displayed in Exhibit 4.1 takes precedent over a ruling from the lower block. In other words, any ruling that is classified as a refinement gives way to another, which is classified as complementary, and so on. However, it would be very useful to think in other dimensions and to develop algorithms that can be beneficial to all people. This is where a new generation of sophisticated, computer-oriented, and analytical scholars will contribute to the science of deriving fatwa (edicts) in the future. It is important to ponder on this approach when making a ruling or developing a model for RF finance in a certain country or region of the world, especially where Muslims are minorities, as in the case of the United States, Europe, and South Asia.

Dr. Riad Adhami included in an article the table of priorities shown in Exhibit 4.1 that is used by the qualified scholars (the issuer of the fatwa, called mufti) in making an edict (a religiously binding edict called fatwa). The table illustrates the concept of prioritization[10] discussed earlier.

For example, ablution (*wudu*, washing to prepare for prayers) is a prerequisite for conducting prayers. However, if the person is ill and cannot use water on the body because it would hurt the health of his skin, the edict would call for allowing the person to do ablution symbolically (in a dry way) by applying what is known as *tayammum* procedure (instead of using the hands to carry the water to wash with, the person would wipe the hands on a dry, clean object like clean sand or surface). In this case, ablution is considered a refinement level in the category of maintaining the faith/religion (priority level B) while health and life are on the top row and are classified as required (priority level A). The same approach can be used when calling a stream of rent in an RF finance scheme by the name *implied interest* or using the word *interest* to satisfy the local laws in a non-Muslim land in order to uphold the laws of that land.

EXHIBIT 4.1 Table of Priorities

Priority	1. Faith/Religion	2. Life	3. Family	4. Intellect and Knowledge	5. Wealth
A Required	1. Required to maintain the faith/religion	2. Required to maintain life	3. Required to maintain family	4. Required to maintain intellect and knowledge	5. Required to maintain wealth
B Complementary	6. Complementary to maintain the faith/religion	7. Complementary to maintain life	8. Complementary to maintain family	9. Complementary to maintain intellect and knowledge	10. Complementary to maintain wealth
C Refined Further	11. Further refinement in the maintenance of faith/religion	12. Further refinement in the maintenance of life	13. Further refinement in the maintenance of family	14. Further refinement in the maintenance of intellect and knowledge	15. Further refinement in the maintenance of wealth

There has been a religious renaissance worldwide. Many people of all faiths are trying to discover the best way to live. They are searching deep within their faiths to find solutions to the many modern-day problems that they face in the twenty-first century and to achieve spiritual fulfillment. The believers who are not well educated in the faith and its rules or in the law (Shari'aa) want to live in a puritan way, conducting a true exemplary life as ordained by God in His books, the examples of the prophets of God, and according to the law. These puritans face many challenges that require a religious edict or ruling, but the resolutions to challenges become a religious opinion first in the public domain. With the advent of efficient means of communication and mass media outlets in the form of hundreds if not thousands of satellite TV channels, many programs have been devoted to answering questions about lifestyles, behavior, interpersonal relations, marital and family problems, financial and business dealings, and the like. This has generated a very high demand for learned religious scholars and leaders who are qualified to issue a religious opinion or edict (fatwa). The person who issues these fatwas, called a mufti, is an elected scholar (*faqueeh*) by a special board of highly qualified and accomplished muftis.

The private fatwa issued by a local scholar or imam (religious leader) becomes, later on, a binding, legal fatwa once it has stood the test of scholarly, legal, and public scrutiny. Al-Azhar Seminary in Cairo, Egypt, the oldest university in the world, is the only Islamic seminary in the Sunni Muslim domain that teaches the Fiqh according to the five schools listed earlier, including the *Sunni* and *Shi'i* schools of thought (*madh'hab*). The seminary contains specialized departments in different disciplines. One discipline is the law (Shari'aa) and Usul Ul Fiqh (the foundations of Fiqh). The graduates develop their skills as faqih through a continual process of supervised research and a long-term track record of interaction with leading and accomplished scholars and the public.

In Egypt, at Al-Azhar Seminary, as well as in other Muslim countries around the world, there is only one final and highest authority in authorizing a public religious edict, or fatwa. This highest authority has the title of the *Grand Mufti,* or the highest scholar in charge of legislation of fatwas after authenticating it by a Board of Supreme Scholars. He presides over this board of accomplished scholars who are classified as distinguished *fuquahaa*. This board holds hearings, conducts and critiques research, and makes recommendations for fatwas (edicts), which are then submitted for the approval of the Fatwa Committee of Al-Azhar Seminary and, eventually, of the Grand Mufti. Essentially the same process is followed in the Islamic republic of Iran (at the *Hawza* in Qum), in Iraq (at the *Hawza* in Najaf), and in Pakistan and India. It is important to note that in Pakistan and India, the elderly scholars, in an effort to train a new generation of Shari'aa legislators, started many colleges that graduate young scholars who carry the title of mufti. It is important to warn the reader here to not being misled by the title mufti as used by many of these Indo-Pakistani graduates, because their achievements in their fields after graduation must be first demonstrated. It is preferred to call them junior mufti, or mufti-in-residence trainees.

Obviously, people are free to choose whose opinions to follow, but it is important to share with the reader the parameters that should be used in recruiting and evaluating (for the fatwa issuing assignment) candidates to serve as advisers on Shari'aa in their institutions. The following is an abbreviated list of the basic qualifications that must be met before a person is qualified to issue a fatwa and act as a scholar in the law (Shari'aa):

- Mastery of the Qur'aanic language, Arabic, as demonstrated by a certificate of graduation from an accredited seminary or university.
- Mastery in the knowledge, meanings, and historic reasons of revelation of the verses of the Qur'aan, as demonstrated by graduation from a recognized institute.
- Formal education in the law (Shari'aa) from a recognized theological seminary or a university that has a reputable department of religion.
- Knowledge of the Jewish Bible and the Christian Bible; this is highly preferred, especially in the West and in Asian and African countries with diversified religious affiliations, but not necessarily required.
- Proven analytical abilities, as witnessed by the guiding scholars, professors, and supervisors who were in charge of teaching; this includes the ability to methodically and scientifically analyze and properly articulate and document difficult issues and legal problems and to debate different opinions in recognized forums and in public.
- Knowledge of computers, word processing, and the Microsoft Office suite (or the like) and of using the Internet.
- Published research in respected media and trade magazines and other outlets, and documented research leading to the development of new legal codes.
- Strong written, verbal, and communication skills, and the ability to speak in public.
- Proven reputation in the community for public service, knowledge, counseling, caring, piety, and generosity.
- Knowledge of family matters, which requires in most cases that the candidate is happily married and that his/her family presents a successful role model to the community.

- Proven track record of issuing fatwas that have been recognized and agreed to by a learned body of scholars and seminary researchers, such as Al-Azhar University (Egypt), specialized universities and seminaries in Al-Madinah and Makkah (Saudi Arabia), Qum (Iran), Al-Najaf (Iraq), and universities (such as the International Islamic University) in Pakistan, Malaysia, Kuwait, and the United States (e.g., Princeton, Harvard, and Claremont) and Canada (e.g., McGill).
- Proven expertise in one of the aspects of living (examples include advanced studies leading to a degree in business administration, economics, and/or finance, for a scholar who wants to practice in the field of RF banking and finance; or expertise in humanities, family law, and psychology, for a scholar who wants to concentrate on matters pertaining to family law).

Obviously, the above list of stringent requirements is what can be called the ideal. It will take time to achieve all these requirements. All students who aspire to become scholars are strongly urged to work hard to achieve a high level of qualification as scholars. This approach is believed to lead to the production of a new generation of scholars for the twenty-first century who will be well positioned to pave the way toward a happier lifestyle in all aspects of life for all people of all faiths, including the RF lifestyle advocated in this book.

THE SHARI'AA BOARD IN AN RF (ISLAMIC) BANK OR FINANCE COMPANY

Despite the fact that the first formal Islamic bank was started in Dubai by Sheikh Saeed bin Lutah in the mid-1970s, there was no record of a formal effort to institutionalize the process of developing a formal body that would research and develop the RF banking and finance legal code according to the law (Shari'aa). Later, three leading financial institutions were started in a formal and dedicated effort to start RF (Islamic) finance and banking. These were: (1) *Dar Al-Maal Al-Islami*, which was started in Geneva, Switzerland, by the son of the late King Faisal of Saudi Arabia, Prince Muhammad Al-Faisal; (2) *Bayt al Tamweel Al Kuwaiti—Kuwait Finance House* in Kuwait, which was organized as a shareholders' Islamic finance company headed by a Kuwaiti of Iraqi origin, Sheikh Bazee Al-Yaseen; and (3) *Dallah Al Baraka Group*, in Jeddah, Saudi Arabia, started by Sheikh Saleh Abdullah Kamel, a former auditor in the Department of Defense in Saudi Arabia and later an important force in the growth and development of a global RF banking movement, with vision and entrepreneurship, who was, in fact, at least 25 years ahead of his time.

They all were faced with the challenge of developing, for the first time in modern history, an RF financial legal code based on the law (Shari'aa). At that time, they resorted to the highest religious authority in the Arabic-speaking part of the Muslim world, which happened to be Al-Azhar Seminary in Cairo, Egypt.

Prince Al-Faisal appointed Sheikh Muhammad Khater, the *grand mufti* of Egypt (a position appointed by the president of the Republic of Egypt), to be the head of a board responsible for developing RF financial tools and methods that are compliant with the law (Shari'aa). The aim was to help with investing—according to the law—some of the vast amounts of "petrodollars" that resulted from the windfall created by the sudden increase in oil price in 1973.

Sheikh Bazee Al-Yaseen chose Sheikh Muhammad Badr Abdel Basset to be his chief scholar in the law. He was an accomplished scholar from the faculty of Daar-Ul Uloom, the House of Knowledge, at Ain Shams University in Egypt, a prestigious college that graduates many high-caliber and recognized leaders of thought and research in the law (Shari'aa) in the Arab and Muslim world. Many of this college's graduates became effective and prominent imams and fuquahaa. Sheikh Abdel Basset helped in the development of the foundation of different RF finance models for use by the Kuwait Finance House.

Sheikh Saleh Kamel appointed a group of the highest religious authorities in many countries to develop an RF financing code based on the law. The group, which was later called—for the first time in modern history—the Shari'aa Board, was given the mandate to develop RF banking products and services that paralleled those available in the riba-based banking and financial services in the West. He appointed significant scholars from Egypt, Jordan, Syria, Sudan, and Saudi Arabia, and later from Malaysia, Pakistan, and India to develop further RF banking and finance models and products and services. He also organized annual seminars and symposia among these scholars and other financial and banking experts to discuss and analyze different riba-based banking products and services available in the West and to develop ways and means to make them compliant with the law (Shari'aa). He was very generous in his investments in the field of new scholarly research in this field. He started a pioneering library of Islamic banking and finance in Jordan, and departments of Islamic banking and finance at the University in Jeddah and at Al-Azhar University in Cairo. In his efforts to develop Islamic banking and finance internationally, he opened a finance company in London and started Al Baraka Bank in London in the mid-1980s. He and his associates at Dallah Al Baraka laid the foundation for communications between some of the top world bankers, financial experts, and business attorneys on one side and religious scholars on the other side for the first time in the modern history of Islam. Over the years, the group developed Islamic banking terminology, rules and regulations, operating standards, financing mechanisms, and products and services that comply with the law (Shari'aa) and that offer an RF alternative to the conventional riba-based ones in the fields of trade financing, auto financing, home mortgages, and business financing, as well as investing in the stock markets.

The Role of the Shari'aa Board

The Shari'aa Board in a typical RF (Islamic) bank is responsible for overseeing the application of different aspects of the law (Shari'aa) in the RF bank or the financial institution.[11] The Shari'aa Board (sometimes called Shari'aa Supervisory Committee), in general, certifies every product, finance model, and service provided by the RF financial institution. It also ensures that all the transactions and operations are in strict compliance with the principles of the law.

The Shari'aa Board is comprised of experts in the research and development of religious rulings by applying the law to financial and banking products and operations. The Board also helps in devising, with the assistance of banking professionals, RF financing models that fit within and compete with modern-day riba-based banking. In some, but not all, RF (Islamic) banks, the Board is empowered with the right of issuing a contradicting religious edict (fatwa) to the position of the bank's board of directors regarding any of the products, services, and/or procedures that violate the law (Shari'aa), if such a violation were uncovered. Some RF banks' bylaws require that the board of directors be obligated to implement the fatwa(s) issued by the Shari'aa Board. In some banks, like the Dubai Islamic Bank, the fatwa is implemented irrespective of whether a unanimous or a majority of the board of directors consensus secures the decision (clause 78 of the Bank's Memorandum & Articles of Association).[12]

Duties of the Shari'aa Board at the RF Bank

The Shari'aa Board (or Council) is looked upon by the RF bank management, board of directors, and shareholders as an expert source on the law (Shari'aa) and its application in RF financial and banking transactions. The board of directors of the RF bank often appoints one of the Shari'aa Board members as a voting member of the board of directors of the bank in charge of overseeing the implementation of the law in the Board. The board of directors of the RF bank may also appoint one of its members to be a member of the Shari'aa Board, to serve as a liaison and a source of hands-on banking operations by a practitioner between the two boards. The following is an abbreviated list of duties for a typical RF bank's Shari'aa Board:

- Detailed documentation of the recorded religious bases and foundations as extracted from the law (Shari'aa), with a complete record of the Shari'aa Board's deliberations and the reasons for and against a specific fatwa (edict) ruling. These proceedings, ideally, should be made transparent.
- Help in the process of innovating, manufacturing, and devising new Shari'aa-based RF banking and finance products and services with the banking professionals.
- Help in devising a detailed set of operating manuals and RF transactional procedures that will make the RF bank services competitive with existing riba-based banking services and products.
- Review and analysis of any contracts and/or agreements related to the services, operations, or outside vendors of the RF bank, to make certain that such agreements comply with the law.
- Participation in the design of the RF bank's training programs, including education about the foundations of the faith, the rules on compassion and honesty, the importance of fair and equal rights without discrimination, and the character of an RF banker who shuns misrepresentation of facts and the culture of pure selling at any cost to meet a sales goal and make a high commission.
- Participation in a hands-on training program on Shari'aa compliance, including the RF finance models used and how these models differ from those offered by the conventional riba-based banks.
- Supervision of the RF bank's day-to-day operations, interaction with the staff and customers, and pursuit of the highest quality of work in processing customers' applications and communicating with the outside world regarding truthful representation of the RF products and services offered by the RF banking staff. This includes random checking of incoming and outgoing mail and faxes, telephone conversations on help lines, and incoming and outgoing e-mails.
- Attention to developments pertaining to Shari'aa issues and new products and services at other competing RF banks, as well as riba-based banks.

The Shari'aa Board is required to submit a complete annual report to the board of directors of the bank, summarizing all the issues referred to the Board, as well as the Board's opinion on the bank's transactional procedures.

Approaches Used to Appoint Shari'aa Boards

The role of the Shari'aa Board in a typical Islamic bank brings to mind the typical role played by a compliance committee within the board of directors of any conventional bank in the United States—but, of course, it is concerned only with issues that pertain to compliance with the law (Shari'aa). It is important to note that two approaches have been used to implement the law in RF banking activities.

1. The first approach is implemented in Malaysia. In this approach, the central bank (Bank Negara Malaysia, BNM) has its own Central Bank Islamic Banking Division with its own banking books and regulations, as well as its own National Bank Shari'aa Board. The National Shari'aa Board of Islamic Banking in Malaysia issues edicts on different products, services, and operating standards and procedures. The opinions and rulings of the National Shari'aa Board of Islamic Banking are binding to all RF banks operating in Malaysia. Then, at the individual RF bank level, each RF bank appoints its own Shari'aa Supervisory Committee to ascertain compliance of the RF bank operations with the rules set by the central bank's Shari'aa Board guidelines. This approach proved to be beneficial. It saves a lot of confusion and resolves conflicts within different Shari'aa Boards. The involvement of the central bank adds credence and weight to the RF banking rules and regulations issued by the central bank Shari'aa Board. In addition, because the Shari'aa Board is operated and supervised by the central bank, there is no potential for conflict of interest because the individual banks are not paying their own hand-picked scholars for their services.
2. The other approach is to allow each RF bank to appoint its own Shari'aa Board. The implementation of this approach has created a lot of confusion and conflicting opinions among the scholars in each of the Islamic banks. It also creates an implicit uneasy feeling of conflict of interest, because the RF bank pays the salaries of its Shari'aa Board members. This approach has also created a large demand for the RF Shari'aa scholars who are scarce and are available in short supply. The net result has been the appointment of some of the "superstar scholars" on the Shari'aa Boards of more than one RF bank. Your author knows of scholars who serve on the boards of more than 50 Islamic banks. This creates another conflict-of-interest situation because these scholars are exposed to the inside information of many competing RF banks. This approach is used mostly by RF banks in the oil-rich Gulf countries and in some Asian countries (except Malaysia).

Concerns of Western Central Bankers and Bank Regulators Regarding Shari'aa Boards

This important issue is very sensitive, and it created some serious concerns in the many efforts invested in trying to implement and popularize RF banking and finance in the West. There are three reasons for these concerns:

1. In most Western societies, especially in the United States, the government and its departments operate with a firm belief in the separation of church and state. Operating a bank with a formal board that has the mission of implementing the laws of a certain religion may be a bit sensitive, especially with consumers who subscribe to other religions, which may result in a fear of religious discrimination disputes that may lead to messy law suits.
2. The existence of two boards in one bank, with one board (the Shari'aa Board) having apparent superiority of control over the other, may create a serious operating conflicts that could have a negative impact on the RF bank's safety and soundness. In addition, there can be further conflict if the Shari'aa Board is paid generously to issue edicts that can create serious conflict-of-interest issues.
3. Most, if not all, of the scholars represented on the Shari'aa Board do not have direct experience in banking and finance, and in most cases, they do not have a proven track record and knowledge of the banking regulations in the West. They may not even have experience in the local area in the West where the RF bank operates. In addition, because many of the scholars live in other countries, it is difficult for them to appreciate local needs, banking regulations, and challenges, and the regulators may find it hard to exercise their regulatory powers on them.

THE DEVELOPMENT OF RF SCHOLARS AND COMPLIANCE COMMITTEES FOR RF FINANCE INSTITUTIONS IN THE TWENTY-FIRST CENTURY

It is the author's deep-seated belief that the public and businesses in the West will gradually become greatly interested in real added value offered by the services and products of the new RF brand of banking. In addition, bankers will be drawn to the concept because it exercises prudence in financing by considering it a true investment and not a mere process to rent money, reduces overhead to a reasonable level, and keeps loan and lease losses to a minimum, and because RF banks deal with those people who are well known to the RF bankers who serve them in the local communities. Hence, the RF banker will be fulfilling the know-your-customer rule of banking and finance. All these and the trust of the community will expand the RF bank's business and increase its profitability. That is why it is important to prepare the groundwork, starting now, for this new brand of banking—RF banking.

My vision of the twenty-first-century Shari'aa Board for an RF bank will be renamed as a *Shari'aa Advisory Committee*, which will not only include Muslim scholars but also scholars from the Jewish, Christian, and other faith-based communities. The idea of a united Judeo-Christian-Islamic approach to RF banking will make it very attractive and highly credible.

The Shari'aa compliance officer, or the Shari'aa Advisory Committee supervisor, will ideally be a scholar who is trained in formal scholarly sciences in an accredited religious studies department at a major institution or seminary, such as Al-Azhar in Cairo, the Hawzah (means seminary) in Qum (Iran), the Hawzah in Al-Najaf (Iraq), International Islamic University in Pakistan, Aligarh University in India, King Abdul Azeez University in Jeddah, McGill University in Canada, Princeton University in New Jersey, or Claremont Graduate University in California. These graduates should not only be well versed in the Islamic law but also in the Jewish Bible, rabbinical laws and traditions, and in the Christian Bible(s) and traditions. These graduates should also have obtained a degree in economics, finance, and/or banking from an accredited university, making them well versed in banking and finance as well as religious law. It is true that it will take many years to achieve this, but the rewards will be worth the investment of time, money, and effort. This process is reminiscent of preparing securities lawyers in the United States. Securities lawyers specialize in the laws of the Securities and Exchange Commission (SEC) in the United States. Many of them start as graduates from universities in the fields of economics, business, or even in the sciences or in history. They often work as financial consultants or stockbrokers in an investment bank to gain hands-on experience for a few years, and then return to college to study for another advanced degree in law to qualify as a securities attorney.

In addition to the requirements listed, an operating license in the field of compliance with the law (Shari'aa) should be made necessary, as is done when licensing a stockbroker, an attorney, or a medical doctor in the United States. There are currently a number of pseudo-regulatory organizations like the Accounting and Auditing Organization for Islamic Financial Institutions (AAOIFI) in Bahrain[13] and the Islamic Financial Services Board (IFSB) in Malaysia.[14] My vision for the process of producing the qualified RF scholar will be the same as that used to produce attorneys, medical doctors, and certified public accountants in the United States. It also involves annual or periodic renewal of licenses by conducting required examination to keep all of them informed of the latest regulations and developments in the field of RF banking in particular and banking and finance in general.

The Central Bank and the Regulatory Shari'aa Compliance Committee

To minimize confusion and conflicting opinions passed by different Shari'aa scholars and different Shari'aa compliance boards of different institutes, the Malaysian model of having one Shari'aa Board appointed, run, and supervised as an independent entity in the central bank of the country involved represents an attractive option to emulate. This central bank Shari'aa Compliance Board is responsible for issuing legal opinions and will be in charge of examining the RF bank's compliance in the same way all operating banks are examined for compliance by the central bank (or the Treasury Department's Office of the Comptroller of the Currency in the United States). However, in this case, testing and examining for compliance will be about adherence to the fatwas (edicts) and legal opinions that comply with Shari'aa as stipulated in the charter of the RF bank.

REVIEW QUESTIONS

1. What is the meaning of the word *Shari'aa?* Where do the roots of the word come from?
2. What are the real goals, intentions, and spirit of Shari'aa (*Maqasid Al Shari'aa*)?
3. What is the law advocated in the book? What does it imply?
4. What are the sources of the law?
5. What is the meaning of Fiqh?
6. Please give three examples that will show that you understand the purposes of Shari'aa.
7. Who is a mufti? What are the qualifications and requirements for a mufti to attain this most revered title?
8. What are the requirements needed to qualify as a person who can issue fatwas?
9. What are the roles of the *Shari'aa Board* in an RF bank?
10. Please indicate which of the answers below is TRUE or FALSE: An RF bank means:
    a. Responsible finance bank
    b. Ribit-free bank
    c. Riba-free bank
    d. All of the above

11. What is the book's position on *Shari'aa* Boards? What is your position on this issue?
12. How do you think the conflict of interest present in current Shari'aa Board members of banks be resolved? How can the Board member be free to oppose the bank that pays him a salary? How can the Board member sit on the Board of different banks with different opinions and with perhaps insiders' information?
13. What is your vision about Shari'aa scholars in America or other countries where you live? From where should they be recruited? How we can develop them locally? Your ideas will be highly appreciated.

NOTES

1. Eric Davis, *Bank Misr and Its Role in the Industrialization of Egypt 1920–1940*. Translated to Arabic and published by Dar Al Shorouk International in 2008, p. 96.
2. Huston Smith, "Introduction," *The Concise Encyclopedia of Islam* (San Francisco: Harper & Row, 1989), 361–363.
3. Riad Adhami, "Maqasid Al Shari'aa." *Islamic Horizons Magazine* (January/February 2006): 48–50.
4. Translations of the Qur'aan were obtained from www.Islamicity.com. Sources used are: (1) Abdullah Yusuf Ali, *The Meaning of the Holy Qur'an, Eleventh Edition,* (Beltsville, MD: Amana, 2009); and (2) *The Qur'an,* a translation by Muhammad Asad (Gibraltar: Andalus Press, 1980). The translation of the Holy Qur'aan by Yusuf Ali is one of the original, and in my opinion, the better translation because it adds to the meanings a wealth of information on historic references and events and especially on links to Judeo-Christian traditions, making it a wonderful foundation for a Judeo-Christian-Islamic future.
5. The following collections of the Hadeeth are regarded as the most authentic:
   a. Sahih Al Bukhari, which were collected, strictly and copiously checked, validated, and compiled by Muhammad Ibn Ismail Al Bukhari (from the City of Bukhara, now in Uzbekistan) (194–256 A.H., 809–870 C.E.).
   b. Sahih Muslim by Muslim Ibn Al Hajjaj (202–261 A.H., 817–876 C.E.).
   c. Sunan Abu Dawud by Sulaiman Ibn Ash'ath known as Abu Dawud (202–275 A.H., 817–888 C.E.).
   d. Sunan Ibn Majah by Muhammad Ibn Zaayid (209-303 A.H., 824–915 C.E.).
   e. In addition to these, Muwatta of Imam Malik (93–179 A.H., 715–795 C.E.).

Mishkat Al Masabih of Abu Muhammad Al Husain Ibn Mas'ud (died 516 A.H., 1122 C.E.) and Musnad of Ahmad Ibn Hanbal (164–241 A.H., 780–855 C.E.) are all well-known authorities.

6. References are as follows:
   a. Imam Jafaar As-Sadiq, founder of the Jafaari or Shi'aa school of thought (madh'hab) in Arabic (80–148 A.H., 699–765 C.E.).
   b. Imam Abu Hanifa Numan bin Thabit, founder of the Hanafi madh'hab (80–150 A.H., 699–767 C.E.).
   c. Imam Malik bin Anas, founder of the Maliki madh'hab (93–179 A.H., 715–795 C.E.).
   d. Imam Muhammad bin Idris Al Shafi'ee, founder of Al-Shafi'ee madh'hab (150–240 A.H., 767–820 C.E.).
   e. Imam Ahmad bin Hanbal, founder of the Hanbali madh'hab (164–241 A.H., 780–855 C.E.).
7. Riad Adhami, "The Goals of Shari'ah." *Islamic Horizons Magazine* (January/February 2006): 48–50; quoted here by permission.
8. Ibid.
9. As ruled by Imam Abu Hanifah.
10. See note 3.
11. Please visit the Dubai Islamic Bank website to read about the role of its Shari'aa Board (www.alislami.ae/en/shariaboard_boardrules.htm); also, read about the Islamic Bank of Britain: www.islamic-bank.com/islamic-banklive/RoleofCommittee/1/Home/1/Home.jsp.
12. Ibid.
13. Please visit their websites: www.aaoifi.com and www.IslamicBanking Network.com.
14. Please visit their websites: www.ifsb.org and www.IslamicBanking Network.com.

CHAPTER 5

Money and Its Creation: The U.S. Federal Reserve System (Central Banks) and Interest Rates

This chapter is about money and, in particular, its use in helping the economic growth and prosperity of the community through providing a medium of exchange and credit. The question is how to fairly reward those who own the money, in order to entice them to invest within the community. Chapter 2 concluded that the RF Judeo-Christian-Islamic law (the Shari'aa law) and lifestyle prohibit the charging of a rental rate or a fee for the use of money (i.e., riba/ribit/usury, which is now called *interest*) and encourages investing in the community to achieve economic prosperity and fair return on that investment. It also concluded that if money is given for helping the poor and the needy, there must not be any increase when it is paid back. In Chapter 3, we discussed how the Judeo-Christian-Islamic Shari'aa law requires that when pricing a service or an item, we should use the RF disciplines of Commodity Indexation (using precious metals or food staples as references to calibrate real value and price) and of Marking to Market (gauging the value of properties and services according to actual leasing values on the local open market).

Any discussion of the riba-free (RF) banking and finance system, as compared to the riba-based system, should be based on a clear understanding of money and how the monetary policies of the leading reserve currency of the world—the U.S. dollar—are designed and handled. This chapter is a must for everyone who is interested in understanding the way modern paper (fiat) money is created and for those interested in popularizing the new RF lifestyle advocated in this book.

THOSE WHO "MAKE" MONEY AND OTHERS WHO "EARN" MONEY

Money is an important factor in our lives. Many of us say that we work in order to "make" money. We try to save money in order to buy the things that bring comfort and pleasure to us. Others spend money to seek personal satisfaction—perhaps through impressing others, by showing off an expensive new car or a designer watch. Money has become so important that people fight over it and hate and love because of it; unfortunately, some would be willing to kill for it. It is amazing to witness all this respect and admiration for a piece of paper that may be green, red, blue, or even have an impressive array of colors and designs. This piece of paper may only be recognized and honored in the place it was printed and issued. Not all currencies in the world are as well known as the major currencies, such as the U.S. dollar, the euro, the Japanese yen, or the British pound. Money cannot reproduce in the way that "money experts" have been leading us to believe. If one seals one's money in a jar for two years and returns to open the jar, one will find the same pieces of paper—except in most cases the paper will buy you less than it did two years before. It is also fundamental to understand clearly that we cannot eat or drink these pieces of paper called money. However, we can use the money to buy food from those who produce it, so that they can take that money and buy their needs—which may include clothes and medicine in addition to the items needed to produce more of that food. Money is not anything but a medium of exchange to conduct transactions in the economy—a measuring device.

To realize the American dream of buying a house for which one has insufficient capital, one can go to a banker to seek financing. The applicant fills out an application and passes a few due diligence checking procedures. After appraising the value of the house based on the price at which the most recent sales in the neighborhood were concluded, the banker will arrange for the applicant to get the money. The bank draws a loan agreement that essentially states that it is renting you the money at a rental rate called the *interest rate*, to be paid back in installments over an agreed-upon number of years. As we learned in Chapter 2, interest rate is the cost of (the price paid for) renting the money from the bank. The bank does this mechanically, regardless of whether the deal of buying the house makes economic sense. A buyer might have expected the banker to advise him/her as to whether he/she should proceed to buy a house because it makes economic sense or rent a similar house or apartment because of a prevalent real estate price bubble being experienced in the community. That does not happen because the banker is interested in getting the customer to rent that money in order to make money for the bank. We realize that this scenario does not happen in most cases because the world is full of honest and decent bankers and wonderful people. Unfortunately, at some time or another, all of us can be blinded by the prevailing culture without stopping to think.

As to the "culture of making money," many have forgotten that there is only one entity that can make (i.e., manufacture, print, or coin) money: the government. That is why we should rethink this concept. Money can be earned only when one offers a service. That is why it is important to ask ourselves every night before we go to bed how much money we earned for the services we have offered. It is also important to respect that earned money, which represents time—which is life. As is said in some proverbs, "Money respects and stays with those who respect it." Money is earned when we offer a product or a service that is needed or when it is invested in a productive project that will make a prudent economic difference in our communities by increasing production and creating job opportunities and economic prosperity. If we discipline ourselves to think this way, we will enjoy a new lifestyle that is more productive and less consumptive—the RF lifestyle. We will enjoy living within our means without a heavy burden of debt. This lifestyle is the lifestyle described at length in Chapter 2: the RF lifestyle.

Another important aspect of money over the years has been its purchasing power and how much that power changes over the years. We all have heard our grandparents tell us how cheap things once were. Members of my generation remember that a gallon of gasoline in Texas in 1971 was 20 cents, compared to $2.50 in 2009 and almost $4 in 2013. This is the same gallon, of the same gas, in the same country, using the very same currency.

The question is: what is money? Is the money revealed in the original Judeo-Christian-Islamic value system and described in Chapter 2 the same as the money we use today? This chapter will focus on this very important issue. This chapter will try, in the simplest terms, to familiarize the reader with paper (fiat) money used today, how it is printed, who decides how much should be printed, and what parameters influence that decision.

What Is Money?

Money is the medium used for the exchange of goods and services. Money is used as a measuring device for the success or failure of a venture that may involve trading, manufacturing, servicing, or construction. Money is also considered fungible because it changes its nature upon using it. Money is fungible because we convert it into goods and services that we buy. The use of money resembles the use of a loaf of bread because the nature of that loaf of bread changes upon using (eating) it. In that sense, we cannot rent a loaf bread because the person who leases that loaf cannot return the same loaf back to its original owner. If we do that, it will be unfair because in that way one would be unfairly paying twice for the title of owning the loaf and for the using of it, while there is only one title of ownership, which is same as the title for using. That is conceptually why money is considered fungible, and that is why it cannot be rented at a price called interest rate. It only can be invested.

The success or failure of an investment is measured in terms of the return reaped at the end of a certain period of time, which is called the *return on investment*. Operators, traders, and investors evaluate the success of their venture by the return on investment. The level of return on investment differs from one locality to another; it is a function of many parameters. A return on investment of 5 percent may be considered a great return in a country with no inflation; however, a return on investment of 15 percent would be marginal and in fact negative in real terms in a country that suffers from 25 percent inflation. Riba banks lend (rent) money to entities at a rental rate called interest. If the interest rate charged on the money is higher than the income generated from the project, to the extent that the borrower cannot pay both the interest (the rental rate on that money) and the principal back, then the project is a failure, and it should not have borrowed money anyway. Conceptually, one can look at interest rate as a red line that defines which projects should be financed. If the projected real rate of return of a project (after allowing for inflation or reduction in purchasing power of money) is higher than the red line, then it makes sense to finance it; if it is lower, financing the project does not make prudent economic sense. The government sets the foundation of that interest rate by deciding on and adjusting the rate of printing of the money. If the government wants to allow only high-return projects to be financed, it will increase rates. As a result, there will be very few projects that make economic sense. Conversely, if the government wants to stimulate the economy, it will lower the rates so that less profitable projects can qualify.

The invention of paper (fiat) money was one of the important human developments in history. Money has helped develop markets in small villages that attracted many traders and merchants, eventually turning these small villages into small towns, cities, large metropolitan areas, states, and countries. The real value of the idea of paper (fiat) money is that it can be transported from one place to another. It can be divided into different denominations, and it can be recognized and accepted by others in the country and in other countries, depending on the country or locality that issued it.

The History of Money[1]

Perhaps one of the earliest forms of money was barter: the exchange of one specific good or service for another specific good or service, such as bartering a bag of rice for a bag of beans. Difficulties with this system arose when the bartering parties could not agree what something was worth in exchange, or when one party did not want what the other person had. To solve that problem, *commodity money* was introduced. In the past, salt, tea, tobacco, cattle, and seeds have all been used as money, because of their importance to local economies. As the world developed it was discovered that using commodities as money presented new challenges. Carrying bags of salt and other commodities was difficult. In addition, commodities might have a short shelf life, after which they perished. Around 5000 B.C.E., metal objects were introduced as money because metal was readily available, easy to work with, and could be recycled. Other countries were soon minting their own coins with specific values. Metals such as iron, copper, silver, and gold were used to make coins. The problem moneymakers had was that some metals change as they rust. Only silver and gold kept their condition; these prevailed as the two main metals used for currencies in the world. The demand for gold and silver was driven not only by their practical use, but also by their role as investments and a store of value. The Roman Empire used gold currency called the denarius (or dinar), while the Persian Empire used silver and called it dirham (or drachma in the Byzantine Empire). The Muslim state used the gold dinar and the silver dirham as the official Islamic currency beginning with the Second Caliph Omar Ibn Al-Khattab (634–644 C.E.). The dinar was defined as the weight of 22-karat gold equivalent to 4.3 grams, and the dirham as the weight of silver equivalent to 3.0 grams. At that time, the caliph established the well-known standard relationship—7 dinars must be equivalent to 10 dirham.

Fiat (Paper) Money

Fiat money is money that has nothing of substance behind it. According to *Webster's New World Dictionary,* fiat money is "currency made legal tender by fiat (sanction) and neither backed by, nor necessarily convertible into, gold or silver." It is a promise to repay nothing, over an unspecified period. This inconvertible paper currency system gives the central bank the power to issue and circulate paper money, which has no intrinsic value except the full faith and credit of the government of a country that has an economic base to rely on. The government adds its full faith and credit to the currency so its citizens and other governments in the world will accept it. This concept of fiat money also allows the government to create (print and/or mint) new money at will to pay off government debts, pay government employees, and use the printed money for any other government expenditure.

The first to introduce the idea of offering money at a less-than-pure gold or silver base were the kings of England, who introduced an idea they branded as the *debasement* of money. Debasement is the lowering of the precious metal content of the currency. Debasements were achieved by *recoinage*. In England during the twelfth century, one pound of silver was minted into 240 silver pennies; during 1666, one pound of silver was minted into some 700 silver pennies, a decline in the value content of almost 292 percent. By means of their debasements, the kings had created what is known today as fiat money. Fiat money is a token of value—its intrinsic value is less than its exchange value. Its exchange value is given to it by *fiat* (order) of the king or the government involved.

Today, precious metal coins are no longer used, and the world deals only with fiat money. The early English bankers produced something of no value (a piece of paper) and gave it the name *one pound*. Some of the earliest known paper money dates to China's Tang Dynasty (618–907 C.E.). During the Ming Dynasty in 1300 C.E., the Chinese placed the emperor's seal and signatures of the treasury on a crude paper made from mulberry bark.

From the time of America's discovery in 1492 until the California gold rush in 1848, silver dominated in common circulation in America and Europe, while gold came into dominance after the discovery of gold in California and Australia.[2] Under the rule of the British Empire, the British pound sterling and the gold standard were adopted around the world. In 1913, the gold cover for Federal Reserve notes was set by 1913 law to be 40 percent. In 1945, the gold reserves against Federal Reserve notes were reduced to 25 percent, and to continue the inflation spiral, this figure (the 25 percent) had to be reduced to zero. Toward the end of World War II, the U.S. dollar and gold became the principal international reserve assets under the Bretton Woods Agreement. The U.S. dollar became the world reserve currency, and it was treated as if it were gold because the agreement defined its value to be $35 per ounce of gold.

American Currency before the Federal Reserve System[3]

The First Bank of the United States (1791) and Second Bank of the United States (1816) were the two precursor banks to the Federal Reserve System in the United States. They were responsible for issuing the small quantity of paper currency that circulated in the early years of the United States. After the Second Bank of the United States closed in 1836, the dominant form of currency became private bank notes issued by state-chartered commercial banks (normally redeemable on demand for gold or silver). The United States did not have a uniform national currency. The system of state-bank issuing of currency notes was confusing and inefficient. By the 1860s, as many as 8,000 different issues of state bank notes were circulating in the United States. With the vast distances to be covered and the lack of efficient means of transportation, banks rarely accepted—at face value—notes issued by banks unknown to them.

During the American Civil War, national bank notes were issued to finance the war and other needs of the different states. Until 1913, these formed the bulk of the nation's paper currency. National bank notes were currency the government gave to nationally chartered commercial banks for them to issue as their own. National bank notes grew out of the government's need to raise money to finance the Union army. Faced with a depleted treasury, and reluctant to raise taxes on northern industry, President Lincoln reluctantly agreed to a plan formulated by his secretary of the Treasury, Salmon P. Chase. Under Chase's plan, the federal government would offer a new type of banking license—a federal, or national, charter. A bank with a national charter would have the power to issue a new form of currency: national bank notes. However, for each note issued, the bank would have to hold a somewhat larger dollar value of government securities as collateral (called a *backing requirement*). The banks could purchase government securities directly from the U.S. Treasury for gold and silver, which were universally accepted money at that time. In effect, the government would receive gold and silver in return for its liabilities (government securities). Chase's plan was embodied in the National Banking Act of 1863. To enhance the prospect that national bank notes would be successful, and to eliminate the competition from notes issued by state banks, Chase also developed a tax that Congress gradually increased until the state bank practice of issuing currency ended. Because national bank notes had to be fully collateralized government securities, the nation's supply of paper currency effectively depended on the government's debt.

The supply of currency expanded and contracted in direct response to changes in the value of government securities in the nation's bond markets, not in response to the needs of the economy. When the government began repaying its Civil War debt, redeeming and retiring securities issued in earlier years, the supply of collateral available in the banking system for note issuance shrank. Currency was inelastic (incapable of adjusting to the public's changing needs and demands), and this led to the money panics[4] that periodically plagued the economy of the United States.

THE FEDERAL RESERVE BOARD OF THE UNITED STATES OF AMERICA[5,6]

The Federal Reserve's power is derived from the Constitution of the United States (Article I, Section 8). The article states: "Congress shall have power . . . to coin money (and) regulate the value thereof . . ." The Federal Reserve Act of 1913 established the Federal Reserve to realize the following objectives:

- Furnish an elastic currency that would respond to the economic needs of the nation.

- Serve as a last resort to defend against any run on the banking system of the nation.
- Establish a more effective and responsive system to supervise banks.
- Improve the efficiency of the national payment mechanism.

The 1946 Employment Act established a number of national goals that must be achieved by the Federal Reserve. These goals were expanded in 1978, when Congress passed the Full Employment and Balanced Growth Act. Following are the expanded goals:

- Full employment
- Increased real income (net of inflation)
- Balanced economic growth
- Balanced federal budget
- Growth in productivity
- Improved balance of trade
- Price stability

The act also required the Federal Reserve to report to Congress twice a year on its monetary policies as they related to the goals outlined in the 1978 Full Employment and Balanced Growth Act.

Function of the Federal Reserve

The three basic functions of the Federal Reserve are:

1. *Implementation of monetary policy.* This is done through the use of three primary control devices:
   - Setting the reserve requirements of the banks.
   - Setting the discount rate at which the Federal Reserve lends the member banks.
   - Setting the monetary growth or contraction through the activities of the Federal Open Market Committee (FOMC); monetary expansion or contraction is done through the purchase or selling, respectively, of government securities.
2. *Providing payment services for the depositories.* These services include loans, check collections, currency insurance, wire transfers, and account settlements.
3. *Serving as a bank for the federal government:*
   - Supervising and regulating banks.
   - Maintaining the U.S. federal government's checking account.
   - Selling and redeeming interest payments on U.S. government securities.

- Establishing relations with foreign central banks and foreign exchange trading worldwide.

The Federal Reserve was created as a branch independent of the politics of governing. Its shares are owned by participating member banks in proportion to their size. U.S. monetary policy, which includes adjusting interest rates and money supply, is designed and implemented without any political interference from the president or Congress. In such a unique setup, the monetary policy would be implemented for the interest of the nation, and not to promote a certain political party, the military, the press, the judiciary, Congress, or the president. However, the president of the United States designs and presents to Congress for approval the fiscal policy of the government, which includes the federal budget, taxes, and government spending. The Federal Reserve's structure as an independent central bank is unique among the world's central banks. This adds to the power of the Federal Reserve to influence the U.S. economy and to bring real creditability to the U.S. dollar worldwide.

Structure of the Federal Reserve Board (America's Central Bank)[7]

The structure of the Federal Reserve Bank is also unique among the world's central banks. It consists of the following:

- A presidentially appointed Board of Governors with general responsibilities for oversight.
- Twelve regional Federal Reserve banks that are private institutions nominally owned by their stockholders (commercial banks that are members of the Federal Reserve System).
- The FOMC, a 12-member policymaking committee of the Federal Reserve. The 12 members consist of 7 governors appointed by the president and 5 regional reserve bank presidents.

The nation's monetary policy is decided at the monthly meetings of the FOMC. To understand how the FOMC operates, let us imagine that people in a community one day find themselves with more paper currency than they wish to hold—for example, when the main Christmas shopping season has ended. If the paper currency is physically convertible (for one ounce of silver, let us suppose), people will return the unwanted paper currency to the bank in exchange for silver, but the bank could head off this demand for silver by selling some of its own bonds to the public in exchange for its own paper currency. For example, if the community has 100 units of unwanted paper money, and if people intend to redeem the unwanted 100 units for silver at the bank, the bank could simply sell 100 units worth of bonds or other assets in exchange for 100 units of its own paper currency. This will soak up the unwanted paper and head off people's desire to redeem the 100 units for silver.

Thus, by conducting this type of open market operation—selling bonds (to take dollars out of circulation) when there is excess currency, and buying bonds (to put dollars in circulation) when there is too little—the bank can maintain the value of the paper currency at one ounce of silver without ever redeeming any paper currency for silver. In fact, this is essentially what all modern central banks do, and the fact that their currencies might be physically inconvertible is made irrelevant by the maintenance of financial convertibility. Please note that financial convertibility cannot be maintained unless the bank has sufficient assets to back the currency it has issued. This is not the case for many countries. For example, during the Asian foreign exchange currency crisis of 1997–1998 many of the Asian countries, such as Thailand and South Korea, experienced a sharp decline in their U.S. dollar and foreign currency reserves when they tried to support the value of their currencies by selling the dollars, the euros, and the British pounds to buy Thailand currency (the baht)—and create fictitious market demand.

The Federal Reserve banks are directed by nine-member boards of directors. Congress also stipulated a unique structure for those boards to ensure that the selection process does not favor bankers and allow them to become a majority on any given Federal Reserve Bank board. Congress, in doing so, wanted to ensure that the views, experience, and concerns of all economic interest groups would be expressed and heard during the development of monetary policy.

The nine-member board of directors of a Federal Reserve Bank is elected as follows:

- Member commercial banks elect three members from the banking community and three members from agricultural, commercial, industrial, services, labor, and consumer communities.
- The Federal Reserve Board of Governors appoints three directors on its own (it also appoints the Reserve banks' presidents).

For a detailed description of the operation of the Federal Reserve and the process used to adjust and manage interest rates, please read David H. Friedman's *Essentials of Banking*.[8]

The preceding discussion clearly indicates that interest rates, especially related to the U.S. dollar, are reflections of the way the Federal Reserve Board manages its monetary policy in response to many other factors.

Who Owns the Federal Reserve Bank?

All national banks in the United States own shares in the Federal Reserve Bank in proportion to their capital. In addition, other financial institutions, like some state chartered banks and other major financial institutions, can own shares in the Federal Reserve Bank if their boards decide to become members of the Federal Reserve System. This way, the bankers in the system can have a voice in the process of developing the monetary policy of the country.

Credit Creation in the Modern Banking System—The Money Multiplier Concept[9]

T-accounts are abstracts of a bank's balance sheet that show only the changes in the bank's assets and liabilities.

For the sake of simplicity, assume, in this T-account example, that:

- All the deposits created by banks stay in the banking system.
- Demand deposits are the only form in which newly created funds are held.
- Banks lend out every available dollar.

These assumptions do not by any means reflect reality. Some deposits created by banks leak out of the banking system into nonbank financial institutions and money market instruments. Consumers and businesses typically convert some newly acquired demand deposits into cash.

Banks do not usually lend (or invest) every available dollar—not because they do not want to, but because the pace with which deposits flow in and out of banks on any given day is often so rapid, the volume so large, and the net effect of check collections so uncertain, that only at the end of the day do banks know just how much they have in net funds to support new loans.

Nonetheless, these simplistic assumptions do not distort the fundamental process by which banks create deposits, which takes place in the following sequence of steps:

1. Assume that Bank A receives a cash deposit of $10,000 from a customer for credit to the customer's transaction account. Under Federal Reserve requirements, the bank must hold an amount of reserves—vault cash or deposit balances at a Federal Reserve Bank—equal to a fixed percentage of its deposits (assume 10 percent). Thus, Bank A must hold $1,000 in required reserves against its new $10,000 deposit, and has $9,000 in excess reserves. These excess reserves can support a new $9,000 loan and the creation of $9,000 in demand deposits entailed by such a loan. (See Exhibit 5.1.)

EXHIBIT 5.1 Assets and Liabilities of Bank A

Assets			Liabilities
Cash assets	$10,000[a]	Demand deposits	$10,000
New loans	$ 9,000[b]	Created for borrowing	$ 9,000

[a] (Created for borrowing) $9,000.
[b] Required reserves $1,000 (10 percent of deposits).

2. When Bank A makes the loan, both its assets and its liabilities will temporarily increase to $19,000, reflecting the addition of the loan to its earning assets portfolio and the addition of the newly created demand deposit to its total liabilities. However, as soon as the borrower uses the newly created funds, Bank A's assets and liabilities will decline to their preloan level as an inevitable result of the check collection process. As can be seen in Exhibit 5.2, if the depositor of $10,000 comes to the bank to withdraw his deposit, the bank will have only $1,000 to give him. If the bank says, "We do not have the cash to give you," the customer will spread the news to the community and all depositors will come to withdraw their deposits and will not use the services of the bank again. This is called a "run on the bank." That is why bankers should adjust their loans and deposits as well as guard their reputation in order for that not to happen.

EXHIBIT 5.2 Assets and Liabilities of Bank A after the $9,000 Cash for Loan Is Withdrawn to Another Bank B of Borrower

Assets			Liabilities
Cash assets/reserves	$1,000	Demand deposits	$10, 000
New loans	$9,000		

3. Assume that the borrower writes a check for the loan amount to a manufacturing company that has an account at Bank B. When the borrower's $9,000 check clears, Bank A will have to transfer $9,000 of its cash assets in payment for the check to the presenting bank (Bank B). Bank A will also strike the $9,000 demand deposit liability carried for the borrower from its books. Thus, after check clearance, Bank A has $10,000 in assets and $10,000 in liabilities. Note, however, that the composition of its assets has changed. Before the loan, it had $10,000 in cash assets; now it has $1,000 in cash assets and $9,000 in loan assets. The $1,000 in cash assets meets the assumed 10 percent reserve requirement ratio against transaction account liabilities. (See Exhibit 5.3.)

EXHIBIT 5.3 Assets and Liabilities for Banks A and B

Bank A	Assets		Liabilities	Bank B	Assets		Liabilities
Cash assets	$1,000	Demand deposits	$10, 000	Cash assets[a]	$9,000[a]	Demand deposits	$9,000
Loan	$9,000						

[a] Required reserves $900—excess over reserves $8,100.

4. The $9,000 in deposit created by Bank A is now a demand deposit on the books of Bank B, increasing that bank's liabilities. Bank B also received a transfer of $9,000 in cash assets when it received payment for the check deposited by the manufacturing company. Bank B, subject to the same 10 percent reserve requirement as Bank A, must keep $900 (10 percent) against the deposit, but can use the remaining $8,100 to support a new loan and the creation of a new $8,100 deposit. (See Exhibit 5.4.)

EXHIBIT 5.4 Assets and Liabilities of Bank B after Granting Loan of $8,100

	Assets		Liabilities
Cash assets/reserves	$ 900	Demand deposits	$9,000
New loans	$8,100		

5. When Bank B makes the $8,100 loan, its assets and liabilities will increase initially and then decline to their preloan level in response to the collection of the borrower's check. Assume that the borrower writes a check for the loan amount to pay for a corporate service and that the corporation deposits the check in its account in Bank C. Bank B's newly created $8,100 will now reside as a liability in Bank C, together with the $8,100 in cash assets Bank B had to transfer in payment for the check. (See Exhibit 5.5.)

EXHIBIT 5.5 Assets and Liabilities of Banks B and C

Bank B	Assets		Liabilities	Bank C	Assets		Liabilities
Cash assets	$ 900	Demand deposits	$9,000	Cash assets[a]	$8,100[a]	Demand deposits	$8,100
Loan	$8,100						

[a] Required reserves $810—excess over reserves $7,290.

6. Bank C, in turn, will now be able to create demand deposits equal to 90 percent of its new cash assets. If it does so, it will give still another bank the ability to create new deposits as shown in Exhibit 5.6.

EXHIBIT 5.6 Assets and Liabilities of Bank C after Granting the New Loan

	Assets		Liabilities
Cash assets/reserves	$ 810	Demand deposits	$8,100
New loans	$7,290		

In theory, this process of bank deposit creation can continue through hundreds of banks, generating, in this example, a total amount of deposits on all banks' books 10 times greater than the $10,000 in cash deposits that started the process. The *multiplier*, or expansion coefficient, is the reciprocal of the reserve requirement ratio. In this example, and under its ideal assumption, because the reserve requirement ratio is 10 percent, the multiplier is 10. This simple multiplier is valid only in the context of this example. In the real world of banking, there are separate reserve requirements for different types and amounts of liabilities. This multiple expansion of bank-created deposits is characteristic of banking systems, but not of individual banks. No bank can create deposits in any amount greater than its excess reserves. If it did, it would find itself in a reserve deficiency as soon as the borrower's check cleared. This act violates the Federal Reserve rules, and the bank would be subject to several federal stipulations, controls, and penalties. Conceptually, banks participate in the process of money creation.

A BRIEF HISTORY OF THE BRETTON WOODS AGREEMENT[10]

By 1944, the political leaders of the West knew that somehow trade protectionism and currency warfare had crippled the world economy in the 1930s and helped bring on WWII. The British government called upon Lord Keynes (1883–1946) to help design a structure of international finance that would help avert WWIII. The Bretton Woods Agreement was the design of Lord Keynes and the undersecretary of the U.S. Treasury, Harry Dexter White (1892–1948). Keynes wanted a world bank, as if there were one world government. Participating nations would have their own currencies, but they would be fully convertible to one another through this World Bank, which Keynes called a clearing union. The bank would issue its own currency, the *unitas*, and would maintain its value not by tying it to gold, but by the "wisdom" of its directors. The Keynesian notion of a world bank that could expand credit without the restraint of a gold standard was rejected. The opposite argument by Undersecretary Harry Dexter White, who believed in the "hard money" approach, using the gold standard rather than the "soft money" approach of Lord Keynes, was accepted because the United States owned $24 billion in gold; the United States got its preferred hard money currency. The Bretton Woods Agreement and U.S. economic might after WWII gave the United States and the U.S. dollar undisputed dominance.

The system would work perfectly as long as the Federal Reserve Board of the United States enforced sound monetary operations by stopping the printing of dollars when people showed up with dollars demanding gold. The U.S. monetary and Federal Reserve authorities naturally would not be able to accommodate a huge run on U.S. gold; however, if such a circumstance were handled promptly and wisely, and if the U.S. authorities could convince the world of the United States' sound policies, then a crisis could be averted. The world economy would always have precisely the right amount of money.

In 1953, when President Eisenhower tried to boost the U.S. economy out of recession, instead of cutting tax rates, he leaned on the Fed to print dollars. Because all currencies were fixed together, the surplus flowed around the world. The printed dollars reduced the U.S. gold reserve by the same amount.

The system did break down. To run a dollar standard, the United States certainly did not need $24 billion in gold bullion, for the value of gold is not as a medium of exchange, which requires tonnage, but merely as an error signal to alert administrators when too many dollars are being printed. By 1965, the United States had depleted Fort Knox of approximately $12 billion of its gold tonnage, mainly to the Europeans and, in particular, France. A media story of the time reported that the weight of the gold accumulating on the second floor of the London Metal Exchange building was so heavy that the floor gave way.

In the spring of 1971, as the Fed tried desperately to expand the U.S. economy by flooding it with dollars, the rest of the world came demanding gold. On August 15, 1971, President Richard Nixon ordered the gold window closed, ending the international currency's link to gold.

An attempt to rebuild Bretton Woods around gold at $38 per ounce instead of $35 was made with the Smithsonian Agreement. Later, the gold-dollar window was shut permanently, and what Keynes suggested in 1944 became a reality. Economists around the world projected a dramatic increase in the price of oil and other commodities; another interesting twist in the accepted folklore that claims that oil prices increased because of the 1973 Arab-Israeli War. It is important to note that the inflation of the 1970s was not caused by the Organization of the Petroleum Exporting Countries (OPEC), but rather was caused by the breakdown of Bretton Woods. No country could escape the impact of inflation. Commodity prices skyrocketed between 1966 and the spring of 1974. Details of the price changes in many commodities like wheat, rice, crude oil, natural gas, and homes in the United States are discussed in Chapter 6. Here are some examples:

- Oil price rose 344 percent, from $2.90 to $10 per barrel.
- The price of rice climbed 375 percent, from $8 per hundredweight (cwt) to $30 per cwt.
- Wheat price rose 322 percent, from $1.80 to $5.80 a bushel.

After President Nixon closed the gold window and currencies started to float, the world changed. Companies with costs in one currency and revenues in another needed to hedge exchange rate risk. In 1972, a former lawyer named Leo Melamed[11] was clever enough to see a business in this; he launched currency futures on the Chicago Mercantile Exchange. Futures in commodities had existed for more than a century, enabling farmers to insure themselves against lower crop prices. But Mr. Melamed saw that financial futures would one day be far larger than the commodities market. Today's complex derivatives are direct descendants of those early currency trades.

This same scenario with different players has repeated itself ever since. The Soviet Union was disassembled in the early 1990s. Iraq invaded Kuwait, and the United States subsequently liberated Kuwait. A heinous terrorist attack on American soil occurred on September 11, 2001. The United States invaded Afghanistan to fight terrorism and simultaneously invaded Iraq to change the regime. In 2008–2009, the financial markets in the United States and the world suddenly collapsed, supposedly because of reckless lending and banking practices. There was a subsequent stock and credit market collapse in October 2008, which led to the U.S. government's rescue of Bear Stearns (a major investment banking company) and AIG Insurance Company by pumping almost $110 billion dollars into them. It also led to the bankruptcy of Lehman Brothers, an icon of investment banking in the United States and the world. Lehman Brothers' collapse took with it the capital of many countries and individuals who had trusted the government to supervise these banks properly. For the first time in the history of the capitalist world, there was a massive government effort to rescue banks by owning them outright (which happened in Britain) or owning a minority share (which happened in the United States and most European countries). Additionally, the United States approved a $700 billion rescue plan for its financial system. After all was said and done, more than $1.2 trillion was allocated to rescue the system. And, of course, we do not yet know what more will come upon us. In November 2008, the Fed started a new program called quantitative easing (QE). It was implemented at least in three stages (QE1, QE2, and QE3) to expand monetary liquid to allow the government to help create liquidity to buy bonds securities like mortgage-backed securities.

All we know is that the only way to come up with the needed amount of huge rescue money is simply to create it by "printing it." In other words, the Fed will increase the money supply in the system, as discussed earlier. If the Fed uses—as an example—wheat, rice, or gold as money, there is no way the Fed can produce that much wheat, because it takes time and effort to produce it, let alone the productivity limits of the land. The same applies to rice and gold. In fact, there is a limit to what we can do to increase the production of agricultural commodities, let alone prospecting, finding, and mining gold. However, it takes almost no time at all to print a lot of money. That has spelled a lot of trouble in the past because this conceptually means that the price of reference commodities (gold, silver, rice, wheat, and others) will have to go up in paper money (dollars) because there are more dollars in the system compared to the limited production and supply of the commodities. That spells big trouble down the road. That trouble is called inflation, as we saw in the 1960s and 1970s.

GOLD: THAT AMAZING METAL

Gold is an important metal that has been used over the years as a reference currency and a store of value. This book is not promoting a return to the gold standard; it intends to familiarize the reader with the gold market and how gold prices are fixed and, in some cases, "stabilized," if not manipulated, by speculators and traders. This brief study should shed more light and give the reader the background necessary to fully understand the RF Commodity Indexation Discipline advocated and promoted by this book. It is sincerely hoped that a new pricing system for world trade will be established, one that is fair to all the citizens of the world.

The RF Institute (the research arm of LARIBA) developed a basic RF monetary rule, which we call the RF Commodity Indexation Rule in which we normalize prices away from fiat (paper) currencies like the dollar and the euro. To bring this rule closer to mind, let us assume that a qard hassan (a benevolent loan to the poor or needy that does not allow any sort of increase over the original value at the time of repayment, as introduced in Chapter 2) of $100,000 was given in March 1971. The agreement to repay this qard hassan back can be expressed in one of the many following options:

- Pay back in U.S. dollars the amount of $100,000 in 2012.
- In case the country is a rice producer only and relies on rice as a reference currency, pay it back in the same amount of rice. In this case, $100,000 would buy, in 1971, a total of 18,868 cwt of rice (rice in 1971 was selling for $5.30/cwt). Based on this agreement, the qard hassan, when paid back in 2012, will be paid back in the exact amount in rice

or 18,868 cwt of rice (which reached approximately $15/cwt in 2012). This is equivalent to $283,000!

- In case the country is a wheat producer only and relies on wheat as a reference currency, pay it back in the same amount of wheat. If we do it in wheat, then $100,000 would buy, in 1971, a total of 70,922 bushels of wheat (wheat in 1971 was selling for $1.41 a bushel). Based on this agreement, the qard hassan, when paid back in 2012, will be paid back in the exact amount in wheat or 70,922 bushels of wheat (which reached approximately $7.90 a bushel in 2012). This is equivalent to $564,000!
- In case the country is a corn producer only and relies on corn as a reference currency, pay it back in the same amount of corn. If we do it in corn, then $100,000 would buy in 1971 a total of 70,423 bushels of corn (which in 1971 was selling for $1.42 a bushel). Based on this agreement, the qard hassan, when paid back in 2012, will be paid back in the exact amount in corn or 70,423 bushels of corn (corn price reached approximately $7.63 a bushel in 2012). This is equivalent to $537,324! Please notice the approximate similarity in value if one uses wheat and corn—two substitutable food staple grains.
- In case the country is a silver producer only and relies on silver as a reference currency, pay it back in the same amount of silver. If we do it in silver, then $100,000 would buy, in 1971, a total of 61,350 ounces of silver (which in 1971 was selling for $1.63/ounce). Based on this agreement, the quard hassan, when paid back in 2012, will be paid back in the exact amount in silver or 61,350 ounces (which reached approximately $34.14/ounce in 2012). This is equivalent to $2.1 million!
- In case the country is using gold as a reference standard for currency, pay it back in the same amount of gold. If we do it in gold, then $100,000 would buy in 1971 a total of 2,857 ounces of gold (which was then priced at $35/ounce). Based on this agreement, the qard hassan, when paid back in 2012, will be paid back in the exact amount in gold or 2,857 ounces of gold (gold price reached $1,700 an ounce in 2012). This is equivalent to $4.85 million!

Gold was the reserve reference currency of the world before the well-known Bretton Woods Agreement set the U.S. dollar as the world reserve currency, in the ratio of 35 dollars to each ounce of gold. Gold has been used as a store of value over the years by central banks as well as by husbands showing their love to their wives, and it is used as a precious metal in industrial applications for its superior conductivity and other physical characteristics. It is well known that every government's central bank, including the IMF, keeps a certain number of tons in gold reserves. Efforts to exert controls on leading economies in the world to keep inflation under control and to manage their money-printing presses have all pointed toward the use of gold (and possibly other commodities). It is interesting also to note that in 1999, at the IMF/World Bank annual meeting, a historic five-point agreement was reached. Fifteen European central banks, including the European Central Bank (ECB), declared their allegiance to the idea of the role of gold in the economy. Willem Duisinberg, president of the ECB at that time, stated that their agreement consisted of the following five items:

1. Gold will remain an important element of global monetary reserves.
2. The 15 institutions will not enter the market as sellers of gold, with the exception of already decided sales.
3. Gold sales that were already decided would be achieved through a concerted program of sales over the next five years. Annual sales would not exceed 400 tons, and total sales would not exceed 2,000 tons.
4. The signatories to the agreement agreed not to expand their gold leasing and their use of gold futures and options during this period.
5. The agreement would be reviewed after five years.

Gold Reserves in the World[12]

Analysis of the official gold reserves reveals very interesting results, which are detailed here to familiarize the reader of the amounts of gold that different countries in the world have set aside as reserves. In addition to these gold reserves, many countries add foreign currency reserves. The following is a summary of some observations about the per capita gold reserves[13] of central banks around the world:

- Switzerland has the highest per capita gold reserve (1,040 tons), at 4.6 ounces of gold for every Swiss citizen, followed by Lebanon at 2.19 ounces of gold per person. This is followed by the following groups:
  a. The Eurozone countries: 1.16 ounces of gold per citizen (total reserves of 10,866 tons)
  b. The United States: 0.86 ounce of gold per citizen (8,133.5 tons)
  c. Japan: 0.19 ounce per citizen (765 tons)
  d. Russia: 0.11 ounce of gold per citizen (523 tons)
  e. China: 0.02 ounce per citizen (1,054 tons)
- Both Canada and Mexico have negligible official gold reserves per capita (each has 3.4 tons).
- The oil-rich Gulf countries' reserves range from 0.84 ounce of gold per citizen (Kuwait—79 tons) to 0.28 (Qatar—12.4 tons) and 0.18 (both Saudi Arabia—143 tons, and Bahrain—4.7 tons).

  In many of the countries with a growing RF (Islamic) banking presence, we find the following reserves in tons and in ounces of gold per capita. (See Exhibit 5.7.)

EXHIBIT 5.7 Gold Reserves in Middle Eastern Countries by Tons and by Tons per Citizen (per capita)

	Tons of Gold	Approximate per Capita Oz/Citizen
Lebanon	286.8	2.19
Algeria	173.6	0.16
Iran	302.3	0.14
Jordan	14.8	0.08
Turkey	116.0	0.05
Malaysia	36.4	0.04
Egypt	75.5	0.03
Indonesia	73.1	0.01
Pakistan	65.4	0.01
Bangladesh	3.5	Negligible

Does the official per capita gold reserve reflect—along with other currency reserves—the economic affluence of a country? This is a question that should be researched in terms of many factors, such as the countries' monetary policies, the contents of the reserves in foreign currency, and the nominal gross domestic product of the countries in terms of their local currencies and how they relate to the exchange rates.

It is believed that the solution to the monetary challenge of defining real value in pricing is not returning to the gold standard, as some may advocate, but to reflect on the purchasing value of the convenient paper (fiat) money in each of the local economies by using the Shari'aa-based Commodity Indexation Discipline presented in this book.

The History of Gold Markets and Prices

It is interesting to note that the gold futures market is one of the smallest-volume markets in the world. Because it is so small, it can be extremely volatile when exposed to massive short-sale activities. The short position in gold, via derivatives, is the one of the larger positions in the world.

As shown in the gold price chart in Exhibit 5.8, the price of gold stayed relatively stable (and in some periods declined) between the early 1980s and 2005. This has been mainly due to the central banks of many of the worlds' countries selling their gold on paper, and using many commodity-trading techniques. In one of these techniques, called *gold*

EXHIBIT 5.8 Gold Prices, 1968–2013

carry, gold is borrowed (on paper and not physically) from the central banks (of mostly third-world countries) at a low interest rate and is used to flood the market to keep the price down or short gold and make money both ways.

Major players have included hedge funds and central banks of major industrial countries and some oil-producing countries, in addition to investment banks and other private banks. As the chart shows, gold prices stayed at $35 per ounce before August 15, 1971, when the official convertibility of gold into dollars was in force. Exhibits 5.9 through 5.12 also indicate that gold is currently overpriced in terms of coal, oil, rice, and wheat.

Setting the Market Price of Gold: Gold Price Fixing

The world center of gold trading is London at the London Bullion Market, operated by the London Bullion Market Association (LBMA).

The practice of fixing gold prices began in 1919. It continued until 1939, when the London gold market was closed as a result of World War II. The market was reopened in 1954. When the central bank gold pool began officially in 1961, the Bank of England (as agent of the pool) maintained an open phone line with N. M. Rothschild during the morning

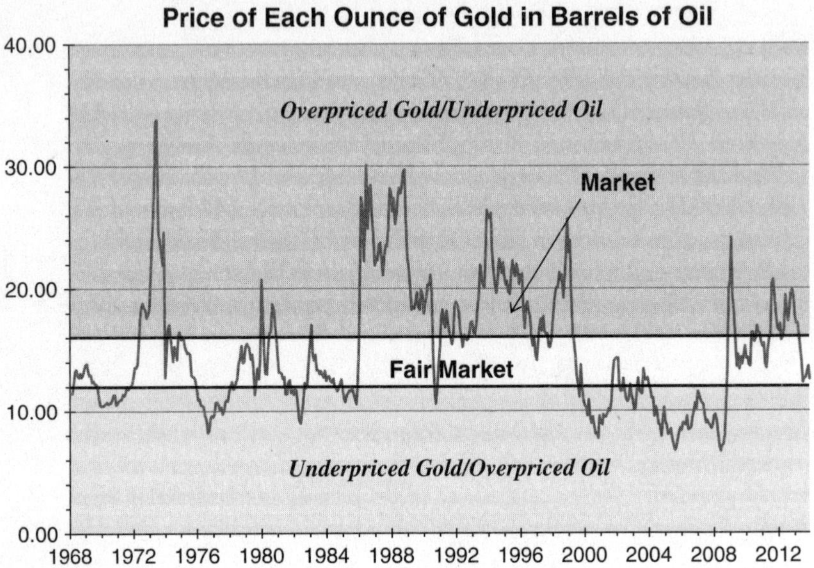

EXHIBIT 5.9 Price of Gold in Terms of Tons of Coal

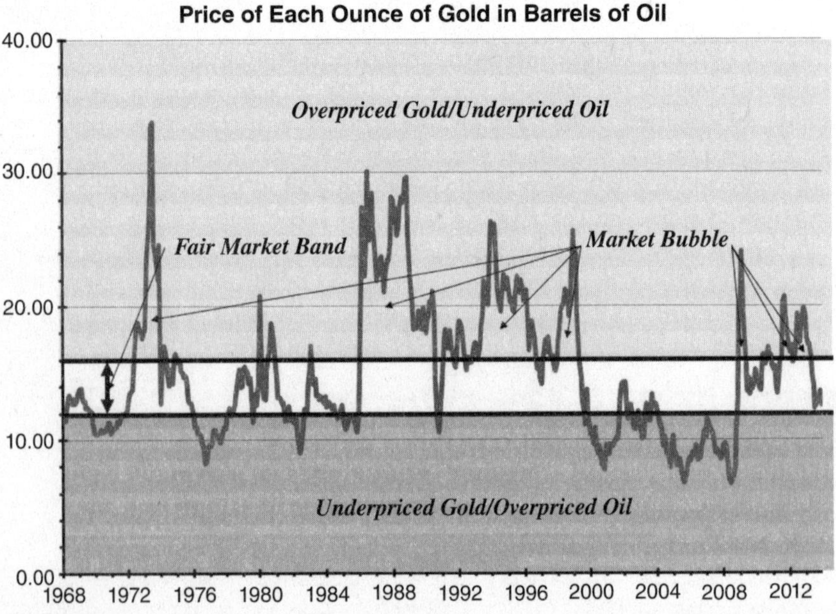

EXHIBIT 5.10 Price of Gold in Terms of Oil

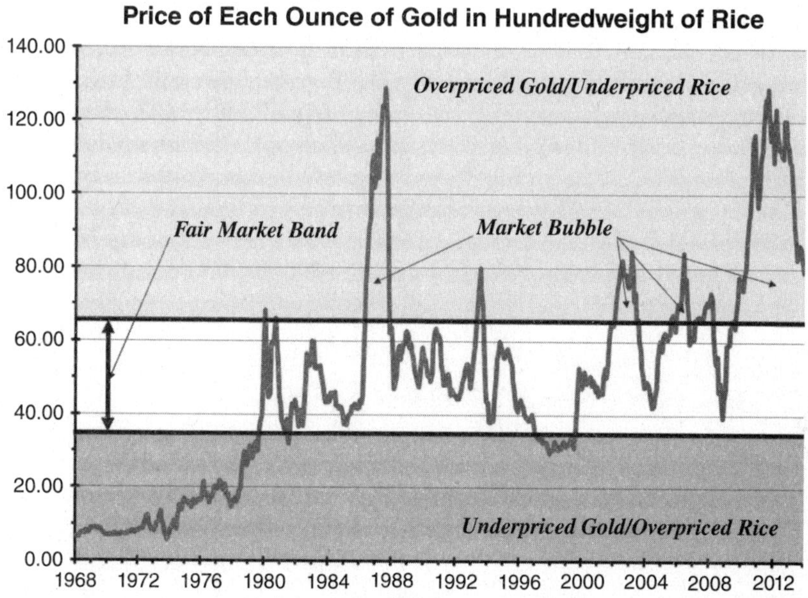

EXHIBIT 5.11 Price of Gold in Terms of Rice

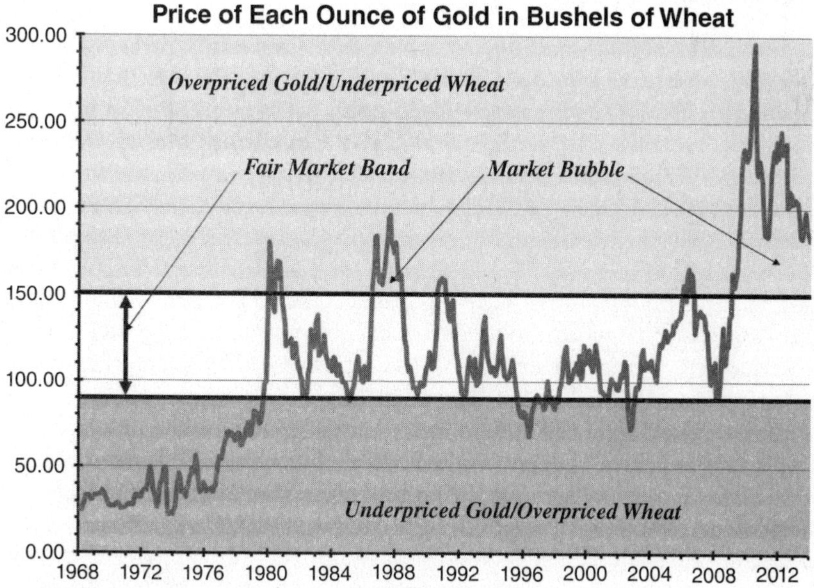

EXHIBIT 5.12 Price of Gold in Terms of Wheat

fixing (there was as yet no afternoon fixing). The objective was to fix the price around the $35/ounce price (as per the Bretton Woods Agreement) within a 1 percent band. In its current form, the London gold price fixing takes place twice each business day, at 10:30 A.M. and 3:00 P.M., in the Fixing Room. Five individuals representing each of the following banks sit at the fixing table:

- Bank of Nova Scotia in Canada, Scotia-Mocatta—successor to Mocatta & Goldsmid and part of Bank of Nova Scotia
- Barclays Capital—Replaced N. M. Rothschild & Sons when they abdicated
- Deutsche Bank—owner of Sharps Pixley, itself the merger of Sharps Wilkins with Pixley & Abell
- HSBC—owner of Samuel Montagu & Company
- Société Générale

Price fixing is based on balancing supply and demand. Usually, the fixing takes less than 15 minutes. In 1979, when the Islamic Revolution of Iran erupted, the afternoon fixing lasted an hour and 39 minutes, due to price volatility.

The Fed Fund Interest Rates Setting Regime: The Taylor Rule[14–17]

This section attempts to summarize how the U.S. Federal Reserve Board decides on a suitable level for the Fed Fund interest rates (the interest rate charged by banks to each other for overnight borrowing to balance their books, which is set by the Fed). The Fed Fund rate is one of the important tools used by the Fed to decide on interest rates, which set the policy of money supply in order to influence U.S. monetary and economic policy. It is important that RF bankers and scholars in RF law understand the foundations on which these decisions are made and the mechanical procedures followed. This information reveals that the Fed Fund rate set by the Federal Reserve is a tool by which the monetary authorities manage the money supply; it is different from the usury or interest prohibited by the injunctions of the RF Judeo-Christian-Islamic Law (Shari'aa).

Professor John Taylor of Stanford University in California formally introduced the Taylor Rule in 1994 to model the process by which the Federal Reserve System sets a suitable Fed Fund rate. He suggested that the two primary factors that drive the model are the gross domestic product[18] (GDP) gap and the inflation gap. This model was improved upon and new models were developed. It is discussed here to introduce the reader to this important monetary management approach.

Intuitively, these two factors have economic bases. This policy rule states that if the economy is growing beyond its potential, or if the inflation rate is greater than the Fed's assumed target of, say, 2 percent, the Fed will increase the Fed Funds. Professor Taylor argued that the Federal Reserve Board can be viewed as setting the target for the Federal Fund rate at a level that is close to, say, 2 to 2.5 percent, with a level corrector mechanism. He recommended that two correctors are added. These are:

1. An *inflation corrector*; called the *inflation gap*. It equals current inflation rates minus the inflation rate targeted by the Fed.
2. An *economic growth corrector*, called the *output gap* (GDP corrector), which is equal to current GDP minus potential GDP.

He also suggested that a most likely scenario is that the impact of the correctors is equally weighted, at 50 percent each. Another scenario might call for a different weighting—such as, for example, the allocation of 70 percent for inflation and 30 percent for GDP, or vice versa. This will depend on the situation, the country involved, and the strategic options available to the central bankers. It is important to clarify further that the interest rate component of the equation is a mere rate or percentage; it is conceptually and materially different from the usury (price charged for using money) or interest (the price for renting money). In this context, this rate is in fact a percentage rate that influences the rate at which fiat—money—should be grown (by printing more) or shrunk (by selling government bonds at high rates to absorb the excess liquidity or by increasing the reserve requirements of the banks). The equation suggested can be written as follows:

Target Short-Term Fed Funds Interest Rate = Rate of Inflation as Measured by GDP Deflator + Equilibrium Real Interest Rate (defined approximately as prevailing interest rate minus inflation) + an Inflation Contribution + an Economic Growth Rate (Economic Output) Contribution

The definitions of the components of the Taylor formula are as follows:

Rate of inflation: As defined by a basket of products and services in the economy.

Equilibrium real interest rate: Interest rate charged by banks and financial institutions minus inflation rate (approximately).

The interest rate charged by banks and financial institutions to their customers is in fact the riba we are talking about; it is prohibited in the Judeo-Christian-Islamic value system because it conceptually represents paying a price for the use or rental of money. This rate, as we discussed in Chapter 3 and will discuss in more detail later, should be obtained using the mark-to-market rule, not the rental rate of money.

Inflation contribution: A percentage of the *inflation gap*, defined as current inflation rate minus target inflation rate, as defined by policymakers. Taylor suggested that we give it a 50 percent weight. However, one can give it a different weight depending on monetary policy goals and strategies.

In the case of the U.S. Federal Reserve System, the policy targets mentioned earlier are discussed and agreed on in a special committee, the FOMC. The committee discusses the trade-off between the Fed's goal of price stability through achieving a low inflation rate and the need to maintain maximum economic growth and output, as well as the highest employment possible. To achieve low inflation, Fed Fund rates need to be raised. However, if the committee wanted the highest employment and economic output, they would adopt a policy that reduces the Fed Fund interest rate. The committee's most important challenge is to try to discover, project, and then decide the most suitable and optimum course of action regarding the Fed Fund rate. In addition, Taylor's equation shows that the Fed Fund interest rate decided by the Fed is needed to adjust the monetary policy in a fiat (paper) money regime, and is far different from the charging of interest prohibited by the RF law (the Judeo-Christian-Islamic Shari'aa), as discussed in Chapter 2. The Fed Fund rate is a percentage sign used to influence monetary policy and to decide how much money to print or withdraw from the system in a world run on fiat (paper) money. In the case of the Judeo-Christian-Islamic value system, there is a world of difference between the renting of real money (as discussed in the six commodity indexes in Chapter 3) and the Fed Fund rate as described clearly by the Taylor Rule.

Real and Nominal Interest Rate

As we read in Chapter 2, the contemporary position of the Roman Catholic Church regarding interest and the time value of money coincides with the position of modern economics and finance. In economics and finance, an individual who lends money for repayment at a later point in time expects to be compensated for the time value of money, or not having the ability to use that money (perhaps more productively) while it is lent, and particularly if it is not returned on time. In addition, owners of capital will want to be compensated for the risks of having less purchasing and investing power when the loan is repaid. These risks are:

- *Systemic risks*. This includes the possibility that the borrower will default or will be unable to pay on the originally agreed-upon terms, or that collateral backing the loan will prove to be less valuable than estimated.

- *Regulatory risks.* This includes taxation and changes in the law, which would prevent the lender from collecting on a loan or having to pay more in taxes on the amount repaid than originally estimated.
- *Inflation risks.* This takes into account that the money repaid may not have as much buying power from the perspective of the lender as the money originally lent, and may include fluctuations in the value of the currencies involved.

Nominal interest rates include all three risk factors, plus the time value of the money itself. *Real interest rates* include only the systemic and regulatory risks and are meant to measure the time value of money. The *real rate* is equal to the *nominal rate* minus *inflation* and minus *currency adjustment*.

The *real interest rate* in an economy is often the rate of return on a risk-free investment, such as U.S. Treasury notes, minus an index of inflation, such as the *Consumer Price Index* (CPI) or *GDP deflator*. This is what we can call the interest rate decided by the Fed, as explained earlier, to run its fiat money monetary policy to the best of its ability. It must be stated that no specific money system is being advocated here because that is not the subject of this book or of the RF banking and finance system presented here. The subject of RF Monetary Discipline will be handled later in detail in a future book. All we want to achieve here is to familiarize the reader with the fact that the interest rate set by the Fed is in fact a monetary policy tool used by the Federal Reserve (the central bank of the U.S. government) and it is, in simple layman's terms, a mechanism by which the government represented in its Federal Reserve decides how much money to print or to withdraw from the market in order to achieve its policy goals about inflation, prices, and employment levels.

As suggested by the Taylor's equation, if all is kept constant and the FOMC wanted to increase the economic production, they would reduce the short-term interest rate on Fed Funds, and hence increase the economic growth rate. Of course, real-life situations are more sophisticated and involve many other factors, scenarios, permutations, and parameters. However, the fact remains that the interest rate that the Feds use is different from the one prohibited in the Judeo-Christian-Islamic Shari'aa law. It conceptually is a calibration tool for designing and implementing the government's monetary policy in a world that uses fiat money. This system, run by the FOMC, adjusts the amount and the rate of flow of money in or out of the fiat paper money system.

All those who believe in Judeo-Christian-Islamic values should focus on two important factors in our development of the RF banking and finance system. These factors are:

- The use of the Commodity Indexation Discipline and approach (discussed in detail in Chapter 3) to ensure fair market pricing by disengaging the monetary effects of fiat (paper) money, as was discussed earlier and will be further developed later in the book.

- The use of the Marking-to-Market Discipline to make certain that we are renting tangible and rentable assets at real market prices, which are obtained, live in the marketplace, and not the rental of fiat (paper) money, in order to ensure that we are investing prudently.

The Fiat Money Economy

The Velocity of Money Concept and the Riba-Based Monetary Principles The velocity of circulation of money looks at how many times a currency unit like the U.S. dollar or any other domestic currency flows through the economy and is used by the various members of a society to transact their business needs. In a simple economy of a developing country, the citizen's needs conduct only to a few transactions like buying food, paying rent for a place to live, paying medical and educational fees, and paying for transportation. In this primitive economic structure, the velocity of money circulation is too low. Compare this with a sophisticated economy that involves a huge matrix of economic and business transactions' activities that may include many needs like food, home mortgages, utilities, durable goods, insurance of different types, construction, entertainment, medical care, maintenance, investing, manufacturing, domestic and international trading, and the list goes on. In this case, the velocity is very high. Obviously, if a country wants to achieve economic vibrancy, one of the most important factors to develop would be an infrastructure that will help increase the number of times the local unit of currency changes hands or to increase the velocity of money. In other words, the velocity-of-money indicator tells economic planners how efficient money supply (M) is used by citizens to create a vibrant local economic activity. The faster money travels—in other words, the higher the velocity of money (V)—and the more transactions in which banknotes are used, the healthier the economy, the richer the citizens, and the more vibrant the financial system. In order to model this, an "Equation of Exchange" was first introduced by Economist Irving Fisher (1867–1947). It should be noted that during his time in 1911, when he introduced this equation, there was no GDP or money supply data.

The Equation of Exchange states an ideal situation of equilibrium between supply and demand:

Aggregate supply side of the Equation of Exchange is expressed by the quantity of products and services offered (Q) multiplied by its price (P). That is, the aggregate supply is equal to aggregate gross domestic production, which equals the quantity of production (Q) multiplied by the average price (P). The outcome of that multiplication process is called the gross domestic product or GDP.

Aggregate demand side of the Equation of Exchange is expressed by the total money supplied to the economy in the hands of the customer (M) multiplied into the velocity of money (V).

The Equation of Exchange, then, can be expressed as follows:

$$V \text{ (Velocity of Money)} \times M \text{ (Money Supply)}$$
$$= Q \text{ (Quantity of Supply)} \times P \text{ (Prices of Goods and Services)}$$

In order to study options available to policymakers, the Equation of Exchange can be expressed as follows:

1. Factors influencing prices (P)
   Using the equation to express prices (P):

$$P = V \times M / Q$$

   So, if policymakers wanted to reduce the price, they would have to devise policies that would lead to reduction in M (money supply) or to the increase of Q (production). Money velocity (V) is assumed constant. Money velocity is a long-term tool because changing it needs fundamental changes in the economic chain like offering new services, opening new stores, opening new cities, and expanding these services to cover a larger number of people and that takes time and may be generational changes.
2. Factors influencing velocity of money (V), as implied by the Equation of Exchange:

$$V = P \times Q / M$$

   Based on the preceding, the velocity of money increases with an increase of production (Q) in addition to other factors like expanding the exchange chain of goods and services throughout the country by, for example, building new shopping centers, transportation routes that connect cities, and new cities. Obviously, it takes years if not generations to make an impact on the velocity of money with the objective of significantly increasing it. This should be an important parameter to follow by governments in developing nations that aspire to grow and prosper.

It is important to note here that the Equation of Exchange is a simplified equation that can be used to model the monetary and economic exchange in a country under equilibrium conditions. There are many other factors that influence the outcome, some of which may not be quantifiable. For example, Henry Hazlitt (1894–1993) criticized the concept of the velocity of money, citing that the equation used to calculate it ignored the psychological effects that also have a significant role in determining the value of a currency. However, the equation can be used conceptually and directionally to discover relationships between monetary and economic factors that can be optimized to lead to a wise central bank policy that fits domestic variables in a particular country.

Another use of the Equation of Exchange is to apply it to two different world economic blocks and use the ratios of the equation to study variations in the parameters to come up with policies that tailor goals for the State Department, the Department of Treasury, the Department of Defense, and the central bank (the Fed).

The U.S. Dollar's Role as an International Reserve Currency and the Developing Nations (Also Called Less Developed Nations)

The U.S. dollar was made a major reserve currency of the world by the Bretton Woods Agreement in July 1944. Nowadays, many countries in the world base their currencies mainly on the value of the U.S. dollar and to a lesser extent of the euro. It is true that we have locally minted and printed currencies in each country with different names like dollar, euro, British pound, Malaysian ringgit, dinar (Kuwait), "geneeh" (meaning a pound in Egypt and Sudan), lira (Turkey, Lebanon, and Syria), peso (Mexico, Argentina, and some Latin American nations), rand (South Africa), riyal (Iran and Saudi Arabia), dirham (extracted from drachma; used in the United Arab Emirates), and drachma (in Greece). The banknotes of the developing currencies are all designed to look unique and different from the way the U.S. dollar and the euro banknotes look. However, many world currencies are in fact tied (pegged) to the U.S. dollar and the euro depending on the local economies and how these economies developed historically, especially in former colonies of European countries, trade relationships, and monetary policies of the particular central bank of the country involved. This reliance on the U.S. dollar (and to a lesser extent the euro) as a reference currency made the U.S. dollar (and the euro to a lesser extent) the currencies of choice in many countries in the world. Transactions in many Asian, African, and some European countries are conducted directly and openly among the public in local currencies and also in U.S. dollars and in euros. That means that the velocity and the money supply of the U.S. dollar and the euro in the world at large have been greatly enhanced because of their status as recognized world reserve or reference currencies by hundreds of million people in the world, in excess of the local populations in the United States and European Zone.

Applying the Equation of Exchange stated earlier once for a developed country (*D*, such as the United States) and another for a developing country (*U*, such as the Central African Republic), and dividing the equation for *D* by that of *U*, one gets:

$$P(D)/PU) = V(D)/V(U) \times M(D)/M(U) \times Q(U)/Q(D)$$

If we assume that the velocity-of-money ratio of a developed country to a developing country ($V(D)/V(U)$) can reach a value of 10 (in fact, it can be much higher), the money supply ratio between a developed country like the United States ($11,000 billion in 2012) and that of a developing country like Egypt ($195 billion in 2012) ($M(D)/M(U)$) is 56; and the quantity-of-production ratio (ratio of GDP in the United States to that of Egypt) ($Q(D)/Q(U)$) is 16,000/195 = 82, then we calculate the ratio of prices in the developed country $P(D)$ to the prices in a developing country $P(U)$ one gets the following:

$$P(D)/P(U) = (V(D)/V(U)) \times (M(D)/M(U))]56 \times 1/82\,(Q(U)/Q(D))$$

That is, if we assume that the velocity of money in the United States is 5 times that in Egypt, which is an extremely conservative assumption, then the ratio of prices $P(D)/P(U) = 3.4$ times. That indicates how the U.S. business-person evaluates the value of local currency in Egypt and the corresponding goods and services supplied there. If the velocity in the United States is 10 times that of Egypt, then prices in Egypt would be one-seventh of that in the United States.

There is one exception to this unfortunate state of affairs in countries like Egypt that does not enjoy a significant natural resources base. If the developing country is endowed with a rich natural resource base (e.g., oil, gas and/or minerals) the situation will be different. In this case, most of the production ratio $Q(D)/Q(U)$ will be much lower than in case of a resources-poor developing country. Let us take the example of Saudi Arabia. In 2012, the Saudi money supply (M2) reached approximately $90 billion while its GDP reached approximately $580 billion (due to the value of the natural resources—oil—on the international market). In this case, the quantity of production ratio for the United States and Saudi Arabia is 16,000/580 = 27, compared to 56 in the case of Egypt, despite the fact that the population of Egypt is almost 90 million compared to almost 25 million in Saudi Arabia. The money supply ratio in Saudi Arabia is 11,000/190 = 58, compared to a ratio of 16 in the case of Egypt. This indicates that the Saudi money supply figures may only reflect the supply in Saudi riyal (tied to the dollar) to meet the liquidity needs of its 25 million citizens. Please note that these figures do not include the vast quantities of dollars transacted in oil sales, military and arms purchases, investments by Saudi Arabia in U.S.-issued government and corporate bonds and other imports by Saudi Arabia and trading in general. In this case and by applying the same Equation of Exchange, we find that at a velocity ratio of 2 (that means the ratio of money velocity in the United States is 2 times that of Saudi Arabia), the ratio of prices in the United States to prices in Saudi Arabia would be a ratio of 1. Please note that if we assume a velocity ratio of 1 to reflect the huge number of transactions in oil only, then the price ratio goes to 2. That is, prices in Saudi Arabia would be half prices seen in the United States. The velocity of money, assumed here to be same as that of the United States, does not have an impact on the domestic Saudi economy because a major portion of the transactions is done outside the domestic economy.

These concepts can be tied up with the recommendation for more creative research to develop an RF Commodity Indexation Discipline, based on the embryonic concepts described in Chapters 3 and 6 to develop a fair value of the domestic currency on the international markets. This RF Commodity Indexation Discipline can be applied to the domestic economy in a matrix that will reflect the domestic production of staple food products and natural resources. This way, the real value of the domestic currency, in addition to being partially tied to the U.S. dollar or the euro, will also be tied to the matrix of products in that country's economy. This way, the fluctuations in U.S. or European monetary policy can be disengaged, and the value of the domestic currency is tied up to domestic production and/or demand depending on strategic issues. This approach may signal the beginning of an RF Monetary Discipline that can be applied as a navigation compass that can be used by economic planners and central bank monetary policymakers to strategically plan for the future of the economy in a particular country by adjusting and fine-tuning the country's products matrix in light of its production, consumption, international trading partners, and its strategic objectives.

Government Taxation Policy and Economic Development It is a known fact that if a government taxes its citizens excessively, the citizens' reaction would be to either not participate in the economy because there would be no economic incentive to do so and/or to try to evade taxes resulting in an unhealthy social fabric in that country. If a citizen decides not to participate in the economy and/or to evade taxes (which is usually coupled with sending money abroad to avoid taxes), this will lead to less money velocity because the currency will travel less. In order to explain this in a simple way, let us consider two countries with a money supply level (M in the exchange equation discussed earlier) of $1 million. Country A, because of its low taxes, has a velocity of money of 10, while country B has a velocity of 2:

1. Country A charges 25 percent in taxes. Every time a dollar is transacted in a business, a tax of 25 cents is charged. In this case, the country will have a GDP of $1 million × 10, or $10 million. The tax collected here is $2.5 million. This would be the money that will be used by Government A to meet its maintenance and growth plans.
2. Country B charges 50 percent in taxes. Every time a dollar is transacted in business, the government keeps 50 cents. In this case, the country will have money velocity of, say, 2, which results in a GDP of $1 million × 2, or $2 million. The tax collected in this case is $1 million.

In this example, one can find that the country that charged less in taxes collected more income than that with higher taxes. Of course, there is an optimization process that must be pursued by planners in economic and monetary policy in order to decide on the most appropriate tax rate that would help achieve government goals and objectives.

Readers who are interested in more details on this subject can search the Web and many of the books and articles in the field of monetary theory for:

- The Laffer Curve (named after Arthur Laffer, who is one of the leading pioneers of supply-side economics in the United States).
- *The General Theory of Employment, Interest Rates, and Money,* published in 1936, by economist John M. Keynes. In this book, Keynes developed his theory of money demand, known as the liquidity preference theory.
- The books and writings of Nobel Prize–winning economist James Tobin (1918–2002).
- The rich contributions of the prominent Nobel Prize winner Professor Milton Friedman (1912–2006), who pioneered the modern quantity theory of money.

REVIEW QUESTIONS

1. What is money? What is fiat money?
2. Answer the following questions about the Federal Reserve Bank of the United States:
   a. What is the Federal Reserve Bank (FRB)? Please be brief but succinct.
   b. What are the tasks the FRB is responsible for, as defined by the U.S. Congress?
   c. Who elects and confirms the chairman of the FRB?

d. What are the most important powers of the chairman of the FRB and the FRB as defined by the Constitution of the United States?
e. What are the basic three functions of the FRB?
f. How many members are there in the FRB board of directors?
g. What is a regional FRB? How many regional FRBs are there in the United States?
h. How are the boards of directors of the regional banks chosen? Why is diversification of the board membership important?
i. How does the FRB setup in the United States differ from that of a central bank in a typical country? Please give some historic examples why the central bank regime is inferior/superior to that of the FRB.
j. Who owns the FRB?
k. What is the meaning of the "Fed Fund rate?"
l. What is the Federal Open Market Committee (FOMC)? How does it function?
m. How does the Fed (FRB) change interest rate in a large economic and banking system like that of the United States? What tools does it use?
n. What is the "Taylor Rule?"
o. How is the Taylor Rule used to estimate the optimum rates of growth of money supply and the Fed Funds rate?
p. How does the Fed manage inflation? Quote an example of how Mr. Volcker, the Fed chairman during the Carter administration, cracked the 1980s' inflation spiral in the United States.
q. Is the Fed Funds rate used by the Fed as a tool for deciding on money supply the same as the riba/ribit/usury defined in the Judeo-Christian-Islamic Value System (Shari'aa) and why?

3. The real task for RF (Islamic) banks: The twentieth century saw a focus of RF bankers on how the loan contracts are written, which was a good beginning. Now, after getting exposed to the monetary world and reading about money and money creation, what in your opinion should be the real most urgent task to define value of different items in the market?
4. Now that you know that banks in the current world banking system can create credit, please answer the following:
   a. Is credit another mechanism of creating money in the economy?
   b. If it does, then how the regulators manage the ability of the banks to do that?
   c. What is the multiplier effect and in your opinion how it affects the monetary base?
5. Answer the following questions about the U.S. dollar as a reserve currency of the world:
   a. Please explain the details and significance of the Bretton Woods Agreement.

   b. Is this agreement still in effect? Please explain what happened and why in the 1970s.
   c. Why has gold price reached the $1,700 in 2011–2012? Is not that contrary to the Bretton Woods Agreement?
6. We hear many analysts making comparisons between the U.S. dollar (the currency of the United States), and the euro (the currency of the European Union). Please enumerate the differences between the two systems and explain why one system may be more responsive and homogeneous than the other.
7. What is the meaning of a country's gold reserves? How does this gold reserve affect the currency of that country in today's monetary regime?
8. What do we mean by the gold standard? Is it applicable anywhere today?
9. Please review the gold reserves of countries in the world:
   a. What two countries have the largest gold reserves, in tons and in ounces per capita, in the world?
   b. What two countries have the lowest gold reserves, in tons and in ounces per capita?
10. How is the price of gold fixed in London? Who represent those entities that fix the price of gold? How many times in a day the price is fixed?
11. What is the conceptual meaning of the velocity of money? How does it impact prices?
12. How does government taxation policies impact the economy and in particular production?

NOTES

1. Glyn Davies, *A History of Money from Ancient Times to the Present Day*, 3rd ed. (Cardiff: University of Wales Press, 2002).
2. J. Laurence, *The History of Bimetallism in the United States* (New York: D. Appleton and Company, 1901), chapter 8.
3. David H. Friedman, *Essentials of Banking* (Washington, DC: American Bankers Association, 1989).
4. These are episodes of irrational public hoarding and runs on banks.
5. Based on Friedman, *Essentials of Banking* (see note 3).
6. Yahia Abdul-Rahman, *LARIBA Bank, Islamic Banking, Foundation for a United and Prosperous Community* (Published by the author, 1994).
7. Ibid.
8. See note 3.
9. Ibid.
10. This section is based on a comprehensive review of history as outlined by Jude Wanniski, *The Way the World Works* (New York: Touchstone/Simon and Schuster, 1978).

11. A short history of modern finance, *The Economist* (October 16, 2008), 79–81.
12. Javier Blas, "Gold Sales Cost Europe's Central Banks $40 Billion." FT.com, May 6, 2009.
13. World Gold Council, Gold Research and Statistics website: www.gold.org/reserve-asset-management.
14. Professor John Taylor, Stanford University. Please visit Professor Taylor's personal home page: www.stanford.edu/~johntayl/.
15. Richard A. Brealey and Steward C. Meyer, *Principles of Corporate Finance*, 6th ed. London: Irwin/McGraw-Hill, 2000), 49.
16. R. Charles Moyer, James R. McGuigan, and William J. Kretlow, *Contemporary Financial Management* (Mason, OH: South-Western Cengage Learning, 2008), 163.
17. For a detailed outline of the many papers, books, and analyses on the Taylor Rule, please visit www.stanford.edu/~johntayl/PolRulLink.htm.
18. GDP is a measurement of the national income and output for a given country. It is a measurement of the total value (in local currency or in dollars) of all final goods and services produced in that economy in a given year.

CHAPTER 6

Towards an RF Monetary Discipline: The RF Commodity Indexation Discipline

In the first five chapters of this book, the reader was introduced to the Judeo-Christian-Islamic foundations of the RF finance and its two pillars: the RF Commodity Indexation Discipline and the Marking-to-Market Discipline. Chapter 5 reviewed the history of money and the evolution of fiat (paper) money and the current monetary system, which is based on paper money. In this chapter, the RF Commodity Indexation Discipline and its use to detect price, economic bubbles, and market excesses will be applied and explained in detail. A call for a new beginning for an RF Monetary Discipline is made.

THE CYCLICAL NATURE OF THE FIAT MONEY ECONOMY

Professor Ahmad Kamal Meera[1] authored an insightful book on the economics of fiat money, bank fractional reserves, and interest, in which he concluded that the fiat money interest-based system causes asset bubbles, particularly after the potential gross domestic product (GDP) levels of an economy have been reached. He described a five-stage process to the creation of cycles in a fiat money-based economy. It is important to state here that the purpose of this discussion is not to criticize the current monetary system or advocate changing it—that is not our goal or the purpose of this book—but rather to throw more light on how the system works, in order to coexist with it and to allow for it—in the short term—while designing, implementing, and operating the RF banking, finance, and monetary system in a world that uses fiat (paper) money. It is believed that this can be done to a high degree of success (as experienced in our operations at LARIBA since 1987 and the Bank of Whittier in the United States since 2003) by applying the screens of the Commodity Indexation Discipline and the Marking-to-Market Discipline. If we know the way the riba-based fiat money monetary, financial, and banking system works, we definitely can—in the short run until a fair RF commodity-based monetary system is developed and implemented—to a better extent and with a great level of success, identify the formation of a pricing bubble earlier, before it grows larger to create a serious economic problem. It is hoped that using this RF discipline will allow those of us who aspire to live by the RF rules and lead an RF lifestyle to have the proper and well-defined early warning signals and the decision-making tools that will allow for the avoidance of or the timely exit from that economic bubble before it bursts and causes everyone in the RF banking and finance system in particular and the society at large a great loss of assets, economic damage, and the loss of stability, reputation, and credibility of the system's financial and banking institutions as experienced during the 2008 financial meltdown. Following are the five stages:

1. A *Period of Money Creation* without significant inflation. In this phase, the central bank or the Feds would allow the creation of more money through the tools at its disposal—for example, lowering interest rates (the Fed Funds rate) and/or reducing the statutory reserve requirements at the banks as explained in Chapter 5. As money becomes available, people begin borrowing money and buying things. This situation creates a period of economic prosperity without inflation, because the excess production and services capacity of the economy goes into an absorption process through that increase in demand.
2. An *Inflationary Period* of excess money supply with cheap (low interest rate) funds. This stage follows the full utilization of available production capacities and the subsequent drying up of supply of inexpensive products, services, homes, and commercial real estate. People still can borrow at low interest rates, which causes demand to rise further and outpace the available supply from the productive capacity of the economy. This situation causes a period of inflation of prices. Excess money in the hands of the public begins going into higher salaries, which means more excess cash in the hands of the public, more savings for retirement, and, in the end, excess cash pouring into the stock market, causing it to heat up and rise sharply. Of course, those in the money market and stock market will always give the impression that there is no end in sight to this spectacular growth. It is the responsibility of a wise central bank or Federal Reserve Board to arrest the money creation machine at this stage to avoid the growth of this economic bubble.
3. A *Period of Destruction of Money Supply*, causing an economic downturn with financial distress and bankruptcies. Here, prices keep rising, but prudent investors start looking at their positions and discover that

the price-to-earnings ratio of certain stocks is too high to be real and the price of real estate is so high that the debt service is much higher than the potential rent. This is where applying the RF Commodity Indexation Discipline and rules and the RF Marking-to-Market Discipline (detailed in Chapters 3 and 5) will be extremely useful to those who lead an RF lifestyle and believe in and apply the RF disciplines and rules of the Judeo-Christian-Islamic Shari'aa law. Many decide to go to cash. This reduces demand and increases supply, causing prices to decline and, in most cases, sharply signaling the bursting of the economic bubble. In most cases, the price of a real estate property, for example, may be lower than the loan the owners obtained to finance it (Americans use the expression "under water" meaning that the value of the home or property is under the level of the loan taken against it)—as many experienced during the 2008 economic meltdown. In most cases, especially in today's culture, that prompts many to declare bankruptcy to run away from their debt responsibility, and the banks proceed to go through the mechanical steps to repossess the properties. Because banks are not allowed by regulators to carry real estate direct ownership on their books for an unnecessarily long time, they are required by the regulators to sell these properties as soon as possible. This causes prices to decline further in a process of capital destruction. The same process happened on the stock market, especially with portfolios that use *margin* financing (borrowing money against the market value of the stock portfolio). Market losses in the Dow Jones Industrial Average—in one day—can reach more than $1 trillion (that is, $1,000 billion). During this process, we witness the destruction of the fiat (paper) money created at the printing press, as described earlier in stages 1 and 2.

4. A *Period of Transfer of the Crisis from the Financial Sector (Wall Street) to the Real Sector (Main Street)*. As the recession sets in, businesses, in their pursuit to cut expenses and overhead, resort to reducing employment and begin laying off employees and reducing production (in industries such as home construction and auto manufacturing, which are the backbone of the economy of an industrialized country such as the United States), with a resulting deep impact on local economies because workers in the backbone industries in the economy—home construction and automobile manufacturing—are laid off in a massive way. This process results in massive economic dislocations and price reductions.
5. A *Period of Recovery that Takes the Economy Back to the First Period* described in stage 1. At this phase, the government starts a recovery program with the help of monetary authorities, and we head back toward the first stage; money creation begins anew.

The five-stage process that ends with the bursting of the bubble has been witnessed during the inflation of the stock market from 1987 to the year 2000 and from 2003 to 2008. The reduction in interest rates that followed the September 11, 2001, attacks caused inflation of real estate prices for a long time, resulting in the 2008 meltdown and the near-collapse of the financial system, not only in the United States but in the whole world.

It is important to note here that one of the responsibilities of the central bankers of the world—including the Federal Reserve of the United States—is to try their best to timely stop the "bubblization" of assets by bursting these bubbles before they become so large that they create a heavy burden on the economy and the whole population when they collapse. It is interesting to note that former Fed Chairman Alan Greenspan (1987–2006) preferred to allow the housing bubbles in the United States to fester for a long time. The bubbles eventually burst a short time before his retirement, causing the huge damage of financial markets worldwide. Unfortunately, in the 2008 experience we have seen that such a *laissez-faire* approach and policy adopted by the Federal Reserve Board invited corruption and fraud (witness the persistent regulatory and legal violations of many of the investment bankers and mortgage bankers). The outcome can be devastating in depth and extent, as we saw in 2008.

The big question is: how can an average citizen or an RF financial institution avoid participating in this bubble-creating banking and finance behavior? The answer is that participation in the bubble can be avoided by applying the following two important RF disciplines and finance rules:

1. Use the RF Commodity Indexation Discipline.
2. Apply the RF Marking-to-Market Discipline.

These RF finance rules make certain that we are investing prudently and not participating in a bubble. True, we may be premature in quitting and exiting a certain market, and we do not participate in some spectacular speculative (gambling) returns, but as RF bankers we are certain that we deliver the most important value of RF banking to our customers who decided to live an RF lifestyle: the preservation of capital and the realizing of prudent returns that, in the long run, will be much higher than such "bubble" and gambling-based returns.

THE PROHIBITION OF RIBA/RIBIT

It would be useful to present here a recap of the Judeo-Christian-Islamic Shari'aa law discussed earlier in the book and to introduce the reader to what can be considered the main contribution of the research that this book presents.

There are two types or classes of riba:

1. *Riba al-nassee'ah* is defined as the time-related increase over the original value of capital given, usually by putting a condition in the loan agreement indicating that the lender would be entitled to an increase over the original value if the borrower asks for an extension of the term of the credit. This type of riba is prohibited by the Qur'aan, the Sunnah (tradition of Prophet Muhammad [pp]), and all scholars, without exception.
2. *Riba al-fadl* is defined as selling (real) money for (real) money, commodity for commodity (e.g., food for same kind food) with an increase over the original value except under special rules, as will be explained later. This practice is also prohibited by all sources (the Qur'aan, the Sunnah, and all the scholars), because it can lead to riba al-nassee'aah, which was described above. It is given the label of riba as a way to attach it to the real reason for prohibiting it: because it leads to riba al-nassee'ah. Prophet Muhammad (pp) said[2]:

   > *. . . do not sell the [silver] dirham (a prevailing currency then) for two [silver] dirhams because I am afraid that you indulge in [the prohibited] Riba.*

The *Hadeeth* (sayings or pronouncements) of Prophet Muhammad (pp) specifically prohibited practicing riba in six items: gold, silver, wheat, barley, dates, and salt. It was reported that the Prophet (pp) said[3]:

> *. . . gold for gold, silver for silver, barley for barley and salt for salt hand to hand [in an on-the-spot transaction without delay to avoid participating of these into options and futures speculative activities because these are used as reference calibrating pricing and valuation tools] those who increase in buying or selling these items or not delivering it at a future date and not immediately [hand-to-hand] they are considered practicing riba. This applies to those who take the increased amount and those who agree to give it.*

In another narration by Muslim (one of the compilers of the sayings of Prophet Muhammad [pp]), it was added:

> *. . . should the kinds [of commodities] differ, then exchange as you wish, provided that the exchange is hand to hand [on-the-spot].*

Reason for Prohibition

The reason for prohibiting riba in dealing with these six commodities is that they represented—at the time—the basic necessities of the citizens; without such basic commodities, they could not live comfortably. Gold and silver, at the time of Prophet Muhammad (pp), were the basic currencies used to buy and sell and to define prices in the market to settle transactions. They were called *tathmeen:* the two commodities used to establish prices in the market because gold and silver represented a way to store value because they do not change over time.

If riba were practiced in dealing with these items, it would have hurt the interests of the citizens and would lead to a breakdown in the fabric of the society. RF law prohibited such dealing as a mercy to mankind and to protect the interests of the citizens by preserving market stability.

The reason for the "hand-to-hand" or spot transaction prohibition in trading reference commodities is to prevent and make it prohibited to create a speculative futures and/or options market in these commodities and changes its use as a reference in calibrating prices. The wisdom of the prohibition in this RF fundamental market rule would eradicate speculation and lead to a credible pricing reference system for measuring fair value.

From the preceding discussion, one can conclude that the reason for prohibiting riba in gold and silver was that gold and silver were used to price things, and riba was prohibited on the other four food items because they were necessary food staples. If these qualifications are found by analogy to apply on other items, the rule applies. Such items are used as reference commodities in the RF Commodity Indexation Discipline discussed earlier.

Based on this determination, the rule can be extended using the discipline of "Measured Analogy" (*qiyas*). The rule can be stated in general as:

1. If the two items transacted are from the same material and are used for the same purpose (e.g., gold for gold, or wheat for wheat), then both riba al-nassee'ah and riba al-fadl are prohibited. The following conditions must be satisfied in order for a like-for-like transaction to be ruled as an RF transaction (riba free):
   a. The quantity on the buy and sell side must be equal, regardless of quality.[4]
   b. The buy and sell must be done on the spot (e.g., hand to hand, as the Prophet [pp] said).
2. If the two items to be transacted differ in their material but are used for the same application, then the rules of riba al-fadl can be invoked on the condition that riba al-nassee'ah is not used. Gold can be sold for silver, or wheat can be sold for barley, and the transaction must be done on the

spot (hand-to-hand), but the quantities do not have to be equal. It was reported that the Prophet (pp) said[5]:

> . . . *it is acceptable to sell wheat for barley and you can get more barley but it has to be hand to hand [an on-the-spot transaction].*

If the two items to be transacted are different in material and in purpose of use, there are no restrictions in applying time in the riba al-nassee'ah and excess over the original amount in riba al-fadl. For example, food can be sold for silver, and one dress for two dresses, or two cups for one cup. In summary, riba al-fadl can be practiced on any item, aside from the reference calibrating commodities: the two metals (gold and silver) and the food staples (wheat, barley, dates, and salt). The Prophet (pp) emphasized this concept when a companion brought to him an excellent type of dates from Khaiber (a city in what is now Saudi Arabia). The Prophet (pp) asked, "Are all the dates of Khaiber like this?" The man said no, but we barter one volume (a volume-measuring unit that was used at that time, called *saa*) of this dates for two volumes (saa) of ours (they were lower quality, smaller dates). The Prophet said: "Do not do that because that is exactly riba and it is forbidden." The way to do it, according to RF discipline, is to sell your dates for money (silver dirham, gold dinar, or another calibrating reference staple commodity except for the same commodity—i.e., not other dates), and buy the good dates with the proceeds.[6] By this rule, one can buy 10 bushels of wheat (food) for one ounce of gold on-the-spot [cash price] or deferred at two ounces of gold after two years. Because the gold is a metal and the wheat is a food, this transaction is halal (divinely allowed). Also, buying 7 bushels of wheat for 10 bushels of barley is allowed on-the-spot, but increasing the price to 7 bushels of wheat for 15 bushels of barley to be paid (delivered) after one year is haram (divinely prohibited) because both are food items. As a more modern example and by using the concept of analogy, if one wants to buy heating oil by exchanging two gallons of fuel oil for one gallon of gasoline, it is not allowed by the RF discipline because both are used as a source of energy and al-fadl can only be applied on two items with different uses. In this case, one can offer to exchange the heating oil for another medium (currency), such as gold or silver, or for a food product such as wheat or rice. Then one can take the proceeds and buy the gasoline with it at market price. This is what we advocate and present for the first time as the RF disciplines in this book; the RF Commodity Indexation Discipline and the RF Marking-to-Market Discipline.

When the Islamic state, with its laws and systems, expanded beyond Arabia, many of the jurists were exposed to different environments, economies, monetary systems, and cultures that used essential commodities that were not known in Arabia. To deal with the intricacies of concluding whether such practices were acceptable to the Judeo-Christian-Islamic Shari'aa law, the jurists used the system of "Measured Analogy" (*qiyas*, as explained in Chapters 3 and 4). For example, this analysis allowed them to add other commodities to the six reference commodities identified by the Prophet (pp), such as rice, which is used in Asia more than wheat, and corn, which is used more as a staple food in Latin America. Muslims continued for centuries to apply these rulings in their dealings.

Application of the RF Law Using the RF Commodity Indexation Discipline

As discussed earlier, the RF law requires that commodities be priced in terms of another reference commodity before being traded for a higher quantity, volume, or weight of the same type of commodity. For example, one cannot trade 100 bushels of good-quality wheat for 500 bushels of lower-quality wheat because it constitutes ribit/riba. However, one can sell the 100 bushels for another commodity (e.g., gold or silver) and use the proceeds to buy the lower-quality wheat. This way, the markets would be used to define the real value of the item traded and that would keep the market in a stable condition and in equilibrium. A transparent RF market system is free from both ribit/riba and *gharar* (deception, speculation, and misrepresentation).

Please note that when it is suggested that one uses gold or silver as a reference pricing commodity along with other food staples, it is not intended to enter into a discussion and get involved in arguments on the subject of going back to the system of the gold standard, advocated by some and vehemently opposed by others. In fact, if we apply the rules of the RF law as detailed in Exhibit 6.1, which was first displayed in Chapter 3,[7] one can make a compelling case that the fiat currencies are not considered as food staples or pricing commodities. Based on that, paper money can be handled as category C, which allows for increase and deferred exchange. That is where the real RF spirit comes in. It is not just about the interest and a percentage sign attached to that charged interest. The RF discipline is indeed about the intent and spirit of the transaction—how prudent and fair it is and whether it is looked upon as an investment or as a mere renting of money and capital. What is strongly recommended here to preserve the Judeo-Christian-Islamic Shari'aa law is to use the RF Commodity Indexation Discipline, which requires that we test the price of things in the economy (e.g., oil, houses, food items) by the use of one of the two types of reference commodities (e.g., precious metals—gold or silver—or food staples—such as wheat, barley, and rice) to detect if they are valued at a fair price. In Exhibit 6.1, the item classified as A would be a reference-calibrating commodity that must be exchanged in equal amounts and on the spot. Items classified as B would be items of different commodities, but the purpose of their use is the same, like a metal or food. For example, gold and silver can be exchanged for more than equal amounts but must be traded on the spot in a hand-to-hand transaction. The same would apply for wheat and rice. Items classified as C can be traded freely. Please read Exhibit 6.1 carefully and attempt to make your own conclusions about paper (fiat) money in contrast to real money.

It is interesting to note that in 1987, the then-secretary of the United States Treasury, James A. Baker III, told world financial leaders during the 1987 fall meeting of the International Monetary Fund (IMF)[8] that the Reagan administration "is prepared to consider" using the price of gold in trying to steer its own and the world's economies. Gold, Mr. Baker explained, could be used in a specially designed index, along with other commodities, to help governments discern inflation and then adjust their policies—by using interest rates or taxes, for example. Professor Robert A. Mundell, a Columbia University economist and proponent of the concept, stated that "this is far from a gold standard." On May 20, 1999, soon after the United Kingdom announced its decision to sell part of its gold reserves, Alan Greenspan, then chairman of the U.S. Federal Reserve, said: "Gold still represents the ultimate form of payment in the world." Dr. Mahathir Mohamad, the former prime minister of Malaysia, also made some very interesting comments in one of his speeches[9] in response to the 1997–1998 Asian currency crises, which resulted from massive hedge fund speculations in Asian currencies. The speculation caused massive devaluation of local currencies in Thailand, South Korea, Malaysia, Hong Kong, Indonesia, and many other countries in the region. Dr. Mohamad discovered that even many of his senior central bankers[10] were not aware of the mechanics of international currency speculation by heavily capitalized hedge funds and other investment banking institutions—or the way to stop such speculation. The "textbook" solution offered by many senior finance officers and ministers of finance of these countries was to support the local currencies by selling hard currencies reserved by the central bank of the country involved like the U.S. dollar, the Japanese yen, and the euro, and buying the local currencies to create new demand for the local currencies to attempt to keep the exchange rate intact. The problem was the huge volume of currencies needed. Many of the countries lost a major portion of their reserves without causing a dent in the exchange rate. The following is a snapshot of what

EXHIBIT 6.1 RF Rules Governing Sale or Exchange of Items in the Marketplace

	Currency Items				Food Items						Anything Else
	Gold	Silver	Currency 1	Currency 2	Barley	Wheat	Dates	Salt	Food 1	Food 2	Other
Gold	A	B	B	B	C	C	C	C	C	C	C
Silver	B	A	B	B	C	C	C	C	C	C	C
Currency 1	B	B	A	B	C	C	C	C	C	C	C
Currency 2	B	B	B	A	C	C	C	C	C	C	C
Barley	C	C	C	C	A	B	B	B	B	B	C
Wheat	C	C	C	C	B	A	B	B	B	B	C
Dates	C	C	C	C	B	B	A	B	B	B	C
Salt	C	C	C	C	B	B	B	A	B	B	C
Food 1	C	C	C	C	B	B	B	B	A	B	C
Food 2	C	C	C	C	B	B	B	B	B	A	C
Other	C	C	C	C	C	C	C	C	C	C	C

Rule Definitions

Rule A	Exchanged items must be of same amount AND on-the-spot sale.
Rule B	Amounts of the items could be different but the sale must be a spot sale (e.g., you may trade one pound of wheat for two pounds of barley on the spot).
Rule C	Amounts of the items could be different and does *not* need to be on the spot (e.g., for whatever amounts you agreed to, you can trade on the spot, or deliver goods now and get payment later, or deliver payment now and get the goods later).

Note: The above rules are based on two Hadeeth of the Prophet (pp) and the explanation provided in "Fiqh al-Sunnah" by Sheikh Sayed Sabiq. The Hadeeth explicitly mentioned six items categorized as food or currency. Scholars' opinion is that it also applies to any food or currency.

happened to some currencies in a very short span of time. The decline of exchange rates relative to the U.S. dollar on February 16, 1998, compared to June 30, 1998, is shown in Exhibit 6.2.

EXHIBIT 6.2 Decline of Exchange Rates in Asian Currencies Relative to the U.S. Dollar

Country	Decline
Indonesia	75%
Malaysia	36%
Thailand	48%
Philippines	36%
South Korea	47%

One interesting but sad and painful case was that of Turkey. The Turkish lira's exchange rate was 108,340 lira for each U.S. dollar in January 1997; it declined by 93 percent to exchange at 1,474,525 lira per U.S. dollar in January 2002. Such massive declines obviously resulted in a reduction in the values of salaries, peoples' savings, pensions, and the meteoric rise in the price of goods and services. Imagine what a poor farmer in the Philippines would do when the cost of rice in his local currency—the only currency he knows about and is using—increases significantly. Such a sudden reduction in the value of local currencies raised the value of short-term debt of the country involved, usually denominated in U.S. dollars or in euros, and increased debt service. As if this were not enough, the sudden currency devaluation reduced the credit rating of the country involved, which resulted in an increase in the cost of borrowing on the international markets; that is the interest rate charged by the international banks on sovereign debt solicited by these countries. All these unfortunate results reduced the country's economic activity, resulting in massive increases in unemployment and poverty.

In an effort to apply the RF Commodity Indexation Discipline by testing the valuation of different commodities in terms of one another in order to conduct sales and trading at a higher price, as stipulated by the Judeo-Christian-Islamic Shari'aa law, we attempted to price different commodities in terms of gold, silver, wheat, oil, and other reference commodities. What was intended in this research was to detect the historic trend of pricing a commodity, say, oil, in terms of gold or another staple commodity, using the RF Commodity Indexation Discipline, for example by asking the question: How many barrels of oil can one buy for every ounce of gold, or how many ounces of gold or bags of rice are necessary to buy a home using average home prices in the United States? We have done the same for commodities such as natural gas, coal, wheat, corn, rice, and soybeans as well as stock market indicators.

In this approach, we conceptually disengaged and tried to neutralize the effects of the use of fiat money, and instead used a reference commodity as stipulated in the RF Judeo-Christian-Islamic Commodity Indexation Discipline detailed earlier. It will be made clear that if we refer the value of each of the commodities to another reference commodity or index commodity, we shall find, in general, that the price or market value would be more stable, less volatile, moving within a narrow band reflecting the normal supply and demand equilibrium patterns, and more fair. Exceptions to this general finding are cases that involve changes in production processes, technological developments, political factors, or significant change in taste and/or lifestyle. The charts also show that regardless of how the price of a commodity changes in terms of fiat (paper) currencies, like the U.S. dollar, the value in terms of a reference commodity are more representative, and that an economic pricing bubble can be detected whenever the band of price fluctuations that reflects normal market forces of supply and demand, for example, seasonal changes, is penetrated to the higher or lower side of the pricing envelope defined by normal forces of supply and demand. In doing so, the reader is encouraged to consider using this RF discipline as a macroeconomic tool to indexing their own products and services to a reference commodity, in order to avoid participating in an economic bubble like those we have witnessed throughout history—from the tulips in the seventeenth-century Holland "tulip bubble" to the year 2000 stock market "dot-com technology bubble" in the twentieth-century United States, to the "housing bubble" at the beginning of the twenty-first century, which resulted in the 2008 global financial and monetary meltdown.

Toward an RF Monetary Theory and Discipline

Money in its banknote (paper) form has been one of the great and historic human innovations that facilitated commerce, industrial growth, and economic development. Our objection in RF monetary discipline is not the use of fiat (paper) money but rather the valuation of these banknotes. The book discussed earlier the two important RF banking and finance disciplines; the RF Commodity Indexation Discipline and the RF Marking-to-Market Discipline. In this section, an important aspect of RF discipline and lifestyle is the monetary aspect of fiat (paper) money and the RF monetary discipline. It is true that very little has been written on the subject and no formal in-depth research has been conducted. The following is a preliminary effort that will hopefully peak the interests of some readers to start a thoughtful research program to develop an RF monetary theory and discipline that will hopefully fix the shortcomings of the current system, which is believed to have been broken in 1971 by the Nixon doctrine and has not been fixed since.

Monetary theory develops the link between money supply and other macroeconomic variables, including the price level and output (GDP). In this chapter, we begin with competing theories of money demand and some empirical evidence about the behavior of money demand. In order to achieve an RF monetary theory and discipline in an introductory way, the following are in a preliminary way the aspects of what can be called the beginning of the RF monetary discipline:

1. The RF Commodity Indexation of products and services in order to disengage pricing in fiat money from its real nature of being a paper banknote used to transact business. This RF Commodity Indexation Discipline has been discussed earlier and the book and will be elaborated on later in this chapter.
2. The concept of the velocity of money, which measures how many times a dollar changes hands in an economy and was discussed earlier in Chapter 5. This concept is important because it gives an indication of two important policies; one is rate of economic growth in the economy and the impact of money supply on that economy and the tax rate applied by governments.

Development of an RF Monetary System to Develop a Fair RF Pricing Discipline

A valuable research on money in Islam was documented in an Arabic language book published by Albaraka and authored by Dr. Omar Kamel.[11]

A Historic Review of the Definition of Money and Monetary Discipline According to the Judeo-Christian-Islamic Shari'aa Law by Many RF Scholars Ibn Khaldun (732–808 A.H., 1332–1406 C.E.), in his book *The Muqaddima,*[12] introduced his recommendations for a sound monetary policy. He stated that he is "against the policies of government authorities to manipulate and play with the value of currency." He also expressed his deep concerns about the economic devastation that occurs "if the authorities are tempted to debase the value of money in order to build palaces for the rulers, the rich and affluent and to finance mercenary armies." He concluded that "these policies will cause inflation and population will lose confidence in the currency." He recommended to government leaders that they should make justice as their prime goal. He stated that "protection of the purchasing power of money has to be implemented as a matter of justice." To reach that goal he recommended that governments devise an independent monetary agency and policy under the authority of the chief justice. He qualified that person to be a "God fearing person who can stand firm to prevent the rulers from carelessly toying with an independent monetary policy leading to reducing the value of currency by debasing it." He concluded that "a stable monetary policy aiming at the protection of purchasing power of money is a must as a matter of establishing justice." He then concluded that what is ultimately needed is less government expenditure on palaces and bureaucracy, less expenditure on mercenary armies, and less taxation. All these policies of establishing and enforcing justice will help in achieving the ultimate goal of a stable currency that will enhance and produce prosperous trading and production in the society.

Ibn Taimiya (661–728 A.H., 1263–1328 C.E.), in his book *The Edicts (Al Fatawa)* stated that money is a calibrating device and is not the thing in itself and it should not be considered for what it is but for what calibrating role it plays in defining prices in the market. In conclusion, Ibn Taimiya states that the purpose of money, gold and silver (at that time), is to be used as a calibrating reference tool for valuing assets through which the value of these assets is defined. Money, gold and silver, is not intended to be used for its commercial use primarily and if exchanged for each other (gold for silver or silver for gold) in transactions that settle later on in the future will make the intention of using it to be in trading and not as a calibrating reference. This in itself contradicts the rule of using it as a standard reference to calibrate value in the open market.

Ibn Qayim Al-Jawziya (691–751 A.H., 1292–1350 C.E.), in his book *Ilam Al Mowaq'ueen Ann Rab'il Alameen* (*Informing Those Who Need to Know about the Rule of the Law of the Lord of the Universe*), stated that money—or silver dirham and gold dinar—is not intended for what it is (in its matter as precious metals), but its use is intended as a reference to value and as a transacting medium in order to transact the exchange of other commodities and products in the marketplace. If these pricing commodities (gold and silver) are used as trading commodities for what they are, then the benefits to the people would be spoiled.

On the matter of the two pricing reference commodities, gold and silver, Ibn Khaldun stated that the Lord, the most supreme, has created the two metals; gold and silver, as a reference tool to calibrate against in order to establish a standardized value for every seeker of assets. These two metals are considered the ammunition (al-zakheera), implying a store of value, and the exchange medium in the market place (al-qunya.) If an individual owns other metals or products, then it is meant that the value of these two pricing metals change in terms of these other products and nonpricing metals in the marketplace. These two metals (gold and silver) are the origin and the reference in calibrating earnings, the medium of exchange valuation, and the store of value.

Ibn Rushd (Averroes) (520–595 A.H., 1126–1198 C.E.), in his book *The Beginning for the Researcher and the End for the User* (*Bedayat Al Mujtahid wa Nihayat Al Muqtasid*), states that prices are stated in terms of gold and silver and the purpose for the use of these pricing commodities should primarily be for calibrating prices and not in using them in different applications that render them to be traded in the marketplace.

Imam Al Ghazaly (450–505 A.H., 1058–1111 C.E.), in his book *Revival (of life) in the Sciences of the Faith* (*Ihia Uloom Al Deen*) states that the two pricing reference metals, gold and silver, were created by God the Supreme in order for exchanging hands as a calibrating reference medium for users in order to define the value of assets in a just and precise fashion. He added that another wisdom and purpose for the creation of gold and silver is to use them as a valuing reference in the market and as a medium of exchange because these two metals are precious and their use is not primarily essential (at that time), and their calibrating valuation of other things in the market are the same. These calibrating metals are in fact a means to store value.

Scholars also made a first attempt to define an RF monetary policy that would help in the preservation of the pricing value of currency:

Al Mawardy (364–450 A.H., 972–1058 C.E.), in his book *Facilitating (and Explaining) the View* (*Tas'heel Al Nazar*), explains the need of the state to fight the tendency of governments to debase currencies (gold and silver) by mixing it with other metals. He states: "The head of state must know that money; gold Dinar and silver Dirham, if handled properly will benefit the state and its citizens. This main purpose outweighs by far the personal benefit to the head of the state. If the head of state allows debasing it, by for example mixing silver with other metals, then the benefit of doing so is overwhelmed by the harm it causes. In addition, this act of fraud produces a currency that tarnishes with time and with transactions from hand to hand resulting in that citizens will refuse to use it for settling transactions. The ultimate result will be that the citizens use bartering instead of these defrauded currencies in their transactions. In addition, if the head of state is known for defrauding currencies by debasing it, then people will use another currency issued by a more credible currency issuer. If the currency is pure and is free from fraud (if it is debased), people will feel that it is a safe currency for storing value and will use it as a currency of choice for their savings and will render it as the preferred currency for transacting trade and business."

Al-Raghib al-Asfahani (d. 508 A.H., 1108 C.E.), in his book *The Excuses that Lead to the Best Application of Shari'aa* (*Al Zaree'aa ela Makarim Al Shari'aa*), says: To know that money, gold and silver, is one of foundations of this worldly life, and if we believe that it does not exist, people will find it difficult to conduct their living needs and will not be able to coexist and work together to benefit mutually from their specific products and services.

That is why it is said that the (silver) dirham is a silent source of governance and of justice, and it is called in Persian the dinar. The word *dinar* means in Persian the debt issued by governments and its rulers. Because of its critical governing role, God has warned those who amass it and do not circulate it in the economy of a grievous punishment on the Day of Judgment as revealed in the Holy Qur'aan, Chapter 9 (Sura Tauba), verse 34:

> *9:34 . . . And there are those who amass gold and silver and spend it not in the way of Allah, announce unto them a most grievous penalty*
>
> *9:35 On the Day when heat will be produced out of that (wealth) in the fire of Hell, and with it will be branded their foreheads, their flanks, and their backs. "This is the (treasure) which ye buried for yourselves: taste ye, then, the (treasures) ye amassed!"*

He elaborates that these grievous punishments have been promised by God because not circulating money in the economy will result in the lack of liquidity, making life difficult for the citizens.

Al Maqreezy (776–845 A.H., 1364–1442 C.E.), in his book about the economy of Egypt titled *The Rescue of the Nation by Uncovering the Setback* (*Eghathatul Ummah be Kashf Al Ghummah*), details the reasons for the crippling inflation Egypt suffered at his time, which destroyed the economy, the decline of Egypt's prosperity, the rise of poverty, and the prevalence of needy people among the Egyptian citizens. One of the main reasons was the minting by the Egyptian government at that time of debased currency. He concluded that there were three causes for the plight of hunger among the Egyptians until 1405 (808 A.H.). The most important reason has been the increase of money supply in a debased form by mixing the silver with another metal to reduce its purity.

The RF Institute[13] started a research program to make modern monetary sense of a well-known Hadeeth by the Prophet Muhammad (pp). This is the Hadeeth of "Gold for Gold"[14] detailed earlier while developing the RF Commodity Indexation Discipline (please see references and quotes in the notes at the end of this chapter). This research was initiated as a result of our original in-depth research about the prohibition of riba/ribit in the Torah, the Bible, and the Qur'aan. The conclusion of this research was that Islam came to reinforce the prohibition, in the Torah and the Bible, of abusing the rights and taking advantage of the poor and the needy through the use of loans given (money rented to them) by the rich. In fact, Islam prohibited all kinds of loans (*qard*, meaning a bite) except one loan: the *qard hassan* (benevolent loan). This RF law prohibited lending (renting) money and using it to take advantage of the poor and the needy that would eventually lead to their enslavement in an effort on their part as forced by the lenders to pay off the loan in terms of work or by confiscating their land and properties.

Further research indicated that the real historic and revolutionary contribution of Islam was the development, for the first time in history, of a fair and well-rooted system for financing commerce and business in an RF format. As it is known historically, Moses (pp) and Jesus (pp) were commissioned in the ages of slavery and agrarian societies. When the Prophet Muhammad (pp) was commissioned, international commerce with trade caravans was flourishing. The challenge was how to fairly calculate the profit and loss of a trade transaction using different local currencies in varying foreign lands like Ethiopia, China, India, Persia, and other communities and countries in the Roman and Byzantine empires. Our research concluded that this may have been the real motivation of what we call the commodities' Hadeeth in order to set fast and firm standards and calibrating reference pricing disciplines in order to normalize the value of the trades using these commodity-based standardized currencies.

The RF Institute developed what is introduced as the beginning of a basic RF monetary discipline, which is called the RF Commodity Indexation Discipline in which we normalize prices away from fiat (paper) currencies like the dollar and the euro. To bring this discipline closer to mind, we reiterate in this chapter what was discussed in Chapter 5. Let us assume that a qard hassan (a benevolent loan with no increase) of $100,000 was given in March 1971. The agreement to repay this qard hassan can be expressed in one of the many following options:

- Pay back in U.S. dollars the amount of $100,000, say, in 2012.
- In case the country is a rice producer only and relies on rice as a reference currency, pay it back in the same amount of rice. If we do it in rice, then $100,000 would buy, in 1971, a total of 18,868 hundredweights (cwt) of rice (rice in 1971 was selling for $5.30/cwt). That is, based on this agreement, the qard hassan, when paid back in 2012, will be paid back in the exact amount in rice or 18,868 cwt of rice (which reached approximately $15/cwt in 2012). This is equivalent to $283,000!
- In case the country is a wheat producer only and relies on wheat as a reference currency, pay it back in the same amount wheat. If we do it in wheat, then $100,000 would buy, in 1971, a total of 70,922 bushels of wheat (which in 1971 was selling for $1.41 a bushel). Based on this agreement, the qard hassan, when paid back in 2012, will be paid back in the exact amount in wheat or 70,922 bushels of wheat (which reached approximately $7.90 a bushel in 2012). This is equivalent to $564,000!
- In case the country is a corn producer only and relies on corn as a reference currency, pay it back in the same amount of corn. If we do it in corn, then $100,000 would buy in 1971 a total of 70,423 bushels of

corn (which in 1971 was selling for $1.42 for a bushel). Based on this agreement, the qard hassan, when paid back in 2012, will be paid back in the exact amount in corn or 70,423 bushels of corn (which reached approximately $7.63 a bushel in 2012). This is equivalent to $537,324! Please notice the approximate similarity in value if one uses wheat and corn—two substitutable staple grains.

- In case the country is a silver producer only and relies on silver as a reference currency, pay it back in the same amount of silver. If we do it in silver, then $100,000 would buy, in 1971, a total of 61,350 ounces of silver (which in 1971 was selling for $1.63/ounce). Based on this agreement, the qard hassan, when paid back in 2012, will be paid back in the exact amount in silver or 61,350 ounces (which reached approximately $34.14/ounce in 2012). This is equivalent to $2.1 million!
- In case the country is using gold as a reference standard for currency, pay it back in the same amount of gold. If we do it in gold, then $100,000 would buy in 1971 a total of 2,857 ounces of gold (which was then priced at $35/ounce.) Based on this agreement, the qard hassan, when paid back in 2012, will be paid back in the exact amount in gold or 2,857 ounces of gold (which reached $1,700/ounce in 2012). This is equivalent to $4.85 million!

In today's economy countries produce a basket of basic commodities that are varied from country to country. That is why we started a research program at the RF Institute to come up with an algorithm that defines the real value of local currencies based on local production of staples and natural resources instead of tying (pegging) these currencies to a major currency like the dollar, which value is defined by a completely different matrix of commodities that relate to the local U.S. economy.

We proceeded to apply this Commodity Indexation Discipline to study prices in the United States of homes, crude oil, food commodities, natural gas, and even the stock market in terms of the reference commodities based on the Hadeeth of the Prophet (pp), and here is a summary of the results:

1. When fiat (paper) money is normalized, in terms of pricing commodities, economic bubbles can be readily identified ahead of time and remedial actions can be taken to avoid participating in or help in taking advantage of the lack of these bubbles. We could identify, ahead of time, the housing bubble in America, starting from the fourth quarter of 2005 to 2006 when the overpricing started to give way, before it burst. We, at LARIBA, using this rule, helped many of our customers not to purchase homes at the peak prices in the U.S. housing market in the states of Arizona, Nevada, Massachusetts, and northern California, as well as Washington, D.C. In fact, based on this RF Commodity

Indexation Discipline, back in 2008, we projected that the depressed prices of homes and undervalued housing market would last for five to seven years and issued our recommendation to buy homes then. It is interesting to note that the housing market in the United States has recovered in mid-2013 as the RF discipline has projected. In fact, because of the housing bubble, the level of housing finance in the bubble period declined, by design, at LARIBA and started to rise sharply, as was recommended to many of our customers, in response to our call to start buying, as shown in Exhibit 6.3 (LARIBA financed a total of $1.25 billion in RF home mortgages from 2000 to 2012).

Let us look at the chart that depicts the history of home prices in the United States in U.S. dollars. We can see that average house prices in the United States kept rising until they peaked around 2006/2007 as shown in Exhibit 6.4.

Exhibit 6.5 shows the home prices in gold after taking away the effect of fiat (paper) currency and using the pricing currency of gold based on the Hadeeth detailed earlier.

In general, we can see that after taking the influence of the fiat (paper) currency away from pricing and using instead a standard reference pricing currency like gold in Exhibit 6.5 or rice in Exhibit 6.6,

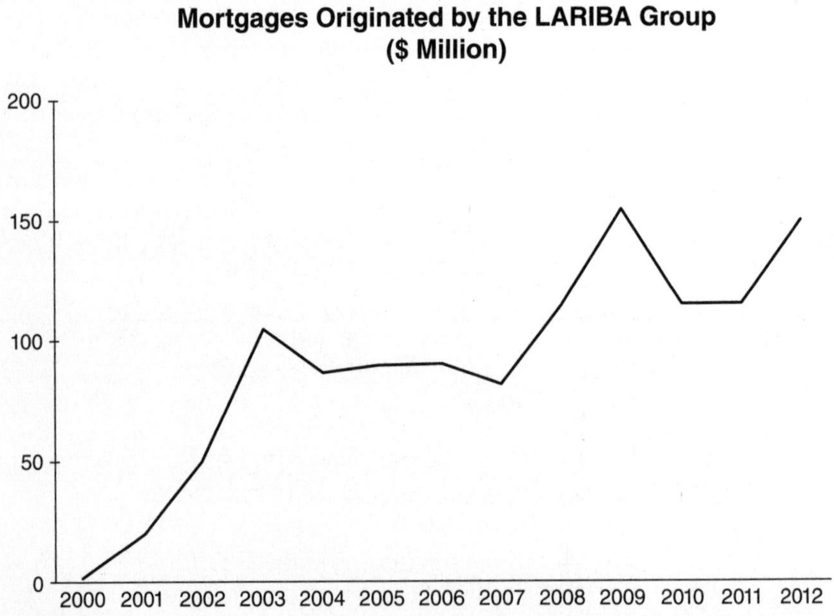

EXHIBIT 6.3 History of Mortgages Originated by LARIBA 2001–2012

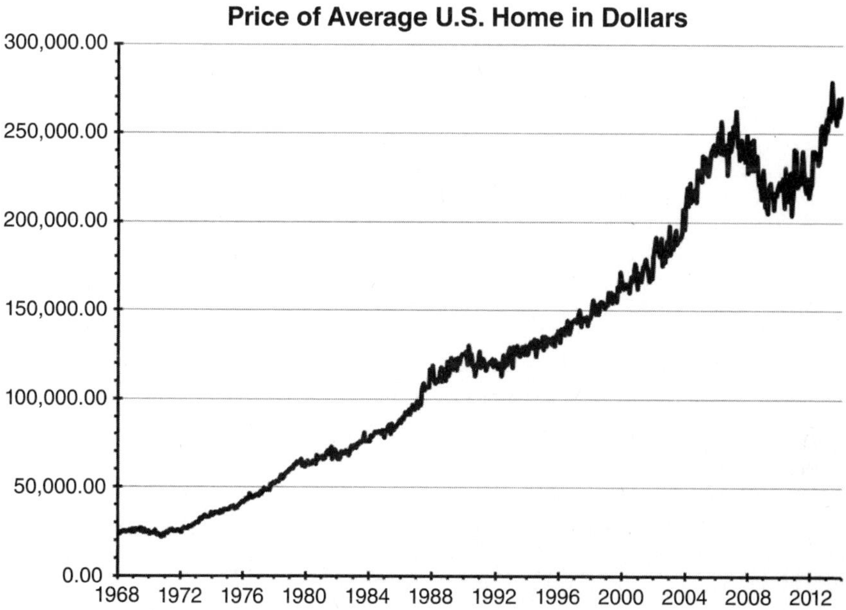

EXHIBIT 6.4 Average Price of a Home in the United States

EXHIBIT 6.5 Price of U.S. Homes in Gold

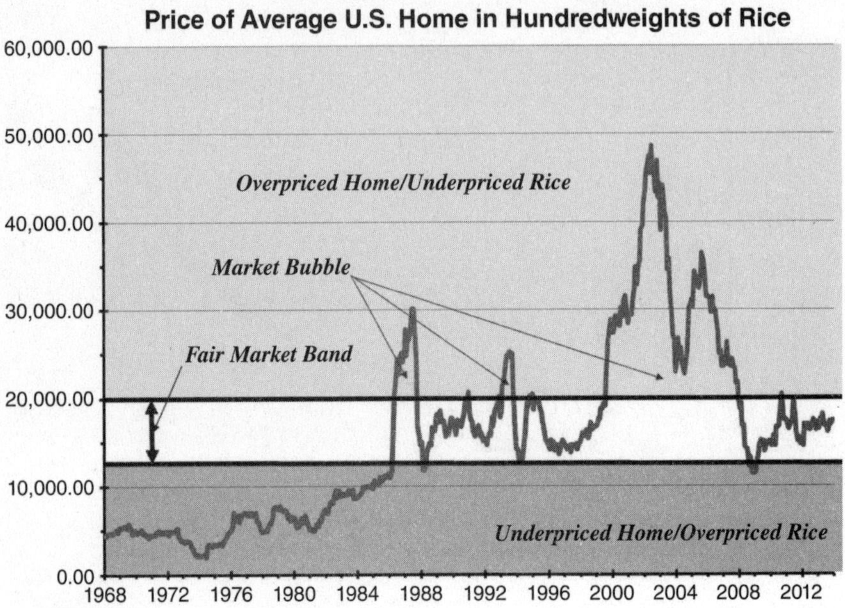

EXHIBIT 6.6 Price of U.S. Homes in Rice

home prices do not show an ever-rising price behavior as experienced in Exhibit 6.4 with the use of fiat money (the U.S. dollar). However, we find that when we use a reference commodity standard calibrating currency, prices fluctuate up and down depending on the market forces of supply-and-demand factors, and prices may drop drastically or skyrocket due to any market manipulations and/or speculation.

To decipher that relationship, we drew a channel—an upper price level and a lower price level—that reflects the range of normal price fluctuations based on the "stochastic technical analysis and charting" techniques of the market forces of supply and demand, which is used in stock market technical analysis. Any time the price is lower than the lower level of the channel, that gives us an indication of an undervalued housing market and it gives a buy signal. Any time the opposite is observed, that is, the price penetrates the upper level of the channel, that gives us a red flag about the overpricing and the beginning of an economic pricing bubble in the housing market created by speculation, and it is taken as an early warning signal of selling and getting out of the market. As can be seen, we noticed this trend to start from the beginning of 2000, and the house price bubble continued to grow until it peaked in 2004/2005 and started its stagnation and decline afterwards. Because of the use the Commodity

Indexation Discipline at LARIBA as an early warning flag, this has alerted our management and underwriters to pay very close attention to the process of investing with (financing of) homes for our customers.

In order to respond to some monetarists in the money marketplace and in academia who may say that this is "another" call to return to the "gold standard," we have studied the pricing of housing and each commodity in terms of other commodities, including gold, silver, rice, wheat, corn, and crude oil. And the results were very educational. Exhibit 6.6 shows the pricing of homes in rice (a staple food) as a standard pricing tool in case the only commodity used in America was rice. The same trend experienced with gold (Exhibit 6.5) is revealed in Exhibit 6.6 when another food staple (rice) commodity is used.

2. Using the same approach described earlier, we can also identify the fair value of crude oil in the market and identify if current prices of gold or crude oil are fair prices based on the market forces of supply and demand or they are hyped through speculation in the commodities' futures and options markets. We at LARIBA, for example, think (as of 2011) that the next bubble to burst will be gold. Based on Exhibits 6.7 and 6.8, we project that the fair market value of gold is between $850 and $1,000 per

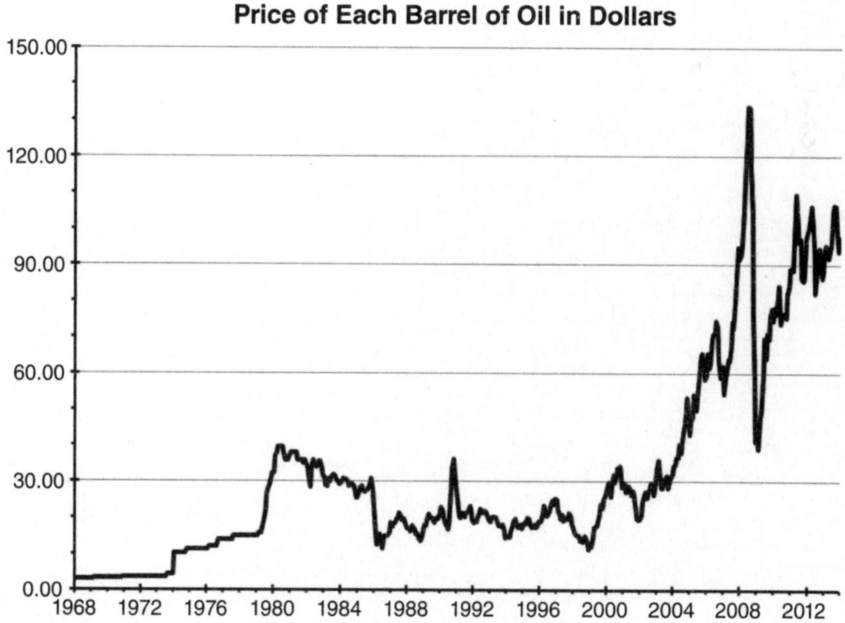

EXHIBIT 6.7 Price of a Barrel of Oil in U.S. Dollars

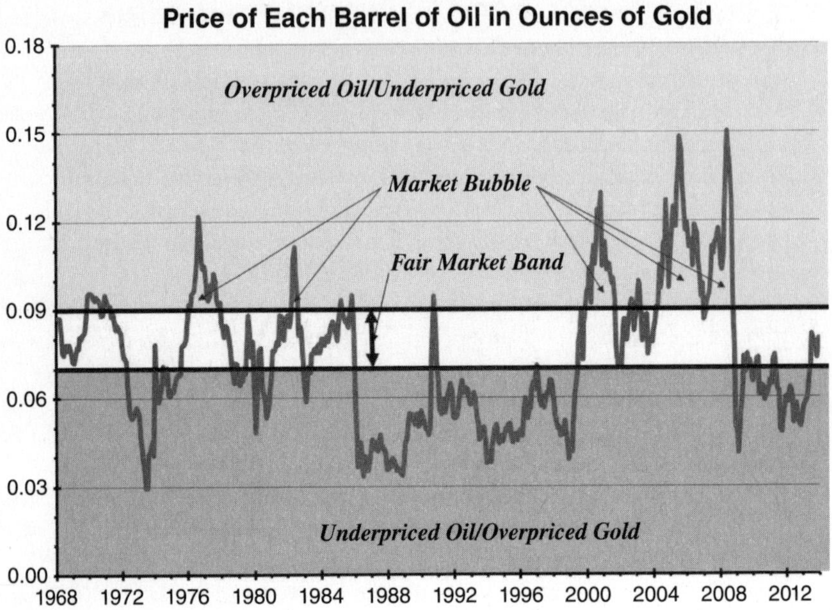

EXHIBIT 6.8 Oil Price in Gold

ounce and that the oil price may range between \$65 and \$80 a barrel in the next two to three years (2014–2015).

3. We also discovered that after taking the effect of fiat currencies away from pricing food commodities like what we see in Exhibit 6.9, the agricultural food commodities prices declined precipitously after the closing of the gold window in August 1971 (by President Nixon) as shown in Exhibit 6.10. Despite higher agricultural food commodities prices in U.S. dollars, as shown in the chart in Exhibit 6.9, their value in terms of other commodities like gold, silver, wheat, and rice have declined precipitously, and as shown in Exhibit 6.10 stayed low and fluctuated between a high and low in a market channel that defines the forces of supply and demand. That explains the reason why farmers worldwide—outside some major economies in North America and Eurozone—have deserted their farms to live in the cities. These farmers also helped train and educate their children to enable them to leave the farm and become city dwellers. It is also interesting to note that the price of one food commodity (say rice in terms of wheat, as shown in Exhibit 6.11) were steady, and that reflected the real exchange value of two food staples as prices fluctuated around a mean market channel that defined the free-market forces of supply and demand.

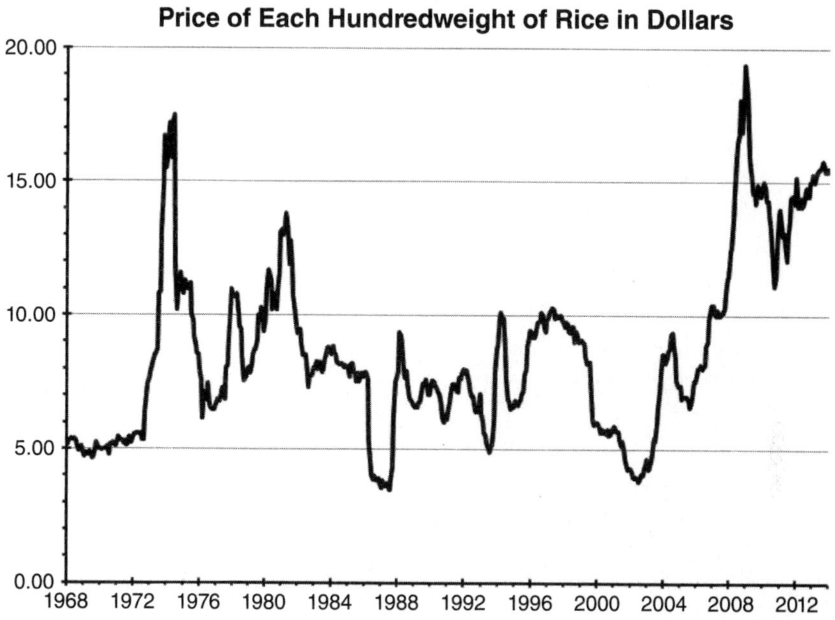

EXHIBIT 6.9 Price of Rice in U.S. Dollars

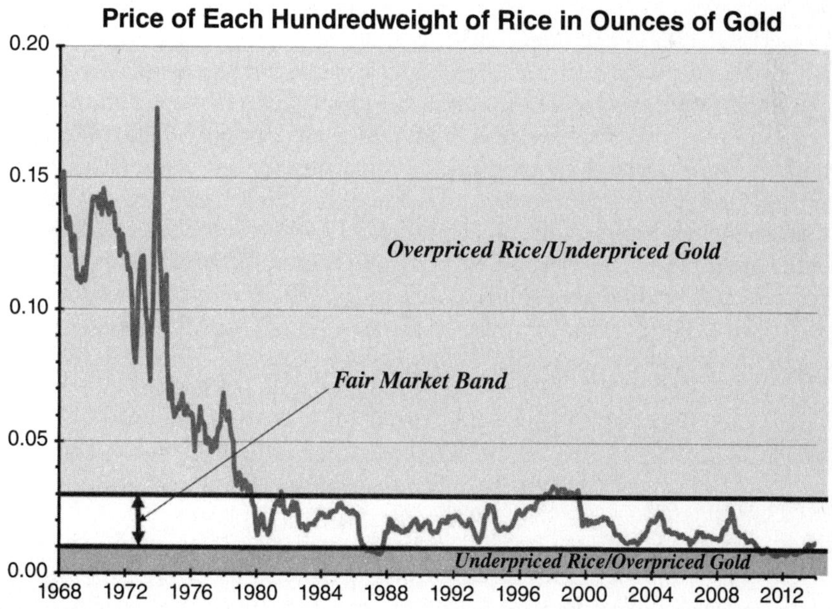

EXHIBIT 6.10 Price of Rice in Gold

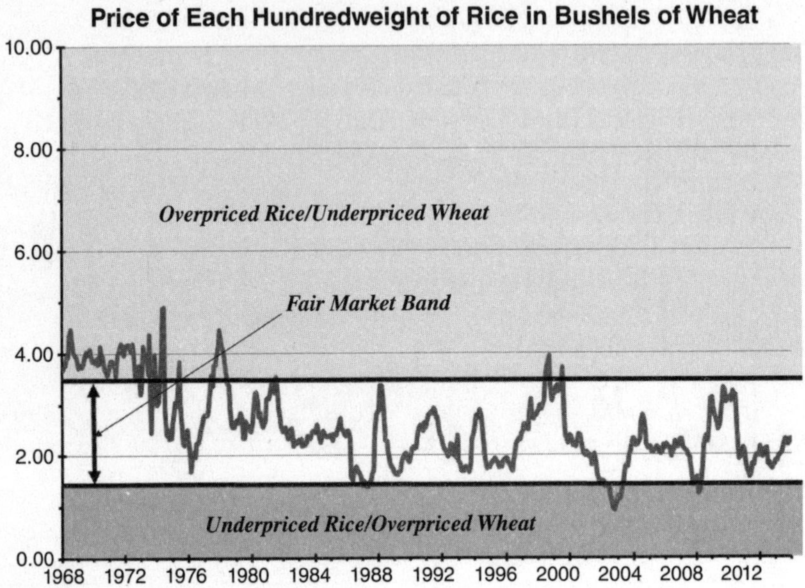

EXHIBIT 6.11 Price of Rice in Wheat

It is believed that the most pressing challenge to RF Shari'aa scholars and RF bankers in the twenty-first century is to develop a comprehensive RF monetary system that will be the foundation of fair pricing in the marketplace and an instrumental tool that can be used to guide central bankers in the stabilization of local currencies and their exchange rates on the international foreign exchange markets. This can be done by using a basket of reference calibrating pricing commodities, metals, and products to normalize prices instead of just using one commodity (food staples), precious metal (gold or silver), or energy sources (oil and gas.) We need to use this beginning as a foundation to start a comprehensive research program in the areas of the RF law and the RF monetary system.

ANALYSIS OF PRICES OF HOMES, COMMODITIES, AND STOCK MARKETS IN THE UNITED STATES USING THE COMMODITY INDEXATION DISCIPLINE

Homes in America[15,16]

As shown in Exhibit 6.4, the average U.S. home prices in terms of the U.S. dollar kept rising and have either stabilized, as they did in the early 1980s; declined slightly, as in the early 1990s; or declined significantly, as happened starting in 2006 to 2009.

Looking at this chart in 2005, one can quickly reach the erroneous conclusion that home prices in America must keep on rising. However, in terms of gold[17] (how many ounces of gold are needed to buy an average-priced home), Exhibit 6.5 shows the true fluctuation in house prices.

The chart shows that prices are relatively more stable when expressed in terms of gold. The chart shows the average house price fluctuating between 200 and 400 ounces of gold. Whenever the price penetrates the lower level of the envelope, it signals that homes are underpriced; this can be considered a good indicator for investing in homes. If the price penetrates the upper boundary of the envelope, it has signaled over the years that homes are entering a price bubble, and we should be careful in our investments as well as in our financing decisions for homes. The chart also shows that houses in the United States began getting pricy around the late 1990s and peaked in 2003 to 2004. It also shows that house prices started to decline after the end of 2005 to reach a bottom, or close to a bottom, in 2008–2009, signaling a good market. It is also important to note that it takes about 7 to 10 years for home prices to start climbing and for a home's owners to reap a good profit on the sale. In general, 2009 home prices in terms of gold indicate that it is a good time to start buying homes and financing the housing industry. Of course, this data is based on general nationwide data. It is recommended that specific data in specific markets should be used in order to reach the correct decisions.

The same correlation can be depicted by looking at the price of a home if we were to pay for it in terms of rice or wheat[18] (if the only product of a community were rice or wheat). We will find that the same correlation applies. The reader must be warned that these charts (as shown, for example, in Exhibits 6.12 and 6.13) are presented here as a directional tool; they are meant to be used by decision makers to gauge the direction of price trends in order to avoid participating in a bubble that may result in significant loss of their investments. It is also important to state that it is hoped that a full research effort be conducted along these lines to refine the analysis, which is admittedly presented here in the form of the art of RF (Islamic) finance. One of the questions that need to be answered is: why did the prices decline drastically, especially the price of agricultural commodities, from their pre-1971 levels when the Bretton Woods dollar-gold parity of $35 dollars per ounce of gold parity was discontinued?

Price of Coal

Coal has been used historically as a source of energy for years. Its production infrastructure, transportation and distribution routes, markets, and uses have matured and are well developed around the world. That is why we see that the relationship between the price of coal (as a basic energy

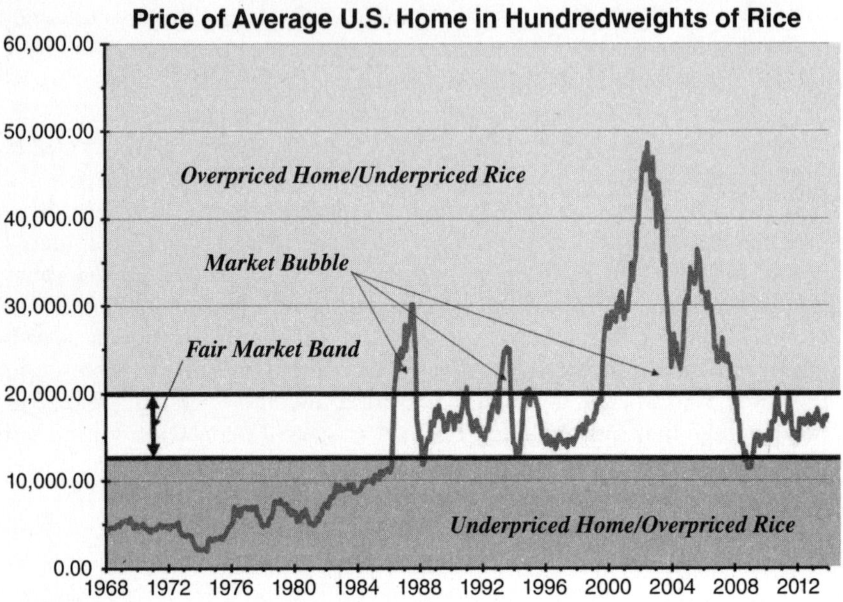

EXHIBIT 6.12 Price of Homes in Rice

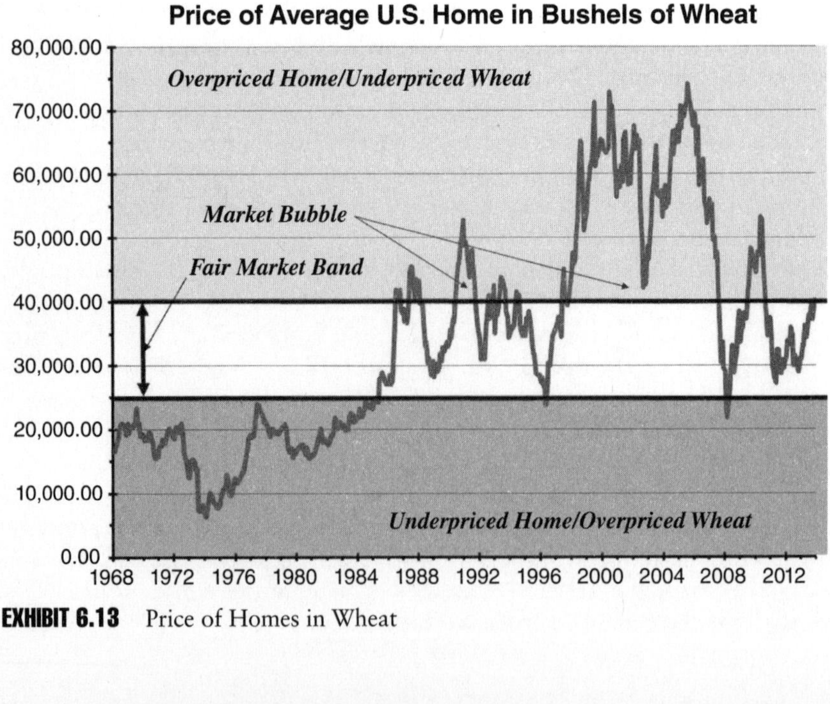

EXHIBIT 6.13 Price of Homes in Wheat

commodity in the matrix of needs of consumers) and the price of other commodities, such as gold, rice, or wheat, fluctuates in a narrower band than that of oil (see Exhibits 6.14 and 6.15).

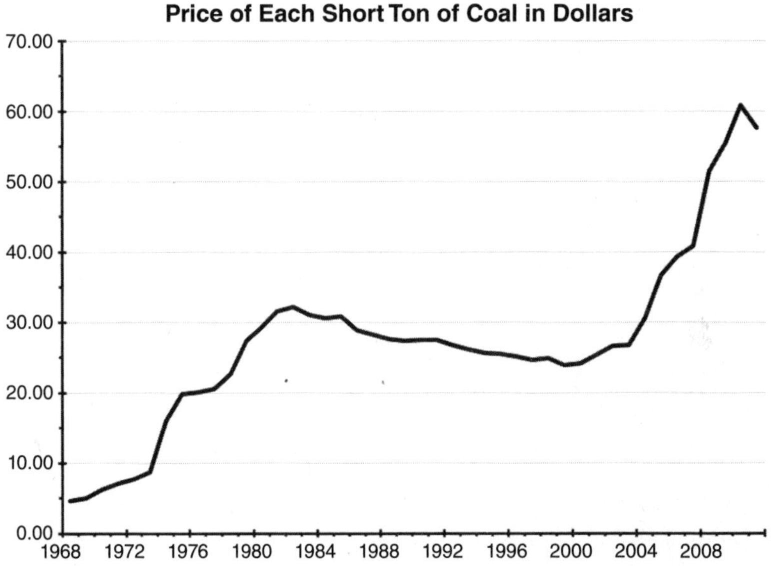

EXHIBIT 6.14 Coal Prices, 1968–2013

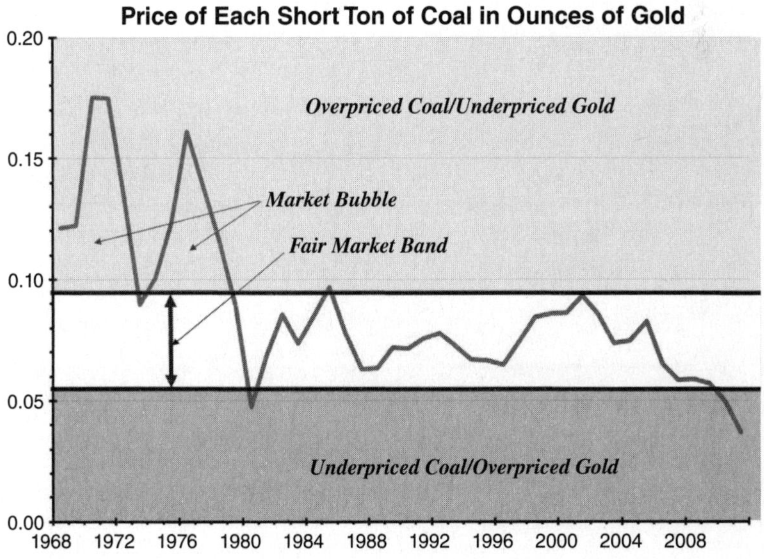

EXHIBIT 6.15 Price of Coal in Ounces of Gold

Based on Exhibit 6.15, the price of coal, which kept rising in dollar denomination, went down in real value—in terms of gold—after 1971, and kept fluctuating in a range of 0.06 to 0.1 ounces of gold for every ton of bituminous coal.

Price of Crude Oil

The oil market followed the same pattern that we saw in the coal market. Crude oil and the refined products markets have also developed and matured over the years. That is why, as we found in the case of coal, we can safely look at oil price gyrations in the market to try to learn the relationship between the price of oil and that of other commodities. The chart in Exhibit 6.16 is intriguing. It shows that despite the large rise in oil prices in terms of U.S. dollars, in normal times, the price of oil in terms of gold is stable, ranging from 0.06 to 0.12 ounces of gold per barrel of oil (10 to 20 barrels of oil for every ounce of gold), with an average price of 0.085 ounces of gold per barrel of oil (12 to 13 barrels of oil per ounce of gold). In fact, based on my 14-year experience in the oil industry—10 of these years were with

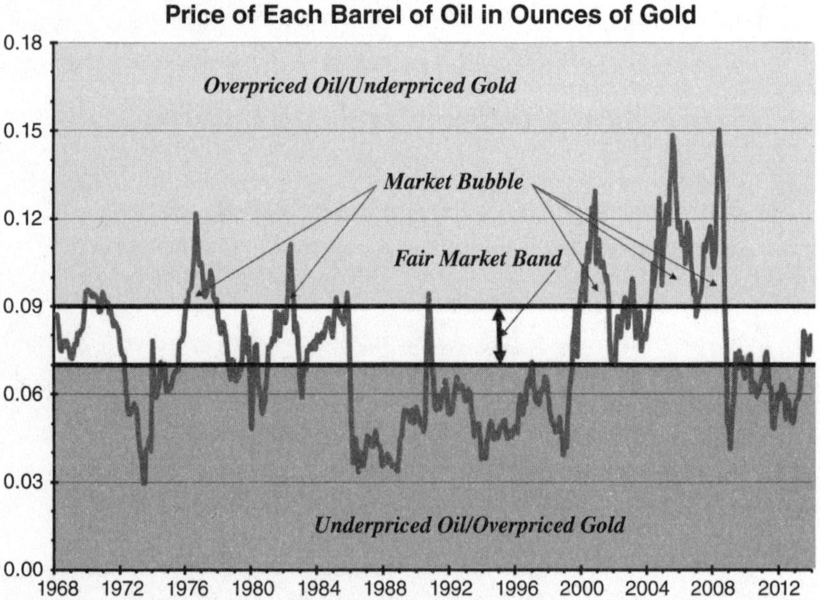

EXHIBIT 6.16 Price of Oil in Ounces of Gold

a major United States–based oil company—we considered 10 to 13 barrels of oil per ounce of gold a fair value. This "technical analysis" was shared by me with some of the distinguished "technical analysts" at Smith Barney/Citigroup in 1999, and they started tracking the relationship and using it as an important indicator for oil price trends.

We can see from Exhibit 6.16 that if the value of oil in terms of gold increases and penetrates the upper boundary of 0.12 ounces of gold per barrel of oil (e.g., 8 barrels of oil per ounce of gold), oil is overpriced and it is an indicator to sell the oil to avoid participating in a bubble. However, if the price of oil is low and pierces the lower level of the envelope at 0.06 ounces of gold per barrel of oil (e.g., 17 barrels of oil per ounce of gold), it is an indicator to buy (go long on) oil. It is very interesting to note that spikes in the oil price in terms of gold reflect political and economic changes that occurred over the course of history. For example, before the first oil shock in 1973, the value of oil spiked from 10 barrels per ounce of gold to approximately 35 barrels per ounce of gold, creating hugely undervalued oil and prompting higher demand—which later created a great supply shortfall, leading to the increase in oil price from $2.50 per barrel to approximately $12 per barrel. Looking into the history of this period, one sees that this was the time when most of the oil-producing countries were renegotiating their oil production participation agreements to increase their share of the production and hence reduce the share that would strategically go to the oil companies. This situation created the incentive, on the part of the producing oil companies, to produce as much oil as possible in the shortest time available, flooding the markets with oil and later creating a supply shortfall that nudged oil prices higher. It is also interesting to note the clear indication of a bubble during major world events.

In the summer of 2008, the oil price had reached a level of approximately $135 per barrel, while gold has reached approximately $885 per ounce. That is, the value of oil reached approximately 6.6 barrels per ounce of gold. Based on the Commodity Indexation Discipline, it was concluded that the price of oil is very high and is overvalued compared to an equilibrium market price. Based on our previous analysis, one expects that this ratio should go back to at least 10 barrels of oil per ounce of gold. At a gold price of $885 per ounce, that would translate to an oil price of $88.50 per barrel. At a gold price of $750 per ounce, and with a most likely oil price index of 10 to 13 barrels per ounce of gold, then one can expect fair value for the oil price to reach $58 to $75 per barrel.

World oil price declined from its peak in the summer of 2008 to as low as $35 per barrel and stabilized at about $50 per barrel in April 2009 and resumed its rise progressively, as shown in the chart. This fluctuation depends on the U.S. dollar's value on the international markets; the price of commodities that underlie the U.S. economy (because it is one of the larger importers of crude oil in the world); and the U.S. government's and Federal Reserve Board's policies regarding the dollar, interest rate, and economic and monetary policies (both in the United States and in the major economies in Canada, Europe, and the United Kingdom). Other important factors are the speculative activities of hedge funds, armed with huge amounts of capital, in the futures and options markets in the oil, gold, and dollar markets. It is interesting to note the cyclical nature of very high oil prices (overpriced oil) followed by another period of very low prices (underpriced oil). Students of history may find a relationship between capital accumulations by the major oil companies during the overpriced stage followed by an intensive record of negotiating new oil exploration contracts in new areas, coinciding with much lower prices.

The prices of some other commodities are charted in the following sections to give the reader a full scope of the validity of the RF Commodity Indexation Discipline. It is sincerely hoped that a group of researchers will take it upon themselves to research these relationships, not only in terms of relative prices but also in terms of stochastic mechanistic analysis, such as determining how much energy is consumed to produce an ounce of gold and how this impacts oil prices. This will not only include the cost of fuel, but also the amount of human energy consumed in exploring for gold, refining it, making it into standardized ingots, transporting it, and storing it.

Price of Natural Gas[19]

Natural gas is believed to be the emerging energy source of the future. Its markets, production, and transportation infrastructure are still developing and are not mature yet. There are huge natural gas reserves in the United States, Canada, and the rest of the world, but these are not fully developed. The natural gas locked into shale deposits started to be produced using a new technique called hydraulic fracturing in which high-pressure fluids are pumped into shale layers in the earth to unlock the natural gas locked within it. In addition, there is tremendous market potential for substituting natural gas as a fuel for trucks and automobiles. Huge investments in the production, liquefaction, transportation, and distribution infrastructure are still in formation. The chart in Exhibit 6.17 shows the price of natural gas in U.S. dollars; it is volatile and tends to reach unbelievable peaks mainly due to efforts by speculators to corner the market (as was done by Enron in the late twentieth century). However, if we apply the Commodities Indexation Discipline, a different picture emerges. For example, the price of natural gas in terms of gold or corn is more stable, as shown in Exhibits 6.18 and 6.19. In addition, one finds that the natural gas price has been stepping up every

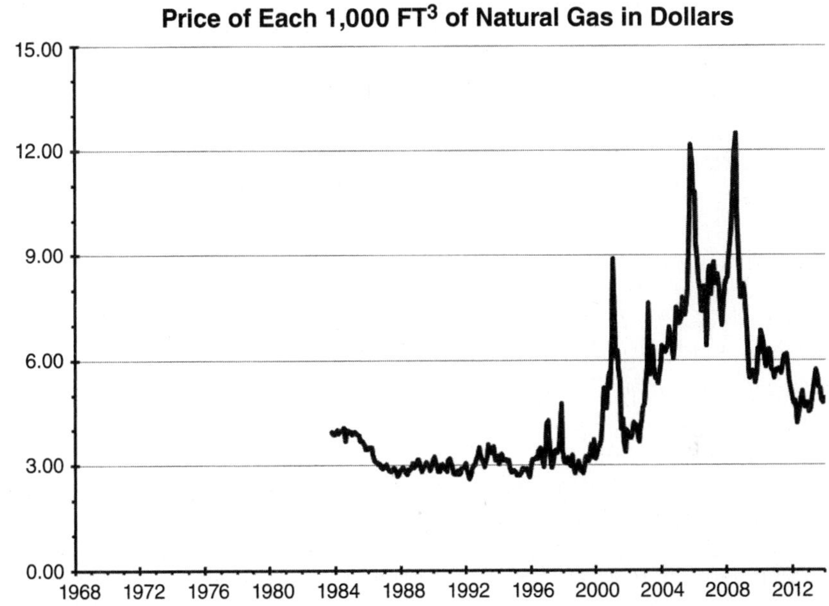

EXHIBIT 6.17 Natural Gas Prices, 1976–2013

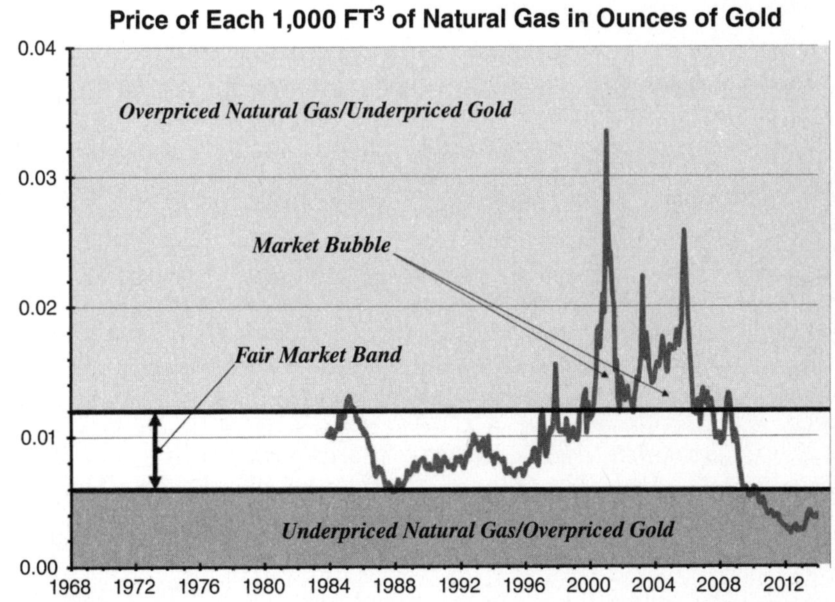

EXHIBIT 6.18 Price of Natural Gas in Ounces of Gold—One Ounce of Gold per MSCF*

* *MSCF* = 1,000 standard cubic feet

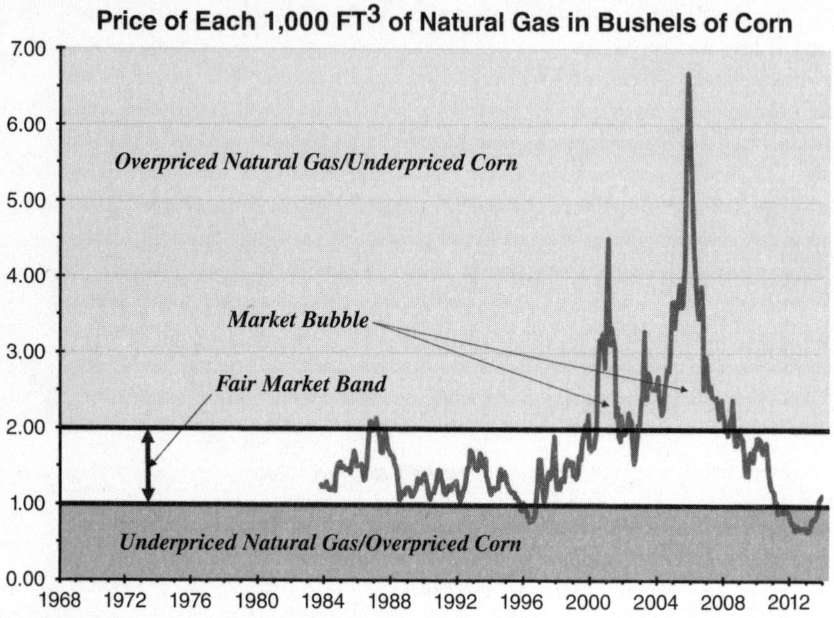

EXHIBIT 6.19 Price of Natural Gas in Rice—One cwt of Rice per MSCF*
**MSCF* = 1,000 standard cubic feet

time there is more development in the infrastructure and hence an increase in demand for natural gas. Research conducted by the RF Institute (the research arm of LARIBA) concludes that one of the best investments in the twenty-first century will prove to be in natural gas–related companies and business. Of course, only God knows best.

Price of Rice[20]

Rice is an important staple food in the diet of mostly all Asian countries and most African countries. Exhibit 6.20 shows the history of the price of rice in U.S. dollars. It is observed that the price in U.S. dollars fluctuated around a mean of about $8 per hundredweight before it rose sharply in 2008. Most of the rice is produced and consumed in Asia. If rice is priced in terms of gold, one would find that the real price of rice declined drastically from its 1969 highs to its lows in the 1980s, and has stayed relatively flat from the 1980s—even with the much-advertised commodity price increases of 2007 and beyond. The real prices of agricultural commodities in the world have been declining. This, coupled with the less expensive agricultural products—mainly wheat—available from the larger developed exporting countries such as the United States, Russia and its former republics, and France, has made it less attractive for farmers in the world to produce basic foods such as wheat. Instead, they prefer crops that will provide more cash, such as some farmers in some parts of the world who prefer to cultivate marijuana and opium over food. Please see Exhibits 6.20 and 6.21.

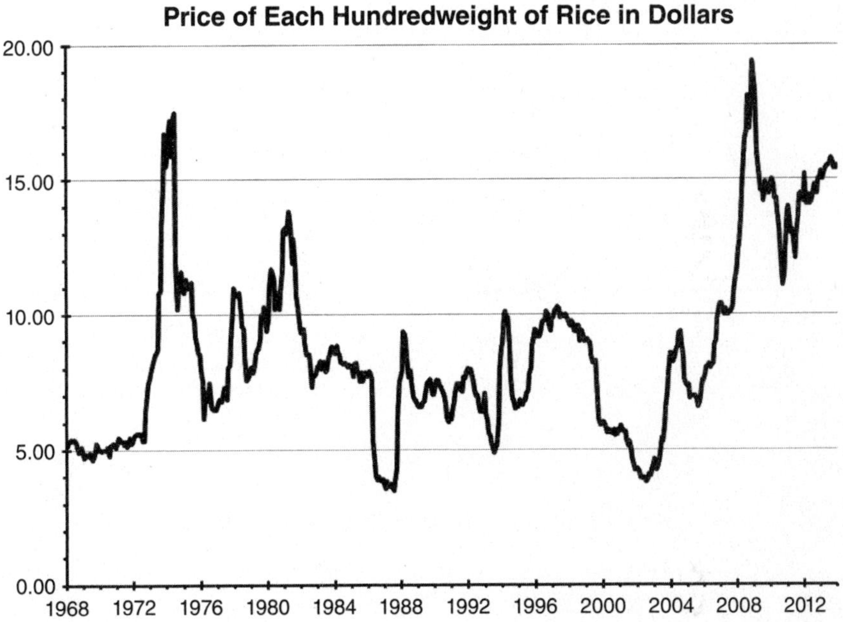

EXHIBIT 6.20 Rice Prices, 1968–2013

However, if we price rice in terms of wheat, we find that the wheat/rice price ratio has been declining. Wheat is mostly produced in Western developed economies, but it is consumed by foreign developing countries. It is recommended that more research be conducted to find out why. See Exhibits 6.21 and 6.22 for a comparison.

The charts in Exhibit 6.22 displaying the price of rice in terms of gold and rice in terms of wheat, respectively, show how the holders of hard currency in developing nations—in this case, the U.S. dollar—feel the real level of prices of such commodities. The users of wheat and rice in many of the developing countries in Asia and Africa see the real escalation and prohibitive high prices of the staple foods on which their lives depend because they use their local currencies, which are pegged or indexed to the dollar and not to gold. This is not the case in the developed economies because their currencies and prices are tied to the value of gold.

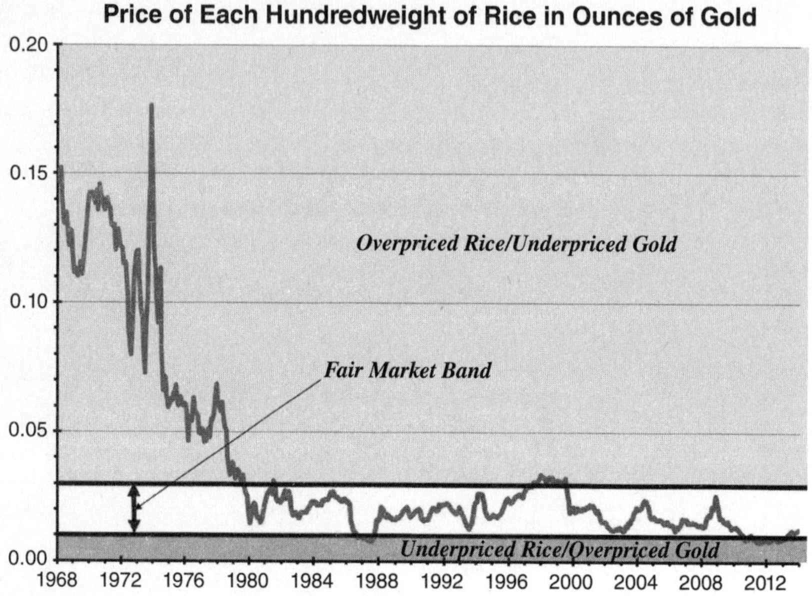

EXHIBIT 6.21 Rice versus Gold

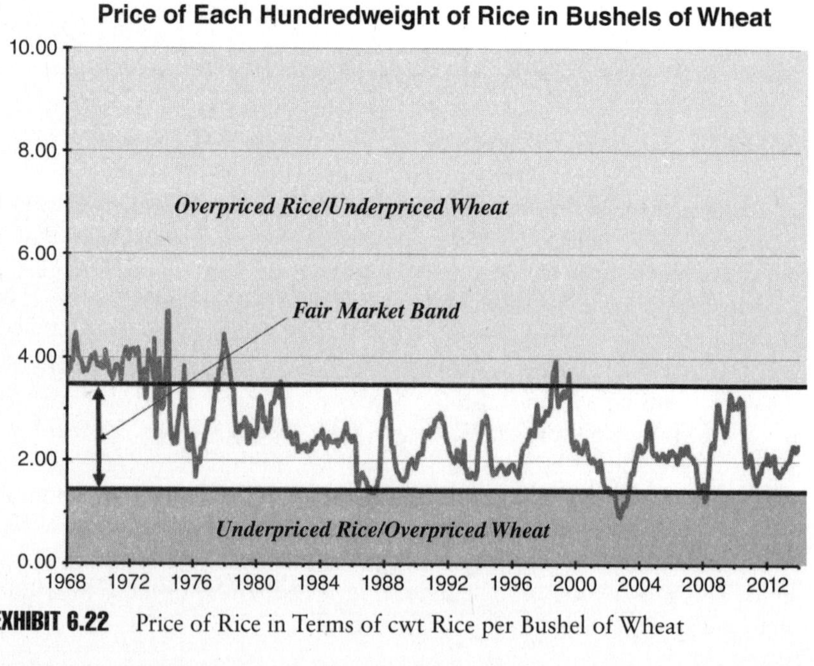

EXHIBIT 6.22 Price of Rice in Terms of cwt Rice per Bushel of Wheat

It is sincerely hoped that this discussion will generate enough interest among world leaders as well as international economists and traders to set up a fair pricing system, using the RF Commodity Indexation Discipline introduced in this book.

A PROPOSED BEGINNING OF A NEW ERA THAT USES THE RF MONETARY DISCIPLINE

In an RF discipline, three important decision levels must be taken into consideration. These are:

1. Normalize prices expressed in fiat money in order to be expressed in the real RF value of that currency in terms of staple food and other commodities that are in that economy. The idea is to produce what one can call the RF currency along the same lines of the basket of currencies used by the International Monetary Fund (IMF), which uses a basket of participant countries' currencies to define a weighted average fairly valued currency called the Special Drawing Right (SDR).

   In case of the RF currency, one would use a matrix of basic staple food commodities, metals, energy sources, and minerals that are considered basic to the economy, in proper proportions based on their contribution to the local economy. This RF currency matrix can be used as a reference calibrating currency. The components of the RF currency are not to be traded or transacted in a riba way (meaning that they cannot be transacted in futures and options markets or speculated with in any other futures and options market, and are kept as a reference-calibrating currency for pricing) as discussed in Chapters 3 and 5.

   Planners can use this RF currency matrix as a foundation to plan, for example, what crops a certain economy should produce because it is considered to have become a staple food for the citizens in the economy and what the share of precious metals should be in that matrix. The objective will be to come up with a local RF currency that would reflect a fair currency value and price in terms of a stable RF currency that can be used to disengage domestic currencies from fiat (paper) currencies and is fairly valued on the international foreign exchange markets.
2. Apply the Commodity Indexation Discipline for the early detection of local or international economic bubbles by using the RF currency to measure prices and disengage price fluctuations due to normal supply-and-demand factors from major changes due to speculation using regular banknote fiat (paper) currencies, as described in Chapters 3 and 5 and as was detailed earlier in this chapter.

3. Devise a fair and intelligent tax policy that will enhance the vibrancy of the economy and create new job opportunities and prosperity leading to peace, happiness, and more production, leading to world peace among all nations. Governments rely on taxes to cover all government services provided to the citizen. According to the Judeo-Christian-Islamic Shari'aa law, the citizen is ritually responsible to pay the ritual alms (zakah), as described in Chapter 2. This zakah income is used by the government to help the poor, the needy, employees who collect and administer it, and other expenses, as described in Chapter 2. In case the zakah collection is not enough, the government is allowed to collect more based on the social and income ladder in a certain community or a country. Tax planning is one of the important government policies because people in general do not want to pay taxes. That is why the Judeo-Christian-Islamic law canonized it as a pillar and a ritual, like witnessing the belief in God and His prophets, prayers, fasting, and pilgrimage, as described in Chapter 2.

REVIEW QUESTIONS

1. Describe the five stages that create economic cycles in a fiat (paper) money–operated economy. How does the macro system balance itself through the process of cycles? Please summarize the five steps the economy goes through in a market cycle.
2. What is the RF Commodity Indexation Discipline? How it can be used as an early warning signal to detect economic pricing bubbles?
3. What is the RF Marking-to-Market Discipline? How it was proposed to apply in the operations of an RF bank?
4. What is the difference between riba al-nasee'aa and riba al-fadl?
5. Using Exhibit 6.1, give us your opinion on the charging of excess fees, in terms of a higher value related to the time of paying it (interest) on fiat (paper) money transactions.
6. What was James Baker III's recommendation on using gold and a basket of commodities to stabilize prices? Why did it rattle the financial and currency markets?
7. What happened during the Asian currency crisis? How did it come about?
8. How did the Asian central banks handle the Asian currency crisis in an effort to rescue their currencies? How did the Malaysian policy differ from that of the policies of the rest of the Asian counties?
9. How did the Muslim scholars define money?
10. What was the Muslim scholars' vision of an RF monetary discipline?

11. If a qard hassan of $100,000 was given to a needy person in March 1971, how much will this person pay back in 2014 if the agreement used different reference currencies?
    a. In U.S. dollars
    b. In wheat
    c. In rice
    d. In silver
    e. In gold
12. Based on the agricultural food products stochastic charts after these price charts have been normalized to decouple these prices in an RF way from the U.S. dollar, what conclusion you can make in light of the sudden drop of agricultural products prices? How did the outcome influence the farmers in the developing nations?
13. Applying the Commodity Indexation Discipline and using the technical analysis applied in the book, what will be the next price bubble?
14. What is the RF currency calibrating reference unit of exchange recommended in this chapter?

NOTES

1. Ahmad Kamal Mydin Meera, *The Islamic Gold Dinar,* (Kuala Lumpur: Pelanduk Publications, 2002).
2. Narrated by Abu Sa'eed Al Khidry.
3. Ibid. Also reported and authenticated by Imam Ahmad and Imam Bukhary.
4. Muslim; the scholar in Hadeeth reported that a person came to the Prophet (pp) to gift him with dates. The Prophet (pp) asked him how he could afford this high-quality, large-size dates and said: "This is not our type of dates." The person said, "Oh Prophet Muhammad (pp), we sold two containers of our dates for one container of the better-quality large dates." The Prophet (pp) said: "This is what Riba is!" He proceeded to tell the person: "Return these dates. Then sell it [our dates] in the market for [real] money and use the money to buy the other dates." In another story reported by the scholar Abu Dawood: A person brought the Prophet (pp) a gold bracelet that had beads woven in it, which he had purchased for nine or seven dinars (gold currency at that time). The Prophet (pp) said: "This transaction must be conducted by separating the gold from the beads. Return it. And price each separately." And the scholar Muslim further reported orders to separate the gold from the beads, and said that the gold should be exchanged for the same weight of gold.

5. By the Hadeeth scholar Abu Dawood.
6. Narrated by Bukhari, one of the recognized authorities on the compiling of the Prophet's Hadeeth.
7. "Islamic Finance and Capitalism: An Introduction," a presentation prepared by Muhammad Yusuf Dadani, Ahmed Naji, Mohamed Osman and M. Hashem Sherif. Presented at the Islamic Society of Central Jersey, 4145 Route 1 South and Promenade Blvd., Monmouth Junction, NJ, May 23, 2010.
8. Peter Kilborn, "Baker Hints at Gold as Guide on Policy," *New York Times,* October 1, 1987.
9. Mahathir bin Mohamad, "The Gold Dinar as an Alternative International Currency," Kuala Lumpur, Malaysia, July 1, 2003.
10. Mahathir bin Mohamad, *The Malaysian Currency Crisis—How and Why It Happened* (Kuala Lumpur: Pelanduk Publications, 2000).
11. Omar Kamel, *Money and the International Monetary System*, Economic Studies Series (Jeddah, Kingdom of Saudi Arabia: Dallah Al Baraka Group).
12. Ibn Khaldun, *The Muqaddima: An Introduction to History*, translated from Arabic by Franz Rosenthal, 3 vols. Bollingen Series, No. 43 (New York: Pantheon, 1958). Cited in a research authored by Hon. Dr. Selim Karatas, Foundation for Science Technology and Civilization under the title "The Economic Theory of Ibn Khaldun and the Rise and Fall of Nations."
13. The RF Research Institute for RF Lifestyle, Economics and Monetary Discipline is part of the LARIBA System. It was established in 1998 by the author in Pasadena, California.
14. Miscellaneous references on the Hadeeth of RF Monetary Discipline:
   - The Prophet(s), said, "Sell gold in exchange of equivalent gold, sell silver in exchange of equivalent silver, sell dates in exchange of equivalent dates, sell wheat in exchange of equivalent wheat, sell salt in exchange of equivalent salt, sell barley in exchange of equivalent barley, but if a person transacts in excess, it will be usury (Riba). However, sell gold for silver anyway you please on the condition it is hand-to-hand (spot) and sell barley for date anyway you please on the condition it is hand-to-hand (spot)."
   - From Abu Sa'id al-Khudri: The Prophet (s) said: "Do not sell gold for gold except when it is like for like, and do not increase one over the other; do not sell silver for silver except when it is like for like, and do not increase one over the other; and do not sell what is away [from among these] for what is ready." (Bukhari, Kitab al-Buyu', Bab bay'i al-fiddati bi al-fiddah; also Muslim, Tirmidhi, Nasa'i and Musnad Ahmad)

- From 'Ubada ibn al-Samit: The Prophet said: "Gold for gold, silver for silver, wheat for wheat, barley for barley, dates for dates, and salt for salt—like for like, equal for equal, and hand-to-hand; if the commodities differ, then you may sell as you wish, provided that the exchange is hand-to-hand." (Muslim, Kitab al-Musaqat, Bab al-sarfi wa bay'i al-dhahabi bi al-waraqi naqdan; also in Tirmidhi)
- From Abu Sa'id al-Khudri: The Prophet said: "Gold for gold, silver for silver, wheat for wheat, barley for barley, dates for dates, and salt for salt—like for like, and hand-to-hand. Whoever pays more or takes more has indulged in riba. The taker and the giver are alike [in guilt]." (Muslim, ibid.; and Musnad Ahmad)
- From Fadalah ibn 'Ubayd al-Ansari: On the day of Khaybar he bought a necklace of gold and pearls for twelve dinars. On separating the two, he found that the gold itself was equal to more than twelve dinars. So he mentioned this to the Prophet, who replied, "It [jewelry] must not be sold until the contents have been valued separately." (Muslim, Kitab al-Musaqat, Bab bay'i al-qiladah fiha khara-zun wa dhahab; also in Tirmidhi and Nasa'i)

15. The United States Department of Commerce, U.S. Census Bureau, www.census.gov/.
16. National Association of Home Builders (NAHB), www.nahb.org/page.aspx/category/sectionID=131.
17. London Bullion Market Association (LBMA), www.lbma.org.uk/stats/goldfixg.
18. United States Department of Agriculture (USDA), National Agricultural Statistics Service (NASS), www.nass.usda.gov/QuickStats/Create_Federal_All.jsp.
19. United States Department of Energy (DOE), Energy Information Administration (EIA), http://tonto.eia.doe.gov/dnav/ng/ng_pri_sum_dcu_nus_m.htm.
20. See note 18.

CHAPTER 7

Civility and Social Responsibility of the RF Banking System

Some of the serious objections leveled against the current banking system are the gambling-like activities in banking that may compromise the safety of the banking system and the exaggerated bonuses system that grants participants huge bonuses that exceed their annual salaries and is based on their production of fees, commissions, and business to their banks without consideration to and paying attention to the risks involved, which may expose banks and financial institutions shareholders' capital, investors, and depositors to significant losses. The objections emanate from the fact that the bankers, acting as sales professionals of investment products, services, and loans may be focused more on their perceived commissions and not the interest of the investors and the borrowers. This takes the bankers' emphasis from primarily having the interests of their clients at heart by making full disclosure about the risks involved before transactions are conducted and the commissions and bonuses they collect based on the volume of business generated.

In the fall of 2013, we at LARIBA, interviewed a promising young graduate, who was 22 years old, from a recognized university for joining our staff. The candidate graduated from a prominent business school with a GPA of approximately 3.7 and has a proven two-year track record as a mortgage banker. We started discussing our business model, which focuses on the ethics of first gauging the benefits realized by the customer from refinancing his or her property. We explained that in order to recommend to the customer to proceed with refinancing the property, the effort must make prudent economic sense to the customer. One way of gauging this, we commented, is that the implied rate the customer will be charged after the refinance process should be much lower than the rate the customer is charged in order to justify the costs involved in closing the refinance transaction (called closing costs). The candidate shared with us that this will limit his "business growth" potential. He said that the culture he was trained on was focused on setting monthly sales goals; meaning how many mortgages he will finance or refinance and how much, in dollars, the fee income is collected by the company. He said that based on these goals, his income and commissions are calculated. He said further that he refinanced mortgages at rates that were one-fourth percent lower. When we reminded him that the closing cost involved will make that transaction not economically prudent and unfair to the customer, he said that this is not his concern. We told him that we understand but respectfully disagree. Obviously, we did not continue with him. This experience—and many like it—was heartbreaking because it involved a bright young banker who had a great potential for a successful future. That potential was spoiled by the culture of "loans (renting money), commissions, and fees production" that is motivated by greed. Unfortunately, experience shows that once the line of social responsibility is crossed, it will be difficult to reverse it.

In the previous chapters, the faith-based business ethics' foundation of the RF (riba/ribit-free) banking and finance system was established. This chapter will discuss the important aspect of bringing these values to life by elaborating on the social aspects of this brand of banking: RF banking and its disciplined commitment to community building, growth, and development. The dimension of civility and social responsibility in RF banking and finance, when implemented on a wider scale, will eventually lead to economic growth, new job opportunities, prosperity, and unity, and hopefully to a future of peace, fairness, and justice for all people. The most important foundation of the Judeo-Christian-Islamic value system is justice for all, as defined by the higher authority we all answer to—that is, God, the revealer of the Qur'aan:

> *4:58 God doth command you to render back your Trusts to those to whom they are due; and when ye judge between man*[1] *and man, that ye judge with justice: Verily how excellent is the teaching which He giveth you! For God is He Who heareth and seeth all things.*
>
> *16:90 God commands justice, the doing of good, and liberality to kith and kin, and He forbids all shameful deeds, and injustice and rebellion: He instructs you, that ye may receive admonition.*
>
> *5:8 O ye who believe! stand out firmly for God, as witnesses to fair dealing, and let not the hatred of others to you make you swerve to wrong and depart from justice. Be just: that is next to piety: and revere God. For God is well-acquainted with all that ye do.*

It is believed that civility and social responsibility in banking and finance is an important foundation for a successful and responsible banking operation.

Perhaps the first well-known dramatization of the character of a true RF banker was in Frank Capra's popular 1940s movie *It's a Wonderful Life*, in which Jimmy Stewart, the lead actor in the movie, plays a Building (Savings) and Loan Society manager who helps build single-family homes to develop a comfortable suburban neighborhood, assisting poorer families to move away from the small, shabby apartments in which they live to a comfortable small home they own. The film was released just after the major runs on the banks in reaction to the Great Depression that started in 1929. An abbreviated version of this movie is used regularly as a basic training resource for all RF bankers in the LARIBA system, as will be explained in more detail later in the book.

In October 2008, the world was shocked to hear President George W. Bush and his secretary of the Treasury, Henry Paulson, talk about the financial tsunami that hit the U.S. and world financial systems. This historic compromise of the financial markets and monetary systems, we were told, was caused by the speculative and casino-like gambling behaviors of some "money managers" and corporate executives. This irresponsible behavior lost $4,000 billion dollars of peoples' retirement money and life savings. The speculative activities and economic "bubbles" such a "casino-like" speculation had been warned against and had been criticized by many. These objections were ignored and quickly marginalized by former Federal Reserve Chairman Alan Greenspan, who was idolized as the "god" of finance from the time of his appointment in 1987 to the time of his retirement in 2006. He was nicknamed "The Maestro"[2] in a book by the famous investigative newspaper reporter and author Bob Woodward. Only a few voices in the media, to be fair, kept reminding its readers and policymakers about the hazards associated with inflating the real estate bubble. These were *The Economist*, a leading financial magazine, and *The Financial Times*, a leading financial newspaper—both of which are published in London, England.

In the 1980s, the Glass-Steagall Act—the most important regulation that translated the lessons learned from the Great Depression into laws that would prevent the repetition of what happened by strictly regulating activities that led to the unfortunate depression—was repealed by Congress. In the 1990s, the Clinton administration and its Treasury secretary, Robert Rubin, celebrated that event by approving the merger of an investment bank (Smith Barney), an insurance company (Travelers Group), and a commercial bank (Citicorp). The move was celebrated as a historic development in the world of finance and as the best thing to happen in the history of the American financial services industry in years because, its proponents thought, it offered service integration that would provide banking, investment banking, retirement planning, and insurance services under one roof.

I was personally in the middle of this, because I worked at Smith Barney at that time. I experienced the process by which the financial consultants at Smith Barney (and the whole industry followed) were retrained to become "asset gatherers," whose first responsibility was to gather people's "excess" savings and retirement money and accumulated assets. The financial consultants at these investment banking firms would then turn these funds over to "big" money managers, who managed billions of dollars in the mutual funds industry or even more in the asset management and hedge funds industry. The entire financial consultants and brokerage community was turned into an asset-gathering machine. The broker or the financial adviser would meet with the customer to define and document the investment objectives, the investment time horizon, and the risk profile of the customer, and then turn the money over to the so-called money management "gurus" to take care of investing it at a flat management fee that ranged from 1 to 2.5 percent of the total value of the managed investment. If a consumer had a bank account at his friendly local branch of a commercial bank, and he objected to the low interest rates on Federal Deposit Insurance Corporation (FDIC)-insured time certificates of deposit (CDs), that client would be turned over to another "investment" representative who offered higher returns by investing in mutual funds but without clearly explaining that these funds are not FDIC insured and that the investor may be exposed to loss of principal due to market fluctuations. This practice is still happening in many bank branches at the time of writing this book. Of course, members of the public were told that the investment adviser disclosed the risks associated with investing in mutual funds and that the customer was advised to read the lengthy and difficult-to-read and difficult-to-follow mutual fund prospectus carefully before they invested. Unfortunately, that was not the experience of many small investors and retired people, who moved their life savings from FDIC-insured time CDs to mutual funds. In addition, the financial consultants were trained and pushed by their managers to sell annuities as a sure investment that would guarantee investors a safe retirement income. The financial consultant was motivated by greed because he was promised to realize out of this sales transaction a commission as high as 5 percent of the amount invested. In each financial sales organization within a bank, financial consultants were rated by the amount of commission they produced. Daily commissions produced by each member of the sales team would be posted daily in front of the manager's office to motivate financial sales representatives to compete and produce more. Financial consultants who produced large fees and commissions were given incentives that ranged from impressive titles like "Vice President Investments" to lavish all-expenses-paid sales' entertainment trips to Europe, Hawaii, and the Caribbean, which costs were deducted by the investment bank as professional education and training meeting expenses.

Wall Street became a large casino instead of an instrument to invest in the long-term growth of the United States and the world (as it was redeveloped to operate after the 1929 stock market crash and the depression that followed it). Talented engineers, medical doctors, technology experts, mathematicians, and scientists quit their jobs, in which they had invested years of hard work to obtain a respectable university degree to work as financial consultants with the branches of many investment banking firms that mushroomed throughout every neighborhood of the country. They left behind the education and training they had earned and a good living they had enjoyed through hard work in the profession they had chosen and worked hard to achieve. This hard work added to the real production and quality of life for the whole community. These professionals preferred to quit all this. They concluded, based on the vast amounts of money made by stockbrokers and bankers, that they could use their talents and time to "make" money through working as financial consultants at investment banking firms or by conducting online day trading of stocks, options, and futures.

It became a national and international obsession to trade stocks online, to wait in big halls with large computer screens showing market movements, with people in Kuwait, Saudi Arabia, Dubai, Hong Kong, China, South Korea, Thailand, Russia, Singapore, Malaysia, Egypt, and many more poor, developing countries sitting and doing nothing but watching and seeing how to "make" more money and how to get around the honorable way of "earning" it through hard work.

As we learned in 2008, the insurance companies that were supposed to protect and safeguard people's assets, retirement funds, and insurance premiums compromised that trust and speculated with people's futures by using structured finance, financial engineering, and loopholes in the laws to avoid the many financial regulations in the United States. We learned that they intentionally broke the spirit of the law while appearing on paper and on official documents to uphold and respect the laws of the land.

In the end, we witnessed the breakdown of the best and most intricate financial system, one that was built in a patient and meticulous way over almost 150 years of America's history. We, the bankers of the United States, had to stand up embarrassed before the world for what a few of us had done. The United States' financial, monetary, and banking system—which was trusted by the world to the extent of making the U.S. dollar as good as gold (as stipulated by the Bretton Woods Agreement) and making the United States the envy of the world—broke down!

As angry citizens in the United States and the world started asking more questions, the politicians running for election in the 2008 presidential campaign explained that more regulations would be needed. However, they approved more of the same. Merrill Lynch (a major American investment bank) and Countrywide (a major American mortgage bank) merged with Bank of America; Bear Stearns was bought by JPMorgan Chase; and both Morgan Stanley and Goldman Sachs were turned into bank holding companies in preparation to make them qualified to become depository banking institutions that would become eligible to receive significant government bailout funds. They started the process of looking for banks to acquire, to realize the model started by Citigroup. Well, we wish them all the luck in the world, because the culture of a traditional banker (who should be extremely risk averse because he/she is assigned the great responsibility and honor of trying to reach a zero risk level to protect the bank's depositors) does not mix well with the culture of risk taking at all levels displayed in the investment banking business. That is essentially what the Glass-Steagall Act was all about.

Another objection voiced by many, especially those who pay their taxes and obey the laws of the land, has to do with the many schemes devised by those who can afford expensive tax planning and structured finance attorneys to "plan" or to "avoid" taxes. *The Economist*[3] discussed a number of corporate structures that help reduce corporate taxes like publicly listed master limited partnerships (MLPs).[4]

Politicians told us that the lack of strict regulations caused this huge catastrophe. In response to these events, the Congress of the United States passed a new act called the Dodd-Frank[5] Act (also called the Wall Street Reform Act). It is the largest financial regulation overhaul since 1930s. The act aimed at preventing a repeat of the 2008 financial and monetary meltdown. The act included sweeping new rules for banks, hedge funds, and derivatives-related investment and speculative activities. The act also called for the establishment of a new regulatory agency—the Consumer Financial Protection Bureau (CFPB). It was established and started working on July 21, 2011. The objective of CFPB as stated in its published mission is "to make markets for consumer financial products and services work for Americans—whether they are applying for a mortgage, choosing among credit cards, or using any number of other consumer financial products." That may be fine, good, and useful, but many, including your author, respectfully disagreed with that sweeping conclusion. All the regulations and laws in the world are good on paper, but good judgment cannot be regulated. These regulations must be respected and applied by the citizens on both sides: the practitioners and the law enforcement agents. If a citizen does not respect the regulations and is not trained to uphold the laws, with ethics and moral conduct at heart, then all the regulations in the world will not be enough. The result will be that the law is taken lightly and looked upon as an obstacle that can be overcome by supposedly "intelligent and smart" structures to achieve what one wants by exploiting loopholes in the laws and regulations. The system then becomes a mockery.

I remember an experience in 1989, after the Islamic Revolution in Iran, when Atlantic Richfield (now part of British Petroleum) lost—through nationalization—250,000 barrels of oil production per day from Lavon Island in Iran. Company upper management put me in charge of trying to secure the supply of as much oil as possible to make up for the loss, in order to meet the feedstock requirements of our refineries. I was fortunate to travel around the world and meet officials at the highest government levels in the oil-producing countries in Africa, Latin America, Asia, and the Middle East. On one of my trips, I focused on an important oil-producing country in Africa. Its name will remain untold to avoid any nationalistic sensitivity by its wonderful citizens. I spent more than six months traveling back and forth to develop working relationships with this country's oil executives, to introduce our company, to understand the organizational chart and decision-making chains of the country's national oil company and its oil sales laws, and to establish contacts with that country's president's office and his personal energy adviser. I understood the wonderful legal and operating system of the land as documented on paper and identified the decision makers. I thought that I had all it takes to consummate a deal.

I forgot to mention, though, that there was one thing missing: the price—or the bribe—needed to get the contract. It is important to share with the reader that one thing I never agreed to or have ever done in my whole life is the use of bribery to get what I want and need. I made that decision early, when I was a young college student at Cairo University. Other students would "bribe" the services and cleaning custodian of the lecture halls to lay down a notebook at a front seat so that the student—who paid him a monthly fee or bribe—would have the advantage of a reserved front seat without having to wake up early in the morning to earn that seat. I disciplined myself to wake up at 5:00 A.M.—a wonderful habit I have maintained to this day—study, and go early to the university to get my preferred seat without taking others' opportunities by bribing people in an unfair and dishonest way. But let us return to the oil story. Because we refused to pay a "commission" or a "fee," otherwise defined in the law and a normal book of values as a bribe, I was surprised to find out later that the contract was given to the Marc Rich Trading Company. Not only had this happened, but to my surprise (one that educated me in the school of "hard knocks" of real life), none of the officials in the wonderful organizational structure of the national oil company were involved. The deal was done in a separate office of a bank run by a tribal leader with the "right" political connections.

Regulations are important if they are well thought out, discussed, and voted on in a proper democratic way within a functioning democracy. However, the citizens and institutions of that democracy should also be socially responsible, civilized, and respectful to each other, and they should uphold the laws of the land.

Professor Stephen Carter at Yale University authored a wonderful book on civility.[6] He concluded that if the adults in a community (i.e., the parents and the leaders in business, media, government, political, and religious communities) do not treat each other with civility, this behavior will be reflected by the community's children. "Our children are mimicking the incivility of the adult world. In one survey, an astonishing 89% of grade school teachers and principals [in America] reported that they 'regularly' face abusive language from students."[7] He concluded:

> *Civility, I shall argue, is the total sum of the many sacrifices we are called to make for the sake of living together. ... Rules of civility are thus also rules of morality: it is morally proper to treat our fellow citizens with respect.*[8]

The moral standard by which the citizens of a community, a city, a state, and a nation live defines the character of that nation. It is also important to note that history has shown repeatedly since its dawn—from the story of Adam and Eve in paradise that not obeying the moral standard set for them by God, which was to not to approach the tree of the knowledge of good and evil, to the story of Cain and Abel, and on to the stories of all God's prophets—that a nation must have a moral standard, ethics, a value system, and a set of rules that are clear to all to live by.

The values of civility, ethics, and morality are taught first at home by the parents, with a spiritual content that is nourished and deepened at the family's place of worship; these values are reinforced at school, by the media, and by the behavior of the political leadership at large. It is unfortunate that many misunderstand the deeply rooted American rule and concept of separating church and state. It is believed that this separation rule means the church or the place of worship cannot run the government—but it should have the full freedom to produce spiritually and morally viable and qualified leaders who have the proper civility, morality, and ethics to run every aspect of the society. When the church, the synagogue, the masjid (mosque), and the temples focus on the substance, they will regain their stature in the community.

THE JUDEO-CHRISTIAN-ISLAMIC VALUES: CIVILITY, MORALITY, AND SOCIAL RESPONSIBILITY

As we know from the Torah, the Gospel, and the Qur'aan, God did not create Adam and Eve as separate individuals who each acts on his/her own. He created them as partners: a husband and wife who were entrusted with the well-being of Earth and with serving Him and populating Earth by multiplying in larger families, villages, tribes, and nations to make the earth a better place to live and enjoy. In the Qur'aan, we read:

> *4:1 O mankind! Reverence your Guardian-Lord, who created you from a single person, created, of like nature, his mate, and from them twain scattered [like seeds] countless men and women;—reverence God, through whom ye demand your mutual [rights], and [reverence] the wombs [That bore you]: for God ever watches over you.*

Humanity (male and female) has been reminded that God is closer to us than our jugular veins. That is, if we are real believers in God, then we have to be careful not to disappoint Him in our behavior because He is much closer to us than many have unfortunately convinced themselves wrongly to know, think, and acknowledge. In the Qur'aan, God reveals:

> *50:16 It was We Who created man, and We know what suggestions his soul makes to him: for We are nearer to him than (his) jugular vein.*
>
> *50:18 Not a word does he utter but there is a sentinel by him, ready [to record it].*

We submit our will to the will of our creator and sustainer, God, and believe in the Judeo-Christian-Islamic values brought to man (male and female) by God through all His Prophets—Abraham (pp) and his children Ishmael and Isaac, descendants and subsequent prophets and messengers, including Moses (pp), Jesus (pp), and Mohammad (pp). These prophets and messengers of God came to train people to better submit to God's will and to assume the responsibility of becoming custodians/trustees on God's property—life in general and the Earth and its resources—and to establish justice on Earth. This system of justice includes social, economic, political, and legal justice.

It has been established historically that human nature, if untamed and not civilized, is characterized by selfishness, violence, and greed. Religions, including the Judeo-Christian-Islamic system brought to the world by Prophet Muhammad (pp) to continue, deepen, legitimize, expand, detail, and seal the teachings of all prior prophets and messengers, focus on training the individual spiritually and ethically to suppress selfishness and greed and to promote goodness.

Success can be defined by different parameters, such as how much money, power, fame, and control one has attained. In an uncivilized world, success is measured only in a material way, which sometimes loses sight of the value of the rest of the society. In a civilized system, and for a socially responsible citizen (and, for that matter, for RF bankers), success can be defined as the progressive realization of a worthy ideal. Civilized and responsible people consider success to lie in both material achievements and in being virtuous. Virtue implies a positive attitude toward life, toward other citizens in the community and the world, and toward all other beings. The results are peace of mind, contentment, and a sense of security. The true image of success is not how much money one has in the bank or the kind of car one drives. Success is realizing a proven track record and reputation as a pious person who serves the community without expecting any rewards or payback, who can be trusted and who is close to God. Success is manifested by a person who feels for the neediest and the poorest in the community and who takes serious steps to improve their conditions, not only through handouts but through training them and through helping by offering opportunities for them to climb the social ladder from its bottom to higher levels over time. God reveals in the Qur'aan:

> *2:177 It is not righteousness that ye turn your faces Towards East or West; but it is righteousness—to believe in God and the Last Day, and the Angels, and the Book, and the Messengers; to spend of your substance, out of love for Him, for your kin, for orphans, for the needy, for the wayfarer, for those who ask, and for the ransom of slaves; to be steadfast in prayer, and practice regular charity; to fulfill the contracts which ye have made; and to be firm and patient, in pain (or suffering) and adversity, and throughout all periods of panic. Such are the people of truth, the God revering.*
>
> *51:19 And in their wealth and possessions (was remembered) the right of the (needy) him who asked, and him who (for some reason) was prevented (from asking).*

The horizon of time in the Judeo-Christian-Islamic value system extends beyond this life to the life after death—the hereafter. Wealth, power, position, and affluence do not come with us to our graves after death. When anyone dies, that person will be remembered by what he or she leaves behind[9]: a family and descendants who perpetuate goodness by following the laws of God; a permanent contribution that will benefit the community, such as a book, a research achievement, a source of income for the poor and the needy, and/or the development of job opportunities for future generations. It is what we leave behind and its contributions to the community and the world at large that will attain us the highest acceptance by God. It is also believed that the globe belongs to God and it is wide open and full of resources and opportunities. Oppression in one location does not justify acceptance. It is the responsibility of everyone who feels helpless and oppressed and who longs for freedom to find another location in this vast and wide world where freedom and human dignity are prevalent. In doing so, a believer, in his/her pursuit of business, carries with him/her the Judeo-Christian-Islamic way of life and values.

A prosperous and healthy society is one that respects hard work and its tangible contributions in terms of quality, creativity, and service. It is a society that discourages and frowns upon gambling, speculation, greed, and fraudulent activities. It is a society that respects the value of education as a means of getting ahead and the value of respecting people's properties, trusts, and assets, and never to speculate with them.

We, the American RF Bankers, need to produce for the United States, and the world at large, a new breed of bankers: the RF banker, who stands on two important pillars:

- The pillar of faith-based moral, ethical, and spiritual fulfillment.
- The pillar of excellence in the quality of products and services offered by the RF bank and its superior operating results, compared to its peer conventional riba-based banks.

We need to see a new breed of American RF bankers who are capable of energetically communicating and articulating the values and messages of the Judeo-Christian-Islamic value system and the RF lifestyle that applies the RF law (the Judeo-Christian-Islamic Shari'ạa law) to the masses in America and the world.

We in the RF banking system should work hard to build a new alternative system, both in content and extent. We want to present to the United States and then to the world the model of patience, perseverance, and respect as well as the elements of a true RF lifestyle for parents, young couples, youths, and senior citizens.

We, the RF lifestyle proponents, want to bring to the United States, and later on to the world, a new banking world vision, one that shapes a new society that lives by RF values:

- A society that is built on intellectual and mental persuasion, in which our mind is the key to knowing God and living by the Judeo-Christian-Islamic values.
- A society that believes in the purity of the soul and body.
- A society that bans drugs, alcohol, and gambling.
- A society that looks at promiscuous activities such as fornication and adultery as filth that should never be condoned.
- A society that believes in respecting promises and that our word is our bond.

- A society that believes in volunteering oneself and one's resources to the cause of serving God by serving people.
- A society that believes in respecting people's properties, dignity, and right to live honorably and freely.
- A society that is disciplined by the RF lifestyle and never allows the individual to overburden himself or herself with liabilities, debts, and promises that cannot be fulfilled.
- A society that never hoards and never uses riba in its financial dealings.
- A society that believes that these goals can all be achieved not through the proletariat of communism and socialism or the selfishness and greed of money changers in an untamed version of what is misrepresented as capitalism, but through the believers and servants of God in the RF disciplined lifestyle.

THE VISION OF AN IDEAL FAITH-BASED JUDEO-CHRISTIAN-ISLAMIC SOCIETY

We need to remember that the road to this RF vision is full of challenges, and we need to prepare to overcome them:

- We need to learn from the success stories and achievements of others in the conventional riba-based banking services in order to analyze those services' success and faults.
- We need to expand within our means and focus on human resources, including well-trained RF bankers and administrators and financial strength enhanced by voluntarism. We need to think of ways of growing the RF banking alternative by expanding the market for our RF services by attracting all people of all faiths to the RF banking services industry. We need to work hard to make sure that the RF banking industry is perceived by the citizens at large and business leaders as the preferred banking system in the marketplace.
- We need to stress the requirement of building true partnerships between the customer and community member, the families in the community, the RF bankers and administrators, and the community at large.
- We need to motivate as many youths in the community to study to be accountants, financial analysts, and business managers and to train them to live an RF lifestyle and to qualify themselves as future RF bankers.
- We need to sign onto a vision of building a standardized nationwide RF banking system that is as good as, and hopefully better than, the conventional riba-based banking system.

NEW TRENDS THAT CAPTURED THE IMAGINATION OF THE PAGANS OF THE ARABIAN PENINSULA—LESSONS TO LEARN FROM

When Prophet Muhammad (pp) was commissioned to assume the responsibility of expanding on and documenting the teachings of all of God's prophets, in particular Abraham (pp), Moses (pp), and Jesus (pp), and subsequently he was commanded to start building the model community of civilization in the city of Yathrib (a small settlement located north of the city of Makkah and the site of the prophet Muhammad's mosque where he is buried). Prophet Muhammad (pp) and his companions started, with the local citizens, to build the new community complete with its constitution and civic laws. The settlement's name was changed to *Madinah*, which means "the model city of civilization." The following is a summary of the way this pioneering Judeo-Christian-Islamic set of values promoted by Prophet Muhammad (pp) has captured people's imagination and changed the history of the world:

- Protection of property rights and title of ownership.
- Abolishment of discrimination and tribalism.
- Enforcement of a new set of equal rights and opportunities regardless of tribal connections, race, national origin, gender, power, wealth, or poverty.
- Recognition of women as equal to men and made both genders complementary in a united community, and viewing women as important contributors to society who are entitled to inherit and own property (for the first time in history).
- Enforcing of the free market system, which was later popularized in the West and the world by Adam Smith.
- Origination of the concept of insurance (*takaful*, which means "mutual benefit and protection").
- Origination of labor rights stipulating fairness to labor and that labor should be paid before the worker's sweat dries from his brow (as pronounced by Prophet Muhammad [pp]).
- Prohibition of hoarding (*ihtikar*), deception, misrepresentation of facts about products and services (*gharar*, which means "trading in risk, fraud, speculation, gambling, cheating, deception, and forgery"), and promotion of transparency.
- Promotion of the concept of living and transacting in an RF way which considers money not as a commodity that can be bought, sold, or rented at a price called interest rate, but instead viewing it as a measuring device (this concept also states that money does not reproduce if left in a safe vault; it only grows when invested in a true and productive economic activity).

- Promotion of the concept that wealth should be circulated and reinvested within the community to help develop that community by creating jobs, economic growth, and prosperity.
- Establishment of the RF Judeo-Christian-Islamic system of economics, finance, and monetary theory, based on four important pillars (described in detail in Chapter 2):
  - Wealth and property (assets) are owned by God; humanity (male and female) is appointed by God in His mysterious and wise ways to serve as trustees and custodians.
  - The system of RF banking and finance.
  - The system of *zakah*, which means alms giving.
  - The system of *miraath*, which means inheritance laws.
- Establishment of a standard for behavior and for an RF lifestyle, calling for followers and adherents:
  - To live below or within one's means.
  - Not to waste, not to live an extravagant lifestyle, and not to overspend, as overspending is defined by the Judeo-Christian-Islamic value system as the work of Satan.
  - To minimize debt obligations and to assume debt only if it is absolutely necessary and it should be done using the RF discipline.

ELEMENTS OF THE RF ECONOMIC SYSTEM

Production

The RF system and lifestyle expects every individual to work and to produce. Prophet Muhammad (pp), as did all prophets before him, teaches: "Never be lazy and helpless." There is no good in an individual who does not want to produce and earn money. It is taught that the unproductive hand is an unclean, impure hand (*najas*). The system also calls for products to be useful and not harmful as defined in the Judeo-Christian-Islamic Shari'aa law.

Distribution

In its efforts to do away with discrimination between people and classes in society based on color, national origin, gender, language, wealth, and affluence, and to reshape the relationship between classes, the RF Judeo-Christian-Islamic system makes the following points:

- God owns wealth, power, and natural resources.
- The individual or the institution is appointed by God as a trustee and custodian to manage them.

- Every being, human or not, has a minimum requirement of being able to live in freedom and dignity. This should be provided by those who are in charge of government institutions to anyone who cannot meet his or her own needs.
- Private property and ownership are sacred rights and must be protected.

The system is paid back and balanced out through the act of ritual alms giving (zakah) as one of the pillars of the RF Judeo-Christian-Islamic system. If these resources are not enough, the government is expected to apply an additional temporary tax on those who can afford it among the rich and affluent to balance the budget; this additional tax is looked upon as a religious duty (*fard kefaya*).

> *9:103 Of their goods, take alms, that so thou mightest purify and sanctify them; and pray on their behalf. Verily thy prayers are a source of security for them: And God is One Who heareth and knoweth.*

Zakah is spent and distributed by the government, as explained in Chapter 2, to help the poor, the needy, the administrators, the oppressed, those who are heavily indebted to meet their basic necessities and pay off their debts, the traveler (wayfarer), and in the way of pleasing God in general.

> *9:60 Alms are for the poor and the needy, and those employed to administer the [funds]; for those whose hearts have been [recently] reconciled [to Truth]; for those in bondage and in debt; in the cause of God. And for the wayfarer: [thus is it] ordained by God, and God is full of knowledge and wisdom.*

The RF banker must be trained to feel socially responsible for others in the community. He/she cannot enjoy life while others are suffering. A government that believes in the Judeo-Christian-Islamic values is responsible for the basic needs of every citizen: food, shelter, clothing, education, jobs, and health care. The RF system also calls for a very basic and fundamental understanding that the only road to wealth and achievement is hard work and the assumption of risk, not through gambling and speculation. That is why the RF law defines exactly how the estate is distributed after death (in a detailed description in the Qur'aan).[10]

> *4:7 From what is left by parents and those nearest related there is a share for men and a share for women, whether the property be small or large—a determinate share.*

The system of inheritance calls for no one to make a will that attempts to alter the predefined and detailed distribution rates as revealed by God in Chapter 4 of the Qur'aan. In addition, if one wanted to include in his/her will a payout to others outside what the Judeo-Christian-Islamic Shari'aa law defines, this is limited to a maximum of one-third of the total estate. To keep social peace among the heirs, this one-third can only be allocated to benefit others outside the inheritance beneficiaries. This way, money is always distributed fairly and is trickled down through the system to rejuvenate the economy perpetually from a generation to the next.

Consumption

The RF Judeo-Christian-Islamic value system believes and preaches that the citizen should seek a life of moderation and a balanced pattern of consumption. Overconsumption is condemned as the work of Satan.

> *7:31 O Children of Adam! Wear your beautiful apparel at every time and place of prayer: eat and drink: But waste not by excess, for God loves not the wasters.*
>
> *25:67 Those who, when they spend, are not extravagant and not niggardly, but hold a just (balance) between those (extremes).*

According to the Judeo-Christian-Islamic Shari'aa law, spending in the wrong way (bribery, illegal business and profits, abusing the legal system, and/or reckless spending) and extravagant overconsumption (even of lawful materials) are not allowed. Everyone is trained to plan for the future and to be careful. The story of Prophet Joseph (pp) in the Torah, the Gospel, and the Qur'aan[11]—in which we are told about the seven productive and the seven lean years, and how Prophet Joseph (pp) attained prominence in the house of Pharaoh in Egypt by implementing and RF disciplined long-range plan of saving for the lean years—is an important lesson in long-range planning for all of us to emulate.

THE RF JUDEO-CHRISTIAN-ISLAMIC SYSTEM AND BUSINESS ETHICS

The RF system calls for profits and services to be maximized legally and fairly in order to realize a better life and living standards, with freedom and independence of the individual without discrimination, by using interdependence and fair interaction with other communities and nations. The

RF system promotes free markets and free international trade as the natural mechanism of getting people to know each other; such interactions will promote mutual respect, peace, and prosperity through communications, trading, and mutual benefits.

> *49:13 O mankinds! We created you from a single [pair] of a male and a female, and made you into nations and tribes, that ye may know each other (not that ye may despise [each other]). Verily the most honored of you in the sight of God is [he who is] the most righteous of you. And God has full knowledge and is well acquainted [with all things].*

RF banks' goal is to develop new and efficient ways and means to improve the quality of life and preserve the individual's most valuable asset, time. Time is life. Protection of the environment, too, is a sacred duty of every citizen who subscribes to the Judeo-Christian-Islamic values. The RF banker should have the passion to focus on a long-term view of investing in the future without speculation, to help generate long-term job opportunities for generations to come. The RF banker should be the catalyst that will provide flexibility in planning for people's futures through strategic planning and training, to prevent business cycles from having a negative impact on the community.[12]

The RF Market System

The RF banker believes that markets are designed to bring a buyer (end user) and a seller (producer) together to consummate a fair, transparent, well-defined, and well-documented transaction that is free of deception (gharar). Speculation or interference with market forces of supply and demand is not allowed. The RF banker should do his/her best to ascertain that markets are free and open to everyone, provided that the Judeo-Christian-Islamic Shari'aa law and the laws of the land are not violated. Information about products, goods, and services should be readily available, complete, and known to all parties. The RF banker believes that misrepresentations are punishable both by law in this life and according to God's judgment in the hereafter. The RF banker lives and operates believing that full disclosure and full transparency are required and that monopoly and hoarding are strictly forbidden and prohibited by the Judeo-Christian-Islamic Shari'aa law and the laws of the land. In an RF system, those in charge do their utmost to make sure that prices are set on the basis of supply and demand using the open market system, and that speculation is strictly forbidden.

The RF Management Ethics

The RF banking manager is looked upon as a custodian of God's trust, given to him/her to manage. However, the RF banking manager is also considered a shepherd of his/her subordinates. He or she is expected to provide guidance, vision, and care for his/her subordinates, to maximize their output, and to keep the values of the faith and the RF system intact. An RF banking manager is chosen with strict qualifications:

- Excellence in professionalism and knowledge.
- Performance, track record, trust, and piety.
- Good interpersonal relationship skills, as manifested by commitment to community service and guided by the ultimate example of all of the Prophets of God and by the role models of proven leaders in the community and business.

An RF banking manager/owner of a workplace is expected to provide employees with maximum job security through continual training, optimization, and community interrelationships and preferably through joint ownership of the business.

Justice and Fairness on Both Sides: The RF Bank and the Customer

It has been the norm of many who call for social justice to only address one side of the issue, and that is the responsibility of the bankers (or, in other words, those who are in control of the money and who decide whether credit can be extended). By the same token, to be just and fair as ordained by God and His prophets and messengers, we need to remind people in the community of their responsibility toward the promises they make by signing the bottom line of that credit agreement—or any agreement. Fulfilling a promise is the backbone of believing in God. In the teachings of all of God's prophets and in the Judeo-Christian-Islamic value system, we are taught that a person is in fact his/her word and that our word is our bond. In this regard, it is accepted that under normal circumstances—meaning under circumstances that do not include deception, misrepresentation, and high-pressure sales techniques—a person who believes in God should never commit to a promise that he or she cannot fulfill.

People should train themselves to be disciplined. They should not try to consider that predicting the future produces certainty. The only one who knows the future is God. We, as RF professionals, can try to project the direction of the future, but we cannot predict it; if we plan our future based on that (usually) rosy prediction, we end up falling deeper into the hole of failure and debt. This is what happened in 2008, as the housing bubble and the subprime mortgage scandals were revealed. It is also important to note that under severe circumstances that are out of our hands, we can use the safety valves provided by the system to reduce the impact of these circumstances on our lives and the community through reorganization and bankruptcy laws (which are clearly outlined in the American laws and legal system.) However, it is not the behavior of a believer in the Judeo-Christian-Islamic system of faith that we sign a promise with the idea that we can get out of it if things do not work out as was "predicted." That is called negotiating and making a commitment in bad faith. I was deeply hurt to watch a television news report depicting a wonderful couple leaving the keys to their home at the front door and said good-bye to their bank. In the Judeo-Christian-Islamic value system, it is the worst offense to not pay one's debt and not to fulfill one's promises and commitments before passing on to our final resting destiny: God's kingdom. It is known that the first question Prophet Muhammad (pp) asked before he offered prayers unto the dead was: "Did he/she pay off his/her debts and fulfill his/her obligations?" If the answer were yes, he would pray. If the answer were no, he would refuse to pray until his heirs make a commitment to settle that debt obligation. That is why it is a standard practice for a Muslim son or family representatives to stand up in the middle of the condolences' gathering event and make a public commitment that all the obligations of the person who died (father, mother, brother, or sister) will be the obligations of those who survive him/her.

BANKING AND INVESTMENT BANKING

In the RF banking system, money is an important tool that must be respected and put to good use by investing it prudently. Growth of this money must not be done by looking at money as something that can reproduce as if it were rabbits without investing it in the community.

The RF bankers and customers believe that money must be earned in a proper way, as defined by the Judeo-Christian-Islamic Shari'aa law. There is one underlying holistic concept of producing income: the difference between *halal*, which means divinely lawful, and *haram*, which means divinely unlawful. "Making" money and eating from haram sources are believed to be the same as consuming hellfire, and those who do this will ultimately not prosper in this life and will be in the depth of hellfire in the hereafter, when we all face God's judgment.

The RF lifestyle, discipline, and banking systems believe that money must be invested in good and productive projects and services that will provide a better, healthier, more productive, more comfortable, and fair RF lifestyle for all.

Unfortunately, some in the community have different ideas about money. Money in the RF system is not considered a commodity that commands a price (interest), as in the riba-based system. It is unfortunate that people are led to believe falsely that money reproduces and gives birth to more money if rented at a price called interest rate. Money is a medium or a measuring device for transacting business. It is used to measure the efficiency of doing business through the use of a yardstick we call in economics the "rate of return on investment."

In an RF banking regime, investment banks are called upon to bring the owner of capital together with the owner of an idea or expertise so that the two may invest together and realize long-term economic growth in the community, resulting in an acceptable return on that investment leading to more job opportunities, better living standards, and prosperity in the community. The investment bankers' role is education, evaluation, promotion, and follow-up for the benefit of long-term growth, not only to realize a commission. The purpose of the RF banking system is to make capital circulate within the community. The RF discipline guided by Judeo-Christian-Islamic value system prohibits trading paper instruments that do not create wealth but rather transfer it through gaming, speculation, and manipulation. The objective should be long-term investing, not day trading as if we were in a gambling casino. Some investment bankers like to attract more money by propagating and selling ideas that resemble going to a casino, trying to make 10 or 100 times what one has committed through gambling and betting (which they misname as "investing"). Others may want to do the same by speculating on currencies in foreign exchange (Forex) markets or day trading in the stock, commodities, and futures market such as what happened during the dot-com stock market bubble, which took the Nasdaq stock market index from almost 1,800 in 1998 to 4,800 in 2000, only to crash to 2,100 in the same year and stay there, with some fluctuations, until it crashed again to almost 1,700 as a result of the burst housing bubble and the subsequent financial tsunami of 2008. Some "investors" made huge amounts of money; others—most of whom, unfortunately, happened to be the average citizens who are classified as small investors—lost their life savings and their retirement assets. Worse still, there are others who can make huge sums of money through destroying the economies of whole nations by speculating against their currencies in the Forex markets, as we witnessed throughout history. This happened to the British pound in the 1980s and to Asian currencies in the late 1990s and in the twenty-first century in some of the promising nations like Brazil and Turkey.

It is important to state clearly that the financial system has honorable, ethical and disciplined men and women who want to do the right thing, but the greed and misguided ambitions of a few have tarnished the whole industry.

In the new brand of banking presented in this book, RF banking, the RF banker answers first to his/her conscience, civility, and social responsibility, because he/she answers to a higher authority (i.e., God). The RF banker is trained to believe in a set of standards as described by the laws of the land and by the Judeo-Christian-Islamic Shari'aa law, as ordained by our Creator. It is God who created us equally, so we might live in peace with each other and care about each other. The RF banker is disciplined to make a difference in people's lives by investing in them and with them. In doing so, the RF banker evaluates his/her progress not only by how much income was made through commissions and fees but by how many households were added to the family of his/her RF bank and the extent of the improvement the RF bank has made to these families by serving them and their financial needs. The RF banker makes sure, before he/she starts the process of financing (notice that the word *lending* is not used here), that the money/credit needed will be used in a productive and tangible project that will benefit the community, that it will not involve speculation and/or deceptive activities, that it does not involve investing in socially irresponsible activities—like operating a casino or taking advantage of the poor in businesses such as check cashing, payday lending stores, predatory lending, and other similar activities—and that it will be used for environmentally and socially responsible investments. The RF banker should have a passion for serving people, should enjoy helping those who need assistance, and, most importantly, should have a vision for improving the lives of those around him or her in the community at large. People in the community expect that when their money is entrusted to a bank, it is treated by the bankers as a sacred trust that will be honored and closely guarded. People's money should be returned intact, as is, when it is demanded by its owners. It also cannot be disposed of in the form of a loan or credit facility to others without the consent of the owner.

VALUES AND BUSINESS ETHICS OF THE RF BANKER[13]

Professionalism

Professionalism is the talent of taking power through our creator, God, the source of all powers, to love what we do, to improve ourselves, to add to our experiences, and to do the best we can at what we promised to do. Professionalism is making promises that can be delivered and, if possible, delivering them better than promised. Professionalism is the act of believing in and bringing to life the values of the Judeo-Christian-Islamic system and in particular the bringing to life a true RF lifestyle and discipline. Professionalism is the pride of doing what we know, the strength of being able to say "we do not know" when we do not, and the determination to learn more.

Concentration

Concentration is the ability to focus, listen, ponder, and reflect. It speaks to us quietly above the roar of our mind. Concentration in prayers, in supplication (*du'aa*), in remembering God, and in our work trains us to ignore the extraneous, dismiss the distractions, and avoid the pessimists, and prompts us to focus at will. Concentration is part of worshipping God (*ibada*). It is clarity. It is what keeps our emotions from getting the better of us. Concentration keeps pressure from becoming paralysis, and keeps us away from diluting our efforts by spreading ourselves too thin. Concentration is what keeps our eyes on our goals, allowing us to turn reaction into action, disadvantage into opportunity, and opportunity into success. Our goals should be crystal clear. We need to build the foundation of a worldwide RF banking and finance system beginning in America, to bring the masses (*alnas*) back to the basic values of trust, humbleness, living within our available means, never stopping to dream and work hard to achieve these dreams one step at a time with sincerity and wisdom.

Consistency

Consistency is a character trait that makes us unimpressed with a single success. Consistency confers medals only upon those who burn brightly with the repetition of achievement. It is more than a promise. It is performance over time. Consistency means never resting, never taking our talents—the precious gifts of God—for granted. Consistency is the practical proof that we are believers in God. The RF banker is trained to be consistent in matching the RF values with an RF lifestyle one person at a time until this lifestyle and RF banking discipline is popularized first in America and then in the world.

Commitment

Commitment is what transforms a promise into reality. We need to promise God and the community to promote and popularize an RF lifestyle and to build the RF banking and financing infrastructure for our customers worldwide. Commitment is the word that speaks of our intentions and the action that speaks louder than words. Commitment is making time when there is none. Commitment is coming through time after time, year after year, for the whole of our life. Commitment is what builds character. It is the power to change starting from the possible in order to achieve what is perceived as impossible. It is the daily triumph of integrity, of belief in God, and of belief in the future over skepticism.

THE 10 GOLDEN COVENANTS OF THE RF BANKER[14]

The RF banker's first and most important responsibility is to serve people in his or her community and to treat them like members of his/her own family. This means knowing the husband, the wife, the children, and the grandchildren. It means that the RF banker becomes familiar with the goals and objectives of the family, who will share with him their dreams and aspirations and view him/her as their financial doctor or expert. It is the responsibility of the RF banker to understand and become familiar with the family's financial situation in great detail, to help the family arrange and position their financial statement (i.e., assets and liabilities and income and expenses), to help the family improve their financial position and status by articulating their dreams and goals and then by restructuring their financial situation when needed. One example is to reduce the family's riba-based debts and liabilities and enhance the value of their assets using the RF discipline to help them lead a true RF lifestyle. It is the responsibility of the RF banker to make sure that the family is well positioned and prepared for a comfortable retirement, for unexpected emergencies, and for saving for college expenses for their children and grandchildren. In doing so, the RF banker's prime passion should be the well-being of the family, not the commission or fee generated from the relationship.

In dealing with our own families of customers, we, the RF bankers will always seek what is best for them. The RF banker would always try to minimize the fees and expenses incurred and charged by the bank and make sure that each transaction is looked upon as an honest-to-goodness investment, with good analysis and prudence exercised to ensure that the purchase of an investment and the taking of credit make economic sense and is based on RF rules. The RF banker also must have in his or her heart the best interests of the community. She/he will be active in all of its civic activities, including its places of worship of all faiths in which he or she is positioned to serve the worshippers, the school Parent-Teacher Association, the city and town services, and other voluntary activities. The RF banker should be a firm believer in speaking the truth, never betraying or compromising trust, and respecting privacy and confidentiality.

At LARIBA, we set a number of covenants, which we called the "10 Golden Rules for an RF Banker." The following is a listing of these rules:

1. *Do not speculate with people's money and trust.* We place people's trust above everything, including our own interest.
2. *Fulfill our promises.* We never promise what we cannot deliver.
3. *Respect money—money "respects" people who respect it.* We are careful with our costs. We keep them to a minimum.

4. *Do not forget our moral responsibility to local communities.* While our most important concern is to achieve the highest return for our shareholders, we never forget our moral responsibility to local communities. We measure our success by return on assets and by the number of households we have helped open up to serve in an RF way and to facilitate their goal of leading an RF lifestyle.
5. *Do not discriminate.* We do not discriminate, regardless of skin color, language, ethnic background, religious beliefs, age, or gender.
6. *Invest in our clients.* We do not look at our business as a money-renting operation. We invest with and in people.
7. *Be socially responsible.* We do not finance alcohol- or tobacco-related businesses, gambling, manufacture of harmful products to people and the environment or any unethical activities.
8. *Be sensitive about who we deal with.* We promise to check our depositors, clients, and customers to make sure of the validity of the sources of their funds and the type and quality of their businesses.
9. *Be conservative.* Our most important RF investment objective is preservation of capital and keeping up with inflation.
10. *Look at our coworkers as our partners.* We aspire to make each one of our coworkers as an important part of the business.

THE RF BANKING DISCIPLINE: WHERE DO WE START AND HOW DO WE REALIZE THE DREAM?

A young professional in our community approached us when American finance house LARIBA was started in 1987, as we were pioneering our effort to implement the values of the RF banking and finance system on a small scale. He said, "I respectfully disagree with your attempt to change the order and the seating arrangements on a *Titanic*-size ship. It will be impossible for LARIBA to do so." We thought deeply about what he said and we wrote to him, stating, "We agree that changing the seating arrangement on a *Titanic*-size ship in one shot is of course impossible and is in fact unwise and of course would lead to failure. However, our approach is very humble and simple. ..."

Our approach is to take a very small area on that large ship, ask those who are responsible for the space for their permission to rearrange things without violating their rules and regulations, and offer the rest of the passengers an alternative way of doing things. If we are right, we shall be able to attract more people to notice our new alternative, ask about it, learn more about it, and eventually subscribe to it. This will eventually lead others to change to a better future, as was tested in this pilot experiment. This description is not a pipe dream. It is, in fact, the lesson of history—of all new civilizations and nations, as described to us in the Torah, the Gospel, and the Qur'aan. All God's prophets started in a small way and grew their base after proving that the new values and systems they were bringing to the community were better. This strategy is articulated in the following sentence, which is used as one of our mottos: "Start from the possible to achieve the impossible." If we have a good idea that we believe is in great need by the people, and if we are sincere in our efforts to introduce it to the citizens—one individual at a time—we, in this RF Movement, shall capture the imagination of all people in the community and in the world, and they will eventually follow and subscribe to the new RF lifestyle and banking system.

But the question is where to begin? The answer is extremely difficult, and in fact was a big challenge for all of us. Our efforts to start American finance house LARIBA in 1987 and the way we developed it to become a recognized institution in the United States and the world were highlighted in the beginning of the book. Yes, capital is an important ingredient of the process. History has shown repeatedly that money does not make people, but people can earn that money and accumulate capital. Experience has shown that the more important factors are belief and trust in God, imagination, and determination to create a clear image of a better but well-defined future. Most important is to attract people who believe in living a new RF lifestyle and use RF banking concepts and services and to capture the imagination of educated professionals who are willing to learn RF lifestyle and banking, leading them to practice it. Our challenge has been to build the morally and ethically qualified RF team players and leaders of the future of a new RF banking movement. We believe that if we are sincere, patient, and wise in our approach, all else will fall in place by the grace of God and the support of our community as well as the superior results we achieve.

REVIEW QUESTIONS

1. What is the definition of civility as presented by Professor Steven Carter of Yale? How does this fit from an Islamic point of view?
2. Speculation and greed have landed the U.S. and world economies in some of their deepest troubles, like in the depression of 1929 and the near depression/recession of 2008. A rule that was enacted by Congress in the 1930s is called the Glass-Steagall Act:
   a. What is the Glass-Steagall Act?
   b. Why was it enacted? And how did it affect the U.S. financial markets?
   c. When was the Glass-Steagall Act put in demise by Congress?
   d. Which institution was the first major beneficiary of the demise of the act?

e. What happened after the breakdown of the Glass-Steagall Act to banks and investment banks in the United States?
f. How did the demise of the Glass-Steagall Act lead to the near depression/deep recession of 2008?
g. Will the deregulation of financial institutions work? Why?
3. Ethically and practically, the book discusses the foundation of RF banking: Please enumerate the two pillars upon which the RF banker stands.
4. The book advocates a new society built on the Judeo-Christian-Islamic values and law: Please enumerate the belief values detailed in the book.
5. In the city of Yathrib, the Prophet Muhammad (s) with the shura (consultation) of the supporters and followers the first ever Covenant or Foundational Constitution in modern history that signaled the dawn of civic life:
a. What was the new name chosen for Yathrib, and what does it mean?
b. What was the name of that constitution?
c. Please list at least six elements of the ideal society covenant of living together.
6. Please list and elaborate on the three elements forming the foundations of Islamic economics based on the theses used in the book.
7. Please list the 10 Golden Rules used by the first RF banking and finance effort in the United States as stated in the book.

NOTES

1. *Man* means male and female.
2. Bob Woodward, *Maestro: Greenspan's Fed and the American Boom* (New York: Simon & Schuster, 2000).
3. *The Economist* (October 26, 2013): Leaders Section, Subterranean Capitalist Blues, page 13.
4. The Master Limited Partnership (MLP) is a corporate structure that combines the advantages of limited liability corporations, the tax advantages of a partnership, and the governance of a private firm to exempt them from taxes while distributing their profits directly to the shareholders. This rendered such MLPs more attractive to invest in because of the higher (pass-through) dividends they pay compared to those paid by regular corporations and time CDs at the banks.
5. Named after its sponsors, Senator Chris Dodd and Representative Barney Frank.
6. Stephen L. Carter, *Civility* (New York: Basic Books, 1998).
7. Ibid., p. 12.
8. Ibid., p. 11.

9. Hadeeth of Prophet Muhammad (pp).
10. The Qur'aan, Chapter 4, Nissaa—Women.
11. Ibid., Chapter 12, Joseph.
12. Ibid., Chapter 12, Joseph.
13. Based on a mid-1980s advertising campaign by Shearson Lehman, but adapted by the author.
14. These are posted on the following websites: www.LARIBA.com and www.BankofWhittier.com.

CHAPTER 8

The Conventional Riba-Based Banking System

THE BANKING SYSTEM OF THE UNITED STATES

The United States has developed the most sophisticated and highly dispersed banking network and system in the world. The American banking system, when it was developed, benefited from the accumulated body of human experience over history, including many religious values, human experiences, and documented and sophisticated solutions to problems faced while developing the system in the United States and other systems in Europe. The system was and continues to be built using the most capable minds, accounting methods and standards, mathematical tools, regulatory disciplines, and analyses available in the world. It is a project in progress. We are reminded that it would be embarrassing to write about the American banking and financial system after what happened in 2008, when the system failed miserably. It is believed that when the lessons learned from the worst crisis since the Great Depression are applied and the system is modified, it will be better: well designed, well positioned, and ready for a better future, not only for the United States, but for the rest of the world. This was proven in the aftermath of the 2008 debacle, as witnessed later on in 2011. History has shown that a country can have the most sophisticated system in the world, but if some people, who are part and parcel of the system, do not respect it and instead indirectly try to sabotage it by trying to get around the laws by taking advantage of loopholes in the regulations, that system is doomed. The United States functioned well with its banking system when Americans at all levels believed in it, respected it, and implemented it, and when we Americans lived within our means.

This chapter covers the U.S. banking regulations, which are considered the most sophisticated banking regulations ever developed in the history of the world. These regulations are included in this book to underline two important facts:

1. These regulations are intended to make sure that every citizen in the United States is treated fairly without the slightest form of discrimination, and that the money deposited in the depository institutions is protected and safe. This is important, because those who are involved in RF banking and its development need not reinvent the wheel; we can use these regulations as a foundation for future efforts, improving upon or adding to this system of regulations in our effort to develop the RF banking and finance system. The United States' banking regulations are built on a huge body of human experience that was meticulously designed and documented.
2. Many of these regulations have Judeo-Christian-Islamic roots. These roots were tied in with the banking regulations.

In addition to the banking regulations, this section attempts to familiarize the reader with the process of regulating and supervising banks in the United States. This chapter will focus on the process used by the U.S. Treasury Department's arm responsible for regulating national banks—the Office of the Comptroller of the Currency (OCC)—and how its "Examination of Safety and Soundness" of the national banks is conducted, including my personal perspectives from firsthand experience running the Bank of Whittier, NA, starting in July 2003. The role of the Federal Deposit Insurance Corporation (FDIC) and the Federal Reserve System will also be discussed. Additionally, the role of the Securities and Exchange Commission (SEC) in regulating the investment banking industry will be explained. The goal is to help the reader understand the processes used by the SEC to ensure that the financially uneducated and unsophisticated citizen is not conned out of his/her precious savings and that the process of selling securities (shares of companies, mutual funds, and bonds) is closely scrutinized by the government through the SEC.

To give a historic foundation to our discussion of how banks work and how Judeo-Christian-Islamic values can be applied to them, we need to know how financial institutions in the United States were built, their contributions to encourage community savings and investments, and their contributions to the lifestyle and the economy in the United States. With nearly 99,160 branches[1] and 415,321 automated teller machines (ATMs), the U.S. banking system is the largest in the world. As of the second quarter of 2013, U.S. banks had $14.41 trillion in assets and $7.35 trillion in total loans. U.S. banking is more diverse than in most Western countries. Despite ongoing consolidation, vigorous competition exists within the vast banking community, which includes financial holding companies that operate nationwide, dominant regional banks, and smaller independent community banks.

In my many personal communications and meetings with finance and banking officials and bankers in the world, especially in the United States, Europe, the former Soviet bloc countries,[2] and the developing countries of Africa and Asia, I was amazed to learn that officials outside the United States are not aware of the real engine of the United States economy: the highly dispersed community-owned (shareholders and board members are from the local community) and operated network of community-based state and national banks, which make it easier for local communities to keep their savings safe and to reinvest these savings in the community. Most of the rest of the world is more familiar with branches of a larger bank that serve local communities.

The American banking system is based on a "bottoms-up" approach as compared to that of the rest of the world, which is designed and built based on a "top-down" approach. This basis, in itself, signifies the ideal of the U.S. banking system, which espouses, to the best efforts possible, the democracy of capital distribution. These, along with the many regulations in the system, aspire to make capital available for those who need it without discrimination of any sort. This in itself is a basic Judeo-Christian-Islamic value and ultimate goal. Compare this to many of the countries in Europe and the developed world, which have huge capital resources but have not yet been able to make it trickle down to the masses despite claims sometimes made by their governments that they are applying the values of the faith and that they are pursuing responsible governance.

It is interesting to report here the results of a survey made by a popular television channel in the Arab world, in which they asked if "Islamic" banks catered to the rich or served the poor and the needy. More than 70 percent of the respondents said that Islamic banks only cater to and serve the needs of the rich. In fact, most banks in the developing world, including Islamic banks, not only cater to the needs of the rich but also invest large sums of their capital and deposits in projects that are outside their countries. It is sincerely hoped that the United States' banking regulations are studied by the regulators, the religious scholars, and the politicians in these countries in order to make a real difference in the fortunes of the future generations at all levels of the social ladder. This can be done through real economic development, prosperity, social justice, and equal opportunity in obtaining credit and in making sure that the huge fortunes accumulated from the sale of the natural resources are invested back in the local communities through a healthy (and hopefully in an RF [riba-free] format) banking industry that believes in making credit available to all people as a basic human right.

TYPES OF BANKING SERVICES IN THE UNITED STATES

The American banking system evolved with the emergence of the United States after the Civil War. There are two types of banks in America: state-chartered banks, which are chartered by the banking department of each state; and national banks, which are chartered and authorized to operate by the federal government through the U.S. Department of the Treasury. One of the reasons Congress created a banking system that issued national currency was to finance the Civil War. Although national banks no longer issue currency, they continue to play a prominent role in the nation's economic life. It is important to understand that banks, be they state chartered or national, are empowered to issue credit facilities that carry the same effect of issuing currency, but only in terms of credit and in the form of a promissory note against the borrowers, as discussed in Chapter 5.

National Banks

Congress has established a number of long-range goals of for the national banking system in America. These are:

- Supporting a stable national currency.
- Financing commerce.
- Acting as private depositories.
- Generally supporting the nation's economic growth and development.

The realization of these goals required a type of bank that was not just safe and sound, but whose powers were dynamic and capable of evolving so that national banks could perform their intended roles, well beyond the Civil War. Key to these powers is language set forth in 12 U.S.C. § 24 (Seventh), which provides that national banks are authorized to exercise:

> *... all such incidental powers as shall be necessary to carry on the business of banking; by discounting and negotiating promissory notes, drafts, bills of exchange, and other evidences of debt; by receiving deposits; by buying and selling exchange, coin and bullion; by loaning money on personal security; and by obtaining, issuing, and circulating notes.*

The national banking system demonstrates the value of applying nationwide standardization by introducing uniform national banking standards to banking activities and products.

State Banks

After the establishment of the United States, each state of the union kept a state-run banking system that was supervised by the individual state banking department. These state banking laws and regulations do not necessarily coincide and are not necessarily similar to the national banking system. However, the state banking laws and regulations are essentially the same as those of the national banks. State banks are usually small in size compared to national banks; however, there are national banks that are small, with capital of as little as $5 million and total assets of as little as $25 million, and state banks that are large, with capital that can exceed $20 million and assets that may exceed $100 million. It is important to note that state banks can, in general, operate only in the state where they are chartered, while national banks can operate, within regulations, in all states.

To avoid the potential of a conflict that would arise from a particular state regulating a national banking institution that is regulated by the federal government, a dual banking system was invented:

> *It has been a bedrock precept of our [the United States'] constitutional law for more than 180 years, since the Supreme Court's decision in M'Culloch v. Maryland in 1819, that states cannot constitutionally control the powers of entities created under Federal Law. Courts have consistently applied this principle over the years to national banks, holding a variety of state laws inapplicable to national banks, and finding that the federally authorized powers of national banks are not subject to state supervision and regulation.*[3]

In 1861, Secretary of the Treasury Chase recommended the establishment of a system of federally chartered national banks, each of which would have the power to issue standardized national banknotes based on United States bonds held by the bank. In the National Currency Act of 1863, the administration of the new national banking system was vested in the newly created *Office of the Comptroller of the Currency*, or OCC, and its chief administrator, the *Comptroller of the Currency*.[4] The law was completely rewritten and reenacted as the National Bank Act.[5] That act authorized the comptroller of the currency to hire a staff of national bank examiners to supervise and periodically examine national banks for safety and soundness. The act also gave the comptroller authority to regulate lending and investment activities of national banks.

Distinctions between the national banking system and the state banking system are rooted deep in constitutional principles and the history of the United States. These distinctions are essential to the vitality of the dual banking system and are encouraged.

The OCC booklet[6] on the dual system states that each component of the dual (state and national) banking system makes different, positive contributions to the overall strength of the U.S. banking system. In defense of the value and contribution of the *state banking system*, state bank supervisors rightly assert that a separate system of state banks "allows the states to serve as laboratories for innovation and change, not only in bank powers and structures, but also in the area of consumer protection." State banks' supervisors argue that state banks put in action the "smaller is better" model of business. State banks are in general geographically closer to state bank regulators. This provides state banks with greater access to state regulators and gives state regulators greater familiarity with the banks they supervise. Nowadays, the OCC has regional and local city offices throughout the United States.

National banks are required by law to become members of the Federal Reserve System. Banks chartered by the individual states are divided into those that are members of the Federal Reserve System (state member banks of the Federal Deposit Insurance Corporation [FDIC]) and those that are not (state nonmember banks). State banks are not required to join the Federal Reserve System, but they may elect to become members if they meet the standards set by the Board of Governors of the Federal Reserve System. Member banks must subscribe to stock (buy shares of the Federal Reserve Bank) in their regional Federal Reserve Bank in an amount equal to 6 percent of their capital and surplus, half of which must be paid in, while the other half is subject to call by the Board of Governors of the Federal Reserve System. The holding of this stock, however, does not carry with it the control and financial interest conveyed to holders of common stock in for-profit organizations. It is merely a legal obligation of Federal Reserve membership, and the stock may not be sold or pledged as collateral for loans. Member banks receive a 6 percent dividend annually on their stock, as specified by law, and vote for the Class A and Class B directors of the Reserve Bank. Stock in Federal Reserve Banks is not available for purchase by individuals or entities other than member banks. The Federal Reserve is responsible for supervising and regulating the following segments of the banking industry to ensure safe and sound banking practices and compliance with banking laws:

- Bank holding companies, including diversified financial holding companies formed under the Gramm-Leach-Bliley Act of 1999 and foreign banks with U.S. operations.

- State-chartered banks that are members of the Federal Reserve System (state member banks).
- Foreign branches of member banks.
- Water edge and agreement corporations, through which U.S. banking organizations may conduct international banking activities.

Details of the Federal Reserve System are found in Chapter 5.

Credit Unions

There is yet another type of depository institution in the United States that is very close in function and services to savings cooperatives. These are called *credit unions*. These are associations of members of a community that are bound together either because they live in the same neighborhood, work in the same company, or worship at the same place of worship. These institutions usually gather assets by selling shares in the credit union and lending to its members at a spread over the dividends paid back to the members. The spread is usually lower than that of larger banks, which yields higher dividends for depositors (credit union shareholders). This is because of the smaller size of most credit unions, the lower overhead, and the very low loan losses because the community knows each other and is close to each other. That was the original concept on which the credit union movement started. By the end of the twentieth century, as it is now, the credit unions are performing depository and financing services that are very close in nature to community banks but with the tax exemption advantage given to the credit unions because it is classified as a not-for-profit organization. However, with the lack of in-depth experience in financing and credit extension, many credit unions have suffered significant losses especially during the 2008 financial meltdown.

Investment Banks

Another important arm of banking in the United States is a category called *investment banks*. They differ from, but complement, the role of depository institutions (i.e., banks). An important role of the investment banks is that they gather funds that are considered "excess liquidity in the hands of the public and other institutions, like pension and retirement plans" and reinvest this money prudently on behalf of the public, mainly in the United States, but also to capture business opportunities worldwide. It is very important to understand this role, because most of the Islamic RF banking discussions, especially concerning attempts to operate in the West, mix the roles of depository institutions—banks—and investment banks together. This has been a major source of confusion and a major problem in developing RF banking and finance services in most if not all of the developed Western world. The lack of an active, sophisticated investment banking institution and investment bankers who understand the intricacies of reinvesting surplus funds in local economies prudently is an important reason for the flight of capital away from many developing countries.

Investment banks are regulated by another U.S. government entity, the SEC, to make sure that the financially uneducated and unsophisticated citizen is not conned out of his/her precious savings, that the process of selling securities (shares of companies, mutual funds, and bonds) is closely scrutinized, and that these activities abide by government rules and regulations.

Licensing a Commercial Bank in the United States

In both national and state banks, an application to start a new bank must detail why there is a need for a banking service in a particular area or neighborhood and the categories of products and services on which this bank will be focusing. This area is called the *assessment area* (AA). The bank charter application should include a detailed outline of the business plan; a description of the capital that will be raised and how, and wherefrom it will be raised; and the identities of the bank's board of directors and key operating staff (mainly the president, chief credit officer, and chief financial officer), with details on their experience, personal and professional backgrounds, and how they will contribute to the bank's mission of serving the banking and financial needs of the community. The feasibility study should also include a thorough and detailed analysis of the competition and a well-thought-out business plan that justifies the chartering of the bank and demonstrates how the community will be better off after chartering and opening the services of this bank. State banks are chartered and authorized to operate by the state regulators, while national banks are chartered and licensed by the federal government through the U.S. Department of the Treasury. In case a group of investors wants to buy a controlling interest in a bank—more than 9.9 percent of the outstanding shares—the group must apply to the regulators for permission to make a change in the control of the bank.

Bank regulators not only review the application in great detail but also perform a detailed check on the background, the police and Justice Department records, and other civil records of all involved to ensure that those who sit on the board or run the bank have a crystal clean reputation before being entrusted with people's deposits and assets. It is preferred that the bank's board members come from diverse backgrounds and business experience so that they will be able to reflect the different interests, needs, and viewpoints of the community. Board members are expected to have received proper training through attending special seminars on banking in general and on how to properly fulfill their responsibilities within the law and the banking regulations in particular. Bank executives and staff members are expected to attend regular training programs to familiarize themselves with all aspects and updates of bank operations and banking regulations. Examples of these training programs will be discussed in Chapter 13. Each board member is required by regulations to risk his or her own money by purchasing at least $1,000 worth of stock in the bank. Many will be surprised to know that members of the board of directors are not highly paid—in most cases—for their services because they are looked upon as volunteers offering their services to the community. The board fees range between $300 and $2,000 (depending on the size of the bank) for each board of directors meeting they attend. Members of the board of directors not only are responsible for supervising bank operations to make sure that the bank is safe and sound but also are responsible before the law for any lapse in performing their duties of oversight and supervision. The details of all these aspects are not the subject of this book. Only a few samples of the important features of a bank structure are mentioned here, in the hope that such features will be studied, improved upon (if needed), and implemented by RF bankers to build on what is available and to achieve a better future for all.

GOVERNMENT SUPERVISION OF THE BANK

National banks are supervised and regulated by the OCC, which is an arm of the U.S. Department of the Treasury. The OCC regulates and supervises all national banks and federal branches of foreign banks in the United States. National bank facilities account for nearly two-thirds of the total assets of all U.S. commercial banks.

The OCC's nationwide jurisdiction over banks—from modest-sized community banks to some of the largest American banks in the world—also contributes to the agency's ability to develop and maintain expert credit examination and risk management capabilities that benefit all banks in the national banking system. The OCC has a nationwide reach, which enables it to take actions to protect customers regardless of the state in which they reside. The OCC's efforts to combat unfair or deceptive practices and its focused approach to customer privacy issues have had nationally recognized consumer benefits.

The Office of the Comptroller of the Currency[7]

The OCC charters (licenses), regulates, and supervises all national banks. It also supervises the federal branches and agencies of foreign banks. Headquartered in Washington, D.C., the OCC has four district offices plus an office in London to supervise the international activities of national banks.

The OCC was established in 1863 as a bureau of the U.S. Department of the Treasury. The OCC is headed by the comptroller, who is appointed by the president of the United States, with the advice and consent of the Senate, for a five-year term. The comptroller also serves as a director of the FDIC and a director of the Neighborhood Reinvestment Corporation, which is mandated to uphold the principal of reinvesting banks' deposited money back in the communities from which they derived their deposits and not outside these communities. The OCC's nationwide staff of examiners conducts on-site close examinations and reviews of national banks and provides sustained supervision of bank operations. The agency issues rules, legal interpretations, and corporate decisions concerning banking, bank investments, bank community development activities, and other aspects of bank operations.

National bank examiners with the OCC supervise domestic and international activities of national banks and perform corporate analyses. Examiners analyze a bank's operations, compliance with the banking regulations, loan and investment portfolios, funds management, capital adequacy, earnings pattern, liquidity adequacy, sensitivity to market risk, and compliance with consumer banking laws, including the Community Reinvestment Act (CRA.) They review and evaluate the adequacy of the bank's internal controls, internal and external audits, and compliance with applicable laws and regulations. They also evaluate the bank management's ability to identify and control risk as well as management's succession plans in order to keep the safe and sound operational continuity of the institution.

In regulating national banks, the OCC has the power to:

- Examine the banks.
- Approve or deny applications for new charters (license), branches, capital, or other changes in corporate or banking structure.
- Take supervisory actions against banks that do not comply with laws and regulations or that otherwise engage in unsound banking practices. The agency can remove officers and directors, negotiate agreements to change banking practices using what is called a memorandum of understanding, and issue cease and desist orders (which would order bank to stop its lending activities and may be requiring the bank to divest

part of its loan portfolio and may limit the bank from taking additional deposits), as well as civil money penalties (called C&D order by OCC).

- Issue rules and regulations governing bank investments, lending, and other practices.

The OCC's Objectives

The OCC's activities are predicated on four objectives that support the OCC's mission to ensure a stable and competitive national banking system. The four objectives are:

1. To ensure the safety and soundness of the national banking system.
2. To foster competition by allowing banks to offer new products and services.
3. To improve the efficiency and effectiveness of OCC supervision, including reducing regulatory burden.
4. To ensure fair and equal access to financial services for all Americans.

OCC Funding

The OCC does not receive any appropriations from Congress. Instead, its operations are funded primarily by assessments (charging a fee) on national banks. National banks pay for their examinations, and they pay for the OCC's processing of their corporate applications. The OCC also receives revenue from its investment income, primarily from investments in U.S. Treasury securities.

Insurance of Bank Deposits by the Federal Deposit Insurance Corporation (FDIC)

The FDIC insures the deposits in all member banks in the United States. The basic insurance amount at inception was $100,000 per depositor, per insured bank until it was increased to $250,000 in response to the 2008 financial meltdown. This was done on a limited temporary basis (until 2013) to prevent customers of "shaky" banks from creating runs on those banks (a run on a bank is an event that occurs when most bank depositors withdraw their deposits from the bank to avoid incurring great losses of their deposits). The FDIC insurance amount applies to all depositors of an insured bank. For more information, the reader is invited to visit the FDIC's website: www.FDIC.gov. One of the FDIC rules requires that every bank should have a clear advertisement of membership in the FDIC.[8]

U.S. BANKING REGULATIONS

This section covers in detail some of the U.S. bank regulations, which are considered to be the most sophisticated bank regulations ever developed in the world. These regulations are included in this book to underline two important facts:

1. These regulations are intended to make sure that every citizen in America is treated fairly without any sort of discrimination, and that the money deposited in the depository institutions is protected and safe. This is important because those who are involved in RF banking and its development need not reinvent the wheel; the existing regulations are built on a huge body of human experience, and it is hoped that RF banks' development efforts can begin by using such regulations as a base for further growth.
2. Many of these regulations have Judeo-Christian-Islamic roots.

In addition to the banking regulations, this section attempts to familiarize the reader with the process of regulating and supervising banks.

Consumer Compliance Management

Every bank in America is required to manage the entire consumer compliance process using an overall *compliance management system*. The system includes a compliance program and a compliance audit function, sometimes referred to as compliance review or self-assessment. The *compliance program* consists of the policies and procedures that guide employees' adherence to banking laws and regulations. After the 2008 financial meltdown, Congress reformed existing regulations and instituted many new banking and finance company regulations through a new act called the Dodd-Frank Act. The act was passed in 2010 and is named after the two representatives who took the lead to issue it. One of the new institutions created to cater to compliance and consumer protection is the Consumer Financial Protection Bureau (CFPB), which is charged with protecting consumers while benefiting from diverse financial services in America.

The *consumer compliance audit function* is an independent testing of the bank's transactions to determine its level of compliance with consumer protection laws and regulations, as well as the effectiveness of, and its adherence to, its own policies and procedures.

Board of Directors and Management Supervision and Administration

Compliance with U.S. banking laws and regulations at every bank is managed as an integral part of the bank's business strategy. The bank's board of directors and management recognize the scope and implications of laws and regulations that apply to the bank. The *compliance management system* should be designed to ensure that the bank's clients and customers are treated fairly and justly, according to the highest ethical standards, laws, and regulations, to protect the bank. Bank resources are expected to be used effectively to minimize any disruptions in daily activities due to compliance issues.

To ensure an effective approach to compliance, the board and management must take the business of compliance very seriously and make it a top priority. The participation of senior management in the development and maintenance of a compliance program is the pillar of the process. The board and senior management should periodically review the effectiveness of its compliance management system in most cases through a compliance management committee that meets regularly. This review includes reports that identify any weaknesses or required modifications due to changes in laws, regulations, or policy statements. Prompt and capable management response to those weaknesses and required changes is the final measure of the compliance system's effectiveness. The bank's senior management is required to assign a well-qualified staff and the necessary resources to properly implement and administer the compliance program. Participation in the compliance management system at all levels is important to its success.

Compliance Program

Each bank is expected to aspire to have in place a carefully devised, implemented, and monitored program that will provide a solid foundation for compliance. The bank's management will continually evaluate its organization and structure and modify its existing program to ensure that the compliance program meets its specific emerging new needs.

A *compliance committee* is appointed by the board and is headed by a *chief compliance officer*, who has specific responsibilities and authorities.

Compliance Committee

The board is required to organize the compliance committee, which is chaired by the chief compliance officer. A typical committee in a small community bank would include the following members:

- Chief credit officer (committee chairman)
- Chief of operations and private banking manager (deputy committee chairman)
- Chief financial officer (deputy committee chairman)
- Manager of loan administration and credit analysis
- Technology coordinator

The bank compliance committee may have the following subgroups, which will focus on specific compliance activities:

- New Accounts, Customer Service, and Information Security and Technology Compliance
- Credit Operations Compliance
- Financial and Accounting Operations Compliance

The committee is expected to meet periodically (e.g., quarterly) or on an as-needed basis.

Duties, Responsibilities, Authorities, and Accountability of the Compliance Committee

The consumer compliance committee will be responsible for the following tasks:

- Design, implement, test, proctor, and certify the compliance program.
- Develop and continually update all bank policies and procedures.
- Develop a continual training and educational program to train the staff, management, and directors on issues pertaining to compliance.
- Develop an internal audit program to self-audit different aspects of the compliance functions using outside independent auditors.
- Perform an annual risk-based audit program to identify areas of the bank operations that need auditing and the frequency needed to perform the audit.
- Develop the compliance audit scope in light of a *risk-based audit program*, and screen outside independent auditors to identify the most qualified entity that can perform the audit.
- Make recommendations to the board of directors regarding the outside independent auditor(s) and scope of each audit; the board of directors has final approval.
- Perform internal auditing of the compliance of each subgroup in a *certification program* to ensure that each department has external oversight (e.g., the credit group would audit the operations group; the operations group would audit and certify the financial and accounting group; and the financial and accounting group would audit and certify the credit group).

Clearly, the formality of the compliance program will increase in direct proportion to asset size, complexity, or diversity (including geographic) of operations of the bank. The board of directors and upper management should discuss these needs as they develop and should promptly take action to meet these needs.

Internal Controls

Internal controls are the systems through which the bank provides and ensures continuing compliance. These generally consist of sound organizational structures, comprehensive policies and procedures, and adequate training.

Organizational Structure

The ability of the compliance committee to implement the compliance program, administer it, and institute effective corrective action depends on that committee's authority, independence, and role, as perceived by other employees, as well as on the support provided by the board and senior management. The compliance committee should be able to:

- Perform audits across departmental lines.
- Access all operational areas.
- Ensure that line management implements corrective actions/changes in policies and procedures.

Policies and Procedures

An effective compliance program includes compliance policies and procedures. Policies provide the framework for the bank's procedures and a source of reference and training for the bank's personnel. Comprehensive and fully implemented policies communicate clearly with all bank personnel the board's and senior management's commitment to compliance. Procedures must be developed to implement the bank's policies. Generally, the degree of detail, specificity, and formality will vary according to the complexity of the issues or transactions addressed by such procedures. Policies and procedures at the bank must be designed to provide personnel with enough information to complete a normal transaction, to the best of management's abilities and taking in consideration the size of the bank. These policies and procedures may include appropriate regulation definitions, sample forms and instructions, and—where appropriate—directions for routing, review, retention, and destruction of the transaction documents.

Training

Education of the bank's personnel is essential to maintaining a sound compliance program. All personnel should be generally familiar with the consumer protection laws and regulations, and should receive comprehensive education in the banking laws and regulations that directly affect their jobs. They must also be trained in the policies and procedures adopted by the bank to ensure compliance with those laws. The faculty of the training program consists of bank board members, senior management, and invited guest trainers from auditing and training organizations. The training program may use videos and training materials obtained from different sources, such as the American Bankers Association (ABA) and other private corporations like Bankers Online (www.BankersOnline.com). The training program is detailed in Chapter 13.

Compliance Audit Function

The other component of a comprehensive compliance management system is a *compliance audit function*. It enables the board and senior management to monitor the effectiveness of the compliance program. The audit function tests the bank's compliance with consumer protection laws and adherence with policies and procedures. An effective compliance audit function should address all products and services offered by the bank, all aspects of applicable operations, and all departments and branch locations. Our team at the Bank of Whittier has developed a pioneering risk-based audit analysis algorithm that was implemented in the form of a computer program, which we use to identify the suitable frequency of conducting each audit in each area of bank operations, based on the many factors that may impact bank operations such as the economy, oil prices, inflation, political developments, staff experience, changes in staff, changes in management, changes in laws and regulations, and the like.

SUMMARY OF FEDERAL BANKING REGULATIONS IN THE UNITED STATES[9]

The following pages summarize some of the important U.S. banking regulations. These regulations are intended to make sure that the financial system in the United States is well regulated and streamlined to prevent any excesses or mismanagement. All these add to the worldwide credibility of the U.S. dollar as a reserve currency of the world. Regulators' main objective is to make sure that the banks' financial services are performed in a universal and standardized regulatory fashion to regulate the banking business in the states of the United States, which in fact resemble 50 different nations. These regulations are improved on a continual basis in the United States, as we have seen, in response to unfortunate experiences of excesses and malpractice. The regulations are built on a vast body of human experience over the years since the dawn of history. As we read in the Qur'aan about justice, discrimination, and fair dealing among people:

> *55:9 weigh, therefore, [your deeds] with equity, and cut not the measure short!*
>
> 10:47 NOW *every community has had an apostle; and only after their apostle has appeared [and delivered his message] is judgment passed on them, in all equity; and never are they wronged.*
>
> *11:85 Hence, O my people, [always] give full measure and weight, with equity, and do not deprive people of what is rightfully theirs, and do not act wickedly on earth by spreading corruption.*
>
> 16:90 BEHOLD, *God enjoins Justice, and the doing of good, and generosity towards [one's] fellow-men; and He forbids all that is shameful and all that runs counter to reason, as well as envy; [and] He exhorts you [repeatedly] so that you might bear [all this] in mind.*
>
> *42:42 blame attaches but to those who oppress [other] people and behave outrageously on earth, offending against all right: for them there is grievous suffering in store!*

One of the purposes of including some of the important U.S. banking regulations in this book is to introduce the respected readers of this book who may be government officials in many of the developing countries. These regulations should also benefit RF (Islamic) banking and finance scholars, executives, and practitioners. It is hoped that they will be motivated to study these regulations carefully and learn from them. If we want to develop a specialized set of regulations for an RF banking and finance system, we will not have to start from scratch. Some of these regulations are also included to draw the attention of the eminent scholars to the fact that it is definitely not enough to "devise a financing model" and issue a *fatwa* (an edict) pronouncing that the RF model used by a certain bank is Shari'aa compliant. Many more aspects of the real spirit of the RF system are based on Judeo-Christian-Islamic values, many of which are catered to by these regulations.

Regulation B: Equal Credit Opportunity

The *Equal Credit Opportunity Act* (ECOA) states that creditors (including banks, retailers, finance companies, and bank card/credit card companies) that regularly extend credit to customers should evaluate candidates on creditworthiness alone, rather than other factors (e.g., age, race, color, religion, national origin, marital status, or sex). Discrimination on the basis of marital status, welfare percipience, or age is generally prohibited (with exceptions), as is discrimination based on a consumer's good faith exercise of their credit protection rights. This regulation is a manifestation of the values of all faiths, including the Judeo-Christian-Islamic faith system, and it forms the foundation of real belief in God. It helps achieve the ultimate goal of the Judeo-Christian-Islamic value system, which requires that credit must be a basic human right.

The ECOA must be translated into a policy of fair lending by the board of directors of each bank in the system. Each bank is required to post a special logo that tells all customers that the bank implements the ECOA.

Fair Lending Policy

The bank should extend (and service) all types of credit consistent with safe and sound operational practices. The bank should also originate loans in such a way as to help meet the credit needs of the communities, including low- and moderate-income neighborhoods. All credit decisions must be based on adequate investigation and the application of sound judgment supported by verified facts. The application of credit guidelines and policies must be uniform for all persons and organizations and never based on race, sex, sexual orientation, color, national origin, religion, age, marital status, disability, or any other prohibited basis. This policy is an integral part of each bank's fundamental mission of providing quality financial services to existing and prospective customers.

Banks must realize that in granting credit, they also build customer relationships, and it is only through these relationships that the banks can achieve sustained, long-term success. A bank must be committed to the principle that every applicant for credit receives fair and equal treatment throughout the credit application and approval process. This principle is embodied in the ECOA and the Fair Housing Act (FHA).

General Policy Statement

Banks must commit to not discriminate with respect to any aspect of a credit decision on the basis of race, color, religion, national origin, sex, marital or familial status, disability, age (provided that an applicant has the capacity to enter into a binding contract), receipt of income from any public assistance program, sexual orientation, military status, or the good faith exercise of any rights under the federal Consumer Credit Protection Act. Every bank in the American banking system is required to fully commit to the principle that all credit decisions should be made without regard to race or any other discriminatory basis that is prohibited by law. Each bank should recognize that affirmative steps must be taken to ensure that this policy is applied consistently and continuously through all aspects of its credit operations, including product design, marketing and advertising, and application and underwriting processes. Each bank is required to regularly monitor its lending activities to make certain that they comply with this policy. When internal and external reviews suggest that a deviation from the policy may have occurred, the bank is expected and required to act expeditiously to investigate and, if necessary, institute corrective measures.

Advertising

Each bank should commit not to engage in advertising practices that would discourage, on a basis prohibited by law, the making or pursuing of an application for credit and should comply with the requirements of applicable laws relating to the nondiscriminatory advertising of credit. Where required, all advertising, press releases, and marketing materials for the bank's lending activities must include a facsimile of the equal housing lender logotype and legend.

Applications and Information Gathering

Oral or written statements that tend to discourage potential applicants on a basis prohibited by law must not be employed with regard to oral or written inquiries and applications. The application process must be neutral in nature and of a type applicable to every applicant desiring the same kind and amount of credit. Credit analysts, private bankers, and other bank employees involved in the loan origination process may not ask prohibited questions regarding:

- A spouse or former spouse
- Age
- Marital status
- Familial status
- Military status
- Sex
- Alimony, child support, or separate maintenance income
- Childbearing
- National origin
- Race

- Color
- Religion
- Sexual orientation

Application Processing and Evaluation and Loan Application Second Review Process

A bank must not use any information it obtains to discriminate on a prohibited basis. No loan application submitted to the bank will be declined unless the decision to decline is supported by sufficient documentation.

Credit Extension

A bank must commit that it will not discriminate on a prohibited basis in the extension or denial of credit.

Notification

A bank is required to provide notices of action taken on loan applications in accordance with the provisions of the ECOA and Federal Reserve Board Regulation B, described earlier.

Record Retention

A bank is required to maintain the following information, as required by law:

- Application form.
- Written or recorded information used in evaluating an application.
- Written or recorded information regarding any action taken concerning a new or existing extension of credit, including a copy of any statement of specific reasons for adverse action.
- Information obtained for purposes of government monitoring.
- Any claim or accusation of alleged discrimination or other violation of law submitted by an applicant or existing customer.

Unless a shorter retention period is permitted by applicable law, the information listed must be maintained for a minimum of 12 months (nonconsumer) or 25 months (consumer) after the date on which the bank notifies an applicant of action taken on an application or of incompleteness of an application.

Government Monitoring Program

As required by applicable law, a bank is required to request and maintain information from loan applicants on race, ethnicity, and sex or any other questions that may create a sensitivity that will lead to discrimination of any sort to allow the government to monitor compliance with nondiscrimination laws.

Fair Lending Training

Bank personnel involved in lending are required to receive appropriate training on fair lending laws and regulations periodically from the bank.

Regulation C: Home Mortgage Disclosure Act (HMDA)[10]

The instinct of owning a place in which to live and to produce a livelihood is a natural dream for every individual and family.[11] The engine that powers economic development throughout history has been the desire to have a place to live and a means of transportation. In today's language, that means owning a house and an automobile. That is why the twin backbones of major developed countries and societies have been the housing and automobile industries. The development of mortgage financing in the United Kingdom, Germany, and the United States has helped propel the economies directly and indirectly:

- Economies are propelled *directly* by increasing demand for the products, industries, and services associated with building homes.
- Economies are propelled *indirectly* by satisfying the citizen's natural instinct for ownership by making him/her feel that he/she owns a house—"a piece of the rock." This feeling of ownership makes the citizen proud of his/her citizenship, deepens the feeling of belonging to the country, and enhances the value of the real estate in general, as owners strive to beautify their owned properties by continually maintaining and improving them. Owning a home strengthens the feeling of responsibility toward the country, the citizens' own families, and the community at large.

One of the important parameters used by the U.S. Federal Reserve System in its decision regarding interest rate and monetary policy is setting the interest rates (as discussed in Chapter 5) and its impact on the housing and automobile industries.

In an effort by the government to monitor home financing activities in every small town, neighborhood, or city throughout the United States, each home mortgage financing participant—including each bank and mortgage finance company—is required to complete a special government form designed to reveal any implicit or systematic discrimination against any minority when it comes to home financing. This act was designed to eradicate to the best possible ability of the government any discrimination activity, such as the most well-known scheme (practiced in the 1970s) called *red zoning*. In this scheme, different areas in a city were red-zoned to indicate that such areas were high-risk areas and that lending there would be dangerous because of the ethnic character of those who lived there. This practice, of course, made the low-income and poor neighborhoods suffer. The *Home Mortgage Disclosure Act* (HMDA) was enacted by the Congress in 1975 (as amended) and is implemented by the Federal Reserve Board's *Regulation C* (12 CFR 203). HMDA requires financial institutions to maintain and annually disclose data about home purchases, home purchase preapprovals, home improvement, and refinance applications involving one- to four-unit and multifamily dwellings. It also requires branches and loan centers to display a special HMDA logo on all its communications, publications, website, and advertising materials.

Purpose of the Act

The purpose of the HMDA is to provide the public with loan data that can be used (1) to help determine whether financial institutions are serving the housing needs of their communities, (2) to assist public officials in distributing public-sector investment to attract private investment to areas where it is needed, and (3) to assist in identifying possible discriminatory lending patterns and in enforcing antidiscrimination statutes.

It was also made very clear in the act that "neither the Act nor this regulation is intended to encourage unsound lending practices or the allocation of credit."

Reporting Requirements

Financial institutions must report data regarding applications for home purchase loans, home improvement loans, and refinancing, whether originated, purchased, turned down, or canceled. HMDA requires lenders to report information on the following:

- The loan, as to its type, amount, and pricing and whether the loan is subject to the *Home Ownership and Equity Protection Act* (15 USC 1639).
- The property, as to its location and type, and the disposition of the application, including whether it was originated or denied; in case of denial, lenders must report the reason for declining.

- The applicant's ethnicity, race, gender, and gross income for mortgage applicants and borrowers.
- In case loans are sold, the type of purchaser for mortgage loans that were sold.

Denial Reasons and Other Data

Financial institutions regulated by the OCC, such as national banks, are required to provide reasons for denials. Providing reasons for denials is optional for financial institutions supervised by the Federal Reserve and the FDIC.

Disclosure

As a result of amendments to the HMDA incorporated within the *Housing and Community Development Act* of 1992, an institution must make its disclosure statement available to the public at its home office within three business days of receipt.

Training and Oversight Responsibilities

Each loan officer is required to attend HMDA training at least annually.

Regulation Q: Prohibition against Payment of Interest on Certain Deposit Account Types

Regulation Q, which was rescinded in 2011 with the new Dodd-Frank Act, prohibited banks, starting in 1933, from paying interest on *demand deposit accounts* (DDAs). Banks, however, were allowed by this regulation to pay interest on *negotiable order of withdrawal* (NOW) checking accounts offered to consumers and certain entities (but not to commercial enterprises, other than sole proprietorships).

This regulation is very interesting for RF bankers because it stipulates *not to pay interest.* I am stating this because in many of the applications made by RF bankers to operate in the West, one of the main negotiation issues has been the payment of interest on some deposits and the requirement of many of the Islamic banking eminent scholars to expose the bank deposits to bank profit and loss, with the possibility of losing depositors' money. We will discuss this issue further in Part Two of this book.

Regulation D: Reserve Requirements for Depository Institutions (Banks)

As we discussed in the summary of Regulation Q, banks were not allowed to pay interest on their DDA checking accounts. Regulation D was devised after the introduction of what are known as NOW accounts, which were allowed to earn interest in order to allow banks to compete with investment banks, whose banking products included interest-bearing money market mutual funds that offered interest on invested cash (deposits that are not FDIC insured). The regulation was devised in an effort to limit frequent withdrawals from these accounts, which may cause the bank to undermine its long-term investment commitment in the community (by keeping a larger percentage of its assets in cash to meet these unexpected withdrawals). Following are the objectives of Regulation D:

- To establish reserve requirement guidelines.
- To regulate certain early withdrawals from CD accounts.
- To define what qualifies as DDA /NOW accounts (please see Regulation Q regarding eligibility rules for interest-bearing checking accounts).
- To define limitations on certain withdrawals on savings and money market accounts.
- To establish that unlimited transfers or withdrawals are permitted if made in person, by ATM, by mail, or by messenger.

In all other instances, there is a limit of six transfers or withdrawals per month. No more than three of these transactions may be made payable to a third party (by check, draft, point-of-sale, etc.).

The bank must close accounts where this transaction limit is constantly exceeded.

Regulation O: Loans to Bank Insiders

This regulation was devised to make certain that bank insiders, such as directors, senior management, and/or principal shareholders, are not getting preferential treatment, over what the consumer is offered, when they deal with the bank (e.g., by receiving higher rates on their deposits than what the bank gives a regular consumer), are not given preferential credit standards when they apply for credit (e.g., by obtaining credit at lower rates and easier loan terms than the public), do not have access to other customers' private information, and do not "front" others in making business decisions based on their preferred position and insiders' information.

Regulations P and S

Regulation P requires all banks and financial institutions to safeguard all personal financial information given by the customer and not to release any such information to a third party, be it an affiliate, an advertising agency, or even a government agency, unless authorized by that customer. In addition, the financial institution is required to mail all its customers a letter—on an annual basis—detailing the institution's *privacy policy*. A copy of the letter sent by one of the community banks is shown in Box 8.1.[12] It is also interesting to note that if a wife opens an account in her name only, her husband cannot get any information about that account without the approval of the wife, the owner of the account.

This regulation is considered to be an important expression of the Judeo-Christian-Islamic value system, which has at its core a fundamental and keen intent to respect and guard private and personal information. In fact, this kind of policy is an important feature of the Judeo-Christian-Islamic Shari'aa law that should be highlighted to RF banking scholars as they expand their efforts to establish a universal set of regulations that will truly express these values of the Judeo-Christian-Islamic system. Many countries claim they apply the law (Shari'aa) as the source of their legal systems or as the foundations of their legal systems, but they have no respect for the private domain of their citizens. In these countries, financial, personal, and corporate information is compromised easily, and privacy is violated without a court order or even allowing those whose rights were violated any legal recourse.

Please see Box 8.1 for a sample privacy letter that the Bank of Whittier sends to its customers.

BOX 8.1 A SAMPLE PRIVACY LETTER SENT TO ALL CUSTOMERS AT LEAST ONCE A YEAR[13]

Bank of Whittier, NA, Right to Financial Privacy Policy

Because Your Trust Is So Important

Your trust is the cornerstone of our relationship. This is why we work diligently to safeguard your privacy. The information that you provide us is kept in the strictest confidence. We have no intention of selling personal information about you, the Customer(s), to any third-party businesses. We are proud to make this commitment to our Customers, because your trust is the foundation of our business. The following privacy policy explains how we use and protect information about our Customers. Please read this very important information carefully.

Notice of Customer's Financial Privacy Rights

The terms *we, our,* and *us,* when used in this notice, are defined as Bank of Whittier, NA.

We define our "Customers" or "you" as having a continuing relationship through the following types of accounts with us:

- Deposit account
- Loan account
- Safe deposit box

As the Customer of the Bank, you will be notified of any sources for nonpublic personal information we collect on you. We will notify you as to any measures we have taken to secure the information. We must first define a few terms.

Nonpublic personal information is information about you that we collect in connection with providing a financial product or service to you. Nonpublic personal information does not include information available from public sources, such as telephone directories or government records.

An *affiliate* is a company we own or control; a company that owns or controls us; or a company that is owned or controlled by the same company that owns or controls us. Ownership does not mean complete ownership, but means owning enough to have control.

A *nonaffiliated third party* is a company that is not an affiliate of ours.

The Bank of Whittier, NA, Privacy Promise for Costumers

While information is the cornerstone of our ability to provide superior service, our most important asset is our customers' trust. Keeping customer information secure, and using it only as our customers would want us to, is a top priority for all of us at Bank of Whittier.

Our promise to our Customers:

We will safeguard, according to strict standards of security and confidentiality, any information our customers share with us.

We will limit the collection and use of customer information to the minimum required to deliver superior service to our customers, which includes advising our customers about our products, services, and other opportunities as well as administering our business.

We will permit only authorized employees who are trained in the proper handling of customer information to have access to your information. Employees who violate our Privacy Promise will be subject to our normal disciplinary process.

We will not reveal customer information to any external organization unless we have previously informed the customer in disclosures or agreements, have been authorized by the customer, or are required by law or our regulators.

We will always maintain control over the confidentiality of our customer information.

Whenever we hire a third party to provide support services, we will require them to conform to our privacy standards and conduct regular audits to ensure compliance.

For purposes of credit reporting, verification, and risk management, we will exchange information about our customers with reputable reference sources and clearinghouse services.

We will not use or share—internally or externally—personally identifiable medical information for any purpose other than the underwriting or administration of a customer's account, or as disclosed to the customer when the information is collected, or to which the customer consents.

We will attempt to keep customer files complete, up to date, and accurate. We will notify our customers on how and where to conveniently access their account information (except when we are prohibited to do so by law) and how to notify us about errors, which we will promptly correct.

The Confidentiality, Security, and Integrity of Your Nonpublic Personal Information

We restrict access to nonpublic personal information about you to only those employees who need to know the information to provide products or services to you. We maintain physical, electronic, and procedural safeguards that comply with federal standards to guard your nonpublic personal information.

The Nonpublic Personal Information that We Collect

We collect nonpublic personal information about you from the following sources:

- Information we receive from you on applications or other forms.
- Information about your transactions with us.
- Information about your transactions with nonaffiliated third parties.
- Information we receive from a consumer reporting agency.

The Nonpublic Personal Information that We Disclose

We do not disclose, nor do we reserve the right to disclose, any nonpublic personal information about our customers or former customers to anyone, except as permitted by law.

Regulation Z: Truth in Lending Act (TILA)

This regulation is one of the most important consumer protection regulations in the United States, and it must be as well to RF bankers around the world. Prior to its enactment, banks lent money at a purportedly low interest rate, but they would charge a number of additional fees that, if added up, would result in a much higher implied interest rate. It was imperative to legal experts and regulators to create a standardized "yardstick" by which the consumer could compare various banks' offers to finance his/her needs. That was the motivation behind Regulation Z, which requires that whenever money changes hands between two persons or entities, the return realized should be expressed in terms of an "implied" interest rate, and that in calculating it, all pertinent fees and costs should be included.

Regulation BB: Community Reinvestment Act (CRA)

The Community Reinvestment Act (CRA) requires banks to define an assessment geographical area in the city or state they operate that they will be serving. Based on this, the regulators monitor the bank's lending activities to make sure that:

- The bank's loan to deposit ratio is at least 50 percent.
- The bank's loan portfolio has at least 50 percent of its loans extended to consumers and entities in the declared assessment area.
- The bank lends to all segments of the community that reside in the assessment area without discrimination and in a way that reflects the demographic nature of the communities residing in these areas including their income. This prevents the banks from only financing the rich and leaving the medium and low income members of the community without credit availability; another important Judeo-Christian-Islamic principle that should be focused on in RF banking. This was clearly expressed in the revelations of all God's books including the Qur'aan.

This is an important regulation that is needed in most, if not all, of the developing countries of the world, including those which have a thriving RF banking industry. One of the most important revelations of God to all of us in all of His messages and through all of His messengers, as taught by the Judeo-Christian-Islamic value system, is to reinvest in the communities to which one belongs and from which banks gather their deposits. This regulation is very important, because in my travels throughout the world, both in the developing non-Muslim and Muslim countries, I was sorry to see that the public banking and credit needs are underserved. The banks collected people's savings and used the money to extend credit mostly to the rich and affluent, and/or reinvested them in financing projects that were only short term in nature; most of the financing was done to facilitate import-related businesses, rather than long-term development and strategic projects. I also discovered that in most of these countries, most banks' loan-to-deposit ratio is 50 percent or less. If this happened in a bank in the United States, the bank would be cited by the regulators for not implementing the CRA and would be required to increase its financing activity in the community. If the bank did not comply within a limited time, its license to operate would be suspended and/or revoked.

Another disappointing fact is that banks in many of these countries invest the excess liquid money left over in their coffers outside the country, which results in two violations. The first is violating our covenant with the higher authority, God, to reinvest in our communities and to change the fortunes of all people to a better future. The second violation is a violation of the CRA. I once was visiting a country in North Africa, and during a meeting with local bankers I shared with them the aspects of the CRA applied in the United States. It was a great revelation to them. I told them that in the United States, according to the CRA, all insured depository institutions are required to reinvest in the communities they serve. It was also suggested that government regulators should require banks there to spend documented efforts with measured acceptable results in an effort to increase banking and credit services to all people, including low- and moderate-income areas, communities, and individuals—of course, without compromising basic safe credit standards. Insured depository institutions in America must display and make available to the public a CRA notice describing their activities and efforts to serve local communities. To meet that requirement, each bank branch must have a current CRA public file or access to it via the company's website. The bank has 10 days to provide the information to any questions on the CRA if asked in person or via mail.

Regulation DD: Truth in Savings Act

Regulation DD requires all banks and other depository, savings, and investment institutions to be truthful when they advertise the interest rate they promise to pay the customer who deposits and/or saves with them and the return on investment realized when a customer invests with one of these institutions. Some banks and financial representatives, in their pursuit to attract as many deposits and investments as possible, quote and/or promise higher "interest" or "returns" in their advertising. Regulation DD requires the bank to be complete in advertising the interest rate based on a universal standard format that is used to calculate the interest on deposits, so that the customer can make a fair comparison. This standard will help the consumer compare "apples for apples" and make an educated decision when he/she decides to invest or save. For example, the bank must disclose the method it used when it calculated the promised rate—for example, whether the advertised rate was a *compounded* or a *simple* rate.

Fair Credit Reporting Act

The Fair Credit Reporting Act requires all financial institutions and banks to exercise great care to be accurate and truthful while reporting their customers' credit history and pattern of paying back their debts and commitments to recognized credit reporting agencies. It is a known fact that consumers' credit ratings are of prime importance when a bank decides whether to extend credit to and/or to do business with a customer. That is why the regulation stipulates detailed methods, ways, and means to ensure protection of the consumer and the timely correction of errors if these errors occur, as well as charging penalties if the credit report was erroneous—particularly if it was done intentionally.

Anti–Money Laundering (AML) Program

To enhance domestic security and eradicate illegal activities that include drug trafficking and following the terrorist attacks of September 11, 2001, Congress passed the USA PATRIOT Act, which contained provisions for fighting international money laundering and blocking terrorists' access to the U.S. and global financial systems. The provisions of the USA PATRIOT Act that affect banking organizations were generally set forth as amendments to the Bank Secrecy Act (BSA), which was enacted in 1970.

The BSA requires financial institutions doing business in the United States to report large currency transactions and to retain certain records, including information about persons involved in large currency transactions and about suspicious activity related to possible violations of federal law such as money laundering, terrorist financing, and other financial crimes. The BSA also prohibits the use of foreign bank accounts to launder illicit funds or to avoid U.S. taxes and statutory restrictions. The U.S. Department of the Treasury maintains primary responsibility for issuing and enforcing regulations to implement this statute.

The U.S. Department of the Treasury has delegated to the federal financial regulatory agencies the responsibility for monitoring banks' compliance with the BSA. The Federal Reserve Board's Regulation H requires banking organizations to develop a written program for BSA compliance. During examinations of national and state member banks and U.S. branches and agencies of foreign banks, OCC (in the case of national banks) and Federal Reserve examiners verify an institution's compliance with the record-keeping and reporting requirements of the BSA and with related regulations, including those related to economic sanctions imposed by Congress against certain countries, as implemented by the Office of Foreign Assets Control (OFAC). It is beyond the scope of this book to detail such regulations.

Bank Examination for Safety and Soundness by Bank Regulators

Every bank in America is examined on a regular basis (if it is a large bank, the OCC would have permanent examiners on-site throughout the year) or on a cyclical basis (in the case of smaller banks, the cycle would be from 12 months in the case of banks that need closer supervision to 18 months for low-risk banks that are known to have capable and wise management and was proven to have a good track record of compliance and low risk to its reputation, safety, and soundness). Box 8.2 presents a typical request letter sent from the OCC regulators to a bank president (in this case, it was me as a president of the Bank of Whittier, NA[14]) to enumerate and prepare all the documents needed to examine the bank. The reader will appreciate the detailed nature of the examination as shown in the large number of requests in the request letter; it is usually conducted by five to eight examiners over a period of three to four weeks—or more, depending on the size, the complexity of operations, bank products and services, and the condition of the bank. After concluding the examination, the bank is rated by the OCC according to each of five important parameters: capital (C), assets (A), management (M), earnings (E), liquidity (L), and sensitivity (S) to market risk (combining each of the first letters of each category gives the acronym CAMELS). A bank with a rating of 1 or 2 is considered superior, and of less than satisfactory status if it is rated 3, which means Needs Improvement. A bank that is rated 4 or below is required to agree to a *memorandum of understanding* with the regulators, in which the bank management makes promises in writing to the regulators about how it will operate and fix its problems according to a preapproved plan and a well-defined time table in the future. Or if the bank is in bad shape, it gets a *cease and desist* (C&D) order, which essentially freezes its operations in a stop and fix format in order to improve its status, and if not fixed, its charter (license) is revoked.

It is also important to note that not all regulations are tested and examined every year. In some years, in addition to the regular examination process, the regulators would also focus their attention on an issue or a number of issues that are considered to be of a high-risk nature (e.g., if there is a high historic risk of flooding in the year of the examination, the OCC examination pays a close attention on flooding compliance). It is also interesting here to recommend that compliance with the RF laws (Shari'aa) could be a part of this examination process in cases when a bank chooses to operate in an RF mode or chooses to include RF banking services as part of its service to the public.

Box 8.2 is a copy of what a bank receives from the regulators in order to prepare for the annual regulatory examination.

BOX 8.2 OCC REQUEST LETTER: FROM THE OCC OFFICE TO THE BANK'S PRESIDENT

In order for us to prepare effectively for this supervisory activity, we are asking you to provide the information listed in digital format. If this is not practical or becomes inefficient for you, please provide copies of the requested documents. Other large items may be provided in hardcopy form for return to the bank. Please indicate which items should be returned to the bank.

Please make available the following upon our arrival on (date of exam). Please forward any items marked by a check (X) to our southern California–North Field Office by [*deadline for submitting the requested documents*].

Management and Supervision

Unless otherwise stated, please provide the most recent information on the following:

- The board packet. Any information included in the packet and requested below need not be duplicated.
- Current organizational chart.
- If any changes have occurred since the last examination, a list of directors and executive management, and their backgrounds, including work experience, length of service with the bank, etc. Also, a list of committees, including current membership.
- A list of officers' salaries and compensation.
- If any changes have occurred since the last examination, a list of related organizations (e.g., parent holding company, affiliates, and operating subsidiaries).
- Most recent external audit reports, management letter, engagement letter, and management's responses to findings (including audits of outside service providers, if applicable).

- The internal audit schedule for the current year, indicating audits completed with summary ratings, and in process.
- Most recent internal audit reports, including management's responses. Include (20XX) audit reports covering loan administration, funds management and investment activities, Bank Secrecy Act program, risk based capital computations, information processing, and any audit areas that were assigned a less than satisfactory rating.
- Brief description of new products, services, lines of business, or changes in the bank's market area.
- List of data processors and other servicers (e.g., loan, investment). The detail of the list should include:

  a. Name of servicer.
  b. Address of servicer.
  c. Contact name and phone number.
  d. Brief explanation of the product(s) or service(s) provided.
  e. Note of any affiliate relationship with the bank.
  f. For example, services provided may include the servicing of loans sold in whole or in part to other entities, including the service provider. OCC examiners will use this list to request trial balances or other pertinent information not otherwise requested in this letter.
- Minutes of board and major committee meetings (e.g., Audit, Loan, Asset/Liability Management, Fiduciary, and Technology Steering Committee) since our last examination.

Asset Quality

Please provide copies of the following [*dated as of* XXXX]:

- List of watch list loans, problem loans, past-due credits, and nonaccrual loans.
- List of the 10 largest credits, including commitments, made since the last examination and the new loan report for the most recent quarter.
- Concentrations of credit reports.
- Policy, underwriting, collateral, and documentation exception reports.
- List of insider credits (to directors, executive officers, and principal shareholders) and their related interests. The list should include terms (rates, collateral, structure, etc.).

- List of loan participations purchased and sold, whole loans purchased and sold, and any securitization activity since the last examination.
- List of overdrafts.
- Analysis of the allowance for loan and lease losses including any risk rating changes from the most recent quarter.
- List of other real estate, repossessed assets, classified investments, and cash items.
- List of small business and farm loans "exempt" from documentation requirements.
- Latest loan review report, including any responses from the senior lending officer, account officers, etc.
- List of board-approved changes to the loan policy and underwriting standards since the last examination.
- The loan trial balance.
- The bank's loan policy including a description of the bank's risk rating system.

Financial Performance

Unless otherwise stated, please provide the most recent information on the following:

- Most recent Asset Liability Committee (ALCO) package.
- Most recent reports used to monitor and manage interest rate risk (e.g., gap planning, simulation models, and duration analysis).
- Most recent liquidity reports (e.g., sources and uses).
- List of investment securities purchased and sold for [*20XX*] and [*20XX*]. Please include amount, seller/buyer, and date of each transaction.
- Most current balance sheet and income statement.
- Most recent strategic plan, budget, variance reports, etc.
- Current risk-based capital calculation.
- Securities acquired based upon "reliable estimates" authority in 12 CFR 1.3(i).
- Securities acquired using the bank's lending authority.

- The prepurchase analysis for all securities purchased since the last examination.
- A summary of the primary assumptions used in the IRR measurement process and the source.
- Current contingency funding plan.
- Investment portfolio summary trial, including credit ratings.
- The list of board-approved securities dealers.
- List of shareholders and ownership.
- Most recent annual and quarterly shareholders' reports.
- Most recent Report of Condition and Income (call report).
- List of pending litigation, including a description of circumstances behind the litigation.
- Details regarding the bank's blanket bond and other major insurance policies (including data processing–related coverage). Provide name of insurer, amount of coverage and deductible, and maturity. Also, please indicate the date of last board review and whether the bank intends to maintain the same coverage upon maturity.
- Summary of payments to the holding company and any affiliates.
- Bank work papers for the most recent call report submitted.

Consumer Compliance

The consumer compliance examination is being conducted under the authority of 12 USC 481. However, it also constitutes an investigation within the meaning of Section 3413(h)(1)(A) of the Right to Financial Privacy Act. Therefore, in accordance with Section 3403(b) of the act, the undersigned hereby certifies that the OCC has complied with the Right to Financial Privacy Act, 12 USC 3401, et seq. Section 3417(c) of the act provides that good faith reliance upon this certification relieves your institution and its employees and agents of any possible liability to the consumer in connection with the disclosure of the requested information.

Unless otherwise stated, please provide the most recent information on the following:

- A list of approved changes to the bank's compliance policies and procedures since the last examination.
- A description of the bank's training programs and criteria for ensuring that employees receive job appropriate compliance training.

Flood Disaster Protection Act

Bank's policy and procedures applicable to compliance with the FDPA:

- A copy of bank contract(s) with third parties performing flood determination services.
- Flood maps used to determine whether a property is in a standard flood hazard area (SFHA), if available.
- A copy of flood notices.
- List of all loans located in special flood hazard areas.

Expedited Fund Availability Act

The bank's Regulation CC policy.

- Copy of your funds availability disclosure.
- Hold reports and/or records from the main office and branch office(s) for the past month.

Privacy of Consumer Financial Information

- Copies of privacy and information security policies and procedures.
- Describe key internal controls that ensure compliance.
- Copies of privacy notices (initial, annual, revised, opt-out, short-form, and simplified).
- List of affiliates and nonaffiliated third parties to whom the bank discloses nonpublic personal information about consumers, customers, and former customers:
    - Outside of the regulatory exceptions (Sections 13, 14, and 15); and
    - Under Section 13, including joint marketing agreements.
- Describe how the bank ensures that nonpublic personal information received from nonaffiliated financial institutions is reused and redisclosed according to regulatory requirements, and describe such sharing activities.
- Any records supporting the bank's categorization of its information sharing practices under Sections 13, 14, and 15, and outside the regulatory exceptions, if available.
- Information sharing agreements and contracts between the bank and its affiliates and between the bank and nonaffiliated third parties.

- A list of consumers who have opted out of the disclosure of nonpublic personal information to nonaffiliated third parties.
- Consumer and customer complaints regarding the treatment of nonpublic personal information.
- Nonaffiliated third-party complaint logs, telemarketing scripts, and any other information obtained from nonaffiliated third parties, if available.
- Compliance and audit work papers related to privacy.
- Training program information and materials.

Right to Financial Privacy Act

- Policies and procedures on the act.
- Requests for customers' financial records received from federal government authorities since the last examination.

Bankruptcy Laws[15]

One important and sometimes abused privilege available to U.S. citizens and businesses is the ability of the person or entity that obtained a credit facility to stand before a special bankruptcy judge in court to present the reasons why the person or the entity cannot meet their financial and other obligations by paying back what he/she owes the bank or the financial institution. These bankruptcy laws are given different titles, depending on the nature of the problem and the solution proposed and adopted by court. If there is an economic slowdown and demand declines, resulting in lower sales and hence lower net profits, the owner of the business can file for a request to the court to protect him/her and his/her business against foreclosure by creditors. The owner of the business would be requested to present the court with a plan to reorganize the business. The reorganization plan usually contains steps that will be taken by management to revive the business like reduction of overhead, increased sales, reduction of raw materials cost, reduction of labor, and a reduction of the monthly payment on a loan, and/or partial loan forgiveness as well as a timetable to get out of this dire situation. Another purpose of the bankruptcy laws is to maximize returns under adverse conditions by providing an orderly distribution of assets and debts.

This facility is considered an important development and a fair "safety valve" in the business of giving credit and in financing. Very disturbing situations and penalties have been reported regarding the failure of a borrower to meet his/her obligations to a bank for good and justifiable causes in other countries—including Islamic countries. Borrowers who do not fulfill their credit obligations are systematically jailed by the government, which resorts to throwing the business owner in jail and taking over the facility. In most cases, the facility is pillaged, the employees are laid off, and the facility is sold for next to nothing. Many developing countries practice such painful and unproductive but revengeful "therapy." I understand that this action can be condoned, and that this approach should be applied to those who defraud others by lying on an application for credit, intentionally misusing and siphoning funds outside the company or country, and/or outright racketeering. Punishment must be done by following due process according to the law and in the courts of law. However, the world has seen wonderful, honorable businesspeople end up in jail in one country or another in Africa, Asia, or the Middle East, and their facilities—along with the households of many of their employees—are shut down just because the economy is in decline or a government official wants to settle a political grudge with a particular family or a businessperson. That is another area that needs pioneering and dedicated work among the RF (Islamic) banking scholars who believe in applying the credible and attractive Judeo-Christian-Islamic value system to the RF banking system that we all aspire to grow. It is strongly recommended that similar provisions be included in the RF law guidelines by which RF banks operate.

REVIEW QUESTIONS

1. What is the difference between an investment bank and a commercial bank?
2. How was the mix-up between the services of investment banking and commercial banks responsible for the confusing state of affairs of Islamic banks?
3. What are the types of banks and cooperatives that are considered depository institutions available in the United States?
4. What is the difference between a commercial bank and a credit union?
5. What is the difference between a state bank and a national bank?
6. What is the FDIC in the United States? How does it operate? What are the levels of insured deposits in U.S. banks?
   a. If a person opens a personal account for himself only, how much is the account insured for by the FDIC?
   b. If a husband and wife open a joint account, how much is the account is insured for by the FDIC?

7. How are national banks regulated in the United States?
8. What is the OCC, and to whom does it report in the U.S. government? How does it operate and how is it funded?
9. What is the bank Examination for Safety and Soundness? Who conducts it for a national bank, and how it is conducted?
10. What is a CAMELS rating, and what does "CAMELS" stand for? Why is it important (but extremely kept confidential) for the bank?
11. With regard to U.S. banking regulations:
    a. What is consumer compliance? What is the premise it is built on by regulators?
    b. What is Regulation B?
    c. What is Regulation C?
    d. What is Regulation D?
    e. What is the TILA, and why it is important when applying RF banking and finance in the United States?
    f. What is the CRA regulation?
    g. What is the GLB Act regulation, and how important it is for safe and sound banking services in the United States?
    h. What is the Bank Secrecy Act (BSA)? How is it implemented in banks in the United States and why?
    i. What is the Anti–Money Laundering Act?
    j. What is the PATRIOT Act in general? As applied to banking?

NOTES

1. American Bankers Association (ABA), Private Communication: As of the end of 2007, there are 42,386 national (commercial) bank branches, 42,895 state commercial bank branches, 9,801 national savings banks, 4,067 state saving banks (savings banks used to be called savings and loan associations and financed homes and apartments), and 11 foreign banks.
2. LARIBA started LARIBA Bank of Kazakhstan in 1994, which offered RF community banking and RF mortgage financing in Kazakhstan for the first time in the history of Kazakhstan. The bank was sold in 2006 due to the increase in capital requirements by the national bank there.
3. Comptroller of the Currency, Administrator of National Banks, "National Banks and the Dual Banking System," September 2003.
4. Ibid.
5. Ibid.
6. Ibid.

7. For more information about the OCC, contact the Office of the Comptroller of the Currency, Communications Division, Washington, DC 20219, via telephone at 202-874-4700, or via the Web at www.OCC.Treas.gov.
8. As stipulated by the authority of regulation 12 U.S.C. 1818(a), 1819 (Tenth), 1828(a): Part 328 describes the official sign of the FDIC and prescribes its use by insured depository institutions. It also prescribes the official advertising statement insured depository institutions must include in their advertisements. For purposes of part 328, the term *insured depository institution* includes insured branches of a foreign depository institution. Part 328 does not apply to noninsured offices or branches of insured depository institutions located in foreign countries.
9. Banking regulations are labeled by an alphabetical letter, starting from A to Z and then AA to, say, CC. For a detailed listing and description of these regulations, please visit the U.S. Treasury Department website.
10. Pronounced "Hamda."
11. Yahia Abdul Rahman and Abdullah Tug, "Towards a LARIBA (Islamic) Mortgage Financing in the United States Providing an Alternative to Traditional Mortgages," Harvard University School of Law, October 9–10, 1998 (presentation).
12. Privacy letter sent annually by Bank of Whittier, NA. This letter is a copy of the 2007 edition of that letter.
13. Ibid.
14. The request letter sent by OCC to Bank of Whittier president in March 2008 to request documents that will help in their examination of the bank.
15. www.uscourts.gov/bankruptcycourts/bankruptcybasics/discharge.html.Chapter 7: The chapter of the Bankruptcy Code providing for *liquidation* (i.e., the sale of a debtor's nonexempt property and the distribution of the proceeds to creditors). Chapter 9: The chapter of the Bankruptcy Code providing for reorganization of municipalities (which includes cities and towns as well as villages, counties, taxing districts, municipal utilities, and school districts). Chapter 11: The chapter of the Bankruptcy Code providing (generally) for reorganization, usually involving a corporation or partnership. (A Chapter 11 debtor usually proposes a plan of reorganization to keep its business alive and pay creditors over time. People in business or individuals can also seek relief in Chapter 11.) Chapter 12: The chapter of the Bankruptcy Code providing for adjustment of debts of a "family farmer" or "family fisherman" as those terms are defined in the Bankruptcy Code. Chapter 13: The chapter of the Bankruptcy Code providing for adjustment of debts of an individual with regular income. (Chapter 13 allows a debtor to keep property and pay debts over time, usually three to five years.) Chapter 15: The chapter of the Bankruptcy Code dealing with cases of cross-border insolvency.

CHAPTER 9

Comparing RF Banking and Conventional Riba-Based Banking: What Is the Difference?

THE RF BANKING BRAND: HISTORY, DEVELOPMENT, AND STAGES OF GROWTH

Riba is prohibited in Judaism, Christianity, and Islam (as detailed in Chapter 2). The RF (riba-free) banking and finance system was started in the time of the Prophet Muhammad (pp); it revived and reinforced the teachings of Moses (pp) and Jesus (pp) in the seventh century and helped the growth of international trading, but it declined over the years and was dismantled completely after World War I and the resulting disassembly of the Ottoman Empire. The RF banking and finance system was left behind as the riba-based banking and finance system grew and developed in a more sophisticated way to meet the ever-growing volume and diversity of world economy and trade. New economic, monetary, political, and social systems were developed in Europe to cope with the changes of the Renaissance and, later, the Industrial Revolution. After World War I, most of the Muslim lands were occupied by the British and the French. It is believed by some that this was God's plan to wake up the people of these lands, to expose them to the Western world and bring them quickly to the latest developments of the nineteenth and early twentieth centuries. As a result, many young men and women were educated and became aware of the new world and its progress in the fields of education, medicine, engineering, technology, social relations, social sciences, banking and finance, and scientific research and development. A new generation of more educated and sophisticated Muslim leaders came in contact with Europe and began dreaming of catching up with its progress. At the same time, many Muslim religious leaders were sent to Europe—mainly to France, after Napoleon invaded Egypt and other Muslim countries in the Middle

East, and to a lesser extent to England—to obtain higher and graduate education and get exposed to the lifestyle and culture there. These students were sent from Egypt and India (now India, Pakistan, and Bangladesh). Many were graduates from religious schools such as Al-Azhar (the oldest Islamic seminary and university in the world) and other religious schools in India. They obtained postgraduate degrees from the leading universities in Europe and went back to their countries, aspiring to build a better future by sharing with their people what they had seen and how they had lived. In the process, they also shared their experiences and dreams about the future of their land. They started motivating people to work hard in order to catch up with Europe and its renaissance. They were assigned responsible posts in the government, such as the ministry of education (to develop a better education system for the future generations) and the ministry of finance (to help streamline and plan state finances and budgets). Many became famous newspaper editors and authors of books in general and about Islam and Prophet Muhammad (pp), using a new research-based approach with documentation and analysis in the way they had learned in Europe. Many of them started new political and civic movements to bring back the long-forgotten glory of the teachings of Islam—which is called in this book the Judeo-Christian-Islamic value system.

One of the first books I read back in 1964 was a small paperback titled *Bonook Bela Fawa'ed*, which means "banks without interest." It was a small book authored by the late Professor Eissa Abdou, a professor of commerce and economics at the second largest university in Egypt, Ain Shams University. I enjoyed reading the book; it was my introduction to a new world of banking. I understood its social objectives, intent, and implications, but I did not know much about its banking applications, because I did not even have a bank account then. Bank accounts were luxuries, reserved only for the rich and affluent professionals and millionaires.

The modern, practical Islamic banking movement started in Egypt around the early 1960s as a micro lending finance operation in a small village in the Nile Delta. It was started by a young German-educated Egyptian—Dr. Ahmad Al-Naggar (this is how it is pronounced in the Egyptian accent, but in the proper Arabic pronunciation it is Al-Najjar), who came back to Egypt with his German wife after finishing his education. He was distressed to see the poor farmers in his small village of Zefta/Mit Ghamr in the Egyptian Nile Delta lacking the funds needed to finance the purchase of seeds, farm animals needed to plow the land, cattle, animal feedstock, and simple pumps—even to finance their subsistence and basic needs until the crop was cultivated and sold on the market. The bank expanded its operations throughout the Egyptian farmland and became very popular until it was nationalized by the government of the late president Nasser[1] and renamed it Nasser Social Bank (*Bank Nasser Al Ijtma'ii*). Dr. Al-Naggar was instrumental in training a new generation of Islamic bankers; he started the Institute of Islamic Banking Training in Cairo and then moved it to Cyprus, which was politically less restrictive to many of the students, who were former bankers and accountants from all over the world. In the last years of his life, as he confided in me during one of his visits to Los Angeles while driving from Garden Grove, California, to Pasadena, California, he became very critical of the direction taken by the Islamic banking industry at that time because it concentrated more on form and less on substance and because it abandoned its social responsibility of assisting the poor and needy, and building the local communities that needed urgent help and instead focused on serving the rich.

The 1973 Arab-Israeli war (*Ramadan War in the Muslim world—the Yom Kippur war in Israel and many Western lands*) instigated the first oil crisis. The increase in oil prices from less than $2.40 per barrel to almost $12 a barrel brought large sums of cash to the oil-producing countries in the Gulf. This money generated a new class of dollars: petro-dollars. Many in the banking industry spoke about the absorptive capacity of the economies of the Gulf's oil-producing countries, describing the inability of their economies to absorb these large sums of money. In an effort to create good use of some of this huge cash flow, King Faisal (d. 1975) of Saudi Arabia set a goal for his country to develop Islamic banking and to develop economic cooperation among Muslim countries. He started the Islamic Development Bank (IDB) and initiated a new vision of an Islamic banking system. In Dubai, a futuristic leader by the name Sheikh Saeed bin Lutah started the Islamic Bank of Dubai. In Kuwait, Sheikh Bazee Al-Yaseen headed a new Islamic finance company called the Kuwait Finance House (KFH). KFH attracted huge deposits and built a strong customer base. KFH started its financing activities with auto financing and later became active in commodity trade finance and real estate financing for homes and commercial buildings.

In Saudi Arabia, two Islamic finance companies were started. One was started by King Faisal's son, Prince Muhammad Al-Faisal. It was registered in Switzerland and named Faisal Finance. Its headquarters were located in a wonderful high-rise blue glass building near the Geneva airport. From Geneva, they invested in commodities like gold (cash and carry contracts as well as commodities funds), and unfortunately lost a lot of money. Prince Muhammad Al-Faisal also received a full-service banking license to operate an Islamic bank in Egypt under the name Faisal Islamic Bank (*Bank Faisal Al-Islami*), which grew into one of the larger banks in Egypt, with more than 700,000 customers and many branches throughout Egypt. The other RF finance company was started by Sheikh Saleh Kamel; he called it *Dallah Al-Baraka*. Sheikh Saleh Kamel started branches, offices, and made investments in London, France, Egypt, Sudan, South Africa, Malaysia, Pakistan, Bangladesh, Turkey, Tunisia, Morocco, Algeria, and the United States. He also received a full-service banking license in Egypt and he called it the Egyptian Saudi Finance Bank (*Bank Al Tamweel Al Misry Al Saudi*). The bank now has many branches in Egypt. In the mid-1980s, he bought a small bank in London and operated it as the first Islamic bank ever in the United Kingdom. The bank was later asked to discontinue its operations by the British Financial Services Authority (FSA) because of noncompliance due to a number of operating shortcomings and because the owners (Al-Baraka) did not have a chartered bank in Saudi Arabia. It is interesting to note that Saudi Arabia did not have a full-service Islamic bank operating inside its territories until the mid-1990s. In the 1980s, Turkey got a new prime minster, the late Turgut Ozal, who had a keen interest in developing the fledgling economy of his country and ridding it of its tight-gripped military rulers. He started by developing strong relations and economic ties with many of the cash-rich Gulf oil-producing countries, especially Saudi Arabia and Kuwait. His government encouraged investments in and export to the Gulf countries. He also helped pass legislation to start what are called in Turkey *finance houses*, a code name for Islamic finance companies that operate like banks but are not called "Islamic" because of Turkish secular politics. The *finance house* name was arrived at in order not to create sensitivities around the long-standing Turkish policy coined by President Kemal Ataturk, the founder of the Republic of Turkey and the many who adhere to his policies. The long-standing Ataturk doctrine that made Turkey a secular and nonreligious country is still in effect today. Two finance houses were authorized. These were Faisal Finance (belonging to Prince Al-Faisal's operation) and Al-Baraka Turk Finance House (belonging to Al-Baraka in Saudi Arabia). All finance houses had a minimum ownership of 50 percent by local Turkish shareholders, as stipulated by Turkish law.

In the 1960s, Malaysia started a savings program to help its Muslim citizens perform pilgrimage (*hajj*). It is interesting to note here a popular religious practice in Malaysia and Indonesia; Muslims there believe that the most successful and blessed marriage is one which is consummated during the *hajj* season in Makkah (close to the *Kaa'bah*, the first house ever built to worship God by Prophet Abraham [pp] and his son [pp], which is close to the port of Jeddah, Saudi Arabia). They started a new savings organization to deposit parents' savings so that they could plan ahead; accumulating the cost needed to finance the *hajj* trip over the years from the time their child is born. This way, when the child grew up and was ready to get married, there would be enough money to perform *hajj* and consummate the marriage. The savings organization, called *Tabung Hajj*, gathered huge savings from devout Malaysian Muslims. It is important to note that most of the Malaysian Muslim religious leaders received their religious education in the 1950s and the 1960s in Cairo, at Al-Azhar University. There, they were taught about the prohibition of riba, which was called also interest (*fawa'ed*). Tabung Hajj began investing these funds in the proper RF way according to the law (Shari'aa) in huge palm tree plantations and in real estate projects in Malaysia and Indonesia; they realized great returns. They started an Islamic bank called *Bank Islam Malaysia*. Since that time, Malaysia has progressively become the leader in RF (Islamic) banking activities. In another development, after Malaysia became independent in the mid-1950s, tens of thousands of Malaysian students were sent for higher education in Egypt, England, Europe, and the United States. These graduates came back with big ideas dreaming of an advanced Malaysia.

I must share with the reader here that I spent at least 25 years of my life traveling extensively to Malaysia and getting to know its people at all levels very well. I was amazed to find out how bold the Malaysians were in their dreams, visions, and aspirations, and how courageous they were in not being afraid of implementing the boldest ideas very efficiently. Their achievement is in fact a manifestation of what people say: "You are as big as your dreams and goals." With these big dreams, the availability of the petrodollars from the Gulf oil-producing countries, and the interest of Japan and the United States in developing the Asian markets, Malaysia became a prime player in the world economic development matrix—and the RF banking movement in Malaysia grew with it. The central bank there—Bank Negara Malaysia (BNM)—pioneered a new approach to help support RF banking. They started to run two books: one book for RF (Islamic) banks and another for conventional banks. The government encouraged teaching RF banking at the International Islamic University Malaysia (IIUM) and started many training and research institutes in the field. They also established a Council of Scholars at the central bank level to establish the central bank's Shari'aa Board to operate and to develop RF banking and finance guidelines and regulations according to the rules and regulations of the RF law (Judeo-Christian-Islamic Shari'aa laws). They also developed new RF banking products and services that complied with Shari'aa and offered alternative RF banking services and products that could substitute and compete with those offered by riba-based conventional banks. The scholars in Malaysia were criticized severely by the scholars in the Arab Gulf countries for, what was labeled then, their liberal views, especially in the area of RF bonds—now called *sukuk*. (The word *check* in English originated from the Arabic word *sak*, or a promise to pay. The plural of *sak* in Arabic is *sukuk*).

In the West, new efforts were initiated to serve the British Muslim communities in the mid-1980s. HSBC and the United Bank of Kuwait (now part of Shamel Bank of Bahrain) started offering home financing services. HSBC called its services (which are now available in many parts of the world)

Amanah. United Bank of Kuwait called its home mortgage finance program Al-Manzil; it is still in use in the United Kingdom. The U.K. FSA authorized the Islamic Bank of Britain (IBB) as a full-service bank with some stiff requirements and guarantees from the shareholders, who come mostly from Qatar with a small shareholders position from Bahrain. In the United States, two companies started operations in 1987 to meet the growing demand among the expanding American Muslim community. These were American Finance House (LARIBA), which financed all community needs serving all Americans, Muslims and non-Muslims, like cars, homes, and businesses, and Muslim Savings and Investment company (MSI), which financed mostly homes. LARIBA grew and its shareholders acquired a full-service bank in 1998, as will be detailed later. MSI experienced significant losses in the housing development business and was later closed down after its contract for home financing was challenged in a Texas court (the case was settled out of court for an undisclosed sum of money paid by MSI). In the late 1990s, the United Bank of Kuwait began to offer its home financing in New York, along the same model it offered in the United Kingdom, but after almost two years of operations it was closed down. In the early 2000s due to a number of issues including noncompliance, HSBC started offering home financing in New York and offered services through a wholly-owned subsidiary they called Amanah, but it was not able to compete because the conventional mortgage staff was not sold on RF mortgage financing and was curtailed. A new home mortgage finance company called Guidance Residential Finance was started in 2001, and with LARIBA, this company became a major home mortgage financing company. Guidance relied in its sales and promotion campaign on the reputation and endorsement of a religious heavyweight adviser who was a chief religious justice and a former mufti in Pakistan.

Perhaps the most historic moment in the operations of RF financing of home mortgages came in 2001, when Freddie Mac approved LARIBA. In 2002, Fannie Mae followed. The support of Freddie and Fannie helped the growth of home mortgage financing using RF finance models in America. Instead of LARIBA being able to finance a home every two or three months, they were able to finance as many as 50 homes per month after the investments from Freddie and Fannie became available. Another first in the history of the United States was the issuing of RF mortgage-backed securities (RF MBSs) by LARIBA with Fannie Mae. These RF MBSs were based on RF mortgages produced by LARIBA with Fannie Mae. In 1998, some of the LARIBA shareholders acquired the Bank of Whittier, NA, and in 2003 a new RF banking team came to run the bank in an RF format. The bank offers financing of cars, homes, commercial buildings, businesses, churches, mosques (*masajid*), and schools. The Bank of Whittier also offers the entire standard banking services offered by any bank in the

United States in an RF format. The bank offers time certificates of deposit (CDs), which derive their income from the RF credit portfolio of the bank. Two other community banks entered the business by offering an Islamic banking window (mostly for home mortgages). These are Devon Bank of Chicago, Illinois, and University Bank of Detroit, Michigan. These banks meet the growing demand for RF banking and finance services in many parts of the United States.

AN OVERVIEW OF RF BANKING

RF banking is a faith-based and socially responsible brand of community banking. It is faith based because it bases its financing models, its operations, and the moral and ethical values of its staff, management, board of directors, and shareholders on Judeo-Christian-Islamic values. It is socially responsible because it applies the values of social responsibility of all those associated with it according to the same Judeo-Christian-Islamic values. For example, it looks at money not as a "thing" that can be rented at a price (called the interest rate), but as a measuring tool to measure the success or failure of investing. It is also concerned with the type of investment in which it invests its money. For example, RF banking does not invest in alcohol-related businesses, gambling and related businesses, promiscuous activities, or in businesses that are not environmentally and socially responsible. It also does not invest in businesses that are unfair to its labor and customers. RF banking does not finance speculative activities that are focused on making money out of money, based on speculations in the different financial, commodities, futures, derivatives, and real estate markets. RF banking is community banking at heart. It believes in community development. It considers its role to be a qualified professional entity that is sound, safe, responsible, and trustworthy to attract the deposits and savings of the community on one side and to reinvest such back in the community projects on the other side.

RF bankers work hard to reinvest these assets in the community by financing projects that will create economic prosperity, job opportunities, and, most importantly, peace and harmony within the community. RF banking does not discriminate, because discrimination in service, in financing, and in dealing with others is a major sin in all Abrahamic faiths. The RF banker is trained to have the interest of the customer and the community at large as his/her prime responsibility and passion. RF bankers are trained to serve their customers from a point of view of a real concern for what is beneficial and good to the family and for the preservation and growth of the family's wealth and assets.

The RF banker believes that his/her role is, in fact, not to generate as many loans and as much lending volume as possible for his/her bank, but rather to consider financing as a process of investing in and with the customer. This approach puts a great burden on RF bankers, because any investment must be prudently conceived, analyzed, and well thought out, and it must make economic sense. That is why all applications for RF financing are thoroughly studied, prudently analyzed, and evaluated in light of the best interests of the family, its nature, and its prior experience, as well as the prevailing economic, social, and political variables in the community and the country at large.

Misnomers in RF Banking

When RF banking was first presented in the early 1950s by Muslim scholars and activists, they attempted to popularize it by calling it *interest-free banking*. The early scholars believed that RF banking's most fundamental requirement was that both parties—the bank and the investor/depositor—participate in the profit and loss of the project they undertake. This made many newcomers who were engaged in the development of this new brand of banking focus on how to resolve two main issues. These were: (1) the removal of the word *interest* from the vocabulary of Islamic (RF) banking and the language of the contracts used, and (2) the restructuring of the transaction to make it appear as a buy/sell transaction, and that the financing institution should own the property—even for seconds—in a back-to-back agreement. An army of riba-based conventional bankers, banking and tax attorneys, and scholars in the Judeo-Christian-Islamic Shari'aa law spent years in the second half of the twentieth century developing contracts and models that were focused on trying to resolve these two important issues. The buy/sell and ownership aspect of the transaction were added later because in the Qur'aan we are taught that riba is not the same as buying and selling. The Qur'aan reveals, as quoted below, that buying and selling is different from riba because God made riba divinely prohibited (haram) and ordained that buying and selling is divinely allowed (halal).

> *2:275 those who devour usury will not stand except as stand one whom the Evil one by his touch Hath driven to madness. That is because they say: "Trade is like usury," but God hath permitted trade and forbidden usury. Those who after receiving direction from their Lord, desist, shall be pardoned for the past; their case is for God (to judge); but those who repeat (The offence) are companions of the Fire: They will abide therein (for ever).*

Many scholars, attorneys, bankers, and practitioners invested valuable resources to fix the form, but not (fully) the substance and spirit of the intent of removing riba from people's lives, as required by the Judeo-Christian-Islamic value system. It is interesting to note that the interest-free banking brand, which was used in the early years of Islamic RF banking, gave consumers the wrong impression and in many cases created a false conclusion. People thought that money would be given away by the Islamic RF bankers to be used to buy homes and businesses without expecting any increase or profit. Many of my friends in the West would ask me how an Islamic RF bank could survive if it did not charge interest. Their questions included: How can the bank pay its employees' salaries? What incentive was offered to the shareholders, who expect to receive decent returns on their investments? In the early days of Islamic RF banking, bankers arrived at an expedient solution: replace the word *interest* with one of a variety of words, such as *service charge, rent, profit,* and the like. This beginning approach may have helped in fixing the form of making the contract and operation "look Islamic," but in fact the charging of interest was still being practiced, just under a different name. Such contracts were devised by well-trained and experienced attorneys in the West and riba-based conventional bankers.

However, when some customers lost the money they had invested with "Islamic" banks, they were told by the bankers that—and I quote—"this proves that there is participation in profit and loss, and it shows that it is Islamic!" In fact, an Islamic finance company that lost the money of its investors in a number of ill-conceived real estate development projects on the East Coast of the United States—because they simply had no prior experience—exclaimed "thankfully" that this proved that the company applies the concept of participation in profit and loss, and the president of the company called it "the cost of being a Muslim"—and even gave it an acronym: *COBM*. This concept and term is still being used by some practitioners of "Islamic" banking, including professional American conventional bankers who in fact know better. These bankers stated many times in public conferences on Islamic banking in America that their motivation was to meet the market demand.

We at LARIBA were privileged to have started a movement in the late 1980s to use the term riba/ribit-free banking—RF banking—instead of interest-free or Islamic banking.

What Is RF (Islamic) Banking?

Some have defined "Islamic" banking as conventional banking minus the word *interest,* with a new contract that does not include the word *interest* and that is structured in a convoluted version of buy/sell, in which the seller changes ownership to the bank or finance company and then the bank sells it to the eventual buyer. Many participants in "Islamic" banking business thought, with good intentions, that these guidelines made the contract Islamic. Others conceptualized "Islamic" banking by using the expression of socialism, minus state control, plus God to give it the needed faith-based credibility.

The following are believed to be the true conceptual fundamentals of the RF brand of banking, which is based on the Judeo-Christian-Islamic value system:

- Believes in the fact that giving credit is a basic human right.
- Is socially responsible and ethical banking, designed to deliver services to the community according to the guidelines of the Judeo-Christian-Islamic value system. For example, RF bankers cannot finance alcohol-related businesses, gaming, gambling, polluting businesses, or other unethical activities. RF banks finance businesses in a fair and just way and serve all customers of all faiths and backgrounds. RF banks scrutinize the businesses they finance to ensure that the business owners treat their employees fairly and without discrimination. RF bankers believe in equal financing opportunities without discrimination, because discrimination is a sin in the Judeo-Christian-Islamic value system. In RF banking practice, no one is too small to serve and work with. Every community member is encouraged to live within his/her means.
- Enjoys the advantages of low overhead, lower risk, and lower loan losses, because the RF banker knows his/her clients, as he/she is active in the community.
- Is built on asset- (and services-)based financing. This requires that a commodity, tangible asset, and/or service must change hands at a fair market value—one that is gathered from the live market—using the discipline of *marking to the market*.
- Is not a money lending operation. It is involved in actual financing of and investing in tangible assets and services. It finances economically viable projects. If the project is not economically viable for the customer, it will not be financed. There is no "name" lending or unsecured lending allowed in RF banking.
- Invests in specific activities and projects to make a difference in peoples' lives. RF financing requires that the RF banker/financier knows what the applicant will use the money for and that the agreement involves the exchange of assets/properties/businesses or the leasing of such.
- Believes that speculation and its tools—like trading in risk (gharar)—and paper trading are divinely prohibited (haram).
- Believes in promotion and financing for community development and reinvestment of its deposits in the community.

- Believes that wealth should be circulated within the community to create jobs, economic growth, and prosperity. It uses the power of congregations and networks in places of worship and in social organizations to enhance its market penetration at the grass roots, thus fulfilling the financing and banking rule of "know your customer." This approach minimizes losses that may be realized due to ill-conceived financing of the wrong project with people who may not meet the needed prerequisites and applicable experience for a successful venture.
- Believes that one of its prime objectives is to remove riba/ribit from people's behavior and lives, one step at a time. RF bankers must start from the possible to achieve the impossible.
- Does not intend to remove, eliminate, or "destroy" riba-based conventional banks and systems. The aim of RF banking is to develop an alternative system that serves all people, regardless of faith or background.
- Measures success by return on investment, the number of households financed, and its achievement in making a difference in the lifestyle of the family and in the community.
- Believes that fiat (paper) money is not a commodity that commands a rental fee (interest rate). It also does not reproduce. Money (fiat—paper money) only grows when invested in an economic activity. Money is a man-made measuring device. It is a "thing." It cannot be rented. It is only useful, as a medium of exchange, if invested. *Riba* can be defined in today's terminology, and in light of riba-based financing activities, as renting money at a predetermined price called interest. RF bankers cannot merely take the interest rate of the day and charge it under the names *rent*, *service charge*, *index*, or *profit*. RF financing should be based on renting assets and services at the actual prevailing market rental/lease rate commanded by the market forces of supply and demand, not on the interest rate—the price of renting money.
- Believes that the value of different things in terms of fiat (paper) currency must be related to one of (or a basket of) the reference calibrating commodities using the Commodity Indexation Discipline, as detailed in Chapters 5 and 6. For example, economic bubbles can be detected by relating prices expressed in fiat (paper) money to a precious metal or a staple food commodity, and investment practices can be adjusted to avoid loss of assets and properties.
- Believes in full transparency as a must. Full disclosure is required as part of the contract, because deception, ruses, and/or attempts to misrepresent (called *gharar*) are haram (divinely prohibited).
- Believes that it must comply with the laws of the land without violating God's law (the Judeo-Christian-Islamic Shari'aa law). RF bankers are not in business to change the laws of the land, to be elected to a high

office using the power of money, to influence, or to discredit others. RF bankers do their best to educate and guide government banking regulators, politicians, and the public at large about the RF system and its values and benefits.

- Prepares and offers to the community RF bankers who are trained to believe that their ultimate goal is not to sell and make commissions, but to serve to earn a decent and humble living and, eventually, win paradise.

What Is the Difference between Riba-Based Conventional Banking and RF (Islamic) Banking?[2]

- *Dominant attractor:*
  - Riba-based: Money
  - RF: Life as prescribed by God in all Abrahamic faiths, as ordained in the Judeo-Christian-Islamic value system and way of life.
- *Defining purpose:*
  - Riba-based: Use money to make money for those who have money.
  - RF: Employs available resources within its means to meet the basic needs of everyone without extravagance.
- *Bank size:*
  - Riba-based: Very large (e.g., mega-banks).
  - RF: Small and medium-sized community-based.
- *Ownership:*
  - Riba-based: Impersonal, with absentee shareholders' role in most cases.
  - RF: Personal, with shareholders playing an active role in bank direction and procedures.
- *Financial capital:*
  - Riba-based: Global, with no borders.
  - RF: Local/national, with clear community reinvestment borders and assessment areas.
- *Purpose of investment:*
  - Riba-based: Maximize private profit and wealth.
  - RF: Increase beneficial output to the community to make it prosper.
- *Role of profit:*
  - Riba-based: An end to be maximized.
  - RF: An incentive to invest productively in the community.
- *Coordinating mechanisms:*
  - Riba-based: Centrally planned by mega-corporations.
  - RF: Self-organizing markets and networks of communities around temples, synagogues, churches, masajid, and other social congregations and networks.

- *Cooperation:*
  - Riba-based: Among competitors, to escape the discipline of competition and in some cases to avoid regulations.
  - RF: Among people and communities to advance the common good for all.
- *Purpose of competition:*
  - Riba-based: Eliminate the unfit and capture markets.
  - RF: Stimulate efficiency and innovation.
- *Government's role:*
  - Riba-based: Protect the interests of property.
  - RF: Advance the human interest, as revealed in all God's messages.
- *Trade:*
  - Riba-based: Free, but for the benefit of mega-corporations.
  - RF: Free, but fair and balanced.
- *Political orientation:*
  - Riba-based: Elitist, democracy of the money (greed is good!).
  - RF: Populist, democracy of persons.

REVIEW QUESTIONS

1. List at least six of the characteristics of an RF bank as listed in the book and please share with us your take on each.
2. List at least eight main differences between riba-based and RF (riba-free) banking and finance as enumerated in the book. Please discuss each and share with us your views and opinions.

NOTES

1. President of Egypt (1956–1970), a leader of the Egyptian Free Officers Revolution of 1952, and a pan Arab leader of Arab Nationalism.
2. This comparison is based on a comparison originated by Professor David C. Korten. It was adapted by the author to compare conventional riba-based banks with riba-free banks. David C. Korten, *The Post-Corporate World*, a co-publication of Kumarian Press Inc. and Berrett-Koehler Publishers, Inc., 1999, p. 41.

CHAPTER 10

RF (Islamic) Banking in the Twentieth Century

The efforts to start RF (Islamic) banking and finance in the mid-1970s resulted in the development of a major model, which became very popular because it was very close to the conventional riba-based financing model. The model is called the cost-plus (*murabaha*) model, which, as described in Chapter 3, includes the following steps:

1. The finance institution buys the item at the order of the ultimate buyer (who wants to finance it) at a certain price.
2. Then the financial institution sells the item back to the ultimate buyer at the original price plus a declared profit element. The profit element usually reflects the accumulated *implied interest*—called profit—that would accrue over the period of financing.
3. The ultimate note signed by the customer includes the total price including the profit. That may impact the credit report of the customer (in the USA) and limit the customer's "borrowing" or financing capacity.

The model focused on the fact that there is a buy/sell transaction and that interest is not charged, as required by the Judeo-Christian-Islamic Shari'aa law. This model was very convenient to the new and emerging RF (Islamic) banking industry, because it was a straightforward application of the interest-based model used in conventional riba-based banks. It was also applied in many of the newly established financial institutions at that time, such as the Kuwait Finance House (KFH), Dubai Islamic Bank, and Dallah Al-Baraka Finance Company,[1] and later in Malaysia. In Malaysia, the model is not called *murabaha;* it is called by what it does, which is to sell at a delayed payment price called in Arabic *al bai' bithaman aajil*, or *BBA*. The murabaha model was later adopted by many of the operating Islamic banks that emerged in many of the Muslim countries.

A number of challenges appeared to the RF (Islamic) bankers who began practicing the murabaha approach. These were:

1. How should one calculate the profit element that will be added to the original purchase price? As a solution to this problem, the finance companies were allowed by some scholars to use the prevailing interest rate as an index to be used to calculate the profit. Because the London money markets were accessed and used by most of the former British colonies in the Arab world (including the Gulf oil-producing countries) and Asia (including Malaysia), the scholars agreed on the use of the London Interbank Offered Rate (LIBOR) or local prevailing interest rates as the reference interest rate. This step was the source of frustration, confusion, disillusion, and disappointment for many young and dedicated RF bankers—Muslim and non-Muslim alike—whom I met all over the world, in Turkey, Malaysia, Egypt, Saudi Arabia, Kuwait, the Emirates, Pakistan, Europe, and the United States. "What is the difference?" they asked. "My boss asks us to survey the interest rates in the market and he ends up using it and we call it a 'profit' or 'rental' rate."
2. What will the "Islamic" finance company or the bank do with the one-step capital gain that results from reselling the item at this huge added "profit" (cumulative interest), which is added to the original price which was paid by the bank to buy that item? In the beginning, the profit was booked on the income statement as an income from transactions, resulting in great performances for the Islamic banks. Later, after the involvement of many international audit (CPA) firms familiar with international accounting standards (like the Financial Accounting Standards Board [FASB] in the United States) and the establishment of AAOIFI (Accounting and Auditing Organization for Islamic Financial Institutions), profit was spread over the life of the facility (amortized) in the same way a loan interest income is booked in a conventional banking operation or as in the case of an origination fee, which is handled by the FASB accounting standards (FASB-91).
3. What will the "Islamic" finance company do with delinquencies in payments? The original conditions (required by the law—Shari'aa) of the cost-plus (murabaha) model were to not increase the profit element added to the original price in case of delinquency or inability to pay the periodic payments or the payoff in time, because increasing the profit would be considered a clear violation of RF values (*riba al-nasee'ah*). This rule was abused by some of the customers of "Islamic" finance companies and banks. To resolve the situation, a number of scholars issued an edict (*fatwa*) that allowed the RF "Islamic" banks and the financial institutions to charge penalties to those who are chronically

late in making their payments without an acceptable, legitimate, and reasonable excuse. A small loophole was left open by the fatwa, and that was to use the principle of mercifulness (*tarahum*) in case the customer had a legitimate excuse. This small loophole created many lawsuits and many legal attempts to help borrowers who dealt with RF "Islamic" banks. In addition, the edicts ruled that the late payment fees cannot be added as an income. These fees—in the form of penalties—are booked in a separate account and are paid as donations to legitimate charities.

When Islamic banking proponents started considering the implementation of the murabaha approaches in the West, they met with many additional challenges. These were:

- The banks (depository institutions) in most Western countries are not allowed by the banking laws and regulations of the land to own properties unless the property was foreclosed on by the bank and was classified as *Other Real Estate Owned* (OREO). In this case, the bank is encouraged to sell OREO properties as soon as practical. This stipulation made it difficult for a bank to buy an item, change the title from the seller to the bank, then sell it to the ultimate buyer by changing title again from the bank to that ultimate buyer to satisfy the buy/sell rule called for by the RF law (the Judeo-Christian-Islamic Shari'aa law), as discussed earlier.
- If the RF financing institution were structured as a finance company, then it could—in some jurisdictions—buy properties and hold title to these properties. However, finance companies in the West discovered that when the company buys a property in its name at a price (X) and turns around and sells it at original price (X) plus a profit (P), then a tax event is created, because the tax authorities considered the profit (P) a capital gain that must be taxed. In addition, in some countries (particularly in Europe), a tax is charged every time title changes hands, creating unnecessary additional expenses.

The real challenge came when the Muslim communities in the West—mainly in the United Kingdom and the United States—wanted to obtain RF financial services. The effort to provide RF financial services in the West was pioneered by Al-Baraka Bank in London in 1988, when it tried to come up with a home financing model and contract that would fit the requirements of the banking laws in the West in general and in the United Kingdom in particular and that would be compliant with the Judeo-Christian-Islamic Shari'aa law. A number of meetings between scholars, attorneys, and bankers were held. This resulted in the birth of a new RF "Islamic" financing model based on the leasing model (*Al Ijara Wal Tamaluk* or *Ijarah Wal Iqtina*—these Arabic terms both mean *lease to own*). This model is now becoming more popular because the RF "Islamic" banking attorneys—most of whom had Western training, experience, and credentials—were able to adapt it in ways that make the financing closer to the requirements of the Judeo-Christian-Islamic Shari'aa law and to expand its use in the development of the RF "Islamic" asset-based bonds (*sukuk*).

RF (ISLAMIC) BANKING MODELS

The following is an analysis of the RF banking models designed to fit the existing conventional finance contracts to make them compliant with the RF law.

The Cost-Plus (Murabaha) Model

This mode of financing (in Malaysia it is called *Al Bai' Bithaman Aajil*, or *BBA*) was developed to finance trade transactions in an RF format. *The Institute of Islamic Banking and Insurance* magazine (London)[2] responds to reservations and criticisms made by many Shari'aa scholars, as well as users of the RF murabaha "Islamic" finance models and contracts, by stating that "we should not . . . ignore that the basic Islamic finance structures adopted today were used primarily in trade in the early Islamic period." The article further states:

> *Murabaha [cost-plus], in its original Islamic connotation, is simply a particular type of sale, not a mode of financing. The only feature distinguishing it from other kinds of sale is that the seller in Murabaha [cost-plus] tells the buyer the cost incurred and the profit (mark-up) on the cost.*

The magazine also quotes retired Justice Muhammad Taqi Usmani:

> *There are two essential points which must be fully understood in this respect: 1) it should never be overlooked that, originally, Murabaha [cost-plus] is not a mode of financing. Therefore, this instrument should be used as a transitory step . . . and its use should be restricted only to those cases where Musharaka [joint ownership with diminishing equity] is not practicable; 2) the Murabaha [cost-plus] transaction does not come into existence by merely replacing the word of "interest" by words of "profit" or "mark up."*

The article further states:

> *Murabaha [cost-plus], though not an ideal model in Shari'aa compliant finance, was adopted initially for home purchase in the UK in the late 1990s, as pure Musharaka [joint ownership with diminishing equity] and other models were not well suited for mortgage transactions.*

In response to concerns voiced regarding the added cost resulting from capital gains taxes levied by tax authorities in the United States for a sale and buy back at a higher price, the scholar Dr. Samy Hamoud issued an opinion to the author when we, at LARIBA, started applying the cost-plus financing concept in the United States in 1987, allowing the company to appoint the customer as an agent (*wakeel*) to buy the property on the bank's behalf. The opinion of Dr. Hamoud was the basis for the fatwa issued by the First Conference of Islamic Banks (Dubai, 1997). *This fatwa—based on an opinion of the Maliki jurist Ibn Shubruma*[3]*—stated that an Islamic financial institution may require its customers to sign a binding promise that he or she will purchase the financed property on credit (with an agreed upon mark-up) once the bank buys it based on his order.* It is important to notice here the use of the term *binding promise* or *waad* in Arabic. The word *promise*, some scholars stress, is different from the word *contract*. The reason for this distinction to be made, with customers signing a promise to buy back rather than a contract to buy back, satisfies some of the scholars' demands. That is because of a clear ruling by the Prophet Muhammad (pp) that prohibits including two contracts (a contract to buy and another contract to sell back to back) in one contract to purchase the property. The resulting contract came to be known[4] as *Murabaha Lil Aamiri bil Shira'aa* (meaning *cost-plus sale to the one who ordered the original purchase*).

The mechanics of a murabaha (cost-plus) financing transaction sometimes blur the boundaries between interest-bearing riba-based conventional loans and credit financing. In fact, murabaha (cost-plus) is sometimes called the bridge between riba-based conventional financing methods and the RF financing domain. Many of the puritans who were looking for RF financing criticized this mode of financing severely when it was first introduced in the United States because it was similar to riba-based financing. This perspective challenged us at LARIBA to research and to try to come up with other methods of financing, which led us to innovate and develop the LARIBA RF financing model.

In murabaha transactions,[5] the customer is appointed as the financier's buying agent (*wakeel*). Thus, the customer may proceed as the financier's agent (wakeel) to purchase the property on the financier's behalf. Subsequently, the ultimate buyer also acts as the financier's selling agent to sell the property to himself. Technically, jurists argue,[6] the financier in fact owns the property during the period of time between the two agency sales and bears the risk, for instance, of its destruction by lightning. Unfortunately, close scrutiny of the process used in this mode of transaction indicates that the bank or the finance company takes all precautions to ensure that the buyer will not go back on that promise, so that the financing entity will not end up owning the property. In addition, RF Judeo-Christian-Islamic Shari'aa law defines the transaction based on the intention (*niyah*) of the transacting party. It is a fact that the financing entity never intends to buy and own that property.

In our efforts to evaluate the murabaha (cost-plus) RF finance model used in the United States for "Islamic" Shari'aa-compliant mortgage financing, we want to share with the reader important glimpses of the procedure used and the contract used by one of the banks in America that advertises its "Islamic" "no-interest" mortgage financing program. The bank uses the murabaha (cost-plus) model. We are deeply indebted to a friend in the community who financed his home using the services of this bank and was kind enough to share with us the details of the process he went through. Here are our observations:

- It is claimed that no interest is charged, despite the fact that the bank uses the prevailing interest rate of the day of the agreement as a base for calculating the added "profit" element in the murabaha (cost-plus) scheme used. We also found that the aforementioned bank uses the same mortgage amortization program that is used in riba-based financing to calculate the "plus" in the murabaha (cost-plus) scheme. Would that be considered a violation of consumer compliance and advertising regulations mandated by the federal and state banking laws?
- It is claimed that the bank buys the property in its name and that the customer promises to buy it back from the bank in a simultaneous back-to-back operation. Upon researching title of the property, we found out that the bank used very restrictive language to ensure that the customer would not change his/her mind and that he/she would proceed with the buyback from the bank. The customer signs a contractual form, not just a promise. We found that the bank places its name on a preliminary title that was never recorded to perfect the claimed purchase step by the bank. This way the bank never changed title of the property to its own name, and the title was recorded in the name of the buyer. In fact, even the down payment was paid by the ultimate buyer and not by the bank, which was supposed—at least on paper—to have been the buyer of the property.

- Upon further investigation and research, we discovered that the bank in some cases has formed a special-purpose vehicle (SPV) in the form of a limited liability company (LLC) that would "synthetically" purchase the property and sell it back to back to the ultimate buyer. In this case, the buyer is charged all the costs associated with this scheme.
- The buyer signs a promissory note for the original price and the accumulated interest together. This makes the buyer liable for the whole amount (the cost plus the profit [interest] charges).
- The bank required the buyer to sign a rider stating that the buyer will be responsible for any capital gains taxes that may be levied by the tax authorities should the buy/sell agreement produce—in the opinion of the tax authorities—an implied capital gain.
- The contract was mostly similar to a regular finance contract, and the note was also mostly similar to a standard note but without the word *interest*.
- The bank charged the customer for the additional expenses involved in this "circumvented" transaction.

Another attempt at Islamic banking was made by a major mortgage finance company which is now owned by the U.S. government, but was then (before the 2008 financial meltdown) classified as a government-sponsored entity (GSE) active in mortgage financing. The GSE was kind enough to seek the opinion of the author about its newly developed Islamic home mortgage financing model and structure. The proposed contract claimed that the customer would be charged zero interest and it had to post, in the contract, a table that translated the "Islamic" finance terms used in the contract to the regular riba-based finance language that is used in standard riba-based mortgage finance contracts. The GSE was informed that this contract should not carry the name of this respected GSE, because it is in fact a regular conventional contract dressed up to make it look compliant with the RF law (Shari'aa). The GSE was also warned that this kind of contract can be challenged in the courts of the law, as happened in other instances in Malaysia, the United Kingdom, Saudi Arabia, and in the United States (with MSI—Muslim Savings and Investment—of Houston, Texas). The GSE did not go further with such a contract.

It is surprising and troubling to experience these attempts at circumventing the law (the Judeo-Christian-Islamic Shari'aa law) using such ruses. Bank regulations in the United States (as well as in the United Kingdom) have plenty of detailed consumer compliance laws that disclose the finite details of the transaction and the total charges levied by the bank in a finance transaction, as required by the Truth in Lending Act (TILA) (Regulation Z) in the United States and the regulation that gives the buyer the right of rescission of the deal. But most amazing of all is the fact that the cost-plus (murabaha) model is used by tens of banks that employ many of the "superstar" scholars on their Shari'aa Boards. Most important of all, it is noted that there is no mention of the method that is used to calculate the markup (profit) in the murabaha (cost plus) model. The fact of the matter is that they use the prevailing interest rate used by all banks in the conventional riba-based system, call it rent or profit, and claim that this interest (usually LIBOR-based) is looked upon as an index.

Financial Engineering and the Law (Shari'aa)

One of the most controversial issues and sources of contention among scholars in the law (Shari'aa) has been the transfer of ownership or title of the property first from the seller to a special-purpose vehicle (SPV), in the form of a limited liability company (LLC) created by the bank in order to create a synthetic buy/sell transaction without violating the banking laws. While many scholars have allowed the appointment of the buyer as an agent (wakeel) in the back-to-back buy and sell transaction, there are a few who refused to accept it. For example, in a murabaha (cost-plus) transaction, the bank or the financial institution would be expected to first buy the house and record title in its name; then it would immediately turn around and sell the house to the real buyer. However, U.S. government banking regulations prohibit banks from owning real estate properties (except those foreclosed on due to nonperformance, which are classified as Other Real Estate Owned—OREOs—on the balance sheet). Regulators press banks to sell such OREOs as soon as practical. To abide by these laws, and to circumvent the law (Shari'aa) in order to have a transaction that appears to be compliant, the bank would start by incorporating a new company (i.e., an SPV in the form of an LLC or a limited partnership) that does the buying and the selling in a back-to-back instant way. This would eventually make the process look—in form—as though it were legitimate with the law (Shari'aa) because the title of the property changed hands (on paper), making it a sale. However, this method forgets the real purposes and spirits of the law (*Shari'aa*), which are:

- Not to rent money at an interest rate.
- To transact a true prudent investment in the property by marking the property to the market.

Many Shari'aa scholars have condemned the use of deceptive financial engineering techniques used to circumvent the Judeo-Christian-Islamic Shari'aa by focusing on the form of the transaction and the contract (on paper) rather than the substance! Dr. Elgamal[7] states:

> *... Al Shatibi [a Muslim scholar in Shari'aa] concluded that cynical adherence to classical contract conditions in order to achieve form and not substance using ruses and deceptive tricks (even if these tricks are classified as Hassan heelah—or a good trick) to circumvent [the Law] Shari'aa may violate it.... "Legal ruses—al-heyal—in religion are rendered as generally illegal. In this regard, legal provisions—al-amaal al-shar' iy'ah—are not ends in themselves but means to legal ends, which are the benefits intended by the Law [Shari'aa]. Thus, one who keeps legal form while squandering its substance and intent does not follow the Law [Shari'aa].*

It is troubling to see the bank or the financing entity form an SPV with the intention of abandoning it just to make the deal look compliant with the law (Shari'aa). Conceptually, this approach is not much different from signing a marriage contract as a matter of convenience with the intention of divorcing after the purpose of that contract has been achieved. It is believed that this renders the contract null and void because it was entered in bad faith. Such an approach stands in fact as a mockery of the real purpose, intent, and wisdom of the prohibition of riba—the culture of renting money. These SPVs cost money to conceive, design, register and to maintain—a cost that some call COBM (the cost of being a Muslim), to our surprise! We believe that wasting money, however small or insignificant, on such kinds of ruses does not fulfill the basic objective of the law (Shari'aa), which is the pushing away of what is harmful and the bringing of benefits to the community, as was detailed in Chapter 4. It is also important to note that such schemes have not yet been challenged in the courts of law or by the tax authorities. It is strongly believed that we should use wisdom to keep our community members out of harm's way by not following such unnecessary ruses.

The Lease-to-Own Models (Al-Ijarah Wal Iqtina or Al-Ijarah Wal Tamaluk)

In response to the many reservations and criticisms leveled against the murabaha (cost plus) model described above, another effort to develop new models was started, based on the lease-to-purchase transaction. The first model was developed by a group of scholars from the Arabic-speaking Middle Eastern countries for Al-Baraka Bank in London in 1990.[8] The second model, which will be detailed in Chapter 11, is the LARIBA model, which improves on the Al-Baraka model by applying the Marking-to-Market Discipline and the Commodity Indexation Discipline, explained in Chapters 3, 5, and 6. The third model was a modification of the Al-Baraka model developed later by (retired) Justice Taqi Usmani and detailed in his book[9] for an "Islamic" mortgage finance company that has operated in the United States since 2001.

The Al-Baraka Shari'aa-Compliant Model[10]

This model was devised to fit the mortgage financing requirements in the United Kingdom in order to offer RF mortgage financing by the first Islamic bank to operate in London, England: Al-Baraka Bank. It was the first serious attempt to offer solutions to the British Muslims' demand for mortgage financing according to the Judeo-Christian-Islamic Shari'aa law. The author was closely involved with the growth of Al-Baraka Bank's operations and experienced at close range the last few weeks before it was closed down by the Financial Services Authority (FSA). The closure was mainly because Al-Baraka Bank owners did not have a chartered bank in Saudi Arabia, its country of domicile, but also due to regulatory violations in its operations. In general, the model calls for three steps:

1. The financing entity and the customer buy the property as a joint venture (*musharaka*).
2. The share of the financing entity in the property is sold to the customer at the outset. This allows the ultimate and real buyer of the property to receive and record title immediately.
3. The financing entity would retain ownership of the "right to use the property" in terms of the lease income the property would produce if it were rented. In lieu of that, the financing entity would receive a lien (implied co-ownership) on the property and collect its share of the rent income as stipulated in the agreement/contract. (In many cases, Shari'aa scholars mistranslate the word *lien* as *rahn*, which means *pawn* in Arabic.) This issue will be discussed in further detail by researching the definition of lien (as an implied co-ownership) compared to pawn (complete arrest of the property usufruct to the pawn holder).

A series of edicts and opinions (*fatwa*)[11] were issued by a group of highly placed and recognized scholars in the Judeo-Christian-Islamic Shari'aa law. These edicts formed a milestone in the "Islamic" finance ways and means. Here are some of the important issues discussed and the edicts issued:

- *The use of the word* interest.[12] The word *interest* can be used in a contract to satisfy local government's legal requirements as long as riba is not practiced during the transaction. The fatwa states:

  Applying the principle for reviewing transactions, stipulating that what matters in contracts are the intentions and the substance—not words and forms—we have reached a consensus that there is no objection to using the term "interest" as an alternative to the term "profit" or "rate of return." In this regard, it is imperative to ensure that the term "interest" in the sense described above is used only in the forms required by entities other than the bank, e.g., tax declaration forms for depositors, or special forms used in various financing cases. However, if the intent is to change the nature of the transaction to make it an interest-bearing loan, then such transaction will be fundamentally impermissible.[13]

- *Developing the lease-to-own model to comply with the banking regulatory requirements of the United Kingdom—The Financial Service Authority (FSA).*[14]
  - *Registering the house's title in the partner's name*, based on trust, from the inception of the contract is permissible under Shari'aa law. Registering the property's title in this manner does not contradict the agreed-upon partnership, especially since the partner's ability to sell the home is restricted until his full ownership of the property is established. In this regard, we took into consideration the fact that this registration of title is a form of documentation insured by the officially established lien on the property, according to the conditions agreed upon with the partner.
  - *Making the partner alone responsible for all [closing costs like] registration, survey, and other documentation costs* associated with the jointly owned property from the inception of the contract, and absolving the bank from responsibility for such costs, is permissible if the partners agreed accordingly. This is particularly appropriate, since the partner will ultimately become the sole owner of the property at the end of the financing contract.
  - With regards to insurance, the default ruling would require that *both partners bear responsibility for insurance premiums* as a shared burden of the jointly owned property. However, the bank may take that into consideration when determining the rental of its share of the property, and include appropriate compensation for the appropriate share of insurance costs.
  - The default ruling in joint ownership is *sharing profits and losses in proportion to ownership*, based on the principle that entitlement to profit must be commensurate with risk exposure. In this regard, since the regulatory framework requires that the bank should not be exposed to the possibility of losses when the partnership is dissolved, the model should be altered such that the order of the transaction proceeds as follows:

- The bank and the customer share in purchasing the home according to the agreed-upon proportions.
- The bank sells its share in the physical property ownership (milk al-raqabah) to its partner, while retaining its share of ownership of the right to use it (haq al-manfa'ah) until the time its partner pays the remaining portion of the price.
- The bank collects an annual rent in accordance with the actually paid portion of the property's price.

If the partner is delinquent in paying the installments for which he is obligated, the bank has the right to keep the sale agreement intact and collect its right to the remaining portion of the price according to the obligatory performance clauses of the lien; or the bank may void the initial sale and take full ownership of the property, if the partner agrees. In the latter case, the bank should pay back to the partner whatever he had paid previously, as a revocation of the sale from its inception. (This item was agreed upon by a majority of the participating scholars.)

The South Asian Diminishing Musharaka Shari'aa-Compliant Model[15]

This model was developed by a retired justice, the eminent Sheikh Muhammad Taqi Usmani, a world-renowned Shari'aa scholar who specializes in Islamic financing. In 1998, he authored a book on the subject.[16] The stepwise approach and methodology recommended by Justice Taqi Usmani were essentially the same as the ones described above in the Al-Baraka model (1990), but without splitting the rights to a property into the right of ownership (title ownership) and the right of using the property (usufruct). Following is a summary of the model based on the book authored by Justice Taqi Usmani, which is titled *House Financing on the Basis of Diminishing Musharaka (Joint Venture)*. The proposed arrangement is composed of the following transactions:

1. Create a joint ownership in the property between the buyer and the financing entity in the form of joint venture (*shirkat-al-milk* in Arabic).
2. Rent the share of the financier in the property to the client.[17]
3. Get the promise (notice the use of the word *promise* and not *contract*) from the client to purchase shares owned by the finance company.
4. Have the buyer gradually buy back the shares of the finance company.
5. Adjust the rental paid by the buyer gradually, in proportion of the ownership by the finance company.

The following is an analysis of each ingredient of the arrangement based on the model description as detailed in Justice Taqi Usmani's book. In general, the steps recommended in this model are not much different from the earlier model used at Al-Baraka Bank in London, but with a number of changes. Contrasting the South Asian model with that of Al-Baraka yields the following:

1. The finance entity leases its share in the house to its client and charges him/her a monthly rent. This is the same process that the Al-Baraka model calls for. But the Al-Baraka model is clearer and more defined, as it divides the rights of the owner in the property to two rights. These are the right to own title (*milk ul raqabah*) and the right to lease or rent the use of the property (*haq al-manfa'aa*).
2. The South Asian model states that the client buys "units" of the "undivided" shares owned by the finance entity, compared to selling all the finance company's shares outright at the beginning as in the Al-Baraka model. This step is a very serious step and has created a number of issues, because:
   a. In this model the buyer and the finance entity continue to own the property, which requires that the title be recorded in both names. This creates many problems. However, in the Al-Baraka model, the buyer buys back all the shares in ownership from the finance entity at the outset, which allows the buyer, according to the law (Shari'aa), to record title in his/her name only.
   b. If the finance entity sells back its shares over a period of time, as the South Asian model calls for, the price of these shares cannot be fixed ahead of time in the beginning of the transaction, because that would be like a sale and buyback at a future date with a fixed predefined price. This type of sale is called in the RF law (Shari'aa) the sale of *eena*. This type of sale is clearly prohibited, because it represents a ruse or a deceptive trick to circumvent the law (Shari'aa). The price in the future must be defined by the market forces of supply and demand prevailing at the time of resale; it can be same, higher or lower. This step may imply that the model proposed accepts that the parties agree that the price of each share is fixed in the future. Sheikh Ali Al-Salous,[18] an established scholar in the field of Islamic finance, recommends that in cases in which the finance entity sells shares to the customer over a period of time in the future, these shares should be sold at the prevailing market price of the property in the open market and the price cannot be fixed ahead of time. After I discussed with him the difficulty and maybe the impracticality of establishing a share price every month, he suggested that when the customer

is billed, he/she should be told clearly—through proper and clear disclosure on the billing statement—that the shares he/she is buying back from the financing entity are offered at a certain price, which may be different from the prevailing market price and that he/she has the right to accept it or refuse it. Of course, the client's refusal to buy the shares at the offered price will trigger other actions as stipulated in the particular contract. Justice Taqi Usmani agrees with this and states so clearly in the conditions listed in the book, but he provides a way out:

It will be preferable that the purchase of different units by the client is effected [affected]on the basis of the market value of the house as prevalent on the date of purchase of that unit, but it is also permissible that a particular price is agreed in the promise of purchase signed by the client.

However, the signing by the client of a fixed price in the future—as done in many of the contracts we have seen—does not make the agreement compliant with the law (Shari'aa) because it makes it a definite *eena* sale. That is why Justice Taqi Usmani states in his conditions that ". . . at the time of the purchase of each unit, sale must be affected by the exchange of offer and acceptance at that particular date."

c. To get around the problem of having two sales contracts in one, the South Asian model uses the word *promise* to describe the action of the customer toward the financier without putting it in writing in the form of a contract. If this occurred, it would again be a sale and future buyback, with a predefined price or eena sale, which is prohibited by the law (Shari'aa). It is important that the steps recommended by the models are done independently, as Justice Taqi Usmani states in his book:

It is clear . . . that each one of the transactions . . . is allowed per se, but the question is whether this transaction may be combined in a single arrangement.

The answer is that if all these transactions have been combined by making each one of them a condition on the other, then it is not allowed in the law (Shari'aa) because it is a well settled rule in the Islamic legal system that one transaction cannot be made a precondition for another . . . the proposed scheme suggests that instead of making two transactions conditional to each other, there should be a one-sided promise from the client, first, to take share of the financier on lease

> and pay the agreed rent, and second, to purchase different units of the share of the financier of the house at different stages. . . . It is generally believed that a promise to do something creates only a moral obligation on the promisor, which cannot be enforced through courts of law . . . [the] most the promise can do is to compel the promisor through court of law to fulfill his promise and if the promisor is unable to fulfill the promise, the promisee can claim actual damages he has suffered because of the default. This makes it clear that a separate and independent promise to purchase does not render the original contract conditional or contingent. Therefore, it can be enforced.

It will be left to the reader to decide if this "promise" is in fact a contractual agreement or not. One fact needs to be made very clear. The contracts used by those banks and financial institutions do obtain clear and firm agreements from the customer to buy back the property—not just a promise. Based on our detailed research and in-depth evaluation of the documents used—at least those used in the United States—no bank or financial institution would act on a mere "promise." The bank or the finance company involved makes sure that the customer not only gives a binding contract, but also pays the down payment on the house he or she wants to buy.

In addition, it is known from the outset that the financing entity does not intend in the first place to buy the property and that it would have never embarked on the step of the "claimed" purchase of the property (as required by the model) without making sure that the client was fully committed and contractually obliged to buy the property back.

We have tried to understand the benefits to the client or to the financing entity of following all these "synthetic" steps, and we found that there are no benefits. It is important to note that this South Asian model requires that the finance entity devise new contracts, mortgage agreements, and promissory notes that may not be different in content, intent, and spirit from the standard riba-based ones, without adding any economic or real legal benefit to the customer. If these newly formulated—nonstandard—contracts are litigated in the courts of law, at least as we are aware in the United States, it exposes the customer to the risk of confusing the court and to liabilities that may be leveled against the financing entity or its parent bank or company. It is understood that this may be a remote possibility, but in the legal system, we learn from history that what may be considered remote today can be messy and greatly complicated and involved when a smarter attorney starts challenging it.

In contrast, the Al-Baraka model solves the above problems in an elegant, straightforward, and more practical way, which is acceptable by the law (Shari'aa). It does not need to resort to establishing the LLC or SPV, because of the direct sale back to back of the bank's share and the registration of the title in the customer's name at the outset of the transaction. It simply states that the finance entity sells all its shares directly at the outset to the customer. The sale proceeds are paid by the customer—without any riba/interest—over a period of time that is agreed upon between the finance entity and the customer. Against this trust, the client proceeds to record title in his/her name and proceeds to share in the rent that the two parties have agreed to in the proportion of ownership. The financing entity keeps a lien on the property. The lien is settled, title is *re-conveyed*, and the implied joint ownership by that lien is released when the shares of the financier have been completely paid back.

Application of the South Asian Shari'aa-Compliant Model

To examine the practical application of the South Asian model, the methods and procedures used by an American-based Islamic mortgage finance company that uses the model will be examined below. This "Islamic" mortgage finance company came to market in late 2001 and was heavily promoted as the real solution to the problem of providing "Islamic Shari'aa-compliant" financing to "Muslims and others" in the United States.[19] In general, the procedure used by the company is based on the South Asian model described in the previous section.

The company advertises and publishes on their website a copy of the fatwa signed by the Shari'aa Board of the company, which includes (retired) Justice Taqi Usmani. The company states that the purposes of the model are to:

- Assist Muslims and others to acquire homes in compliance with Shari'aa.
- Help buyers to enjoy tax benefits.
- Allow the company to securitize their ownership investment in homes.

The company explains that the financing process goes through the following steps:

1. The mortgage company forms a limited partnership as a special purpose vehicle (SPV) with the customer. They agree to purchase the property together and to record title in the name of the customer and the SPV company jointly. The cost of forming the SPV is charged to the customer (approximately $1,400 to $1,500) and its monthly maintenance cost (usually $18 to $20) is also charged to the customer. The company makes the following disclosures about the use of a "Bankruptcy—Remote Limited Liability Company" (LLC—a special-purpose vehicle) as co-owner: ". . . the LLC [has a] separate legal entity that

prohibits co-owner from incurring debt other than the financing of the property." This may be an advantage, in that it limits the customer's ability to use his home as a credit card. Despite that fact, we have seen in practice customers who have still taken a home equity line of credit on homes financed by this model—but only from that company, because it has the customer captive through its joint title ownership. In fact, the company that uses this model has been advertising to encourage members of the American Muslim community to take a home equity line of credit to finance *hajj* (pilgrimage). It is known that the law (Shari'aa) requires that the Muslim pays off all debts (except in many cases the mortgage necessary to live in a house) before he/she goes on hajj and not to borrow more to go on hajj. It is not clear whether the Shari'aa Board approved such an invitation to take a loan to go on hajj, which first stands opposite to the condition required by Justice Taqi Usmani and second is in violation of the law (Shari'aa). The LLC that serves as co-owner may also serve as co-owner with other consumers in up to 10 separate properties with 10 separate consumers.[20] The LLC mortgages the property to the financier ("the company"). The company also discloses that there will be an ongoing LLC fee of $18.75 per month to be used to pay for unaffiliated third-party expenses. The company also states that it may adjust the ongoing monthly LLC fee in the future to reflect any increase to the current fee. The LLC fee is part of the financing costs.

2. The SPV would proceed to rent the property back to the customer at a rate agreed between them using the prevailing (interest) rate as the rent of the property—making it, in fact, a process of renting money and not the property. This rent is exactly the riba interest rate charged in the market. In fact, if a customer called the company representative, that representative would proceed immediately to tell the customer that the rental rate is, say, 6 percent, which happens to be the interest rate on mortgages at that time. It is well known that renting a property depends on the location of the neighborhood, the specifications of the house, and any other special features the house may have. The actual rent of the property on the market can in fact be drastically different from what the company defines as rent using the interest rate at that time. The name of the SPV company stays on title until the buyback is completed. At that time, title is transferred to the customer. This feature limits the freedom of the customer to act without the approval of the joint holder of title. In other cases, it may represent a liability to the customer, for example, if the company faces challenging times.
3. The buyer would agree to buy back shares from the partnership, representing the payback of the principal. Since the units of property will be

purchased by the consumer under this arrangement at cost and without increase, the company claims that there is no element of *eena* in this arrangement. As stated earlier, *eena* is defined as a sale with a promise to buy back at a later date at a pre-agreed-upon price. According to the law (Shari'aa) the buyer should be offered these shares at the prevailing market price, and the customer should be given the choice of accepting or rejecting that sales price offer, but that is not what happens.

4. The company states that the consumer will make monthly payments composed of *profit payments* and *acquisition payments*. The acquisition payments, the company states, represent the consumer's payments for his/her acquiring the co-owner's interest in the property. It is noticed here that there is a lack of full disclosure as required by Justice Taqi Usmani. As stated earlier, the scholar makes the condition that for the model to be compliant, the company must offer its shares in the joint venture for sale at a true prevailing market price, and not just bill the customer to pay the acquisition payment (principal).

The company that uses this model discloses that this model or mortgage product conforms both to the practices of the U.S. mortgage regulation and the principles of the law (Shari'aa). Therefore, the use of the terms *interest*, *principal*, *borrower*, and *lender* are mandated by law, and the model is subject to the same disclosures as a regular mortgage loan, such as a good faith estimate (GFE), TILA disclosure, and so on.

It was also noticed that the company claims that both parties benefit and bear the risks of their respective shares in the property throughout the contractual arrangement ("term of the financing"). The customer benefits from the fact that he/she is participating in what is presented as a "Shari'aa-compliant" contract. However, in doing so, the customer has to go through a number of extra steps without reaping any economic or religious benefits—like joint venturing with an LLC, paying extra costs for the SPV, and accepting a joint title ownership with the SPV that may result in future undefined risks. One of these risks, for example, is a case in which the company—the joint owner of the title—experiences legal difficulties. The other concern that can be made about this model is the claim that this model allows both the customer and the company to bear the risks of their respective shares in the property. Upon further detailed analysis, it can be safely concluded that the risk carried by the company is even less than the risk assumed by a conventional bank or a financing entity doing a riba-based transaction. It is also concluded that this method exposes the consumer to many risks, especially the risk of getting involved in a nonstandard mortgage structure with nonstandard contracts and promissory notes that has not been tested in the U.S. courts of law yet, as compared to the standardized mortgage finance contract offered in the United States. The other risk is the unfamiliarity of judges and participants in the legal system with such contracts, let alone the extra legal expenses that would eventually be incurred by both the customer (who has much less means than those available to the company) and the company in case a lawsuit is brought to court as compared to a standard and simple administrative legal process in the case of a standard mortgage contract.

It is important to state that regardless of the objections voiced about the contract and the circumventive ruses and deceptive tricks used, it is believed that God will reward those who have made an attempt to develop it in good faith and those users who trusted these claims and were willing to pay more to avoid participating in riba because He, our Creator and the Ultimate Judge, knows that their intention is not to deceive people or to violate the Judeo-Christian-Islamic Shari'aa law.

COURT CHALLENGES TO THE SHARI'AA-COMPLIANT "CONTRACT FITTING" USED BY SOME ISLAMIC FINANCE APPROACHES[21]

It is important to note that the use of RF (Islamic) banking as a financing alternative was challenged in many courts in the United Kingdom, Malaysia, the oil-rich Gulf countries, and the United States. Many of the lawsuits were settled outside the court, and the details on all of these cases may not be readily available. Many of these lawsuits were brought to the special courts of the law (Shari'aa courts) in Muslim countries in which such courts operate—in most cases—outside the realm of the civil laws that prevail in many countries of the world. Such courts exist, for example, in many of the Gulf oil-producing countries, such as Saudi Arabia, the United Arab Emirates, and Kuwait. Details of the lawsuits and how such suits were settled are not available because they were not made public. However, in most cases, and based on reports from friends who live and work in these areas, a religious judge presiding over a Shari'aa court may rule that the interest owed on a loan is forgiven because it is considered Riba.

Malaysia and the U.K. courts have litigated many of these Islamic finance cases. Most of these cases involve financing deals that used the cost-plus model (murabaha, or BBA in Malaysia). Philip T. N. Koh, Esq.,[22] a practicing attorney in Malaysia, has documented a number of cases that were brought to British and Malaysian courts.

These cases are quoted here to alert those who think that RF (Shari'aa-compliant) financing in the United States may not one day be brought to and challenged in courts to please think again. All these LLCs and SPVs and sophisticated structures present a smarter attorney with wonderful opportunities to challenge all such schemes, ruses, and claims. A most important and messy claim is that the "*Shari'aa* compliance" description can be coupled with a religious discrimination claim. These claims can cause damages ranging from expensive settlements that may bankrupt the institution to negative publicity that may have far-reaching negative effects on the operation of the RF institution(s) involved and maybe the RF industry altogether.

The following are examples of such cases.

Cases Litigated in the U.K. Courts

In *Shamil (Islamic) Bank of Bahrain v. Beximco Pharmaceuticals*,[23] the defendant (Beximco) argued that obligations on them are enforceable only if valid under both Shari'aa and English law. They argued further that the cost-plus (murabaha) arrangements were merely a disguise for interest-bearing loans, which are unenforceable under Shari'aa.

The court held that reference to the law (Shari'aa) was intended to mean that the bank held itself out as doing business in accordance with Islamic principles and was not intended to trump the application of English law.

There have been many other litigations and court cases in Malaysia regarding the same subject.[24] In a case that involved the application of the different schools of thoughts—*Sunni* and *Shi'aa*—the judge,[25] after conducting a survey of differing sects of branches of *Sunni* and *Shi'i*, described the issue as "a mind-boggling minefield awaiting lawyers and judges alike."

Resolutions Taken by "Islamic" Banks to Avoid Lengthy Trials

In response to these cases, and to reduce the confusion of the judges in different courts and in different countries (especially non-Muslim countries), many Islamic banks and finance companies have resorted to modifying their "Islamic" contract to include some of the following sample articles[26]:

- "This Agreement shall be governed by and be construed in all respects in accordance with the laws of the State of Malaysia not being Islamic Law (Shari'aa) and the parties submit to the jurisdiction of the Courts . . . (not being the Shari'aa Courts or any Courts implementing Islamic law or Shari'aa) in all matters connected with the obligations and liabilities of the parties under the security document."
- "Nothing in this Agreement shall be invalidated and no rights, powers, remedies and security of the financier created under the Security Documents shall be affected in any way if any of the provisions herein . . . or the enforcement thereof contravenes or is prohibited by Islamic Law, Islamic tenets and/or 'Shari'aa.'"

It is also interesting to note that in many of the "Shari'aa-compliant" contracts that are supposed to be "Islamic," we find similar statements, most famous of which is: ". . . this is a finance contract and in case it is brought to court it will be handled as a regular interest-bearing financial transaction!"

CONCLUSION

RF financing is a discipline with a spirit and not a set of legal documents that can be prepared and fixed to fit a certain set of requirements. An interesting way to visualize the dilemma of money with all what it entails including monetary theory, economic theory, finance and economics is to make it metaphorically resemble a big elephant. Many have attempted to improve the health of that elephant but they started from the tail without paying attention to the huge body of that elephant and its head. With all due respect and sincere appreciation for all the sincere, dedicated and pioneering work accomplished in the second half of the twentieth century in the field of RF (Islamic) banking and finance, it is believed that we, in the twenty-first century, must handle the head of that elephant; that is, its monetary discipline with its paper (fiat) money regime and its body (i.e., the huge network of banking and finance institutions and its riba-based culture, sales techniques, and products).

It is regretful to observe that the Islamic Banking Movement in the twentieth century—out of sincere and well-intentioned efforts—has gone through all these religious claims, models, and references, in addition to the hundreds of millions of dollars spent and the valuable energy invested to develop such models and "compliant" contracts, to end up traveling a full circle. As we read earlier, in a court of law, the contract is to be handled as a regular (riba-based) contract. This is the same good old riba-based contract that many of the Shari'aa-compliant efforts made since the 1970s and spent extensive efforts to change! There is another amazing observation having to do with the complete and deafening silence about two very basic aspects of the RF financing discipline. These are the Marking-to-Market and the Commodity Indexation Disciplines, which were discussed in Chapters 3, 5, and 6.

REVIEW QUESTIONS

1. How did the name of RF banking develop over the years from the 1950s until now, and how do you feel about that?
2. How did "RF" banks start in Malaysia? How have these RF banks thrived and grown compared to, for example, what happened in Saudi

Arabia? What course of action was taken by the Malaysian authorities to promote and enhance RF (Islamic) banking?

3. Describe in a step-by-step approach:
   a. The process used by a bank to finance a home using the murabaha (cost-plus) model. Please enumerate the features and give your opinion.
   b. The process used by Al-Baraka model when the first RF bank was opened and operated in the United Kingdom in the mid-1980s. Please share with us your opinion.
   c. The process used by the South Asia model and your opinion of it.
4. Compare each of the models. What is the real added value that the model contributes to the customer?
5. Quote examples of lawsuits that involved "Islamic" finance in Malaysia and the UK. Please describe how these cases were settled and how "Islamic" banks arranged to protect their businesses. What do you think?

NOTES

1. The cost-plus model was used by American Finance House (LARIBA) in the southern California area in the United States when it started its operations in 1987; it was used until 1989. However, after severe criticism from many of the community members based on the fact that it was very similar to riba-based transactions, LARIBA started searching for another model. In late 1989, LARIBA started using the new model, which was based on a lease-to-own approach developed for home financing for Al-Baraka Bank in London. However, it was further developed by the author to include in it the Marking-to-Market Discipline, as will be discussed in a later chapter.
2. *Institute of Islamic Banking and Insurance (IIBI)* magazine: New Horizon, www.NewHorizon-IslamicBanking.com, issue 170 (January–March 2009), 38.
3. Cited in Mahmoud Elgamal, *Islamic Finance—Law, Economics and Practice* (Cambridge, England: Cambridge University Press, 2006).
4. Ibid.
5. Ibid.
6. Muhammad Taqi Usmani, *An Introduction to Islamic Finance* (Karachi, Pakistan: Idarutul Ma'arif, 1998), 152–153.
7. Elgamal, *Islamic Finance—Law, Economics and Practice*, pp. 44, 129.
8. Fatwa of Al-Baraka available at www.lariba.com/fatwas/index.htm and in Arabic at: www.lariba.com.eg/karadawy.htm.
9. Usmani, *An Introduction to Islamic Finance*, pp. 85–91. Also available online at: www.lariba.com/fatwas/usmani.htm.

10. See note 8.
11. *Al-Baraka Annual Edict (Fatwa) Meeting of Islamic Finance Scholars—Meeting Number* 6 (pp. 77–78) Algeria 5–9 Sha'baan 1410 A.H./2–6 October 1990 C.E. Sha'abaan is the eighth month of the Islamic calendar, and A.H. (which stands for After Hijra) denotes the Islamic calendar system. (*Hijra* means immigration of the Prophet Muhammad [pp] from Makkah to a northern city in the peninsula called Madinah, where the early pioneering Muslims started the foundation of the Islamic civilization and where the Prophet Muhammad is buried.) The Islamic calendar has 12 months, but it is based on the lunar system, which is 11 to 13 days shorter than the Gregorian system. That is why, for example, the month of fasting—Ramadan—rotates through all seasons. The calendar does not have a "short" month concept, as in the Jewish and Asian lunar calendar, to adjust for the seasons. For more information, please visit: www.islamicity.com/science/islamic_calendar.shtml.
12. Ibid., pp. 81–82.
13. Ibid. The fatwa also states: "This opinion is based on the view that what is intended here is not to effect riba, which is forbidden in the law (Shari'aa). Thus, following our deliberations, we reached the following conclusion: 'Despite the fact that interest, as conventionally used in banking transactions, coincides precisely with the riba that is forbidden in the law (Shari'aa) to pay or receive, and regardless of whether the underlying transaction is a consumption or production loan, we have found that there is no objection to the use of the term "interest" in the cases related to those dealing with Al-Baraka Bank, London, aiming to benefit from the financial advantages given to interest in various cases of deposits and financing.'"
14. Ibid., pp. 84–87.
15. See note 9.
16. Ibid.
17. Ibid. Justice Taqi Usmani states of the Shari'aa foundation: ". . . there is no difference of opinion among the Muslim jurists in the permissibility of leasing one's undivided share in a property to his partner. If the undivided share is leased out to a third party, its permissibility is a point of difference between the Muslim Jurists. Imam Abu-Hanifa and Imam Zubair are of the view that the undivided share cannot be leased out to a third party, while Imam Malik and Imam Shafi', Abu Yusuf, and Muhammad Ibn Hasan hold that the undivided share can be leased out to any person. But so far as the property is leased to the partner himself, all of them are unanimous on the validity of 'Ijarah.'" It is interesting that he does not call the leasing its proper classification and name as the "right to use." He also stays silent about his position on the subject of dividing ownership into the title and the right to use.

18. During a number of meetings with him at his home in Cairo and via telephone conversations.
19. Guidance Residential Finance.
20. It is interesting to note that company representatives claim that the LLC monthly fee is paid to the state, that it costs $35 in the state of Florida, and that the customer pays half of it and the company pays the other half.
21. Philip T. N. Koh, *Islamic Financial Instruments: The Civil Law and the Sharia Confluence or Conflict?* Presented at the fifth Islamic Finance Conference, Monash University, Kuala Lumpur, Malaysia. Philip T. N. Koh, FCIS, is an advocate and solicitor (equivalent to an attorney in the United States) for the High Court Malaya; his degrees include: LLB (Hons) (University Malaya), LLM (London), MA (Theology) (Australian Catholic University).
22. Ibid.
23. Ibid. *Shamil Bank of Bahrain v. Beximco Pharmaceuticals* [2003] 2AllE R (Comm) 849 (Ch); [2004] 2 Lloyd's Rep 1 (CA).
24. *Bank Kerjasama Rakyat Malaysia Berhad v. EMCEE Corporation Sdn Bhd* [2003] 2MLJ 408; *Affin Bank Bhd v. Zulkifli b Abdullah* [2006] 3MLJ 67; *Bank Islam Malaysia Bhd v. Adnan B Omar* (1994) 3CLJ 735; *Bank Islam Malaysia Bhd v. Shamsudin bin Hail Ahmad* [1991] 1 LNS 275; *Arab-Malaysian Merchant Bank Bhd v. Silver Concept Sdn Bhd* [2005] 5 MLJ 210; *Tahan Steel Corp Sdn Bhd v. Bank Islam Malaysia* [2004] 6MLJ 1, 33, 34.
25. J. Suriyadi, in *AMMB v. Silver Concept.*
26. See note 21.

CHAPTER 11

RF Banking Model for the Twenty-First Century: The LARIBA RF Model

Developing the Shari'aa-Based Finance Model

This chapter will detail the unique financing model that was pioneered at American finance house LARIBA, which is based on the Judeo-Christian-Islamic Shari'aa law, in contrast to the "Shari'aa-compliant" riba-based contract fitting to make these contracts "compliant," as discussed in Chapter 10. This LARIBA RF finance unique and pioneering model is believed to embody the true spirit and substance of the RF (riba-free) value system.

In 1987, we started a humble community-based effort by establishing LARIBA (American Finance House). We started our finance operations by using the cost-plus (*murabaha* or BBA in Malaysia) model, because we did not know better. We simply started with the interest rate of the day, calling it a "profit" index based on opinions and edicts (*fatwas*) by some of the early Islamic finance Shari'aa scholars at that time. We would calculate the value of the dollar amount to be borrowed and compound it at the "index" (interest rate) to create an equivalent sale price at the end of 15 or 30 years, depending on the term of financing. The company would agree to sell the house back to the ultimate buyer at the original price plus a profit element, so that the total cash paid would be equal to the compounded value arrived at—just as if it were a regular interest-based transaction.

Many of us were not very comfortable with this approach, despite the fact that it was sanctioned by most of the well-known Islamic finance Shari'aa scholars at the time. At this juncture, the values of the educated and sophisticated believers in the Judeo-Christian-Islamic value system became useful. The educated and analytical God-loving members of the community objected to the murabaha system because it did not make sense to change names, use the same exact approach used by riba-based conventional banks, and then claim that we are providing RF (Islamic) finance services just because the name was different. We at American Finance House were severely criticized by many of the puritan and educated members of the community, who asked repeatedly: "What is the difference?" In fact, we concluded that they were right—there was not much difference. Within our first year of operation, we began to develop a model that is truly beneficial to the user and that follows and abides by the Judeo-Christian-Islamic Shari'aa law. We call it the Shari'aa-based model or the LARIBA model, as it is known worldwide.

Through our development of this model, we asked a fundamental question: "Why does the RF discipline prohibit riba or the act of renting money for a price (the interest rate)?" We reasoned that if we stopped renting *money* and started looking at the rental rates of utility offered by the *items* financed in the actual marketplace, then we were in fact investing in rent-producing cars, properties such as homes, apartments and commercial buildings, and businesses. If the transaction is profitable because of the rent it generates, then it makes prudent economic sense to invest in it with those who come to us for finance. We also concluded that based on the fact that money is a fungible thing (changes its nature upon use as does an apple or a loaf of bread) that cannot be rented, then giving it to a customer in the form of debt financing (the word *financing* produces a *dayn* [indebtedness] in Arabic, compared to *qard*, or *loan*, as explained in Chapter 2) is actually as if we are investing with this customer.

THE PUZZLE AND THE CHALLENGE OF DEVELOPING RF BANKING AND FINANCING

It is useful to document the many challenges we at LARIBA faced while trying to meet the challenges of developing an RF finance and banking operation and of solving the many puzzles that appeared before us with the humble tools and the limited resources we had available to us at the time. The intention of this review is to document what our team did for the record and for the benefit of future generations.

When we started LARIBA, our goal was to come up with a solution to the problem of living a full American life without violating the laws of our faith as ordained by the Judeo-Christian-Islamic Shari'aa law and to uphold the laws of the land without participating in the culture and practices of riba/ribit. It may have been easy to articulate that goal; in practice, though, it was a big and daunting challenge and a hard dream to realize!

The following sections comprise a review of the many currents we at LARIBA faced while developing an RF financing and banking operation and discipline.

Legal and Financial Categories

First, let us review what we learned so far in this book by touching on each category of the subject that had an impact on the development of the RF financing and banking brand.

The Law (Judeo-Christian-Islamic Shari'aa Law)

- Shari'aa has as its main goal the protection of the self, the family, the assets and wealth, and the faith in the community.
- Shari'aa focuses on the intent and not the form. The real test is the outcome.[1]
- The main objective of Shari'aa is to maximize the benefits to the family and the community at large while pushing away what is harmful.
- Shari'aa requires those who make edicts (*fatwas*) to be knowledgeable of the faith, the community, and the local conditions and systems where the edict is solicited and applied.
- Shari'aa states that if it (the law) cannot be applied in full, that does not give believers an excuse to abandon it completely without attempting to the best of one's abilities to apply whatever is possible.[2]
- Shari'aa does not allow the use of ruses (deceptive tricks, *heelah*) or circumventive structures that may look as Shari'aa compliant but in fact ignore the intent and spirit of Shari'aa.

Money

- Money is a thing and is fungible, like an apple or a loaf of bread. Fungibles cannot be rented because the minute they are given to another person, they will be used. When these fungibles are used, they change their nature and cannot be returned in the same exact original shape, form, and condition as stipulated in a rental relationship. When a fungible is handed over to another, it becomes an "investment" that is entrusted with those who accept it. Money is a fungible thing.
- Money cannot be rented by paying a price for using it. In the past, the payment of a price (rent) for the use of the money was called *usury* by the Catholic Church; now it is called an *interest rate*.
- Money is a measuring device and is useful only if invested. It can only be invested in a useful activity, such as the purchase of an asset, a service, or a business. Money does not grow on its own if not used. It must be invested in a productive activity that produces a useful outcome.

- Money cannot be loaned, except in the form of a good benevolent loan (*qard hassan*) to those who need it. A loan is conceptually looked at as a bite (*qard*) given to those who lend the money out of the assets of those who borrow it because they do not have money; it is to be given to the poor and needy without expecting any increase.
- Money is a measuring tool that is used to measure the value of the product or service produced by this economic activity. The success or failure of that activity is measured by how much value—measured in money—is produced by that asset. The concept of *return on investment* is a measurement of the success or failure of that investment.
- Money must be real money that can be used as a calibrating measure of value, and real money must be a base commodity. It can be gold, silver, a basic energy or mineral source or a basic food staple. Paper (fiat) money can be used as a convenient tool of exchange and trade, but it must be related and indexed to these basic real money reference commodities. That is, one can use U.S. dollars, British pounds, the yen, and/or the euro, but such currencies must be referred and indexed to a calibrating standard and reference commodity to be fair to all by keeping fair pricing and free and balanced markets without deception (*gharar*).
- When basic commodities—that is, gold, silver, and food staples like wheat, rice, corn, salt, or dates—change hands, they must be exchanged for the same amount if they are of the same element. That is, gold is exchanged for the same amount of gold, and corn for the same amount of corn. The exchange must be done on the spot, hand-to-hand, and the trade cannot be delayed or settled at a future date. That implies that these calibrating reference commodities (pricing metals and food staple commodities) cannot be included in futures and options market speculative activities. If the exchange involves two commodities that are different but used for the same purpose—for example, gold and silver, which are used as a pricing reference (real money), or corn and wheat, which are used as a food staple—the exchange can be made with an increase, but it must be done on the spot and should settle hand-to-hand without delay. This makes trading these calibrating reference pricing commodities in the futures market prohibited by the Judeo-Christian-Islamic Shari'aa law. For example, it is allowed to exchange one ounce of gold for seven ounces of silver because both are used as pricing commodities or one bushel of wheat for three bushels of barley because both are used as a food staple. The exchange must be done on the spot. No delayed delivery is allowed. If the two commodities are different in element and in use, they can be exchanged for an excess amount, and the exchange can be done on the spot or for delivery at

a later date for a different price. However, if delivery is not completed at the agreed-upon date for a legitimate reason (such as a change in the economic environment or climate conditions), no increase over the agreed future exchange ratio is allowed to compensate for the delay in payoff, because it is considered riba (time-dependent nassee'ah riba). For example, an ounce of gold can be exchanged for 7 bushels of wheat hand-to-hand; subject to agreement between the two parties it can be exchanged for 15 bushels of wheat after one year. If the wheat is not available after one year for reasons that are considered *force majeure*, no further increase is allowed. This concept was introduced in Chapters 5 and 6 as the *Commodity Indexation Discipline*.

- In case one wants to exchange an item for another item of higher quality—for example, exchanging small oranges for larger, higher-quality oranges—the exchange must be done in equal quantities. However, to perfect the exchange as a legitimate exchange according to the Judeo-Christian-Islamic Shari'aa law, the small oranges should be first exchanged in the market for a different element, such as gold or corn; then the gold or corn can be used to buy the larger oranges. This way, markets are kept fair. Transacting business this way ascertains that fair pricing is achieved without deception (*gharar*). This concept, called the *Marking-to-Market Discipline*, was introduced in Chapter 3.

Interest Rates

- Interest can be defined as an excess or an increase—riba (in the Qur'aan) or ribit (in the Jewish Bible and the Old Testament)—over the original amount of the capital given as a loan (*qard*). The increase is divinely prohibited (*haram*) in case of a qard to the poor and needy. Any increase in whatever form—be it in the form of excess money, compensation through free and unpaid labor, the free use of the borrower's facilities, or publicizing the borrower's indebtedness—is considered riba and is not allowed.
- In a *fiat* (paper) money regime, the interest rate used by central bankers to decide on the policy of how much money to print or to withdraw out of the market—called the Fed Fund rate in the United States—is different from the riba prohibited by the Judeo-Christian-Islamic Shari'aa law.
- Interest charged as a price for renting money to those who do not have it (because they are poor or because of lack of capital available to business owners) is what the prohibition of riba (interest and usury) is all about. Interest charged for a transaction that implies the renting of money to a user of money for credit (*dayn*) without marking it to market is considered riba or ribit, and is not allowed by the Judeo-Christian-Islamic Shari'aa law.

Money and Commercial Transactions

- The original teachings of the Judeo-Christian value system focused on the abuse exercised by the rich against the poor in agrarian societies in order to expropriate their land, crops, and properties and render them slaves in their own originally owned land. The Judeo-Christian-Islamic value system reinforced that ruling and made it into law, which prohibited *usury* (or *interest*)—the act of charging a rent for the use of money, which is considered an act of riba or ribit. The system encouraged helping those who need money through the application of a benevolent lending system of *qard hassan*, meaning a good and benevolent loan that does not charge any increase over the original amount in any shape or form.
- With the development and growth of trading and commercial businesses, owners of these businesses needed money not because they were poor but because they wanted to expand their business and their capacity to transact more business. A historic revolutionary development in business financing was brought about by Islam under the leadership of Prophet Muhammad (pp) by developing RF disciplines and pricing valuation disciplines using reference commodities (the Commodity Indexation Discipline). This system brought about a currency calibration mechanism that brought a standardized calibrating reference pricing commodities that can be used for defining the real value of different currencies used in various countries.
- As commerce developed and grew, the Judeo-Christian-Islamic system expanded upon the Judeo-Christian system to allow buying and selling at different prices as dictated by fair and open markets, but not renting the use of money (*usury*, now called *interest*). Buying and selling transactions that involved an increase due to profit making, in an open and fair market, are not like charging riba by charging a rent for the use of money, as revealed in the Qur'aan. For buying and selling to be perfected, the title of the item to be acquired must change hands from the seller to the buyer in a documented buy-sell agreement. Different models developed to put this rule in effect were used during the Muslim reign and adapted in the 1700s by the rabbis in the eastern European areas in their *hetor iska* models (also known as *musharaka* or joint venture in Islamic RF banking applications).
- To perfect the buy-sell transaction, the two parties must participate in all risks (including profit and loss) as defined by the buy-sell contract.
- The buy-sell contract must be fully documented, free from any deceptions or undefined parameters and risks, and should be transparent. The concept is called *gharar free* (which means deception free). *Gharar-free* rules also require that trading in risk, as in cases of sale with a guaranteed

buyback at a future date at a predefined price (called *eena* in Shari'aa law), uncovered short sales, naked options, and futures, as well as financial derivatives, involve major aspects of *gharar*, and they are prohibited.
- Future sale prices cannot be set ahead of time because such practices interfere with the free and fair market system as defined by the Judeo-Christian-Islamic value system. Only God knows the future. That is why a contract that includes two sales (i.e., buying a property from someone at a price and promising to sell it back to him/her at a future date in the same contract at another prefixed price—an eena sale), is prohibited. Contracts of this type are considered divinely prohibited (*haram*) contracts and a means of gharar.
- If the person who was entrusted with the money cannot make the payments for legitimate reasons, such as unexpected changes in the economy or a sudden war—*force majeure*—foreclosure is not allowed unless one of the parties committed fraud or deception. In this case, the asset is sold and the proceeds are distributed between the contracting parties as per the partnership agreement.
- In a joint venture, a predefined profit is not allowed. However, the percentage participation in profit and loss, or the rent for the use of the property, or the service between the parties can be agreed upon between them.
- One cannot sell what one does not own.
- Ruses and circumvention (*heelah*) of the rules of the Judeo-Christian-Islamic Shari'aa law are not allowed.

Banking and Securities Laws and Regulations

- In the United States, these regulations are rooted in the Judeo-Christian-Islamic value system of fairness, nondiscrimination of any type, transparency, full disclosure, truthfulness, trust, and preservation of people's assets and properties. These regulations encourage the people to reinvest their savings in the community, thus generating job opportunities and economic prosperity and allowing equal opportunity for all, regardless of faith, skin color, gender, marital status, language, national origin, social status, and/or relationships.
- The laws and regulations are designed to supervise, identify, and discover abusers of the system and to examine the safety and soundness of the financial institutions entrusted with people's hard-earned deposits, investments, and assets.
- The laws and regulations are based on the vast body of recorded human experience throughout history.
- The laws are designed to prevent fraud by those who attempt to defraud people in the marketplace and those who want to take advantage of people who do not have knowledge, are not educated in finance and

risk, or are not well informed, by insisting on full disclosure, transparency, and fair representation.

- The regulations are in continual development because they are adapted to correct previous and newly uncovered faults and loopholes in the design of the system, with an objective to reach perfection as closely as is humanly possible.
- The laws and regulations require that any financial transaction must be translated into an implied interest rate (as required by Regulation Z in the United States, called Truth in Lending Act [TILA]) that includes the effect of all fees and expenses so that the consumer can make a fair comparison between different offers and an educated decision in his or her financial dealings.
- The regulations do not allow depository institutions (i.e., banks) to own properties except in cases where these properties are owned by default, such as foreclosure (this concept is known in U.S. banking as *Other Real Estate Owned*, or OREO). Banks are encouraged to dispose of these properties as soon as practically possible.
- The laws and regulations include a safety valve that gives borrowers who cannot meet their obligations ways and means to restructure and reorganize in an orderly fashion without destroying their facilities or their investments, which might cause the loss of jobs and create more problems (U.S. bankruptcy laws).
- The laws prohibit the payment of interest on bank demand deposits (Regulation Q in the United States, which was suspended, as stated earlier). Interest-paying accounts are allowed only with strict conditions and limited withdrawals (see Regulation D in the United States).
- The U.S. banking regulations offer standardized, frequently used, and fundamentally needed consumer finance contracts, such as those used to finance home mortgages or automobiles. This cohesiveness helps maintain quick settlements of disputes and avoids lengthy and expensive legal proceedings.

Participants in the Development of Modern RF Banking

It is important to recognize all the wonderful people from different professions, with diversified training in many fields, Muslim and non-Muslim alike, who did and are still doing their best to bring full life back to the "Islamic" RF banking industry. This effort has not been attempted since the nineteenth century, in a world that has seen quantum leaps in the business of riba-based banking and finance since that time.

The following is a listing of the different professionals and customers who have actively and sincerely participated in the development or the use of services of modern Islamic RF banking and finance since it was first conceived in the second half of the twentieth century.

Muslim Puritans

The word *puritan* is advisedly used here because of its American roots.[3] It was used first in England to describe a group of early American settlers who immigrated to America so that they could apply the true spirit of the Judeo-Christian values as articulated by the Protestant reform leader Martin Luther to their daily lives. The Muslim Puritans emigrated from many Muslim countries around the world to the United States to escape persecution in their own former lands and/or to seek new opportunities in America. It is believed that the first responsibility of the RF banking brand is to help this category of citizens solve the problem of living the American dream without the use of riba/ribit. The challenge that RF bankers have to resolve is how to convince these puritans that an RF banking approach is acceptable, in order to bring them into mainstream America and get them to move out of small apartments they do not own and into a nice home that they do own in a nice neighborhood. This, it is believed, could help them and their families become viable and effective U.S. citizens, because they will get to know their neighbors, send their children to neighborhood schools, and become fully involved in the American way of life. They would eventually transform, becoming owners of a "piece of the rock." We at LARIBA have had the honor of meeting wonderful professionals who have lived a puritanical life in the United States, without borrowing with riba (interest) or depositing their money in conventional riba-based banks to earn interest on a time certificate of deposit, because they believe that doing so is haram (divinely prohibited). Many of these families lived in humble, crowded apartments for more than 20 years to avoid taking a loan with interest to buy a home. They went on saving as much as they could to pay for their dream home. In fact, when we started LARIBA, some of these wonderful new Americans had saved up to 80 percent of the price of their home and contacted us so they could finance the rest riba free. Because of their meticulous attention to detail regarding the RF models and procedures used, and their commitment to not participate in any religiously prohibited transaction, many of these puritans wanted proof that the techniques used were sanctioned by a fatwa (an edict) from a recognized and trusted scholar or a group of well-placed scholars. We were happy, patient, and delighted to meet that challenge.

To satisfy the needs of these customers, we wanted to expose them to all the edicts and Shari'aa opinions (fatwas) by displaying these fatwas in full on the www.LARIBA.com website. We urged our customers to read these edicts carefully before they decided to use our services. We also made it clear on the website that including these edicts on our website did not mean that these scholars have given us an edict to sanction our own model, and that we shall never use the names of the scholars to sell our products and services. In addition, we made our Shari'aa supervisor available to answer any questions from these customers. The Shari'aa supervisors used to spend approximately 3,000 minutes a month on their mobile phones answering questions about Shari'aa and the details of the LARIBA RF finance model. This strategic decision proved to be an important one, because it made us serve and meet those highly analytical, deeply religious, and intellectual customers who are interested in reading and analyzing. They are disciplined to reach their conclusions on their own, without being influenced by superstar scholars' names or persuasive marketing and advertising. It also was very fortunate that they were so well disciplined because of the highly diverse nature of the many scholars (some of whom are self-appointed), who have opinions that in many cases differ from one scholar to another, depending on their country of origin and the religious subgroup they represent. This situation made us address the customer base in a direct and transparent way.

Monetarists[4–6]

These research-oriented Muslim (and non-Muslim) scholars in the field of monetary theory believe that the use of *fiat* money and credit creation in the modern banking system through the multiplier effect, as explained in Chapters 5 and 6, are the main reasons for the ills of the international riba-based conventional monetary and finance systems, and that truly Islamic RF banking should not be part of these. They sincerely believe that RF Islamic banking scholars and practitioners should start a serious effort to use gold as a monetary base. Efforts toward that goal were attempted in the late 1980s with the introduction of the gold dinar in Malaysia. The prime minister of Malaysia, Dr. Mahathir Muhammad, was one of its supporters. Many of these monetarists believe that RF Islamic banking in a *fiat* monetary regime is in fact a mere change of names and brands without resolving what they believe to be the fundamental problem of the *fiat* money regime and riba-based conventional banking monetary expansion techniques. It is believed that resolving this major concern will take a very long time, and it would not be practical to wait until it is resolved because it involves major structural changes in the world's monetary and political systems. It is the duty of RF bankers to develop wise solutions that can be applied now—in the short and medium term—to benefit all people by applying the tenets of the Judeo-Christian-Islamic Shari'aa law in an intelligent, prudent, and productive way. This approach will achieve our goal of helping people transact their business in an RF way, according to the values of the Judeo-Christian-Islamic system, and hopefully in a way that will normalize the effect of such a variable and major concern on the real market value and market prices in a standardized unit of currency using the Commodity Indexation Discipline.

To attempt to meet this important challenge without having to wait for a solution that may take many years to achieve, we followed what is believed to be two wise solutions that are based on the law (Shari'aa). One was an ideal solution in which we would apply the *Commodity Indexation Discipline* described in Chapters 3, 5, and 6. The approach was to replace *fiat* money with a reference commodity (or a matrix of commodities which are basic to the economy), such as gold or silver or even a staple food commodity like wheat, rice, or soybeans—or a combination of all of these, as James Baker III recommended in 1987, and which is detailed in Chapter 3, 5, and 6. However, this solution would be complicated and impractical. It would take years and the support of many of the countries that command strong economic, diplomatic, and military power—exactly as happened in 1948 in the Bretton Woods Agreement.

That is why it was decided to use these reference commodities as a tool to decide, in a macro way, whether an economic pricing bubble is perking in the type of asset we intend to finance (by this we implicitly mean "to invest in"). The other solution we use is to *mark the property to market* using the Marking-to-Market Discipline described in Chapter 3. Applying the Marking-to-Market Discipline normalizes the effect of *fiat* money and its growth by evaluating the return on the investment in the property at hand based on its actual lease or rental rate in the marketplace. Doing it this way—going to the live market and researching the lease that such a property or a business could command in the open market—enables us to evaluate the economic viability of the capital investment. This way, we can ascertain that the actual market rent or lease rate of this property is used, and not the interest rate, which is the rent of money.

Religious Leaders

We deal with many categories of religious leaders. These differ not only by their role but also by their country of origin and the school of thought in the Judeo-Christian-Islamic Shari'aa law they subscribe to.

Popular Thought Leaders in the Muslim World These recognized leaders write extensively on many religious, social, political, international, and jurisprudence issues that have to do with Islam in general and business transactions and finance in particular. They have become recognized and highly respected stars in the field of religious leadership over the past 60 years. Because of their status, they were the first to be contacted by those who wanted to develop RF (Islamic) banking practices. These leaders did the best they could, based on the knowledge on hand at the time, to start the RF "engine" and get it going. Their biggest challenge was their lack of understanding and education in the fields of banking and finance. However, their religious knowledge was complemented by the Muslim and non-Muslim professionals who worked in the riba-based conventional banks as bankers, attorneys, and entrepreneurs. They were able to lay down the foundation of what is now documented as a set of opinions that are based on the law (Shari'aa).

Perhaps one of the more significant, pioneering, and influential efforts was the Annual Fiqh (Jurisprudence) Symposium that was pioneered by Dallah Al-Baraka[7] to "Islamize" different banking products and services. The annual symposium pioneered by Dallah Al-Baraka was by invitation only and was attended by most of the recognized religious, banking, and Shari'aa experts in the world. Sheikh Saleh Abdullah Kamel, a visionary leader in the field of RF finance and the founder of Dallah Al-Baraka in Jeddah, Saudi Arabia, must be recognized for the historic effort that laid the foundation for the growth and globalization of RF banking and finance. Many of the tools, techniques, edicts (*fatwa*), and research centers at Al-Azhar Seminary, Al-Azhar University in Cairo, and other universities in Saudi Arabia, Malaysia, and Pakistan that are available today were pioneered and generously financed by the important and historic efforts of Sheikh Saleh Abdullah Kamel. Most of the invited scholars came from the Arabic-speaking world in Egypt; the Sudan; Tunisia; Jordan; Syria; the Gulf oil-producing countries, such as Saudi Arabia, Kuwait, and Bahrain; and the English-speaking countries like Pakistan, India, and Malaysia. These scholars have since served as active members of the Shari'aa Boards; a new profession pioneered by Sheikh Saleh Kamel in most of the RF (Islamic) banks around the world. As these scholars became involved, their reputation increased and respect for them grew, from the wealthy banks in the oil-producing nations of the Gulf to the masses at large (particularly in the Indo-Pakistani subcontinent and Bahrain). Their services were solicited by 40 to 70 different RF (Islamic) banks around the world. As a result, it became both difficult and expensive—if not impossible—to obtain a famous name (superstar) religious scholar to sit on the Shari'aa Board of an RF (Islamic) bank, to approve a product, or to issue a fatwa (an edict) that would sanction and legitimize the activities of a new RF (Islamic) bank or finance company.

Local Community Religious Leaders or Imams The imams are the leaders of the community masajid (mosques). *Imam* means a *prayer leader*, and in particular the leader for Friday congregational prayers. Imams are also considered religious and religious conscience leaders who act as counsels for the community. Most of them are qualified scholars in the Qur'aan and the *Hadeeth* (pronouncements and sayings of Prophet Muhammad [pp]), but few of them have a good command of the details of the law (Shari'aa), especially in topics having to do with riba, business transactions, banking, and financing. They rely on the easy and noncontroversial way out by honestly stating that riba is haram (religiously forbidden) and that they cannot recommend a certain model or an RF bank or RF finance company because they are not familiar with the details. Others rely on the opinion of the scholars discussed in the previous category. Some of these local leaders are first-generation immigrants from the Muslim world, and they usually resort to checking with their teachers in their home country. Communication, translation, and familiarity with the local norms, cultures, and ways of doing business in the United States, Europe, and the West in general are a real challenge with this group. Others, who can be considered the new generation of American (Western) imams, are either raised or are born in the United States. It is our sincere hope that these imams will bring a new dimension to the study and implementation of the Judeo-Christian-Islamic Shari'aa law that will be useful and beneficial to all.

Community Leaders These are professionals who took a keen interest in organizing the communities in general and religious services for the communities in particular. These professionals became the heads of the national Islamic organizations in America and in the European countries, and the heads of the local communities in major American states and in countries such as the United Kingdom, France, Germany, and the rest of Europe. They mostly are self-educated in religion and are well read. Some of them have even decided to go to religious seminaries to learn more about the Qur'aan; in some cases, they memorized all of it and decided to be further educated in the law (Shari'aa). They usually take a neutral, well-advised position of not sanctioning any commercial activity, business, or company because they are afraid of the repercussions that may impact the whole community if the RF company or RF bank they recommend fails or uses practices that result in the loss of the community's investments and assets.

Academics and University Professors of Economics and Finance

These university professors and recognized research scholars in the field of finance and economics have invested their life in research in the field[8] of finance and economics at the highest academic levels. Some of them, by the nature of their discipline in research and analysis, have attained a very high level of proficiency and scholarship in the field of Shari'aa and in particular the science of RF commercial transactions and business. Many have been critical of the models used in some RF Islamic banking (the Shari'aa-compliant models developed in the twentieth century) as it is practiced in the world. They concluded that the methods and contracts used may fulfill the requirements of the law (Shari'aa) on paper and in form, but these solutions do not achieve what the spirit and intent of RF financing was instituted to do.

Dr. Abdul Hamid Ahmad Abu Sulayman,[9] formerly rector of International Islamic University–Malaysia and a Saudi Arabian religious scholar, stated:

> *Islamic Banking is a good example of a field where basically the Western system has been partially "Islamized," but in many aspects "Islamic" names have been given to various transactions that do not truly reflect the goals or vision of Islam. The result of this frame of mind is called al–hiyal al-shar'hi'aah, [Shari'aa tricks], where forms, terms, and words are changed rather than the substance when the need is really for a new vision.*

In fact, a new term was coined by one of the distinguished academic researchers in the field and the first professor to hold a Chair in Islamic Finance and Economics at Rice University, Professor Mahmoud Elgamal.[10] The term he uses is *Shari'aa arbitrage*, by which he means that a new arbitrage has been created for Shari'aa scholars' sanctioned models. Such arbitrage does not really add anything to the transaction. It only adds an increased cost due to the additional fees and added cost of legal maneuvers and ruses (*heelah*) used—let alone the cost of Shari'aa advice to make the existing riba-based contracts compliant, at least in form, with Shari'aa. Professor Elgamal complains bitterly about the added cost and sophisticated financial engineering structures that have been used with one benefit in mind—keeping the form intact without trying to preserve the spirit and intent of the RF value system. As a matter of fact, legal fees may have been very high for the first few deals, but as the contracts were standardized and used in a large number of transactions, the costs became much lower. It is believed that the concern should not only be about the cost, but about the real economic benefits of going through the many sophisticated steps and various ruses, deceptive tricks, and special-purpose (SPV or special-purpose vehicles) limited liability companies (LLCs) that have no economic or even structural or legal benefit except to make things look Shari'aa compliant. It is the responsibility of the academics to reveal, through dedicated and thorough research, the real benefit of the RF system to rescue all people from a lifestyle that may mean a bleak future for all of us and pave the way for them to lead an RF lifestyle. We need to focus on the spirit and intent of the RF value system.

Politicians

The attitude of political leaders toward RF (Islamic) banking varies depending on the country, the region, and the political orientation of the leader and his government. In many of the Arabic-speaking Middle Eastern countries, RF (Islamic) banking has been a big challenge to many of the politicians. Some are afraid of giving the Islamic political groups or political parties (representing the opposition to their political rule) added legitimacy and power that may undermine their ability to rule. Others have resorted to allowing it as an expedient political solution, but with many limitations and restrictions. Other politicians in the West have been sensitized by politically motivated lobbyists who are interested in casting the Muslims as terrorists and as disloyal citizens. Another concern has been the creation of a back door to implement the law (Shari'aa), which is frequently criticized as being backward and medieval. In the oil-rich Gulf countries and in some Asian countries (e.g., Malaysia, Indonesia, Pakistan, and Bangladesh), RF (Islamic) banking is offered side by side with riba-based banking to meet the growing market demand for Islamic banking services.

To meet this challenge, LARIBA started the tradition of organizing an annual seminar on RF financing, which included a prestigious awards dinner, the LARIBA Award for Excellent Achievements in RF Banking and Finance, to recognize outstanding contributors to RF banking from all countries in the world. We invited local and national politicians to the dinner, as well as religious and community leaders, diplomatic core representatives, and the press in Los Angeles, California, and in Dallas, Texas. At one of these galas, we recognized the prime minister of Malaysia, the honorable Dr. Mahathir Muhammad, in Chicago, Illinois, for his unique efforts to rescue the economy of Malaysia during the 1997–1998 Asian currency crises and for his support of RF banking in Malaysia. These efforts have helped us introduce many in the political arena in the United States to what we are trying to do, increase their understanding of RF banking, and help them feel comfortable about the integrity and worthy ideals of RF banks and its leaders and practitioners. This effort has had a definite positive impact on the acceptance of RF financing in the United States.

The Media

We were contacted and were covered by many media outlets, including television, radio, newspapers, and magazines. These outlets included organizations such as ABC News, National Public Radio, Voice of America, Malaysian TV, the *Wall Street Journal*, *Time* magazine, the *Los Angeles Times*, *USA Today*, the *Dallas Morning News*, the *Washington Post*, the *New York Times*, the

Chicago Tribune, *Bloomberg Finance*, and many other news wire services, newspapers, and magazines. It was very difficult to explain to the reporters what we do because it is very involved and required a lot of attention and concentration on the part of the correspondent. We learned that reporters are looking for "sound bites" and simple, fast statements. We also learned how to do that, but we insisted that they get a piece of paper and a pencil, and we went through the LARIBA RF finance model from A to Z. Many of them were impressed. In fact, the coverage we received was the envy of many in the field. Our competitors asked who our public relations officer was. The fact of the matter is that we never had one. We received all these calls from all these reporters without even seeking or expecting them. They must have been a gift and recognition from the "Higher Authority—God."

The most interesting experience was a call we received from a senior business reporter, Elliot Blair Smith, at *USA Today*. The newspaper had published at least three articles about LARIBA. When we took the call, Smith explained that he had spent more than a year in Pakistan investigating money laundering and transfers involving terrorists. He wanted to investigate and know more about LARIBA. We explained to him in great detail what LARIBA is and what we have done at LARIBA, as a responsible American finance company that abides by the Judeo-Christian-Islamic values and the American laws. The phone call lasted more than 60 minutes. At the end of the call, he said, "Can I come to visit you?" He flew from Washington, D.C., to meet everyone at LARIBA in Pasadena, California. Over lunch, he told us that he was looking for "blood" and illegal activities and that he was extremely impressed with what he experienced. He published a wonderful article about us at LARIBA in *USA Today* on the front page of the Money section.[11]

Bank Regulators

Bank regulators are required by law and their job description to make sure that the depository institutions (banks) under their jurisdiction operate according to regulations and that the laws of the land are upheld to the fullest in a safe and sound way to preserve the assets of the citizens and the reputation of the system. Regulators have been willing to listen graciously and with great interest, and to entertain new products and service ideas.

The first attempts to engage the banking regulators in the West were made in the United Kingdom, when Al-Baraka Bank was started in London in the mid-1980s. The charter was withdrawn later by the U.K. bank regulators because of a number of violations and the fact that the owner entity—Dallah Al-Baraka in Saudi Arabia—though licensed there to operate as a finance and investment company, did not have a licensed operating banking institution that was chartered by the central bank of the country of origin, Saudi Arabia.

Another attempt was later made by a Kuwaiti bank (United Bank of Kuwait) at its U.K. branch in London and its U.S. branch in New York. The New York branch representatives explained to the regulators—the Office of the Comptroller of the Currency (OCC), in this case—how their finance scheme and model for home mortgages, called *Al-Manzil*, worked.[12] After long evaluation, research, and deliberation, the OCC concluded, based on the detailed supporting documentation supplied by the applicant, that there was no difference between the proposed scheme and the regular interest-based contract, and pronounced it acceptable.

When an entity (like Fannie Mae, Freddie Mac, the IRS, or the OCC) decides that a new product or scheme looks fine, they list it under the category of *exceptions to the norm*. This term was used by Fannie Mae and Freddie Mac in order to accept the modified Shari'aa-compliant contracts. That is well and good in good times, but that "exception" can be taken away any time, rendering the RF bankers' many years of effort worthless. That is not what we are aiming to do. The challenge, for those who believe in RF banking and way of life, is to devise legal documents that abide by the laws of the land, using ways and means that comply with the regulations and the laws of the land while not violating the basic values of the Judeo-Christian-Islamic value system and Shari'aa law.

Professionals Who Serve and/or Benefit from the New Islamic Banking Industry

Shari'aa Scholars RF Shari'aa scholars come from diversified backgrounds; they have accumulated a respectable body of knowledge and command the respect of all. The demand for RF (Islamic) finance Shari'aa scholars has outstripped the available supply, which elevated many of the scholars, especially those who have a good command of the English language, to the level of "superstars." In RF banking, the RF Shari'aa scholars serve three important operating functions:

1. Developing the proper RF finance models to be used.
2. Developing Shari'aa-qualified banking products and services.
3. Ensuring that the RF bank operates according to the law (Shari'aa); religious compliance.

The RF Shari'aa scholars also serve another important function, and that is the marketing of the bank they represent. The RF (Islamic) bank with the most superstar scholars on its Shari'aa Board will carry more credibility to its operations and will attract more depositors and customers. RF Shari'aa scholars also participate in and attend seminars, symposia, and international conferences to represent the RF banks they work for and the products they helped develop and sanction. They hold training courses, give television and radio interviews, and go on talk shows (some are beamed live to the United Kingdom and the United States), which brings a lot of customers to do business with the RF banks they represent. For example, as a prerequisite for their success and their ability to sell their shares to the public, new RF (Islamic) banks make sure that their Shari'aa Boards include some of these superstar RF scholars. A typical Shari'aa Board member commands an annual retainer of approximately $50,000 (or more) and a first-class plane ticket and accommodations when he travels. Scholars with this superstar status sit on the Shari'aa Boards of an average of 50 to 70 RF banks. This raises very serious conflicts of interest, confidentiality, and insiders' concerns and issues. It is hoped that a major effort will be designed to increase the supply of these RF scholars by producing a new generation of localized RF scholars to serve in the future.

Attorneys Many Western attorneys became involved in the field of RF (Islamic) banking because world banking laws and regulations are set according to Western standards. Most of the attorneys involved specialize in tax planning, business structuring, and financial engineering. These disciplines are important because the attorneys invited to "Islamize" the banking agreements, finance contracts, deed of trusts, promissory notes, and arbitration articles in the contracts were requested to improvise these legal documents so that they would be acceptable to both Shari'aa experts and to Western countries like the United States, the United Kingdom, France, Germany, and other countries in Asia and the Middle East that use these laws. I have participated in, attended, and was exposed to many of the meetings that were held between representatives from Islamic banks or finance companies and specialized lawyers. The time spent by the lawyers, and the fees charged, was unbelievably high. Once one of my attorney friends telephoned me from San Francisco after concluding one of these contracts—"Islamization" programs—and earned a handsome seven-figure fee. He asked me, "Why are you Muslims doing it this way? You end up with a contract that looks Islamic on paper but it does exactly what any other standard conventional riba-based finance contract does—but, of course, it costs a lot more just to remove the word *interest* from the contract to make it look as if it is a buy/sell agreement, which it definitely is not."

Riba Bankers Riba bankers are professionals with a proven track record and experience. In the early stages of the development of RF "Islamic" banking, they brought the products, services, and techniques of the riba-based conventional banking system to the RF (Islamic) banking arena. They are useful in explaining the conventional banking business to the scholars, which helps them create Islamic RF products and services that comply with the law (Shari'aa). They also brought their experiences in conducting efficient banking operations.

Organizers for Seminars, Industry Group Conferences, and Training Programs In the beginning of the RF (Islamic) banking movement, seminars were organized by semigovernment and government organizations—mainly in Malaysia and Bahrain—to discuss, promote, popularize, and present papers on new products and services that are RF qualified. Professionals who were known to make true and pioneering contributions to the field of RF banking and finance based on their research work were invited to present their papers at these conferences, seminars, and workshops.

As the business of training conventional bankers on RF banking grew, and demand increased from many RF banks throughout the world, commercial seminar organizing companies took over the business. These seminar and training companies organized educational training programs and promotional conferences in the field of RF (Islamic) banking and finance. These conferences were run for profit, which is why the organizers invited a predefined roster of superstar scholars and speakers to attract participants, who paid thousands of dollars to register for these seminars. These seminars were turned into marketing forums for large investment banks and conventional commercial banks, which paid to speak or participate in a panel. Fees paid to include the name of the company on the program and to invite the company to speak in the conference ranged from $10,000 to $100,000. These entities would present their new, "revolutionary," and extremely profitable "Shari'aa-compliant" products, which were designed and approved by no less than the superstar scholars, who were, of course, present at the conference as speakers and as supporters of the "marketing and sales" cause.

After this practice became the norm, LARIBA's board of directors decided not to participate in any conference that required that we pay to speak. Our position has always been and still is that we do not believe in the practice of "pay to play." We consistently told the organizers that if they thought we could add value and substance to the seminar or the conference because of what we achieved, we would be happy to participate. The result was, of course, that not many of these organizations invited us to such conferences.

RF Banking Consumers and Potential Users

Four types of customers contact us for RF financing:

1. *The puritans.* These customers "shake in their boots" when the word *riba* is uttered. They contact us because they are looking for an RF solution to a financing situation. They are willing to pay more to save themselves from participating in the haram (divinely prohibited) act of dealing in riba. These are the best customers any financial institution would hope to add to their books. They have some of the best credit scores and are devout customers who are the best in fulfilling their contractual

obligations. However, it takes extreme patience and knowledge of the law (Shari'aa), RF products and services, as well as a long time and extreme patience, to explain the RF finance models used and to convince them of (and make them comfortable with) the true RF nature of the transaction.

2. *Average consumer.* These are customers who would be interested in RF financing if it were made available at competitive prices, costs, and terms as compared with conventional riba-based banks. These customers can be Muslims or non-Muslims. At LARIBA and the Bank of Whittier, we have had the great honor of adding many of these customers, who come to us from all faiths and backgrounds through referrals because they appreciate the unique, sincere, and high-quality service as well as the added value of the RF banking and RF bankers.
3. *Customers who claim that they are coming to RF banks because they want RF financing*, but after further investigation it is discovered that they have been to every bank to seek financing, and after they failed to get it, they came to us, the RF bankers, to see if we could help. These customers need to be handled with great care, prudence, and scrutiny. One such experience was a potential customer who had a printing shop. He stated that he liked RF financing because the RF bank "participates" in the profit and loss. After scrutinizing the application and exercising prudence, we found out how much loss he had in his business. We declined the financing (i.e., the investment).
4. *Educated and sophisticated customers.* These are the young American-educated and trained professionals who are used to asking the right questions and who are keen on getting straight, convincing answers that make sense. They respect the opinion of the RF scholars, but they want to know why things are done in a certain way and how the RF scholars arrived at their edicts (*fatwa*). They want answers that appeal to the mind and to the intellect. They demand answers that prove that RF financing makes economic sense and offers advantages over the alternative conventional riba-based system. They are savvy, Internet-conversant, and sophisticated in analysis and in reaching conclusions. These customers are, in fact, the best customers for a bright RF banking future.

THE SHARI'AA LAW AND THE LAWS OF THE LAND

The many different and sometimes opposing undercurrents, mainstream constraints, and varying participants detailed earlier make the process of developing a true RF banking operation a huge challenge. These challenges had to be met and resolved wisely, and all the pieces of the puzzle had to be put in place to pioneer *The Art of RF (Islamic) Banking and Finance* in the United States. It was a huge challenge. Here is a list that gives an overview of the major issues:

- Where should we start? We did not have the capital to apply for a bank charter, and even if we did, how could we apply for the charter of a bank run without riba in a business environment that only knows and recognizes riba-based conventional banking and finance transactions?
- Who would run the RF bank or the financial institution? There are very few experts and practitioners in the field of RF banking and finance. It was also challenging to know that those with banking experience are employed by established banks and are paid high salaries. Bankers with RF (Islamic) banking expertise are employed with very high salaries by the well-capitalized and rich RF (Islamic) banks in the Gulf oil-producing countries.
- Where could we find an attorney who had the necessary RF expertise and was affordable, given our limited resources?
- What RF financing model should we use, and would it comply with the laws and regulations of the United States—our country—without violating the Judeo-Christian-Islamic Shari'aa law?

Developing the Art of RF (Islamic) Banking and Finance

The Art of RF (Islamic) Banking and Finance is the process by which all of the undercurrents described earlier are put together to come up with a new brand of banking. The RF banking brand merged all of these undercurrents to produce a banking service that would be able to satisfy the market demand. The goal was to develop the RF banking system as an optimum and meaningful financing approach that would benefit all people and help them to live a life free from riba (the RF lifestyle).

The Approach Used to Develop the Art of Islamic RF Banking

The challenge we faced, at LARIBA, was how to develop an RF bank (with the limited knowledge we all had then; please note that in 1987 we called it *interest-free Islamic banking*) that would abide by the law (Shari'aa) and at the same time would comply with the laws of the land. In trying to do so, a prior experience I went through in 1972 in Dallas, Texas, was useful. At that time, I was the chairman and one of the imams (religious leaders) of the first organized Islamic Center in Dallas (and maybe one of the first in the state of Texas), the Islamic Association of North Texas, or IANT. I also was nominated to be the southwestern regional representative and board member of the Muslim Students Association of the United States and Canada (now called ISNA—Islamic Society of North America). One of my responsibilities was to perform weddings according to Islamic law (Shari'aa). The board of the association asked me to start working on getting Texas state officials to recognize an Islamic wedding contract, instead of the state-sanctioned civil marriage license. Our group talked to lawyers, state officials, and the clergy in the Christian (Catholic and Baptist) and Jewish faiths. Soon, we learned that other faith leaders had tried earlier, but it was not possible. A wise religious leader shared with us the fact that the civil marriage certificate carries with it the weight of the law of the land in order to protect the two parties in the marriage contract. In addition, the civil marriage contract can be signed by a civil official (e.g., a justice of the peace), which makes it civil, or by a religious leader, which makes it religious. Without the power of the state's legal system, law enforcement systems, and legal codes, this leader pointed out, no institution would be able to prevail in case of a dispute.

It was a personal experience that made us see the light. One day I performed the wedding of a wonderful young lady who had come to the United States from a Muslim country to study. She met a young man, and they decided to get married. I officiated the wedding using a "homemade" Islamic wedding contract. Six months later, the young lady contacted me with tears in her eyes and told me that her husband had left her and disappeared. We tried to help by calling the police. I showed the police the "Islamic" marriage certificate. We were told that it might be a useful document, but it did not carry the weight of an official civil marriage certificate issued by the municipality involved. After searching my heart, I concluded that we should use the civil marriage contract. We concluded that what makes a marriage Jewish, Catholic, Methodist, Protestant, or Islamic is not only the religious vows and the signature of the religious leader on the civil marriage contract. What makes it any of these things is what the parties do at the time of a dispute. The couple can go to the religious leader (e.g., the rabbi, priest, or imam) to preside over an arbitration process that is conducted according to the tenets of the faith involved, and that will make it religious. Or they can go to a civil court and that will make it civil. After this experience, which deeply touched us all, we recommended to all Islamic Centers in the United States and Canada that no imam or certified community leader be allowed to perform a wedding without a civil marriage certificate, in order to protect each party. This ruling stands today.

Our team at LARIBA reflected on this experience when we started looking for ways to bring RF banking to America, in order to solve the puzzle and optimize the process of merging the many currents and players in the field as detailed earlier.

We were concerned and troubled by the standard approach used by many "Islamic" RF bankers who were interested in establishing an Islamic RF banking operation in the West. It is sincerely hoped that this frank discussion will not offend any of the wonderful, well-intentioned, and believing RF (Islamic) bankers in the world—Muslims and non-Muslims—who want to use this approach.

The standard approach used starts by requiring local authorities in other non-Muslim countries to change their laws, regulations, and procedures to fit the requirements of the Shari'aa Board of those RF banks. I was privileged to have been exposed to many of the detailed discussions that led the U.K. Financial Services Authority (FSA) to license an Islamic bank (the Islamic Bank of Britain [IBB]). The legal costs involved, the compromises arrived at, and the monetary guarantees offered could be done only by a very rich entity that could afford it and would be capable of providing the guarantee from the central bank of the country involved. We respectfully ask those who use this approach to reverse roles. Imagine that a bank in the United Kingdom comes to a Muslim country, presents itself as a Christian bank, and calls itself the "Christian Bank of Country X"—and demands that the laws of the Muslim land be changed in order to transfer large sums of money and open that bank. It does not require much imagination to project the reaction of the country. It is hoped that this attitude will be changed because it may be temporarily accepted by some non-Muslim countries' officials to achieve a short-term goal, like securing "Islamic" funds for an "Islamic" bond (*sukuk*) in a European city. Alternately, it will be accepted from those who happen to have the funds to spend today, but after the funds dry up, then there will be no more guarantees and the license is withdrawn or the special conditions are removed. It is also important to note here that complying with the U.S. banking regulations and satisfying the regular periodic examinations conducted by the bank regulators is a very important and essential aspect of running a viable bank—both RF and conventional—in the United States and most other Western nations, as well as other nations in the world.

In our efforts to establish a viable RF banking operation in the United States, we started by realistically listing the facts. Here is a list of what we came up with:

- The OCC[13] ruled that the Islamic banking models of cost-plus (*murabaha*) and lease-to-own (*ijara wa iqtinaa*) proposed by the United Bank of Kuwait—which follows the Shari'aa-compliant model—are in fact regular interest-based finance transactions with different names.
- Almost all Shari'aa-compliant contracts we reviewed and analyzed were in fact similar to the regular finance contracts, but with different names and procedures that make them look "Islamic" on paper. In fact, the

contracts stated implicitly that they are indeed regular finance contracts in case they are brought to the courts of law.

- There is sensitivity associated with the mixing of religion with business and also the stereotyping of Muslims in many Western societies. These sensitivities intensified after the heinous attacks of September 11, 2001.

While developing an RF finance model in the United States, we decided that our goal was to find a workable solution that would abide by the Judeo-Christian-Islamic Shari'aa law and would not violate or attempt to change the laws of the land. We drew on our experience in developing the Islamic marriage procedures and contracts in the United States. There were many reasons for us to adopt this strategy. The first is that we do not have the money, the human resources, or even a standardized and universal working RF legal code that we could present as a foundation.

The basis of our strategy was to achieve small successes in our endeavor to prove the viability of this new RF banking and finance system, and not to limit our growth and success potential by trying to achieve impractical and unrealistic goals. We started from the fact that the United States has, as described earlier in the book, the most sophisticated and fair banking system representing the fruits of many years of improvisation; it is rooted in the fairness of the Judeo-Christian-Islamic set of values. In our efforts to develop RF banking and finance, we decided that we should not start from ground zero and reinvent the wheel, but should draw on the huge body of human experience in banking and finance, which cannot simply be ignored or thrown away, as that approach would not be fair and wise and indeed would have been counterproductive. Our priority was to prove to ourselves first that we had a working concept with proven success and to chart a track record for applying this new RF brand of banking and finance. We knew that this approach would require a lot of hard work to raise capital; to put systems in place; to locate, identify, recruit, and train human resources; to clearly understand how conventional riba-based banking works; and to develop RF models and products that are easy to understand by the RF bankers and customers and that comply with the law (Shari'aa) while at the same time upholding the laws of the land. Most importantly, we wanted to develop an investment (loan) portfolio that proved that we have a small but viable and proven RF banking and finance alternative. We firmly believed that American Muslims as a minority—and, for that matter, the minority of all minorities in America—must be humble, respectful, and understanding in this effort to develop RF banking and finance without violating the law (Shari'aa) but while also upholding the laws of the land.

An important aspect of the RF banking business is its faith-based credentials. History has shown us time and again that religious fervor, when instigated, can be very strong; it can be the source of great emotional energy, which can be used for marketing products and services. It has happened in the United States, when religious groups (including some Muslims) raised capital from innocent and trusting members of their faith-based communities, promising them great returns in this life and God's acceptance in the hereafter, only to see the trusting customers lose everything when the promoters disappear. One recent episode was the Madoff hedge fund, which attracted money from many Jewish nonprofit organizations as well as many wealthy investors and banks all over the world. It turned out, apparently, to be a type of Ponzi scheme that lost its investors billions of dollars.[14] Another episode was that of Sunrise Equities, a Chicago, Illinois, company that not only offered "Islamic" investments but also had its own "Shari'aa Board," which the company had imported from India to add legitimacy to its operations. In one of the financing applications we received from a customer, we noticed an investment certificate from Sunrise Equities that promised the investor 15 and 20 percent annual returns on investment. We met the founder and the representatives of the company during a New York conference in October 2007, took them to the side, and told them that what they were doing was wrong, illegal, and damaging—not only to themselves and their victims but to all of us in the new and emerging RF banking and finance industry in America and the world. They shrugged their shoulders and walked away smiling. Earlier that year, a delegation from LARIBA had flown to Chicago to discuss the matter with their imported and company-financed "scholar" and his team and to alert them to what was being done in the name of religion. We were discounted. It was saddening to learn that in September 2008 the Indian- and Pakistani-American Muslim community—mostly from Hyderabad—lost all of its investments, and the "bearded" and "turban-dressed" religious business "leader" who founded the company disappeared with his staff. Episodes like these have also been experienced in Egypt, Turkey, and many other places. We at LARIBA have disciplined our operations from the time we began in 1987 to go slowly; to exercise prudence; never to use faith in our advertising; to learn systems, techniques, and operations from the pros in conventional banks; to attract professionals to join our team; never to promise what the return will be, because only God knows the future; and to always try our best to underpromise and overdeliver. These are, in fact, some of the aspects and character foundations of the Judeo-Christian-Islamic value system that make RF banking a uniquely positioned brand name in banking.

In conclusion, we decided to first understand the laws of the land and to try to apply these laws in the same way that the Islamic/civil marriage process was developed in the United States.

MAJOR OBJECTIONS OF RF SHARI'AA SCHOLARS TO THE CONVENTIONAL RIBA-BASED FINANCE CONTRACT

Most modern RF (Islamic) finance scholars who reside in some of the Muslim countries made the following recommendations to change the riba-based conventional banking system:

1. The contract must be changed to fix some of the noncompliant features it suffers from. The Shari'aa-compliant contract (as ruled by these scholars) must:
   - Not show the word *interest*. As discussed in Chapter 8, this stands against Regulation Z (TILA). As discussed in Chapter 10, there is a clear edict (*fatwa*) from the most senior and respected scholars that states that if the laws of the land require using the word *interest,* then it can be used. This fatwa (edict) is conditional on not using interest—money renting—in the actual process of financing.
   - Show a buy-sell transaction in which the bank buys the item from the seller, and then sells that item to the buyer. As discussed in Chapter 10 and in many parts of this book, U.S. banking regulations stipulate that banks cannot act as buyers of properties. In addition, in most Western systems, any buy-sell transaction triggers a tax event, and the profits are taxable. In addition, as was concluded in Chapter 10, all the buy/sell schemes are synthetic in nature and are in fact ruses and deceptive tricks (*heyal*) used to get around and circumvent the law (Shari'aa).
   - Late payment fees cannot be applied unless the payments were intentionally made late without an acceptable excuse. These late payment fees should be paid out to a charity, and should not be added to the bank's profit. This was an easy requirement to implement.
   - Any income realized by the bank due to an unavoidable interest source must be paid to charity and not added to bank profit. This condition is also achievable.
   - In a lease-to-purchase model, insurance premiums must be shared by the two participants in the transaction in proportion to their ownership. Most scholars suggested that the monthly payment of the buyer be increased to reflect that cost, and add the portion of the insurance premium to the monthly payment. Per U.S. bank regulations and for the sake of transparency and straightforwardness, the bank must disclose in full the payments made and what they were used for. In response, it was decided that if an RF bank uses the LARIBA Shari'aa-based RF finance model, the bank must tell the customer openly that he or she is responsible for the insurance; because he/she owned the

shares from the beginning (as will be discussed later in the LARIBA RF Finance Model) and that he/she is the one benefiting from the use of the facility in an operating lease.

- Maintenance must be shared. Again, because the buyer uses the facility, regular maintenance is not only required but must be paid by the user to keep the property in the best of all shapes.
- Customers' deposits must be exposed to bank profit and loss. Investment products cannot guarantee a certain interest rate or return. It is believed that it is unfair, in a banking scheme that offers FDIC insurance on deposited funds, that peoples' hard-earned savings and deposits are exposed to the risk of loss. We are aware of the scheme used in the United Kingdom (at the IBB), in which the customer must be offered the guarantee *and* offered the option of refusing it in order for that condition to be applicable.
- The bank should have a supervisory board that specializes in Shari'aa to ensure that the bank's products, services, and operations are compliant with Shari'aa. The Shari'aa Board is given the power to render bank operations not compliant. That condition can be implemented as a part of, and a complement to, the annual on-site regulatory examination conducted by the concerned regulatory authorities. As discussed earlier in the book, many of the aspects of the regulatory onsite examination ensure compliance to regulations. It must be frankly admitted that the bulk of the regulations, which are in fact Judeo-Christian-Islamic in nature, are not even considered by the Shari'aa Boards of some of the RF (Islamic) banks in many of the Muslim countries. As an example, the fairness of treating expatriate workers needs to be closely examined and evaluated by the Shari'aa Board of the RF bank or finance company before dealing with such companies. Another example is applying the basic human right, pertaining to nondiscrimination, when a guest worker applies for obtaining credit in a host country. The Shari'aa Board in the setting we propose should complement the onsite regulatory bank supervision to make sure that the RF models used are in fact the same as advertised and that these models comply with the Judeo-Christian-Islamic Shari'aa law and that the RF bankers and their representatives apply that law (Shari'aa) when they promote and "sell" these products and services. Unfortunately, the extent of the Shari'aa Board's involvement in the operations of many RF (Islamic) banks has been minimal, and their job mostly ends at sanctioning a particular RF model or an RF product. Unfortunately, it is observed that many of the "Islamic" bankers use the names of these respected scholars to advertise and seek acceptance in the market. The question we have is: Does every light bulb

we buy have to have the signature of Mr. Thomas Edison to make it an acceptable light bulb?

2. It is interesting to note that the focus of the scholars was concentrated on the legal aspects of the contract but did not include some of the basic requirements that define the substance and spirit of the true RF banking and finance system. For example:
   - Very little is mentioned about the aspect of social responsibility of "Islamic" RF finance. It is true that the rules put forward by many Shari'aa Boards and scholars prohibit participation in financing religiously prohibited (haram) businesses like the manufacturing or selling of intoxicants, gambling, illegal activities, or promiscuous activities, as well as businesses that involve socially irresponsible activities such as environmentally damaging industries, businesses that do not treat their employees and customers fairly, and institutions that use false advertising to con their customers. However, one would notice little or no mention of the responsibility of the RF banker to local communities by investing the deposits gathered from a community back into that community—as in the U.S. Community Reinvestment Act (CRA)—before allowing bank deposits to be invested outside the communities (and in some cases, outside the country), depriving the local communities of the opportunity to reinvest these accumulated deposits in order to help the economic growth of local communities and create prosperity for the citizens by creating new job opportunities. Also, it is noticed that there is no mention of treating people equally, without discrimination based on national origin, wealth, tribal ties, skin color, gender, or language.
   - There was no significant sign that the scholars of the RF Shari'aa and the "Islamic" bankers tried to benefit from the vast body of bank regulations, especially in the United States, that deal primarily with fairness and respect of human rights in the communities, as well as to protect those who experience unexpected and unfortunate circumstances beyond their control, as we see in the bankruptcy laws and codes in, for example, the United States.
   - It is peculiar to note the posture of most of the Shari'aa RF finance scholars, who ignore what is believed to be the basic revolutionary aspect of the RF finance system: the Commodity Indexation Discipline, which neutralizes the effects of *fiat* money fluctuations (leading eventually to a new, fair, accurate, and revolutionary RF Monetary Regime), and the Marking-to-Market Discipline, by which each of the items to be financed is marked (compared) to the market to identify any market pricing bubbles and help investors make prudent investment decisions. We believe in prudently evaluating the potential

investment in terms of *return on capital* invested, by pricing, for example, cars, homes, businesses, or equipment based on the actual market-measured lease rate they would command in the open market system. It is believed that these rules are the most important, and add fundamental unique aspects to and provide real added value of the RF financing approach. There is no mention, for example, of paper (*fiat*) money and how it may lead to unfair and deceptive pricing aspects and unfair valuation of a transaction.

In conclusion, it is believed that in a fair and viable RF banking regime, all the banking regulations that were discussed in Chapter 8 should in fact be part of Shari'aa Boards' requirements. It is the real intent and not merely the words in a convoluted contract that in fact makes the RF banking and finance system unique and beneficial. Many of the Shari'aa-compliant contracts are in fact designed by force-fitting the conventional riba-based contract into language that "complies" with Shari'aa in form, but that in most cases does not satisfy the real spirit and substance of why Shari'aa prohibited riba.

I want to share with you, the reader, a personal experience that we hope will shed more light on the unfortunate practice of some of the "RF scholars" who have in fact risen to positions of fame despite very little being known about their education, training, research, scholastics, and/or any proven track record of documented, debated, and critically reviewed research.[15]

At LARIBA, we once decided to engage a well-American-educated economist who had completed a PhD in economics in one of the respected universities in the United States, had authored a number of books on "Islamic" economics, presented himself as a scholar in the law (Shari'aa), and acted as an adviser to some of the most prominent law firms active in "Islamic" finance legal services. We wanted this economist to evaluate the LARIBA Shari'aa-based RF finance model as a foundation for true RF banking and finance and develop a set of documents that he would feel satisfied with what he believed to be the law (Shari'aa). We gave him the fruits of our many years of research since 1987, supported with references and research papers to read. He came back with a big smile on his face, saying, and I quote, "This is really unique and is different. I think you have something that will be very useful in the Islamic banking industry." We agreed on the scope of work he was assigned to perform, which consisted of making sure that the research we documented was included and articulated in his efforts and ensuring that we had followed the laws of the land and the norms required by the U.S. banking regulations—something we later discovered that he knew very little, if anything, about. He asked us to supply him with copies of the standard deed of trust and promissory note used in standard banking transactions. After a few weeks, he e-mailed us his products. Upon investigation, and after matching the Microsoft Word documents using the edit-tracking facility, we can summarize what he did as follows:

1. Replaced the word *interest* with *rent* or *profit*. We had told him that we take care of that in the process of RF finance preparation, and that doing it his way creates a completely different set of documents that will require us to obtain an exception from the regulators in order to receive complementary approvals, which would expose us to a lengthy and expensive process that is not permanent. We also stated that this approach might compromise the interests of the customer, especially in a court of law, where it would result in utter confusion among the judge, the prosecutors, the defense attorneys, and the jury. We also stated that it does not matter—based on many references in the law (Shari'aa)—what you call that percentage sign (denoting interest) as long as it does not imply the "renting" of money, indicating a riba-based transaction.
2. Made the process look like a buy/sell agreement. We told him that in a buy/sell transaction—based on the laws of the land and Shari'aa—we should include a documented and properly recorded transfer of title from the seller to the bank (the buyer), which violates U.S. bank regulations and credit policy. This step must be followed subsequently by a sale from the bank to the ultimate buyer. In addition, this claimed buy/sell step is, in reality, synthetic, because we know that the bank never intended to buy the property and that the process is done this way to make it look "Islamic." We told him that metaphorically, it reminded us of a man who wanted to enjoy a few nights with a lady. He proceeded to marry her with the intention of divorcing her after he got his pleasure—definitely a deceptive trick designed to make the process look religiously and socially acceptable on paper, though the intention was anything but! We also told him, based on our long-time banking experience, that this approach might open the bank (as a buyer of the property) to punitive actions by the regulators and a potential capital gains tax that could be significant. He said, to our amazement, that changing title (of ownership) was not necessary, because at the time of Prophet Muhammad (pp), there was no change of title, let alone the concept of title altogether! We told him that we obviously were no longer living in that age. We also told him that it would be counter to our claims to be trying to uphold the law (Shari'aa) if we did not tell the truth, which is one of the most important foundations of any faith, let alone the Judeo-Christian-Islamic value system.
3. Included in the documents was a very interesting disclosure, in which he stated, and I quote: "This is a finance contract . . ." Our response was,

"If this is the real intent, what is the point? Why go through all these changes and maneuvers?" He said that we needed this to be done in order to be compliant with Shari'aa.

We canceled his consulting contract. He reacted by saying that he was not surprised because he felt that we had no respect for scholarship! He is still being invited to teach scores of European and Western bankers in training seminars, short courses, and conferences on how to structure "Islamic" contracts that would "comply" with Shari'aa. These are the same seminars organized by the same groups that have controlled the "Islamic" banking promotion domain with one goal in mind: presenting scholar participants who will help promote the "Shari'aa-compliant" banking that conforms to the methodology promoted and signed on by the very Shari'aa scholar "superstars" created by such promoters.

In another experience, one of our staff members was sharing the challenges we face as a minority in the United States with another "scholar." The staff member shared with the scholar that we all should be wise, honest, and creative in order to offer true RF banking that would be based on the law (Shari'aa) without violating the laws of the land and the U.S. banking regulations, while at the same time offering real economic substance and an advantage to the user of RF financing techniques. This scholar's advice was that we get ourselves a good lawyer who is well connected with the regulators and/or a retired regulator—as they had done earlier, in another European capital—and all would be taken care of. We shared with this scholar that in the United States, it is not the usual practice to buy your way in; even if you were successful in the beginning, it would cost you a lot of money and result in many restrictions—as happened in the aforementioned European country—that would render RF financing a "joke," something that satisfied the form but not the spirit and the substance of the Judeo-Christian-Islamic value system based on Shari'aa.

While developing this LARIBA Shari'aa-based RF model, we had to come up with solutions to the many challenges discussed previously in this book and we had to merge many of the opposing undercurrents. The following is a list of the major guidelines used to develop the model:

- It should reflect and embody the real spirit and substance of the Judeo-Christian-Islamic Shari'aa law.
- It should be based on Shari'aa (notice here the phrase *based on*, not *compliant with*) and not force-fitted, as is done in the Shari'aa-compliant approach.
- It must reflect the added value and benefit to the user when compared to the models used by the riba-based system and the Shari'aa-compliant system.

- It must enforce and abide by the laws, regulations, and standards of the banking and financing system in the United States. The most important task here is to design the RF alternative product and service such that it can easily be compared with the riba-based product and service to enable the consumer to make a well-educated decision.
- It must be appealing to all users, regardless of their faith, skin color, national origin, ethnicity, gender, marital status, or language.
- It must be convincing to the educated and sophisticated users, offering a real economic advantage and benefit and not relying solely on the reputation of a famous religious scholar's endorsement.

BUILDING THE SHARI'AA-BASED LARIBA RF FINANCE MODEL

After a thorough analysis of the Islamic finance models available on the market and used mostly in the oil-rich Gulf countries and in Malaysia, it was concluded that these "Shari'aa-compliant" models were in fact not much different from those used by the riba-based conventional banking system. What reinforced our conclusion was the ruling passed by the Office of the Comptroller of the Currency (OCC) in response to the application of the New York branch of United Bank of Kuwait to allow the bank to offer "Islamic" banking using the cost-plus (*murabaha*) and lease-to-own models. The OCC concluded that these products were the same as interest-based financing. This fact made us conclude that we do not need to obtain special government approvals and exceptions that require a huge investment of time, money, and effort. We felt that what was needed was a system that would truly implement the Judeo-Christian-Islamic values of Shari'aa to benefit all.

Many attempts were made to devise a model that would satisfy our requirements at LARIBA. After a long search and extensive analysis, the effort focused on an analogy to our community's experience with the development of marriage procedures and contracts in the United States. A marriage contract is considered in the Judeo-Christian-Islamic system as the most solemn, most binding, and "thickest" of all contracts (Qur'aan 4:21). Based on our community's earlier experience with the development of an Islamic Shari'aa-based marriage system and procedures that utilize the civil marriage contract, we can draw a wonderful parallel with our efforts to develop a Shari'aa-based RF finance system. As is normally the case in marriage, a standard process is used. In this process, a number of preparatory steps must be followed before signing the standard civil marriage contract. For example, the two families would meet and agree on the details of the marriage agreement (e.g., the dowry), and the wedding details (e.g., the religious leader [the rabbi, priest, preacher, or imam] who will officiate the wedding). Then, the couple to be wedded would apply for a standard civil marriage license that has a space in it for a religious leader's signature. The religious leader would meet with the two families and the couple to be wedded to explain in full detail the meaning and obligations of the marriage contract according to the rituals and processes of the faith and to consult with and agree upon the details of the process. It was also reasoned that what makes a contract Islamic, Catholic, or Jewish is not only the religious ceremony and the religious wedding vows and rites pronounced, but also where the couple goes if they have a dispute. If they seek religious arbitration, that makes it a real faith-based marriage; if they seek the civil courts, that makes it a civil marriage.

There are two important considerations that need to be included in the development of the Shari'aa-based RF finance system:

1. That money is not rented. This stipulation is met by ensuring that the property is marked to market.
2. That, in the case of a dispute, the contracting parties use a board of arbitration that abides by the law (Shari'aa). This makes the contract "faith based," depending on the faith involved.

Another important parallel experience of the American Muslim community and its development was our 1969 attempt to make available to the American Muslim community *halal* (divinely permissible) meat products from chicken, cattle, and animals in general that are slaughtered according to the rules of the law (Shari'aa). In 1969, as the community prepared for the second nationwide Annual Meeting of the Muslim Students Association of the United States and Canada (MSA) in Green Lake, Wisconsin, I, acting as the chair of the conference, tried to arrange for the famous Oscar Mayer meat company in Madison, Wisconsin, to give us beef that was slaughtered according to Islamic rites, as it is conceptually done for kosher meat.[16] I went to Oscar Mayer's general slaughterhouse and participated in making the slaughtering according to the law (Shari'aa) and witnessed firsthand a rabbi doing the same for kosher meat. In an effort to systemize this process, one can state that the meat production involved a number of subsequent steps. These are:

1. *The Preparation* of the animal. It had to be clean, clear of any illness, and able to pass the standard regulatory tests of the veterinarian.
2. *The Faith-Based Action* to slaughter the animal, which differs by faith.
3. *The Processing*, which includes proper slaughtering and cutting and complete drainage of the blood; the details of this process also differ by faith.

4. *The Packaging* can include the label *kosher* (for Jews) or *halal* (for Muslims) in addition to the U.S. Department of Agriculture (USDA) label and emblem, which are required to sell the product according to the laws of the land as described in the universal standards set by the USDA.

Our strategic group reasoned that this process, too, could be copied and used in the development of RF financing without the need to incur huge expenses in trying to reinvent the wheel.

Applying this vision based on the analogies and the stepwise approach described above, we reached the following process as it pertains to RF financing:

1. *The Preparation.* This step includes taking an application from the customer and processing it by evaluating the customer's resume and personal data to get to know his achievements and his family, credit scores to check on his/her credit character profile, to learn where the property is in order to be ready for an appraisal, and to learn the customer's financial details.
2. *The Faith-Based Qualification.* This step includes the application of the LARIBA Shari'aa-based RF finance model to decide whether investing in and buying the property makes economic and prudent sense.
3. *The Processing/Underwriting.* This step includes the analysis of all the information gathered, the assembly of all the documents needed, and the decision as to whether we should join in investing in the property with the customer.
4. *The Documentation.* This step includes documenting the agreements according to the standard and universally used documents that follow the banking laws and regulations of the United States. To record the process we used, we developed what we call the LARIBA Agreement. It is a rider that is added to the agreements and contracts. It describes in detail the prohibition of riba, the process that was used, and the U.S. banking regulatory reasons why the phrase *implied interest* was used.

We are aware that others in the field of Shari'aa-compliant "Islamic finance" in the United States and other parts of the world—in their sincere attempts to comply with Shari'aa—have used expensive lawyers and costly and sophisticated structured corporate vehicles for the purpose of "financial engineering." We are also aware that others use ruses (*heyal*, or deceptive tricks and practices) to make the financing agreement look Shari'aa-compliant on the surface, but when the intent, the fine print, and the methods used are investigated, one can clearly and readily conclude that the contract is intended to circumvent the law (Shari'aa).

Based on thorough research in the original sources, on our consultations with many scholars in Shari'aa since 1987, and our soul searching, we decided to be fully transparent about the LARIBA RF finance model methods and not to mislead or misrepresent facts by using "financial engineering" techniques such as the use of an SPV, as discussed in Chapter 10.

It was also decided never to use the names of the eminent scholars in Shari'aa for advertising purposes to make it easy to "sell" our RF products and services. We feel that doing so takes away respect and eminence from those respected scholars and, in fact, is counterproductive because it is important that educated and sophisticated users understand the concepts used in order to be responsible for their actions and decisions in this life and the life after.

The Unique Features of the LARIBA Shari'aa-Based RF Finance Model

As described earlier, in today's banking terminology, one can conceptually define riba as the rent on money and/or lending to rent this money at a price or rate called interest rate. Riba-based conventional financing may involve unsecured and noncollateralized credit that is not asset or service based. The riba-based conventional financing system uses an index called interest to define the cost of "renting" money to the customer. In an RF finance setting, the bank's financing activity is looked upon as an investment by the bank in the individual (or company), in order to help that entity acquire tangible assets and/or services. In this capacity, the RF finance officer makes sure that the finance facility has economic merit by measuring the return on investment using the prevailing market rent of the facility, the service, or the business. Please note that in RF financing, we prefer to use the word *finance*, not *lend*, because the financing is looked upon as a true investment with the customer. The only loan in the law (Shari'aa), as detailed earlier, is *qard hassan* (a loan that is returned with no additions to the original value, which is made for a good cause).

The other important aspect of an RF banking transaction is that there is no predetermined value measurement for the renting of money, called *interest* in riba-based conventional banking transactions. In an RF banking transaction, the return on investment is obtained as a result of the investment process or the leasing process of the asset in question. That return on investment is the real measure of the value of the investment activity, with its unique characteristics. In doing so, the RF banker marks the item to be invested to the local market, instead of using a unified interest rate to rent money at a predetermined level throughout the country. For example, a house rent should reflect the value of that house and not a *capitalization* rate, as is done in most leases and in many models used by some "Islamic" bankers. The rent of two similar homes—one in Alabama, which has a smaller economy, and another in California, the eighth-largest economy in the world—should be different, because of the difference in the economic characteristics of each state. That difference should be reflected in the financing process by the lease rate of the item to be financed in each state, as dictated by the market forces of supply and demand.

The following are some of the unique features of the LARIBA Shari'aa-based RF finance model:

1. The RF model is based on a belief that can be articulated by our motto: "*We do not rent money; we invest in you.*" Applying this model requires that the RF banker approach each transaction as an investment (using the Declining Participation in Usufruct [DPU] Model) instead of lending. The RF banker advises the customer, to the best of his/her abilities, as to whether the transaction is a good investment or it is better for the customer to rent until the economic situation changes. This process prevents the buyer and the finance company/bank from participating in an economic pricing bubble and from buying an overpriced facility or business.
2. The RF finance model requires that the RF banker does not calculate the monthly payment by starting from an interest rate, as is done in riba-based finance transactions. Homes, cars, and businesses can be rented at a fair market value that is defined and agreed upon by the RF banker and the customer after studying the market. The monthly payment is based on the market rental value of the property to be financed. The rental value is determined by going to the market—both the customer and the RF bank finance officer independently—to measure the rental rate of a similar property in the same neighborhood by asking real estate agents in the area and checking data available on the Internet. The fair rental value is determined by mutual agreement between the customer and the RF finance entity. In this process of marking to the market, the house buyer calls three different real estate agents to get the actual market value of the rent of a similar house (in dollars per square foot), as if it were to be used as an investment property. In addition, the RF bank finance officer does the same. This way, the RF bank obtains an average marked-to-the-market, agreed-upon property market rent that the RF bank finance officer subsequently uses in its calculation of the rate of return on investment to decide whether buying the property makes prudent economic sense. Prudence in investing is an important ingredient of the spirit of RF financing.
3. The RF model requires that the RF bank or finance company work with clients in a humane, merciful, and fair way (*tarahum*) in times of trouble. To do this, the RF bank helps families that are in trouble by

counseling them and offering them the facility of an RF *qard hassan*, a "good benevolent loan," without any increase or interest, from a nonprofit organization that can assist in making part or the whole of the monthly payment until the difficulty is eased—for example, when the husband gets a new job to enable him to resume the payments.

The Stages Used to Implement the Shari'aa-Based LARIBA Model of Financing

The LARIBA Shari'aa-based RF finance model is based on the original and pioneering fatwa and model developed for financing homes in the United Kingdom by Al-Baraka Bank in London. However, the model has been modified and expanded by the author to include in it the two basic foundations of the true spirit of removing riba from financing transactions: the Commodity Indexation Discipline and the Marking-to-Market Discipline.

The process consists of three major stages:

1. Formulating the RF (riba-free) Shari'aa-based agreement.
2. Documenting the RF financing for compliance with U.S. laws and banking regulations by transforming the agreement into a U.S. government–sanctioned and standardized financing (mortgage) note and contract.
3. Signing the *LARIBA Agreement*, which explains the prohibition of riba, the terms in the standard U.S. contract, and the process used to mark the property to the market so the transaction is Shari'aa based.

Formulating the Financing According to Shari'aa

Fatwa There are a number of edicts (*fatwa*) issued by some of the highest-placed scholars in RF banking and financing (detailed in Chapter 10). The edict used by the LARIBA model is based on that developed for use by Al-Baraka Bank of London. In this model, the scholars divided the property rights of an item into two rights: The first is the right to own title of the property (*milk ul raqabah*), and the second is the right to use/operate the property—such as the use of a home, a car, or a business (*haq al manfa'aa*, meaning usufruct).

The procedure used by the model goes through the following stipulations:

1. The model allowed the RF finance institution or the RF bank to assign the buyer to act as an agent (wakeel) of the bank and to proceed to negotiate the purchase price and other conditions on behalf of the RF bank.

2. The RF bank, in one approach recommended by scholars, agrees to form a conceptual partnership with client to buy the property together, with the following stipulations: Registering the title of the item to be financed (home title, for example) in the partner's name, based on trust, from the inception of the contract is permissible under Shari'aa. Registering the property's title in this manner does not contradict the agreed-upon partnership, especially as the partner's ability to sell the home is restricted until full ownership of the property is established. In this regard, the scholars took into consideration the fact that this registration of title is a form of documentation insured by the officially established lien on the property, according to the conditions agreed upon with the partner.
3. The bank, in another approach recommended by scholars for transactions in Europe and the United States, would finance the purchase jointly with the buyer in the form of a joint ownership (musharaka):
   a. The RF bank would sell its entire share back to the buyer immediately and record the property (the house or the car) in the buyer's name.
   b. The RF bank would exercise and perfect a lien that makes the RF bank a lien holder, and get a contractual promise from the client to pay back the RF bank's share over a certain period of time (the term of the buyback) by the customer. In this step, the buyer would be the owner of the title (milk ul raqabah). The customer can register the title of the property in his name from day one.
   c. The RF finance company or the RF bank would participate in and share in the benefits of using the property (haq al manfa'aa)—in the case of a car, it is the lease rate of the car; in the case of a house, it is the lease rate of the house—over the years in the proportion of its changing implied ownership of that usufruct (the RF bank's implied co-ownership of the usufruct—through the lien—and hence the share in the usufruct declines as the buyer progressively pays back his owed part of the purchase price).
   d. The RF bank or the RF finance company can use the word *interest* to satisfy the laws of the land to describe the payments share of the rental of the property. However, the opposite (taking interest and calling it profit) is not allowed.

During the initial stages of developing an RF banking and finance knowledge base for the Shari'aa scholars the word *lien* has been mistranslated to Arabic as *rahn*, which means *pawn*. There is a world of difference between the two in legal definition. In general, in case of *rahn*, or pawning the property, the property itself and its use are both arrested and placed in the custody of the pawn holder. That means that the right to use the property (haq al manfa'aa) is confiscated until the riba loan is paid back. If it is not paid, then the rahn-holder would take over the property (milk ul raqabah) without legal action, as agreed in the rahn agreement, because it is in the possession of the rahn-holder.

Below are definitions for pawn and lien:

- Pawn[17]

  Verb: To deliver personal property to another in pledge or as security for a debt or sum borrowed.

  Noun: A bailment of goods to a creditor as security for some debt engagement; a pledge; a deposit of personal property made to a pawnbroker as security for a loan. That sort of bailment when goods or chattels are delivered to another as security to him/her for money borrowed of him/her by the bailer. Also, the specific chattel delivered to the creditor as a pledge.
- Lien

  Lien is defined as the right to take and hold or sell the property of a debtor as security or payment for a debt or duty.

  It is also defined as a claim, encumbrance, or charge on property for payment of some debt, obligation, or duty.[18] Additionally, it is defined as a *qualified* right of property which a creditor has in or over specific property of his debtor as security for the debt or charge or for performance of some act. It is further defined as a right or claim against some interest in property created by law as an incident of contract. It is also defined as:
  - Right to enforce charge upon property of another for payment or satisfaction of debt or claim.
  - Right to retain property for payment of debt or demand.
  - Security for debt, duty, or other obligation.
  - Tie that binds property to a debt or claim for its satisfaction.
  - A charge against or interest in property to secure payment of a debt or performance of an obligation.

The Meaning of Establishing a Lien Based on the definitions of pawn and lien, one can establish that liens, which could not have existed without a searchable title database in order to make sure that the property is free and clear and that there are no unknown claims against it, are a form of ownership right that is different from the classic pawning (*rahn*) contract. Here are some facts to support our conclusion:

- A lien is defined in the dictionary[19] as "a conveyance of title to property that is given to secure an obligation—as a debt or promise to perform a financial obligation—and that is defeated upon payment or performance according to stipulated terms."

- An acid test of the preceding consists of the response to two events: The first is that when the house experiences damage of some sort, the insurance company issues the check in the name of the title owner and the co-mortgage—or lien—holder. Second is the fact that the process of releasing the lien is called "reconveyance" of title.

Based on these facts, the conceptual definition of a mortgage and the perfection of a lien in favor of the RF bank is like a *diminishing partnership* (*musharaka mutnaqisah*) in usufruct between the two entities—the property (home or business) buyer, called the mortgagee, and the RF bank or RF finance (mortgager) entity. The perfection of that lien also allows the implied co-owner of usufruct or lien holder to distribute the rental income that pays for the usufruct between the two co-holders in the proportion of the co-ownership as the customer pays down the capital owed.

As a result, it can be concluded that there is no need for the creation of an SPV or the incurring of additional expenses and significant legal complications and confusion that would render RF financing more expensive and liable to complicated legal suits in case of a dispute.

We significantly modified the Al-Baraka model described in Chapter 10. This modification produced the model known as the Shari'aa-based LARIBA RF finance model; also known as the Declining Participation in Usufruct Model, which is based on Shari'aa in contrast to the other approach and models, called *Shari'aa-compliant*, which uses financial engineering tools and ruses to force fit the RF principles into the existing riba-based finance models to make it appear as if it complies with the Judeo-Christian-Islamic Shari'aa law. As discussed earlier, this Shari'aa-compliant model approach has been used since the latter part of the twentieth century. In contrast, the LARIBA Shari'aa-based RF finance model uses the Commodity Indexation Discipline to normalize the valuation and pricing effects of paper (*fiat*) money regimes (to avoid participating in an inflated economic bubble and ascertains to the best of our efforts the prudence of the investment as discussed earlier) and the Marking-to-Market Discipline to introduce, for the first time in the history of RF banking and finance, the real spirit, intent, substance, and wisdom of modern Islamic RF banking to the finance field. RF financing is not a money-lending operation that rents money; it is a true prudent investment process with and in the customer. Following are the modifications introduced by the LARIBA model to the Al-Baraka model:

1. *LARIBA Model Modified Step 1.* Apply the RF Marking-to-Market Discipline. In this step, the actual market-researched rental rate of a

similar property (a car, a home, or a commercial building) or a business in the same neighborhood and with similar specifications (in the case of a home or a commercial building, in terms of dollars per square foot) is used. These rental/lease rates are researched in the market by contacting automobile rental companies or real estate agents active in the area as well as checking Web-published local market data. The customer and the RF finance officer each come up with three documented estimates. The average of the six rent estimates, or a mutually agreed-upon rental value, is used. This rent is used to evaluate whether the rate of return on the investment is attractive, using the patent-pending LARIBA RF finance algorithm and computer model. This way, the RF bank and the investor think and act as if the purchase of the car, the home, or the business is an investment. In this context, the buyer is disciplined to think about the process as a prudent investor and not just a borrower or renter of money to buy his or her needs as is done in the riba-based finance approach. This will be discussed later in further detail.

2. *LARIBA Model Modified Step 2.* The costs, including recording fees, maintenance, and other fees are booked to the account of the customer, who now owns the facility and is its operator. The insurance is not shared because the customer owns the title to the property (milk ul raqabah). This is also helpful because of the strict consumer compliance requirements pertaining to what is labeled predatory lending when the finance company also offers other services like insurance at a preferred rate. U.S. consumer compliance laws and regulations demand full disclosure of the items involved in every payment as well as giving the consumer the freedom to choose. This way, the customer will have the freedom to choose his/her own insurance provider.

Monthly payments include an installment to repay the capital forwarded by RF bank and a rental component:

1. The monthly repayment of the RF bank capital invested with the buyer is paid back, on a monthly basis, on an agreed-upon schedule and on a riba-free (interest-free) basis. This component is called the *repayment of capital* and was given the acronym *RofC* (pronounced "rofsee"), which is called in riba-based financing the payment of principal.
2. The rental component is the RF banker's share in the mutually agreed market-obtained rent, based on the proportion of the capital returned to the RF bank. This component represents the profit or income the RF bank collects as a benefit in co-owning the right to use the property—the usufruct. This is called in the RF finance model *return on capital*, and its acronym is *RonC* (pronounced "ronsee"), which is called in riba-based

financing the payment of interest. It is important to note here that the value of RonC is based on the actual market rent of the property, not the rent of money (riba, interest rate), in contrast to the portion of payment in a riba-based conventional banking setting in which the interest is really calculated using the rent on money (riba), which is prohibited by the Judeo-Christian-Islamic Shari'aa law.

It is important to note that the preceding steps are done independently without preconditions, and none of the steps is a precondition for the other to take place. If the process is not done this way, it will not be based on the law (Shari'aa) because it may be considered as "two sales contracts in one contract," as explained in case of the sale of eena in Chapter 10.

Calculation of the Economic Viability and Prudence of the Investment An important and truly unique aspect of the LARIBA Shari'aa-based RF finance model is prudence in investing one's assets. It is the responsibility of the RF banker to act as a wise and prudent investment adviser, protecting the customer from digging a deeper hole of debt for himself and his family by imprudently investing in a property, a business, or a house and/or by overstretching his repayment capacity. If the house, for example, would not make prudent economic sense to invest in, in case it were rented to a third party as an investment, it would not make prudent sense for the customer to own it.

Appraising the Property or the Business There are two approaches to appraising the property. The first approach is that obtained by the standard appraisal methodology, based on the last few sales in the neighborhood. But this approach may be extremely misleading in an inflated market, like the ones experienced in Houston, Texas, during the 1980s housing and commercial real estate bubble, in Silicon Valley in the 1990s, and during the nationwide bubble experienced in the United States for housing and commercial real estate, which reached its peak in 2006 and burst in 2008.

This is the real spirit and real intent of the prohibition of riba/ribit in the Torah, the Christian Bible, and the Qur'aan. In fact, based on the LARIBA RF finance model, LARIBA may be the only finance company that would decline financing a property or a business if the return on investment based on the actual market rent of similar properties in the same neighborhood were not attractive, using market parameters as will be detailed later.

Applying the Discipline of Marking the Property to the Market Each property has a market value, which is best defined by what its lease value would be if it were leased on the open market. The LARIBA RF finance model assumes that the property is leased at fair market value, as defined by the location and specifications of the property, and as mutually agreed upon between the client and the RF bank. Here is the detailed procedure:

1. The customer is asked to research the actual long-term rental of a home, car, property, or businesses with the same specifications and in the same neighborhood. This can be done, in case of buying a house for example, by calling three different real estate agents in the area and documenting the findings. The RF bank officer does the same.
2. Based on the six data points collected above, the customer and LARIBA agree on a *fair market rent* value of the property.
3. The RF bank calculates the customer's monthly payment using the proprietary LARIBA RF algorithm and computer model. This monthly payment consists of two parts: the RonC (portion of the rent that belongs to the RF bank for renting its share of the usufruct of the item) and the RofC (repayment of the capital paid as interest-free credit to the customer).

The Unique Features of the LARIBA Shari'aa-Based Model In a riba-based conventional banking setting, the customer will approach the bank to ask, "If I take a loan of $240,000, and repay it over 20 years (the term can be 5, 10, 20, or 30 years) to finance the purchase of a house, how much would the monthly payment be?" The riba-based banker would look at the bank's interest rate tables (the rental rate of money) of the hour on that day and tell the customer if he or she qualifies. The loan representative of the riba-based conventional bank informs the customer that the bank can lend them $240,000 at an interest rate (money rental rate) of, say, 7 percent conditional on many requirements like good credit rating and other bank conditions. The riba banker would quickly reach to his or her laptop computer and start an amortization computer program. He inputs the amount to be financed, the number of years to repay the debt, and the interest rate (the rental rate of the money). The unknown here is the monthly payment. Most, if not all, citizens have been trained to think and ask: if I borrow so much, how much is the interest rate and how much will the monthly payment be? In fact, most customers would proceed to negotiate a lower interest rate to feel good, but they do not know that small reductions in interest rates do not make much difference in the monthly payment. Customers should be retrained to think about prudence of the investment and the fair valuation of that property price in the market. That is what we mean when we preach about a riba-free lifestyle and way of thinking and arriving at an investment decision. It is not just a mere process of renting money, as is done in the riba-based lifestyle.

In contrast, when an RF banker is called for a financing transaction, the customer will—as he or she is trained—be asking about the interest rate and the monthly payment. The RF finance officer is trained not to deal with renting money but renting properties. The customer will be told that the RF bank cannot calculate the monthly payment before we know the location of the property, its specifications, and its rental/lease rate on the open market—based on the rent of comparable properties in the same area—because we do not rent money (which is riba/ribit), but we rent properties and businesses. In order to allay the fear of the customer about the RF bank overcharging him or her, the RF banker is trained to assure the customer that if the investment makes economic sense based on our LARIBA RF finance model, the monthly payment will be made competitive with that offered by the conventional riba-based banks. To evaluate the economic viability of owning a property in contrast to not buying it and instead renting a similar property, the RF banker does exactly the opposite of what the riba-based banker does, as described above. The RF banker goes through a lengthy and tedious process unique only to LARIBA. The RF banker asks the customer about the address of the property and its specifications, and proceeds to obtain three rental estimates in addition to the three rentals estimates requested from the customer. Notice how long this process takes the LARIBA RF banker compared to the instant response of the riba-based banker by looking at the interest rate tables. The LARIBA RF banker inputs the monthly rent obtained from the market survey process described earlier, the number of years to pay back, the purchase price, and the down payment into the patent-pending and copyright-protected LARIBA model computer program. The unknown here is the rate of return on invested capital, which is called the *implied interest rate.* Contrast this with the unknown in the case of the riba-based banker, which is the monthly payment. In the case of the LARIBA RF banker, the monthly payment is obtained based on the real live market research by applying the Marking-to-Market Discipline. In the case of the LARIBA RF finance model, we look for a percent sign. This sign does not represent the interest rate or the rental rate of money, but it actually is the rate of return on investment for this property. As the process continues, the LARIBA RF banker compares the calculated rate of return with the expected rate of return by the investors in the RF bank or RF finance company. There are three possible outcomes:

1. *The rate of return on investment, based on the actual market rental value of the property, is higher than the RF return on capital expected by investors.* In this case, the LARIBA RF bank would inform the property buyer that the property purchase makes economic sense and that because the investors (those who invest with the RF bank and its shareholders) are looking for a lower return to compete with the riba-based conventional banks, the RF bank will unilaterally reduce the agreed-upon market rent of the property so as not to hurt the community

member who wants to abide by the law (Shari'aa). This makes RF financing competitive with the riba-based banks in the rest of the market as was demonstrated since LARIBA started in 1987.

2. *The rate of return on investment, based on the actual market rental value of the property, is very low compared to the return on capital expected by investors.* In this case, the LARIBA RF bank officer advises the prospective buyer that the property market prices in this neighborhood are extremely inflated and experiencing an economic price bubble. The LARIBA RF banker informs the customer that it cannot finance the property and that the customer is advised to back off this investment. In fact, applying the LARIBA RF finance model has allowed our RF bankers discover that some markets in northern California; Arizona; Nevada; Washington, D.C.; and Massachusetts have been suffering from the problem of price bubbles since late 2005 to mid-2006. Our LARIBA RF bankers found that the appraised value obtained by using the standard appraisal technique based on sales comparisons is acceptable, but by applying the model they concluded that the economic viability based on the unique LARIBA Marking-to-Market RF finance model is not valid and advised against investing. The LARIBA RF finance model may make the RF bank unique due to the fact that it may be the only RF finance institution that would reject financing, despite the fact that the buyer may be a great customer for any bank to deal with. It is important to state that we at LARIBA have saved many customers in the aforementioned states (Massachusetts, Arizona, Nevada, northern California, and Washington, D.C.) from participating in the 2008 real estate bubble. In fact, because of this feature of the model, we have realized the following achievements at LARIBA and the Bank of Whittier:
   a. The RF mortgage portfolio originated by LARIBA and the Bank of Whittier was rated as one of the 64 best-performing portfolios in the United States during the bursting of the 2008 real housing bubble. This was reported to us by United Guaranty Insurance Company.
   b. Fannie Mae informed us right after the 2008 bursting of the housing bubble that our RF mortgage portfolios with them were one of the 10 best-performing portfolios in the western U.S. region, which extends from Colorado to Hawaii.
   c. The delinquency and foreclosure rate was one-tenth of the national average.

   It is interesting to share with the reader the experience we had when LARIBA's bankers first met with Freddie Mac in 1999 to allow their business development representatives and analysts to inspect and look into what we do, so that Freddie Mac could proceed with its fact-finding and approval process to invest in the homes we finance. We explained our model to the four representatives. The head analyst asked us, "Do you really mark the house to market?" We said yes. He asked to review the files. We supplied him with the files. He was impressed, and LARIBA was approved toward the beginning of 2000. It took Freddie Mac six weeks to approve LARIBA, compared to the national average approval time needed of six months. Later, in 2001, Fannie Mae followed Freddie Mac's lead.

3. *The rate of return on investment, based on the actual market rental value of the property, is marginally lower than the return on capital expected by investors.* In this case, the LARIBA RF bank officer and/or credit committee would advise the prospective buyer to try to renegotiate with the seller to reduce the price by a recommended amount as suggested by the LARIBA RF model results. This reduced price will eventually render the investment economically viable. At LARIBA, we have had a number of successful experiences where we helped a number of community members in Washington D.C., Arizona, and Nevada by suggesting they renegotiate a lower purchase price for their perspective home purchases.

The LARIBA RF finance model allows our customers to sell the property at any time they want because they own the title of milk ul raqabaah and pay back the remaining capital owed to LARIBA (the balance of the financed amount). Partial prepayment may also be made at any time. Partial repayments are applied against the purchase installments in inverse order of maturity, and the rental component is reduced proportionately.

Documentation of RF Financing for U.S. Compliance

The banking and financing laws and regulations in the United States are among the strictest in the world. RF financing in America is offered using two approaches:

1. Start with the conventional riba-based banking product and devise ways and means to dress it up and to "force"-fit it to an "Islamic" solution that would comply with (or at least look like it complies with) the Judeo-Christian-Islamic Shari'aa law, using intellectual and expert help from experienced riba bankers, structured finance and financial engineering attorneys, and ex-regulators. One of the techniques used is the creation of a special-purpose entity (SPE) or an SPV, which would buy the property and either sell it back, in a cost-plus (murabaha) scheme, or lease it back, in a joint venture with declining equity (musharaka mutnaqisah) scheme. The other idea, used in declining joint venture models (musharaka mutnaqisah), is to register the title of the property in both the financial institution's affiliate offshore LLC company name and that of the customer or business buyer to make the transaction appear to be a true joint venture.

2. Start with the LARIBA RF finance model to test the prudence of the investment and to calculate the monthly payments, based on the actual rental value researched in the market (by applying the Marking-to-Market Discipline). In the LARIBA RF finance approach financing contracts and documents are drawn up according to the U.S. federal banking laws and regulations and we keep the word interest as allowed by the edict detailed earlier. The contract is supplemented by a LARIBA propriety "rider" called the LARIBA Agreement. The LARIBA Agreement explains the prohibition of riba and the process used by LARIBA to achieve an RF financing which adheres to the law (Shari'aa) and to the standard U.S. regulations and laws.

It is believed that this second approach, the LARIBA RF finance approach, is a true manifestation of the Judeo-Christian-Islamic values because it is based on the Judeo-Christian-Islamic Shari'aa law. Here are the reasons why:

1. The LARIBA RF finance model uses the standard mortgage documentation required by the laws and banking regulations of the United States. This documentation and its associated contracts have been in continual development by the U.S. banking and finance authorities since the Great Depression of the 1930s.
2. It can be easily compared by the parties involved, including their attorneys and the courts of law, to the conventional riba-based approach. This way, the customer can make a fair comparison (apples to apples) in his/her pursuit to make the right decision.
3. It offers protection of the customer, because it conforms to standard U.S. financial and banking industry norms rather than to special considerations that may require lengthy court deliberations to settle in case of a dispute as experienced in cases involving Islamic finance in Bahrain, Malaysia, and the United Kingdom.
4. In the case of RF mortgage financing, the LARIBA RF financing model offers the customer the advantage of being able to deduct the rent-based payments from the gross annual income of the family in order to help reduce taxes, as implied interest, using the statutory mortgage reduction laws in the United States. In comparison, the Shari'aa-compliant model uses an Internal Revenue Service (IRS) Opinion Letter, which does not carry the weight of the law and is usually temporary in nature. It can be withdrawn and/or nullified at any time.
5. Because the LARIBA RF Shari'aa-based finance model records title in the name of the customer, it protects the customers' ownership rights and satisfies consumer compliance regulations and laws. Companies that use the Shari'aa-compliant models require that the title be in the

names of both the buyer and the financial institution. Recording title in both the name of the customer and the finance company or bank may expose the customer to any risks assumed by the finance companies.

The LARIBA RF finance model uses the following documents:

- *Promissory note* that indicates the amount of financing, the agreed-upon monthly payments, and the imputed (implied) interest rate of the transaction as calculated by the LARIBA algorithm and computer model (in order to satisfy Regulation Z or the TILA).
- *Deed of trust.*
- Other required regulatory documentation relating to truth in lending; nondiscrimination; servicing of the financing; necessary disclosures, which vary depending on the state involved; and so on.
- The unique, copyright-protected rider; *LARIBA Agreement.*

The LARIBA Agreement

The RF Shari'aa-based financing process (as is done at LARIBA) uniquely supplements the above standard documents, which use the word interest, with a specially devised rider called the LARIBA Agreement. This agreement documents the process used in the LARIBA Shari'aa-based RF finance model to calculate the monthly payment using the market measured rental value agreed upon between the customer and the RF bank or RF financial institution. The LARIBA Agreement clearly declares that riba/interest charging and/or receiving is divinely prohibited (*haram*). It also summarizes the proprietary process and the LARIBA RF finance model used. In addition, it states that the calculated and agreed upon rate of return, using the actual market rental rate of the property, is called an *implied interest rate* in order to comply with the U.S. Regulation Z (TILA, detailed in Chapter 8). The RF bank issues U.S. IRS tax form 1098 to allow for the deduction of the rental portion of the payments (as an implied interest) in the case of home mortgages, which is calculated at the beginning of the transaction and converted to an implied interest rate on the promissory note, as previously explained.

Monthly Billing LARIBA has created a new billing format (for both American Finance House [LARIBA] and Bank of Whittier) that, we believe, is a historic development in the RF movement. LARIBA's monthly billing breaks down the monthly payment in terms of RofC (called principal payment in the riba-based finance industry) and RonC (called interest in the riba-based industry). A copy of the monthly billing is shown in Exhibit 11.1.

LARIBA
American Finance House

750 EAST GREEN STREET STE 210
PASADENA, CA 91101
PH: (626) 449-4401
FAX: (626) 449-5319
LARIBA@LARIBA.com

Account Information:

Account Number:	
Statement Date:	3/18/09
Payment Due Date:	**4/1/09**
Property Address:	

Balance:

Principle: (Unpaid Capital)	459,217.80

Year-to-Date Summary:

RofC* Paid (Repaid Capital):	1,328.92
RonC* Paid (Implied Interest):	8,051.84
Late Payment Expenses Paid**:	.00

Payment Information:

RonC* Paid (Implied Interest Rate):	7.00000%
Monthly Payment (RofC* plus RonC*):	3,126.92
Escrow Payment (Taxes, Ins. or PMI)	.00
Number of Past Due Payments:	0
Past Due Payment Amount:	.00
Unpaid Late Payment Expense**:	.00
Unapplied Payments:	.00
Total Payment Due:	**3,126.92**

www.LARIBA.com

Please call us to save on "Shari'aa-Based" refinancing and please tell a friend.

For information on President Obama's initiative to help homeowners, please call us at 1 (888) LARIBA 1.

Please call to open a Riba-Free (RF) Checking or RF CD account with the Bank of Whittier (www.bankofwhittier.com). Bank of Whittier is owned by our community. It offers Riba-Free; FDIC insured accounts including IRAs and 401k. We thank Allah for his helped to make the Bank among the top performing and rated banks.

Please remember us in your du'aa

For Billing Inquiries Please Call:
1-888-LARIBA-1 Ext.112
1-888-527-422-1 Ext.112

***Late Payment Expense (Late Charge) of 62.54 will be applied if payment is not received by 4/15/09 (as explained in the Financing Note). This is the estimated administrative cost to LARIBA for handling overdue payments.*

***The RofC amount stated on this invoice represents the Repayment of Capital using our conceptual Lease-to-Purchase model of financing. The RonC amount represents the Return on Capital calculated using our conceptual Lease-to-Purchase model of financing. It is presented as an interest rate for purposes of conformity with Federal and State laws, and is intended to be mortgage interest under the Internal Revenue Code and similar tax laws.**

Please detach and return the bottom portion of this statement with your payment using the enclosed envelope. **(Allow a minimum of 5 days for postal delivery.)**

PAYMENT COUPON

LARIBA
American Finance House

***Please include your account number on your check**

Account Number:	
Statement Date:	3/18/09
Due Date:	**4/1/09**
Total Due:	**3,126.92**
Additional RofC:*	________
Additional Escrow:	________
Total Amount Enclosed:	________

AMERICAN FINANCE HOUSE - LARIBA
750 EAST GREEN STREET STE 210
PASADENA, CA 91101

Return portion

- ☐ **AutoPay** check here and fill out the back to pay all your future payment automatically
- ☐ **Change of billing address** Check here and make change on the back

EXHIBIT 11.1 LARIBA Monthly Billing

Servicing the Financing Facility—The Loan Servicing of the credit facility (called loan in riba-based banking) is the process of maintaining the finance facility after it has been funded. It includes recording title with the concerned local government authorities, billing the customer on a monthly basis, responding to customer inquiries, resolving any issues faced by the customer, escrowing (depositing monthly payments to accumulate enough savings to pay taxes and insurance) taxes and insurance for the property, and maintaining records according to consumer compliance government regulations. Many finance companies and banks "sell" the servicing to outside banks and servicing companies, some of which are located outside the United States, for a handsome sum of money. This practice may expose the customers in general and the RF customers in particular to customer service personnel and managers who are not from the community members who financed their properties, are not familiar with RF finance, and are not trained in the moral authority required by the Judeo-Christian-Islamic value system. It is believed that this may not be permitted by the law (Shari'aa). The Shari'aa-based LARIBA RF finance model requires that the RF institution services the RF facilities it originated and that it cannot sell the servicing of those facilities to another company. Metaphorically, one cannot sell the children he has produced! When the RF institution services its facilities, community members who are well trained and who understand the RF finance and banking concepts, community values, culture, and languages are not only ready to serve and respond to inquiries, but they are also trained in the important Judeo-Christian-Islamic value of mercifulness and kindness (*tarahum*) to those in need.

Sources of Funds Used in RF Financing One of the biggest challenges to our effort to popularize RF financing in the United States has been the availability of capital. When we started LARIBA in 1987, it was very difficult to raise the necessary capital. We were faced with many challenges. The first and most important challenge was the novelty of the effort. Many members of the community had talked about having a bank or a financial institution that serves our community, which is one of the most underserved by the banks and financial institutions because of the prohibition of riba. However, when many of these community members were contacted to invest, they politely declined, with many excuses. We understood their position and prayed more.

The other approach we thought of trying was to start a public drive to raise capital. That option was very expensive because it required the use of very expensive attorneys and U.S. Securities and Exchange Commission (SEC) registration, which required exorbitant expenses that can reach more than $1 million in legal, application, consulting, auditing, operating, and other fees. It was quickly concluded that we could not afford this approach. In addition, we did not have a proven track record of a working model with tangible results to include in our application for SEC registration to raise funds to capitalize this RF effort. It was simply a venture capital project that needed high-risk capital—and it is known that high-risk capital comes at a very high price.

We also thought of starting or acquiring a bank. This would have been a wonderful solution, because all depository institutions are allowed to take deposits that can be used to finance different projects. However, that was a formidable task because we did not have the capital or the qualified staff that could be certified and accepted by the regulators.

On another front, we went through the process of applying to start a credit union and we were very close to receiving a charter. However, after reading the details of how a credit union works, we found that every depositor is considered a shareholder. We found that regardless of the size of the deposit, each individual represents a vote. We became very concerned due to prior experiences in the field of political manipulations of elections and voting in many nonprofit organizations. We discussed the matter and decided to back off.

We finally decided to start a small finance company, organized as a small—Subchapter S (the S stands for Small)—corporation. This option had its advantages and disadvantages. The main advantage was the flexibility of raising the capital needed and the avoidance of double taxation. The avoidance of double taxation means that the company's profits are not taxed at the company's level as in the case of regular corporations, which are taxed at a high rate that can reach 42 percent for state and federal taxes. In a Subchapter S corporation the profit is not taxed at the company's level and is distributed to the shareholders, and the shareholders subsequently pay taxes according to their own income tax situation. The disadvantages were many, but we had to start from what was possible in order to eventually achieve what is impossible. The first disadvantage was that the number of shareholders was limited to a small number (it was 35 members when we started in 1987; as of 2013, it was set to 100 shareholders). In addition, a Subchapter S company cannot solicit funds from the public because that would not comply with the conditions of the Subchapter S articles.

We started American Finance House (LARIBA) in 1987 with a small capital of $200,000, which we had gathered from close, lifelong friends in the United States. We had humble means, but our dreams and aspirations were much greater. We started a website (www.LARIBA.com) that became very popular throughout the world. We financed cars, homes, and small businesses. It is true that we only did one or two financing deals per month, but those deals helped us to start a balance sheet, an income-expense statement, a financial ledger, and a successful track record for the company. The biggest challenge was the huge demand for RF financing applications we at LARIBA received from the community. We were heartbroken to say to prospective customers, "We are sorry, but we do not have enough capital." We asked our friends whom we knew could afford to participate in our efforts to increase our capital, but they refused. They indicated that they would be more comfortable if their funds were federally insured by the FDIC, something that was impossible at the time. We used to finance homes with a 40 percent down payment and a term of seven years. This financing term could be afforded by only a few, who were mostly the believing affluent puritans. However, we reasoned that one has to start at any level possible.

It may prove useful to share with the reader the size of the problem of raising the necessary capital by focusing on one aspect of the business of mortgage financing. If we wanted to finance only 50 homes a month at $200,000 each, that would require that we come up with $10 million a month or $120 million per year. Knowing the community, we did not have this kind of money available. Some recommended that we contact the oil-rich countries. We tried, but the competition had gone ahead of us, promising investors in these countries the wonderful American dream and returns of 20 to 50 percent rather than the more realistic numbers we, as responsible bankers and businesspeople, projected with no guarantees. Of course, many of the rich Gulf countries' owners of capital put tens of millions of dollars into the companies that promised high returns but not into us at LARIBA. We decided to remain patient and never to compromise our standards and values.

Around the turn of the century, in 1999, demand for our services was so large that we could not meet it because of the lack of capital. One of our executives suggested that we close the company down because we could not meet the demand. My reaction was simple. I told him, with tears in my eyes, that all God asks from us is to do the best we can with what we have. In a few months, we received an e-mail from Ahmad Elshal, who used to work with Freddie Mac. He told us that he had visited our website and that he liked it. He called me to inquire about the details of what we do at LARIBA. He asked one of the Freddie Mac executives at that time, Saber Salam, to contact us. The rest is history. As stated earlier, LARIBA received early approval from Freddie Mac, and we were elated. New problems erupted but they were much sweeter. Now, our problem was not capital but how to organize ourselves to serve the growing demand.

Freddie Mac and Fannie Mae were originally organized as government-sponsored public companies (GSEs) by the U.S. government to provide necessary liquidity to the housing market in the United States. To accomplish this goal, Fannie Mae and Freddie Mac provide the liquidity to the institutions that finance homes (called mortgage companies) and banks, by authorizing the companies to act on their behalf to finance homes according to universally set but strict guidelines, and proceed to exchange the note for cash. The GSEs assemble the notes in the form of asset-based fixed-income securities (bondlike) called mortgage-backed securities (MBSs). The GSEs offer these securities for investment to institutions looking for high-quality asset-based bond-like investments that yield a higher interest rate. This way, the GSE generates cash to turn around and reinvest that cash in mortgages. Buyers of these MBSs were U.S. institutions, banks, and retail savers, as well as international banks and investment banks.

In April 2001, LARIBA was the first ever RF finance operation in the West to be approved for investing Freddie Mac's money using the LARIBA Shari'aa-based RF home finance model. In 2002, LARIBA became the only U.S.-based Shari'aa-based RF finance company to be approved by the largest mortgage investor in the world, Fannie Mae. Later, LARIBA became the only RF finance company that issued—with Fannie Mae—RF MBSs. In 2003, the Bank of Whittier was approved by both Freddie Mac and Fannie Mae.

It is also important to state for the record that LARIBA—and, for that matter, any RF finance company or bank—is not allowed by the Judeo-Christian-Islamic Shari'aa law to borrow money with interest (riba) from Freddie Mac, Fannie Mae, and/or other investors. Freddie Mac and Fannie Mae are looked upon as investors in the RF LARIBA Shari'aa-based mortgages. In fact, we evaluate the financing of each home as an investment, and we offer it to Freddie or Fannie online as investors in the LARIBA-financed homes. If approved, they indicate to us the expected return they need to realize as investors. This is the rate we use to measure the economic prudence of the investment (using the rate of return on investment based on the actual market rent, as explained earlier). If approved, LARIBA forwards the money from its own funds to purchase the house and is paid back within a week or less by Freddie Mac or Fannie Mae. Freddie Mac and Fannie Mae were the real major source of capital for all "Islamic" finance companies and banks in the United States. We were fortunate at LARIBA to have acquired a national bank—the Bank of Whittier, NA—which accumulated the deposits needed for financing.

Another important aspect of dealing with Freddie and Fannie has been the documentation used in the RF financing process. Such documents must follow the same standards called for by the industry and regulations. Our LARIBA Shari'aa-based RF finance model paid us a wonderful dividend, because we did not have to receive a special exception from the GSEs or regulators to be approved. The risk of receiving an approval with an exception is that this exception can be taken away when times are not suitable, as it started to emerge in 2012 and 2013 with the GSEs trying to cut down on the mortgage companies they deal with and scrutinize RF banks and Islamic mortgage companies in particular. While others went through expensive legal maneuvers to make the documents look "Islamic," then turned around and diluted the Islamic content to bring it back to the standard codes, we at LARIBA started on the right and straightforward track. It is important to note here that the LARIBA Agreement described earlier is a required part of the documentation called for by the GSEs. Many of the RF "Islamic" MBSs produced by RF finance companies, which are based on Shari'aa-compliant models, were designed for sale to the "Islamic" banks in the Gulf and Malaysia. In contrast, the LARIBA RF MBSs were designed to be offered for investors and all entities in all markets, and are of the highest quality. These RF MBSs are "produced" by us at LARIBA with Fannie Mae. That is why they, to us at LARIBA, are not a mere "black box," like other MBSs, because we simply know the mortgage components of each of the LARIBA RF MBSs.

Other sources of capital are the share capital of the company and investments from accredited and qualified high net worth and sophisticated investors. It is important to note here that, by the grace and blessings of God, not a single investor or shareholder has lost a penny since we started our operations at LARIBA in 1987. In addition, we consistently distributed dividends and profits that were at least 1 to 2 percent higher than what any riba-based institution would offer on CDs.

Advantages of the LARIBA RF Shari'aa-Based Finance Model and Procedures

1. It applies the fundamentals of the RF law (Shari'aa) of the Judeo-Christian-Islamic system.
2. It does not use ruses (*heyal*) nor financial engineering and structuring techniques that are usually used in the Shari'aa-compliant models.
3. The LARIBA Agreement clearly spells out the bases from Shari'aa upon which the relationship, the process of financing, and the process of calculating the monthly payments are built.
4. It is universal and designed to benefit all people of all faiths.
5. It is not based on renting money at a price called interest rate. It is based on the Marking-to-Market Discipline, which requires the use of the actual market-measured rent of the items to be acquired as measured—live—in the marketplace by the customer and the RF finance company/bank finance officer in charge. It helps the customer make the decision to buy a property—or not to buy it, and instead rent until it becomes more economically sound to buy it.
6. It normalizes the monetary problem of paper (fiat) money by using the Commodity Indexation Discipline, by marking the property to the

market, as called for by the Marking-to-Market Discipline. Using this approach helps us to identify economic and price bubbles before they fester and become speculative bubbles. In this way, we at LARIBA help the customer avoid participating in such a bubble. It is important to note that we at LARIBA detected the real estate bubble in many states in the United States as early as 2005 and 2006. This raised a red flag that stressed to our underwriters the necessity of exercising strict diligent and being cautious when evaluating the merits of the "investment" based on the Marking-to-Market Discipline and the Commodity Indexation Discipline.

7. It benefits the customer and the financing entity, because its method is based on investing in a property or a business and not on renting money when using an interest rate. It reveals the economic value of the purchased property, which ensures prudence in investing and protects against participation in an economic bubble.
8. It relies on arbitration using experts who are well versed in the Judeo-Christian-Islamic Shari'aa law that are chosen by each side.
9. It uses the standard financing documents and notes. This makes it fulfill the U.S. banking regulations, meet the requirements of bank examiners, and make it seamless in case other government requirements are implemented. This also helps the consumer and the RF financing entity settle any dispute before U.S. courts without confusion or misinterpretation that may cost a lot of time, money, and frustration. Using the standard finance document and notes allows the customer to declare its finances in an understandable and U.S. government–compliant way that benefits the customer in preparing and reporting their taxes and in reporting and complying with government agencies like the Labor Department's regulations pertaining to pensions and/or retirement plans.
10. It records the title of the property in the name of the customer directly. The model does not call for the title to be recorded in both the customer and the company's name, as is required in some Shari'aa-compliant schemes. Doing it this way may expose the customer to the unknown liabilities and unknown corporate future of the riba-based financing entity or riba-based bank, and it limits the freedom of choice of the customer.
11. It services the financing facility (servicing means among other things billing, collection of monthly payments, escrowing of insurance and tax payments, and resolving any problems) and it does not sell servicing to an outside servicing company. The LARIBA RF Shari'aa-based model requires that the RF finance entity or RF bank keep the servicing in house, with the work done by local community members. This practice

helps the customers if a problem occurs, especially in cases when the customer loses his/her job or is temporarily disabled. The concept of mercifulness (*tarahum*) is applied. The customer who has developed loss of income, health and/or other family problems is turned over by the experienced and merciful attitude of the servicing department to a specially formed nonprofit assistance organization (the Miskeen Fund—meaning the Needy Fund—which is known as the M-Fund) to help meet the temporary needs of the family until the problem is resolved and saves them the devastation of losing their home and the pain and damage of being foreclosed on.

THE RESULTS

The most important feature of the LARIBA Shari'aa-based RF finance discipline and principles is that the investment decision is based on the actual market rates of rent of the property or the business, as measured by both the customer and the finance officer in the open market. The process does not simply take the rental rate of money—riba—and use it to calculate the monthly payment as is done in riba-based banks. Using the LARIBA RF finance model, the process of buying a home, a car, a business, or a service is looked upon as an investment that must be prudent and must make economic sense, not just as a buying exercise that obtains (rents) money by incurring debt at an interest rate (rental rate of money.) In this regard, the RF finance company or RF bank considers itself as an implicit coinvestor in the activity, as implied by the application of the lien and the participation in the usufruct in a declining way, as described earlier.

That is why investing according to the Shari'aa-based LARIBA RF finance model has had superior results compared with the results experienced by conventional riba-based banks and other "Islamic" finance organizations that use the Shari'aa-compliant model. This success is because the LARIBA RF bank relies on evaluating the prudence of the investment. It is clear that due to using the LARIBA Shari'aa-based RF finance model, delinquencies are essentially nonexistent—almost 10 in 1,000—compared to a delinquency rate as high as 10 percent—100 in a 1,000—in some cases, as experienced by riba-based banks and financial institutions.

One day, after the revelations of the economic meltdown of 2008 and the subprime mortgage debacle, I received a call from the assistant editor of a major U.S. news magazine.[20] She had been following our progress since her first interview with LARIBA in 2002 (she called in 2002 to interview me about LARIBA from New York while I was on a business trip in Singapore). She asked about the LARIBA mortgage portfolio performance and how we were doing in the difficult meltdown of the housing market and weak financial conditions faced by the United States and the world. I told her that we were doing very well, and I shared with her the fact that LARIBA mortgage portfolio delinquencies are a small fraction—one tenth—of the national average.

Fannie Mae representatives were impressed by the performance of the home mortgage portfolio underwritten using the RF LARIBA Shari'aa-based model and process. In 2009, Fannie Mae analysts explained to us that our portfolio is among the top 10 performing portfolios in the western region of the United States. We told them that the reason for our success is our disciplined approach of marking every home we attempt to finance to the market. If the investment does not make economic sense based on the actual market-measured rental rate of a similar home in the same neighborhood, then we discourage the customer and we do not proceed with the financing, as explained earlier in the book. It is also interesting to note that a representative of a private mortgage insurance (PMI; the insurance required by industry standards if the down payment of the customer is less than 20 percent of the appraised value, as called for by standards and underwriting requirements)—company, United Guaranty, came to visit us, asking how we at LARIBA could increase the size of our portfolio that is insured with them, because our portfolio—based on their analysis—is one of the best-performing portfolios among the top 64 U.S. mortgage companies and banks they underwrite for private mortgage insurance. In addition, the Bank of Whittier, which uses the LARIBA Shari'aa-based RF financing model, was rated a five-star bank for many years (the highest rating by Bauer Financial; www.Bauerfinancial.com) because of its performance at a time when major banks were failing due to the 2008 economic meltdown.

REVIEW QUESTIONS

1. The book enumerates in great detail the many different undercurrents that may enhance, impede, or destroy the quest for RF banking in the world with special focus on the West.
   a. Please give us a summary of at least three of these factors and how they may impact the development and growth of RF banking.
   b. Please explain how you would personally recommend resolving these difficulties.
2. Regarding the RF finance model proposed by LARIBA in this book:
   a. Please explain in a step-by-step approach the LARIBA RF model.
   b. How does it differ from the other three models used in the twentieth century as detailed in Chapter 10?

c. What added value does it bring to the customer? How does this compare to the other models?
d. What is the unique feature(s) of the model, and how do you feel about the model, its compliance, and its usefulness?

NOTES

1. The Prophet pronounced in the Hadeeth: All deeds are dependent on the intentions (Niyat) and each will realize his/her real intention.
2. A well-known rule in Shari'aa (*mala yudraku Kulluhu la yutraku Julluhu*, in Arabic).
3. Yahia K. Abdul Rahman and Abdullah S. Tug, "Towards a LARIBA (Islamic) Mortgage Financing in the United States—Providing an Alternative to Traditional Mortgages." Paper presented at the Islamic Finance Program, Harvard University School of Law, October 9–10, 1998; and Yahia Abdul Rahman, Mike Abdelaaty, and Gary S. Findley, "The Challenge of Offering a LARIBA Financial Services Window in an American Bank." Research paper presented at the Harvard Islamic Banking Symposium, Harvard University, October 1, 1999.
4. Tarek Diwany, *The Problem with Interest* (London: Kreatoc Ltd., 2003). This is the most useful and educational book on the problem of charging interest and paper (fiat) money. The book has published two editions and was translated into Turkish, Bhasa Malaysian, and Arabic. Dewany is a thought-provoking researcher and a prolific author who disagrees with the approach that uses form over substance in Islamic banking.
5. Tarek Diwany's website is www.Islamic-Finance.com.
6. Ahmad Kamal Mydin Meera, *The Islamic Gold Dinar* (Kuala Lumpur: Pelanduk Publications, 2002).
7. For example, Fatwa of Al-Baraka, available at: www.lariba.com/fatwas/index.htm.
8. For example, M. Nejatullah Siddiqi, *Muslim Economic Thinking* (Leicester, England: Islamic Foundation, 1981). Professor Siddiqi is a distinguished Indian Muslim Scholar who was responsible for this highly praised work, which included for the first time some 700 references of works in English, Arabic, and Urdu in the field of RF (Islamic) Economics. He is a prolific author and was the recipient of the first annual LARIBA Award and later became a LARIBA Fellow in Islamic Banking and Finance at UCLA, California.
9. Philip T. N. Koh, "Islamic Financial Instruments: The Civil Law and the Sharia Confluence or Conflict?" Presented at the 5th Islamic Finance Conference, Monash University, Kuala Lumpur.

10. Mahmoud Elgamal, *Islamic Finance—Law, Economics, and Practice* (Cambridge, England: Cambridge University Press, 2008). Professor Mahmoud Amin Elgamal holds the first ever Islamic Economics Chair at Rice University. He is a gifted researcher in economics, mathematics, game theory, Islamic law, economics, and practice. He authored a pioneering book in the field. His bitter frustrations about the practices of scholars have landed him a lot of resistance and, in many cases, isolation by many conference organizers. In fact, some scholars refuse to appear in the same conference programs in which his name appears. He coined an interesting term, *Shari'aa arbitrage,* by which he means the added premium charged in Islamic banking and accepted by some banks and customers that create an arbitrage between the Islamic banking techniques and the conventional banking methods. His thesis has been that the methods used in Islamic banking sanctioned by many Shari'aa scholars focus on form and lack the real spirit and substance of the original Shari'aa sources, and that these methods are inefficient and costly while in fact they are the same as conventional banking.
11. *USA Today* website, posted February 24, 2005, and updated February 25, 2005: www.usatoday.com/money/perfi/general/2005-02-24-islamic-finance-usat_x.htm.
12. OCC, Interpretive Letters #806 (1997) and #867 (1999). Please visit www.OCC.treas.gov. These letters were written regarding the United Bank of Kuwait's Al Manzil Program: The OCC has issued two opinion letters, one on murabaha and the other on ijara home financing by the United Bank of Kuwait (UBK), which has since been merged into what is now Shamel Bank in Bahrain; the federal branch was closed in the early 2000s, only two years after it started offering these contracts.
13. Ibid.
14. Bernard Lawrence "Bernie" Madoff (b. April 29, 1938) is an American businessman, and former chairman of the Nasdaq stock exchange. He founded the Wall Street firm Bernard L. Madoff Investment Securities LLC in 1960 and was its chairman until December 11, 2008, when he was charged with perpetrating what may be the largest investor fraud ever committed by a single person. Prosecutors accused financier Madoff—the alleged mastermind of a $65 billion Ponzi scheme—of intending to transfer up to $100 million worth of assets to protect them from seizure, and they wanted him locked up immediately. Madoff was sentenced in June to 150 years in prison after admitting the fraud—the largest in history.
15. I had the good fortune of moderating a session on Shari'aa that was attended by some of the superstar scholars. As customary, I asked them to give me their bios or CVs. I am sorry to state that some of them did

not have enough formal education in Shari'aa to qualify them to assume that role. I am sorry but I cannot name them out of respect for their privacy.

16. This occurred when I was in charge of the Muslim Students Association (MSA of the United States and Canada, now called Islamic Society of North America, ISNA) near Madison, Wisconsin, in 1969.
17. Henry Campbell Black, MA, *Black's Law Dictionary*, 6th edition (St. Paul, MN: West Publishing Co., 1990), 1128.
18. Ibid., p. 922.
19. *Black's Law Dictionary* editor, Bryan A. Garner.
20. Ms. Temma Ehrenfeld, *Newsweek*, private communication, April 16, 2008.

CHAPTER 12

Putting the RF Finance Movement and Discipline Together

A Step-by-Step Application of the RF Finance Procedure

This chapter is designed to give the reader an integrated view of how the different concepts and disciplines discussed in the book so far are applied in the unique financing process used in RF financing at LARIBA–Bank of Whittier. It is important to stress that what this book is presenting and advocating is a movement; we call it the RF Movement. The goal of this movement is to invite people of all faiths and beliefs to a new lifestyle; we call it the RF lifestyle. It is based simply on:

- Living within one's means.
- Redefining happiness and satisfaction in life to make happiness measured and felt not in terms of appearance and looks—as is promulgated in advertising campaigns which are designed to sell more and to entice people to consume more—but in terms of real things based on living humbly, helping those who need help and making a difference in the lifestyle of the community at large.
- Abstaining from thinking about borrowing money as a rental process of money at a price called interest rate. This includes the use of credit cards as a source of renting money to extinguish consumptive instincts promoted by slick advertising campaigns. Credit cards, which were first introduced to market as "charge cards," should be used as charge cards to facilitate the purchase of consumer needs and the settlement of consumer obligations with the commitment to pay off the balance by the end of the month of the billing period.

- Approaching every expense we embark on as an investment that must be prudently evaluated in light of:
  - The macroeconomic status of the market after disengaging the confounding valuation effects which are introduced due to the use of paper (fiat) money. This is done by using the Commodity Indexation Discipline as explained in Chapter 3.
  - The microeconomic analysis of the actual value of the utility of what we want to buy in terms of its market rental (lease) value using the Marking-to-Market Discipline, as explained in Chapter 3.

The following is a summary of what the LARIBA System's efforts toward bringing to market a new banking and finance brand name: RF banking and finance and the format LARIBA presents itself in the market.

LARIBA'S MISSION AND BACKGROUND

LARIBA has pioneered and is actively popularizing and supporting the RF (riba-free) Movement to introduce the unique features of RF principles and lifestyle to people of all faiths and walks of life. This movement represents an important tool for inviting people to a new lifestyle through RF finance and banking. It is a comprehensive approach that includes reaching out to customers in all communities and sharing the LARIBA vision through words and actions.

The company background is offered here for our readers in order to guide all those who want to start the same effort in their communities. Experience at LARIBA has shown that it is indeed possible to start small community-based RF finance companies that will offer RF financing to assist the community members to live an RF life style. The building and loan societies (later called savings and loan) and the credit union movement started in a similar fashion but lacked the RF discipline and vision. They slowly emerged as another category of riba-based banks competing with the riba-based commercial banks.

LARIBA was founded in 1987 by a group of American community members in southern California. It is the first ever RF finance company in the history America. In 1987, your author (also known as the Father of Islamic banking in America) started the company with a humble investment of $200,000 collected from close friends who invested $10,000 to $20,000 each.

The company represents a new and pioneering RF American Movement to popularize a new liberating lifestyle—the RF Lifestyle—to all Americans, which includes a new brand and culture of banking—RF finance and banking. The following are some of the RF finance services featured by LARIBA:

- LARIBA derives its capital and financial resources from shareholders and investors in America within its community. There are no investments from outside the United States.
- The LARIBA RF finance model is unique in that it does not start from the use interest rates and use it as a process to "rent money." We start from the actual rental value of a similar property in same location to establish the prudence of the investment.
- LARIBA has created a new domain in RF financing—RF mortgage financing, with its brand new nomenclature, algorithms, programs, and disciplines.
- The staff members of LARIBA and Bank of Whittier are graduates from the better local universities in our communities. They come from multicultural backgrounds with proven track records as professionals with solid family background, community servants, and distinguished students. They share an unwavering commitment to the belief in living an RF lifestyle and in serving the community.
- LARIBA conducts the whole RF finance process in-house, including credit application accepting, processing, underwriting, funding, and, finally, servicing the relationship. LARIBA does not sell the servicing of the credits (loans) originated.
- LARIBA, as a community service company, ensures that its customers and prospects are able to access any of the company's team members at all levels, from finance officers, underwriters, servicing managers, senior executives, the president, and the chief executive officer to Shari'aa scholars.

The LARIBA RF Finance Model[1,2]

The LARIBA RF finance model allows the following:

- The title to the property is to be held and recorded directly in client's name from the beginning of the transaction. This is known as holding the right of ownership; or *milkul raqabah* in the Shari'aa law.
- The share of the investment advanced by LARIBA becomes a debt (*dayn*) assumed by the client, who pays it back over a period of 120 to 360 months (for the payback of LARIBA's capital) and is called rofsee (RofC).
- The right of usage of the property is to be shared proportionately by both the client and LARIBA. The proceeds from the right of usage, that

is, the estimated rental value based on the actual market rent of similar homes in the same neighborhood, are to be jointly shared by both LARIBA and the client in an amount that is proportionate to their shares.
- The share of the income generated from the use of usage right received by LARIBA (called return on capital [RonC]) decreases each month as the client repays his capital advanced.

Summary of the Model

The LARIBA RF finance model is unique in the following ways:

- It follows a *disciplined* process that starts from macroeconomic evaluation of the housing market using the Commodity Indexation Discipline, followed by applying the Marking-to-Market Discipline based on actual market rent of a similar property in the same neighborhood.
- It does not start by taking the interest rate of the day or an index such as the London Interbank Offered Rate (LIBOR) and calls it the "rent." It is believed that this process is akin to renting of money at a price called interest rate, which is "riba." The model starts from the actual rent of a similar home in the same neighborhood, which is researched by both the client and our finance representatives. The rental research information is used to agree with the client on a true "marked-to-the-market" rental value for the property.
- It uses a unique and proprietary computer program to calculate the monthly payment and the rate of return on investment from the agreed-upon rental value of the property, starting with the market rent to calculate the return on investment.
- It uses a genuine "investment" approach to advising the client and approving the financing requests. By calculating the rate of return on investment, we can advise the customer *not* to refinance if the rate of return is low. We may be the *only* entity (Islamic or conventional) that refuses financing based on the lack of prudence of investing based on the rate of return.
- LARIBA, for the first time, introduced two new terms in the modern RF finance industry: repayment of capital ("RofC," pronounced rofsee) and return on capital ("RonC" pronounced ronsee) to respectively replace the interest-based terms of principal and interest used by riba-based conventional banks and finance companies. These are now used regularly in the LARIBA and Bank of Whittier statements.

At the LARIBA System we insist on retaining the servicing relationship of each transaction, which allows us to apply the Judeo-Christian-Islamic

Shari'aa law principle of mercifulness (*tarahum*) in the relationship with the financially distressed clients.

The Process

The RF finance model takes a much longer time to process than the conventional riba-based financing, which consists mainly of using an amortization computer program by plugging in the loan amount, the number of years, and the rent of money to come up with the monthly payment in less than five minutes. At LARIBA, we follow certain steps, as called for by the LARIBA RF finance model described in this book, in order to make sure that money is not rented at the interest rate of the day, which is riba. These steps include:

1. *Test for the presence of inflated price/economic bubbles using the Commodity Indexation Discipline.* The first step called for by the LARIBA RF finance model is to apply the Commodity Indexation Discipline, pioneered by Prophet Muhammad (s) as detailed in Chapter 3. The Prophet (s) developed the system for standardizing the measurement of value of objects using precious metals and staple commodities. This allows an investor to study the real value of an investment to see if priced appropriately in the marketplace or overvalued. This Commodity Indexation Discipline is used to study the price of homes, cars, businesses, and any other tangible item that need to be financed against real commodity price indexes. For example, viewing the median U.S. home price in terms of dollars would reflect the following picture:

   Based on Exhibit 12.1, and as detailed in Chapters 5 and 6, one can clearly determine that homes started to penetrate the upper fair market price channel level in the year 2000 and peaked in around end of 2005 and 2006 compared to periods of relative bargain prices for homes in 1979 to 1983 and 2010 to present, and in relation to overpriced homes in the period from 1968 to 1973 when homes were overpriced. As further evidence, one can do the same analysis of median U.S. home prices compared to the value of hundredweights of rice, as shown in Exhibit 12.3. Because rice is not a staple commodity in the United States, the conclusions are different. Here, we see that, in terms of rice, homes were underpriced between 1968 and 1984. However, after the coupling of rice and including it in the commodity speculation portfolios of many hedge funds along with other commodities, the 2000–2006 bubble can be revealed easily. It is also important to note that after the bursting of the price bubble, home prices once again became a bargain, as indicated by Exhibits 12.1 and 12.2. In fact, we at the LARIBA System issued recommendations to our customers late in 2008 to start looking into buying homes again.

EXHIBIT 12.1 Price of Average U.S. Home in Dollars

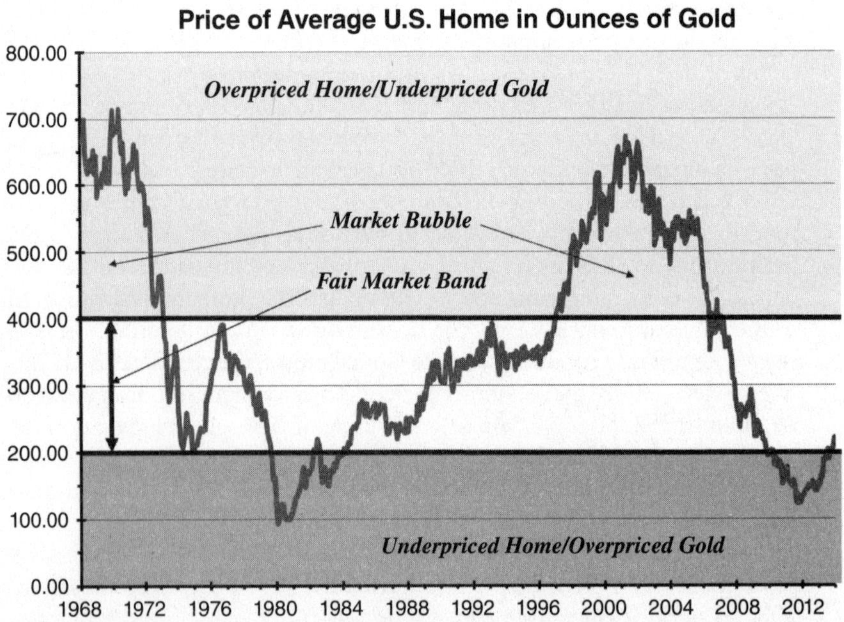

EXHIBIT 12.2 Price of Average U.S. Home in Ounces of Gold

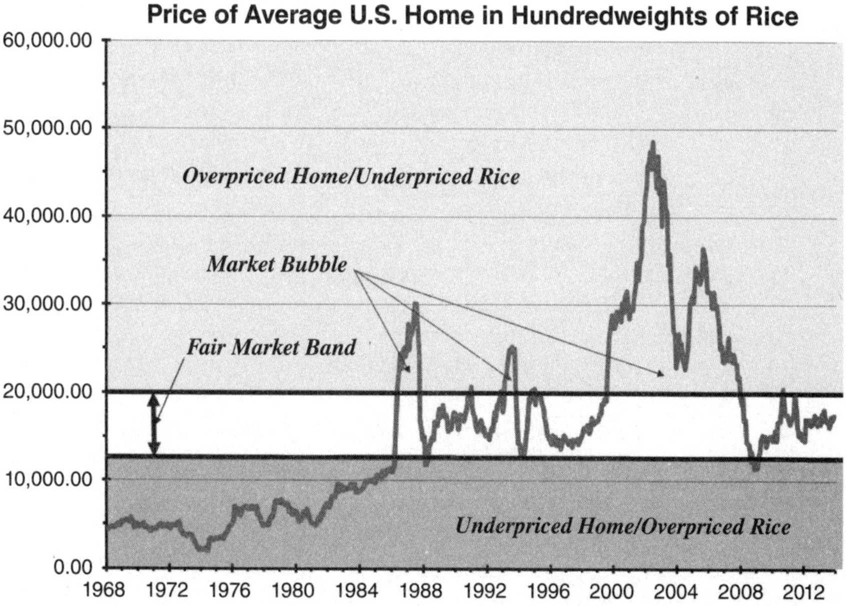

EXHIBIT 12.3 Price of Average U.S. Home in Hundredweights of Rice

Applying the RF finance model at LARIBA has helped in saving many community members in Arizona; Nevada; northern California; Washington, D.C.; and Boston, Massachusetts, from participating in the 2008 monetary and financial meltdown. Our nonperforming and troubled loans level is a tenth of the national average.

2. *Define the rental value of the property in the local market area to apply the Marking-to-Market Discipline.* The LARIBA RF finance model's next step is to test for the economic prudence of investing in a home, a car, a business, and other items. It uses the Marking-to-Market Discipline pioneered by Prophet Muhammad (s), which was described in detail in Chapter 3. This discipline is based on the story of the Khaybar dates. Prophet Muhammad (s) advised his companion Bilal that he should have established the value of a small, low-quality dates by selling them for another reference commodity in the market, then using the proceeds to buy the higher-quality Khaybar dates.

   Applying this discipline to homes, for example, is done by establishing how much this home can be rented for in the open market based on similar homes in the same neighborhood. That is why when a finance officer at the LARIBA System receives a call from a perspective customer asking about the current mortgage interest rate and how much the monthly payment would be, the LARIBA finance officer is trained to consistently tell the customer that we do not rent money and we do not deal in interest (riba). The officer asks the caller about the address and the specifications of the house in order to estimate how much it would rent for in the open market in that particular neighborhood.

The research of the actual market fair rental value of the property is done by both the client and the LARIBA System's representative in the same geographic location. The sources of rental information are leasing agents, real estate brokers, newspaper advertisements, and online resources. The client and LARIBA System's representative each provide three documented estimates (for a total of six estimates). The goal here is to determine a range of available market rental values, in U.S. dollars per square foot, from similar properties in the same neighborhood. The client and LARIBA System's representative compare their findings and agree on a rental value to be used in our proprietary LARIBA RF computer algorithm and model.

3. *Test for the economic prudence of investing in the proposed property using the LARIBA RF proprietary algorithm and computer model/program.* Once the agreed-upon rental value is achieved as discussed above, the LARIBA RF algorithm and computer model calculates the rate of return on investment (ROI) in the property. The computer model inputs are: the property value (total investment value), amount to be invested (financed) by LARIBA, the number of years the client wishes to pay back, and the monthly rental value obtained from the market, as discussed earlier. The unknown, which the RF computer model solves for, is the ROI.

   This contrasts with the procedure used by the riba-based banks, whose payment calculator, called the mortgage amortization program, starts with an interest rate and the unknown is the monthly payment at this interest rate or the rental rate of the money rented by the bank to the customer (riba). These mortgage amortization computer programs used by the riba-based banks input the amount to be financed, the number of years to pay back, and the rent of money (interest [riba]) and solves to estimate the unknown, which is the mortgage monthly payment.

4. *Evaluating the results of the ROI calculated by the LARIBA RF computer model.* There are three possible outcomes:
   - *The ROI is higher than the return expected by the LARIBA (or finance company or bank) investors.* In such a case, the LARIBA System's finance officer advises the customer that investing in this property makes prudent economic sense and that LARIBA will be happy to co-invest with the customer (finance the property). In order to offer a most competitive monthly payment in the marketplace, LARIBA

voluntarily reduces the agreed-upon market rent in order to be able compete with the monthly payment offered by the riba-based banks.

- *The ROI is much lower than what our investors are expecting (say 2 percent) while our investors expect to match what can be realized by investing in the competing investments, including those offered by riba-based banks (which are expected to yield, for example, 6 percent).* In such a case, LARIBA declines to coinvest in (finance) the property and the LARIBA System's officer advises the client not to purchase such a property because it is believed—based on the LARIBA RF finance model—to be overpriced. This very part of the RF finance process and discipline shows the real unique value of applying the LARIBA RF finance model. Applying the RF finance model has been the main reason why LARIBA warned many of our customers and raised the red flag about purchasing and financing homes in overpriced properties in Arizona; Florida; Massachusetts; Nevada; Washington, D.C.; and parts of California during the period 2006 to 2008. Applying the LARIBA RF discipline and financing process has saved many of customers from participating in the 2008 real estate price bubble.
- *The ROI is marginally lower than the expected return by our investors (say, for example, 5 percent and our investors expect 6 percent).* In such a case, the LARIBA finance officer, in his capacity as a trusted family financial adviser and not just a "seller" of a loan, advises the client to consider renegotiating the price lower. This was done a few times, and the clients were successful in renegotiating a lower price.

APPLICATION OF THE MODEL

Steps for Implementing the Model

1. The bank (finance institution) and the customer share in purchasing the home according to the agreed-upon proportions: The finance institution conceptually purchases the property jointly with the client by authorizing the client to act as its agent (*wakeel*) to select, negotiate the price of, and execute the intent to purchase the property.
2. Out of his/her own free will, and because of the customer's ultimate intent, the client offers to buy, and finance institution accepts to sell its shares that it owns (*milk ul raqabah*) immediately to the customer at the same price (without increase). Based on this understanding, the finance institution authorizes the client to record the title (register it with the local authorities) directly into his or her name. The client becomes the owner of title of the house or the owner (milkul raqabah). The

finance institution and client agree to perfect a lien (implied co-ownership of usufruct) on the property in favor of the finance institution. This lien evidences finance institution's co-ownership share of the usage right (in the case of a house, it is the rent due to pay for living in and using the house, and in the case of a car, it is the rent of that car in order to use it) and is to be "reconveyed" back to the client once the entire RofC is fully completed. Please note that some mistranslate the word lien as rahn (the word *rahn* in Arabic literally means pawn). In a rahn situation, the ownership is suspended until the loan is paid back and the right of use of the property is arrested completely like in case of pawning a watch for money. In a lien, the right of use is not arrested and the ability to share the right of use is allowed. The value of the sale of the institution's ownership share becomes like a riba (interest)-free debt called an RF "dayn," meaning an RF debt, to be paid by the client to the financial institution in monthly installments over a period of time up to 30 years without adding any riba/interest. The monthly repayment, as detailed earlier in the book, is called RofC.

3. As the client gradually pays back his/her RF loan (dayn), the finance institution's shares less in the usufruct (*haqul manfa'aa*). That way, by the end of the repayment period, the client's share of the usufruct will reach 100 percent.
4. The agreement and the lien imply that the client and LARIBA agree to share the income from the usage of the property proportionately (the agreed-upon rental value of the property, as discussed earlier) based on their shares. This income is called RonC.
5. As the client pays back his riba-free loan, LARIBA releases a proportional share in the usufruct. That way, by the end of the repayment period, the client's share will reach 100 percent.
6. The monthly payment due, to be paid by the client over the financing period, consists of a portion of the unpaid RF obligation/loan (RofC) and an amount equal to finance institution's proportional share of the agreed upon rental value (RonC). The proprietary LARIBA RF computer model does the arithmetic calculations using the proprietary RF algorithm.

The Algorithm and Computer Program

The LARIBA System has developed its own proprietary payment calculation computer program to calculate the monthly payment and the rate of ROI based on the live market researched and the agreed-upon rental value of the property. The LARIBA RF computer program inputs are shown on the left-hand side of the table shown in Exhibit 12.4. The RF computer program results are on the right-hand side.

The LARIBA RF computer program is different from the standard mortgage amortization program used by riba-based banks. The LARIBA RF

EXHIBIT 12.4 The Output Generated from the LARIBA RF Valuation Program

Program Inputs		Program Calculations	
Purchase price	$400,000.00	Scheduled payment	$1,520.06
Finance amount	$300,000.00	Customer equity	25.00%
Monthly rent	$ 1,500.00	Number of payments per year	12
Loan period in years	30	Scheduled number of payments	360
Start date of loan	3/1/2014	Actual number of payments	360
		Total rent	$247,220.13
		Return on capital	4.45500%

computer model does exactly the opposite of what the riba-based mortgage amortization program does. It starts with the market measured rental rate of the property to calculate the percentage of ROI, while the riba-based amortization program starts with an interest rate (riba), that is, the percentage of interest rate charged, which represents the cost of renting money (riba) as a given. In the RF program, the return on investment in percentage is an important output that is used to evaluate the prudence of an investment, as explained earlier.

Mortgage Finance Servicing Policy

Servicing a loan is an important aspect of the any financing process. Some in the riba-based banking and finance domain think that the financing process ends with dispensing the money and closing the loan. That is not true. An important pillar of the financing process is the servicing of the loan. That is a relationship that can last from 3 years, in the case of financing a car, to 30 years, in the case of financing a home. Servicing of the loan includes monthly billing and collection of the payments, dispensing the collected payments to investors, receiving inquiries from customers and from investors, and collection and payment of annual taxes and insurance payments, as well as handling situations of financial distress faced by the customers. These are serious relationship responsibilities that must be handled by officers who are well connected to the customer and to the community and who understand the financing transaction in great detail, especially if it is an RF financing transaction. Most finance companies and banks "sell" the servicing of the loan portfolio to servicing companies for a fee. These finance companies handle thousands, if not millions, of loans, and the customer is suddenly transformed from being a community member into a loan number that is handled by a person who answers a toll-free

800 number, who is seldom accessed twice in a row because of the huge number of calls and the agents who are assigned to answer such calls.

One of the cornerstones of the LARIBA RF finance model is the insistence on retaining the servicing relationship of each financing transaction originated by LARIBA. Metaphorically, the RF financiers believe that the child produced by marriage should be catered for and not sold to others. This allows the RF finance institution to apply the Judeo-Christian-Islamic Shari'aa law and the RF value system in its relationship with the clients by having community members who are trained to be RF servicing agents, who directly communicate and deal with the clients, and who are trained to help them as their circumstances may warrant. The clients can speak with their RF servicing agent, the finance officer who helped them close their financing, the chief financial officer, the president, the chairman, and the Shari'aa adviser, in contrast to other companies both in RF and riba-based domains, which sell the servicing to other companies that have no knowledge of RF financing or the community.

One of the examples of the benefits of dealing with clients directly, as is called for by the LARIBA RF finance and servicing discipline, is manifested in the issue of charging late payment fees. In the LARIBA RF finance and servicing discipline, late fees are usually waived except for those chronic delinquent clients that are clearly trying to take advantage of the system. Finally, to make sure that the RF finance institution has no incentive to profit from late fees, all late fees collected are donated to a special charity fund called the "miskeen fund" (*miskeen* means "the needy" in Arabic) abbreviated as the "M-fund." Details of the M-fund are explained next.

The Needy (Miskeen) Fund

The LARIBA RF finance and servicing model long ago stipulated that any late fees collected from chronic and abusive customers of the compassionate posture of the RF system be used to help others who are needy and are struggling to honor their obligation. As such, the M-fund was established as a nonprofit entity that supports charitable causes. One of such causes is to help people who have lost their jobs or have endured an unexpected financial hardship that prevents them, despite their best efforts, from making their payments on time. These customers apply in confidence to the M-fund and receive a charitable benevolence loan (a *qard hassan* basis) to the amount of their needs to help stay current on their obligations and not adversely impact their credit until their fortunes improve. The benevolent loan is paid back without any increase when the customer is in a position to do so without impacting their financial well-being.

At the LARIBA System, many needy customers have been discretely helped to help them overcome adverse financial situations. Circumstances in which the M-fund came to the rescue include medical emergencies, unemployment, and family emergencies.

Loan Documentation Philosophy and Approach

The LARIBA RF finance model has designed the processes, the documentation, and the legal processes to comply with the laws of the land without violating the Judeo-Christian-Islamic Shari'aa law. It should be clearly known that it is not our mission in the RF finance domain to change the laws of the land. We are challenged by offering RF products and services that comply with the laws of the land while not violating the Judeo-Christian-Islamic Shari'aa law. The LARIBA RF finance model is also designed to be keen on protecting the rights and obligations of RF clients in case of adverse situations. In order to apply our mission of providing RF financing to all people, we do not wish to create unnecessary structured and engineered financial products that do not add any value or legal advantage to the transaction but, in fact, cause excessive legal fees, unnecessary limited partnership fees, and in most cases insert unusual language in the contracts that could make them look "Islamic" but renders these contracts irregular and difficult to pursue legally.

The documentation package was designed to be seamless and not different when it is compared to a regular mortgage package to make sure that client rights are protected in case of legal dispute. To supplement the regular loan documents, which include the word *interest* as allowed by many highly placed moderate and conservative scholars in the law (Shari'aa), a rider called the LARIBA Finance Agreement is used:

1. The LARIBA Agreement (rider), which describes the LARIBA RF finance process followed and the development of and arrival at the agreed-upon rental value used as the basis for our LARIBA RF finance model application and calculation of the monthly payment.
2. Late fee rider, which describes the guidelines and rules of the charging and dispensing of the late fees.
3. Standard American mortgage industry and regulatory sanctioned financing note and deed of trust/mortgage.
4. Standard industry and legal disclosure forms.

REVIEW QUESTIONS

1. What is unique about the LARIBA RF finance model? What do you like about it, and what you do not like and want to improve when compared with the prevailing riba-based conventional finance model?

2. What is the advisory role of the RF finance officer, and how it is contrasted with the role of the traditional loan officer at a riba-based conventional bank? What is the advantage?
3. What is the difference between the riba-based approach to financing and the LARIBA RF finance model?
4. What is an amortization computer program, and how does it differ from the LARIA RF computer algorithm and program? What added value does the LARIBA RF finance model bring?
5. What is the meaning of "servicing a loan"? How is it usually handled, especially in the cases of mortgage loans and Small Business Administration (SBA) loans? How does the RF finance Judeo-Christian-Islamic value system look at servicing? How does the RF servicing discipline impact the future of the financing facility and relationship?
6. What is the M-fund and how is it used? Whom is it funded by?
7. What is the general guideline for charging late payment fees in a riba-based bank as compared to an RF bank?
8. What is a deed and what is a note? Does the LARIBA RF finance model allow for using such in the financing (loan) package? Do these documents include the word *interest?* How can it be RF (Islamic) while containing the word *interest?*
9. What is the LARIBA Agreement rider? Is it considered by the laws of the land as an important part of the consumer's financing package?

NOTES

1. The LARIBA RF finance model was pioneered and patented by Dr. Yahia Abdul-Rahman in 1988. The LARIBA model is based on and follows the same steps outlined in a series of fatwas (edicts) issued by a panel of distinguished scholars, including their eminences Sheikh Yusuf Al-Qaradawi, Sheikh Al-Dhareer, Dr. Samy Hamoud, and Sheikh Dr. Abdul Sattar Abu Ghuddah. These fatwas were published by Dallah Al-Barakah, a pioneering Islamic Finance and Banking Company (fatwas are available on www.LARIBA.com under Fatwa ans Shari'aa). The fatwas were issued for use at the Dallah Al-Barakah bank in London, the first Islamic bank in the history of the United Kingdom. The model described in the fatwas relies on the fact that tangible (nonfungible) properties have two rights: (1) the right of ownership (milkul raqabah) and (2) the right of usage (haqul manfa'aa).

   The LARIBA RF finance model improved on the original Al-Barakah model by applying two important disciplines based on the teachings of Prophet Muhammad (s): the Commodity Indexation Discipline and the

Marking-to–Market Discipline, as will be more fully discussed in the following section.

The LARIBA model was also modified with consultations during two meetings held between Dr. Yahia Abdul-Rahman and his eminence Sheikh Dr. Aly Alsalous, a prominent Shari'aa scholar in Cairo, Egypt, in July 2006.

2. The LARIBA RF finance model has been progressively updated, and the last update was done in 2013 by Darul Hikmah, a U.S.-based Islamic law (Shari'aa) consulting firm that was established to serve the financial jurisprudence needs of riba-free finance and banking. The chief scholar of Darul Hikmah is his eminence Sheikh Dr. Mohamad Adam Elsheikh, who has served as LARIBA's chief Shari'aa scholar since 2001.

   Dr. EI Sheikh graduated with honors from the faculty of Shari'aa and Law, Omdurman Islamic University, Sudan, in 1969. He was appointed by the Department of Justice in Sudan to serve as a judge for the Shari'aa courts. In 1978, he was approved for scholarship to study in the United States, where he obtained an MS in Comparative Jurisprudence (MCJ) from Howard University (Washington, D.C.) in 1980, an LLM (Master of Laws) from George Washington University (Washington, D.C.) in 1982, and a PhD in 1986.

This chapter was co-authored by Mr. Mike M. Adelaaty, President of LARIBA.

CHAPTER 13

Starting an RF Bank in the United States

Acquiring and Restructuring a Troubled Bank and Operating It Riba-Free

INTRODUCTION

This chapter covers the efforts we at LARIBA went through to acquire and operate a full-service national bank in the United States. This chapter is a must for anyone who may be interested in buying and operating a bank in America. It also can serve as a useful stepwise discussion that should benefit those who want to restructure a troubled bank and bring it to a healthy and a profitable condition. Finally, this chapter is important for those who are interested in operating a riba-based bank in America and the West in a riba-free (RF) format without having to go through the lengthy and expensive process of trying to obtain exceptions from the regulators, as was done by other Islamic banks in Europe. As was stated earlier in the book, RF banking is not about changing words and names of products and services, and it is not about using circumventive techniques to make the contracts look "compliant" with the Judeo-Christian-Islamic Shari'aa law.

RF banking is a new brand of banking that applies the spirit and substance of Judeo-Christian-Islamic values. It is about the use of principles that would save the consumer and the businesses from living an extravagant life style on "rented" money, from making an unwise purchase and financing decision and from participating in an economic bubble like that of 2008.

One of the options we considered in 1987 when LARIBA was started was to organize it in the form of a depository institution (meaning a bank). We reasoned that this option would offer us the ability to take deposits and to offer insurance on deposits through the Federal Deposit Insurance Corporation (FDIC). However, we knew nothing about the business of starting a bank in the United States. We were told by many of our friends that the process of starting or buying an existing bank (which is called the application for change of control of that bank) is difficult. Acquiring an existing back is an expensive, involved, and lengthy process. In addition, it requires the organizers to be well known to the banking regulators and the founding shareholders to have sufficient capital. As detailed earlier, we did not satisfy many of these prerequisites:

- We did not have a lot of money to capitalize the bank.
- We did not have a lot of money to spend on preorganization and preoperating expenses, such as legal, organizational, administration, and application fees and expenses.
- We were not known to the regulators; we were offering a new brand of banking, which at the time was foreign to all people, including the banking regulators. For that matter, the RF banking and finance system was not only foreign to the banking regulators but also to Muslims and non-Muslims in general.

We simply did not know where to start. That was why we started by licensing LARIBA as a finance company regulated by the State of California Department of Corporations.

After operating LARIBA for almost three years and interacting with customers and users of our services, many of our customers and community members indicated that they would love to transfer their bank deposits to us, but they could not, because deposits at LARIBA are not insured, as are banks, by the FDIC. We told them that we at LARIBA could not accept deposits anyway because LARIBA is not a U.S. government-chartered depository institution; it would be illegal for us to accept deposits. However, this thought planted the seed of the idea of owning a full-service bank in the United States that would serve the community in an RF mode. The dream we had was to start or buy a small community bank that would eventually be operated according to the Judeo-Christian-Islamic Shari'aa law, while upholding the laws of the land.

Our strategic vision was to design the operation and services of this bank to serve people of all faiths, and not Muslims only. That is why, later on, when we developed the bank, its advertisements, its business development campaigns, the website, and the presentations we gave were all designed for people of all faiths. In our focus groups, people in the community were asked a simple question: "Would you prefer to go to a small, crowded Asian or Middle Eastern grocery store or to a large, clean, well-stocked and -organized supermarket that offers international foods?" The answer has always been the supermarket.

Another important strategic decision made was how to present our services. Many others that came to the market focused only on the Muslim community. We decided to focus on the U.S. market first, and hopefully the world. Calling something Islamic does not necessarily make it so. It is the way one conducts business, deals with people, and conducts his or her life that defines who that person and that institution are. Calling a model of financing by a "foreign" name like *murabaha, musharakah,* or *mudharabah* does not make it Islamic; what makes it Judeo-Christian-Islamic is the substance and spirit by which it offers unique and measured advantages over other conventional riba-based banking and finance models. In summary, we made sure that we do not "wear our religion on our sleeves."

BOX 13.1 BENEFITS OF OFFERING AN RF BANKING ALTERNATIVE IN AMERICA

1. It applies the strict conventional U.S. banking regulatory and supervisory environment and practices enjoyed by U.S. banks to RF banking practices, products, and services. This adds more credibility to the RF banking approach and will make its products more reliable and acceptable in the market.
2. It creates a larger pool of bankers of all faiths, training, and experience who are well versed in both conventional riba banking and RF banking. This will bring a large pool of banking experience, expertise, and creative abilities to "manufacture" new products and services for the RF banking industry. It will also provide the emerging RF banking industry with RF bankers who can show the real difference by the mode of service they offer and be able to explain it well. This will help us achieve our long-term objective of creating the foundation for a new banking service and brand name, RF banking, that is offered nationwide.
3. It offers consumers the choice between conventional riba-based banking services and RF banking products and services. The consumer will enjoy the ability to choose from a wide variety of banking, financing, and saving products and services.
4. It encourages the members of the faith-based communities that believe in a riba/ribit-free lifestyle, including the American Muslim community, to participate fully in the U.S. economic system, integrate with it, and become important contributors to American

life without violating their religious beliefs. This will have a great social impact on the growing American Muslim community and the American faith-based communities at large, and will encourage savings and entrepreneurship.

5. It creates an atmosphere of healthy competition between the riba-based conventional banking products and services and the RF banking products and services. This competition should be beneficial to the consumer and to both riba-based and RF banking systems.

RIBA-BASED CONVENTIONAL FINANCING VERSUS RF FINANCING

To contrast the approach taken in a riba-based conventional financing with RF financing, let us consider a case study.

A family wants to buy a car for $30,000. They have only $6,000 of the purchase price. They want to approach a bank to help them finance the car. The following is a comparison between how the process would likely go in a riba-based banking setting as compared to RF banking setting.

Riba-Based Conventional Banker

1. Evaluates the application form.
2. Concludes that the family derives a good income and that they have a good balance sheet and a good credit history. Also, the banker finds that the family's cash flow could help them pay for a larger car or even to take a bigger loan without putting the $6,000 down. The reason the banker thinks this way is that the banker is interested in "selling" a larger loan to increase his loan sales volume and achieve his loan sales target set by management, to help increase the profitability of the bank and eventually to generate his commission or sales credit.
3. Decides to lend the family (i.e., rent them) money at a certain rate (interest rate) over a period of time. In fact, the banker may encourage the family—especially if they have a good credit history and good income—to stretch the repayment period for a longer time. The repayment period defined by the banker can even be longer than necessary, because (the banker says) he or she wants to help improve the family's cash flow. In fact, it also helps the bank derive more interest income from a good, qualified family as the loan repayment is extended.

4. The riba-based conventional banker may convince the family to buy a bigger and better-equipped car complete with many options that may not be necessary. This is because the larger loan amount, when amortized, will represent only a small addition to the monthly payment, and it will be taken care of by prolonging the financing period (term of the loan).

RF (Riba-Free) Banker

1. Evaluates the application form.
2. Concludes that the family derives a good income and that they have a good balance sheet, good credit history, and good tax returns. Also, the banker finds that the family cash flow is enough to cover the monthly payment for the car purchase.
3. Calls around to ask car leasing agencies—such as Hertz and Enterprise, as well as manufacturers' leasing agencies, such as the Toyota, Ford, and GM fleet leasing divisions—about the utility value of the car measured by the lease rate charged in the market.
4. Draws up an agreement with the family that complies with the RF finance legal requirements.

In this agreement, the family acts as the agent of the RF bank to buy the car. The transaction is structured such that the family would own \$6,000/\$30,000, or 20 percent, of the car, and the RF bank would (temporarily) own 80 percent of the car. The family agrees out of their own will to buy the bank's share of the car for the same value, or $\$30,000 - 6,000 = \$24,000$. This way, the bank does not own the title of the asset (*milk ul raqabaah,* as explained in Chapter 11 and based on the Shari'aa law) and is in compliance with the U.S. banking rules and regulations. The family, based on their cash flow, agrees to pay back the bank's share, interest-free over a period of, for example, three years, or \$8,000 per year. This is called the *return of capital (RofC)*. In lieu of the promise to pay back RofC, the family gives the RF bank a lien on the car. In lieu of the joint ownership of the right (perfected by the lien) to use the property, the family and the RF bank divide the income (the usufruct) from the lease among themselves in the (changing) proportion of unpaid capital.

The family and the RF banker independently survey the market to find a fair leasing rate for a similar car in the same market; the family and the finance officer each come up with three documented lease rates offered in the market. The family and the finance officer, based on the six data points about the car lease, can take the average or can negotiate a fair lease and agree to it. Here, the lease is divided in the beginning between the family (20 percent in the beginning, rising to 100 percent over three years) and the bank (80 percent in the beginning and declining to 0 percent over a three-year term). This is called the *return on capital (RonC)* for the RF bank.

The proprietary RF finance computer program developed by LARIBA is mechanically not much different from a regular amortization schedule. The real difference is that the variable in the LARIBA program is the car lease rate defined by the market, while the riba-based amortization schedule uses interest rate—the rental rate of money—as an input parameter. In other words, in the riba-based conventional banking model, the unknown is the monthly payment. In the RF banking service, the monthly payment is calculated based on the lease rate using the declining participation in usufruct (DPU) model, and the unknown is the rate of return on investment (ROI).

The family and the RF banker, in order to satisfy the laws of the land, sign a promissory note that documents the repayment of the debt (*dayn*—no time value of money) and the declining participation in the lease rate in a total monthly payment. To comply with the laws of the land, the RF banker plugs in the monthly market measured and agreed-upon rent of the facility representing the lease rate, the purchase price, the down payment, and the number of years to pay back into the LARIBA proprietary computer program. The program calculates the rate of return on investment, which is called in the RF system "implied" interest rate. This rate is disclosed to the client to comply with the Truth in Lending Act (TILA, or Regulation Z).

Please note that the resulting "implied" interest rate is not uniformly the same. It differs from one car to another, based on the leasing rate the same car would bring in the relevant market. If the rate of ROI is higher than the rate of return expected by the RF bank's shareholders and investors, the RF banker encourages the family to buy the car and would unilaterally and voluntarily reduce the monthly rental rate obtained from the market so that the monthly payment would compete with that offered by riba-based conventional banks. If the rate of ROI were calculated to be much lower than that expected by the RF bank's shareholders and investors, the RF banker would inform the family that buying this car is not a good investment, and the financing would be declined.

In the RF banking environment, the RF banker encourages the family to pay their car off as quickly as possible in order to reduce the burden of debt on the family's cash flow and free more money to save for the future and to make the family's excess cash flow a source of capital to reinvest in the community, leading to the creation of new job opportunities and economic prosperity.

LOOKING FOR A SUITABLE BANK TO ACQUIRE

In 1989, we started searching for banks available for sale. We stumbled into a report called the *Findley Report*,[1] which is published by a prominent banking law firm in southern California. The firm was started by a leading

California attorney who specialized in helping communities obtain charters (licenses) for community banks. The *Findley Report* was an amazing source of banks' financial information and great reading material for me. We all pored over it and studied the financials and profitability of many banks.

In 1989, after feeling more comfortable that the concept of RF financing works and that there was demand for RF financing—and knowing that we were really hurting for more capital—we began to consider buying a small bank. We called for a meeting with Mr. Findley Sr. He invited us to his rather humble office in the city of Yorba Linda (the city is located in Orange County, California) and sat us down. After the niceties of introducing ourselves and briefing each other on what we do, he looked us in the eyes and shocked us by saying, "There are three reasons that I know why someone would like to own a bank: The first is that he/she is stupid, the second is that he/she wants to put his/her hand in the 'cookie jar' and taste from it—" (by this, he meant using the bank's money for personal benefit) "—and the third is that they are genuinely interested in serving people in the community without expecting any rewards or recognition." I was quiet for a few seconds and came back directly by saying that we belonged to the third group. We told him that our passion was to build a bank that will serve the needs of the community. He apparently believed us and introduced us to his son, who was also an attorney in the same field—the honorable Gary Steven Findley, Esq. who runs the firm today. We became good friends and developed mutual trust and rapport.

Throughout my life, I can attest to the fact that when God wanted to help me achieve a goal, He would create an event that made a change in the scene or brought a certain person in my life to help me do so. When I started thinking of LARIBA, God created the reasons for me to meet, by mere coincidence, without any effort to do so, the distinguished pioneer Sheikh Saleh Abdullah Kamel, the founder of Dallah Al-Baraka Group in Saudi Arabia. This man was then (when I met him in 1987)—and still is today (in March 2014, the time the second edition of this book is being written)—one of the most influential, visionary, and busy RF (Islamic) bankers in the world, and one of the most difficult people to get an appointment with. He happened to be visiting Los Angeles in mid-1987 and attended a congregational prayer, which I was leading as an imam. He liked my ceremony, approached me after I finished, and he said that he wanted to get to know me. He introduced himself. I had no idea who he was and what he did. He politely asked that we meet. I agreed—as I always do with people who approach me. Later, I asked about him and the person who briefed me did not believe that this influential RF (Islamic) banker had asked me for an appointment. We became very close family friends. Our mutual respect and appreciation for each other continues today. I learned a lot about the concepts of RF (Islamic) banking and finance from him and from the many distinguished and highly accomplished and qualified scholars he was able to assemble from most of the countries in the Muslim world to get RF financing off to a good start in the Gulf, Europe, and the United States. As if God wanted to add to that gift to help us in our efforts to realize the vision of popularizing RF banking in America, God created the reasons for me to meet the father and son banking-attorney team of Mr. Gerald Findley, Esq., and his son Mr. Gary Steven Findley, Esq.

When we started looking to buy a bank in America, we considered offering an RF finance window into a regular riba-based conventional bank. This idea was extremely controversial when it was first implemented in Malaysia. The issue of major concern was how one could justify, from the point of view of the Judeo-Christian-Islamic Shari'aa law, the "sin" of owning a financial institution that dealt with the religiously forbidden riba/ribit, while at the same time claiming to be active in offering an RF banking window. In fact, many of the puritans and strict Muslims believe that this is a clear case of hypocrisy that should never be allowed. It was first investigated in Malaysia and then in the Middle East.[2] This problem has been investigated at length by a number of jurists and scholars and many scholars allowed it as a step toward the popularization of RF banking. However, after many conversations and "spot" opinion checks with leaders in the community, we decided to abandon the idea of opening an RF banking window in a riba-based bank. The problem of dealing with riba-based (conventional) and RF financing models in the same institution troubled many of the Muslim scholars of the Judeo-Christian-Islamic Shari'aa law and many members of the American Muslim community.

The U.S. banking system has emerged from a community-based banking network to become the most sophisticated banking system in the world.[3] The system offers products and services that meet the traditional needs of the community. At the same time it is active in many other services, such as in developing new products that are technology-based or focused on expanding the type and quality of financial services and products. While the U.S. banking system is primarily based on tradition, to a certain extent this banking system has only recently recognized the financial and banking traditions of a significant segment of the American population—the American Muslim community. The faith-based communities of all faiths have been endowed with a reservoir of highly qualified professionals, entrepreneurs, business executives, successful scholars, and distinguished students. Most of the community members are compelled to violate one of the most basic requirements of their faith: dealing with interest, or riba/ribit. The Community Reinvestment Act (CRA), which played an important part in the American banking system in the twentieth century, was originally introduced to allow community banks to gather community savings and reinvest these savings back into the community and not outside it. CRA has helped many communities develop their housing, consumer, and business needs and has also helped in creating job opportunities for the members of the community.

MAKING HISTORY: ACQUIRING THE BANK OF WHITTIER, NA

To look for a bank, we sat down to list the characteristics of the bank we wanted to acquire in order to offer in it RF banking and finance services. The following is the list we came up with:

1. *Capital* required to buy the bank should not exceed \$1.5 to 3.0 million. We did not have much money for capital.
2. *Loan portfolio* should be very small so that it could be reviewed thoroughly by our team on a loan-by-loan basis. We could not afford the consulting fees of an expert who specializes in loan portfolio review.
3. *Type of charter* we preferred was a National Association (NA) charter, which would enable us to serve other states in addition to California.
4. *Bank location* should be somewhere in the center between Los Angeles County and Orange County (in California).

It took us almost eight years to locate the Bank of Whittier as our target bank for purchase. During this long time, we would identify a bank, and then Gary Findley and our group would go to visit its president, to get a feel for the bank management's reaction to the idea of its being acquired, and to take a closer look at the bank. Upon our return, we would assemble a team to evaluate our impressions from the first meeting and to make a decision as to whether we should proceed. We looked at six banks in the period between the years 1990 to 1997.

At the end of 1996, we took another look at a bank we had considered earlier. The Bank of Whittier, NA, was chartered in December 1982 and was owned by a holding company structure called the Greater Pacific Bancshares (the letters NA stand for National Association, which means that the bank is chartered by the U.S. Treasury Department's OCC—the Office of the Comptroller of the Currency).

In March 1997, Gary Findley and I went to meet the chairman of the Bank of Whittier at that time, Mr. N. Ghannam (87 years old at that time), who was a first-generation American of Lebanese descent. His father had immigrated to the United States after World War I. Mr. Ghannam was in the printing business. He told us that he owned a few shares of the bank, but the share price kept going down because the bank was not run well and the shareholders wanted out. He went on buying more and more shares in the bank. He had assembled a small board of directors to help him run the bank. As a result, at the time we met him, Mr. Ghannam owned about 55 percent of the shares. We had a number of meetings with him and agreed that he would sell the bank. What he did not understand clearly was the meaning of the word "sell." He thought that he would be selling his 55 percent share. We advised him that there are many rules and restrictions regarding fairness to his other shareholders, and that fiduciary responsibility required that he sells his other shareholders' shares first before his. He impulsively said that meant all the bank's shares must be sold. We (some of the shareholders of LARIBA) agreed to buy the shares, and ended up owning almost 93 percent of the shares of the holding company.

The Bank of Whittier offered us the best opportunity to meet the strategic parameters we set for ourselves.

- It is a national bank.
- The bank was wholly owned by a holding company, Greater Pacific Bancshares. The holding company is (theoretically) traded on the stock market. Of course, at that time, it was traded as a *pink sheet* item. But we reasoned, as we improved it, increased its capital, increased the number of shareholders, assigned it to a good market maker, and started introducing it to the investment banking community, that it would be a good publicly traded stock that investors are attracted to.
- Its assets amounted to approximately $29 million. In fact, it was one of the last few small, independent banks left in southern California that had not been acquired or merged.
- Its capital was approximately $2.3 million.
- Its loan portfolio had been cleaned regularly during the bank and savings and loan crisis of the 1980s and early 1990s. In fact, the bank had stood the test of the 1980s banking crisis and was still in operation.
- It is located in a city in the center between Los Angeles County (about 25 minutes driving time from downtown Los Angeles) and Orange County (about 40 minutes driving distance from Irvine, California), which makes it accessible to many community members who live in the area.
- The bank's senior staff was essentially out because of their bad performance, but not all were replaced. This situation helped us to participate in the selection of the new management (while waiting for federal approval for change of bank control).

The Bank of Whittier had been in business since December 1982. It offered a unique service environment, with "sit-down" teller stations, and a good location on Whittier Boulevard, a major commercial street, in the same complex with the Whittier Community Hospital and at least two medical doctors' professional buildings.

In December 1997, we signed an agreement with the board of directors of Greater Pacific Bancshares and Bank of Whittier to purchase up to 100 percent of the shares of Greater Pacific Bancshares. The bank was operating under a memorandum of understanding (MOU) from the regulators. The MOU required that the management and board of directors improve the board of directors committees and supervision, hire necessary senior staff, increase capital, and not distribute dividends or acquire new companies/banks until approved by the authorities. After reviewing the OCC's most recent bank examination results, we concluded that it was good to note that the examiners were now increasingly positive about the bank because of its new management and the new loan cleanup and classification system installed by the new management. In addition, the feeling was that the MOU might be removed very shortly. The total of adversely classified items, as a percent of the total assets, was 6.6 percent. Out of that, total past-due and nonaccrual loans and leases were 5.8 percent of the total gross loans and leases. *ALLL* (the allowances for loan and lease losses) were adequate and the analysis used was reasonable. The ALLL totaled approximately $796,000 in mid-1997 and was 4.6 percent of the total loans.

In general, the new management continued its efforts to improve credit quality, credit administration, and risk management. Based on the public information and the audited financial statement of the bank and bank holding company, we came up with the following:

- *Capital ratios.* Tangible equity capital as a percent of total assets was estimated at 7.8 percent, indicating that the bank passed the capitalization test and was considered well capitalized. However, more capital would be needed to strengthen the bank earnings by deploying new loans into the assets. It was recommended that at least $1 million in fresh capital be injected immediately after takeover. However, a $3 million capital increase (total capital of approximately $5.3 million) would greatly improve the bank's earnings.
- *Earnings analysis.* Net income (after tax) was expected to be 0.64 percent of total average assets. Return on average assets (ROAA) was lower than it had been in 1996 (0.86 percent) due to the aggressive loan write-off by the management (in coordination with us while waiting for the approvals). Earnings analysis indicated that the bank had a strong *net interest margin* (NIM). But this NIM continued to be offset by weak asset quality and high overheads. The NIM was 6.95 percent, which compared favorably to peer banks. However, loan losses and deterioration in the

Small Business Administration (SBA) and business manager (factoring meaning accounts receivable financing) portfolios resulted in ALLL provisions of at least $380,000 by the end of 1997. Despite this, the bank was expected to be able to earn at least $165,000 in 1997. Overhead expenses, particularly consulting fees, had been very high historically. However, they declined 18 percent in the first six months of 1997 compared to the first six months of 1996, and were expected to decline further under the new management. Many unnecessary overhead expenses were curtailed or were on their way out; the SBA loans had been brought to a halt, and the business manager (underwriting factoring or accounts receivable financing) had been canceled and the loan officer in charge was terminated. It was expected that monthly profitability would improve as a result of management's decision to increase loan volume, primarily through carefully selected loans (we hoped and expected these loans to be RF loans).

- *Liquidity.* Bank liquidity was satisfactory, and liquidity risk was low. Short-term investments were 24 percent of total assets and included approximately $4 million in Fed Funds sold and approximately $2.4 million in CDs. The loan-to-deposit ratio was 67 percent. This indicated the need for new high-quality loans added to the portfolio. We thought that this was an excellent entry point for our LARIBA portfolios in Pasadena. The fund management and investment strategy needed to improve upon the bank's operating results by establishing a good investment portfolio in which to invest the bank's liquid assets without sacrificing risk and liquidity, while earning the highest RF-based return possible.
- *Interest rate risk.* The bank's interest rate risk position was good. The bank's balance sheet was asset sensitive, with rate-sensitive assets (RSAs) of $27.2 million, higher than its rate-sensitive liabilities (RSLs) of $17.8 million within a one-year period. The RSA/RSL gap was 1.72 at 60 days and 1.33 at 1 year. The goal was to keep it at 1 to 1.5. A sensitivity analysis showed that with a 100–basis point decline in interest rates, annualized net interest income exposure was $82,000.

We signed the preliminary agreement to be approved by the bank's board and shareholders. We obtained these approvals. We then set out to take a very close look at the details of the bank's operations, its assets, and in particular its loan portfolio. We evaluated the financial statements, the existing lawsuits the bank is involved in (if any), the loan portfolio (loan by loan), and the operations of the bank. We discovered more about the MOU signed with the OCC that the bank was operating under, and the details of the special restriction from the OCC as detailed in the MOU. One of the criticisms the OCC had was that the bank did not have a detailed set of operating policies; there were other criticisms about the bank's operations, its policies, and its profitability. Placing an MOU on a bank is not an action that can be taken lightly. The bank management is required to operate according to a plan approved by the OCC, and the bank management must go to the OCC for any significant decision including management changes. This slows down management operations and limits management flexibility, but it is the price that must be paid when a bank's management does not abide by the rules and regulations. This MOU was removed in the early 2000s after fulfilling the requirements of the OCC.

If you think that was the end and that we now owned a bank—please think again.

The next major and most demanding step was gaining the approval of the United States government's banking authorities for us, the buyers, to assume control of the bank, a process called "change of control." In the case of the Bank of Whittier, government regulators were represented by three entities. These were:

1. *The Office of the Comptroller of the Currency (OCC)* because the OCC supervises national banks. That is why we—as buyers of the shares who would become the control persons of the bank—had to file a full application with the OCC.
2. *The Federal Reserve Bank of San Francisco and the Federal Reserve Board (FRB)* because the Bank of Whittier was owned by a holding financial services company that was supervised by the FRB.
3. *The Federal Deposit Insurance Corporation (FDIC)* because the bank was a member of the FDIC system, which insures customer deposits up to $250,000 for a single account holder and $500,000 for a joint account (say for a husband and wife).

The application process took a long time, almost 15 months. The application forms to change control of the bank required full background information and disclosures that might go back to the childhood of the applicants, their place of birth and origin, their education, their financial details, their criminal records, and their business history, in detail. The application also called for a complete description of the reasons why the new control persons wanted to take control of the bank, how they would operate the bank, what their business plans were for the bank, and how they would serve and improve the bank's service to the community. The regulators also required that the new control group prepare a complete business plan for the bank's future budget and financial projections.

In an effort to reduce legal expenses and the preacquisition costs in order to fit our rather humble financial means, our team first took the applications from Mr. Findley's office and then would spend very long nights completing them and preparing the plans and reports the application called for. In many cases, some of us were traveling out of the country and would operate via telephone and fax because the Internet was not popular yet. We would send the completed forms and reports to Mr. Findley, who would edit them and pass them on to the regulators. The regulators would respond with more questions and inquiries for Mr. Findley, who would pass them on to us. We would again prepare the detailed answers to these questions. The word *detailed* here sometimes worked to our detriment because, as we learned from Mr. Findley's office, when we got a question from a government agency, that question had to be answered in a specific fashion, in full and clear details, and in a direct way, without opening new topics or subjects. Not abiding by these rules and course of action triggered more questions. The process took approximately 15 months of back-and-forth communications that culminated in a telephone meeting in January 1998 (during the holy month of *Ramadan*) that was attended by representatives from:

- The OCC in California and in Washington, D.C.
- The Federal Reserve Bank in Washington, D.C., and the Federal Reserve Bank of San Francisco.
- The FDIC in Washington, D.C.
- Gary Findley and his associate.
- Our team.

The government agents thanked us—the applicants—for our "... patience, perseverance, detailed answers, and your posture as humble professionals. . . ." We, in return, thanked them for their wonderful and refreshing due diligence. I wanted to lighten the atmosphere, so I told them that they now knew more about us than our parents and family ever did. This experience is shared here in great detail to reassure the reader of the quality of the U.S. banking system and the meticulous detail the system goes through to make sure that the regulations of the system are put in effect. What happened in 2008 and before was due to a group of irresponsible bankers who violated the law, violated the trust placed in them, and ended up hurting all of us. They should not have been in this honorable business.

We thought that this was the end of our challenges and that we now finally had a bank. The local community paper published the news, and we all were delighted. Frankly, we were expecting the whole community to rush to transfer their accounts to the bank. Well, that did not happen! We also thought that we could run the bank in the same fashion we ran LARIBA, for the benefit of the whole community. We did not know what we were getting ourselves into. The community banking fraternity, we discovered, is an interesting group, to say the least. Please enter the new domain called community banking. Many of the community banks were run by veterans who prided themselves in front of others—visitors, customers, other bankers, and auditors—as to how many years of "banking" experience they had. You heard them bragging about their "40 years of banking experience." We ended up with a few of them. I developed an interesting sensitivity scale, in which I raised a big mental red flag whenever I heard that claim uttered. I once asked one of them, who really did not have much to offer except that claim to fame, "Did you ever consider the possibility that you were making the same mistakes for 40 years but did not know about it?"

The reader may also find interesting a request made by one of the candidates for president of the bank. After stating his huge salary and benefits request, he asked for two SLX automobiles. Frankly, I did not know what he meant. I asked him why he needed two cars. He said that he wanted one for him and another for his wife. I obviously told him no! I then called my young daughter to ask her what an SLX car was. She said, "Dad, I thought you did not like expensive cars. An SLX is a Mercedes Benz that can cost $120,000." A story like this should give the reader an insight into the state of affair of a few bankers and how it changed compared to the community building and loan society banker we watched Jimmy Stewart portray in the movie *It's a Wonderful Life*.

We tried to work with at least two consecutive bank presidents to convince them of the responsibility to reinvest in the community, to care for people, to go out and mix with the community, and to serve people. It was very difficult. We were not treated nicely because we were looked at as outsiders to the community banking fraternity and as people who did not have "enough" banking experience. We also discovered that any time we shared some of the successes we had experienced at LARIBA, they would directly come back to tell us that it is not doable, because the regulators would not approve. We would come back and show them that other successful banks in the business were doing the same as we recommended.

Around the year 2000, a bank president sent to the OCC a letter claiming that I was interfering in the management of the bank, which was in complete violation of the banking regulations because I worked at the time for another investment bank—Citigroup/Smith Barney. I voluntarily committed in writing to the OCC that I would not step foot in the bank again. In fact, from that time until I took early retirement from Citigroup and started managing the bank, I did not set foot in the bank—as I promised—until our management came to run the bank. That was for a total of 30 months.

It is also interesting to share with the reader what happened to us when we arrived at the Bank of Whittier on July 10, 2003, to take over bank management. Most staff had resigned and we were left with two employees. The bank's total assets were approximately $26 million, and the bank had been losing money. We could not even find an insurance company that would agree to insure our executives and officers against any business mishaps. The bank was going from bad to worse. There were no written policies in any of the bank's operations, and the bank treasury and accounting systems were not well taken care of. There was no experienced operations manager, there were no manuals for the computer systems, the financial ledgers were not properly balanced by the person in charge, and customers had no respect for the new team. One day in our second week of running the bank, two contractors arrived at the bank to cash some checks, and we were very busy. One of them made a loud and noisy scene. I approached him politely to ask him to please lower his voice and to tell me what the problem was. He said, "In this country, American customers expect immediate service," and he proceeded to make some references to the fact that I am an immigrant. I smiled at him and asked him and his partner to step into my office. Then I closed the door and gave him a real piece of my mind. I told the man that I was proud to be a first-generation American—but I want to assure you that in this great country, I started with nothing, I must have paid much more in taxes than he did, and that he should never demean or put people down again because of their accents or national origin. The man was shocked. His partner looked embarrassed and apologized, and he followed. His partner is still the bank's customer to this day.

After arriving at the bank we decided to clean it up—to refurbish the bank facilities to give the customers who come to the bank the feeling of a private community bank with a "family living room" atmosphere. We also obtained board approval to improve the technology and systems so that we could have a fully automated banking operation that would be ready for the twenty-first century, in addition to a very user-friendly website (www.BankOfWhittier.com).

We started looking for associates who could help build up the bank management and staff. Another person who was also a gift from God was a young man I met by mere coincidence in one of the community centers. Mike Abdelaaty was a banker with Bank of America at the time, where he had spent 7 years of his career. He then moved to Sanwa Bank (now Bank of the West) for 10 years, and he spent 3 years in one of the Gulf oil-producing countries. While in Los Angeles, I always solicited his support in the banking and finance work that we did at LARIBA. After his return to the United States in 1999, he contacted me and decided to do only RF banking. He joined LARIBA as its president.

Another interesting experience we went through was dealing with the audit firm that audited the finances of the bank. We noticed the sloppiness of the representatives who came to collect the bank's information and documents. We went through with the audit in the first year, but were not satisfied; many of us were not comfortable with the results. It was felt that the certified public accountant (CPA) who signed our financial statements did not do his due diligence and did not know the financial condition of the bank. I shared this information with Gary Findley and the board, and they authorized a change. We commissioned another CPA firm that we were very happy with and we are using the firm until now.

We started with a very small staff. We had to spend long and hard hours to put together a full set of policies by which the bank would operate. In addition, we started to look for outside auditors who could come and audit—on behalf of the board of directors—bank operations, bank compliance with government regulations, the bank loan portfolio, and *Bank Secrecy Act* (BSA) matters. We went through our first-ever OCC examination as a new team and we received wonderful results and compliments. From this humble beginning, we have come a long way. The Bank of Whittier, NA, was rated a five-star bank by Bauer Financial during the 2008 financial meltdown and beyond (until the time of this writing in March 2014, it is rated a five-star bank).

OPERATING THE FIRST RF BANK IN THE UNITED STATES

As explained in Chapter 2, in today's banking lingo, one can conceptually define riba/ribit-based financing as renting money for financing, secured and unsecured (noncollateralized credits that are not asset or service based). In RF banking, a bank's financing activity is conceptually looked upon as an investment by the bank in the individual (or the company) in order to help that entity acquire tangible and productive assets and/or services. In his capacity as an investor of the bank's money—which is the community's money—the RF bank credit officer makes sure that the financing facility is used for a specific purpose and that the investment is prudent and makes economic merit.

The time has come to publicize and popularize the new *RF banking* brand as a complementary community banking and financing service, to allow the community to make a choice. The free market system will be the judge of the real value of this RF finance and banking system to the average consumer in the United States.

Our Strategic Approach to Restructure the Bank of Whittier

On July 10, 2003, our team of three associates arrived at the Bank of Whittier to take over the management of the bank. We found that the bank was in a very sorry state of affairs. In addition, the OCC requested that we submit to them within a few weeks a detailed plan that documented how the new team would change the fortunes of the bank.

The Bank Restructuring and Workout Plan: Turning the Bank Around

To begin, the management team developed a number of goals that had to be achieved in order to turn the bank around and start operating it as an RF bank. The following is a list of these goals:

1. Rectify any regulatory concerns as soon as possible.
2. Increase the bank's capital.
3. Stress quality in services, and use a new slogan that identified our character as an RF bank: *We Do Not Rent Money—We Invest in Our Customers.*
4. Control bank expenses in a tight, micro, and detailed way. For example, we used both sides of the copier paper and recycled paper in the copying machine to save on paper.
5. Hire highly educated and qualified staff.
6. Use the best banking and service technologies available.
7. Improve bank facilities to give a feel of a private bank and a living room ambience in order to attract new clients who would feel like members of our new and expanding bank family.
8. Achieve reasonable and competitive profitability, compared to the bank's peer group.
9. Increase loan (credit) portfolio to 70–75 percent of total deposits, and then increase deposits and loans in a parallel mode.
10. Improve quality of credits (loans) and expand the bank's loan portfolio using RF financing policies, values and discipline.
11. Do not allow speculation-oriented lending.
12. Do not do business with intoxicant sellers, bars, check cashing, pawn shops, gambling casinos, or individuals deriving their income from socially irresponsible sources and activities.
13. Popularize the RF concepts that require that we do not "sell" or "buy" loans. We invest with the customer, and we do not sell our relationships. We service all the financing that we originate.
14. Be fair to all.
15. Be active in serving the community.
16. Offer new RF products and services to attract new deposits and customers looking to finance their facilities and projects.
17. Offer a Bank of Whittier credit card service through a bank that specializes in credit card services, because the bank did not want to be involved in an interest-based charging activity, does not have the staff available

to administer credit card services even if it were RF, and it cannot compete with the mega-bank issuers of credit cards. These conditions would drastically reduce the credit risk exposure to the bank, while offering an important facility to our customers without the bank getting involved in any prohibited interest charging. The card is a Visa network card that offers credit, but the bank advises the customers to pay within a month to avoid paying riba (interest). This advice is posted in red letters on the front page of the bank's website. We may be one of the few banks that strongly encourages its customers *not* to use credit cards as a means of borrowing and use it in offering its original service when it was first introduced—a charge card. The other card is a regular Visa-linked *automatic teller machine* (ATM) debit card that only dispenses money or credit up to the deposits in the account and can be used throughout the world at one million ATMs. It is known that some in the RF banking domain call the debit cards *Islamic* credit cards! We insist that we call it what it really is: a charge card. As the RF scholars became more flexible, credit cards were allowed as a means of "Islamic" lending, something that created many heavily indebted customers during the bursting of the real estate bubble in Dubai and some of the Gulf countries.

Specific Action Plan and Steps Taken by Bank Management

After a number of intensive brainstorming sessions attended by the new management and the board of directors the new management recommended (and the board of directors approved) the following list of actions:

1. *Continue to develop a sound corporate image and reputation in the local community, with the business community, and with the regulators.*
   - Better and professional facilities.
   - Socially responsible, educated, experienced, friendly, humble, and professional staff.
   - Deeper community involvement by communicating with civic associations, faith-based organizations, and surrounding universities.
   - Training bank staff on bank regulations, RF banking and finance, RF credit, business development, communications, appearance, and customer service at the newly innovated RF Bank of Whittier Open University.
2. *Develop strong roots and community relations to increase the bank's client base and its RF credit (loan) and deposit activities.*
   - Call on existing bank holding company shareholders, friends, and our network of customers and potential customers to bring their business to the bank.

- Call on medical doctors and professionals in our building and surrounding buildings, including Whittier Hospital, Presbyterian Intercommunity Hospital, churches, synagogues, and neighborhood fast food restaurant franchises.
- Call all existing deposit and loan clients and bank shareholders.
- Actively ask for referrals.
- Hold in-person meetings with existing clients and prospects, in order to act as their trusted bankers.
- Hire staff from the bank's immediate service areas and through neighboring universities and business colleges.
- Participate actively in the local chamber of commerce.
- Develop personal working relationships with city and county elected officials.
- Broaden and stress the offering of diversified RF banking services.
- Cross-sell bank products and services.

3. *Review all bank policies and develop a new set of bank policies and train staff through the new and innovative training program administered by the Bank of Whittier Open University. The following is an abbreviated list of policies developed by the new management team and reviewed and approved by the board of directors:*
   - Employee handbook
   - Credit policy
   - Consumer compliance policy
   - USA PATRIOT Act policy
   - BSA policy
   - Customer identification program, used to open new accounts
   - Anti–money laundering policy
   - Large currency transactions and kiting detection policy
   - Availability of funds policy for out-of-town and area checks
   - Audit policy
   - Funds management policy
   - Liquidity policy
   - Wire transfer and automated clearinghouse policy
   - Investment policy
   - Information technology and information security policy
   - Emergency preparedness plan and procedure
   - Disaster recovery plan
   - Privacy policy and procedure (Gramm-Leach-Bliley Act)
   - Vendors' management policy
4. *Improve and enhance the security of the bank facilities, systems, and operations.*
   - Equip the bank with the most up-to-date alarm and security systems.

- Run drills and emergency tests for different disaster scenarios, such as fire, earthquake, loss of power, loss of computer connection to the central computer processor, loss of server, and loss of Fed-line connection, which connects the bank with the Federal Reserve System.
- Continue to implement frequent risk-based outside audit programs in all bank operations, loans, consumer compliance, BSA activities, accounting and finance, and technology.

5. *Continue to improve bank quality of services and operating efficiency.*
   - Assemble a strong team of RF bankers and instill a conservative, highly analytical, professional, helpful, and friendly operating culture.
   - Continue to hire highly educated, computer-literate, and professionally sound team members.
   - Hire part-time trainees from surrounding business colleges to prepare candidates for future employment at the bank and to fulfill the bank's social responsibility of training future generations.
   - Train staff on systems and on high ethical, moral, and professional standards.
   - Streamline management by focusing on specific job functions and the measurement of staff achievements against the board of directors' approved budget, joint planning, goal setting, and comparing results with budget.
6. *Improve the computerization and automation of bank operations and services.*
   - Start using a standard client and prospect management information and communications maintenance system on all staff's computers, to keep track of customers, prospects, loan renewals, and reviews.
   - Improve the quality and security of the bank's computer network.
   - Improve the quality of the hardware used by staff.
7. *Increase bank deposit base.*
   - Continue to improve facilities to increase efficiency and attract new customers.
   - Continue to improve service quality.
   - Tap existing network of community members and friends to open new accounts and to add new RF credits (loans).
   - Diversify bank RF products and services without having too many products that would confuse customers, using the "Keep It Simple Stupid" (KISS) approach.
   - Expand customer base through better involvement with family, including children and grandchildren, to keep an evergreen book of clients.
   - Expand customer base through asking for referrals.
   - Continue to carve and deepen a unique corporate image and culture and promote social responsibility in lending and services.

   - Continue to advocate, enhance, and implement a bank policy of cultural diversity among employees and bank customers.
8. *Continue to reduce bank operating expenses.*
   - Control expenses on all fronts by paying attention using a micro-expense review approach.
   - Motivate and reward team members by using productivity-based and bank profitability-based salary and bonus review programs.
   - Insist on thorough and prudent credit (loan) analysis to reduce loan losses.
   - Develop steps to achieve close scrutiny and follow-up of existing credits (loans) in order to solve any problems and fix them, if possible, before they occur and become seriously troubled and nonperforming and become a loss.
   - Conduct weekly comparisons between actual expenses and budgeted expenses.
9. *Increase bank income.*
   - Actively pursue the prudent growth of the credit (loan) portfolio through deeper penetration of current depository customers and cultivation of new customers through referrals and community involvement.
   - Introduce RF mortgage financing based on the long years of experience gained at LARIBA finance company.
   - Preserve and retain existing credits (loans).

The following includes strategic steps that were implemented to improve the management process of bank operations.

1. *Open and review all incoming and outgoing mail and faxes.* The first step taken by the new management was to find out where the bank was, and what was going on in its day-to-day operations. It is important that we share our management experience with the reader, because this was one of the important steps that helps in understanding what is going on in a newly acquired institution. The new chief executive officer (your author) asked that all incoming and outgoing mail and faxes be brought to his office so that he could open the incoming mail with another bank manager, review the incoming faxes, approve the outgoing faxes before they are sent, and read the outgoing mail before the envelopes are sealed, stamped, and mailed. This is done always in the presence of another officer. The management needed to know how the bank was connected to the outside world by, for example, reviewing the incoming invoices and engagement contracts with various vendors to know who the bank is dealing with. This step gave us—in

three months' time—a great and comprehensive feeling for the bank, its pulses, and its operations.

2. *Hire new employees.* We started looking for new employees to build our team. We needed at least two tellers, a highly qualified credit analyst, and a good accountant to start with. We contacted some of the tellers and loan administration officers who had resigned from the bank before we took over, to see if they would come back. Only one teller accepted our offer; all the rest declined. In fact, some of them did not care to return our calls.

   We then started thinking about a way out of this dilemma. One of the management team came up with the idea of hiring business school students from the surrounding colleges and training them on the job. This proved to be a great idea. We appointed juniors at the business schools of the colleges and universities surrounding the bank as tellers and administration personnel. Later, these part-time student workers became candidates for full-time positions as operations manager and supervisors. As part of our training of these new employees and the existing staff we thought that if we engaged high-quality qualified outside auditors of bank operations would give the staff a useful hands-on and on the job training. We started looking for a high-quality and experienced auditor of banking operations and compliance. We wanted an auditor who would critique and at the same time coach and train the new staff as he audited the bank. We found an experienced and dedicated retired banker who was passionate about compliance, regulations, and quality of bank operations. We engaged him with instructions to play the dual role of an auditor of our bank operations to uncover deficiencies that need to be fixed and to provide hands-on training for our staff. We asked him to come on a quarterly basis and to make himself available for consultation. We instructed all employees to be open to any comments and recommendations on lack of compliance discovered by the auditor. We also instructed the staff to take advantage of the knowledge and experience of the auditor and not to be defensive and quick to justify why things were not done right. We assembled the staff before the audit started and asked them to look at the auditor as a teacher and a coach and to be truthful and open when answering any questions. The management team also had a meeting with the auditor and told him that the management and the board of directors wanted to learn in great detail what was wrong in the bank, not simply what was done right at the bank. We also assured the auditor that we intended to promptly fix any problems he found as soon as they were recognized.

3. *Familiarize management and staff with computer systems and outside service providers.* Management also started to familiarize the staff

with the computer operating system and with the bank check processing and technology providers in order to know how the business is conducted.

4. *Review all financial ledgers and financial operations.* On the financial front, the new management went through the bank financial statement and ledger in great detail with the chief financial officer (CFO) and asked a lot of questions. This step was the most important, because we discovered many violations and nonposted transactions. For example, every time the CFO had not been able to balance the financial statement (assets and liabilities), he had assigned the discrepancy to a new bank control account. We discovered more than 30 such accounts and many tens of thousands of dollars that were not properly accounted for. It took us many months and long hours to try to reconcile these accounts and we still were not able to reconcile all of them. That meant that we had to add such discrepancies to the bank losses.
5. *Evaluate the quality of the bank auditors.* After discovering the unfortunate state of affairs of the treasury function and the professional quality of the financial officers involved at the bank and the fact that the auditors/CPA of the bank never questioned it or mentioned anything about it in their annual audited financial report, management was very disappointed in the quality and authenticity of the CPA audits. We contacted the chief CPA auditor of bank's CPA firm and complained about the unprofessional way the bank accounting and auditing system had been handled. He did not have the time, he said, because he was busy with bigger and more important banks. He relied on two young accountants who would come to the bank to pick up the statements from the CFO and leave without even spending a few minutes to discuss these statements with the officer. This shows what happens when the culture in an organization is to operate on "automatic pilot" and hopes for the best to happen. In fact, the worst happens because the quality of the operation deteriorates quickly as it did with the bank. Management conferred with the board and the bank's lawyer. We had some concern about changing the bank CPA auditor. We were worried that the regulators, the shareholders, customers, and people in general might suspect that the CPA auditor may have been in disagreement with bank management on some issues and that is why the bank management and board of directors were motivated to change the CPA auditor. Management finally decided to push hard to change the auditing firm. It took us a long time to find an audit firm that would accept a bank that was losing money and had a new unproven management. I called Mr. Findley, and he helped us to find a CPA firm that accepted the job. He kindly put in a very good word about the bank's new

management. However, the new firm had a condition: they first wanted to review the bank's condition and then contact the existing audit firm to make sure that there is no irregular activity involved at the bank. They did. After numerous contacts and interviews, they decided to become our auditors. We were all very impressed by the quality and depth of their work, and we felt comfortable about this most important bank activity.

6. *Develop the unique RF niche at the Bank of Whittier.* One of the most important steps in rescuing and restructuring the bank was to develop a strategic vision for a niche that would characterize that bank. The following gives a summary of the process we used to articulate our RF finance system under difficult and challenging conditions.

Strategies Designed and Steps Implemented by the New Management

The following is a list of the strategies developed and the steps that management took to achieve its goals of restructuring the bank and operating it as a successful and as a preferred RF bank.

1. Determine the appropriate optimum size of deposits needed for the bank to serve its clients while reducing the cost of retaining expensive-to-keep deposits. In doing so, we reduced deposits and at the same time gradually increased the credit (loan) portfolio to improve profitability and operating ratios. The strategy called for reducing the rates paid on all existing interest-bearing accounts first, and then, as the credit (loan) portfolio grew, we could grow the deposits accordingly. This strategy resulted in the closing of all those accounts that were classified as interest-rate-sensitive liabilities. In a matter of a few months, asset size had decreased from $29.2 million at December 31, 2003, to $25.0 million at December 31, 2004, resulting in reduced interest expense and positioned the bank to start and chart a new RF path for the Bank of Whittier.
2. Renovate the bank's facilities and automate its operations to improve the bank's image and operating efficiency.
3. Improve the bank's website and offer full Internet banking, online bill pay service of the highest quality, and mobile phone banking, free of charge. Here, it is worth giving the reader our intent of using the Internet at the bank. We were aware of the many risks involved with using the Internet to open accounts, transfer money, and/or to provide loans online using the Internet. That is why we decided to use the Internet in a different way than the way it has been used by major banks. We

observed that the objective of the major banks is to drive customers away from the bank lobby at the branch to reduce in-branch traffic and overhead. In order to achieve this, the major banks used high-tech ATMs outside the branch, remote capture check-scanning machines for customers who process large volume of checks, and the other Internet banking facilities. We at the Bank of Whittier, as a small community bank, had a different goal and vision. That goal was to use the Internet to encourage our customers and prospective clients to know who we are and what products and services we offer, and encourage them to call us in person and to come and visit us if they live close to the bank. That was why the Internet was used as a means of connecting with the customers. Our website was designed to fulfill that goal. Internet banking was used to serve customers and make it easy for them to bank without the risk of compromising their accounts. The Internet banking service was highly rated by our customers when compared with that of larger size banks.

4. Prohibit board members and senior managers from taking loans or benefiting directly or indirectly because of their position. In this way there would not be the slightest concern of violating Regulation O, which requires close proctoring and disclosure of any insider activity in the bank operations. That voluntary restriction approved by the board of directors of the Bank of Whittier reinforces the goal of the bank's board and management to underline its commitment to serve the community and not to personally benefit in any way from that service.
5. Offer new Bank of Whittier products and services, like the FDIC-insured certificate of deposit (CD) accounts, which are insured up to $50 million through a strategic alliance with the Certificate of Deposit Account Registry Service (CDARS).[4]
6. Employ highly qualified and educated professionals with extensive banking experience, and train a new generation of bankers by hiring new business school graduates, preferably from the immediate neighborhood and the local universities around the city. In addition, hire tellers who are business school students. They are hired as part-time employees and are cultivated by management to be future bank employees to meet our long-term growth plans.
7. Provide exceptional banking services by splitting the traditional bank function of a "loan officer" into two functions.
   - *RF private banker.* This function was designed to provide each customer with a well-trained and seasoned RF banker who is well educated professionally trained to become the point of contact between the client and the bank. In addition, the RF private banker is responsible for knowing the family and its members, understanding their

aspirations, and articulating their financial state of affairs and specific short- and long-term goals. This allows the RF banker to integrate its services with the client's needs. The RF private banker aspires to add new family members to the RF Bank of Whittier's expanding family. The services of the RF private banker are available to customers 24 hours a day, 7 days a week.

- *RF credit analyst.* The analysts hired at the bank are among the better educated in the field of financial analysis; some have MBA degrees, and all hold business school degrees from some of the better business schools in the United States with a grade point average that is higher than 3.5 and preferably 3.75. The goal of the RF credit analyst is to conduct a thorough analysis of the financing application at hand, to perform sensitivity analyses with different assumptions and to develop a number of scenarios and recommendations for whether or not to finance the proposed financing using the RF discipline. We train our RF credit analysts not only to protect bank interests but also to be sensitive and caring about providing what is in the best interests of our customers. During the Bank of Whittier Open University training program, we drill the candidates to understand that we are in service not to rent money and produce loans and pay commissions. All of our associates—the staff of the Bank—are salaried employees who are not motivated by collecting a commission on a sale of loan or banking service. We are in the business of investing in our clients.

8. Provide all bank employees with the best training available through in-house training programs conducted by expert bank executives and senior managers, video training programs, Web-based programs, and live training presentations by outside experts. Training also is done continually on a daily basis through direct encounters, meetings, joint analysis sessions and discussions with the chief executive officer and senior management. It is the team work that will produce positive results. In addition, we train our employees on being socially responsible. Our simple focus is to train every one of our staff to watch RF banking in action and to emulate the ethics, service, attitude, and commitment of the first RF banker in America George Bailey in the movie *It's a Wonderful Life*. In fact, every employee is required to watch a 20-minute short version of this movie at least once a year, and it is discussed in bank training forums to improve the spirit of serving our clients in an RF way and at the same time share with our clients the aspects of RF lifestyle. In addition, the bank encourages and in some cases finances further continuing education of distinguished and promising staff contributors in the area of special banking topics as well as in MBA banking programs at some of the best schools and universities in the nation.

9. Expand bank services through a strategic alliance with a major bank. This alliance allows our business customers to access the services of the Bank of Whittier at any of the hundreds of the major bank branches in the United States.
10. Expand our business hours; we are open from 9:00 A.M. until 5:00 P.M. every weekday except on Friday, when we close at 6:00 P.M. On Saturdays and Sundays we are ready to open by appointment for customers who are interested in applying for credit (loans) or for financial advice.
11. Develop bank policies for all aspects of bank operations, as well as a procedures and an operations manual.
12. Focus on improving the quality of the credit (loan) portfolio. Perhaps this is the most important aspect of the strategy in order to reduce losses and to transform the portfolio from a riba-based portfolio into an RF portfolio. This was done by:
    - Contacting our community members in our CRA assessment area, especially those who have been underserved.
    - Closing and declining renewal of those loans which were below our conservative credit underwriting standards, and increasing the size of the bank's RF credit (loan) portfolio through RF marketing and promotion by cross-marketing the existing customers and our existing network of personal and business contacts.
    - Developing new RF credits (loans) using strict and conservative RF underwriting standards.
    - Activating RF mortgage financing to attract new customers and increase bank income. The bank pass-through mortgage business has been an important contributor to its income and turn around.
13. Offer integrated banking services on both the asset and liability sides of the customers' ledger. This is done through the services offered by the bank's private bankers and business development managers.

THE STAFF AND EMPLOYEE POLICY

In my new capacity as the chairman of the board and the CEO at the Bank of Whittier, I felt fortunate but immensely challenged due to the staff situation when I arrived at the bank on July 10, 2003. I essentially had to staff a new bank, which was good, but the challenge was where to begin, where to find the staff, and most importantly what to look for.

One approach anyone in my situation would do is to contact an employment agency or to put an advertisement in the business papers like the *Wall Street Journal* or the *Financial Times*. However, that was not an option because of the type of bankers that would be expected to apply. They would ask for very high salaries, which the bank could not afford, and in general they would not agree to join a bank that was losing money and was in the shape that Bank of Whittier was in at the time. The other approach I tried was to contact friends in the banking industry to help recommend good bankers. I interviewed a few of them. I felt that they wanted a job and a big salary, which they knew was too large for the bank to afford in its state of profitability.

During a quiet moment our team sat down to ponder, brain storm, and think. It was reasoned that the bank could continue to use the services of the chief financial officer (CFO), but with very close supervision and a lot of patience to accommodate his negative and pessimistic "energy-sapping" remarks and attitude. We would also seek some of the wonderful hardworking associates at LARIBA to come and help. I asked my deputy at LARIBA and the secretary of the board to act as the chief credit officer on a part-time basis because the loan portfolio was very small. We all started also to look for a smart, sophisticated, and highly analytical credit analyst. It was reasoned that this person did not have to have any banking experience but must have demonstrable financial analysis skills. To do this, I called a friend and he recommended a person who was a perfect fit. He had an undergraduate degree in aerospace engineering (which meant to me that he has a very careful and deeply sophisticated approach to analysis), an MBA, and was working on his Certified Financial Analyst certification. He had a very heavy accent, and you had to either listen carefully to him or to ask him to repeat the words slowly in order to understand his English. I mention this to share with you the value of a person and the talents that person may have that can be uncovered regardless of this/her accent, national origin, faith, skin color, or gender.

In this regard, it would be useful to share two personal experiences. That experience happened to your author when I was training at Shearson American Express (predecessor to Smith Barney/Citigroup) for a cold-calling financial consultant job (cold calling is an American innovation). A cold call is a phone call initiated by the finance development representative, which is made to a person whom the financial officer has never met, hence the use of the word *cold*. The cold call is intended for the finance officer to meet that person on the phone, get to know that person, and offer one's services to that person on the other side of the call based on the experience and the service the finance firm or the bank offers. Cold calling requires excellent communication skills and sound intellect to be able to respond intelligently, spontaneously, and convincingly in an honest way and clear expression. During my cold call training, a co-trainee approached me in a sincere way and said that he wanted to give me an advice. He said that because of my accent, I needed to apologize to the person I cold-called, telling him or her that if he/she did not understand my accent they can feel free to ask me to repeat what I said. I looked at him for a minute and said to him that he must be crazy. He thought that he had offended me and started to apologize. I told him that he had not offended me and I thanked him for his advice and concern. I told him that if I had a scar on my face, I was not going to apologize for having it to every person I met. There are things that people cannot do much to change, and that should never be an impediment to their progress and acceptance by others. In fact, feeling rejected, ignored, discriminated against, marginalized, or isolated is all in the mind of the person who has the problem. If he/she accepts who he or she is and tries to improve himself or herself, he or she will be successful. If he/she feels sorry for himself/herself and feels that he/she is failing because he/she is discriminated against, he/she will certainly fail. The mind is like a fertile soil. If one sows rose seeds in it, roses will grow, and the person will enjoy the smell and the beauty of the roses; but if one sows the seeds of poison ivy, one will be harmed by that ivy's poison. In my case, I went on to become the top achiever in the training class and eventually became a trainer in the Financial Advisory School at Shearson (a predecessor investment bank to Smith Barney/Citigroup), where I specialized in training people on how to make a cold call!

Another experience I had was with a customer at the bank. A prominent lady who belongs to a prominent family in the city had an account with the bank. I knew that the bulk of her money was at another bank. Our private bankers at the bank and I personally tried very hard to encourage her to transfer her banking service to us because she appeared on the NSF (nonsufficient funds) list every morning. I finally had a private meeting with her. I asked her to tell me frankly why she was not expanding her relationship with us. She said the first thing she thought I needed to do was to hire employees who speak English without an accent. I thanked her for her feedback. She continued to be on the NSF list. At a meeting of the operations department, they all complained about the disrespectful way she treated them when they called her respectfully to tell her that she had written a check without sufficient funds to cover it. We all were surprised because she never apologized but was always rude. We decided to ask her to close the account. During my account closing exit interview, I told her that I was sorry about the "accent" problem, but asked her to remember that the United States was founded and built and still is being built and refreshed by hardworking, sincere, and wonderful people who speak English with different accents, and I wished her the best.

We also decided to home-grow our own RF bankers using two approaches. The first was to advertise for banking entry-level positions in the business schools in the universities located in the cities surrounding Whittier. We looked for fresh graduates with excellent scholastic achievements, with a grade point average (GPA) of at least 3.5 (out of 4) and preferably 3.75. We asked not only for a resume/CV, but we also asked for the transcripts in order to carefully review the course work covered and the grades achieved. Experience has shown that this reveals a lot about the character of the applicant. We also advertised for part-time tellers in the same business schools. The idea was to train these tellers at a young age (sometimes as young as 18) and watch their progress closely in order to recruit from among them our future staff. We knew that this strategy and approach would need time, but it was reasoned that this would be the best investment for the future.

To train all of these new and fresh bankers, we pioneered the "Bank of Whittier Open University." The classes are held at least once a year for 45 days from 8:00 A.M. to 9:30 A.M. and all staff members, including senior management and those with prior banking experience, are required to attend. The training program will be discussed in detail in Chapter 14. In addition, the bank started an intensive training program for the board of directors where we covered one topic of training on regulations and policies in each board meeting.

The decision to groom our own RF bankers fresh from universities proved to be the most important decision we ever made to change the fortunes of the bank. These smart fresh graduates were like sponges, hungry to absorb information and apply that information to their practice, to learn new banking regulations and techniques and strictly following them, and to create new solutions to the problems we faced. They brought with them vibrancy, fresh ideas, loyalty, challenges that made me feel younger, and most importantly the ability to be molded to believe in, operate, and serve people in our new brand of banking—the RF banking way.

THE AUDIT POLICY

At the Bank of Whittier, NA, we pioneered the use of a risk-based audit program that helped management establish which areas of bank operations needed to be audited in light of the risks associated and the extent of those risks as well as the frequency of conducting that audit (monthly, annually, or biannually). Management innovated and developed a computer-based program that helped institutionalize this risk-based audit function and determine the frequency of each audit area.

All board members, management, and staff of the bank sincerely believe that the various internal and external audits and the on-site government (OCC) examination are processes of discovery, cleansing, training, and coaching of bank management and staff that will help to improve the quality and effectiveness of bank operations and that will result protecting its safety and soundness as a first-rate banking operation. As to dealing with outside or inside auditors and examiners, bank management trains bank staff to listen carefully, to not argue, to not act defensively, and to learn. They are also trained to take prompt and immediate action to correct any oversight or error pointed out by the auditors, preferably before they leave the bank premises. Bank management asks bank auditors to point out specifically what needs to be fixed so that we can attain the highest level of compliance.

The board of directors' *audit committee* is responsible for establishing and maintaining an effective audit function that satisfies statutory, regulatory, and supervisory requirements and professional credibility.

As stipulated by the standards of government regulators, directors cannot delegate these responsibilities. However, they may delegate the design, implementation, and monitoring of specific internal controls to management and the testing and assessment of internal controls to auditors and other outside vendors. The board of directors' meeting minutes should reflect decisions regarding audits, such as external audit engagement terms (including any decision to forgo an external audit), the scope of audits to be performed, or why an audit of a particular area is not necessary.

Members of the bank's board of directors are specifically responsible for:

- Reviewing and approving audit strategies, policies, programs, and organizational structure.
- Monitoring the effectiveness of the audit function.

Following are the audit functions to be executed by the board's *audit committee:*

- Facilitation of the appointment and work of the internal and outside auditors.
- Analysis and evaluation of their findings.
- Recommendation of corrective actions with a specific timeline.
- Reporting of all findings and recommendations in the board's meeting minutes.
- Review of financial content of the bank's financial reports to be submitted to stockholders, the public, and/or regulatory agencies.
- Recommendation and/or initiation of an investigation of adverse operation results or trends, where applicable.

The formality and extent of a bank's internal and external audit programs depend on the bank's size, complexity, scope of activities, and risk profile. The board of directors must carefully consider how extensive the audit program must be to effectively test and monitor internal controls and ensure the reliability of the bank's financial statements and reporting.

The board of directors must strive to ensure that the bank's audit system is efficiently capable to test internal controls in order to be able to identify:

- Inaccurate, incomplete, or unauthorized transactions.
- Deficiencies in the safeguarding of bank assets.
- Unreliable financial and/or regulatory reporting.
- Violations of laws and/or regulations.
- Deviations from the bank's policies and procedures.

The board of directors is expected to do its best to be aware of all risks and control issues for the bank's operations, including risks in new products, emerging technologies, information systems, and Internet banking. Control issues and risks associated with increasing reliance on technology include:

- Increased user access to information systems.
- Reduced segregation of duties.
- Potential unidentifiable errors resulting from the shift of operations from paper to electronic audit trails.
- Lack of standards and controls for end-user systems.
- Increased complexity of contingency plans and information system recovery plans.

Engagement Letter for External Auditors

In its efforts to prudently identify the most capable auditing entities for its various audits, the bank's board of directors must invite and request external auditors to submit engagement letters before commencing audit work. Such a letter is expected to reflect preliminary discussions between the bank's board and/or senior management and the external auditor(s).

The engagement letter(s) will stipulate, among other things, the audit's purpose, its scope, the period to be covered, and the reports the auditor will develop. Schedules or appendixes may accompany the letter to provide the board with more details of the proposed audit. The letter may briefly describe procedures to be used in specific areas. If the scope of the audit is limited in any way, the letter may specify procedures that the auditor will omit. Additionally, the letter would specify if the auditor were expected to render an opinion on the bank's financial statements and/or other bank functions, depending on the type of audit being conducted.

Types and Scope of Various Audits

1. *Risk assessments and risk-based auditing.* Risk assessment is defined as the means by which the board of directors identifies and evaluates the quantity of the bank's risks and the quality of its controls. An effective risk-based auditing program will cover all of the bank's activities. The frequency and depth of each area's audit will vary according to the area's risk assessment and how serious the impact of that risk is on the bank. All areas of bank activities are included in order to establish the frequency of the audit necessary to mitigate any risk in bank safety and soundness and its reputation.
2. *External audit function.* The primary role of the external auditor is to independently and objectively review, evaluate, and document its findings about bank activities in order to help the board of directors of the bank and its management maintain and/or improve the efficiency and effectiveness of the bank's risk management, internal controls, and corporate governance.

   External auditors must understand the bank's strategic direction, objectives, products, services, operating philosophy, strategy, and processes. The auditors will communicate their findings to the board of directors and to senior management.
3. *Objectives.* The objectives of external audits are:
   a. To provide reasonable testing, review, and analysis of the bank's operations to ensure the effectiveness of internal controls over financial reporting, the accuracy and timeliness in recording transactions, and the accuracy and completeness of financial and regulatory reports.
   b. To perform an independent and objective view of the bank's activities, including processes relative to financial reporting and bank operations.
   c. To determine whether the bank complies with laws and regulations and adheres to established bank policies and whether management is taking appropriate steps to address control deficiencies.
4. *Types of audits.* The type of audit commonly referred to as a directors' examination entails specified and/or agreed-upon procedural reviews of the adequacy of internal controls and accuracy of financial information. The independent audit parties can be public accountants, certified internal auditors, certified information systems auditors, bank management firms, bank consulting firms, and/or other parties knowledgeable in banking.

   Please note that the frequency of the audits is determined in light of the risk-based audit discussed earlier.
   - *Financial statement audit by a certified public accounting firm, CPA.* An independent audit of financial statements should be designed to

ensure that the bank's financial reports are prepared in accordance with generally accepted accounting principles (GAAP) and that the independent financial statements are performed in accordance with generally accepted audit standards (GAAS). The scope of the audit will be sufficient to enable the CPA to express an opinion on the bank's financial statements.

The following list represents areas for which the board of directors requires an annual audit.

a. Cash and due from banks
b. Credits (Loans)
c. Allowance for loan and lease losses (ALLL)
d. Premises and equipment
e. Other assets and liabilities
f. Deposits
g. Notes payable
h. Non–interest income
i. Expenses
j. Equity (holding company, if applicable)
k. Tax return

- *Operational, USA PATRIOT Act, Bank Secrecy Act (BSA), and Office of Foreign Assets Control (OFAC) audits.* These types of audits include a review of policies, procedures, and operational controls to determine whether risk management, internal controls, and internal processes are adequate and efficient. Operational audits generally include procedures to test the integrity of accounts, regulatory reports, and other aspects of operations. These audits may also include a review of management and employee compliance with bank policies and procedures. The operational, BSA, and OFAC audits should be scheduled annually at specific times.
- *Compliance audit.* This type of audit determines whether the bank is complying with bank procedures and internal and external regulatory regulations. This audit should be scheduled at least annually—or as frequently as the risk analysis may call for—preferably in the first quarter of the year but no later than the second quarter of the year. It focuses on the bank's adherence to consumers' compliance regulations to ensure that the bank has adequate systems and control procedures to avoid any violations.
- *Credit (loan) review audit.* This type of audit is conducted to assess the quality of the bank's loan portfolio and provide an early alert of problem loans or negative portfolio patterns or trends, as well as the adequacy of and procedure used to calculate allowance for loan and lease losses (ALLL). The ALLL estimation process at the Bank

of Whittier is conducted, as discussed earlier, by following a unique risk-based method and a proprietary computer program pioneered by the bank to include in the calculation all risk factors that may have an impact on the various credit facilities. The process will be detailed in Chapter 14.

- *Information systems, technology, and security audits.* These types of audits assess the controls over the bank's electronic data processing and computer-related areas. These audits focus on management, development, support and delivery, data security, and physical security. Information system and technology audits also include a review of computer and client services systems, end-user reports, electronic funds transfers, and service provider activities. This type of audit should test the architecture of the system and should be completed annually in the first quarter of the year. It also helps review and critique security systems used by the bank.

5. *Treasury, financial, operations, and loans management monthly certifications.* The responsibilities of the operations and loans departments are to certify all general ledger accounts as provided by management to the application—DDAs (demand deposit checking accounts), savings, time deposits, and loans. For example, operations staff will be responsible for certifying all loan systems to the general ledger, and the loans department staff will certify all operations applications to the general ledger. The certifications will be completed according to the certification listing and provided to the CFO monthly before the tenth day of every month.

Audit Response by Management

Management will prepare a written response to the board of directors within 21 days from the date of the submission of the particular audit report and its findings. The management response will outline any deficiencies or concerns outlined by the audit, list the corrective actions already taken, and identify specific recommendations, plans, and the expected time of completion for responding to such recommendations to fix the problems discovered by the audits.

The management response will be sent to the firm that completed the audit. In addition, the OCC (usually during the exam time) and other related regulatory bodies, if needed, will be notified by the bank's chairman of the board of directors as to the different audit findings, the corrective actions already taken, and the actions that will be taken, including expected time of completion.

REVIEW QUESTIONS

1. What does the term *change of control* mean when it applies to a bank?
2. What are the advantages of structuring and offering RF banking in America compared to other parts of the world? Please state at least three advantages.
3. How is an RF banker trained to think and operate compared to a riba-based trained banker?
4. When one attempts to purchase a national bank, which entities take care of reviewing and executing the application?
5. Please list at least five of the goals set by the RF bankers who purchased Bank of Whittier in order to turn it around.

NOTES

1. The founder of the Findley Company was Gerald Lee Elmer Findley who, from 1952 to his retirement in the late 1980s, was responsible for chartering more than 120 banks in California. Gerald and his son Gary have organized almost 200 banks in their 50 years of business.
2. The Central Bank of Malaysia (Bank Negara Malaysia) sought the views of three jurists on the permissibility of establishing an RF banking window as an additional but unique service offered by a conventional riba bank. The Shari'aa scholars involved were the late (Almarhoum) Tan Sri Professor Ahmad Ibrahim and Professor Dr. Mahmoud Saedon Awang Uthman from the International Islamic University, Malaysia, and Tuan Haji Mohammad Shahir Ahmad from the Department of Islamic Affairs in the Malaysian Prime Minister's Office. These scholars' view was that "a conventional riba-based bank, whose operations are conducted on the basis of interest, *is not prohibited* from operating an RF banking window." The conclusion was based on foundation of Shari'aa. Many jurists and scholars around the world have concluded that owning and operating a conventional riba-based bank that offers RF banking products and services, such as lease-to-purchase financing, is not only acceptable but is encouraged (Dr. Saleh Malaikah, in a private communication dated May 17, 1999; the opinion is based on research conducted by Dr. Malaikah). Scholars like Dr. Al-Qari, and Dr. Abdul-Rahman Serri have concurred with this opinion. This, however, does not make riba-based finance activities permissible according to Shari'aa. The ownership and operation of a conventional bank by Muslims is desirable and encouraged if the intention is to offer riba-free products as a unique service

that can compete with the conventional banking products. The gradual approach with a clear plan will allow riba-free banking products and services to be tested by the consumers who will ultimately make the final decision about which products and services they like to use.

3. Yahia Abdul-Rahman, Mike Abdelaaty, and Gary S. Findley, Esq., "The Challenges of Offering a LARIBA Products and Services Window in an American Bank," presented at the Harvard University Seminar on Islamic Banking, 1999.
4. CDARS stands for "Certificate of Deposit Account Registry Service," which offers CD investments insured up to $50 million by capitalizing on the network of member banks accepting tranches of the deposit and swapping it with a deposit from that bank in the originating bank. This allows the originating bank to access the FDIC coverage of the corresponding bank.

CHAPTER 14

RF Capital Markets

Developing the RF Capital Market Investment Products

The sophisticated and highly diversified capital markets that have been developed and systemized over the past century are riba-based. This chapter is not intended to be a comprehensive study of the global capital markets, the way they operate, their regulations and their systems. It is hoped that this chapter will create an interest in some of the readers to study these markets by researching the vast body of literature available in specialized books and by reviewing the vast information available in many books and research papers available in abundance on the Web.

THE CHALLENGE OF FINANCING NEW BUSINESSES AND GROWING EXISTING BUSINESS

One of the important challenges faced by entrepreneurs and businesspeople is how to raise capital in order to finance their new business start-up and/or to attract new capital investments to help in the growth of existing successful businesses. As explained earlier in the book, the real revolution that was brought to the commercial and business world by Islam and systemized by the Prophet Muhammad (s) was to develop riba-free (RF) disciplines and solutions to the problem of: how to finance a business in an RF way.

Businesspeople and corporations continually need fresh capital not because they are needy and poor but because they want to finance the growth of their existing business or the financing of a new business venture. When the Prophet (s) was commissioned, as it still is today, the challenge was to develop RF regulations, business structures, disciplines, markets, and systems to supply capital to those businesses that need it in a fair and equitable fashion, using the RF disciplines, to both the financier and the business owner.

A number of basic business rules were developed based on prior human experience that resulted in the development of world capital markets. These rules require that the businesspeople or corporations who are soliciting capital investments disclose to the prospective investors, in a clear and transparent way, the details of that business, the reason for the addition and solicitation of new capital, how this capital will be utilized, the projected and expected future of the investment and the risks involved with the investment. In this regard, investors can be classified in two categories:

- *Accredited investors.* This is a sophisticated and well-informed class of investors with high income and high net worth. The investors in this group have accumulated prudent business acumen over the years through practice in the local marketplace. They can be financially independent individuals and families as well as large investment companies and investment funds. These entities are considered by capital markets' regulators to be knowledgeable in the intricacies and risks of investing. That is why the investment disclosures required to be made by the solicitors of capital investments must be reported but various detailed information are not required to be scrutinized by the regulators. Remember that the word used here is not that these investments are not regulated but they are less stringently regulated compared with those disclosures required by regulators when raising capital from the next category.
- *The public.* This group includes small investors from the public who are not financially sophisticated. Any public investment solicitation of capital of any type from this group of investors must be detailed and fully disclosed. Capital market regulators require those who solicit capital investments from the public at large to prepare a detailed document called a prospectus. The prospectus must include detailed disclosures about the risks involved with that proposed investment as well as full disclosures about the business, its major investors, its existing and/or proposed management, its proposed management prior experiences, its proposed management potential areas of conflict of interest, its prior audited operating and financial results and its market potential. An important sentence used in the prospectus about prior results states clearly that *"prior investment results are not a guarantee for future investment performance and results."* The investment prospectus must be registered with a government regulatory body; in the United States this regulatory agency is the U.S. Securities and Exchange Commission (SEC). Please remember that the SEC attorneys' and capital market experts' responsibilities involve the close and prudent review and analysis of the accuracy and the adequacy of the information provided in the investment prospectus. Disclosures are tested by the SEC to ascertain

that the public is adequately informed and educated about the investment and is fully warned about the risks that may lead to losing that investment in order to comply fully with the applicable laws and capital markets' regulations. After the offering prospectus is registered with SEC, the SEC makes sure to disclose that its registration does not mean that the SEC approves the investment. The SEC discloses very clearly in writing that its role was to only make sure that the prospectus is in compliance with the capital market regulations and that registration is not an approval or an implicit guarantee of the business performance or future results. It should be noted that going public to solicit and raise capital is an expensive process not only during the registration stage due to legal and preparation expenses as well as registration fees but also for the continuing detailed disclosure and required annual reporting to the government and the public as required by capital market regulators.

Before discussing the RF capital markets, it is important to briefly and generally familiarize the reader with the basic conventional instruments used to raise capital currently in the riba-based capital markets. Readers who are interested in the details and specifics about capital markets in general should refer to the wide body of literature available in many books and research papers available on the Web.

Private Direct Investment

An important aspect of this category of capital investments is that they are usually not liquid (there is no open market for trading these investments) and may result in a huge profit or a complete loss of the original investment.

These rivate direct capital investments are made in the form of:

- *Direct participation in new venture capital projects.* A venture capital (VC) project is classified as highly risky because it involves new businesses, products and conceptual new ideas, services, and products that did not come to market before or that have no prior operating experience and market penetration records like in the case when Microsoft and Apple Computers were just embryonic ideas. Based on the high risk involved, the venture capital investor would demand realizing his or her return on the capital invested into a big share, equity ownership of the venture or a big share of the profits generated from the venture because the probability of full loss of the investment is very high. The well-known rule applicable here is an investor who accepts a high-risk investment also expects a higher return than the return on an established ongoing business.

If the venture capital investment is in the form of shareholder ownership and that it would not involve lending (or renting) of money at a specific interest rate then it is considered RF provided that the venture deals into activities that are not prohibited by the Judeo-Christian-Islamic Shari'aa law like alcohol-related businesses, gambling, and prohibited foods.

- Lending (renting money) to projects with a certain interest rate, which is usually excessively high to compensate for the high risk involved. Hence, the offering of Venture Capital fixed income bonds is not considered RF and are not allowed by the RF law. It was demonstrated in RF bond offerings since the 1990s and is still happening today, albeit to a lesser extent (at the time of writing this book), that a clever structuring attorney can come up with a sophisticated business structure that can make such riba-based bonds look like and satisfy, at least on paper, the RF law (Judeo-Christian-Islamic Shari'aa law), disciplines, and guidelines. I respectfully disagree with such attempts. The real test here is to examine if the spirit of RF values and disciplines are met by such instruments.

Fixed-Income Debt Instruments in the Form of Riba-Based Bonds

Nowadays, fixed-income bonds represent an important source of funds to meet in a large way the capital needs of different entities. Bonds provide an investment vehicle for those investors who feel more comfortable and secured because they offer investors a predefined return in the form of riba-based interest rates.

Bonds are debt certificates—IOUs (which stands for *I Owe You*)—that represent a contract between the individual or investor and the company or the entity that needs the capital. The contract defined in the riba-based bond prospectus defines the nature of this capital contribution as being a debt that rents money in the form of capital that is to be paid back in full (called the face value of the bond) within a certain period of time (called the *term* of the bond, which can be paid back in full in a few months or in 1, 5, 10, or 30 years or more) at a specific date (called the *maturity date*), and while this debt is active the company that issued these bonds would pay the investor (the bondholders) a fixed rental rate called interest (defined as the interest rate of the bond). Riba bonds are classified as short-, medium-, or long-term bonds, depending on their maturity. Generally, short-term bonds mature in 1 year or less, medium-term bonds mature in 5 years or less, and long-term bonds mature in 10 or more years (can be as long as 30 or 40 years). The financial industry standardized the face value of a bond to be US$1,000 (or in general 1,000 units of the local currency) and the interest rate is expressed in percentage and is usually paid quarterly to the bondholder to coincide with the quarterly financial statement report of the bond-issuing entity. The issuing entity can be a government or a company.

There are three types of bonds, depending on the purpose of the intended use of the proceeds and on the issuing entity, which are discussed next.

Government or Sovereign Bonds These are issued by the government involved and are either collateralized by a certain income stream that may be generated from taxes for example or from a certain facility owned by the government like an airport facility, a highway, or a water supply project. These bonds can be designed for subscription by local citizens. These bonds are called domestic government bonds, which are mostly denominated in domestic currencies, but in some other cases can be issued in international currencies like the U.S. dollar or the euro. The prospective buyers are nationals of that country. Other government bonds can be designed to attract foreign investors and can be in domestic currency or in most cases in an international currency like the U.S. dollar or the euro. In such a case these bonds are made available to investors to buy in outside international capital markets. If the bonds are issued by a sovereign government they are called sovereign bonds. In the United States, these bonds are called Treasury bonds or "Treasuries" for short. There are 1-year, 10-year, 15-year, and 30-year bonds. In addition, the U.S. Treasury issues inflation-indexed Treasuries, which are indexed to inflation in the United States. The market value of these bonds is used by market analysts as a good indicator of the perception of the financial markets about the future of inflation in the United States. U.S. Treasuries are purchased by U.S. citizens and in a large way by other world governments that have foreign currency surplus with the issuing government as in the case of China and Saudi Arabia, which accumulate significant U.S. dollar trade surpluses. An interesting reflection on the politics of such bonds was offered by the famous capitalist Steven Forbes[1] regarding the vast Chinese government holdings of U.S. Treasuries. Forbes states that "China holdings in U.S. Treasuries, which reached record levels in 2013, are setting off alarm bells. They shouldn't. They underscore that Beijing is becoming more dependent on the United States and the rest of the world for its strength and prospects." The following are some points made by Forbes to keep in mind:

- If the United States and Beijing ever engaged in a mortal confrontation, how much would China's holdings in American government bonds be worth if we in the U.S. government said that the paper was no longer valid? Beijing is a hostage to our U.S. government's willingness to honor these obligations.

- China has not been a big buyer of U.S. government paper for several years because of its concern about the dollar's integrity.
- What would happen if China, to damage us in the United States, decided to dump its trove of Treasuries? Prices might wobble, but not for long. There are trillions of dollars' worth of investors who would hunt for a chance like this.
- If China sells U.S. Treasuries, it would be paid in dollars. So what? They would buy yens and euros. In this case, the Fed, in coordination with the Japanese and European central banks, will plan to keep the currency ratios in check.

Municipal Bonds In the United States and other nations with sophisticated capital markets, local governments in states, counties, and cities can issue bonds for the capitalization of municipal local authorities' needs such as the building of a certain number of schools in a city, county, or state; the building of an airport that will help enhance the local economy; and the building of a new sewage and water treatment system for a city. In America, these bonds are called municipal bonds. In order to encourage investors to buy these bonds, the U.S. federal government law has rendered the interest paid by these municipal bonds to bondholders exempt from federal and state taxes. That is why these bonds are called "double-tax-free bonds" meaning the interest paid is free from federal and state tax. Municipal bonds are usually floated in the market after their approval by a vote in a referendum by the people in the state or municipality involved. Capital investment comes from high-net-worth families, usually retired persons or families and entities that need to reduce their tax liabilities (i.e., reduce their income tax payments). Capital investment in municipal bonds can also come from mutual funds that are designed to invest in these municipal bonds (called municipal bonds' mutual funds) to help smaller investors invest in a diversified municipal bond portfolio to derive tax-free fixed income.

Municipal bonds can be structured as RF municipal bonds if the quarterly income generated is based on a market-based rental or lease rate of the facility financed by the bond proceeds and is conditional on the fact that these bond investments have been invested in specific assets and the investors have acquired a lien on these assets using the LARIBA RF finance model as described in this book. One of the pioneering RF municipal bonds was structured in Malaysia to build the Kuala Lumpur International Airport and some large highway projects.

Corporate Bonds These are debt certificates that are issued by the company involved to raise capital that would be used by the company to help finance its operations and growth. Most companies prefer direct equity investments, especially in times when the prevailing market interest rates are high. However, there are situations when company organizers prefer not to dilute direct ownership (equity ownership) by complimenting their capital needs by issuing fixed-income bonds. This is usually the case when interest rates in the market are attractively low. Interest payments on corporate bonds are senior to the payment of any dividend on equities (shares or company stocks). In addition, it is important to note that in case of the liquidation of the company bondholders' liabilities are junior only to federal and state tax liabilities of the company.

Corporate bonds can be structured as RF bonds if they are structured as asset based, where the acquisition of an asset using the RF (asset-based) bond proceeds is involved (as in the case of a power generation plant inside a factory, a group of drilling rigs that operate in a field by a drilling company, or a fleet of trucks that are part of a shipping company). The income stream used to pay the bond holders comes from the rental or lease rate income generated from the leasing of that particular asset. Structuring these RF bonds can be easily done using the LARIBA RF finance model described in this book.

Position of the Catholic Church on Usury (Interest) from Riba Bonds and the Church's Changing Position over Time At this juncture, it is thought that it would be useful to review the history of the Catholic Church position regarding interest-based riba bonds (usury-based bonds) during its strict prohibition of charging usury (the culture of renting money; *usury*, as defined by the Catholic Church then, is now called *interest*).

The charging of interest on borrowed money was clearly prohibited by the Catholic Church and was slowly relaxed and then was allowed in the sixteenth century.[2] This resulted in the development of debt securities (riba bonds) and the beginning of what is called today the financial capital markets. The following is a brief review of the history.[3]

The lending function by banks was suppressed by the Catholic Church ruling that prohibited lending money with interest (which means renting the use of money at a predefined rate called usury—now interest). This delayed the introduction of debt securities—now called bonds—into European commerce and also led those who adhered to the Jewish faith and some of the Protestants in Europe to specialize in the money-lending business and earn huge profits. The Church also permitted the development of what was called *bills of exchange*. These were negotiable contracts that allow the holder of these bills of exchange to exchange one currency for another at a future date.

The debate about interest (originally called usury by the Catholic Church) did not extend to equity investing, which means ownership of shares or part of a business since the Catholic Church prohibited only the charging of interest on money. The focus of the Church was on the usurious (interest-bearing) receipt of a certain profit as a part of a contractual agreement. The receipt of profit—and not interest (usury) from an uncertain venture—which might either turn out to be profitable or not was regarded acceptable by the Church because money was not rented and the shareholder was exposed to the risk of profit or loss as his co-shareholders. This is not much different from the basic premise of participation in profit and loss found in all RF (Islamic) banking literature. It is also interesting to note that promising a certain return (income) from the beginning may also be misused as a ruse to charge "hidden" usury.

By the seventeenth and eighteenth centuries, the Church's influence regarding usurious transactions in northern and western European commitment diminished.

The following is an overview of the stepwise growth of the interest-based riba debt securities issued[4]:

1. The first project finance using debt started to appear alongside share ownership in industries like mining and shipping. The historic Dutch East India Company was financed by share ownership and by riba debt securities.
2. The second type of need for debt financing was to finance governments using riba debt contracts (now called sovereign bonds). Countries ranging from major European states to smaller city-states could only be debt financed in order to often finance their military campaigns to expand the territories under their control by acquiring neighboring countries by force or to defend themselves against an upcoming war to confiscate that country's territories. Investors in such transactions were motivated by the high interest rates promised by the bonds. In addition, other investors (mainly foreign governments) were motivated by the strategic political influence that will be achieved after the success of these military acquisition campaigns. The two nations of Holland and England were the greatest beneficiaries of issuing riba debt contracts with interest to finance their shipping and acquisition and development of their new colonies around the world.

Lenders to governments would make a written contract—now called bonds—with either a king or a government. In the seventeenth century, loans were frequently secured by pledging specific assets of that country or king. These bonds are now called asset-backed sovereign bonds. By the eighteenth century, debt contracts started to rely on liens on streams of income or state revenue from customs, taxes, or service facilities. These bonds are now called revenue bonds.

An interesting view that should be always kept in mind about such on riba debt financing was the discussions that surrounded the riba debt financing of governments by the Meiji Emperor in Japan in 1881.[5] His remarks are worth quoting because it records the serious concerns of many wise governments of being forced into compromising their national goals and aspirations due to the accumulation of debt in the form of foreign governments buying sovereign bonds. It was that some of his government officials suggested the idea of issuing foreign loans to raise capital in order to help support the country's external currency reserves. The emperor decided against the recommendation. He quoted advice he has received from then–U.S. president Ulysses Grant. Grant told the emperor during a visit to Japan: "Look at Egypt,[6] Spain, and Turkey. . . . Some nations like to lend money to poor nations very much. By these means they flaunt their authority and cajole the poor nation. The purpose of lending money is to get political power for them." Along these lines of strategic lending by issuing sovereign bonds, Samuel Hayes and colleagues enumerate the following historic sovereign riba bond lending cases[7]:

- The Berlin to Baghdad railway during the reign of the Ottoman Empire (riba bond investment from Germany).
- The South African Cape of Good Hope to the north railway.
- The Canada Pacific railway.

In addition to public financing of these countries, the lending countries were often exporting capital equipment and construction services on a deferred-payment (another form of debt financing) basis. These techniques are still in use today in the twenty-first century.

The challenge faced by bond-issuing investment bankers was to create a regime and a market that can easily provide cash liquidity when needed by selling these bonds to other investors. That was the challenge that had to be solved in the twentieth century by the creation of liquid markets in London and in New York primarily. It is interesting to note here that these same challenges were faced by the RF bonds (*sukuk*) markets in Dubai, Bahrain, and Malaysia.

VALUATION OF BONDS: BOND RATING AND RATING AGENCIES

An important question by bond investors that need to be answered by the entities that solicit capital is the entity's financial and operating record and future projections and its future prospects. This is called the entity's *creditworthiness*. Some of the questions that need to be answered by the entity that offers a bond issue in the market are: How good is the quality of this bond-issuing entity? In case one invests, what is the possibility that the entity will default on payment of interest and the risk associated with the entity's ability to honor its contract to pay back the principal?

In order to enable investors to make that judgment, there was a need to establish a neutral and highly analytical body to facilitate and standardize the process of evaluating the creditworthiness of the bond-offering entity. To meet that challenge, *rating agencies* were created. Bonds (and their issuing entities) are rated by these specialized rating agencies at the time they are issued, and the evaluation of the quality of these bonds continues after the issuing. Both bonds and their issuers are periodically reevaluated to see if a rating change is warranted. These rating agencies are established to ascertain institutions to be neutral, independent, and highly qualified institutions. These rating agencies are required to not be influenced directly or indirectly by the issuing entity or the investment banking companies involved in the issuing and/or promoting these bonds and other capital investments in the market. Rating agencies' staff consists of highly qualified, sophisticated, and experienced professionals in financial business intelligence and analysis, accounting, business valuation, government regulatory laws and policies, and fiscal policies with a proven and demonstrated track record. The rating agency's objective is to issue a neutral and most accurate valuation of the entity that is measured and the financial instrument issued by this entity, like a bond, by designating it by an alphabetical letter–based rating. Bond ratings are important not only for their role in informing investors, but also because they affect the interest rate that companies and government agencies pay on their issued bonds. Ratings can range from the highest (AAA) or the lowest rating (D). Examples of globally respected and reputable rating agencies are Standard and Poor's (S&P), Moody's, and Fitch. For example, Standard and Poor's highest rating is AAA. Once a bond falls to BB+ status, it is no longer considered an investment-grade bond, and if the lowest rating (D) is assigned, that indicates that the bond is in default, meaning that the issuer is delinquent in making interest and principal payments to its bondholders.[8]

Since the 2008 financial and monetary crisis, rating agencies have been criticized for not identifying all of the risks that could impact a security's credit worthiness, particularly in regard to mortgage-backed securities (MBSs) that received high credit ratings but turned out to be high-risk investments. Since that time rating agencies tightened their standards and even lowered the U.S. Treasury's investment rating due to the high deficit in the U.S. budget. That is why it is advised that these ratings should be supplemented by a thorough analysis by the investors.

Investors are also concerned about a possible conflict of interest between the rating agencies and the bond issuers, since the issuers pay the agencies for the service of providing ratings.

Because of these and other shortcomings, ratings should not be the only factor serious investors rely on in assessing the risk of a particular bond investment. The investors should employ a trusted financial adviser to be consulted in order to sift through the rating agencies' reports and conclusions in light of the specific investment objectives of the investor and the investment temperament and risk appetite of that investor.

The rating of the company, the entity or the government will have a direct impact on its ability to access the capital bond market and to borrow money and the interest rate that it can pay to bond holders. If a company is rated AAA and can pay 4 percent to bondholders, then another company rated lower, with an A rating, has to pay a higher rate to bondholders to compensate for the inherent risk, say 6 percent, and another rated even lower at BBB can offer to pay, say 8 percent, in order to satisfy the higher risk associated with buying that entity's bonds. It is also interesting to note that if one invests in a AAA-rated company and its rating is lowered by one of the rating agencies the market value of that bond may decline to 90 percent or 80 percent of its face value ($1,000) or even lower to reflect the fact that the implied rate in the market should be higher.

Outside the United States and Europe, there are now a number of rating agencies in Asia and in particular in Malaysia. One of the oldest and most respected in Asia is a Malaysian company, RAM,[9] which also rates RF bonds (*sukuk,* which are asset-based bonds).

Bonds' Pricing in the Secondary Market

Impact of Variation in Market Interest Rate Environment on Bond Market Value If one holds a total of 1,000 bonds ($1 million capital investment value) issued by a company and the bond carries a coupon rate (interest rate) of 5 percent, this means that this investor would derive annually $1 million multiplied by 5 percent or $50,000. Suppose the market has changed and interest rates have, for one reason or another, increased to 10 percent. If the same company goes to the market to issue new bonds it will have to mark the coupon interest rate higher to 10 percent. That is if one invests $1 million in the new bonds then the investor would expect to derive an interest income of $100,000. This amount of interest income is double the amount received from the first bond issue with a 5 percent coupon. If one goes with the 5 percent coupon bonds to the secondary market to sell them and create cash, then the buyer will reason that if he invests in any of the new bonds in this 10 percent environment his income will be 10 percent or for a $1 million annual income should be at least $100,000. That is, in order for the holder to sell the 5 percent bonds and for the buyer to produce an income of $100,000, it must sell for a value of $500,000. This new value is derived simply and in general by dividing the perceived interest income of $50,000 obtained from the 5 percent bonds by the $100,000 that can be received from the new 10 percent bonds. If one multiplies the result or 0.5 by $1 million, this produces the new value of the 5 percent bond on the market and the resulting fair calculated value would be $500,000. That is, due to the increase of interest rates in the market from 5 to 10 percent, the value of the 5 percent bond declines by 50 percent. Such a decline has an effect on the value of the bond in the market in case its holder wants to sell these bonds for cash. Of course, there are other factors in the market that may change that price to an even lower value or a higher value. However, if the company, the government or the entity that issued these bonds is still in a good operating and financial condition and can pay back the bondholders at maturity, they will be paid the face value or $1,000 a bond at maturity date. That is why market players try to buy bonds at a discount in order to earn a handsome capital gain at maturity. This occurs especially in the case of sovereign government bonds when some of these bonds sell at deep discount at 10 percent of face value or even at a much deeper discount due to political, economic, social, or environmental instability. High-risk investors gamble by assuming and projecting that these particular governments will not risk their market creditworthiness at maturity and will pay the full face value, resulting in a huge profit windfall for the investor.

Liquidity of Bonds

As discussed earlier, investors are most concerned about the creditworthiness of the entity that they will invest in either in the form of equity or in the form of fixed-income securities (bonds in general). The question is: if we own shares or bonds in this entity can we readily go to the market, sell them, and receive cash? This is called *market liquidity*. This market liquidity is defined by the size and liquid capacity of the secondary markets. Such liquidity is enhanced by having market makers who facilitate the functioning of the market and act as a catalyst to encourage buyers and sellers to participate in the market.

It is worth noting that the RF bond (sukuk) markets are still thin and are not readily liquid. The Malaysian capital market officials are doing their best to enhance the liquidity of the sukuk in the Malaysian market, which is the largest sukuk market in the world.

THE RF CAPITAL MARKET AND ITS RF INSTRUMENTS

One of the important challenges that faced and is still facing the RF Movement was how to develop and "manufacture" RF products and services that will become RF alternatives to the conventional riba-based instruments, as well as creating liquid secondary markets to handle the liquidation of these products when necessary. These RF instruments and products, if developed correctly, would enhance and facilitate the development of a complete and integrated RF capital market. This RF capital market would offer a total alternative to the well-established and sophisticated riba-based capital markets. Malaysia, through its national bank (Bank Negara Malaysia) and the Malaysian Securities and Exchange Commission (Malaysia SEC) has achieved great strides to achieve that goal.

In the mid-1980s, a group of RF finance pioneers started thinking of developing rules and guidelines about investing in the stock market and develop an RF stock investment portfolio and the associated RF guidelines that are derived from and are based on the Judeo-Christian-Islamic Shari'aa law. In addition, other pioneering groups, mainly in Malaysia and to a lesser extent in Bahrain, started developing guidelines to issue an RF bond alternative to the interest-based bonds, that is, sukuk. The original few sukuk issues produced in Malaysia were severely criticized by the Arabic-speaking Gulf scholars, but Malaysia and its RF scholars took the strategic and political decision to forge ahead with the development of the fundamental blocks of the RF capital market. The strategy was based on gradualism in building the RF capital market structure and show that it works. Malaysian central bank (Bank Negara Malaysia) enhanced the process further by developing the building blocks that included rating agencies, a securities commission, a Central Shari'aa Scholars' Board at the central bank and the Malaysian SEC. The Central Shari'aa Board would issue unified rulings and edicts (fatwas) that would be universally applicable throughout Malaysia. In an effort to popularize RF banking, Malaysia's central bank allowed riba-based investment and commercial banks to open up RF (Islamic) banking windows. One can say that with the stroke of the pen that allowed these RF windows to open, hundreds of RF bank facilities were initiated with the least capital commitment. The judiciary in Malaysia started developing laws and regulations that would solidify many of the financial regulatory institution into becoming credible and respectable institution that have the same credibility and of the same caliber as those in the United States, the United Kingdom, and Australia.

In the 1990s, Malaysia started reaching out to London to popularize its RF services and RF legal structures and to the oil-rich Gulf countries to familiarize its financial practitioners and RF scholars and leaders with the Shari'aa foundations, strategies, and methodology used in its RF activities. In London, many capital market leaders have taken a note that there is a serious competitor now to the London "Islamic" banking market. In the oil-rich Gulf countries, a newer generation of RF scholars were willing to study and evaluate the quantum progress and solid achievements made by the Malaysians in RF capital markets. These scholars, with the support of Malaysia scholars and specialized institutions, bridged the gaps that existed.

The result was a wider and universal acceptance of many of the achievements made in Malaysia. Today, Malaysia represents the prime RF capital market destination, followed by London, Bahrain, and Dubai.

The following is a brief overview of the main ingredients of the RF capital market instruments: RF bonds (globally known as sukuk) and RF stocks.

RF (Asset-Based) Bonds—Sukuk

The following is a brief and conceptual description of sukuk, which will not go in the details and specifics of structuring a sukuk financing deal. The intention here is to give the reader the fundamentals of RF bonds (sukuk) in order to equip those who are interested with the fundamentals of the Judeo-Christian-Islamic Shari'aa law and guidelines. This way, the interested reader can let his or her creative imagination go in order to devise the model and structure in the design of the sukuk issue while upholding both the RF laws while adhering to the laws of the land. It is important to remind the reader that the market has seen the issuance of many sukuks, especially in the beginning during the early 1980s, which are structured by smart, able, and experienced financial engineering and financial structuring attorneys and investment bankers. At that time, the extent of Shari'aa research and Shari'aa scholars' knowledge of the various riba-based financial instruments were not adequate enough. The result was the issuance of many sukuk deals that were designed to be RF on paper but when checked for their adequacy to fulfill the real spirit of RF discipline and the RF law, they failed. It is recommended that those who want to live riba free by applying the RF disciplines to their lifestyle consult their heart and conscience as well as to conduct a thorough review of the particular sukuk or RF investment in order to conclude for certain that it is indeed RF disciplined—in other words, if the financial instrument or investment is called Islamic, riba-free, or RF, but it in fact looks like riba-based, feels like it actually uses ruses, and is a structured deal that involves the renting of money at a price called interest. Some of these RF products use words like *rent, profit,* or *service charge* in order to make it look riba free when it is in fact riba-based. Since its inception in the early 1980s, the RF Shari'aa discipline in general and sukuk research and development in the area of RF law (Judeo-Christian-Islamic Shari'aa law) has intensified, and various laws and regulations have been issued and are now recognized mainly in Malaysia and to a lesser extent in the oil-rich Gulf countries and Pakistan.

In the next chapter, you will be exposed to an example of a sukuk structure that was designed to meet the demand of the moment using the LARIBA RF finance model. The Shari'aa advice was rendered by the author and a Malaysian RF scholar when the authorities of Singapore required the development of a number of Islamic trust (*waqf*) properties owned by MUIS, the government-sponsored organization in charge of the Singapore Muslims' affairs. Two sukuks were issued, the first valued at S$25 miliion and the second at S$35 million.

Riba-based bonds have been the motor of raising large amounts of capital to finance industrial growth, industrialization, and modernization of society and military expeditions that help in the geographical and political influence expansion of rich nations. In an RF environment, the manufacturing of these bonds must be done carefully in order to make sure that money is not rented at a rate called interest rate and that the purpose of raising the money is abiding by the law (Judeo-Christian-Islamic Shari'aa law). Riba-based bonds are looked at as an IOU contract that promises the rental of the principal capital at a price called interest, and the owner of the capital is looked upon as a lender and is entitled to an interest income on a quarterly basis. In contrast, RF bonds are in fact asset based, and they are looked upon as a real investment to help in the purchase of leasable assets and/or productive assets and services. The income distributed to the RF bond (sukuk) holders is not based on the rent of money at an interest rate, but rather on the cash flow generated from the rent of an asset, the cash flow from production of a product or the cash flow of the sovereign entity from taxes.

The origin of the word *sukuk* is "sak" (sukuk is the plural of the word *sak*) as defined by the Arabic dictionaries as "to strike or officiate using an official seal," implying that a sukuk is an official and authentic contract. The word *check,* used globally in banking (as in checking accounts) is derived from the Arabic word *sak.* A sukuk can be called an RF debenture or Islamic income security. These RF debentures or bonds are issued by those who need the capital, called *borrowers* in a riba-based discipline. The relationship between the issuer of the RF bond (sukuk) and the capital investor is defined by the RF investment model used. For example, if it is a joint venture RF model, then those who issue the RF bond are looked upon as a joint venture participant and co-owners of the financed facilities. If the capital raised by the RF bond is used to buy a piece of equipment like a compressor or a production unit to lease to those who needed it and issued the RF bonds, then the relationship is that of a lessee (the issuer of sukuk) and a lessor (the holder of sukuk).

RF bonds or sukuk are defined as certificates of equal value that evidence undivided ownership or investment in the assets using the RF law (Judeo-Christian-Islamic Shari'aa law). RF finance principles and concepts must ideally be approved by a recognized government entity for fulfillment of the Judeo-Christian-Islamic Shari'aa law as defined by the recognized government Shari'aa Boards, as well as the requirement that they must comply with the laws of the land regarding full disclosure, transparency, and wholeness. Malaysia has been active in developing such RF institutions and frameworks. In Malaysia, the securities issued must first be approved by the Malaysian Securities Commission, its own Shari'aa Board and the Shari'aa Board of the national (central) bank of Malaysia—Bank Negara Malaysia.

In the same way riba-based bonds were classified earlier, sukuk can be classified in two ways. The first is based on the issuer's status if it is a government agency (or one of its agencies), or a commercial company as follows:

- Sovereign sukuk, which are issued by sovereign governments to finance airports, freeways, municipal projects, and government buildings.
- Commercial sukuk are issued to finance the capital needs of commercial projects.

Sukuk can also be classified by the RF finance model used to finance the company facility using RF discipline. The following is a comprehensive and useful inventory of the different types of sukuk. The detailed classification was published by the Malaysian Securities Commission[10] and is expanded on to explain the meaning of the name given to each sukuk model and to elaborate on its features and particular circumstances:

- *Sukuk BBA or sukuk al-murabaha.* These are sukuk that are based on the pricing of the item financed at a revealed acquisition cost by the RF finance entity and selling it back at that cost plus an agreed-upon profit. The payback is to be over an agreed-upon period of time. The following are the varieties of such sukuk, which are available in the market:
  - *Sukuk BBA.* These are known in Malaysia. The letters or acronym "BBA" stands for Bai [sale] Bi (with) Thaman [a price] Aajil [in the future.]
  - *Sukuk al-murabaha.* The word *murabaha* (cost-plus) means that the RF finance entity or the financier would purchase the item (title for that item will transfer from the seller to the RF financier). Then the RF financier, now the owner of title, would proceed to sell the item to the ultimate buyer at the original and fully disclosed purchase cost plus an agreed upon profit element. That is where the name of this model, cost-plus, came from. As explained earlier in the book, if for any reason the buyer cannot make the payment due to a legitimate reason the "plus" in the "cost-plus" stays the same; otherwise, it would be considered time dependent and becomes classified as a riba-based bond.
  - *Sukuk istisnaa.* In the area of financing manufacturing activities, the sukuk issued are conceptually called sukuk istisnaa. The word *istisnaa* means financing an order to manufacture. The word *istisnaa* is derived from the word *yasnaa* (meaning "to manufacture" in Arabic), and it means that the manufacturer would accept an investment from

the RF financier or finance entity to manufacture and make available in the future a certain supply of a specific product at a certain agreed-upon price. This is closely similar but not exactly the same as working capital or raw materials finance or what is called factoring, which are all riba-based financing techniques (some, if not most, of these riba-based techniques can be classified as loan sharking). However, the RF istisnaa sukuk represents an actual investment in the production of a certain product that meets agreed-upon and well-defined specifications. Istisnaa sukuk are certificates of equal value, which evidence an undivided ownership of the certificate holders to the asset including the rights to the receivables arising from the underlying contracts of exchange.

- *Requirement of an underlying specific asset.* Under contracts of exchange (such as BBA, al-murabaha and al-istisnaa) an asset, whether tangible or intangible, must be made available for sukuk to be issued subject to the following as defined by the Malaysian RF Shari'aa bodies:
  - The underlying asset and its use must comply with the Judeo-Christian Islamic Shari'aa law. That is, such RF bonds' proceeds cannot be used in any forbidden activities as defined by the law (Shari'aa).
  - An encumbered asset, such as an asset charged to a financial institution, or an asset that is jointly owned with another party, can be used only as an underlying asset provided that the issuer has obtained consent from the owner.
  - In case of expected future receivables for goods and services, that is where receivables are used as the underlying asset, they must be established and certain and transacted on a cash basis on the spot.
  - *Asset pricing*:
    - The purchase price should not exceed 1.51 times the market value of the asset. This multiplier figure (1.51X) is an arbitrary number that most likely was based by the Malaysian authorities on considerations that have to do with overcharging the consumers in light of the prevailing economic conditions when the ruling was issued.
    - In cases where the market value of a particular asset could not be ascertained, a fair appraised value by a professional and licensed appraiser must be applied.
- *Sukuk al-ijarah.* This means those RF bonds that are based on leasing. These are certificates of equal value that evidence undivided ownership of the certificate holders to the leased asset and/or usufruct and/or services and rights to the rental receivables from the said leased asset and/or usufruct and/or services. In this case, the application of the LARIBA RF finance model is most appropriate.

- *Sukuk al-mudarabah.* Meaning those sukuk that are based on an investment that is managed by an investment manager called the mudarib. These are certificates of equal value which evidence undivided ownership of the certificate holders in the mudarabah venture. Proceeds from mudarabah bonds are conceptuality used to finance RF investment companies or RF investment funds that are managed and operated conceptually in the same way as those known as hedge fund investments in the riba-based investment banking domain.
- *Sukuk al-musharakah.* Meaning those RF bonds or sukuk that are based on the RF joint venture model (musharakah meaning "joint venture participation"), which are certificates of equal value that evidence undivided ownership of the certificate holders in the musharakah venture (joint venture).

Requirements of the Judeo-Christian-Islamic Shari'aa Law in the Issuance of Sukuk

The following is a summary of the principles and requirements published by the Malaysian Securities Commission, which are applicable to the RF discipline of developing, manufacturing, and production of all types of RF sukuk. As will be seen, the type of sukuk and the name given correspond to the RF finance model used in the financing.

Shari'aa rulings applicable to specific types of sukuk include:

IJARA (Leasing) Sukuk

- *Rate of lease rental and lease period.* These should be determined upon the contract called in Arabic *aqd.*
- *Usage of leased assets.* These assets should be used for Shari'aa-compliant activities only.
- *Sublease of leased assets to a third party by the lessee.* It may be allowed provided that the sublease period should not be longer than that of the initial lease.
- *Sublease of leased assets to a third party by the owner of assets.* The owner cannot and is not allowed to lease the assets to a third party while the same assets are being leased to another party during the lease period.
- *Maintenance of the leased asset.* The lessor is responsible for maintaining the leased assets. However, the maintenance of the asset may also be determined as agreed by both parties as stated in the terms and conditions of the lease (ijarah) agreement. The lessor can also assign the responsibility to the lessee as service agent at the lessor's cost.

- *Forward lease* (called in Arabic ijara mawsufah fi zimmah):
  - A forward lease is a permissible contract for the issuance of sukuk.
  - A forward contract is an ijarah contract for an asset that will exist in the future like in the case of constructing a plant and then leasing one of its components. The lease rate, the nature of the leased asset, the lease period, and the method of the lease payment are to be clearly stated in the contract as agreed between the contracting parties.
  - If upon delivery the lessor fails to deliver the asset based on the specifications detailed in the agreement, the lessee is entitled to reject the asset and has one of two of the following choices:
    - Demand replacement of the asset that conforms to the agreed specifications; or
    - Terminate the lease (ijarah) contract, and if the lessee has paid advance rental, the lessor should refund the amount paid and in some cases legitimate costs incurred by the financier.
- *Variable rate mechanism.* The lease rate may be based on fixed or variable rates. In case variable rates are used, the effective lease period and the lease rental compensation must be agreed upon in the contract and the index used to define the variation in the lease rate.
- *Transfer of ownership of the leased asset.* At the end of the lease period, the ownership of the leased asset may be transferred from the lessor to the lessee or to any third party through one of the following methods:
  - By way of selling the leased asset at an agreed price, or
  - By way of giving it as a gift (called hibah in Arabic).

Sukuk Al-Musharakah (Joint Venture)

- *Musharaka (joint venture) capital.* Capital contributed by each of the partners should be in the form of cash, in kind or a combination thereof.
- *Guarantee (kafalah in Arabic) on musharaka capital.* Guarantee of musharakah capital can be provided by way of a third-party guarantee with or without imposition of fees.
- *Musharaka (joint venture) partners.* There should at least be two partners to form a musharaka. However, there is no maximum number of musharakah partners (sukuk investors) in the secondary market.
- *Profit and loss.* The profit from the musharaka venture will be distributed among partners according to the preagreed profit-sharing ratio. However, any loss should be shared among the partners according to the respective capital contribution.
- *Waiver of rights (tanazul in Arabic).* A partner may waive his or her right on the profit payment from the musharakah venture, if he or she so desires.
- *Management of the venture.* One of the partners or issuer or a third party may be appointed as the manager to manage the venture.

Sukuk Al-Mudaraba (Money Management)

- *Capital.* Capital contributed by owner and provider (*rabbul maal* in Arabic) should be in the form of cash, in kind or a combination thereof.
- *Guarantee (kafalah) on capital.* It may be provided by way of a third-party guarantee, with or without imposition of fees.
- *Collateral* (*rahn/lien*—please note our discussion on liens and pawns, meaning rahn in Arabic in Chapter 11). The capital owner may request the money manager/entrepreneur to place collateral as a protection from the possibility of loss on capital that may occur as a result of negligence and conducted by the mudarib.
- *Profit and loss.* The profit should be distributed between the capital owner and the money manager/entrepreneur as agreed. Loss should be borne in its entirety solely by the capital owner.
- *Waiver of right (tanazul).* A partner can waive his rights to profit if he so desires.
- *Venture management.* It can be conducted by the mudarib (money manager) or by a third party appointed by the mudarib. Consent of capital owner to approve third party may or may not be necessary depending on the contract (aqd).

TRADING OF SUKUK ON SECONDARY MARKETS

Supplementary RF Finance Definitions and Principles Pertaining to Sukuk Trading

Following are some of the concepts and terms used in the sukuk trading activities. It should be stated here that the trading of sukuk has represented a major challenge to Shari'aa scholars and RF bankers because it is a known Shari'aa rule that debt cannot be traded unless a number of strict requirements have been met. Following are some definitions offered by the Malaysian Securities Commission in its regulations of sukuk issuance:

- *Debt trading (bai' dayn).* A transaction that involves the sale and purchase of securities or debt certificates that conforms to the law (Shari'aa). Securities or debt certificates will be issued by debtor to creditor as an evidence of indebtedness.
- *Open market bidding trading (bai ul muzayada).* An action by a person to sell his asset in the open market through a bidding process among potential buyers. The asset for sale will be awarded to the person who has offered the highest bid/price. This is also known as the sale and purchase transaction based on tender.

- *Guarantee transfer (kafalah/dhaman).* A contract of guarantee whereby a guarantor underwrites any claim and obligation that should be fulfilled by an owner of the asset. This concept is also applicable to a guarantee provided on a debt transaction in the event a debtor fails to fulfill his debt obligation.
- *Ownership rights (haq tamaluk).* An asset in the form of ownership rights as classified by Shari'aa, which are tradable.
- *Gift (hibah).* A gift awarded by an owner to a person voluntarily.
- *Remittance (hawalah).* A contract that allows a debtor to transfer his debt obligation to a third party.
- *Rebate (ibraa).* An act by a person to withdraw his rights to collect payments from a person who has the obligation to repay the amount borrowed from him.
- *Preagreed contract (ittifaq dhimni).* A sale and repurchase of the underlying assets of which the prices are agreed by the parties prior to the completion of the contract. This is an external agreement that must be reached before the contract can be concluded to allow for the bidding process (*bai ul muzayadah*) to take place.
- *Collateral (rahn/lien).* A valuable asset is made by this act as pledge for debt. The collateral can be used to settle the debt when the debtor is in default.
- *Fee (ujrah).* A charge made to pay for the effort made and the utilization of financial services (*manfa'aa*). It can be in the form of a salary, allowance, commission, and/or any permissible for of assets.

Trading of Sukuk

The Accounting and Auditing Organization for Islamic Financial Institutions (AAOIFI[11]) is a recognized Islamic banking regulatory and supervisory body located in Bahrain. AAOIFI issued a "Resolution on Sukuk" based on the discussions conducted in the meetings of June 27, 2007; September 8, 2007; and February 13 and 14, 2008:

The AAOIFI resolution states that in order to be able to trade Sukuk:

- They must be owned by a sukuk holder with all rights of obligations and ownership, in real assets, whether tangible, usufructs, or services, capable of being owned and sold legally. The manager issuing the sukuk must certify the transfer of ownership in its underlying assets in the books and must not keep these assets under his own assets.
- They must not represent or include in their underlying assets receivables or debts, except in the case of a trading or a financial entity selling all its assets, or in the case of a portfolio with an outstanding financial

obligation in which some debts which are incidental to physical assets or usufructs were included unintentionally.

- The sukuk manager who acts as an investment manager (*mudarib*), as a partner (*shareek* in Arabic), or as an agent for investment (*wakeel* in Arabic) is not permitted to:
  - Undertake to offer loans to sukuk holders when actual earnings fall below expected earnings. However, it is permissible to establish a reserve account for the purpose of covering shortfalls to the extent possible and the policies used to establish and fund this reserve account must be clearly stated in the offering prospectus.
  - Undertake to repurchase the assets from sukuk holders or from one who holds them for its nominal value when the sukuk are extinguished at maturity. It is permissible to undertake the purchase on the basis of the net value of assets at its market value, fair appraised value or at a price to be agreed between the parties.
- It is permissible for the lessee to purchase the underlying leased assets at their nominal value in the special case of sukuk based on the lease to purchase model provided that the lessee is not also acting as the sukuk manager, agent, or partner.
- The Shari'aa Supervisory Board should not limit their role to the issuance of fatwa (edict) on the structure and permissibility of the sukuk. That responsibility should be extended to cover all aspects of the issuance, handling, trading, and accounting and auditing of the issuer.

Equity Investments According to the RF Discipline

This represents investing in RF qualified shares that are issued by a company either during the initial public offering (IPO) of the shares for the first time to investors in the capital market or by buying it in the secondary markets when these shares have already been issued and are offered for trading on one of the world stock markets like the New York Stock Exchange or Nasdaq stock market (also called over the counter) or local national stock markets like those of China, Singapore, London, Kuala Lumpur, Kuwait, and other countries.

Soliciting investments in an IPO offering of company shares is a tool that gathers and accumulates capital that would go into financing the company's capital needs. These needs include financing company start up requirements, expansion plans and/or continuing operations. After the IPO shares are issued and a calm period elapses to help stabilize the share market value to allow the market forces of supply and demand for that stock to settle, these shares can be resold in a market called the secondary market like the New York Stock Exchange or the over-the-counter market. The secondary market cash proceeds from the sale of the shares go to the owner of these shares and not to the company. However, the market (sale) price per share will define the company's market value (equals the price per share multiplied by the number of outstanding shares) and will produce an impact on the company's ability to obtain loans and credit facilities from the banks and other investors.

A company that has been in operation for some time can go back to the capital market for a new round to raise new fresh capital through a "secondary offering." This capital goes directly to finance the company needs in the way described in the issued prospectus to raise that capital.

There two types of company shares:

- Shares that are listed on one of the many stock market exchanges. This is called in the market "liquid shares." That means that the shareholder can go to the market—through a stock brokerage firm or directly in person or on line to sell the shares at a market price that is publicly disclosed and updated continually in an open market operation and receive cash, or
- Shares that are considered to be public but not listed on a public stock exchange. These shares are sold by arranging a buyer and a seller outside the market and that renders these shares illiquid. That is, these shares cannot be readily sold for cash in the open market.

Investors invest in shares to achieve one or more of the following objectives:

- Receive a dividend—that is, the amount of income per share the company announces it will pay out to its shareholders on a quarterly basis,
- Realize a handsome capital gain upon the sale of the shares using the "buy low–sell high" trading principle, or
- Realize a combination of both of the objectives listed above.

Investors in IPO's are mostly interested in capital appreciation, while investors who purchase shares in the secondary market are interested in either capital gains or dividend income or both depending on the stock involved and/or the investment objectives of the investor.

Because of the risks involved, investing in the stock market in general and in a certain sector or a certain company carries a certain level of risk with it. Investors have different levels of risk tolerance. Some would not mind high risk hoping for higher returns and others would like to keep a very low risk while investing. Professional portfolio managers, who are educated, well trained, and experienced investment professionals with an accumulated track record of investment results over a long period of time, can provide an investment advisory service that would tailor a portfolio of shares that would meet the investment objectives and risk tolerance accepted by a specific investor.

GUIDELINES FOR RF INVESTING IN THE STOCK MARKET

The spirit of investing according to the RF law (Judeo-Christian-Islamic Shari'aa law) is to participate in equity investing and not in debt-type investing. Equity investing means owning equity in the company (or companies). Debt investing means lending money to the company using a riba-based instrument, such as a direct loan, an interest-based (renting money) promissory note, or a predefined interest-based bond.

Investing in equities is highly encouraged by the law (Shari'aa). RF financing is all about equity participation in business activities that need financing. I was part of a group of scholars and experts who started the structuring of the first RF stock investment portfolio in the world in 1988 in a $250 million portfolio according to the law (Shari'aa). The portfolio performed much better than the market averages. A number of guidelines were developed as early as 1988 to regulate investing in stocks based on the law (Shari'aa) by using RF discipline. The following is a list of these RF guidelines:

- It is preferred to invest in companies that operate in local communities to generate economic growth and prosperity that would create new job opportunities, peace, and harmony in the community.
- Investing should be in socially responsible companies with a management dedicated to high ethical and moral standards. Investing cannot be in companies which are involved directly or indirectly in divinely prohibited (*haram*) businesses, such as:
  - Alcoholic beverages, intoxicants, bars, nightclubs and associated activities, casinos, hotels that operate bars and casinos, airlines that serve alcohol on their planes, or other promiscuous activities. For example, Walt Disney Company provides family entertainment and theme parks, but it also owns movie divisions and trade names that may violate the promiscuous activities rule. Coca-Cola, in addition to its huge soft drinks business, has a thriving alcohol-related wine business. RF discipline and rules may not allow investing in either of these companies.
  - Pork and pork products industries.
  - Tobacco products.

  - Any other unethical activities and businesses that are not fair to their employees and customers or are environmentally irresponsible.
- The company capital structure should have minimum debt. This has generated a lot of research and debate. The first issue was how to calculate the debt structure of the company. Should it be based on the company's book value or the company's market value? And how to define the market value, is it the total number of shares multiplied by market price? Or is it the fair market value of the company's shares and assets?

  In the beginning, most scholars and Shari'aa committee members preferred using the book value as a conservative basis for calculating the debt as a percentage of total company capitalization and preferred to keep debt as low as possible.[12] Later on, as demand for RF (Islamic) mutual funds started to grow in the market, the RF scholars' regulation was relaxed to replace book value with market value defined as the number of shares outstanding in the market multiplied by the closing price in the market, which has allowed practitioners in the highly inflated market prices to expand the list of company stocks from which they can choose.
- Equities in the U.S. market were screened. As part of the research,[13] more than 10,000 companies were analyzed. The percentages of RF noncompliant stocks (in 2000) were as follows:
  - Prohibited business line: 22 percent
  - Excessive borrowing: 62 percent
  - Excessive interest income: 8 percent
  - Other exclusions: 3 percent

  The total percentage of companies excluded was 95 percent. Out of 10,000 companies, only 500 were RF Shari'aa compliant.
- The maximum debt allowed is 33 percent of the market capitalization, not the balance sheet capitalization (originally the ruling was to use the balance sheet capitalization).[14] However, in an RF regime using the Marking-to-Market approach, along with the Commodity Indexation principles discussed in Chapter 5, a corrector should be used that reflects the overpriced assets in case a bubble is detected. For example, if oil price reaches $150 and, based on the Commodity Indexation principles, the oil price should be $50 to $70, that means the market valuation of that stock should be reduced to about one-third to one-half of its value, leading to a decision to sell out of the position to avoid participating in the bubble.
- Company accounts receivables should remain at 45 percent of total company assets.
- Interest income should be less than 5 percent of total revenue.

- Investment should be in actual stocks backed by an operating company and not just a paper index. Indexes are only used for measuring performance results.

These foundations for RF stock market investing according to the law (Shari'aa) were adopted by the Dow Jones Company to develop the Dow Jones Islamic Market Index (DJIMI).[15] Later, Standard & Poor's[16] introduced its own S&P Islamic index. These indexes formed the bases for many Islamic RF mutual funds available in the market today. Amana Funds,[17] one of the most successful funds, developed its own parameters and screens. Its two funds, the Amana Income Fund and the Amana Growth Fund, realized a five-star rating on the Morningstar rating system. The company was successful in getting some of the major brokering companies, like Charles Schwab and T. D. Waterhouse, to distribute its fund for retirement plan and general investors. This has increased the assets under management from approximately $65 million in the late 1990s to almost $1 billion in 2006 and over $3.5 billion in 2012.

REVIEW QUESTIONS

1. What is the real major revolutionary contributions brought by Islam to the world of finance and monetary theory as stated in the book?
2. Capital can be solicited and raised in the market to finance new projects and expand existing ones. What are the regulatory guidelines that regulate this process of soliciting capital from the public? What entity in the United States regulates that process and how?
3. Capital can also be raised from a class of investors who are sophisticated and who can make educated decisions about risks involved in investments. What are these investors called by the regulators? What are their qualifications as stated by the regulators in the United States?
4. Capital can be raised by soliciting companies, governments, and organizations. In what categories and types? Please enumerate the capital market's investment vehicles that can be used.
5. What is the SEC, and what are its responsibilities in the capital markets?
6. What is a private direct investment? Can a private direct investment be structured as an RF investment and how?
7. What is a venture capital (VC) investment? What is the risk level associated with it? How can investors be rewarded for taking this risk?
8. What is the difference between capitalization using a bond issue and a stock/share issue?
9. What is a riba-based bond?

10. What is a government security? What kinds of guarantees and collaterals can a government offer to support a government bond issue?
11. How were bonds used by colonizers to enhance their interests? Please give two country examples and the details on what happened?
12. China and Saudi Arabia are two of the largest holders of U.S. government debt securities/paper (U.S. Treasuries). What happens if China decides to cash off these debt securities? Please share with us the views of Steve Forbes. What is your opinion?
13. What are the different types of riba bonds available in the market?
14. What is a municipal bond? What steps should a municipality or a city follow in order to issue a municipal bond to finance a municipal project like an airport, a water plant, or a highway?
15. What are advantages offered by municipal bonds to investors?
16. What is a corporate bond? If a company is liquidated what is the position of seniority of these bonds compared to government and local taxes and to dividends owed to shareholders?
17. The Catholic Church started with strict prohibition of riba/ribit (the charging of rent for the use of money called usury), then it started relaxing these restrictions. Please discuss what were the motivations that prompted the Church to follow that course of action? How the relaxation was done and the steps followed?
18. How are bonds rated and evaluated in the market? Please explain what a rating agency is. What does a rating agency do? Please discuss the strict regulations necessary to ascertain that the recommendations of these rating agencies are made credible.
19. What is the impact of higher market interest rates on the market value of a bond when liquidated?
20. What is the meaning of a secondary financial market?
21. What is an RF bond, or sukuk? How do these RF sukuk differ from riba bonds?
22. What are the two categories of sukuk?
23. What are the different types of RF financing models used for issuing RF sukuk? Please select three types and explain how these models are used to issue these types of sukuk.
24. What are the conditions used to ascertain that the underlying asset that a sukuk is issued to RF finance are in fact not pledged or encumbered?
25. Trading debt is a very sensitive and highly research issue in RF financing and markets. Please summarize the rules of trading sukuk in the secondary market in order to create liquidity in sukuk markets.
26. What are the RF disciplines and guideline required for investing in a company stock?

27. One of the RF disciplines and required parameters for RF screening of company stocks is the ratio of debt to company value. The company value can be valued using two methods: book value and market value. Please define and then explain the difference between book and market value. What does the book advocate for establishing company value, and why do you think this may be a true expression of RF discipline?
28. What is the Dow Jones Islamic Index? Please explain, and discuss its RF credentials based on what you read in the book.

NOTES

1. Steve Forbes, "China Is Dependent on Our Fiscal Health." *Forbes Asia* (February 2014), 11.
2. Samuel L. Hayes III and Philip M. Hubbard, *Investment Banking: A Tale of Three Cities* (Boston, MA: Harvard Business School Press, 1989).
3. Ibid.
4. Note that after the January 25, 2011, revolution and the election of President Morsy, the government tried to introduce a law that regulates RF bonds or sukuk. The major objections voiced by Al-Azhar scholars had to do with pledging national sovereign assets as collateral to these sukuk.
5. Hayes and Hubbard, *Investment Banking: A Tale of Three Cities.*
6. Ibid.
7. Ibid.
8. For a good overview on rating agencies, please visit www.investopedia.com/terms/b/bond-rating-agencies.asp.
9. RAM Holdings (formerly known as Rating Agency Malaysia Berhad) was established in November 1990 as Malaysia's first credit-rating agency. RAM's shareholders comprise both local and foreign financial institutions.
10. Securities Commission Malaysia (Suruhanjaya Sekuriti), *Islamic Securities Guidelines* (Sukuk Guidelines, revised July 12, 2011, effective August 12, 2011).

    Basic RF finance models, definitions, and concepts:

    - Deferred-payment sale (BBA—bai' bithaminin aajil in Malaysia and cost-plus or murabaha in the Arabic-speaking countries and South Asia): A contract that refers to the sale and purchase back of an asset on a deferred and installment basis with a preagreed payment period.
    - Cost-plus sale (murabaha): A contract that refers to the sale and purchase of assets whereby the cost and profit margin (markup) are made known.
    - Sale with immediate repurchase at a preagreed price (bai ul einah): A contract that involves a sale and buyback transaction of an asset

by a seller. A seller will sell the asset to a buyer on a cash basis. The seller will immediately buy back the same asset on a deferred payment basis at a price that is higher than the cash purchase price. It could also be applied when a seller sells the asset to a buyer on a deferred basis. This type of transaction is not accepted by many RF scholars because the repurchase price should be at the prevailing market price at that time.

- Supply sale (bai ul istijrar in Arabic): A contract between a client and a supplier, whereby the supplier agrees to supply a particular product on an ongoing basis, for example monthly, at an agreed upon price and on the basis of an agreed mode of payment.
- Advance purchase (bai ul salam in Arabic): A sale and purchase contract whereby the payment is made in cash at the point of contract but the delivery of the purchased asset will be deferred to a predetermined date.
- Sale and repurchase (bai ul wafa in Arabic): A contract with the condition that when the seller pays back the price of goods sold, the buyer returns the goods to the seller.
- Leasing (ijarah in Arabic): A contract whereby a lessor (owner) leases out an asset to a lease at an agreed leasing rate for a predetermined lease period. The ownership of the leased asset shall always remain with the lessor.
- Lease to purchase (ijarah montahiyah bil tamaluk in Arabic): A contract that begins with an ijarah contract for the purpose of renting out a lessor's asset to a lessee. Consequently, at the end of the leased period, the lessee will purchase the asset at an agreed price from the lessor by executing a purchase contract.
- Declining participation in usufruct—DPU (al-musharaka fi haqul manfaa, also known as the LARIBA RF finance model): The ultimate buyer buys back the share of the finance entity immediately at same price of its purchase and proceeds to register title in his name. A lien is perfected by the finance company to participate in the usufruct and protect its return of the original capital by the customer.
- Finance future production—purchase order (istisnaa): A purchase order contract where a buyer contracts with a seller or a contractor to deliver or construct the asset completed in the future according to the specifications given in the sale and purchase contract. The payment term can be agreed by both parties in the contract.
- Capital management and profit sharing (mudaraba): A contract between two parties to enter into an RF investment business venture. The parties consist of the capital owner (rabbul maal in Arabic) who shall contribute capital to finance the venture, and the money manager

(mudarib) who will manage the venture. If the venture is profitable, the profit will be distributed between the capital owner and the money manager based on a preagreed formula. In the case of a business loss, the loss shall be borne solely by the provider of capital.

- Joint venture profit and loss sharing (musharakah): A partnership agreement between two or more parties to finance a business venture whereby all parties contribute capital either in the form of cash or in kind for the purpose of financing the said venture. Any profit derived from the venture will be distributed based on preagreed profit sharing ratio, but a loss will be shared on the basis of capital contribution.
- Benevolent loan (qard hassan): A loan contract between two parties on the basis of social welfare or to fulfill a short-term financial need of the borrower. The amount of repayment must be equivalent to the amount borrowed. It is however legitimate for a borrower to voluntarily pay more than the amount borrowed as long as it is not stated or agreed at the point of the contract. However, when the qard hassan loan is made the giver of the loan gives it with the expectation that it may not be paid back and then it will be a loan for the sake of God. The conditions of this loan are detailed in Chapter 2.
- Tripartite sale (tawarruq): Purchasing a commodity on a deferred price and then selling it to a third party for cash. Many RF scholars have objections and serious reservations about this type of financing.
- Agency (wakalah): A contract where a party authorizes another party to act on behalf of the former based on agreed terms and conditions as long as he is alive.

11. Please visit AAOIFI website for information and updates on RF banking and finance: www.aaoifi.com/en/about-aaoifi/about-aaoifi.html.
12. Saleh Jameel Malaikah, presentation at the LARIBA 2000 Seventh Annual Symposium on LARIBA (Islamic) Banking & Finance and Awards Dinner, Pasadena, California, April 29, 2000.
13. The original opinion was to minimize the debt so that it would be as close to zero as possible. With the resulting small number of companies in which one can invest, the scholars and financial experts agreed to use analogy, with the conclusions used to limit the change in inheritance distribution to be a maximum of one-third. The scholars used this as a foundation to limit the debt of a company that can be invested in to one-third of the capital at first, then relaxed the ruling to be the company's market value on the market. Another major issue erupted with the minimum debt. The issue had to do with the dot-com and technology companies that were sizzling in the market in the late 1990s and early 2000s. These companies had essentially no debt and were included in the Islamic indexes. With the bursting of the dot.com bubble in 2000,

many of these indexes lost a major percentage of their value. Islamic mutual funds that started in the late 1990s ended up losing more than 50 percent of their value.

14. See Note 13.

15. The Dow Jones Islamic Market Indexes (DJIMI) were introduced in 1999 as the first benchmarks to represent Islamic-compliant portfolios. Today, the series encompasses more than 70 indexes and remains the most comprehensive family of Islamic market measures. The indexes are maintained based on a stringent and published methodology. See the website for more information: www.djindexes.com/mdsidx/index.cfm?event=showIslamic.

16. The S&P Shari'aa Index series is designed to offer investors a set of indices that are Shari'aa compliant. The S&P 500, the leading measure of the U.S. equity market, was one of the first S&P indices to offer a Shari'aa-compliant version. Modeled after its U.S. counterpart, the S&P Europe 350 and the S&P Japan 500 indices also offer their respective compliant versions. See the website for more information: www2.standardandpoors.com/spf/pdf/index/ Shariah_factsheet.pdf.

17. Amana Mutual Funds Trust is designed to provide investment alternatives that are consistent with Islamic principles. Generally, Islamic principles require that investors share in profit and loss, that they receive no usury or interest, and that they do not invest in a business that is not permitted by Islamic principles. Some of the businesses not permitted are liquor, wine, casinos, pornography, insurance, gambling, pork processing, and interest-based banks or finance associations. The funds do not make any investments that pay interest. In accordance with Islamic principles, the funds shall not purchase bonds, debentures, or other interest paying obligations of indebtedness. See the website for further information: www.amanafunds.com/amanx.html.

CHAPTER 15

Case Studies

Developing the RF Banking Investment Products

This chapter is designed to apply the RF (riba-free) banking principles discussed in the book to different financing situations. Portfolio managers are trained to diversify an investment portfolio between different asset classes to optimize the expected return in light of the risk level that fits the particular situation of each investor. The portfolio manager is trained to construct an *investment pyramid* (see Exhibit 15.1). Because the conventional riba-based banking system has been in existence for hundreds of years, serves some of the major world economies, and is standardized worldwide, the portfolio manager can tap many asset classes to build a certain portfolio. This is not the case in RF banking. This brand of banking has lagged behind the conventional system for about 600 years. The challenge ahead for RF bankers is to develop such a menu of diversified RF products that can help RF investors build a diversified RF investment portfolio that can be designed to deliver an acceptable return with commensurate risk. In designing these RF products, RF bankers must try to fulfill the following two important guidelines:

1. The RF investment product must comply with the Judeo-Christian-Islamic Shari'aa law and the laws of the land.
2. The RF product, at least in the beginning, must have the same feel and purpose as those offered by the conventional riba-based banks to enable the customer to conduct a fair and equitable comparison—and it must be at least of the same (or superior) quality.

In this chapter, the reader will be exposed to a number of real-life examples of RF financing case studies conducted by the LARIBA System. These cases are presented as an example of how to apply the RF principles to serve

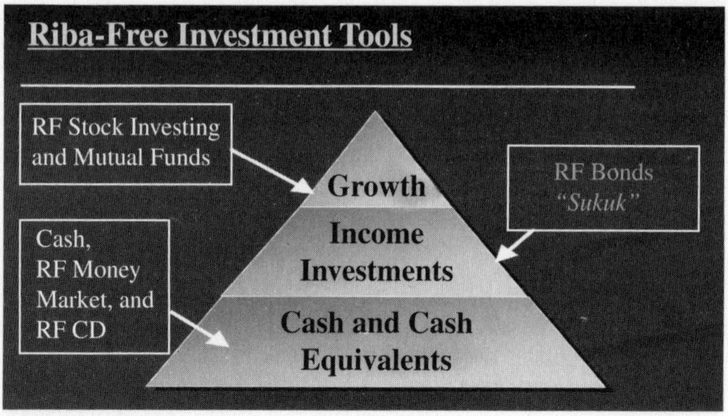

EXHIBIT 15.1 RF (Riba-Free) Investment Tools

different financing needs. These case studies also offer examples of the RF investment products that can be produced for the benefit of RF financial adviser to help him in structuring efficient investment portfolio for clients who seek to invest in RF portfolios. It is hoped that these "case studies" will make the RF financing and banking principles and discipline clearer and encourage you, the readers, to come up with new ideas, approaches, and products that are based on the RF principles and disciplines discussed throughout the book and that will certainly introduce those who try and succeed to the RF banking domain by offering superior new, less risky, and more rewarding financial services and products in the marketplace.

THE INVESTMENT PYRAMID

When a financial adviser attempts to construct an investment portfolio for a customer, that portfolio is usually built using what is known as the *investment pyramid*. The pyramid consists of three basic layers (other layers of investment classes can be added), of which the foundation has the least risk and the top has the highest risk. Exhibit 15.1 displays the characteristics and nature of the products that fit each layer.

Cash and Cash Equivalents

At the bottom of the pyramid, the adviser allocates a certain percentage of the customer's wealth in the form of cash and other cash equivalents. The cash equivalents in a riba-based domain are monetary instruments that can be made readily available in the form of cash, such as money market funds. The challenge we present here to you is to develop a much-needed

RF product, in the slate of products needed in the RF financial and capital market industry, like an RF product that is equivalent to the money market fund, an RF short-term instrument that will offer RF customers an alternative to the riba-based money market instruments.

At an RF bank, this layer will include the demand deposit (deposit in trust, also known as DIT or *Amana*) accounts as well as other Fed Fund deposits with the Federal Reserve System.

Short-Term Investments

The next layer of investments is a longer-term investment that can mature in three months to three years. Riba-based conventional banks offer time certificates of deposit (TCDs) that mature in three months to three years or more.

In an RF regime, this category includes short-term RF financing instruments that are structured by using the RF finance principles and disciplines such as a one- to three-year RF financing of an automobile or a piece of equipment.

RF Bonds: Sukuk (RF Asset-Based Income Instruments that Replace Riba-Based Bonds)

The next layer is a higher risk investment category, which includes the investment in fixed-income securities (riba bonds) in the case of riba-based conventional banks.

A new RF asset-based bond was developed by the RF industry to substitute for riba-based bonds. The RF bonds are called *sukuk*. (The word *sukuk* is the plural of the word *sak*, which is the origin from which the word *check* was derived.) The sukuk or RF bonds were discussed in Chapter 14. In this layer, the LARIBA RF finance model offers, as an example, two products developed with the participation of your author:

1. The first project was to develop an RF stock investment portfolio for Al-Baraka in Bahrain and Saudi Arabia in 1988. The goal was to develop the guidelines, rules, and disciplines needed to invest, for the first time in history, in an RF disciplined portfolio of stocks in the United States, Europe, and Asia.
2. The other was a to develop an RF bond (sukuk) to raise fresh capital through:
   a. The securitization of RF mortgages financed using the LARIBA RF finance model to develop RF mortgage-backed securities (MBSs) that can be used as substitute for riba-based bonds as applied in the United States and fixed-income securities.

b. The development of another type of special sukuk called *waqf sukuk*. These RF bonds were issued to help to unlock the financial potential of long-term religious trusts (waqf) in a pioneering way that is acceptable by the Judeo-Christian-Islamic Shari'aa law and the laws of Singapore, where it was done for the first time in history.

RF ASSET-BACKED BONDS (SUKUK)

RF Mortgage-Backed Sukuk Securities

An RF MBS uses the RF mortgage financing contracts developed by LARIBA to finance home mortgages according to the Judeo-Christian-Islamic Shari'aa law. The first RF MBS ever in the history of the United States was issued by LARIBA with Fannie Mae in 2002.

An MBS is an investment which represents an individual interest in a pool of home mortgages. Payments on the underlying pool of mortgages[1] that back an issue of MBS are *passed through* each month from the servicer of the mortgages (the entity responsible for administering the collection of the mortgage monthly payments, ensuring tax payments and sufficient insurance coverage and other needs) to the security holder (the MBS investor). In the United States, a unique security identification number is assigned by the Federal Reserve to each MBS and is maintained and transferred on the Fed's book-entry system.

In these RF MBS pools, the RF mortgages are assembled in $1 million packages, given a CUSIP number (CUSIP refers to both the Committee on Uniform Security Identification Procedures and the nine-character security identifiers that they distribute for all North American securities for the purposes of facilitating clearing and settlement of trades), and are bought by the bank, which uses them as a source of RF income for longer-term RF investors, who seek monthly or quarterly income. The income is generated from the rent stream of income paid—for example—by the house owner, as described earlier in the LARIBA RF finance model.

The Development of a Religious Real Estate Trust RF Bond (Waqf Sukuk)

The MUIS[2] Waqf Sukuk[3]: RF Asset-Based Bonds Used to Unlock the Value of Real Estate Trusts This example is a product of a very interesting circumstance that has helped the Singapore Muslim Community (MUIS[4]) unlock the tremendous value of the real estate holdings of different religious trusts. These real estate trusts were pledged to serve the interests of the Muslim community hundreds of years ago (these are called w*aqf*, which means pledged trusts that can only be used for the service of the faith as defined by its objectives). This example shows how MUIS was able to generate critically needed liquidity from the trust in an RF way using RF bonds (sukuk). The capital generated by investing in these RF bonds (sukuk) was used to develop old and undeveloped real estate properties which happened to be located in downtown Singapore into highly valued and market-rated properties. In turn, these developed real estate properties produced a sustained respectable income to help further the growth needs of the Singapore Muslim community.

The world is full of goodhearted people who want to leave a legacy by giving back to society in the form of donations or by pledging a productive asset that can produce enough income to help finance the operation of a place of worship, like a temple, a synagogue, a church, or a *masjid* (mosque). In the United States, donations of this sort are often motivated by reduction of taxes, retirement planning, and asset transfers to future generations to keep the family legacy alive in addition to making a contribution to the community. The foundations left behind by Ford, Carnegie, Rockefeller, and Kennedy are examples of such efforts.

In Islam, and for that matter the Judeo-Christian-Islamic value system, there is a similar system for giving which is motivated only by the interest of the donors to please God by donating assets that can be used as facilities for worship, education, health care, and administration of peoples' affairs, or that produce income to help the poor and the needy. Donations can also include income-producing assets. The income of these assets would be used to fund education, health care, research, and other public projects and needs. These trusts are called *waqf*. The word *waqf* literally means that the title of the asset has been "arrested." In today's lingo, a waqf is a *public charitable trust*, in which the assets are pledged to God. The title of the asset is treated as that of a ceased property that is pledged to God. This asset can be a prayers place (masjid), a hospital, a research center, a library, an oil-producing territory or well, a school, a farm land, an orchard or any other income-producing asset, producing a stream of rent, crops, minerals, and oil and gas. These tangible productions can be sold to produce cash income that can benefit the beneficiaries and maintain the asset; if there is a surplus, it can be used to benefit other waqf assets. History shows that charitable waqf giving escalates with economic prosperity; the opposite is also true. Charitable waqf properties are usually not well maintained and are left to run down during times of economic and political decline. According to the Judeo-Christian-Islamic Shari'aa law, assets that can be pledged as *waqf* can be classified in two types:

1. *Immovable:* For example, real estate, including land, buildings, and other location-specific assets, such as fruit orchards, trees, water wells, and oil and gas wells.
2. *Movable:* For example, cash and investments in stock portfolios.

An interesting situation came up during one of my visits to Singapore. The community had lost a prime multimillion-dollar property in one of its most expensive prime neighborhoods in downtown Singapore because they did not have the money to develop it and they were not allowed by the law (Shari'aa) to borrow money with riba. The big dilemma was that two more properties in prime downtown areas were required by the municipality before a certain approaching deadline, to be modernized and renovated; otherwise, those properties would be lost as well. I had a meeting with the leaders of the community and we developed an RF approach to solve the problem. The approach involved the issuing of *RF waqf bonds* (sukuk) for the first time in the history of Singapore, and the world for that matter. This approach enabled us to unlock the real value of a religious trust (waqf) to generate capital using RF sukuk to develop the real estate properties further.

The following is a summary of what was done, especially in this field of unlocking the vast economic and financial potential of the frozen assets of waqf, which had not been researched for a long time. This approach is now being implemented in many Muslim countries, and a special waqf bank is being sought to focus on this large market demand. The details on the two projects involved will follow.

The Judeo-Christian-Islamic Shari'aa law states that, in general, the pledged assets of a waqf (public charitable trust) cannot be sold, granted to others, nor inherited by others. It must be used always for the purpose it was pledged to fulfill.[5] However, historians and scholars in the law (Shari'aa) have documented some exceptions, which were practiced under unusual circumstances that required modification of this rule.[6] For example, the second Khalifa of the Muslim State (Umar Ibn Al-Khattab 584–644 C.E.) approved the change of use of a masjid (mosque) when he ordered that the old *Kufah* (a city in Iraq) masjid moved to a new location to improve the services. The old location was changed from a masjid to a market for date sellers. In addition, history records that both the second Khalifa (Umar Ibn Al-Khattab) and the third Khalifa (Uthman Ibn Affan 577–656 C.E.) did approve the expansion of the original masjid of the Prophet Muhammad (pp) in the city of Madinah (a city in Saudi Arabia). This opened to us some very useful and creative ideas.

One of the two Singapore properties was a historic masjid (mosque) in the center of downtown proper and close to the world renowned and prestigious Singapore Management University (SMU). The problem was that the waqf consisted of a masjid in a prime area, and that it also had attached to it a prime piece of undeveloped real estate. The challenge was to see how it could be developed—as required by the local municipality—into a prime commercial building that could generate income for the waqf without violating the law (Shari'aa) conditions regarding the assets pledged as a waqf.

Naturally, the community would be up in arms if the leadership decided to demolish the historic masjid and build a modern and more efficient one along with a high-rise building that could produce enough income to enhance the fortunes of the community. After in-depth discussions with the architects and the developer, a plan was created to keep the masjid intact and to attach to it a long-term-stay hotel for professionals who come to work on special projects for periods ranging from 1 to 12 months. The problem was how to generate the money needed to finance this development. The solution offered was formulated by two Shari'aa advisers, Dr. Mohamad Daud Bakar (from Malaysia) and your author. The solution involved using the LARIBA RF finance model of forming an entity that would raise the capital and appraise the value of the waqf asset. The combination would form a joint venture between waqf and the sukuk investors. The capital raised would be used to develop the property, lease it, and share the rental income while the waqf bought back the shares of the venture from the sukuk investors, using the LARIBA RF finance model in the same way as was described in Chapter 11. In this way, the waqf asset could be kept intact while its real value was unlocked to generate the capital needed to develop the property.

The Structuring of the Singapore MUIS Waqf Sukuk[7]

The effort involved the rescuing of two properties. The first was a high-rise building called *Fusion* that required S$25 million to renovate in order to bring its specifications up to the required city standards.[8] The property is located on the corner plot of the famous Raffles Hotel landmark and Shopping Arcade block. The other was a masjid property called *Bencoolen*, in a high-traffic market area close to the prestigious business school, the Singapore Management University (SMU). The property had a vacant piece of land which needed to be developed into a high-rise residence hotel and required an investment of S$35 million.

As discussed in the book, charging, paying, receiving, and dealing in interest (riba) is clearly prohibited by the law (Shari'aa). The sukuk (asset-based RF bond) issue is in fact a musharakah (joint venture) agreement between MUIS and United Overseas Bank (UOB), which uses the LARIBA RF finance model (the declining participation in usufruct [DPU] model) and approach to formulate such an asset-based bond (sukuk). Following is a description of the four steps we followed:

1. MUIS Waqf Fund (the owner of the property) and UOB entered into an agreement to jointly own the property. The property was appraised at S$34 (S$ is Singapore dollar) million. UOB agreed to forward S$25 million to MUIS in order to own 73.52941 percent of the joint venture (obtained by dividing $25 million by $34 million). MUIS retained the balance, or 26.47059 percent, of equity in the property. The title of the property is held by MUIS, and a lien is placed on it for the benefit of

the joint venture to utilize its usufruct as described in the LARIBA RF finance model. This way, the rule of not compromising or transferring the title of a waqf property is not violated.

2. The joint venture participants (musharaka partners) agree to sign a five-year lease of the property at a fair and mutually agreed-upon lease rate which conforms to the prevailing market rate as required by the LARIBA model's Marking-to-Market Discipline.
3. UOB agrees to immediately sell its share back to MUIS at the same price, or $25 million, and to get paid after five years. The lease income, after expenses and applicable taxes (income from the usufruct), will be distributed between MUIS and UOB in the same proportion of ownership.
4. To abide by the laws and monetary regulations of Singapore, and to benefit from the tax advantages of issuing a bond in the state of Singapore, the return on invested capital for the sukuk (bond) holder may be called *implied interest*.

The transaction is depicted in Exhibit 15.2.

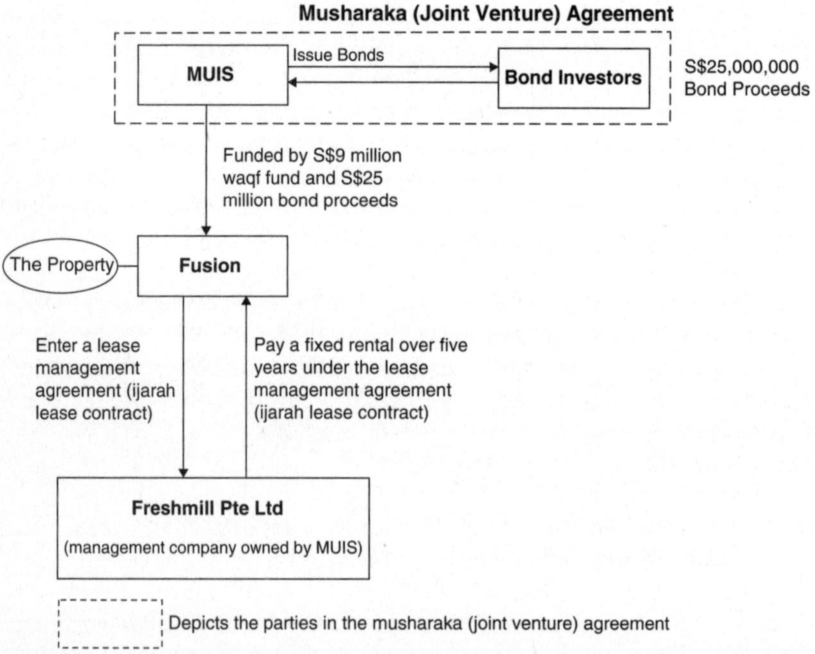

EXHIBIT 15.2 A Pictorial Diagram of the Transaction Structure

RF Investment Discipline in Stocks

This layer represents a higher return, but also a higher risk. The RF guidelines for investing in the stock market was summarized in the previous chapter and detailed below.

This section will detail how the RF discipline and parameters for investing in stocks were developed for the first time in 1988 by your author and another pioneer; Dr. Saleh Jamil Malaikah, who is now one of the leading executives of one of the larger RF insurance companies (takaful); RUSD investment banks (http://www.rusdbank.com). In addition, many of the principles of RF financing and investing disciplines will be discussed in order to avoid participating in a stock market bubble that would waste the hard-earned wealth of the customers and investors involved.

The following are the RF disciplines and guidelines that were developed for RF investing in the stock markets.

Guidelines for RF Investing in the Stock Market

The spirit of investing according to the Judeo-Christian-Islamic Shari'aa law is to participate in equity investing and not in riba-based debt-type investing. Equity investing means owning equity in the company (companies). Riba-based debt investing means lending money to the company using a riba-based debt instrument, such as a direct loan, an interest-based (renting money) promissory note, or a predefined interest-based bond.

Investing in equities is highly encouraged by the law (Shari'aa). RF financing is all about equity participation in business activities that need financing. I was part of a group of scholars and experts who started investing according to the Judeo-Christian-Islamic Shari'aa law in 1988 in a $250 million stock portfolio. The portfolio performed better than the market averages both in total return and in its lower volatility. A number of guidelines were developed as early as 1988 to regulate RF investing in stocks based on the law (Shari'aa). The following is a list of these guidelines:

1. It is preferred to invest in companies that operate in local communities to generate economic growth and prosperity that would create new job opportunities, economic prosperity, peace, and harmony in the community.
2. Investing should be in socially responsible companies with a management dedicated to high ethical and moral standards with demonstrable results and track record.

3. Investing cannot be in companies that are involved directly or indirectly in divinely prohibited (*haram*) businesses, such as:
   a. Alcoholic beverages, intoxicants, bars, nightclubs and associated activities, casinos, hotels that operate bars and casinos, airlines that serve alcohol on their planes and their first class and business class lounges, or promiscuous activities. For example, Walt Disney Company is known worldwide to be a company that provides family entertainment and theme parks, but it also owns movie divisions and trade names that may violate the promiscuous activities rule. Coca-Cola, in addition to its huge soft drinks business, has a thriving alcohol-related wine business. We could not invest in these companies.
   b. Pork and pork products industries.
   c. Tobacco products.
   d. Interest-charging and/or -paying entities, such as banks, finance companies, payday check cashing companies, investment banks, insurance companies, and related businesses.
   e. Any other unethical activities and businesses that are not fair to their employees and customers or are environmentally irresponsible.
4. The company's capital structure should have minimum debt. This has generated a lot of research and debate. The first issue was how to calculate the debt structure of the company. Should it be based on the company's book value or the company's market value? In the beginning, most scholars and Shari'aa committee members, including our pioneering group, preferred using the book value as a basis for calculating the debt as a percentage of total company capitalization and preferred to keep debt as low as possible. Later on, as Islamic mutual funds started to grow in the market, the regulation was relaxed to replace book value with market value. (Market value is obtained by multiplying the number of outstanding shares in the market into the closing share price on that day. Of course, in an inflated, overheated, and "bubbly" market, the market capitalization is so high that the debt on the company books when divided by that market value would give a misleading low debt to capitalization ratio.) This decision has allowed practitioners to expand the list of company stocks from which they can choose.
5. Equities in the U.S. market were screened as part of the research[9]; more than 10,000 companies were analyzed. The percentages of noncompliant stocks (in 2000) were:

   Prohibited business line: 22 percent

   Excessive borrowing: 62 percent

   Excessive interest income: 8 percent

   Other exclusions: 3 percent

The total percentage of companies excluded was 95 percent. Out of 10,000 companies, only 500 were Shari'aa compliant.

6. The maximum debt allowed is 33 percent of the market capitalization, not the balance sheet capitalization (originally the ruling was to use the balance sheet capitalization).[10] However, in an RF regime using the Marking-to-Market Discipline and approach along with the Commodity Indexation Discipline discussed in Chapters 5 and 6, a corrector should be used that reflects the fiat-money-denominated overpriced assets in case a price-bubble is detected. For example, if oil price reaches $150 and, based on the Commodity Indexation Discipline, the normalized oil price after applying the Commodity Indexation Discipline by using a reference calibrating commodity like gold, silver, or a food staple should translate to a fair oil price of $50 to $70, that means the market valuation of that stock should be reduced to about one-third to one-half of its value, leading to a decision to sell out of the position or a portion of it (depending on the level of risk acceptance by the investor) to avoid participating in the bubble.
7. Company accounts receivables (A/R) should remain at 45 percent of total company assets.
8. Riba-based interest income should be less than 5 percent of total revenue.
9. Investment should be in actual stocks backed by an operating company and not just a paper index. Indexes that are not backed by tangible assets and that reflect the performance of an index based on prices are used in an RF regime only for measuring performance results.

These foundations for stock market investing according to the law (Shari'aa) were adopted by the Dow Jones Company to develop the Dow Jones Islamic Market Index (DJIMI).[11] Later, Standard & Poor's[12] introduced its own S&P Islamic Index. These indexes formed the bases for many Islamic mutual funds available in the stock market today. Amana Funds,[13] one of the most successful funds in general and the better RF fund in particular, developed its own parameters and screens. Its three funds, the Amana Income Fund, the Amana Growth Fund, and the Amana Developing World Fund, realized a four-star rating (2013) on the Morningstar rating system. The company was successful in getting some of the major brokering companies, like Charles Schwab and T. D. Waterhouse, to distribute the investment in its RF funds through its trustee capacity for custodianship over fund saved for retirement plans and for investments by general investors. This has increased the assets under management from approximately $65 million in the late 1990s to almost $1 billion in 2006 and over $2 billion in 2013.

Normalization of Various Stock Market Indexes Using the Commodity Indexation Discipline

Perhaps one of the riskiest factors in valuing the stock indexes, including the Islamic stock indexes, is that the market value of the stocks is included in the index without allowing investors to detect any bubble formation due to speculative market forces created by options and derivatives and excessive hedge funds market speculation techniques. In the case of the Islamic Shari'aa-compliant indexes, the use of market value to screen for the debt a company has on its balance sheet to be a maximum of one-third of total market capitalization can be particularly hazardous, because of the gyrations in the market value of stocks on the market, especially in the case of speculative market bubbles.

It is recommended that the index be normalized using a reference commodity like gold, silver, a staple commodity (as described in Chapters 5 and 6) or a combination thereof, depending on the market in question. In this approach, it is recommended that we relate the market index, say, to gold, and follow the gyrations in terms of gold to detect for price bubbles and to reduce investment positions and exposure to the market accordingly. This approach is still in its infancy and requires more intensive research.

As an example, let us study the value of oil company stocks in the volatile period when oil prices skyrocketed to almost \$150 per barrel in 2008. At the time, many analysts expected the price to reach \$200 per barrel and recommended the purchase of more oil company stocks. However, based on the gold price and oil relationship and applying the Commodity Indexation Discipline described in Chapters 5 and 6, the data indicated to us that oil was extremely overpriced and suggested that oil prices were experiencing a serious price bubble. This should have prompted the RF-disciplined investors not to invest more in oil company stocks, but rather to liquidate their positions in oil and energy company stocks, because the commodity price RF Commodity Indexation Discipline suggested that the oil price must decline to around \$55 to \$75 per barrel. However, when oil prices reflect an extreme low in terms of gold, as happened in February 2009 when oil reached \$35 per barrel, RF-disciplined investors should have accumulated more oil company stocks in their portfolios.

This approach can be generalized to the whole market by applying the Commodity Indexation to the stock index. Exhibit 15.3 shows the relationship of the index in terms of gold price. The chart shows the relationship between the Dow Jones market indexes (DJIA), the Nasdaq market index, and the S&P 500 market index in terms of gold price.

Please note that these techniques are not to be taken as predictive tools but rather as tools that would be used as a guide to directional movements in the market into overpriced (bubble) or underpriced (value) territories.

The charts indicate that:

- *Exhibit 15.3.* The DJIA value divided by the price of gold fluctuated in a channel in the range of 4 to 10 times the price of gold with a mean of seven. That means if gold price is $950 the fair value of DJIA would be in the range of 3,800 to 9,500, with a mean fair value of 6,650. The important level beyond which the DJIA starts to be overpriced based on the commodity indexation rule is 9,500. However, if gold reaches $1,500 an ounce, the fair value of the market would fluctuate in a channel that has a low value of 6,000 and a high value of 15,000. Any time the value of the Dow Jones index crosses over 15,000 (at $1,500 an ounce gold price), that should raise a red flag about the overpricing of the market.

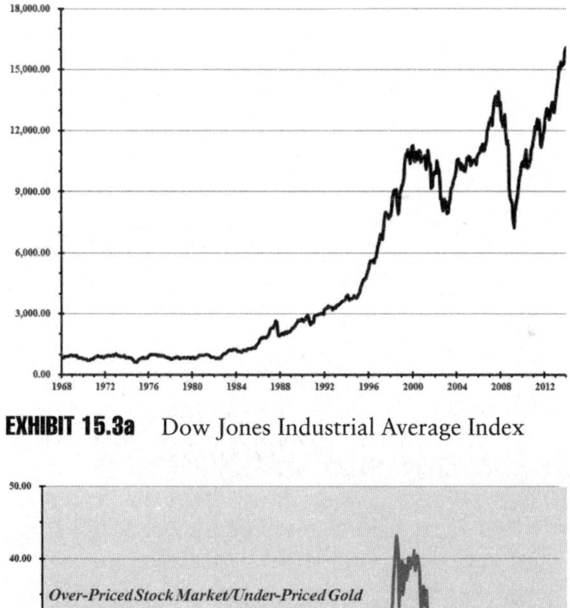

EXHIBIT 15.3a Dow Jones Industrial Average Index

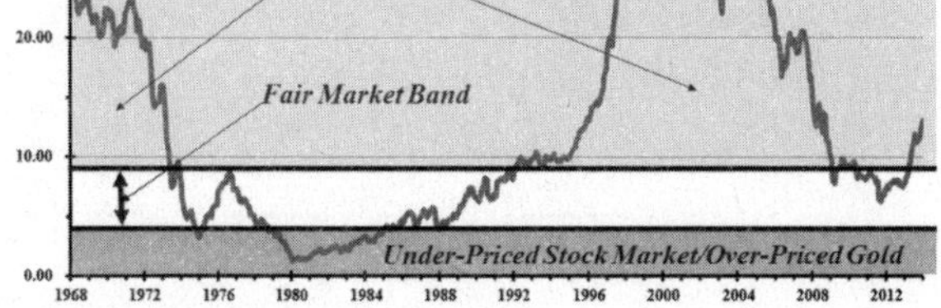

EXHIBIT 15.3b Dow Jones Industrial Average in Ounces of Gold, Units of Dow Index per Ounce of Gold

- *Exhibit 15.4.* The Nasdaq value divided by the gold price fluctuated in a channel ranging between one and four units of Nasdaq for each dollar of gold price with a mean value of 2.5. That implies that if gold price reaches $950 per ounce that Nasdaq's fair value would fluctuate between 950 and 3,800, with a mean of 2,375. The important level beyond which Nasdaq starts to be overpriced based on the commodity indexation rule is 3,800. However, if gold reaches $1,500, then it is expected that the Nasdaq market index fluctuate between a low of 1,500 and a high of 6,000, with a mean of 3,750. Any time the index crosses over 6,000 (at a gold price of $1,500 an ounce), a red flag should be raised and decisions about liquidation out of the market should be discussed seriously.

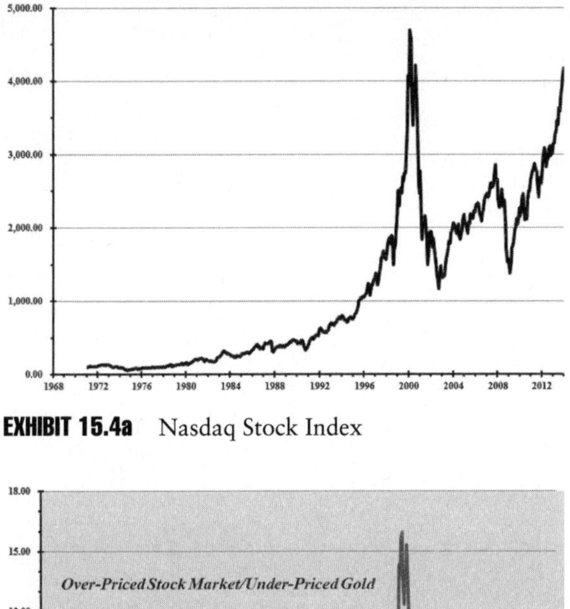

EXHIBIT 15.4a Nasdaq Stock Index

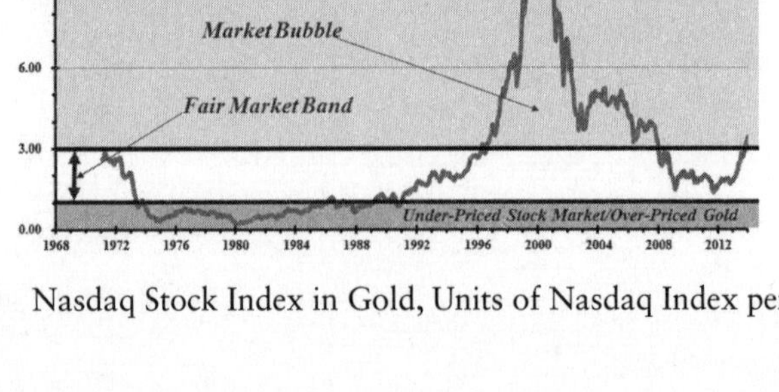

EXHIBIT 15.4b Nasdaq Stock Index in Gold, Units of Nasdaq Index per Ounce of Gold

- *Exhibit 15.5*. The S&P 500 value divided by the gold price fluctuated in a channel ranging between one half and one unit of S&P 500 for each dollar of gold price with a mean value of 0.75. That implies that if gold price reaches $950 per ounce that S&P 500's fair value would fluctuate between 475 and 950 with a mean of 712.5. The important level beyond which the S&P 500 starts to be overpriced based on the commodity indexation rule is 950. On the other hand, at a gold price of $1,500 an ounce we would expect the S&P Index to fluctuate between 750 and 1,500. Any time the upper range is violated caution must be exercised to avoid an overpriced market situation.

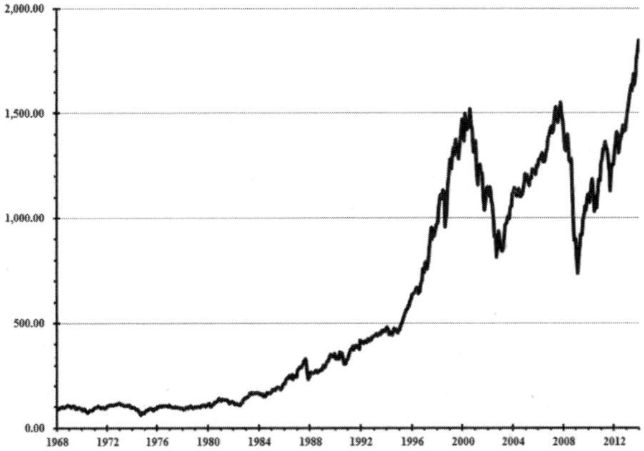

EXHIBIT 15.5a S&P 500 Stock Index

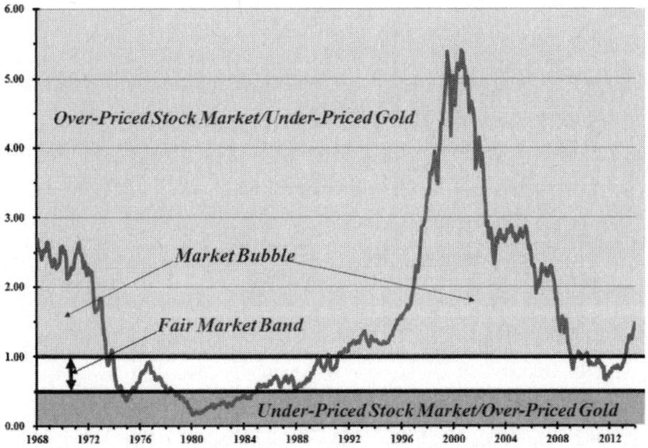

EXHIBIT 15.5b S&P 500 Stock Index in Gold, Units of S&P Stock Index per Ounce of Gold

It is clear that definite signals of a serious inflated market bubble have loomed since 2006. I would be the first to admit that this is an art—based on technical analysis—and not a science, but two important points must be considered at this juncture:

1. This "technical analysis" approach using the Commodity Indexation Discipline should be one of the factors considered in making investment decisions in the stock market.
2. The application of this technical analysis approach requires more research and strategy development by qualified data-mining experts.

Many may argue that this approach of Commodity Indexation may lead to premature selling, which happened to me while managing my portfolio, when I got out of the market in 2006. However, it is better to err on the conservative side and miss 20 to 35 percent of the market's move to the upside than to sit in the market and lose 60 percent of the *entire value of the portfolio*. Many investors do not realize that if the market declines by 50 percent, that means that the market must appreciate by 100 percent in order to return to where it was before it declined. This is a move that will require many years to achieve.

REVIEW QUESTIONS

1. What is financial engineering, and what is a structured deals attorney? What is his task in structuring Islamic products and services that are Shari'aa compliant?
2. What is the difference between the terms *Shari'aa compliant* and *Shari'aa based*?
3. What is the investment pyramid?
   a. What are the common layers that represent the building of that pyramid from the floor to the top of the pyramid?
   b. Please explain how we can use RF products and services in order to build a portfolio of investments that would be based on Shari'aa investment disciplines.
   c. Please explain how much of a percentage of the total portfolio a retired individual at age of 70 years can invest in mutual funds or stock market and why.
   d. What is the meaning of the word *sukuk* and from what was it derived?
4. What is the meaning of waqf? What are the restrictions of the Judeo-Christian-Islamic Shari'aa law about the sale and pledge of the waqf?
5. How were the restrictions on dealing with the waqf resolved while developing the waqf properties in Singapore?

6. Please choose a waqf property in the country you live in and tell us about the potential capital that can be unlocked using the same approach used in Singapore. Please tell us how that can be done and what project your vision leads you to develop in order to develop that waqf property.
7. Please look at the levels of the Dow Jones Industrial Average, Nasdaq, and the S&P 500 and tell us if the values are overpriced or fairly priced and why by applying the Commodity Indexation Discipline.

NOTES

1. A pool of mortgages is a loan or group of loans with similar characteristics. Minimum pool submission size in case of single pools is $1 million for fixed-rate mortgages with monthly payments and $500,000 for fixed-rate mortgages with biweekly payments.
2. MUIS, also known as the Islamic Religious Council of Singapore, was established as a statutory body in 1968 under the Administration of Muslim Law Act, Chapter 3, of Singapore (AMLA). Under the AMLA, MUIS is to advise the president of Singapore on all matters relating to Islam in Singapore.
3. Yahia Abdul-Rahman, research presentation at MUIS WAQF Conference, Singapore, March 6–7, 2007.
4. MUIS is the abbreviated name of the body that serves the needs of the Singapore Muslim community: "Majlis Ugama Islam Singapura."
5. Based on a saying—Hadeeth—of Prophet Muhammad (pp).
6. The two scholars, Abu Hanifa and Ibn Taymiya, allowed it with the condition that one must prove that there will be benefit to the public as a result of such modification. However, the scholar Imam Al Shafi disallowed it because it is the property of God.
7. Based on Yahia Abdul-Rahman, *A Memorandum of Understanding and Agreement, Musharaka Bond Issue by Majlis Ugama Islam Singapore (MUIS)*, which was authored in preparation of the first RF sukuk to be issued by MUIS in February 2001, to be arranged by United Overseas Bank, Asia.
8. MUIS—UOB Asia Ltd. Bond (sukuk) issue of S$25 million in 2001, due in 2006.
9. Saleh Jameel Malaikah, presentation at the LARIBA 2000 Seventh Annual Symposium on LARIBA (Islamic) Banking & Finance and Awards Dinner, Pasadena, California, April 29, 2000.
10. The original opinion was to minimize the debt so that it would be as close to zero as possible. With the resulting small number of companies in which one can invest, the scholars and financial experts agreed to use analogy,

with the conclusions used to limit the change in inheritance distribution to be a maximum of one-third. The scholars used this as a foundation to limit the debt of a company that can be invested in to one-third of the capital at first, then relaxed the ruling to be the company's market value on the market. Another major issue erupted with the minimum debt. The issue had to do with the dot-com and technology companies that were sizzling in the market in the late 1990s and early 2000s. These companies had essentially no debt and were included in the Islamic indexes. With the bursting of the dot-com bubble in 2000, many of these indexes lost a major percentage of their value. Islamic mutual funds that started in the late 1990s ended up losing more than 50 percent of their value.

11. The Dow Jones Islamic Market Indexes (DJIMI) were introduced in 1999 as the first benchmarks to represent Islamic-compliant portfolios. Today, the series encompasses more than 70 indexes and remains the most comprehensive family of Islamic market measures. The indexes are maintained based on a stringent and published methodology. See the website for more information: www.djindexes.com/mdsidx/index.cfm?event=showIslamic.
12. The S&P Shari'aa index series is designed to offer investors a set of indices that are Shari'aa compliant. The S&P 500, the leading measure of the U.S. equity market, was one of the first S&P indices to offer a Shari'aa-compliant version. Modeled after its U.S. counterpart, the S&P Europe 350 and the S&P Japan 500 indices also offer their respective compliant versions. See the website for more information: www2.standardandpoors.com/spf/pdf/index/Shariah_factsheet.pdf.
13. Amana Mutual Funds Trust is designed to provide investment alternatives that are consistent with Islamic principles. Generally, Islamic principles require that investors share in profit and loss, that they receive no usury or interest, and that they do not invest in a business that is not permitted by Islamic principles. Some of the businesses not permitted are liquor, wine, casinos, pornography, insurance, gambling, pork processing, and interest-based banks or finance associations. The funds do not make any investments that pay interest. In accordance with Islamic principles, the funds shall not purchase bonds, debentures, or other interest-paying obligations of indebtedness. See the website for further information: www.amanafunds.com/amanx.html.

CHAPTER 16

RF Credits (Loans) in Contrast to Types of Riba-Based Loans

Over the years the conventional riba-based banks developed a number of lending products to meet the market demand and to diversify product features in order to compete with each other to meet market needs and to attract new customers. These loan products are all based on the idea of renting money and using it for different uses by the customer to finance his or her financial needs. In this chapter, the different types of riba-based loans available on the market will be discussed and their RF applicability will be analyzed. The types of loans discussed in this chapter will include some of the popular types used by riba-based banks and will not include every type. As the reader develops a good grasp of the basic concepts, he or she can let their imagination and analytical capabilities go in order to develop RF credit products and services that comply and are based on the Judeo-Christian-Islamic Shari'aa law.

OVERDRAFT PROTECTION FOR HOLDERS OF CHECKING ACCOUNTS

Most banks in the United States offer their customer a credit facility called *overdraft protection.* It was designed to cover deficits in the checking account when a customer writes a check that is not covered by the balance available in the account. The bank, by applying this service, would honor the check, create an overdraft loan to balance the deficit in the account and charge an overdraft service fee that can range between $20 and $50 plus interest, which can be excessive compared to the prevailing fair market interest rates. At the LARIBA Bank of Whittier, overdraft credits are not available because it is the ultimate example of renting money (riba). To offer superior service to the RF customers, the LARIBA RF Bank of Whittier representative calls the customers who have NSF (nonsufficient funds) status early in the morning to inform them about the NSF. The RF Bank of

Whittier representative would allow the customer until noon to cover the deficit in order to avoid returning the check unpaid.

LINES OF CREDIT

These are loans given to customers as an open bank account in which the bank approves a certain maximum level of credit. The customer can draw money out of that line to meet his cash flow needs like for example a trader who wants to buy products and the proceeds of selling these products will take time to be paid to the trader. The customer withdraws the money needed out of this line of credit and uses it in his activities and when money is collected, he pays it back to the account and is charged for renting that money for that period—interest. The customer does not make principal payments throughout the term of the line until it matures or is called (terminated) by the bank. When the customer receives the money he can pay back the line. He can continue this process where the line is drawn and paid back. As an example, a customer can obtain a million dollars line of credit and all he has to pay is the interest; the renting cost of the money (riba), on the million dollars. If the rent of money; interest (riba) is given at an interest rate of 5 percent, the rent will be $50,000. The client does not pay the principal until the line is called.

Lines of credit can be given for a certain period of time, say one year, after which the customer has to pay it back in full. It can also be given as an open line of credit that can be renewed from year to year until called off by the bank in case the conditions of granting the line, the policies of the bank, and/or the economic environment change. The customer can either pay it back from his own funds or he can go to another bank and start a new line of credit. The problem is that in most cases these solutions would not be available to that customer whose line of credit was canceled because of financial problems. Experience shows that in most cases the customer whose line of credit is called would not be qualified and able to get another line from a different bank to pay back the first line and the bank ends up classifying that line as a nonperforming loan or a loss.

Lines of credit are generally not fitting in an RF bank because it is exactly what riba is all about. It involves the pure rental of money, which is the prohibited riba. However, line-of-credit facilities can be useful in a number of RF applications. The following are examples of RF lines.

Working Capital RF Lines of Credit

These are useful for operating companies which may need financing of purchases of raw materials or paying salaries but do not have the money yet because the product is still being manufactured or is sold to a customer and the payment is due after the time the cash has to be made available. In this case, the RF bank can provide a line of credit with the needed amount of money and whenever the customer pulls money out of that line the finance company or the bank would apply the murabaha RF finance model on the raw materials needed or in case of salaries the RF bank would use the istisnaa RF finance model or can conceptually buy a share in the company and use the LARIBA RF finance model to do the rest.

Construction Financing Lines of Credit

These are useful in cases when the customer wants to build a house but does not have the money to pay the contractor. If the customer has a business, then arrangements can be made to provide this RF line, which would represent a purchase of a the needed material like lumber, concrete, and other items using the RF murabaha model. Another approach is to apply the LARIBA RF finance model where the bank can buy a share of the business based on a share value that is evaluated by the bank or financial institution and agreed upon by both parties. Every time the customer pulls money out of the line that would trigger a conceptual purchase of a number of shares in the business. The return to the bank can be valued using one of two methods. The first would be a joint participation in the profit derived from the business or by renting back that share in the business at a fair rental rate. The concepts used in the LARIBA RF finance model can be applied further.

Unsecured Loans

These are riba-based loans given to high net worth individuals based on the fact that these individuals are well to do and have a strong balance sheet and financial position as well as a good credit report and good standing in the community. The idea is that these individuals own significant assets and have developed a long-term relationship with the bank that a loan can be given without going through the normal process of thoroughly evaluating the assets and liabilities and the prudence of investing the money and most importantly the purpose of taking the loan. Experience has shown that most of the unsecured loans underperform and many of them are not collected leading to classifying the loan as a nonperforming loan. The unfortunate part of this situation is that there is no specific collateral that the bank can attach and revert to in case of nonperformance. That makes the situation very complicated, the legal transactions more involved, and the cost of legal settling may end up being excessive and the end result will be a complete loss of the loan to the bank.

These types of loans cannot be offered in an RF bank because the RF bank is not in the business of renting money, which is the prohibited riba. The customer should provide a full application and the purpose of using the funds. The RF bank should formulate an RF finance model to consummate the finance. That is why these loans are not offered in an RF bank.

Ballooning Loans

These loans are offered to finance customers who cannot make a large payment if the loan is fully amortized (paid back with interest) over a period of 7 years, for example. The solution is to amortize the loan over a long period of time like 15 to 20 years. This way, the monthly payment will be much lower than if it were amortized over 7 years and the balance will be due in full on the seventh year. Naturally, the loan principal will not change much over 7 years. Some bankers believe that the 7-year period will give the bank a chance for recourse in case the customer situation or business conditions change. In fact, in some cases the customer after 7 years will attempt to refinance with his current bank or another bank. If the customer's financial condition is still viable the bank will be able to renew the loan. If the customer is not creditworthy, the bank will not be able to refinance that loan. In many cases, that customer may not be bankable at other banks and will resort to defaulting on the loan.

In an RF banking environment the structure of the LARIBA RF finance model requires that each loan is participated in fully until the end of the period. This will give the customer a clear view of the overhead and other costs as well as the sharing of the income generated from the leasing or rent of the facility. In an RF bank, it has been our experience to structure the LARIBA RF finance model over a period of 7 years but not more than 10 years. The reason for the 7 to 10 years is that things change; for example:

- The product life cycle of the business product may be entering into a declining phase.
- The economy may be slowing down.
- The business owner/customer changes his or her values due to life and business pressures and ends up trying to leave the business in a way that may reduce the business profit.

That is why it is recommended that in an RF bank the RF financing of businesses should range from 7 to 10 years in duration and should not be done in a balloon payment format and the financing should be structured in a true RF way using the LARIBA RF finance model.

Automobile and Equipment Leasing

Automobile and equipment leasing offer many advantages like the acquisition of the car or the piece of equipment without having to pay too much of a down payment. The lease contract can be structured by a specialized attorney to take advantage of the lease as a tax deduction or a business expense, plus the important advantage of showing a better balance sheet because some of the lease commitments can be kept by creative accounting as an off-balance-sheet commitment.

The riba-based lease is structured based on three important factors:

1. The prevailing interest rate.
2. The purchase price at the beginning of the lease, which is taken as the current market value at the beginning of the lease.
3. The projected value of the car or the piece of equipment at the end of the lease which may be in two, three, or five years. This value is obtained by assuming a depreciation schedule for the car or the equipment.

Most leases, if not all, are riba-based financial leases. The finance company owns title to the car or the equipment and keeps its name on the title. It leases it to the user at a monthly rate that will include a finance charge portion based on the interest rate used to calculate the monthly payment. At the end of the lease, the customer returns the car or the piece of equipment and he walks away. However, the customer may be responsible for any excessive wear and tear over and above what was expected by the leasing company, the owner of the item leased. Examples are excessive miles driven over and above the agreed-upon limited miles per year, any paint and/or body damage, and any damage to the tires, car engine, and car systems over and above usual use.

The problem with leasing (also called financial leasing) in RF finance is the problem of renting money and not renting the use of the car. That rent of money at an interest rate does not change from car to car or from a geographical location to another—one with a vibrant economy and another with a weak economy, depending on the supply/demand and utility factors but it is dependent on the going interest rate on the day of the agreement. In the LARIBA RF model, we use the prevailing market lease rate from sources such as national car rental companies. The other problem is the projection of the depreciated car price three years or five years in the future on which the future value of the item is estimated. Only God knows what the price of an item will be a few days later, let alone if it is three or five years later. RF discipline requires that the price should be marked-to-market at the time of the termination of the lease and that should be the price used to figure out the monthly payments using the LARIBA RF finance model.

With the LARIBA RF finance model, the monthly payments over a five-year period would not be much different from the lease rate but at the end the customer owns the car or the equipment and does not have to go through the cost and inconvenience of estimating the item over utilization and the cost of replacing the overused items and the excess miles driven.

Mortgages

The most popular two types of mortgages are fixed-rate mortgages and adjustable-rate mortgages (ARMs).

The LARIBA RF finance model can be used to offer the same services. RF mortgages with a fixed long-term lease can replace the riba-based fixed-rate mortgage finance. In a riba-based mortgage, money is rented, but in an RF finance situation, the two important disciplines of Commodity Indexation and Marking-to-Market are applied, as detailed earlier in the book, to ascertain that the purchase of a house is not just a process of follow-the-herd mentality and renting money, but it is a process of investing wisely and prudently based on the actual rental rate derived from market research. This way, the home buyer will be saved from participating in a price bubble.

If the rental rate agreed upon is fixed, then that will offer the consumer a RF alternative to riba-based fixed-interest mortgages. If the rental rate agreed upon varies based on an index, then that will offer the consumer an RF alternative to the ARM that uses the renting money (riba) at a variable interest rate.

In addition to the preceding, the mortgage industry came up with a number of new product innovations. These are discussed next.

Home Equity Line of Credit (HELOC) These loans are designed to generate cash for the homeowner based on the fact that the house value on the market has appreciated and that resulted in a higher equity position for the homeowner. For example, if a homeowner bought a home in Texas for $150,000 and he invested 20 percent or $30,000 in 1985 and later on in 2000, his house value has appreciated to $250,000, that means that the owner now owns at least the $30,000 in original equity, the capital paid back over the years and the appreciation of the house. That means that the owner now owns at least $130,000 in equity.

If the owner wants to take advantage of this large equity to cash out funds that he needs he can apply for a line of credit that is collateralized by his home with a second lien on it. This loan can be in one of two forms. The first is a line of credit called a home equity line of credit abbreviated and is known in the industry as HELOC. These HELOC lines are usually approved based on the value of the house on the market and in relation to the equity accumulated in the house. The purpose of the HELOC does not have to be fully disclosed.

The other is a home equity loan that is fully amortized over a certain period of time and is analyzed and the purpose of applying for it is fully disclosed. As explained earlier, the line-of-credit approach allows the customer to withdraw money out of the bank and pays it back whenever he has the money. Customers pay interest on the money only for the time they used it. Many homeowners took advantage of these line-of-credit facilities called HELOCs; to finance the renovation of the house by adding an extra room, remodeling, and the like, which helps appreciate further the value of the house. Others used the money in speculative activities like buying more homes with as little equity as possible in order to repeat his own experience of home appreciation. This has contributed to the acceleration of the growth of the housing prices' bubble. Others simply took the money and speculated with it in the stock market or simply used the money to live a lavish life by extinguishing all those needs created by slick advertising about owning an expensive car and the like.

In summary, the consumers ended up using the excess home equity as a credit card because the interest rate charged was much lower than those charged by credit cards. The problem came when the HELOC is called by the bank and the resulting payment shock. Unfortunately, these HELOCs were called during the time of the bursting of the price housing bubble when the unthinkable occurred coupled with many homeowners losing their jobs. The net result was the inability of the homeowner to pay off the HELOC and the loss of the house through foreclosure.

HELOCs are not offered in an RF bank because these lines are in fact a clear process of renting money, which is the prohibited riba, encourage homeowners to spend more unnecessarily and drive the consumer in a deeper pit of debt that can result in consumers losing their homes at the time when the line is called off by the bank.

Home Equity Loan Home equity loans are loans granted by the bank in response to a formal loan application, which discloses the reason for applying for the loan and analyzes the capacity of the applicant to pay back the loan within his income and his obligations. In many cases bank policy can limit the loan to market value to 70 to 80 percent. In fact, some states, such as Texas, prohibit the cashing out of equity that would make the loan to value of the house exceed 80 percent. Further, Texas, as well as some other states, have installed many brakes to discourage and limit the use of the house as a credit card.

These home equity loans are acceptable in an RF bank as long as they are processed using the LARIBA RF finance model.

Reverse Mortgages Reverse mortgages are mortgages that were designed to meet the cash needs of retired persons who need the cash to meet their living needs in an economy that pays less than 1 percent on savings. The idea is that many retired members of the community have accumulated a significant equity in their homes because they have lived in these homes for 10 to 30 years or more and the mortgage owed on the house is either relatively very small (loan to value is 20 percent or less) or has been paid off. This loan was made attractive because if a retired person applies for a cash-out home equity loan, he may be denied because the income of that retired person does not give him enough capacity to repay the loan.

Reverse mortgages are loans given out and paid back not in cash monthly payments but in the form of adding the monthly payments to the loan, resulting in an increase in the loan to value. The proponents of reverse mortgages reason that by the time the retiree dies or vacates the house to a senior retirement or nursing home, the loan to equity would have increased to 80 percent. The financier sells the house and collects back the loan and a handsome capital gains profit due to the home price appreciation.

These loans may be useful in some special cases like meeting medical care bills, children's and grandchildren's needs, as well as the retiree's basic living needs. However, these loans can be used to take advantage of the retirees and to encourage them to spend more, especially when their emotions are more sentimental as they age. Many fraudulent abuses against the elderly have been perpetrated in the United States using reverse mortgages and resulted in the retiree and elderly community members ending up losing their life investment in their homes.

Reverse mortgages are not offered in an RF bank because of the many problems these loans create and again the concept of renting money and not regulating and managing the purpose of using the generated cash from the reverse mortgage loan. It is true that the reverse mortgage loan can be structured perfectly legitimately using the LARIBA RF finance model by selling shares of the house systematically to the financier. However, here the wisdom leans toward the purpose and the benefits as compared to the harms and not the mechanics of executing a financing process. Financing retired persons to meet their cash needs should be done in a careful and prudent way to define exactly what the cash needs are and the purpose of using this cash in light of the capacity of the elderly to pay back. That is exactly what RF banking and finance is all about.

Commercial Buildings Financing of a commercial building can readily be done in an RF finance format using the LARIBA RF finance model. If the commercial building is owner occupied, then the financial and credit analysis is made easier because the process involves the person applying for the financing. However, if the commercial building involves leasing it or units of it to others, the task becomes more tedious and involved. The analysis should involve the evaluation of each lease, the company that is leasing that space from the owner and its capacity to make lease payment as well as the length of the lease. Another important aspect in an RF bank financing is the nature of business conducted by those companies or individuals who are leasing the space to make certain that there are no violations of the values and tenets of RF financing and lifestyle, such as leasing to night clubs, liquor stores, payday check cashing, and lending stores that take advantage of the distressed and pawn shops.

Prudence in an RF bank recommends that the loan term should not exceed the length of the lease and that the total income collected from the leases should be 1.25 times the monthly payments of RofC and RonC in a LARIBA RF finance model.

Business Financing

Business financing in an RF setting does not only require the use of the LARIBA RF finance model but also the implementation of the Judeo-Christian-Islamic Shari'aa law that includes restrictions on dealing in prohibited businesses like alcohol, unfair commercial activities that take advantage of those who are in need, like payday lenders, pawn shops, professionals who take advantage of their customers, and businesses that are not fair to their customers and their employees.

Business financing in an RF setting requires that the business has accumulated documented operating hands-on experience complete with its documented financial results for at least two to three years. RF financing of start-up businesses is discouraged in an RF community bank because of the risks involved. Such start-up businesses are classified as potential subjects for RF venture capital financing using an RF investment bank setting where the risks are higher and the rewards as well as losses can be much higher.

Business financing to professionals like medical doctors, pharmacists, and entrepreneurs can be conducted in two ways. The first is the financing of the building that houses the business if applicable. That can be easily done using the LARIBA RF finance model. As to the business itself, thorough analysis based on at least two to three years of business operations, results and future potential should be conducted. The RF financing is done using the LARIBA RF finance model by conceptually sharing in the ownership of the business and sharing in the profits realized by the business as detailed in the LARIBA RF finance model.

Another important category of businesses is restaurants. Experience has shown us that private-label family restaurants can be a wonderful investment but require three important conditions to be realized:

1. A unique service environment, service style, product, recipe, and/or taste.
2. Enough private capital to keep the restaurant going for at least five to seven years because it takes that much time to develop repeat customers who get used to the service style and taste.
3. Experienced hands-on operator who runs the business personally with the family.

Financing such facilities can be classified as a venture capital type of investment and cannot be financed in an RF community bank setting. These can be financed only by an RF investment bank or RF finance company.

Franchise fast food restaurants can be a great foundation for building a community of entrepreneurs. These restaurants, which are operated by a national organization, have established a proven operating and financial track record and can be financed in an RF community bank. However, there are many guidelines that we have learned at the LARIBA System in our practice since 1987. These are:

- Many restaurants can be involved in selling or serving items that are prohibited by the Judeo-Christian-Islamic Shari'aa law like pork, bacon, and wine. Proper edicts (fatwas) must be obtained regarding each of these cases. Also, practical solutions can be offered. Examples are the use of halal (properly slaughtered) turkey bacon and sausages instead of regular pork-derived products and the suppression of advertising for pork and wine-related products in the menu with the consent and approval of the area manager of the franchise, which will eventually lead to no sales of these prohibited products.
- The operator of these franchises must have had at least three years of proven hands on operating experience in all aspects of the restaurant operation.
- The term of financing of such franchises should not exceed seven years for two important reasons:
  - The first is that the popularity of a certain franchise may decline over the years.
  - The second is that the character of the operator and business ethics may change over the years. That is why an RF community bank using the LARIBA RF finance model uses a maximum term of seven years to finance such facilities.

- The loan to business value for these facilities should be at least 40 to 50 percent in order to ascertain that the franchisee will give the business his or utmost best to make it a success.
- It is also preferred that the franchise operate in a real estate building owned by the franchisee.

Nonprofit and Religious Centers and School Financing

One of the goals of RF financing is to assist individuals and communities in their efforts to pursue and live an RF lifestyle. That includes worshipping and educating its followers and their children in the faith each community believes in. In that regard, RF banking is committed to facilitating the process of worship and assembly to perform worship practices and rituals in sanctuaries like temples, churches, masjids (mosques), schools, and community centers. In addition, RF banking and finance is keen to help facilitate the establishment of schools and educational institutes that enhance the process of general education with moral and ethical values derived from the faith these communities believe in without the slightest form of discrimination.

At LARIBA Bank of Whittier, we financed many worship and educational facilities like churches, masjids, and schools. In the process, we have perfected a methodology for RF financing of such nonprofit organizations. To start with, it should be acknowledged that operating a nonprofit organization is largely a voluntary activity that can change from time to time depending on the mood and motivation of the persons involved, the interpersonal relations and homogeneity of the leaders involved, the community, and the religious leaders involved. I was actively involved in this work for over 45 years since coming to the United States in 1968, when the American public knew very little about Islam and the Muslims. The lesson learned is that it is extremely challenging to manage such nonprofit organizations. Another important factor is the sensitivity and sometimes the religious restriction regarding the foreclosure of a place of worship or a religious school, let alone the reputation risk and challenge met by the RF bank when it forecloses on such places. The other challenge in that regard is that the RF bank is not in the business of operating such facilities knowing that it is prohibited, by regulations, for banks to enter into the operation of other nonbanking activities.

The first step in the process of financing these nonprofit organizations is to establish the size of the community that uses these facilities by asking questions like:

- How many worshippers come to the weekly congregational prayers and how much money in donations are collected on a weekly basis?

- How many attend the annual feast prayers and celebrations (like Christmas, Hanukkah, Eid-ul-Fitr, and Eid Ul Adha)?
- How many fund-raiser events are conducted annually, and how much money in donations is raised?
- Who is the religious leader in charge and his or her background and character?
- Who are on the board of directors and those who are the real responsible "movers and shakers" in the community?

After evaluating the community, interviewing its leaders and key members, and analyzing its operating and financial data, the RF bank's credit department decides if this is a community that the RF bank can proceed to look into financing its facility. If the answer is yes, the next step is to ask the leaders to look for three to five significant members of the community who are willing to cosign the financing documents as coborrowers. The RF banker makes it clear to each of the cosigners that he or she will be personally responsible for the financing they signed on, and that will appear on their credit report and will affect their borrowing ability in the market. For example, if the financing required is a $1 million, the community can find five members who will be responsible for $200,000 each to apply with the center or school for financing. The reason we recommend three to five and not one person or more than five is based on experience. Practical experience showed us, at the LARIBA System that if one is involved, that person may be accused and may in fact be tempted to act as if he owns the community and singularly decides for it. This eventually creates community breakdown, and that is not what we at the community RF bank are working hard for. However, if there are too many cosigners, the chance of infighting becomes greater and leads to the same bad results. Another important and fundamental value of involving cosigners is to test the commitment of the community leaders to the cause by signing their names on the bottom line of the credit facility. In fact, this "acid" test reflects, based on experience, the seriousness of the community leaders about the project that is under financing consideration. In fact, about two to three centers out of seven applying centers pass the test and are considered for further financing.

Finally, it should be stated that financing nonprofit faith-based organizations is a great enriching experience and the financial performance is impeccable—this is, of course, depending on whether the structure of the RF financing is done correctly.

Construction Financing

Construction financing in a community bank has to comply with regulatory requirements, which include many expensive procedures like assigning a construction consulting engineer or engineering firm that will be responsible for the follow-up and inspection of each step of the construction process. Funds allocated for construction financing are dispersed in stages. After the completion of each stage, the consulting engineer inspects the satisfactory completion of that stage and authorizes the disbursement of the funds necessary for the following stage. For example, after land preparations of the site, it has to be inspected by the engineer before funds necessary for funding the pouring of the concrete slab are approved for disbursement and so on. In a small community bank, that process can prove to be expensive for the bank and the customer. This may render the cost of financing a construction project in a small community bank more expensive than that for a large bank that has its own construction engineering department. That is why a creative solution to this problem was necessary.

The solution lies in analyzing the customer's particular situation. For example, if the customer is a medical doctor who runs his own business out of a medical services office, the value of the medical services business is appraised and the financing is done to create cash as a participant in that business using the LARIBA RF finance model. In an RF bank, the bank conceptually would buy shares in the business for a certain sum of money that can be used for construction. The customer becomes responsible for the construction and the quality of execution on his own. The risk to the bank is transferred from the bank to the customer and the cost of engineering supervision by the bank is drastically reduced. The building is inspected for occupancy by the customer through his own inspection engineer and confirmed by the local city inspectors. The shares that are conceptually bought by the bank are immediately sold back to the medical doctor and the income generated from the business is shared between the bank and the business until the principal is paid back and the construction is completed as stipulated by the LARIBA RF finance model is used. After the completion of construction, the building is financed using the LARIBA RF finance model. Another approach to the construction financing problem is applicable in the case of an RF finance company. In this case, the contractor needs of concrete, wood, drywall, plumbing supplies, and the like are purchased for the contractor and sold back to him using a murabha (cost-plus) RF finance model. At the end of the construction, the building would be financed using the LARIBA RF mortgage finance model.

In conclusion, the RF banker is called upon to find solutions to specific financing challenges as long as the RF banker understands the basics and foundations of the LARIBA RF finance model and the RF financing disciplines of:

- Not to get involved in a money renting scheme that is riba.
- Using the Commodity Indexation Discipline.
- Using the Marking-to-Market Discipline.

REVIEW QUESTIONS

1. What is overdraft protection offered by riba-based banks? Can it be offered in an RF bank? Why?
2. What is a line-of-credit, and how does it work? What is the downside of offering a line-of-credit?
3. What is a revolving line-of-credit? Please explain its features.
4. What is a working capital line of credit in a riba-based bank? Can it be offered in an RF bank? Please elaborate how it can be offered in an RF bank.
5. What is a construction financing line of credit? Can it be offered in an RF format?
6. What is an unsecured line of credit in a riba-based bank, and how it is done? Can it be offered in an RF bank?
7. How is auto and equipment leasing conducted in a riba-based format? Can it be done in an RF bank? How?
8. What are the types of mortgages available in a riba-based bank? How are mortgages offered in an RF bank?
9. What is an ARM mortgage, and can it be done in an RF platform?
10. What is a reverse riba mortgage? How does it work? Why is it offered? Can it be offered in an RF format? What wisdom should be implemented while conducting a reverse mortgage financing?
11. What is a home equity line of credit (HELOC) in a riba-based bank? Can it be offered in an RF format, and what guidelines should be taken in consideration?
12. What is a home equity loan? Can it be offered in an RF platform and how?
13. How is a commercial building financed in an RF format? What parameters should be carefully considered in the RF financial analysis while financing an owner-occupied commercial building? What are these parameters in the case of financing a commercial building that leases to a number of companies and practitioners?
14. How are businesses financed in an RF format? What precautions should be taken in the RF analysis of financing a private-label family restaurant as compared to a franchise restaurant?
15. How are nonprofit organizations like places of worship and schools financed by the LARIBA System?

CHAPTER 17

The RF Approach to Handling Troubled and Nonperforming Credits (Loans)

One of the unpleasant experiences in the banking and finance business is a nonperforming credit (loan), meaning that the customer does not make the monthly payments on time and eventually stops making these payments altogether for a number of reasons like his financial inability to do so. In this chapter, I will share with you case studies that will hopefully show the benefits of the RF culture, mentality, and approaches that have been employed while operating the LARIBA System since 1987 to resolve this challenge.

Nonperforming credits (loan) represent a significant drag on the profitability of the bank and the financial institution. These nonperforming credits may eventually result in reducing the bank capital, which may lead to the need to raise more capital or the closure of the bank.

The standard approach to nonperforming credits in a riba-based bank is to notify the customer and remind him of the covenants of the credit agreement and ending with transferring the loan to the legal department to take action. In most cases, the attorneys in the legal department start by filing a lawsuit to recover the assets using the collateral pledged against the credit facility or the other assets owned by the customers in order to recover as much as possible of that loan. Legal proceedings are necessary and useful but should be used as a last resort and in a wise way based on analyzing the reasons the customer is not keeping the contractual commitment as well as balancing the costs and benefits of recovering the nonperforming loan using legal proceedings. Nonperforming loans are due to one or all the following reasons:

- Imprudent credit analysis.
- Character of the customer.
- The change in the general economic environment in the community and the country.

The challenge of handling a nonperforming credit (loan) is one of the real trying experiences when the RF banking and finance values claimed by its proponents are tested. In conventional riba-based banking, money is rented. The main concern of the conventional banker is to collect the monthly rental due as calculated on a daily basis. In RF banking, the payments represent the participation of the RF bank in the income generated from the usufruct of the asset financed. If the asset financed does not produce income due to economic factors that are outside the control of the customer or due to other reasons, it becomes the responsibility of the RF banker along with the customer to wisely analyze and evaluate the situation and come up with a well-thought-out plan to resolve that unfortunate situation. That brings in the most important rule in banking in general, in both conventional and RF banking, which is the Know Your Customer (KYC) rule. This rule requires the banker to intimately know everything about the customer not only when the credit is granted but on a continual basis.

In RF banking, this is considered a must and as part of the regular audits performed to ascertain that the values of RF banking are implemented in full. The process of granting credit starts with evaluating the character, experience, lifestyle, value system, and reputation of the customer. Every customer is required to submit a detailed CV/resume to allow the credit department to evaluate the customer's achievements, employment history, and stability. In addition, a thorough knowledge of the customer's family and family lifestyle is assessed. The credit department interviews the customer and, if possible, the family. In the case of financing a business, the credit department requires at least a three years of hands-on experience in operating or working in a similar business. The main objective here is to make the customer a true family member of the RF bank's community. This is enhanced by sharing with the customer the RF values and the RF bank's main goal of assisting community members to live an RF lifestyle. The credit department evaluates the reaction of the customer and his commitment to these values.

After approving the financing, the RF banker is trained to stay in close and continual touch with the customer so that he can detect any financial or operating problems before they grow and become difficult to resolve. The RF banker is trained to come to the rescue of the customer in a timely manner. That is why RF banking is designed to be community based and does not aspire to become a mega-bank where the customer is reduced from being a member of a family and is treated as such to becoming a number in a computer database. In difficult circumstances that are usually faced in business and in life, the value of an RF banker's acting as a coach, a partner, and a sincere participant trying to offer ideas and solutions and the value of dealing with an RF bank becomes most apparent and useful. That is not enough because a conventional riba-based bank may be able to offer the same service, but what is important in RF banking is the mentality of that RF banker, which leads him to believe that he is a real partner in that business, and that he is responsible for that credit personally because he is the one that initiated it and was responsible for its existence. In addition, the RF bank is designed as a smaller-size complete unit with its private RF bankers who developed the business, RF credit analysts who have participated in analyzing and evaluating the business, and the RF bank managers who approved the credit are all present in person to assist the customer in case of trouble. The RF banker is not trained to get even, to run away claiming irresponsibility for the bad performance of a credit, or to try to squeeze as much as he can to get as much money as possible back to the bank. The mentality is simply to help, to decide if that business was troubled because of the general economic conditions in the community, the country, or the world or because of operating problems within the business to decide if that business can continue, if it can be restructured, and what plans should be implemented.

RESOLVING THE PROBLEM OF NONPERFORMING CREDITS (LOANS)

In RF banking and finance, nonperforming loans are the result of sudden changes in the economic conditions that may be out of control of the customer and the bank. In an RF bank, the challenge becomes not how to take the customer to court in order to recover as much as the bank can of the balance of its credit (loan), but rather to work with the customer in order to help him or her in meeting his or her commitments without destroying the future of that honorable customer. The reason the customer is described here as honorable is the fact that the relationship between the customer and the RF bank was developed after a thorough evaluation of that customer's ethical and moral values, character, and professional capabilities. This approach can be challenging because the accounting standards and the regulators have set rules and regulations to go by. For example, if a customer stops making the monthly payments for six months, this credit must be charged off. The challenge faced by an RF banker is immense because the banker has to comply with the laws and regulations and, at the same time does not want to destroy the future of the customer who has gotten into problems because of factors that are in most cases in an RF platform outside his control and not of his own doing.

The strategy used in our RF banking practice consists of the following steps:

1. Reserve enough funds to meet unexpected nonperforming loans. The allowance for loan and lease losses (ALLL) is not only evaluated as a percentage of the size of the loan portfolio, usually taken as 1.5 to

2 percent of the loan portfolio, but by using historical loss experience of the RF bank plus a probabilistic approach to the changing factors that may impact the different types of political, economic, and environmental factors and the loan sectors in the loan portfolio. The probabilistic approach lists all environmental parameters that may impact the loan portfolio like the direction of the economy, energy price projections, expected levels of unemployment, occupancy expectations of commercial buildings, and so on. Executives, credit managers, private bankers, and credit analysts are supplied with a critical analysis and review of the economic factors and how they may unfold. The economic salient features report is based on reviewing economic research by specialized research institutions, respected publications like the *Financial Times,* the *Economist*, the *Wall Street Journal,* and other, similar publications. Each member of the group is asked to fill out a matrix that includes his or her expectation of the direction of change of each economic parameter. These matrixes are integrated and a weighted average is obtained, with weights allocated based on the experience of each group member. These probabilistic values are applied to calculate the projected loss factor and subsequently a conservative estimate of ALLL is calculated. In an RF bank, ALLL can be as high as 3.5 percent of the loan portfolio. This has been a real important factor in sailing our RF bank through the financial meltdown of 2008—the most difficult economic downturn since the depression of 1929.

2. Maintain a civil and family-based relationship with the customer, and never treat that customer as a bad person because he or she cannot make the monthly payments. The issue of character in an RF setting is moot because it was settled during the thorough evaluation process that preceded the granting of the credit. The problem here is to continue to discover ways and means to help the customer to come back to his normal life as an honorable and respected citizen while insisting on recovering the bank's credit. When good and sincere will is expressed and implemented, and the customer is treated as an honorable family member, that customer will cooperate and return that goodwill with sincere cooperation to recover the credit fully.
3. Offer help to resolve customer's chronic needs especially in cases when the customer is laid off or the customer loses a major contract that may be the reason for nonperformance. In an RF bank setting, a special fund called the M-fund (M stands for miskeen, which means "the needy"), which is an assistance organization, may be able to offer interest-free loans to the needy. This fund is capitalized from donations by members of the community, unavoidable interest income that is earned by the RF institution, and late payment fees and penalties charged to chronic abusers of RF facilities.

4. Exercise extreme patience, sympathy, and understanding. Resolving a nonperforming credit can take two to three years because that is the time needed for the economic cycle to start an upturn.
5. Do not resort to a lawyer unless all efforts fail and the customer tries to get away from meeting his or her commitment. Attorneys are expensive and lawsuits are difficult and time consuming, drain the valuable time of the bank's staff, and usually the return on that investment is negligible except in cases that involve intentional fraud or bad faith.

CASE STUDIES

The following are real-life cases that were faced during the financial and monetary meltdown of 2008. These cases are detailed in order to present to the reader another aspect of RF banking and finance as a new brand of banking. In many of these troubled loans, the reader will feel the compassion and passionate mercifulness of the RF banking brand and the role of the M-fund.

The first loan involves an inventor who lost his orders due to the economic meltdown. This impacted his ability to make payments on his loan to finance the manufacture of his product. Please read how the situation was handled by the well-trained RF bankers.

The second case involves what the RF bankers did with the many customers who lost their jobs and could not make monthly payments. Please note how the number of those customers was minimized through prudent RF finance model valuation and through proactive assistance of the RF bankers.

The third case involves a significant and successful automobile dealer with many showrooms around the area. His business was hit by the economic slowdown, and he said that he simply had no money to help him pay the credit he received from the RF bank in a timely manner. Please read how the RF banker and RF bank managers handled that situation in an amicable way that did not incur any litigation cost and that brought back the customer's credit and the RF bank's money. It is true that it took about three years, but the long wait was worth it.

The fourth case was for a significant and successful professor of medicine and practitioner with significant assets. He and his partners bought a good-sized hospital in Orange County, but he faced many challenges of corruption and lawsuits. Please read how the patience, determination, and respectful passion helped recover the loan.

1. A customer started a new business to manufacture a new generation of lightweight video cameras that can transmit live video reports from the scene. The customer applied for a $100,000 financing for his company's

capital needs. The contract he signed with a major U.S. government entity was canceled due to budget cuts associated with the 2008 financial meltdown. We met with the customer and discussed with him solutions to resolve the problem. We found that he had a $50,000 equity in his house. We proceeded to RF mortgage finance a home equity loan collateralized by a second lien on the house using the LARIBA RF finance model. He could not make payments on the remaining $50,000. The $50,000 balance was charged off. We recommended that we can help him through the M-fund by paying $200 per month until his fortunes changed. It is important to note that this customer was not a Muslim. He was deeply touched. He voluntarily proceeded to make a $200 payment for 18 months, and he voluntarily increased the payments to $400 a months. He has been consistent, and he intends to pay off the balance of $36,000 soon after a new contract is signed with another entity.

2. During the 2008 financial meltdown, a number of homeowners were laid off. Many of these were accomplished information technology (IT) engineers who had RF mortgages with LARIBA. Instead of starting foreclosure proceeding against them, they were contacted by an RF resolution specialist. They were asked how much they could pay without straining their budget. The M-funds helped them compliment what they could afford and helped them make the monthly payment on their mortgages. Many of them found a job within two to three months and paid the M-fund RF (interest-free) loans in full. They told us that they would never forget that favor. We told them that we asked the reward from God, and we asked them to remember us in their prayers and in their supplications.
3. A major and significant new car dealer who operated a number of large car dealerships for Chrysler, General Motors, and Volvo was forced to close a number of his dealerships because the car manufacturer was deeply impacted by the 2008 financial meltdown. He owed us $450,000. He came to visit us and was really devastated. We sympathized with him. We told him that he had proven to be a successful and honorable entrepreneur before, and he definitely would recover and be successful again. This customer was not a Muslim, and he is a devout believer in Jesus. We charged off the credit (loan). We worked with him for three years. When he settled his major financial problems, we identified a real estate property that had enough equity to finance it using the $450,000 credit he owed us. The financing was completed, and the full credit was recovered.
4. A successful medical doctor and a professor of medicine had a credit balance of $350,000 with us. He had over $15 million invested in a local hospital. Unfortunately, he faced major fraudulent challenges while trying to run the hospital. He took the perpetrators to court.

> In the meantime, he could not make the payments. He belongs to the Hindu faith. We charged off the loan, but we never stopped to stay in touch with him and his wife to help heal the pain he and his family suffered. He was told by our RF bankers that we believe in him, his professionalism, and his moral values and commitment to his promises. After two years, he won the lawsuit and paid his credit in full.

The preceding cases detail the successes we achieved and were blessed with. That does not mean that we have not had a few setbacks. These setbacks were not created by insufficient and improper prudence in evaluating and approving the credit. It was based on an important and significant factor that has to do with people. No one can predict when, why, and in what direction peoples' character and values will change. That is why we learned not to finance small businesses for more than seven years—because people change. We also learned that a balloon credit given to a business is not a wise idea because no one can predict the product life cycle of the product they sell at that business. One important thing we disciplined ourselves on doing was documentation of experiences and sharing with staff in order to build a unique banking experience: the RF banking model.

We are thankful to have been able to recover all these nonperforming loans without spending any money on attorneys, which kept our costs to a minimum, preserved our relationship with our customers without burning any bridges, and reassured ourselves of the value of RF banking disciplines and culture.

One last comment regarding reduction of overhead in an RF bank or financial institution. We all know that in difficult economic periods, many troubled organizations resort to reducing overhead, starting by laying off a portion of their staff. We at the LARIBA RF banking system do not believe in this solution. We believe that when we employ a staff member, we make a commitment to him or her to become a member of our family and to allow him or her to start a family and feel secure. During the difficult years after the meltdown of 2008, we started voluntarily reducing the wages of our executives and not our middle managers and staff. We figured that the executives have enough flexibility and resources to help them meet the reduction of their salaries, but not the younger staff who have limited resources and who have families to take care of and households to maintain.

We at the LARIBA RF finance system firmly believe that this attitude, culture, and faith in our Creator are the reasons for the great blessings showered on us as a reward from God, leading to the successes we have achieved with the humble resources that are available to us. We thank God immensely for His guidance and for the best of all gifts we ask Him to maintain: the gift of wisdom with humbleness.

REVIEW QUESTIONS

1. What is a nonperforming credit (loan)?
2. What are the reasons behind a loan's becoming nonperforming?
3. What procedure does the riba-based bank use to recover nonperforming loans? How do these procedures compare to those used by RF bankers?
4. What is ALLL? How is it calculated in a riba-based bank?
5. How is ALLL estimated in the LARIBA RF System?
6. What are the procedures and processes used by the LARIBA RF System to resolve non-performing loans?
7. What is the unique process used for troubled loan recovery at the LARIBA RF System?
8. Please share with us a situation of a nonperforming loan you have encountered and how it was handled by a riba-based bank. Please share with us how this situation would have been handled using the RF strategies discussed in this chapter.

CHAPTER 18

Visions for the Future of RF Banking

THE 2008 GLOBAL ECONOMIC AND FINANCIAL MELTDOWN

As I started writing the first edition of this book in 2009, the world was experiencing the deepest economic and financial meltdown since the Great Depression of 1929. This meltdown has touched every citizen in the world because of the efficient communication systems that have successfully interconnected the world's financial and banking systems. It is unfortunate and sad to experience the laying off of many employees who had nothing to do with what happened; the loss of their homes through foreclosures; the decline in living standards, not only in the developed world but also in the developing countries; and the increase in poverty worldwide.

The core reason for what happened has been a culture of "making" money on money by renting it with interest (ribit/riba) and speculating with it instead of working hard to earn it. The financial and banking system in the United States is well designed and regulated. Unfortunately, it has been abused by some who claimed that they could create money by using hedge funds, financial speculation, and gambling. The unfortunate thing is that many pension funds joined the party because they were impressed by the high returns realized by these speculative investment funds. These pension fund managers should have known better; they were entrusted with the future retirement funds of millions of Americans. Many of those who speculated and gambled with people's money and life savings as well insurance premiums paid by the public to insurance companies to protect against unexpected catastrophes in the future did not abide fully by the regulations. They had the wrong idea about money and what money is all about. They believed that if you have a lot of money, you can make a lot more—not necessarily by investing in productive activities, but by using options, derivatives, and financial gambling techniques that speculated on what the future holds. The 2008 meltdown proved that this was the wrong way to look at and invest money. It is unfortunate to report that as I am writing this second edition of the book in 2014, the situation has not changed much. The government successfully rescued many mega-banks and insurance companies, as well automobile manufacturers, using creative monetary policy. However, banks are still using derivatives and options to hedge against fluctuations in interest rate and to earn money through fees, spreads, and commissions on trading stocks, bonds, and commodities. Major banks are using interest rate hedging to give loans at artificially reduced interest rates for periods of 5 to 10 years. Mega-banks have the capital, staff, and know-how to do this. Small community banks do not have this luxury available to them, which allows larger banks to charge a fixed interest rate for 7 to 10 years. Small banks cannot fix rates for such long periods of time and end up losing customers to the larger banks.

It is interesting to note that only 25 employees in the Financial Products division at AIG (AIGFP)—the huge international insurance company that employed 113,000 professionals worldwide and was rescued by the U.S. government in 2009 and recovered fully three to four years later but as a smaller-size company—were responsible for bringing the whole company down. One of their tools was a product they designed to speculate on the movements in the levels of market interest rates. For example, one of their bets would result in a profit or a loss of $500 billion if interest rates changed by a small percentage in either direction. This loss, realized by the company, is equivalent to paying for the loss and damage caused by 62 California-size earthquakes.[1] Unfortunately, AIG grew so big that even with the most sophisticated management and supervisory tools and techniques, no one could regulate the activities of this small group of employees.

What is most sad, concerning, and disappointing is the fact that we all were warned many times about the outcome of such speculative activities in the market. Those who were in charge used a bandage approach to fix these problems temporarily. No one took the time or spent the effort needed to meticulously and permanently fix the root causes of the problem. Here is a list of some of the small earthquakes that introduced us to what was waiting to happen in 2008:

- The savings-and-loan junk bond crisis ($240 billion loss in 1989).
- The German commodity and metals company Metallgesallschaft ($1 billion loss in 1993).
- Barings Bank (speculation by one of its traders in Asia cost more than $410 million).
- Procter & Gamble (loss of $160 million in 1994).
- Orange County, California ($1.7 billion loss in 1995).
- Long-Term Capital Management Corporation ($4 billion loss in 1998).

- Global Crossing Corporation (billions lost in 2001).
- Enron Corporation (billions lost in 2001).
- WorldCom Corporation ($3 billion lost in 2002).
- Société Générale unauthorized trading ($7 billion lost in 2007).

Analysts in most of these cases concluded that the main reasons for not avoiding these losses were management's lack of clear and thorough understanding of the products and the risks involved, and the faulty assumptions used in structuring these speculative financial products.

THE MEGA-BANKS AND FINANCIAL INSTITUTIONS

The primary reason for these mega-losses is believed to have been the lack of good and responsible judgment by those who were in charge. Many reasoned that what happened was due to the lack of suitable government regulations. That may be partially true, especially in the cases of hedge funds and derivatives and associated speculative financial products. The real fact of the matter is that the prevailing culture of renting money prompted many money managers to believe that money can reproduce and become productive if it is placed in speculative and "smart" products. As we detailed in this book, money is only a tool—a measuring device—and it does not reproduce unless it is invested in a productive activity that adds value to the economy of the community and the country. Theirs was an ill judgment because speculation and its tools are a zero-sum game. Those who outsmarted other money managers came away with huge profits at the expense of huge losses by others who made the opposite bet. As the hedge fund industry grew bigger, it dabbled in currency speculation, as happened in the 1997–1998 Asian currency crisis, which brought down the Asian economies and many Asian countries are still feeling its economic ripple effects until today in 2014. When the leaders of Asia complained bitterly about the need to stop these huge gambling activities and the way these activities were impoverishing their economies and other small and developing countries' economies, they were lectured by the self-appointed and self-serving "free market" advocates appearing in popular TV networks and major financial newspapers and magazines and were marginalized. As the problem grew even bigger, these hedge funds did the unimaginable by bringing down the economies of the United States and the world in 2008, followed by many countries in the European Union like Greece, Spain, Portugal, and Italy.

No government can issue regulations that would guarantee good judgment. Good judgment has to do with a value system taught at home by the parents, by the values taught as families worship and become enriched spiritually, by the standards set by the school system and its teachers, and by the university professors who teach finance in business schools. Judgment has to do with the prevailing culture, which is nurtured by the media that defines the norms of what is considered an acceptable behavior and lifestyle.

THE CULTURE OF RENTING MONEY WITH RIBIT/RIBA

As we sort out and sift through the events that led to the financial earthquake of 2008 and the various remedies used to fix it in the United States—the most important of which was the quantitative easing (QE) programs, which are built on printing more money to buy fixed-income securities to create market activity—we conclude that there must be an optimum size for a company or a bank, beyond which the company becomes inefficient and difficult to manage and may become a great liability to the economy as a whole (as in the cases of AIG and Citigroup in 2008 and JPMorgan Chase and many European banks in 2013). The towns and cities of the United States were built by community building-and-loan societies, which gathered the community's savings and invested them prudently back in these communities to finance the building of homes, cars, home mortgages, businesses, and other community needs for people who live in the community and who are known to the community bankers. Many of these savings-and-loan local community banks were taken over by the big banks like Citibank, Bank of America, and JPMorgan Chase. The progression of growth in the size of these banks tempted management to make more money by controlling more money. It was done first by becoming the large and certified banker of the government and then the preferred bank of the large corporations because they offered larger loans at lower interest rates and costs through their vast networks worldwide. Instead of large corporations supporting the local communities by using the services of their local community banks, savings-and-loan associations, and credit unions, they all migrated to the big banks.

As these big banks ran into no other areas for growth, they started to focus on the local communities and the small investors by essentially gobbling up most of the small community banks and savings-and-loan branches. They lured the gullible and simple law-abiding citizens to do business with them through slick advertising and marketing tools that included one of Chase Bank's promotion campaigns paying $200 as a reward to those who opened a checking account with them. Of course, the bank turned around and charged a hefty service charge and fees for nonsufficient funds checks in order to collect this bait money back and more. Another example is credit cards, which were originally designed and introduced to the market to facilitate the day-to-day buying needs of the consumer and were changed into instruments to encourage small-size consumers to borrow money and consume more—without being told the truth about the high costs of borrowing via credit cards. University and high school students were offered credit cards. Many of them did not qualify on their own merit; they were sent credit cards by mail because the companies knew that their parents would foot the bill. Many parents were surprised to receive their children's large credit card bills, which had to be paid to save their sons' and daughters' financial reputation and future credit.

Credit cards were also used to lure consumers by offering zero interest charges for six months. In fact, many who looked for RF financing options fell for that advertisement and signed up because on the surface it appeared to be interest free. However, the card issuers did not make it clear to the consumer that after six months the interest rate would go to, say, 8 percent, and that if there were a delinquency, the rate would reach as high as 28 percent. All of these "unimportant" details were printed in tiny letters that could hardly be read, to "comply" with strict consumer compliance regulations. The new Consumer Finance Protection Bureau (CFPB) has since issued regulations to credit card issuers to print disclosures in the same size font as the rest of the monthly invoice, and the disclosure should be placed in a spot that can easily draw the attention of the consumer. The only reason a credit card company would change interest rates arbitrarily and charge a lot of fees is that the company is in the business of renting money that borders on defrauding people, by seducing them to spend more so that the companies can make more money. It is surprising to observe that an average citizen with humble income and assets is allowed to own 10 credit cards (and maybe more) and accumulate a debt of more than $100,000, as we experienced with the many decent fellow citizens who called us at LARIBA and the Bank of Whittier to help them sort out their personal financial problems.

Perhaps the saddest of all has been the way major banks handle overdrafts (nonsufficient funds checks written by customers who do not have enough money in their accounts). In 2009, U.S. banks and credit unions made over $38.5 billion in overdraft fees, 90 percent of which was paid by 10 percent of customers, according to a Moebs Services survey featured in the *Financial Times*.[2] This number has not changed much in 2014.[3] The survey of more than 2,000 depository institutions found that the national median overdraft fee rose by one dollar to $26 in 2009, with larger institutions charging a median of $35 per overdraft. It also found that 44.5 percent of all institutions have overdraft income greater than net income. The highest overdraft fees were charged by the largest banks, said Moebs. At banks with assets greater than $50 billion—a group including Citigroup, Bank of America, JPMorgan Chase, and Wells Fargo—the median overdraft fee is set at $33. At Bank of America, a customer overdrawn by as little as $6 could trigger a $35 penalty. If the customer does not realize they have a negative balance and continues spending, they could incur that fee as many as 10 times in a single day, for a total of $350. Failing to repay the overdraft within a few days results in an additional $35 penalty. Conceptually, banks can be looked upon to be officially in the business of renting money (riba/ribit) and not in the real business they were created to do: investing in the real economy of the local communities.

As if that were not enough, a wonderful government program designed to help students who are in dire need to finance their education at low interest rates was also abused by those who love to rent money. The student loan program became an easy outlet for students to live it up, to spend more, and in some cases use the money as a down payment for a car or a house by also using the subprime home mortgage facilities. The daughter of a friend of mine, who was only 26 years old, graduated with a law degree from a prime university that cost her $350,000. She financed this huge debt with a student loan. The sad part of the story is that she could not find a job. One can only wonder at how university graduates can start their careers and a family while owing these huge sums of money.

It must also be said that the student loan facility has helped inflate tuitions at universities and costs on campus. The culture of renting money and of spending today to pay later (with interest) has taken over our American and for that matter world cultures. The American lifestyle that once called for students to work hard while going to schools and colleges, taking part-time jobs as dishwashers, distributers of the morning papers on different routes using their bicycles early in the morning before school starts, cleaning crews, waiters at restaurants, and tutors to help finance their education has largely gone by the wayside.

Perhaps the saddest part of this culture of renting money was accepting speculation and gambling techniques as a legitimate way of "making" money without having to work hard to "earn" it. These techniques were given fancy names and legitimate theories by distinguished professors at very prestigious universities. Investment bankers on Wall Street hired the brightest mathematicians and statistical analysis experts who graduated from the best universities in America and the world, such as Caltech (the California Institute of Technology, Pasadena, California, where Einstein was a visiting scientist), to work on these schemes and algorithms of gambling and speculation techniques, using the same theories, algorithms, and solutions that are applied in the gambling casino industry. These talented graduates were recruited to devise more sophisticated tools to outsmart others with money in order to win and "make" more money, instead of using their wonderful talents and education to design, for example, a better and more energy-efficient lifestyle, to develop ways to eradicate poverty and to teach the future generation.

The son of a friend of mine is a gifted mathematician. He was offered a multimillion-dollar-per-year job at a major investment bank in New York to work on these mathematical models. As he explained it, one can only wonder at the way the stock market and the bond market were turned into a large gambling casino. It is puzzling to learn that an investment bank could justify this large salary for a young university graduate who has no hands-on practical experience and who did not even have to assume any risk—personal or otherwise! This culture proliferated throughout the economy in America and the world, including developing countries. Medical doctors have to charge their patients and insurance providers a lot of money, which they turn around and largely pay back to (possibly) the same insurance company, to protect them and their families against malpractice lawsuits.

Probably the saddest part of all is the mirage of wealth that many thought they had on paper for years, only to discover that it was just paper wealth. Unfortunately, that discovery came a bit late for the majority of the Baby Boomer investors, who were preparing to retire just as the bubble burst in 2008.

THE RF LIFESTYLE

The Lifestyle of the Judeo-Christian-Islamic Value System

As has been stressed throughout this book, the Judeo-Christian-Islamic value system prohibits us from participating in the culture of renting money. Perhaps one of the most important prohibitions in the Jewish Bible (*Exodus: Chapter* 22, *verses 24–26*), the Christian Bible (*Exodus 22:25, Leviticus 25:35–37, Deuteronomy 23:19–20, Nehemiah 5:1–13, Psalm 15, Proverbs 28:8, Ezekiel 18:5–18, Habakkuk 2:6–7, Luke 6:27–36*) and the Qur'aan (*Chapter II—Al-Baqarah 275-278, Chapter III—Alee Imraan—The Family of Mary & Jesus (the family of Imraan): 3:130, Chapter IV—An-Nissa'aa (Women): 4:161, Chapter XXX—Ar-Rum (The Romans): 30:39*) is the prohibition of *ribit* (Old Testament) or *riba* (the Qur'aan).

As explained in Chapter 2, we know from the original Jewish teachings that a person of the Jewish faith who participates in ribit cannot stand as a witness in a Jewish court; the Old Catholic teachings (before the fifteenth century C.E.) held that a person who deals in ribit is denied a Catholic burial. In the Qur'aan, charging of ribit/riba is one of the most severe offenses against God.

As discussed in great detail throughout the book, ribit/riba, according to Judaic, Christian, and Muslim teachings (which this book has pioneered calling Judeo-Christian-Islamic values) can be defined as the act of renting money at a price called *interest rate*. In the old days, the word *usury* was derived from the act of paying a price (interest) for the use of money. We also know that today's money is a thing, a man-made currency. It is fungible, just as an apple is. One cannot rent an apple from another, and the same applies to money. The minute money is handed over to another person, it becomes that person's responsibility to invest it prudently, and it is the responsibility of those who give it in trust (the bankers and investors) to users (the borrowers) to handle it prudently.

That is why today's culture, which emphasizes spending as much as you can today by renting money with interest from banks, by using credit cards, and by using the family's home as a credit card (home equity line of credit and home equity loans), is frowned upon and prohibited by all faiths, especially those in the Judeo-Christian-Islamic value system. Money is a measuring device that quantifies the success or failure of an investment. It is not for hire or rent to the highest bidder (at the highest interest rate), and it can be used for food to survive. If we had evaluated the purchase of each item, based on its utility as measured by its actual market rent (rent of a car, a house, or a business, according to the Marking-to-Market and Commodity Indexation Disciplines (discussed in the book), we would have been saved from the wrath of speculation and from the deep holes of debt many of our community members and our beloved country and countries of the world are suffering from. That is why Jesus (pp) took it upon himself to drive the money changers out of the temple.

It is believed that one of the important elements in solving the unfortunate financial meltdown—which started in 2008, and its ripple effects are still felt in all corners of the world in 2014—is to simply reverse the trend of mergers and acquisitions that caused the financial institution to grow so large that it became difficult to manage and regulate. It is sincerely believed that it is the responsibility of the government regulators, through their periodic examinations, to decide whether an institution has outgrown its ability to manage risk. Time and again we were taught—by the hard school of loss of people's money and assets—that the investment banking culture is completely different from that of the commercial banker. Based on my own experience while working with Smith Barney and Citigroup, it is evident that investment bankers and commercial bankers have two different temperaments, risk tolerances, and professional purposes. It was proven that the two cultures cannot be merged or mixed. Bank of America tried it with Charles Schwab and failed in the 1980s; Citibank and Smith Barney tried and failed to succeed at the dawn of the twenty-first century; and now Bank of America, after merging with Merrill Lynch after the 2008 meltdown, is once again finding out that what we learned in the late 1970s and early 1980s still holds true. Perhaps we should respect the experience that led to the *Glass-Steagall Act*, which installed a thick wall between the two activities after the Great Depression.

SOME ADVICE FOR THE NEWCOMERS TO THE RF LIFESTYLE

It would be useful to bring to the attention of all people who have decided to join the RF lifestyle a few recommendations as to what to do. We need not to overindulge. We need to live within our means, to stop over borrowing. We should not use credit cards as a means of borrowing, but should use credit cards judiciously and pay off credit card purchases within a month to avoid paying interest. We need to save (for a "rainy day") 10 cents of every dollar we earn. We should not panic and sell stock portfolios "low" nor invest in the stock market once we are too old for the risk required. (The formula recommended is to subtract your age from your family's life expectancy—for example, if your family's life expectancy is 75 and you are 65 years old, the maximum exposure to investing in stocks should be 75 minus 65, or 10 percent of your total assets.) We should learn and teach our children that life and coexistence with others should bear personal sacrifices and not selfishness. These attitudes of "me first" have been the root causes for the reduction of birth rates in developing countries, the alarming rates of breakup of families, and the high divorce rates in many communities worldwide. Furthermore, we should strictly advise our children to stop taking excessive student loans to live it up. It is better for a student to graduate in six years with a part-time job and no debt than in four years with $120,000 in student loans. We need to help each other, to buy within our communities, to reinvest in our communities, and to do business with our local community banks and credit unions. We need to help the elderly, who were forced to take a huge income cut because of the reduction of interest rates on CDs, their major source of living income, from an average of 5 percent before the meltdown in 2008 to an average of 0.65 percent. That is, if a retiree had saved $300,000 for retirement, his annual income before 2008 was approximately $15,000 a year ($1,250 a month) compared to approximately $2,000 a year ($162.50 a month!) after the meltdown and the reduction of rates on CDs until today in 2014! It is sincerely hoped that the elderly Americans who built the American dream, and who live on Social Security and the few dollars they get from that reduced "interest" on their small savings, will be helped and taken care of by their children and grandchildren—the younger generations. After all, they are the ones who built the America we all enjoy today.

The RF bankers, RF bank branches, and Internet services should also become very active in the popularization of a new lifestyle—one that believes in minimum debt and in paying off that debt as soon as possible, in saving for the future, in living within our means while consuming less, in offering healing and helping hands and resolution plans to those who need help, in encouraging students to do without student loans unless it is absolutely necessary. As RF bankers, we should lead a compassionate life that cares about others and can be taken as a model for others to emulate. For example, RF bank offices should be efficient and well-appointed but not luxurious, the cars driven by RF bankers should be energy efficient and humble, the RF bankers' entertainment and business expenses should be simple and kept low, and the attitude should be humble. This can most effectively be done in collaboration with local community and religious leaders in a wonderful interfaith cooperation that will lead to peace, prosperity, mutual respect, and a wonderful life for all.

REVIEW QUESTIONS

1. Explain the difference in the meaning of "making money" and "earning money."
2. How did large banks participate in the meltdown of 2008? Have these banks learned the lesson or are they still using the same techniques?
3. How did AIG fail in 2008?
4. Please enumerate the warning signals, listed in this chapter, since 1989.
5. How can large banks afford to give loans below market rates and fix these rates for 7 to 10 years?
6. What was the original name used for credit cards when these cards were first introduced? What was the purpose of introducing these cards first?
7. What does the new name "credit cards" imply? How are they used by consumers today?
8. What is an NSF account? How did banks use this to generate fee income for their operations?
9. What are student loans? How did student loans participate as an important factor in inflating tuition fees at U.S. universities?
10. How do you feel about student loans?
11. Please explain what is intended by the RF lifestyle advocated by this book. Please enrich this discussion by reflecting on the RF lifestyle, and please give us more ideas on the subject.

NOTES

1. The highest insurance cost paid by AIG for a California earthquake was around $8 billion.
2. Saskia Scholtes and Francesco Guerrera, "Banks Make $38bn from Overdraft Fees." *Financial Times* (August 10, 2009).
3. Huff Post Business Online, March 16, 2014.

CHAPTER 19

RF Banking: A New Banking Brand for the Twenty-First Century

As we journey into a new century, the dream is to popularize the RF banking brand and the RF financing methods using well-trained and dedicated RF bankers, branding experts, and media specialists. Judgment of a person, a manager, an investor, a banker, a board of directors, a politician, or a community leader cannot be regulated by a government decree or a set of laws. Judgment is personal and depends on the prevailing culture. Making a judgment depends on the way people were raised by their parents, their value system, and their deep-seated belief that a higher authority—a much higher authority than government regulations and laws—is watching over them.

The RF banking brand has been tested in the United States since 1987 at American Finance House (LARIBA), since 1994 at LARIBA Bank of Kazakhstan (before it was sold in 2006 due to government request to drastically increase capital) and at LARIBA Misr (in Egypt from 2004 until 2010) with great success and a proven track record. Later on in the United States, we branched out to test it on community banking operations, to see, first, whether it could be implemented and, second (and most importantly), whether the consumers in a small, conservative city like Whittier, California, since 2003 and later in Richardson (North Dallas), Texas, since 2011 would accept it. We are very pleased to report that the principles of RF banking and finance were accepted and proven to be successful not only by our auditors and bank examiners but also by many of our customers, including most churches and the Jewish community leaders in town who all have chosen to become our customers. These varied satisfied customers kept referring their neighbors, friends, and associates to do business with us. It was proven also that in 2008 and beyond, in the midst of the worst banking and economic meltdown in America's history since World War II, RF banking and finance disciplines rescued both LARIBA and the Bank of Whittier from becoming a participant in that meltdown. The results show it.

Strategically, it is important to make sure that we learn from the mistakes and errors in judgment of the twentieth century that led to the 2008 meltdown. The option of acquiring other banks has proven to be unsuccessful, especially in the area of creating a cohesive RF banking culture that trickles down even to the newest teller. RF bankers have to be trained from scratch, and these RF banking pioneers should be prepared to lead in the effort to produce more RF bankers who believe in the cause and the culture of RF banking and RF lifestyle. The other option of building a "brick-and-mortar" branch system has proven to be very expensive and difficult to manage, especially for this new RF banking brand that needs to be popularized with the lowest expenses in a vast country like America and later on in the world.

To plan for the future, one must take a peek at and articulate a vision of that future. With the growth and sophistication of the Internet, it is a fact that most people seldom go to their bank branches after opening the account. A new generation—not only in the United States, but all over the world—is now Internet bound. That is why the new RF banking system should benefit from the latest trends in Internet banking and Internet communications, without sacrificing security and privacy, by using the most up-to-date and sophisticated systems and techniques. We have attempted to do that at LARIBA and the Bank of Whittier, and we were very successful, not only in serving the cities of Whittier (a suburb of Los Angeles), California, and Richardson (a city approximately eight miles north of Dallas), Texas, and its surrounding neighborhoods in southern California and Texas, but also all 50 states.

One very serious hurdle would limit the expansion of our RF banking service to achieve our dream: the variation of banking laws from one state to another in the United States. For example, a bank charter or license must be secured in almost every state to practice depository services in that state. It is true that a national bank can serve from one location, but there is another layer of regulation that limits the expansion outside that area—the Community Reinvestment Act (CRA). This is a very big challenge that has to be resolved in a smart and strategic way.

As we proved that the pilot experiment worked, we have been contacted by many who believe in the RF banking and finance brand and its values and methods. They invite us to open branches in their communities. The standard response we give is: "We would be happy to do so, if we can establish that there is real demand for our services." We usually propose the following steps, in order not to be hasty, not to waste money, and not to compromise our reputation:

1. Start a virtual branch in our computer system by creating a soft branch in the financial ledger. In the branch's ledger, we keep track of the new accounts and deposits made from that community, as well as the

financing facilities (loans) invested in that community. When the level reaches a certain critical mass, we go to the next step.

2. Open a loan production office (LPO) that is responsible for promoting the financing of community needs; it is not allowed to take deposits in the LPO, but bank representatives can encourage the use of Internet banking and ATM depository abilities.
3. Open a small branch and encourage Internet banking. If the branch is in the same state where the bank is chartered, local leaders of the community are invited to become shareholders and advisers. This adds local content and contribution, in terms of money (capital), intellect, and reputation, to the effort. In addition, a small local executive board should be formed to give the effort a local feel and legitimacy. If the bank starts operations in a different state, shareholders from that state must be added as a prerequisite to opening that branch.

About the Companion Website

Another innovation we present with the Second Edition is a dedicated website for the book. Go to www.wiley.com/go/islamicbanking2e (password: wiley14).

The website includes:

- All charts from the book.
- Quarterly updates of price history of all the commodities, houses, and financial markets in the form of updated price charts.
- Answers to end-of-chapter review questions.

The RF financial and banking disciplines pioneered in this book (Chapter 3) will be applied to study fair pricing in the marketplace. The analysis will be used to warn users to be careful in case an economic price bubble materializes and to encourage them to take advantage of situations when prices in the market reflect undervaluation.

The reader can contact the author by e-mail at yarahman@msn.com or yarahman@whittierbank.com with any questions or discussions regarding the information discussed in the book and on the website.

Index

Note: Page references in *italics* refer to boxes and exhibits.

B

D

L

S